By the Same Author

THE FRENCH REVOLUTION
by Claude Manceron

Blood of the Bastille

1787–1789

Blood
of the
Bastille *1787–1789*

From Calonne's Dismissal to the Uprising of Paris

by CLAUDE MANCERON

Translated from the French by Nancy Amphoux

SIMON AND SCHUSTER
New York Toronto London Sydney Tokyo Singapore

SIMON AND SCHUSTER
Simon & Schuster Building
Rockefeller Center
1230 Avenue of the Americas
New York, New York 10020

Manufactured in the United States of America

1 3 5 7 9 10 8 6 4 2

Library of Congress Cataloging in Publication data

Manceron, Claude.
[Sang de la Bastille. English]
Blood of the Bastille. 1787–1789 : from Calonne's dismissal to the
uprising of Paris / by Claude Manceron ; translated from the French
by Nancy Amphoux.
p.   cm.—(Age of the French Revolution ; v. 5)
Translation of: Le sang de la Bastille.
Includes bibliographical references.
1. France—History—Revolution, 1789–1799—Causes.   2. France—
History—Revolution, 1789–1799—Biography.   3. France—Intellectual
life—18th century.   4. France—Politics and government—1774–1793.
5. Bastille.   6. Calonne, M. de (Charles Alexandre de), 1734–1802.
I. Title.   II. Series: Manceron, Claude. Hommes de la liberté.
English (Simon and Schuster Inc.)
DC145.M3513   1989
[DC138]
944.04'092'2 s—dc20
[944'.035]   89-21916
                                        CIP
ISBN 0-671-67848-5

Contents

Contents

Contents

Contents

Contents

To François Mitterrand,
President of the Republic
for which the Men of Liberty strove,
and to Danielle Mitterrand

The blood of the Bastille cried out all over France.
—SAINT-JUST

We may be permitted to hope that human history is beginning with us.
—MIRABEAU

The Situation
at the Beginning of This Book

1787.

The word "revolution" is in the air. But it is in the air of many other countries more than that of France, where the meeting of Notables convened by Louis XVI at Calonne's suggestion ought to—as the Court is fully convinced it will—wipe out the deficit without encroaching upon the venerable preserves of the privileged.

Most of the states of Europe are in danger of making history. As a consequence of a network of intermarriages among close kin, the incumbents of most of the thrones that are occupied belong to a single, far-flung tribe of degenerate princes protected by a sort of semideification. The kings of Portugal and England are plain crazy; those of Spain, Naples and Sweden, and the emperor of Germany (Frederick II's nephew, who has just succeeded him in Prussia) have distinctly shaky nervous systems. Taking them all in all, the soundest of the lot are Louis XVI in France—despite a pathological inability to make up his mind, now being aggravated by ethylic pickling— and even more the little German princess Catherine, whose blood is too fresh to have turned sour and whom chance and the assassination of her husband have seated on the throne of the greatest empire of the day, Russia.

In America, people have already stopped talking about revolutions; there, the word these days is "structure," meaning the creation, by hard work, of a republic in which everything has to be invented from scratch.

After a series of preliminary whirrs and ticks, it is a French clock that is finally going to chime in the new age.

CONDORCET

I

DECEMBER 1786

Taking the Plunge

On December 28, 1786, as the new age is dawning, Condorcet marries Sophie de Grouchy. It's all so beautiful. Here we have a marriage of love taking place, almost the very day of the convening of the Notables by Louis XVI, between France's greatest scholar and the cream of Vexin nobility. It is attended by a little crowd of overjoyed guests culled from the top drawer of the French Enlightenment, oh what a lark is life, tra-la-la! You'd think it was a banquet of politics, illumination and fine feelings scheduled centuries earlier.*

In the front row of the spectators, of course, is La Fayette.

On twenty-eighth December one thousand seven hundred eighty-six, after publication of the banns in this church [in Gondecourt, a small village nestled in a green valley perpendicular to the Seine northwest of Paris] and in that of St. André des Arts in Paris, among the announcements at the parish mass; the betrothed having obtained a dispensation as regards the two further banns and the time condition; between Marie-Jean-Antoine-Nicolas de Condorcet, adult son of Messire Antoine de Caritat de Condorcet, chevalier and captain in the Brabançon regiment, and of Marie-Magdeleine-Catherine Gaudril,† his wife; and Marie-Louise-Sophie, not-yet-adult daughter of Messire François-Jacques de Grouchy, chevalier, seigneur of Villette, Sagy, Gondecourt and other places, and of Marie-Gilberte-Henriette Fréteau, his wife . . .[1]

I, the undersigned Cuillin, parish priest of Gondecourt, after the betrothal

---

*The King announced the convening of the Notables at Versailles on December 29, 1786. In the last volume, I promised to begin this one, as a sort of prelude, with Condorcet's wedding—a curtain raiser to the Revolution. The opening dates of this volume accordingly overlap, very slightly, the closing ones of *Toward the Brink*.

†The proper spelling of Condorcet's mother's name is Gaudry. Both his parents were dead.

performed the same day, and in consequence of the permission granted by His Grace the archbishop, recorded their mutual consent to the marriage and bestowed the nuptial blessing* upon them in the presence of Monsieur and Madame de Grouchy, father and mother of the bride, and of Marie-Paul-Joseph-Gilbert du Motier, Marquis de La Fayette, camp marshal, major general in the service of the United States

. . . which means that, five years after the victory at Yorktown, he's listing this rank among his essential claims to fame. La Fayette "the American" is a senior officer in the New World army and wants the fact to appear in public documents, alongside his French military title.

Dispensation from the banns, betrothal and wedding the same day— why are these two newlyweds, on the day of the Feast of the Holy Innocents, in such a rush to tie the knot? The only rush is to get the fuss over with. The gentry can afford to simplify the actual wedding; at their level of society it's the negotiations between families prior to the signing of the contract that tend to draw things out. But once those are finished, it's all pull together, mates, and oil the bell ringers' ropes to hurry things along, if need be.

After La Fayette's name in the marriage act comes a tidy lapful of Grouchys, du Patys, Fréteaus, Pontécoulants, Arbouvilles and Puy-Montbruns— all nobles of gown or sword but, for reasons of tradition, pride and almost deliberate boycott, quite separate from the Court (except for La Fayette). This is a wholly independent, self-sufficient little world, in which Condorcet will feel perfectly at home. The great bachelor of the academies has finally been hooked. His far-flung colleagues shake their heads and marvel; in the end, they had come to regard him as some kind of monk.

But Nicolas is not a minute older than his years, and why, with his extreme good looks, and so tall he has to stoop a little, but still full of a sap that has been bottled up since childhood, should he start acting the dotard at forty-three? If anybody is making fun of him, it's only because they're jealous. "Last week† the Academy of Sciences received notice of the marriage. Delegates were appointed to present the body's official congratulations, one from the geometry group, one from astronomy, etc.

" 'Gentlemen!' exclaimed Dionis du Séjour [the wit of the company]; 'it is not from among these persons that our choice should be made; the person we should send to our colleague is the one who is best and strongest in anatomy!'

"The laughter raised by this jest rang out all the louder, as Condorcet

---

*In the chapel of the château de Villette.
†According to Bachaumont's *Mémoires secrets.*

is the young lady's senior by twenty years* and she is pretty, tall and strong, and a morsel not to be so easily digested by such a newlywed as this."[2]

How delicate! Proof that on some occasions the erudite are the equals of any musketeer. Lagrange, the mathematician, showed a more subtle spirit, by reverting to the letter he had received from d'Alembert twenty years before, when he had taken the same step: "I hear you have done what is known among us philosophers as taking the plunge. Above all else, a great mathematician should be able to calculate his own happiness. I have no doubt that, having done your sums, you find marriage to be the true solution."[3] The sparkling d'Alembert, the matchless friend who made Condorcet his executor, would have been happy to be there, too, beaming his mournful monkey's smile—the smile of one who never tried this experiment himself—over all the perfectly curled and powdered guests in their gorgeous array and the troops of peasants, hat in hand, who belong to the château de Villette. This is where the match between Sophie and Nicolas was made last summer, out by the double row of old limes that slopes gently down to the court of honor with the château at the end, its two wings reaching out in half circles. On the right stands the chapel, connected to the main building by a gallery that looks like a cloister. On the left, the outbuildings, teeming with plebs in their Sunday best. The guests pass each other ascending and descending the double-horseshoe staircase that rises out of the domed entrance hall, which can contain three or four times the number gathered here today. The Grouchys have held both land and château since the beginning of the reign of Louis XV, when their forebear, Nicolas-Pierre, a captain of the King's ships, married a rich young woman named Cousin who brought Villette as part of her marriage-portion. A marble bust of old Homer faces the guests. The entrance hall opens onto the drawing room with its six windows, the dining room containing monochrome piers adorned with rococo grottoes and various other suites of rooms. This is more than affluence; it's regulated opulence. The lackeys have just brought up a large basket "filled with sword bows, knots, fans, and green and gold cords for the ecclesiastical hats that were to be handed out among the guests. This custom was extremely expensive."[4] Defying the wintry weather, the more warm-blooded members of the group venture a few steps onto the terrace "overlooking the grounds and streams, which are the crowning glory of this noble residence."[5] The bride's aunt, Adélaïde du Paty, née Fréteau, assures us, in the "Villette style"—the parlor-pastoral chatter held dear by the clan—that "Flora, Ceres and Neptune amused themselves embellishing this dwelling, whose owners have contrived

---

*Condorcet was born on September 17, 1743, at Ribemont in Picardy, where his father was garrisoned; Sophie de Grouchy was born at Villette in March 1764.

to make it into a little earthly paradise" in the hollow of the region called the French Vexin, where the Seine sweetens and grows tame before venturing into Normandy after the rigors of Champagne and changing moods of Paris. Is this a parable for Condorcet, whose hitherto harsh life is also bending gently in the direction of sweetness?

The nearest city is Meulan to the south on the Seine, three leagues downstream from Poissy and upstream from Mantes; not so much a city as a big village, its white houses clinging to the hillside that tumbles down to the river and the little island on which the relics of St. Nicaise, the bishop-martyr of Rouen, are preserved. "The rest of the island, and the fortress of Meulan, belong to the see of Chartres, although the town itself belongs to that of Rouen,"[6] a situation that fuels many a canon's quarrel. North of Gondecourt lies another little estate, called Rueil,* and from it, on August 22 the previous year, escaped a dog, foaming at the mouth and quite conceivably an agent of rabies and death. As it turned out, however, it was the dog that made the match, by serving, to use the chemist's lingo, as "precipitating factor."

One presumes that Condorcet had already noticed Sophie, in the course of his frequent calls upon the Grouchys, or more exactly upon his friend Councillor Fréteau,† a kinsman and habitual guest of theirs, one who could do his own inviting at Villette. But he will never forget the moment when the girl stepped permanently into his desire as she ran across the lawn to rescue a little boy who had been savaged by the dog from Rueil. The child was Charles du Paty, a budding seigneur, the *Président*'s only son. With his quick eyes, set off by the fair skin of the du Patys, and his appealing fragility, he bids fair to deserve his name, and his father would die if anything happened to him; and here's the little fellow rolling in the grass, trying to protect his face from the large hairy ball with the sharp teeth. Underlings brandish sticks, but from a safe distance, and the whole household, all the Grouchys and Fréteaus united, comes tumbling out of the drawing room and lurching up with the awkwardness of people who have forgotten how to run. As for

---

*Not to be confused with Rueil-Malmaison, also to the west of Paris but much closer to the capital.

†This volume makes much greater use than previous ones of the titles of various officials, connected primarily with the courts. Their hierarchy and organization are bewilderingly complicated, and not only to us in the twentieth century. Following some (but not all) authorities, this translation leaves a number of terms in French: *parlement* (both more and less than a court but less than a parliament), *président, procureur du roi,* for example, and translates others: advocate (*avocat,* a lawyer who pleads and has more education and a higher status than the *procureur*), attorney (*procureur*), tipstaff (*huissier*), state councillor, master of requests, farmer general, etc. I crave the reader's indulgence; if full explanations were given in every case, the whole character of the book would be distorted.—*Trans.*

Condorcet, he looks like some great bird flapping its wings. But Sophie, who acts as a second mother to her nephew and never lets him far from her sight, streaks ahead in her white gown and tackles the dog, hitting at it with her bare arms and screaming so loudly she drives it away. Then, while everybody is fluttering ineptly around the young victim, she reassures him, calms them all and silences the blatherings of Aunt Fréteau, who is saying that the animal must be rabid and the child must be sent to the seaside to bathe at once, before being treated with mercury.[7] Sophie's twenty-two years shame them out of their panic. A strong woman, our little Grouchette, as her family still calls her here, using the nickname she had in childhood. Did she catch Condorcet's gaze upon her just then? With a little soldier like her on one's arm, a man might brave the storms he feels are coming tomorrow, he hopes will be coming tomorrow. . . . That may well have been the day he made up his mind to marry her.

Beaumarchais, too, is delighted by the tale; yes, he's been here, of course, and will be here again. Beaumarchais, ferret-extraordinary among the men of liberty, who became an associate of all progressive men of law at the time of his trial, and is therefore a close friend of du Paty, to whom he wrote, back at the beginning of September, "My friend, the appalling news of your son's mishap brought a frightful spasm to my heart. . . . I am told there is hope that the dog was only in a temper and not rabid. Has the animal been captured? But although the skill of Monsieur Sabatier [the doctor] may restore your dear child to you, I warrant I know the French well enough to assure you that this double misfortune will have rendered you doubly dear to them,"[8] the first of du Paty's misfortunes being that for years he has been the victim of covert persecution by his peers in the Bordeaux magistracy, partly on the grounds of his patent and deliberate nonconformism, but even more out of pure class intolerance toward the son of a tradesman. He's in "a condition of unhappiness," an exile in his own homeland—as though the mortifications of Louis XVI weren't enough!

Du Paty is the Voltaire of French justice, and wasn't it Voltaire who called him "the Socrates of Bordeaux"? It was he who brought Condorcet and the Grouchys together, who introduced his blushing niece to the scholar so alert to anything emanating from him. Condorcet could not have coveted royal blood more ardently.

Young Charles du Paty's wounds have healed without necessitating recourse to baths in the sea, and he plays his part of Young Master at his cousin's wedding with all the requisite seriousness. He pays her a well-turned compliment, heartfelt and appropriate, as he leaves the pseudo-Gothic chapel in which, flanked by his father and mother, he has observed the proceedings. Because they're both there, too, of course, and the *Président* is stared at by the guests no less than is Condorcet himself. At the end of this year, which seems to some as though it may also be the end of the old world, the consummation for which both du Paty and Condorcet have been fighting for many years, du Paty stands out as a figure of quite special interest.

From the way people look at the newlyweds, stepping aside to let them pass; from the universal consideration and concern surrounding them like a moving stage set, one can plainly see that this is no ordinary wedding. Condorcet is radiant, in his pearl-gray coat with—for once—impeccably ironed ruffles at the wrists. People observe that he is not only mild-mannered and intelligent but handsome, too. They attribute to him the graces with which the public tends to invest all cult figures. At last, he is emerging from his gilded lair in the Hôtel des Monnaies, to which the course of events has relegated him these past ten years.

It was no coincidence that he published his *Vie de Turgot* last year. Tomorrow, perhaps, Turgot may finally return to power—through his disciples, like so many of history's great dead—and who among them more faithful than his friend of every hour, including the last? How far will the little ripple of Notables who are about to converge upon Versailles from the four corners of the realm carry Condorcet, his *Vie de Turgot* in his hand like a missal? This girl at his side, in her white crepe gown trimmed with *point de Bruxelles* lace, a paragon of steadfastness of spirit, might well be the new Eve of the age of learning, the daughter of the *Encyclopédie*. Now Sophie has replaced her ceremonial bonnet* with "a lovely toque set off with white plumes, to which the bouquet of orange-blossom was fixed."

Is she happy? So it would seem. In love? Yes, in a way. But a few of the more expert witnesses, her close relatives, intimate friends and that cat, Adèle Suard, the gossip-in-chief of the literary salons, who will subsequently make a whole novel out of it,† note a small cloud dimming the dazzle of her smile and find that her gaze pauses a trifle too often upon "her beloved little uncle."

---

*Brides in those days did not wear a veil.

†On the Suards' *petit ménage,* which becomes the meeting place for one wing of the progressive intellectuals, see Volume IV.

2

DECEMBER 1786

Her Love of Balls Had Passed Away

"The admirable perfections of a superb body. . . . Features full of mischief and wit; arched brows indicative of a powerful will; large dark eyes, a graceful chin, slightly upturned nose with flaring nostrils; the mouth a trifle wide, but accustomed to smiling; an oval face framed by a mass of fine hair; in repose, the look of those women who used to gather periwinkles with Jean-Jacques": that is how Marie-Louise-Sophie de Grouchy[1] is described at the time of her marriage, and that is how Condorcet sees her.

The road she traveled in her first twenty years is retraced later by their only daughter, with the precision of a miniature:

> She spent her childhood and youth with her father and mother, who was a good and witty woman, but [*sic*] very pious. My mother often told me that she was never able to believe in the Christian religion, that she never could reconcile the idea of such a vast number of damned and such a small number of elect with the existence of a God who was good; that, to please her mother, she prayed regularly for six months asking for faith, but to no avail.
>
> Until the age of eighteen or nineteen she spent no more than two or three winters in Paris with her father and mother, who lived extremely quietly when there; she was not permitted to read anything but devotional books, and a very few history books: *Télémaque* and Marcus Aurelius. At nineteen she was sent, with a companion, to the Neuville chapter near Mâcon to be received as a canoness. There, after attending the balls for six consecutive weeks, she fell ill. She took to her bed plain and homely, and of no more than average height, and she rose from her illness exceptionally beautiful, tall and wonderfully elegant. The transformation was so total that upon her return from the chapter her own mother did not know her. Her love of balls had passed away. During the two years she spent at the chapter she rented books,* read Voltaire and Rousseau,

*From the Mâcon reading room; such places existed, on the fringes of the numerous

and concerned herself seriously and constantly with her mind. When she returned to the château de Villette, her mother, heartbroken by her lack of religious feeling, burned the few books she brought with her. But she remembered what was in them. She applied herself to deeds of charity toward all the peasants thereabouts; from childhood on, and throughout her life, these were a source of much joy to her. She often told me it was in those days, going over in her mind everything she had read, that she brought it all together and reflected upon it all.[2]

She found her guide, in "bringing it all together," at just the right time, as so often happens to us somewhere around the age of twenty; the person who helps us to see ourselves, at last, from head to foot. And for her, as for so many others, the illumination was filtered through first love. She couldn't have chosen a better man. "*Président* du Paty [Condorcet's daughter goes on] had married my grandmother's sister."

To be exact, in the middle of the reign of Louis XV, four Fréteau children were born to a family of Parisian magistrates. The eldest and only boy followed in his father's footsteps and lengthened his name, as everybody else was doing in those days, by adding on to it the name of a piece of land purchased near Paris. By 1786, he was Councillor Fréteau de Saint-Just in the Paris *Parlement*.* One of the three girls married a fashionable member of the Bordeaux *parlement* named Jean-Baptiste du Paty, while the other two married "sword" aristocrats: an Arbouville and a Grouchy. A good example of the osmosis between the nobility of the gown and the other sort. Sophie was the child of the remarriage, in 1760, of François-Jacques, seigneur of Robertot, Marquis de Grouchy, onetime page of Louis XV, cavalry officer and childless widower, to Henriette Fréteau. Forty-six years to her eighteen. Ebenezer Scrooge and Dora Copperfield. He was considered "cold and reserved," she overflowing with charm and goodwill.

And it was this sugar-sweet Mummy who nearly drowned her daughter in holy water. Grouchette had to endure the same lonely battle of an intelligence besieged by monsters as a Manon Phlipon or a Comtesse de Monnier.†
She emerged from it with a mind as well tempered as theirs, at the end of her long and pleasantly withdrawn adolescence at Villette and her period as canoness at Neuville-les-Dames, the nickname given to Neuville-en-Bresse on account of all those distinguished young ladies who used to spend a few months there playing at being the Good Lord's little dolls in the Dombes

---

intellectual societies and clubs founded, beginning in the 1750s, by "enlightened" Notables in towns of substance.

*No connection with our Saint-Just.

†Manon Phlipon, later Madame Roland, and Sophie de Monnier, most famous of Mirabeau's mistresses. Their progress toward atheism is observed in Volume I.

before coming of age in the great world. There was small danger of their falling into either chastity or poverty; the institution of the canonesses, typical of that age of privilege-made-sacred, was more like a finishing school combined with a little conventual social life.

In the reign of Louis XVI there were twenty-six "chapters" in France, open to five or six hundred girls who must as a rule be able to show eight quarters of blue blood, eight generations "of military and chivalric nobility"[3] on both sides of their family tree. Sophie's mother did not meet these requirements, and that is why they had to look around until they found the Neuville priory, which belonged to the less stringent diocese of Lyons; there, one could get away with only three noble quarters on the mother's side. In this way the Grouchy girls, Sophie first and then her younger sister, Charlotte, were able to acquire a sort of ecclesiastical nobility.

So Condorcet is marrying a canoness. In 1784 and 1785, Sophie wore the amice, or almuce, an odd, squirrel-lined headpiece, when she sang in the choir at mass. She was already being called *madame.* Out of church she could dress as she liked, in the latest secular fashion, augmented only by a gold cross dangling from a moiré ribbon. She had had to bide her time "in a conventual apartment," a three-room suite, for the duration of a "nonprebended" canoness's novitiate, paid for by her father at the rate of two thousand livres a year. Then she got a little house of her own, and servants, like the "prebended-countess-canonesses" of the priory, who included a Damas, no less, and a Durfort, a Saint-Phalle, a Polignac, a Lévis-Mirepoix, etc. But soon, having duly acquired an *estate,* it was time for Sophie to go home to her parents and give her place to Charlotte. Even if she didn't catch a husband, she would always be entitled, providing only that she remained celibate and made a few brief tours of duty at Neuville, to a portion of the seven hundred thousand-odd livres of income divided annually among the canonesses of the realm. As for marriage, it was perfectly in order for her to prefer that, as an estate, and toss her almuce over the windmill whenever she felt like it.

Sophie's early twenties were named Neuville, thus, a place of contradictions where she read Voltaire and Rousseau between masses against a background rumble of partying laced with waves of incense. That was where her already latent atheism grew stronger, as she edged nearer to the machinery of the Holy Roman Church. At vespers on the day of her "introduction" into the chapter, she was made to kneel down and ask the Reverend Mother Superior "for the bread and wine of St. Catherine," patron saint of the priory, "to serve God and the Holy Virgin." She was given a wafer to eat, she moistened her lips in a goblet of wine, the twist of ribbon with the cross at the end was put around her neck, she was wrapped in a long ermine cloak and the almuce and black veil were put on her, a *Te Deum* was sung; "then the procession returned in the same order, and a ball began."

She never danced so much in her whole life; week after week of un-interrupted partying took her to death's door in June 1785, in the form of a "fever of exhaustion" that affected her sight. Her mother's sister, the Aunt du Paty who often came to visit her, had written to her husband the *Président:* "The canoness is still displaying all her talents, despite her trouble with her eyes. She is translating Tasso and the sublime Young.* Her eyes are her one great torment. No remedy but rest can be prescribed, but how is one to inculcate rest into souls as ardent and active as that of my niece? . . . She has taxed her strength too high, has that young woman, and these overexertions are always paid for in the end."[4]

In August 1785, a long-anticipated visit from du Paty himself was to make a lasting impression upon her and consolidate her self-confidence. "I am hoping for my little uncle sometime this month. I should so like him to give me two or three days. An exiled hermit is surely worth as much as one or two rare buildings or a few masterpieces of painting,"[5] of the type du Paty has just been admiring on a trip to Italy in the manner of the *Président* de Brosses and from which, like his predecessor, he would send back letters that were to give him, too, a name as a writer. Here he is, here he is, the little uncle, coming from Turin, all rattled from the jolts of the Grand Saint-Bernard Pass: Charles-Marguerite-Jean-Baptiste du Paty. Just turned forty, something jolly and fun-loving about him, a sort of great cleanliness stamped on a smooth face marked only by quotation marks of humor around the mouth, his hair impeccably rolled above a high, round forehead and an already receding hairline, an aquiline nose spreading as it descends, the better to sniff life with, my dear.[6] It makes one feel good just to be in the same room with his kind of man, and the canonesses read the signs aright from the start. Du Paty, meanwhile, is almost ready to believe he has strayed into Thélème: "How good it feels to be here! What a pleasant retreat! What charming conversations! I eat, sleep, put on weight, I rest, I love and am loved, and may even have some small success. Or at least, the ladies here are kind enough to make me think so. . . . My heart is beginning to open up and revive."[7] This was written in response to the caressing gaze of a Sophie whom he had last seen a child and was now meeting as a young woman. "I found my niece more interesting than ever. There is nothing to be added to the house—save, perhaps, to take something away from it, for she does too much. Her life is nothing but solitude, isolation, books, all manner of learning,

---

*Torquato Tasso (1544–1595), Italian poet, author of *Jerusalem Delivered.* Edward Young (1683–1765) was the author of *The Complaint; or, Night-Thoughts on Life, Death, and Immortality,* published in London in 1742 and immediately translated throughout Europe. This ten-thousand-line saga of melancholy reeks of the cult of woefulness that was to become a major component of the Romantic sensibility.

and, alongside that, Villette, her family, our family, in short, her heart and our hearts. . . . Your niece is loved, esteemed, honored; she is unique here, do you hear?" he told his wife, who retorted, a touch briskly, "I have no wish to disturb your pretty committee with my niece. Embrace her, in the way of friendship."[8]

Sophie was as though carried out of herself by it all. Will she ever come back? "Can you conceive how these conversations, so full and interesting, came about, dear little uncle?* . . . For my part, I am still touching them [*sic*] and shall go on touching them for a long time to come, because I never yet relished so delicious a blend of soul, wit, love of philosophy and literature,"[9] as they strolled arm-in-arm along the network of canals and streams criss-crossing this waterlogged region, just around the corner from Châtillon-sur-Chalarosse, where Vincent de Paul was parish priest a hundred years before. You can't walk three feet there without bumping into one of those roving ponds that the peasants are constantly shifting from one place to another, flooding their fields in alternate years so that they can harvest fish and eels like some kind of vegetable crop. The weather was sultry that August; the damp air shimmered with heat and the first dead leaves were slowly adding their yellow hue to the tapestry of waterways. There was a rumble of thunder almost every evening.

On their walks, Jean-Baptiste and Sophie would meet the other canonesses, who waggled their sunshades at them and uttered little shrieks of goodwill.

It was hard for Sophie to detach herself from the Grouchy world; she was still upset by the marriage of her brother Emmanuel,† in May 1785, to a young lady named Pontécoulant, whom she called "Pontécouleuvre." [*Couleuvre* = common grass snake; but to "swallow a *couleuvre*" is "to swallow anything, to be gullible."—*Trans.*] Good Uncle du Paty, full of indulgence where all young ladies were concerned, scolded her a little about it: "That little grass snake is worth more than any of you have seen in her. I have been able to catch several glimpses of her soul and mind through her timidity, which is extreme, I beg you to believe, and have been charmed by them." He talked to her about his own family, too, about little Charles, his firstborn, his heir, whom he would like to put into her hands for a while so that she might polish off the rough edges and act as a Mummy-sister to him while he was away on his travels next year, 1786, as though the boy's mother, poor

---

*Written to du Paty on September 4, 1785, just after he left. "She writes like Madame de Sévigné," the *Président* said.

†Emmanuel de Grouchy becomes a soldier. We shall see him again in the Revolution, which he supports. He becomes a marshal of the empire but only during the Hundred Days; and it is he Napoleon awaits in vain at Waterloo.

Aunt Adélaïde, were some sort of aged matriarch. Sophie would like nothing better: "I promise, dear little uncle, to take care of Charles and undertake to prepare his soul for the constant activity which alone can enable him to make the most of his position, his years, his gifts and your example. . . . How charmed I should be if, in these trying times [of du Paty's very relative persecution], I might truly serve your affection and help to shape a soul worthy of yours; I mean a soul that resembles yours."[10]

Du Paty introduced Sophie to his own favorite mentor, the master of integrity and equity. "I love Montesquieu even more since I heard you reading him, no doubt because you read him as he must have read himself."[11] He "carried her through Italy with the eyes of the soul and good taste," and in a spirit that accorded, as lute and oboe, with the conclusions she had reached from her own reading. The customs and usages of the Papal States had forti-fied the *Président*'s tranquil agnosticism: "Two things contribute signally to the good fortune of the Romans. Religion, with its absolutions, always cleans away their past, and with its promises, adds color to their future. They are the people who have the blindest and at the same time the most accommodating of religions. Let them only regularly attend some religious ceremony, some entertainment, that is, and utter certain words, and heaven is theirs."[12]

When he talked like this, he was not speaking as some more or less amoral aesthete. Du Paty was full of fire and enthusiasm, and still so young, in spite of the hard knocks life had given him, so quick to switch from mockery to anger, from superficial to essential, from the court of Rome to the whole of Europe of degenerate sovereigns! "What a theater for eloquence, that Basilica of St. Peter! . . . I should so like the voice of a Bossuet to burst out there, in the midst of all that pompous paraphernalia! To cast down upon an audience of kings the sovereign word of the King of kings, who would call to account the awakened consciences of these pale, trembling monarchs, for all the blood and all the tears that are flowing at this very moment, by their doing, over the whole surface of the earth."[13]

When she heard him speak such words, his niece devoured him with her eyes. The revolt expressed in the testimony of the man of experience confirmed the revolt of the adolescent girl. She thought the young lawyers of Bordeaux were blessed indeed to be able to learn this kind of eloquence in his shadow; young Justinien-Pierre Vergniaud, for instance, who had been du Paty's secretary for the last five years and was now cutting a swathe with his own winglike sleeves back there.*

Most of all, she got him to talk about himself, which he did without too much twisting of his arm. He has had the hounds at his heels for sixteen

---

*The most famous of the future Girondins. See Volume II for Vergniaud's youth in Limoges and the causes for his removal to Bordeaux.

years and more. Du Paty is the great persecuted magistrate of the end of the reign of Louis XV and the whole of that of Louis XVI, although less visibly of late. And if he will go on knocking himself out and shaking up the entire kingdom just to save three men from the wheel, people are not likely to make things much easier for him yet awhile.

PRÉSIDENT DU PATY

3

DECEMBER 1786

So Long as It Shall Please God . . .

Seventeen years before, Diderot had taken notice of someone named du Paty, "advocate general at the *parlement* of Bordeaux," a young magistrate who had pleaded the case of a widow versus public opinion:

> Among our laws there is one that is most notorious. More often than not, it is a woman's fortune, not her misfortune, to become a widow. If, in the course of her year of mourning, she is convicted of having intimate commerce with a man, the law deprives her of all her rights of widowhood.
>
> M. du Paty has undertaken to defend a widow who stands in a slightly better case, against grasping heirs.
>
> His pleadings still seem those of a young man. There is bombast and some irrelevance in his style. One could wish him more muscle, precision, stringency. Yet with all these shortcomings, one can hardly credit that at the age of twenty-two or twenty-three (for M. du Paty is no more than that) it is possible to possess so much knowledge, eloquence and logic.[1]

What connection could there be between our du Paty of nearly twenty years later and the actors in a backwoods squabble in Champagne? Yet at the time of Condorcet's wedding, du Paty has gone to bat for "the three men on the wheel." Here history and the news item brush wingtips.

January 29, 1783. A farmer and his wife, the Thomassins, go to sleep in their little cottage at Vinet, a hamlet near Troyes. The wife is fifty, the husband sixty. Two rooms, a stable, a few sheds.

The next morning their oldest son, aged thirty, comes galloping up to the nearest gendarmerie brigade, in Arcy, as fast as his nag can carry him. He notifies the "marshalsea" that his parents were attacked during the night by three evildoers, who beat them with sticks and, he claims, committed an outrage upon his mother. The assailants disappeared, according to him, bearing "a small gold cross, a sum of 120 to 140 livres, some linens and items of food."[2]

January 31, 1783. After recording a brief summary of the victims' accusation, a local gendarme* arrests two "layabouts" within easy reach: an epileptic named Guyot, who was a scissors grinder of sorts; and "a beggar with neither passport nor certificate" named Lardoise. Both offer alibis, but no effort is made to check them.

In the ensuing days, on the strength of denunciations by local people, a third man, called Bradier but nicknamed Malbrough, "squat and red-bearded," is also arrested, along with his brother-in-law, named Simare; both are occasional horse traders.

They are searched on the spot, and on one of them some broken bits of jewelry are found, not at all like the cross stolen from the Thomassins, it appears; then they are taken to prison and given into the charge of the *lieutenant criminel* [a lawyer who assisted *baillis* and *sénéchaux* in the performance of duties relating to criminal affairs] who, in the inextricable tangle of French customs, also turns out to be the judge. Depending on the seriousness of the offense, he can punish, either alone or with some vague assistance, anyone from a poacher to a murderer.†

So the four accused men are interned in May 1783 in the prison of Chaumont-en-Bassigny, a town of some importance to the establishment of royal authority in Champagne. Five thousand inhabitants, on the banks of the Marne. There is a "magnificent church belonging to the Carmelite nuns, the altar of which is all of marble and jasper. . . . It is rather hilly country, and the chief commerce is in wheat, rye and the sheep which are fattened there. . . . The townspeople are rightly considered to be very well mannered."[4]

The prisoners find themselves in the keep of the square tower, "built

---

*The gendarmerie, also known as *maréchaussée* or marshalsea, was a body of men formed gradually, and not without difficulties at the local level, all over the French territory, starting in 1670. It was commanded from afar, by the King's Household, but local units were composed, as here, of a few men from the vicinity.

†"The lesser courts are the most severe; their judges would hang a man just to show they have the power to do it. I have witnessed this a hundred times in our presidial sittings." (From an anonymous pamphlet by a Béziers magistrate.)[3]

of stout stones" before the reign of Louis XII and now starting to fall to pieces.

And there they await someone's gracious pleasure . . .

In December 1784 Guyot, the epileptic, dies in prison.

June 1785 (or twenty-eight months after being charged). The three surviving prisoners are transferred closer to the scene of the crime and, at last, brought face-to-face with their alleged victims in the presence of an emissary of the *lieutenant criminel* of Chaumont. The Thomassins formally "recognize" them. Now they can be tried.

August 11, 1785. The three men spend a few hours on the "seat"* in Chaumont, at a "hearing" held without benefit of witnesses, audience or, of course, counsel.

As far as criminal justice is concerned, this is an age of no more than ordinary cruelty. That same year, in Toulon, a mass desertion of seamen returning from America produces a certain amount of agitation on the Aix-en-Provence highway. They had been given no leave and no money and were utterly exhausted. "Starvation led them to waylay passersby. Six were caught, taken to Aix, sentenced and broken alive. They said on the scaffold, 'If we had been paid what was owed us, we would not be here now.' "[5]

The registrar doesn't even write down the words spoken by the accused in their defense. The trial is over in a day. They are taken back to prison, where they are not to be told their fate. Three judges, the *lieutenant criminel* being one of them, consider the case without further ado and sentence them to the galleys for life.

One might have supposed that now they were at least sure of their lives; but according to the customary law of the time, appeal to the Paris *Parlement* was mandatory in any provincial ruling awarding less than the maximum penalty. So they are stuffed into a vehicle and driven, prison by prison, to Paris, where they are incarcerated in La Conciergerie of the Palais de Justice.

The magistrates of the Paris *Parlement* have the reputation of being among the fiercest of France, and they deserve it.

On October 20, 1785, the three wretches are summoned to another "hearing" in the Chambre de la Tournelle, before *Président* Gilbert des Voisins, assisted by eleven councillors. The dreaded Advocate General Séguier calls for harsher punishment, once again in the absence of the accused. Nine councillors vote for the wheel, two are content with life in the galleys, and only one asks for further information.

But the name of that one is Emmanuel Fréteau de Saint-Just.

---

*A wooden seat on which the accused person sat in a painful and humiliating posture during the trial.

The case is closed in less than two hours; the registrar writes out the final ruling:

> Having considered, the chamber, ruling in the appeal lodged by the said Nicolas Lardoise, Claude Bradier, also known as Malbrough, and Jean-Baptiste Simare, known as Pierrotot, quashes the former ruling and sentence absolutely and sentences the said . . . to have their arms, legs, thighs and backs broken alive by the executioner of high justice on a scaffold to be erected for the purpose on the public square of Chaumont-en-Bassigny; this being done, each to be placed on a wheel with his face turned to the sky, there to remain so long as it shall please God to grant him life; pronounces all their goods confiscate to the King or to whomsoever it shall appertain, in either case a fine of two hundred livres having been previously deducted for the said King, in the event that he be not the beneficiary of the confiscation . . .
>
> Done in *Parlement* at the sitting of October 20, 1785.
>
> Gilbert Lambert.[6]

Fréteau . . .

He is appalled. His entire professional life leaps out at him in fury with this sentence, passed in front of him, and in spite of him.

He tells his brother-in-law about it, the one they're already starting to call "the great du Paty." Together they rush to Versailles and get the keeper of the seals to order the three condemned men brought back from Chaumont to La Conciergerie in Paris. When minutes count, even this brief respite could save their lives.

February 1786. A literary torch is lit in Paris[7] and sets fire to the rest of the country, on no greater matter than a criminal trial—just the way Voltaire did twenty-four years before, writing on the Calas affair.

After arguing against the second trial condemning the three men to the wheel, *Président* du Paty relates his visit to the condemned men in prison, as he told it to his niece:[8]

> I arrive at the prison; I ask for the three poor wretches; they are brought to me in the room in which I am waiting; there they are. Well! I say to myself, so here are these three men, who are innocent and who have been sentenced to the wheel by a court judgment.
>
> "Well, my friends, are you not Simare, Bradier and Lardoise?"
>
> "We are."
>
> "Which is Simare?"
>
> "I am."
>
> "Bradier?"
>
> "That's me."
>
> "Lardoise?"

"I'm Lardoise."

"Take heart, my friends, I am sent to assure you that your misfortunes are being looked into. Alas, it has been three years now! You must have suffered much in these three years?"

"You're asking if we've suffered!"

Then, raising his voice, Simare told me that a dreadful epidemic broke out in the prisons of Chaumont only a short time after their arrival and that it was the death of seventeen prisoners, including the unfortunate Guyot. "It was so bad," Simare told me, "that the jailers were afraid to come near us to bring us our bread and water and our straw every morning; I got off with thirteen months of stiff legs; all last winter I had to pull myself over the snow by my hands."

"And," Bradier said, "half my body was swollen up for six months."

"I didn't catch it, thank God," said Lardoise; "but the imprint of my irons [I should think so, after thirty months] hurt my leg so badly that it got gangrene in it and they almost cut it off."

They also told me that when they were sent to Vinet from the jurisdiction of Troyes, they were questioned in the Ramerupt prison in front of the Vinet judge, and that Simare, who was down with the fever, had to be carried to the hearing on a stretcher, and that the judge said to him, "Simare, I believe you are malingering."

"But, friends, there was no mention at the trial of this hearing by the Vinet judge!"

"There was a hearing at Ramerupt!" exclaimed all three of them.

They further assured me that when they were removed from the Chaumont prison to the prison at Piney, they were not questioned.

"But, friends, the trial documents refer to a general questioning dated from Piney."

"We were brought before the judge only once at Piney, and then it was to be seen by the Thomassins."

Then I recollected that it would have been very hard indeed for the Chaumont judges to make this whole voluminous inquest at Piney, comprising four hundred rolls, in seven days, and to perform all the acts and verifications, to ascertain all the facts and hear all the people and make comparisons between their statements, not to mention the visit to the Thomassins' house and the report on it, which alone took two days.

After these initial questions I asked them, one by one, about different points of the trial, about their status, way of living, families. Simare has three children; he has been married twice; his mother is still alive, nearly eighty years old. He lived with his mother, wife and children and a sister in a little house at Champfleury. Bradier has six children. They all described to me their proceedings and whereabouts and movements prior to the fatal January 29th and up to the moment of their arrest. They named forty people who could confirm their alibis; why were these people not heard, they asked; let them be heard!

"If," Lardoise said, "the farmers at Porte deny that I slept at their place on

January 29, deny that they said they had had things stolen a short time before, deny that I sat up with them until midnight, then I'll stand condemned!"

"But, friends, the Thomassins recognized you at the hearing in the presence of the parties!"

"Recognized!" they cried.

Lardoise spoke up then. "The judge asked the Thomassin woman, 'Do you recognize that man?' and she said, 'How's that? How's that? Very unpleasant, what's happened to us. Yes, I recognize him.' 'You hear what that woman says,' I told the judge; 'let that be written down, write it down!' The judge began to laugh; 'but, Milord, I told him, we're not talking for fun, here!' "

Bradier said, "I said to Thomassin, 'You say you've got a knife wound in your left arm; then show it!' 'Ah,' says he, 'it's healed now!' 'But what about the scar?' He didn't dare show it. I begged the judge to mention that, but it was no use."

"And I," said Simare in turn, "I said to the Thomassin woman, 'Where did you buy your cross?' 'At Troyes,' she said. And I called out, 'Write it down! Because mine was bought at Sézanne-en-Brie and there's the stamp and hallmark that will decide between us.' "*

All of this was spoken between us so peacefully, so tranquilly, with such conviction, that I was shaken to the depths of my soul.

"Let the gentleman speak," they would say from time to time. "Turn and turn about!"

And so we were, the four of us, all sitting around a table with a light in the middle; and I (for I never felt so much at peace as with these "three murderers"), as they spoke with the lamplight flickering over their features, I sought their innocence in their pale brows, their lean features, their hollow eyes in which a ray of hope was burning, their countenance, beneath their rags; and in all those places, I found it.

"How secure they feel!" I said to myself, with my gaze fixed upon them! "See! Under the fatal sword hanging over them at this moment (which I alone perceived, for they know nothing of the sentence and decree), every night, thus, they sleep! Every morning, they awake! All day long, they breathe! . . . See!" I further said to myself, with a shudder, "what if someone were to come of a sudden to tell these men, so innocent and serene, who could not even imagine it possible to believe in the crime of which they stand accused; what if, suddenly, they were to hear, like a thunderclap falling into the certainty of their innocence, 'All three of you are to be broken on the wheel!' " I imagined what those same faces would be like then. Ah, poor wretches!

Fréteau to du Paty, du Paty to Condorcet: in them, the France of the Enlightenment is rekindled. In the very months when he is marrying Sophie

---

*It seems likely that Victor Hugo, a great lover of eighteenth-century texts, was familiar with this one; there is an echo of it in Les Misérables.

de Grouchy, Condorcet cannot separate his own cause from that of the three wretches. He has just published a series of articles defending the "Three Men on the Wheel."

CHATEAUBRIAND

4

FEBRUARY 1787

My Heart Swelled with Vanity

In February 1787, the Chevalier François-René de Chateaubriand is presented to the King.* He is nineteen years old. He has just lost his father and firmly turned down the career in the Church for which his status as a younger son seemed to destine him.

He's everything and nothing at once, as he emerges from an almost uncivilized adolescence on his ancestral estates: he's the heir to an ancient lineage of Breton nobility and he's also the fellow citizen of the little peasants of Combourg and Saint-Malo.

His brother, the only other surviving male out of a horde of children, many of whom died in infancy, is the cock of the walk. He has found a place for his younger brother as second lieutenant in the Navarre regiment garrisoned in Cambrai. So from Combourg to Cambrai he goes, with a detour by way of Paris and Versailles, where his brother has also arranged for him to be presented at Court.

Seven months ago he was still in his little Breton noble savage's lair, where he had wrung from his dreaded father René-Auguste, and his sweet neurasthenic *maman,* their consent to his renunciation of the priesthood, for which he was so definitely unsuited. At first, to his stupefaction, his father had even fallen in with his idea of setting sail from Saint-Malo to serve some chimerical prince somewhere in the Indies or Canada.

But that was the only possible similarity between the destinies of this father and son. Forty years before, René-Auguste had lived the life of the "warrior merchants," unleashed upon the high seas like so many marine

---

*See Volume I for the day of his first communion.

wolves, whose sole responsibility—and at their own expense—was to transport all manner of cargo including that direst of all, "ebony," as the slaves
deported from Africa were called.

So Chateaubriand's father had been a slave trader, with all that the term
implies in the way of a moral context. Perhaps that's the reason for those
fits of mutism that came upon him in his old age, his twitches and tics, and
the feudal arrogance with which he treated his belongings. But when he
heard that his younger son had a fancy to live the same life of adventure . . . who knows?

The fantasy lasted two short months. One morning at eight, at Combourg, his father called him into his study:

" 'Monsieur le chevalier, you must give up your wild ideas. Your brother
has obtained a commission for you in the Navarre regiment. You will go to
Rennes, and from there to Cambrai. Here are one hundred louis; take care
of them. I am old and ailing, and have not long to live. Conduct yourself as
an upright man and never dishonor your name.'

"He embraced me. I felt that stern, wrinkled face pressed feelingly
against mine. It was my last paternal embrace."[1]

It may also have been the first.

In September 1786, some form of paralysis carried René-Auguste de
Chateaubriand to his grave. His son arrived too late for the funeral, but had
a fleeting reunion with the woods of Combourg, "where I began to feel the
first pangs of that *ennui* that I have carried with me my whole life long, and
the sorrow that has been both a torment and a blessing to me."[2]

More fleetingly still, he had a reunion with his favorite sister, the Lucile
of his youth, whose image has been enough, thus far in his life, to satisfy the
tuggings of his emotions, and will add a hint of incest to some of his subsequent loves.

So here is the lost child flung into the great whirlwind. "The fatal day
arrived; I had to leave for Versailles, more dead than alive. . . .[3] I went to
the chateau alone. Whoever has not seen the pomp of Versailles has seen
nothing. . . . Louis XVI was still there."

François-René is small of stature and has a proud and unapproachable
air; his dress, although ceremonial enough, is not in the latest fashion and
he does not possess the art of conversation; when he enters the famous Salle
de l'Oeil-de-Boeuf amidst a throng of courtiers, many of whom, in comparison with his own ancestry, are parvenus, with lineages a scant century long,
every possible complex of age and indigence fastens itself to his steps like
so many vultures. "I was observed; I heard people asking who I was."[4]

However, "when the King's rising was announced, all those who had not been presented withdrew; my heart swelled with vanity. . . . The doors to the King's bedchamber opened; I saw the King, as was the custom, completing his toilette; that is, taking his hat from the hand of the First Gentleman of the Bedchamber."

The King is going to hear mass; where else would he be going? As he passes, the Maréchal de Duras pulls the young Breton forward:

"Sire, the Chevalier de Chateaubriand."

Long afterward, he said that at that moment his shyness evaporated and he felt quite prepared to engage in conversation with Louis XVI on matters of the greatest moment. "It was the sovereign who, being even more embarrassed than myself, and finding nothing to say to me, moved on."

What's surprising is that he should have been surprised; he must be one of the very few aristocrats not to know about Louis XVI's acute shyness and difficulties of communication.

However, he returns to his furnished rooms in town feeling mightily pleased to have come out of it so well, and also to have observed, as a bonus, a noble curtsey of the Queen returning from chapel, "surrounded by a radiant and numerous cohort; she seemed to be enchanted with life."[5] He nevertheless feels, or so he swears, a deep aversion to the Court and all its ways, and is terror-stricken at the thought of being compelled, in his capacity as a young debutant, to attend the Day of Carriages on February 19.*

But attend it he does, in a gray coat with scarlet vest, breeches, riding boots, a hunting knife at his side and a small hat trimmed with gold braid on his head.

A procession of carriages containing those who have been newly "presented" falls into line behind the royal coaches in the forest of Saint-Germain. The custom was for the horses used for this ceremony to be lent to the debutants by the King's stables. François-René is given a "temperamental and skittish" mare called l'Heureuse. Despite all his riding experience, she nearly breaks his neck and runs away with him on the trail of a fallow deer that has just been brought down, and by the side of which there suddenly appears, at the same time as himself—the King!

Now, all the debutants had been told and told again, before the hunt began, how they were to behave and how, in no circumstances, were they ever to "cut the King's hunt," for that might easily trigger one of his towering rages.

Catastrophe! Chateaubriand is already imagining himself disgraced for the rest of the life he has not yet started to live. "I leap to the ground, pushing my mount back with one hand and sweeping my hat very low with the other. The King looks, and sees nothing but a debutant who got to the animal's last

---

*A very official royal hunt in the neighborhood of Versailles.

moments before himself; he had to say something; but instead of losing his temper, all he said to me, in a jovial tone and with a loud laugh, was, 'Well, that one didn't last long!'

"Those were the only words Louis XVI ever spoke to me."[6]

CALONNE

5

FEBRUARY 22, 1787

In an Agricultural Kingdom

Did François-René de Chateaubriand not know what was about to take place at Versailles, five days after the royal hunt? Apparently he did not.[1] In that respect, he was no different from most of the people in France. The gathering of the Assembly of Notables was creating much ado in the little world of Versailles and Paris but would not reach the ears of the rest of the kingdom until later, in the form of newspaper articles for the learned and Sunday sermons for the illiterate.

. . . And here we are back in the hall of the King's Menus Plaisirs, on February 22, 1787, the opening day of the Assembly.*

A hundred or so of the privileged among the privileged, seated around three sides of the hall, stare coldly at Charles-Alexandre de Calonne, comptroller general of finance, to whom they were still paying court only yesterday. But now, everything is different. According to the rumors that have been circulating all this long month of delay, he may be about to attack some of those precious privileges.

Him? Calonne?

Him. He's starting to do his job.

Sitting at a large table in the austere garb of the higher magistrates, he makes the speech of his life. He knows, he feels, behind him and three steps

---

*We now pick up the thread left dangling at the end of the previous volume, *Toward the Brink,* just as Calonne was beginning to speak.

up, the presence of the King and princes. He believes that the dignitaries to whom he is speaking, and who have been carefully selected by himself, are going to hear and approve him. So he goes ahead "with the confidence of a man sure of victory. His speech, perfectly written and spoken with all the graces of the most ingratiating declamation," is going to be "enthusiastically applauded by the very people who had previously sworn to bring about his downfall."[2]

With his opening lead, he blocks all opposition by hiding behind the pseudowill of Louis XVI:

"Gentlemen,

"The fact that the views which the King has instructed me to put forward to you in a body have become wholly his own makes it an even greater honor for me to perform what is demanded of me."[3]

In other words I, Calonne, have succeeded in persuading His Majesty to adopt my vision of things. "Three years have been spent in these essential preliminaries, and those three years have not been wasted.

"When at the end of 1783 the King deigned to entrust me with the administration of his finances, they were in the most critical condition." (Here come some red-hot cannonballs, aimed at Necker.) "The coffers were empty, public securities devalued, circulation at a standstill; alarm was widespread and confidence had been destroyed."*

Fortunately, St. Calonne was at the ready. He balances Necker's hair-raising summary with an idyllic tableau of the present situation. The navy has been restored; France has given birth to America and is trading, by treaty, with Holland, England and Russia; all treasury debts have been repaid; the port of Cherbourg is being built apace, as are those of Le Havre, La Rochelle, Dunkirk and Dieppe; canals are being cut in "several provinces"; the new East India Company "has redoubled the product of its efforts, since the King has permitted it to double its budget."

But "His Majesty has not lost sight of that which, in an agricultural kingdom, may be called the first and foremost of all manufactures: the cultivation of land. . . . Rural associations have been formed among landowners, churches and enlightened farmers, to carry out experiments and offer country populations the only lesson that will convince them, namely the setting of an example."

And he goes on to list the new quays in Marseilles and the new great square in Bordeaux, the rehabilitation of the center of Lyons, the restoration

---

*This is in flagrant contradiction to Necker's famous *Account Rendered*, which was bubbling over with optimism; its publication, in January 1781, brought about Necker's dismissal. See Volume II.

of the arena of Nîmes, the law courts of Aix, the clearing away of the houses that had been cluttering up the bridges of Paris . . . So is this Heaven? We're getting to the middle of the speech.

Oopsy-daisy. It's as though a gilded coach had overturned in the ditch. "I must admit, the annual deficit is very substantial." What does that mean? The word "deficit," by which France is going to be haunted from this moment on, simply means that the royal treasury is spending more than it receives. A shiver of fear runs through the Assembly when Calonne reveals that the public treasury collects only 475 million livres a year, but spends 600 million. The word is out; but perhaps he's going too far in his efforts to humiliate his predecessors. "The deficit stood at 37 million at the end of 1776; since that date, and until the end of 1786, 1,250 million have been borrowed."

This switch from the dreamiest of rose-colored visions to the promise of a quick march into the abyss makes his listeners' heads spin. At this stage in his speech, believing he could be sure of the outcome, Calonne moves without transition to a statement of the reforms he considers to be most urgently needed.* He declares war on the *abuses,* you heard him, of the most privileged members of society and proposes a relatively egalitarian allocation of taxes on a territorial basis; he wants produce to be allowed to travel freely within the kingdom, which can only lead to the abolition of certain provincial prerogatives (he calls it "relocating the fee-offices at the national frontiers"); he would like to see "the alleviation of the burden of the *gabelle,*† which I have never mentioned to His Majesty without his soul being feelingly moved to regret his inability to relieve his subjects from this charge altogether."

Having said what he has to say, Calonne closes with a clever curtain line: "Others may recall this maxim of our monarchy, 'As the King wills, so wills the Law'; His Majesty's motto is rather, 'As the people's happiness wills, so wills the King.' "

After talking for an hour and a half, the comptroller general of finance goes to kneel at the feet of his King, who looks extremely hungry and clearly seems somewhat overwhelmed by the extent of the good intentions being imputed to him. The sovereign, princes and ministers withdraw, leaving the Notables to gape.

Calonne is sure he's put a fast one over on them all. Wanna bet?

---

*Except, of course, that he never utters the inadmissible word "reform."
†The compulsory purchase of a certain quantity of salt at a fixed price.

6

FEBRUARY 1787

His Prostituted Name

Calonne has already received one shot in the legs: the pamphlet by Mirabeau*
which is making many "informed" tongues wag in Versailles and Paris.

One indication of the size of his audience is the heavily sarcastic noti-
fication of princes and powers throughout Europe, appearing in Grimm's
Correspondance littéraire, that "among the blessings attaching to this great age,
France will soon be able to count the joy of embracing to its bosom the
illustrious author of so many fine pamphlets against the Water Company, St.
Charles Bank, the Caisse d'Escompte, etc."[1]

Mirabeau has an itch for public action. He can't bear the thought that
the fate of France, and the rest of the world, should be determined without
help from him. He has scrambled in and out of hired coaches, leaving his
beloved Yet-Lie behind in Berlin, but for want of money and deftness in
human relations, he gets to Versailles too late to be used. He was hoping
to be first secretary of the Assembly of Notables; the job has been given to
Dupont de Nemours. In Calonne's pay only a minute ago, he was hoping
to gain some toehold on the ladder to a national role through the minister,
who, following an unexpected metamorphosis, has now become a reformer.

But he doesn't even get through the door. Like many of history's other
adventurers, he is kept pacing up and down in the waiting rooms. His false
friend Talleyrand has interposed himself as a screen between Mirabeau and
Calonne. So, as on so many previous occasions in his life, the only recourse
left him is to pick up his pen and write. In three weeks, he produces his
Dénonciation de l'agiotage au Roi et à l'Assemblée des Notables. At last, a text
signed "by the Comte de Mirabeau." In the days of the Notables' first sittings,
it's selling like hotcakes in the shops of a few Parisian booksellers.

---

*Left in Berlin at the end of Volume IV acting as a secret agent, more or less in the pay
of—Calonne!

His hangman of a father, the eternal marquis of hatred-for-his-son, still playing the same old part, informs his brother the *bailli* that people are paying as much as nine livres a copy for this 143-page booklet: "You know that since this person has been printing his prostituted name all over the place, he has assumed a tone of hauteur and insolent dignity, combined with the overcoat of the honest man and citizen; it's enough to make you vomit, laugh, or weep, to see the impudence with which he abuses the art of speech."[2]

This is not one of Mirabeau's best efforts—far from it. He obviously wrote it at a headlong gallop.

He starts off with a fanfare: "I had been in Berlin for nearly a year and expected to stay there several months more when I learned of the convening of an Assembly of Notables. I said to myself at once, On this solemn occasion you will pay the tribute of your feeble talents to your country, to your King."[3]

He continues in a mode of sustained polemic and denunciation, attacking the entire financial system of the realm. His first target is stockjobbing, market speculation [in French, *agiotage*—*Trans.*], which, according to him, "comes from *agio,* a corrupt Italian word meaning 'added, additional, supplementary.' The word was originally applied to any price in excess of the original, natural value of things and in particular to one currency in comparison to another of the same denomination; paper money, for example, as compared to specie."[4]

First of all, then, Mirabeau is getting at the great capitalists of his day, the people who have what he has always wanted: fortune, influence, means. He goes around in circles, he quotes himself with smug satisfaction, he pummels almost every page with stevedore's roars, "Aha . . . Hey there! . . . Really!" etc. The text reads more like the rough draft for a speech than a piece of writing. Sometimes one wonders what he's aiming at. Does he know himself? Is he trying to demolish Necker? No doubt, because when Necker was in power, he paid no attention to Mirabeau. But he might as well slaughter Calonne, too, while he's at it.

Is personal disappointment his only motive, the result of the minister's patent contempt for him? Informed by Talleyrand of Mirabeau's grudge against him, Calonne shrugs it off with "Bah, I'll fix him with money."[5] This comment, promptly carried back to its unfortunate object, sends him into a frenzy. He writes to Major Mauvillon, his new friend in Brunswick, "that there is still some juice left in the lemon the minister has thrown away and if Mirabeau was there for the taking, he may find a very different man when it comes to the leaving."[6]

So much for Calonne, then. Ever since his hand has been on the throttle, his policy, like that of Necker before him, has been to borrow rather than tax, and Mirabeau ranges around and around the arena in which he has already charged his adversaries several times, like a runaway bull:

"Spain sent us shares in the St. Charles Bank, which is not a bank; Cabarrus, its founder, was imitated in France; we have had an India Company that was compelled to place its hopes in fire insurance; another insurance company that makes a profit, by stockjobbing, for those who are prepared to insure themselves, and which exchanges shares that earn one hundred fifty percent for insurance premiums of ten sols per thousand livres. All these business absurdities, these obvious snares, are sustained, fed and inflated by the administrators of the relief bank, which discounts floating paper, for the use of which banks charge money and which they then lend to the ravening gamblers, fools or rogues who make up the army of stockjobbers that seeks to destroy what little wisdom, prudence and honesty we have left."[7]

Only those in the know can understand that this and many other passages in the text are aimed at the comptroller general of finance, whose policy has been founded on borrowing and discount facilities. As it happens, however, the author has chosen the wrong moment for his attack, since, in his speech to the Notables, Calonne is about to do an about-face and propose that the royal budget be salvaged by taxation instead of borrowing. But it's too late. Mirabeau has the bit between his teeth; in three pages he switches from high politics to a denunciation verging on blackmail, and this is why his pamphlet has become a best-seller, to the feigned disgust of his father.

He has found a scapegoat in the person of the Abbé d'Espagnac, a wealthy young priest who is vicar general at Sens and who, like Talleyrand himself, was one of those younger sons of rich families who would have been happier as plain and simple speculators instead of being compelled to operate through a Church in which they no longer believe. So it is, however: D'Espagnac has just made a kind of name for himself by reaping extravagant profits on market transactions.[8] His influence over Calonne is considerable, not because the minister is dishonest, which is unlikely, but because he is gullible. D'Espagnac has made a fortune by buying thousands of fictitious shares in the India Company and other similar bodies and selling them to the Treasury before they were ever in his possession. Who gave Mirabeau the confidential document setting out the details of this swindle?* Possibly Talleyrand, but there is no proof.

In any event, here he is tearing the Abbé d'Espagnac to shreds and, through him, Calonne, at the close of a few pages on recent developments on the world political scene:

"So it was for an Abbé d'Espagnac that the India Company was set up! It was for a stockjobbing priest that industrious ships' outfitters, hardworking

---

*D'Espagnac will go on, despite Calonne's dismissal, speculating and horse dealing in the corridors of power, even with the National Constituent Assembly. As army contractor, to Du Mouriez in particular, he will be arrested for fraud and guillotined in 1793.

merchants, respectable men, have been despoiled! Yes, it is for the sake of his insatiable greed, his conceited ignorance, his culpable presumptuousness, his criminal intriguing, that a commerce which was formerly conducted on true principles has been put in the hands of a monopoly with headquarters in Paris! It is the Abbé d'Espagnac, it is this pure man, this useful and virtuous citizen, who is now sharing with the state the rights abandoned to this monopoly, of which he has contrived to become the proprietor!"[9]

As a bonus, he publishes, at the end of his pamphlet, the *Plan des opérations de l'abbé d'Espagnac, pour soutenir et continuer le monopole des actions de la nouvelle Compagnie des Indes,* and a highly detailed plan it is, too, disclosing the names of a fair number of speculators.

His job done, Mirabeau finds himself stranded once again, although it's true that he is also becoming famous. In all modesty, he writes to Mauvillon that "the book has been prodigiously successful and may deserve to be so, as a public service rendered with courage and dignity. Most of the Notables, corporation leaders, honest people of all classes, have congratulated and thanked me. From the notaries' offices to the fair ladies' boudoirs, I've been read, praised, preached."[10]

Maybe; but Calonne is beginning to be sorry he was so contemptuous and would be much happier not to have a scandal raging in these critical days. Shares in the India Company are plummeting, the Caisse d'Escompte is shaky. Compelled by public opinion to condemn the Abbé d'Espagnac to a nonviolent exile, the minister is also compelled to allocate twelve million livres to him—from state funds—"for damages."

Will he let the lonely denunciator get away with it? Two men knock at the door of the furnished rooms in which, for want of any better accommodations, Mirabeau is camping out at Versailles. Why, it's Talleyrand and Dupont de Nemours—his dear friends . . . who tell him that at the behest of the King, who is infuriated by all this agitation, the Baron de Breteuil has just signed a *lettre de cachet* (another one!) relegating him to Saumur or the fortress of Ham, they're not quite sure which.*

Mirabeau panics; with no protectors and less money, even the last resort of hiding out with his father is no longer open to him. One more hope crushed. In the days when the Notables, whose inspiration he had wanted to be, are beginning their conclave, he finds himself back on the road to exile again, heading for Liège in the Austrian Low Countries, where he writes

---

*This letter did exist but remained in the archives of the King's Household. It was found preferable, no doubt on the advice of Calonne, who was compromised on both sides, to intimidate Mirabeau without actually imprisoning him. In its issue for Friday, March 30, 1787, the *Gazette de Leyde* mentions Pierre-Encise. The name of the governor and location of the prison are left blank in the text of the *lettre de cachet*.

mournful letters to his sweet Henriette de Nehra, always on the horizon of his emotional life, asking her to leave Berlin and join him as soon as possible. But neither of them has enough money to pay for the trip.

At his heels runs a pure Parisian epigram, broadcast by Grimm:*

O weighty Mirabeau, may your
    potent homily
Bring down the rogues who're
    spoiling all our trade!

The thief converted now must
    hangman be,
Preaching as his erstwhile mates
    upon the rack are laid.[11]

GOETHE

MRS. GOETHE (NICE LEGS)

7

FEBRUARY 1787

Everything Is Rising Up in Me at Once

This same month, February 1787, while a few bigwigs in Versailles are starting to rattle the bars, one man, a long way off in body and in spirit, is changing the thread of his life. Johann Wolfgang Goethe has just run away from Weimar, to Italy.†

Running away, running out, all of it.

He's thirty-eight years old and has prepared for this trip the way a convict prepares for an escape attempt. Does that mean he was unhappy in Weimar? That's not the real question. For the past eleven years he's been pretending he was alive. He is one of the most important figures in the little German Court and has just been ennobled by the Emperor, at the request of the Grand Duke of Weimar: now people have to call him "von Goethe." Maybe that's why he wants to get off the merry-go-round.

His record of his travels in Italy is kept in the form of letters to an

---

*And attributed to Rivarol.

†See Volume I for Goethe's beginnings; I left him just as he was appointed adviser to Grand Duke Charles Augustus of Weimar and was starting to concern himself with politics.

imaginary beloved. On February 24, at Sant' Agata near Naples, his pen
exudes relief:

> Just as we were leaving Fondi it began to grow light and we were instantly
> greeted by oranges hanging over the walls on both sides of the way. The trees
> are as weighted down with them as can be imagined. Their young leaves are
> yellowish at the top, but at the bottom and in the middle, the richest green. . . .
> The road went on through the valley, between stony but well-plowed wheat-
> fields of the finest green. In a few places one saw special spaces, round and
> paved, surrounded by low walls: the grain is threshed there on the spot, not
> brought back to the house in sheaves. The valley narrowed, the roadway
> mounted, bare limestone boulders rose up on either side. The wind blew in
> fierce gusts behind us. Hail fell, and melted very slowly. . . .
> Then we caught sight of Vesuvius, with a cloud of smoke at its summit.[1]

For the last six months Goethe has been in the throes of his one true
love affair, the discovery and embracing of Italy. Italys, one ought to write:
one Italy in Verona and another in Venice, one in Rome and another in
Naples.

> One can have no idea, if one has not seen it, of the beauty of a walk through
> Rome under a full moon. Every detail is drowned in great masses of light and
> shadow, and only the most grandiose and universal images confront the gaze.
> For three days we have well and fully rejoiced in the brightest and most mag-
> nificent nights. One particularly lovely aspect is that offered by the Coliseum.
> It is shut at night; a hermit lives there, near a little church, and beggars huddle
> beneath the dilapidated vaults. They had made a fire on the ground and a breeze
> drove the smoke toward the arena, shrouding the lower part of the ruins while
> above emerged the dark bulk of the massive walls; we stood outside the iron
> gates and watched the phenomenon; the moon was shining brightly, high in the
> heavens. Little by little, the smoke passed between the partitions and filled all
> the interstices and openings, and the moon illuminated it like fog. It was a
> ravishing sight. It is in this light that the Pantheon, the Capitol, the square
> outside St. Peter's basilica and the other great streets and squares should be
> seen.[2]

In passing, he had contracted one of those ambiguous relationships that
suit him so well: "And just now as I am about to leave Rome, I am forging
delicate bonds of friendship with kindly intentioned persons. I feel an emotion that is both pleasant and painful, when I begin to believe that someone
is sorry to let me go."[3]

Early in February, at Candlemas, he went to the Sistine Chapel "for the
ceremony of the blessing of the tapers. I immediately felt very ill at ease and

was not long in taking my leave, with my friends. I was thinking that these are the very tapers that for three hundred years have been muddying those splendid paintings, and this is the very incense that, with holy impudence, not only hides this unique sun of art from view but is obscuring it year by year and will ultimately turn it completely black."[4]

On this trip, he has one of the supreme experiences of his existence. On February 17 the weather was "unbelievably and indescribably fine; apart from four days of rain, the whole month of February has been pure, clear skies, and almost too warm at noon. Now we want to go out into the countryside, and although thus far one's mind has been taken up solely with gods and heroes, suddenly the landscape is coming into its own again, and one is becoming attached to one's natural surroundings, which are animated by the most splendid daylight."[5]

"I have seen the sea twice, first the Adriatic, then the Mediterranean, but as though in passing. We must become more closely acquainted in Naples. Everything is rising up in me at once."[6]

And will go on rising. He had to get to Naples, it was his pagan pilgrimage. On February 25,

> at last, we reached the plain of Capua and shortly thereafter Capua itself, where we lunched.
>
> Vesuvius was still on our left, throwing up dense smoke, and I was silently rejoicing to see this remarkable sight at last with my own eyes. The sky grew lighter and lighter and at last the sun sent piercing rays into our cramped moving quarters. The weather as we came into Naples was utterly serene; and then we found ourselves truly in another country. The flat-roofed houses indicate a different climate; perhaps they are not very nice inside. Everybody lives out of doors and sits in the sun as long as it is pleased to shine. The Neapolitan believes that heaven is his and has a very grim notion of northern lands: *Sempre neve, case di legno, gran ignoranza, ma dinari assai.* That is his picture of our lot. For the edification of Germanic peoples, here is what the words mean: "Snow and more snow, wooden houses, great ignorance, but piles of money."
>
> At first sight, Naples itself looks gay, free and lively; countless people are hurrying in all directions, the King is hunting, the Queen is expecting an heir, so all is for the best.[7]

What's got into him? He is already in the middle of his life; as he has just written to his parents, he has risen as high as a "Frankfurt burgher" can rise. He has no money problems and has been living, for the moment, without attachments. All the more reason, then, to indulge that yearning for escape that haunts most creators, and many other human beings too.

Weimar? It's worth an escape attempt: a town of six thousand souls, the houses are all plain, or just plain hovels, chickens and swine wander down paths of beaten earth and the wagons meet nothing but a few Court carriages. The center of a microscopic set of provinces, the most important among them being Jena. The town belongs to the Emperor, it buzzes with the agitation of a Court that is more bourgeois than aristocratic. Goethe has tried to introduce a few modest reforms, aimed in particular at improving the status of the peasantry, "the marrow of the country, good people, hard-working and simple, dressed in shirts with no buttons, held together by leather thongs. They are too poor to buy buttons, and cut their own thongs to fit their bodies."[8]

But how could a man actually survive there, even if he belonged to the upper echelons of the Court? The rest of its members are all "toads and basilisks. If one attempts to step outside one's house, all one puts one's feet in is shit."[9]

> In the narrow streets, you could look out your window and see your neighbor looking back at you from his, and most of the windows had no curtains. You could identify every step, even at night; the streets were unlit, one had to grope one's way through the dark holding a lantern in front of one's face. Everybody knew everybody, the Court society was the object of the most prying curiosity. All the servants, from cooks to footmen, told everything that went on. People knew (and this was an affair of state) when Charles-Augustus had slept with his wife, and they knew even better that he did not often do so. They knew every detail of the lives of the ladies and gentlemen of the Court, and of their loves. They themselves wrote and chattered about all these matters with the greatest freedom, and took enormous pleasure in doing so.[10]

So the town itself is sufficient reason to run away. What about its sovereign? The days are long gone when Charles Augustus, the reigning Grand Duke, would piss on decent folks' doors when he was out on a spree with his friend Goethe. "With his short, thick head, his broad short nose and heavy jaw, he looked like one of his own gamekeepers."[11] The era of wild oats is over for him and for Goethe, too, and now Charles Augustus has persuaded his powerful neighbor Frederick II to give him a regiment to lead in the Prussian armies.

Goethe, always hovering around the fringes of a kind of pederasty, was undoubtedly pained by this development. He resisted. He struggled, especially for the renovation of the Ilmenau silver mine, the great government scheme on which he was counting to eliminate Weimar's perpetual budget deficit.[12] And which ended, in a shipwreck of mud and rocks. The only food his political appetite has given him to eat thus far is thistles.

Even so, he has managed, in the last ten years, to write seventeen hundred letters to a lady-in-waiting of the Duchess Louise of Weimar—

Charlotte von Stein, the wife of a Master of the Horse who saw his spouse no more than three times a year at most. Did Goethe really love her? Did they ever even make love? She was small, she was dark, she was withered. But she was a second mother to him, better than the one in Frankfurt. She remade him. "Drop by drop, you poured moderation into my overardent blood."[13] At the end of ten years of romantic friendship, when the time comes to look at the bottom line, he will cherish a strong grudge against Charlotte for having turned him, or so he believes, into an old man.

Five years before the break, or at the halfway mark, Charlotte was already telling a friend that "we can no longer speak together without hurting each other."[14] But Goethe went on writing screeds to her, talking about himself even when his subject was the whole world. Charlotte was a convenient mirror.

"My opinion of women does not derive from actual fact; it was inborn in me, or grew in me, God knows how. That is why the female characters I have created have been successful: they are all better than the women one can meet with in real life."

She's well aware of this, and never forgives him.

As time passed, he came to feel justified in his fear of and contempt for women, even if an occasional gala soirée found him flirting gallantly with one or another of them. He was growing increasingly open in his preference for masculine camaraderie, and what he had appreciated most about Charlotte was that she had given him her adolescent son, Fritz von Stein, for three years. During that time, Goethe tried to turn him into a sort of improvised scribe, part whipping boy, part spoiled brat.

When the youth was old enough to live on his own and had succeeded in escaping, at top speed, into the army in Prussia, Goethe "adopted" a retarded lad, whom he rebaptized Kraft [= Power]; then, when that one died prematurely, he acquired a half-savage Swiss lad with whom he was very much infatuated. "The boy belongs to me now. I am going to see if I can make what I hope to of him."[15] But this ungovernable youngster also rebelled, and also disappeared. Goethe never loved wisely, if he loved at all.

Another indication of his preference for boys is his cohabitation in Weimar with his factotum Philip Seidel, part servant, part secretary, part coachman. Seidel often slept on a straw pallet in his master's room. They would have endless conversations, some echoes of which have survived in Seidel's notes. On the subject of Corsica, for example, when the whole of "enlightened" Europe, following in Rousseau's footsteps, was thrilling to its armed combat, first against Genoa, then against France:*

*In this connection, see the opening of the chapter on Bonaparte's childhood in Volume II.

We skipped from one subject to another. . . . We roughhoused until about four in the morning. The question we were debating so vehemently all that time was this, whether a people is happier free or under a sovereign's dominion? I had said, the Corsicans are truly unhappy. He [Goethe] said, "No, it is the good fortune of themselves and their descendants to have the chance to become refined and civilized and to learn about the arts and sciences, whereas in the past they were coarse and uncouth."

"My master," I said, "what the devil good would it do me to be civilized and learnèd if I lost my freedom, which is precisely what gives us happiness? Except for those who live in the mountains, the Corsicans cannot really be savages; otherwise, they would not have so high a sense of freedom and they would not have shown so much courage. They used to be happy. They could satisfy all their own needs without any fuss, because their needs were not imaginary. Now they have more needs than before and they are unable to satisfy them, because none of us can dress and eat and drink and entertain himself as much as he would like. They had everything they desired because they did not require much, but could enjoy what they had in freedom.[16]

During all this time Goethe has created nothing, except a conventional *Iphigenia* and a few essays on a developing discipline in which he has already acquired some expertise: science. He has developed such a passion for prehistory and anatomy that he has sent, at prodigious expense, for the skull of an elephant, which he has hidden away in the most remote room of his lodging "in order that I may not be thought mad. My landlady supposed that the huge crate it came in contained porcelain."[17]

He's convinced he has discovered the human intermaxillary bone, which would provide a missing link in the chain of the evolution of species.

But nobody is paying any attention to him.

Outwardly, he has never been so well off. He has five servants to take care of him and his pretty house. His word is law at Court, even in the Grand Duke's absence. He is honored, enriched, gorged. So it is high time that he should yield to that impulse rising out of his inner depths, his ten-year-old dream "of a clandestine voyage."[18]

He has made exhaustive preparations for his departure; only Seidel knows what is up. He asks the Grand Duke for a leave of absence for an indefinite period of time, without mentioning that his destination is Italy, a Mediterranean land, whereas he himself is purest Teutonic. At 3:00 A.M. on September 3, 1786, he slips into a post chaise accompanied by a belt purse and one suitcase, and the pseudonym Jean-Philippe Möller. Bound for Verona, Venice, Rome, Naples.

A few days later, going through the customary social routine expected of distinguished guests, he meets one of the most alluring women of the day* in the rooms of Lord Hamilton, the English ambassador to Naples, and the impression she makes upon him is lasting:

> Lord Hamilton, who is still living here as ambassador of England, has now, after so long a career as a lover of art and so long a study of nature, found the summit of the pleasures of both nature and art united in one pretty girl. He has her in his home, she's an Englishwoman, about twenty years old. She is extremely beautiful and shapely. He has had a Greek costume made for her that suits her perfectly, and when she wears it she lets her hair loose, takes a pair of shawls and abandons herself to such a variety of attitudes, gestures and plays of expression that at the end one really does think one is dreaming. What so many thousands of painters would have been mightily pleased to execute is seen performed here in motion and with astonishing versatility. Standing, kneeling, seated, lying down, serious, sad, mischievous, lascivious, contrite, provocative, threatening, fearful etc., each attitude follows the last and grows out of it. For each expression she knows how to choose and vary the folds of her veil, and she produces a hundred different headdresses with the same scrap of material. The old knight holds the lamp meanwhile; he has given himself up to this object with all his soul.[19]

Soon she will be Lady Hamilton. . . . Goethe seldom spends so much time on a woman, in this case one who is spoken of by everyone in Naples as a high-class tart. At the moment, she goes under a false name, Emmy Hart, but she is in reality the daughter of "Henry Lyon, a blacksmith in England, and his wife Mary, and was born on May 12, 1765."[20]

Her father probably died soon after her birth; her mother lived on in Flintshire. At thirteen, picked up on the streets of London, she was already being noticed by painters, financiers and men of the world, through whom she gained a small celebrity.

A lucky stroke brought her into the orbit of Sir Charles Greville, an aging beau in search of a companion. She was promoted to the rank of "kept woman." Like a miniature Comtesse du Barry, she came to preside over a great household and was received in London society; people began talking about her on the continent.

In 1784, she entertained, among others, Charles Greville's uncle, Sir William Hamilton, the English ambassador to Naples: "He was a well-built man with a comely face indicative of intelligence and the elegant refinement

---

*She plays a political role, as well as providing food for gossip, in the affairs of the Kingdom of Naples and the Two Sicilies. Bisexual in nature, she exerts considerable influence over Marie Antoinette's intimidating sister, Queen Marie Caroline, but also, at the end of the century, over Lord Nelson.

of aristocratic breeding. At that time he was over fifty, but did not look his age. A skeptic in all things save where women were concerned, he had been a widower for the past nine years" . . . And he seems to have "bought" young Emma in a transaction "between men," with his own nephew.[21]

Now, still going under the name of Miss Hart, she is Lord Hamilton's official mistress.

SAINT-JUST

8

FEBRUARY 1787

The Only Remedy in My Power Is the Future

At a time when the third estate is finally beginning to have a voice in the fate of the nation, the son of one minor dignitary of the Soissonnais region finds himself having to eat crow.

For the last five months Louis-Antoine de Saint-Just has been shut up, at his mother's behest, in a sort of reformatory at Picpus.* More than enough punishment for the "theft" of two or three pieces of family silver, and the youth who was refusing to sign his statement to the police last autumn is now prepared to bow to superior forces. He wants so much to get back to the forest of Blérancourt again, and his friends and his loves. He writes a letter of submission and repentance to the Chevalier d'Evry, the local gentleman and friend of his mother who was responsible for getting him locked up:

Paris, February 26, 1787.

Sir,

On bended knee I crave your forgiveness for not answering more promptly the letter you were kind enough to write me. I caught a fever about a fortnight ago and have been unable to hold a pen. It was nothing serious, however, and I am almost as fit now as I was before.

---

*See Volume IV for the circumstances of Saint-Just's flight and imprisonment. He has not yet turned twenty; his father, a career officer, died a year before.

Thank you for your advice; a determination to do the right thing preceded it, and I shall follow it if I do not deviate from the plan I have worked out for myself. I have just written to *maman* and sent her a letter for Rigaux.* I trust this effort will be successful, unless someone else has stepped in ahead of me. You notified me in your letter that the reply was to be sent to *maman* so that she could send it on to you. That was my intention, for although I did not at all wish to give her my address, I thank you all the same for your advice, because it may be that I was acting only in my own interest in this matter and you have made me act decently. That proves that you see much better and more astutely than I. I can, however, assure you of all my esteem and gratitude, because they do not necessitate any astuteness. . . .

I have the honor to be, sir, your most humble and obedient servant.[1]

To the bitter end, his mother and two younger sisters have been writing loveless letters to him from Blérancourt. At the end of October Marianne Robinot, Saint-Just's widow, was still writing to her dear "friend," the Chevalier d'Evry, that he was not to pay any debts her son might have contracted in "the house of Madame de Sainte-Colombe": "He has already caused me sufficient useless expenditure, without the least return, for me to have nothing further to do with his wild extravagance [*sic*]. It will be for him to deal with, when he comes of age to enter into his rights. . . . I did not expect that anything much would ever be recovered of the things he took from my home."[2]

Her only remaining recourse was to fall ill of her own hysteria, which she duly did that winter. "If my son has any feelings left at all, he must be reproaching himself for the sorrows he has given me, as in my present circumstances they may well cause my death. It is a poor way of repaying all the tenderness and affection I have always felt for him."[3]

Louise, one of the younger sisters, sends the soon-to-be-liberated youth a proper dressing-down:

> Dear Brother, I should have liked to give you more comforting news of maman, but can only tell you, to my pain, that she is in the same situation as before. An obstinate fever and incoercible aversion weaken her daily. My sister is also sick, and has been for the same length of time. Judge of my hardship, especially that of seeing what is most dear to us in such a state. She was waiting for M. Rigaux's reply before writing to you, she is fully satisfied with it. There is no point in my telling you what it says, since I am forwarding it to you.
>
> There must be no other thought, dear brother, than that of progressing in the condition which you are to enter upon, in order to restore maman altogether.

*A young advocate in Soissons who was prepared to take Saint-Just on as a clerk.

She has great need of such consolation because not only her fever but the sorrows she has been through have put her in this state. Her situation alone should be enough to encourage you to reflect wisely.*[4]

He may as well make a good job of it, while he's at it; so before climbing into the stagecoach for Noyon, Louis-Antoine abases himself a little further to the Chevalier d'Evry: "Maman, according to all I hear, is going from bad to worse. It is sad for me to be unable to hide from myself the fact that I have some share in her illness, because of the grief I have caused her; but what is done cannot be undone. The only remedy in my power is the future."[5]

Louis-Antoine now has two personalities, as is often the case with young people whose worth has not been recognized: one, that of a young man who has been brought to heel and is about to become, unenthusiastically, the second of four clerks in Advocate Rigaux's firm; and the other, that of the secret author of an extended and baroque poem in twenty cantos, which he has long dreamed of writing and which his period of detention has just enabled him to get on paper. No one knows of it yet, but he himself is reveling in it, avenging himself by completing it, consoling himself with the thought that at the age of twenty he has been capable of producing *Les aventures du chevalier Organt*.†

A hodgepodge. A bizarre medley of verse, the lines often halting, the rhymes approximate, that sweeps the reader along into a torrent of images and ideas but gives no hint where the author wants to go. Clearly, he doesn't know himself, and to give free rein to his obsessions, he simply hides behind a curtain of historico-legendary parable. We're in the days of Charlemagne, it seems, but the screen soon becomes transparent because Charlemagne is Louis XV, or Louis XVI; a woman named Adelinde is Madame du Barry; a cruel queen shows hints of features then being attributed to Marie Antoinette.[6] There's much more in the grab bag, behind various pseudonyms, from Beaumarchais to d'Estaing, from the senior prelates to the actors of the Comédie-Française.

The one sure thing is that Organt is Saint-Just himself, as he tells us by giving his own name, Antoine, to this alleged bastard son of Turpin, arch-

---

*On March 30, 1787, the lieutenant general of police signed the order releasing Louis-Antoine, "at the gracious pleasure" of the Baron de Breteuil, minister of the King's Household.

†At the risk of repeating myself I must again, as at the end of Volume IV, draw attention to the originality of this odd work and the riches it contains, and I would point out that none of the main figures of the Revolution had written anything comparable before it. Saint-Just published *Les aventures du chevalier Organt* in 1789.

bishop of Sens, who sets off down all the highways of heaven and earth, in the company of his guardian angel, to fight, philosophize, polemicize and abundantly fornicate. Some of the passages of this epic are so untrammeled and crude that they would have put Saint-Just back inside Madame de Saint-Colombe's establishment the moment they were published, if they had been published when he wrote them. There's a touch of Sade here:

In his cynical fury the monk in rut
Puts a lascivious hand on her charms so round,
With eager arm lays her out on the ground,
While she cries out in tears, "But Holy Father, Oh, but—!"

All in vain: his rough mustachio nips,
Pursues and presses the elusive lips.
With excitement and also with rage she is fraught,
She curses him but with cunt writhing hot,
And at times her virtue is quite forgot.[7]

So debauchery skims the surface of the work from start to finish, often embodied in an ambivalent creature, now donkey, now monk, who has little time to spare for refinements. He "most tenderly claims"

The donkey's rights, the lover's rights too.
How sweet, though, are donkey's rights at these games—

In the arms of one's fainting lover to woo.[8]

When the pace steps up, the influence of Rabelais becomes more perceptible:

The pope in heat, armed with official stole,

Catechized from the heights of the Capitol,
And all for a farting saint.[9]

He's got it in for saints, in fact, "who play at learning and heat his bile":

There's nothing can stop me; for
   me, sin's free!

And what's it to you if a sinner
   I be?[10]

References to both legend and contemporary history abound, giving
Organt a prophetic tone:

The bleeding Rhine calls me to
   its bed;

We'll sing of honor, of folly, of
   the dead.[11]

And since he's writing in 1786, how could he fail to mention the
"Queen's necklace"?

From all this din it is easy to
   guess
That the matter is crucial and
   nothing less.
If our trustworthy chroniclers
   are telling true
The cause of all the cries and
   shrieks
Was the theft, milords, of a
   woman's jewel.
You must know that for six unending weeks

The talk of wise man and the
   talk of fool
Was of naught but the jewel,
   the jewel, the jewel.
It was talked of at table *chez*
   Monsieur the Prince,
In every boudoir in the whole
   province;
This one jewel raised more hul-
   labaloo
Than a thousand crimes of state
   could do.[12]

But he doesn't spare Louis XVI either:

The King! The King! Whose
   dire indolence

Knows nothing, alas! of the
   woes of France.[13]

That France that he loves:

For our ancestors, too, like us,
   were vain,
Fine fellows and gay; and with
   greedy maws

Gobbled up the fumes of fame.
To the last man among them,
   such are the Gauls.[14]

When he has a moment, Organt muses about the possible fate in store
for him, producing an abundance of utopian imagery:

I want to build a lovely dream;
It will fill my leisure, and myself
　with mirth;
For that while, I am King of the
　earth.[15]

I pity those who are put to
　shame

By chance and fate, a simple
　game;
I fear naught. When once I've
　breathed my last,
If against its blows my soul
　stands fast,
Dead I may be, yet at death I'll
　laugh.[16]

At the beginning of Canto XVII there's a surprise in store for the historian who can see things coming. Here we can leave Louis-Antoine's vengeful manuscript in his suitcase as he emerges from his term of detention; we'll see it again. It will be published. Just be patient . . .

Long he gazed at those quaking
　stones,
Mt. Etna's searing guts and
　bones,
The dire debris where *la Ter-
　reur** holds sway.
Above the abyss you see her
　stray,
Plumbing the depths, girt round
　by hosts
Of goblins and ogres, shades
　and ghosts.
Close by, flights of dreams flut-
　ter and wheel:

Each night *la Terreur* her flocks
　she drives,
A deathblow to tyrants' sleep to
　deal,
With flaming stakes and blood-
　ied knives,
And the gashing vulture that
　flags, she revives.
The heartless she makes, as in
　bed they toss,
To feel some friend has be-
　trayed them, and loss, and
　loss.[17]

*Author's italics.

9

APRIL 1787

Like M. Restif de la Bretonne

In the spring of 1787 another man of liberty—in Saint-Just's generation—publishes a "licentious" novel, the smug success of which, throughout enlightened Europe, is assured by a squib in Grimm and Meister's *Correspondance littéraire: "Une année de la vie du chevalier Faublas,* five small volumes":

> This relates one year in the life of a young man of condition making his debut in the world; he is sixteen, comes to Paris and falls desperately in love with Sophie de Pontis, a young person living in the same convent as his sister. But his grand passion does not prevent him from indulging in fresh illusions daily; he spends his time reconciling his true love with his amorous conquests. . . . The fair Marquise de B —— is the happy enchantress who undertakes to educate our young Hercules; she is a woman of twenty-four or five who knows how to make the most of everything, has no scruples about anything, and combines the most imperturbable presence of mind with infinite sophistication, intrigue and seduction. Her husband is just as one might wish him, as smug as he is stupid, a true comic figure. It is true that in the end his eyes are opened and he attempts to avenge his honor, but most unsuccessfully. He is killed, and although the chevalier is obliged to flee after the duel, he takes his dear Sophie along with him for consolation. She turns out to be the daughter of his father's best friend, and he marries her.
>
> The author of this novel is Monsieur Louvet,* a young man of twenty-six or seven who, like M. Restif de la Bretonne and the celebrated Richardson,†

---

*Jean-Baptiste Louvet de Couvray is born in Paris on June 12, 1760, and dies there, of illness, on August 25, 1797. Between these two dates he is famous twice; once for his *Faublas* series and once because of the not negligible role he plays in politics after 1789, and even more after 1792, as one of the main figures in the Girondin group in the Convention, which Robespierre is opposing. He falls with them, narrowly escapes death, and remains loyal to the Republic.

†Samuel Richardson (1689–1761); the English author, some forty years before, of two highly successful novels, which were still much in fashion in Europe: *Pamela* and *Clarissa Harlowe*.

started out in life as foreman in a printing shop. Like his hero, he has found a Sophie; he has married her, and it is her modest dowry that enables him, it is said, to devote himself entirely to his literary pursuits.[1]

Faublas is beginning to pass from hand to hand. It's one of the first libertine books ever published under its author's own name; and although biographical material is scarce, it is possible to rectify one or two of Grimm's approximations. Louvet was born in Paris on the rue Saint-Denis, the son of a stationer or paper manufacturer who seems to have treated him rather harshly. "He was a stern and brutal father whose coarser constitution could never divine the secrets of the constitution of his son."[2]

He made his own way to adulthood. He may have worked in the offices of Dietrich the ironmaster,* then as a clerk for Pruault the bookseller. At that stage, like Beaumarchais and many others, he ennobled himself for nothing, by adding a place-name, Couvray, to his own name. In the bookshop, he soaked up the atmosphere of the age; he was an avid reader, full of imagination and desires. "At seventeen, dressed in women's clothes, he could have slipped under the guard of a jealous husband,"[3] but he soon matured and turned into a slender little fellow "with weak eyes and untidy dress;† he is unnoticeable to the common person, who does not see the nobility of his brow and the fire that burns in his eyes and features whenever he encounters some great truth, fine feeling, ingenious repartee or subtle jest."[4]

Such as he is, and even before acquiring the somewhat blurred reputation that comes to him as a result of his first *Faublas,* he loves and is loved; which is what Grimm is alluding to. She is a woman named Cholet, who found herself mismated to a jeweler living near the Palais-Royal and has presumably known Louvet since childhood. She has "regular features, a simple and noble bearing. From the habitual composure of her physiognomy one might readily infer a lofty soul and a strong will."[5] She is firmly anchored on the horizon of this most sedate author's heart and senses, however much his contemporaries are about to suppose him a rampaging Don Juan.

What a gulf between himself and his novel! And what an abyss between the genius of a Laclos or a Restif‡ and the honeyed facility of Louvet! A lazy reader might easily spend a year on the *Année de la vie de Faublas.* It was highly courageous of Grimm to produce his succinct résumé of such a verbose, lachrymose muddle, positively incoherent at times, in which the author

---

*During the Revolution, Dietrich is mayor of Strasbourg; Rouget de Lisle first sings *"La Marseillaise"* in his home.

†According to Madame Roland.

‡See Volume III, on the anonymous publication in 1782 of *Les liaisons dangereuses,* by Choderlos de Laclos; and Volume I, on Restif de la Bretonne, the first author to come from "the people."

wavers between trashy eroticism and Rousseauian elegiacs. The "pure girl" he loves at first sight through the screen of a convent parlor is the young Sophie, yes, and it is she he will marry in the fullness of time. But his initiator is a handsome young woman of the liberated persuasion, ten years his senior, whom Faublas' naturally calls Maman, "la Marquise de B ———."

A typical instance of this incessant switching from the platonic to the sensual is the passage below, which occurs somewhere around the middle of *Faublas:*

> It is time to return to Sophie. At last it dawns, the third day! I can go to the convent to see my fair cousin. Oh, how much more beautiful she has grown in the last three days!
>
> For quite two months, it was my joy to converse with her regularly twice a week in the parlor. O prodigious power of virtue and beauty united! When leaving my Sophie I always imagined that it was impossible I should love her more, and each time I saw her I felt that my love had increased.
>
> I must confess, however, that during those two months I often saw the fair Marquise who, still resolved upon the scheme of reform which she had indeed adopted, was so sparing of our pleasures as sometimes to refuse me the bare essentials. I must also confess that my pretty little Justine,* who knew perfectly well where I lived, would come to see me incognito, to reap the benefit of her mistress's parsimony.[6]

These adventures proceed in an agreeable atmosphere of gilded idleness, a condition of which the young printer's foreman from Saint-Denis must often have dreamed. Here's Faublas out on a foray, accosted by an officer of the peace:

> "Here, friend, who are you?"
> "Sir, I am the Chevalier de Faublas, your very respectful servant."
> "Ah, so sorry, sir! Where are you staying?"
> "With my father, the Baron de Faublas, rue de l'Université."
> "What do you do there?"
> "Precious little, like so many young men of quality."[7]

Now and then a ripple skates across the stagnant waters of the tale. For instance, Faublas's entrance into Paris, at the age of sixteen, where his doughty father has brought him to sow his wild oats:

> We entered the capital in October 1783, by the faubourg Saint-Marceau. I was looking out for that splendid city of which I had read such brilliant

---

*The Marquise's maid, who is, of course, in on everything.

descriptions. I saw ugly, high-thatched huts, long, very narrow streets, wretches clothed in rags, a horde of half-naked children; I saw the great population and the appalling misery. I asked my father if this was Paris; he coldly replied that this was not the finest part of town.[8]

Faublas does, thus, have a few redeeming features, such as this persiflage on "the noble art of warfare": "I diligently applied myself to the study of geometry; above all I trained myself in that noble trade that makes one hero at the expense of one hundred thousand unfortunates, and that men, more vainglorious than humane, have called the great art of war."[9]

In this vein, if Louvet-Faublas had wanted, had been able . . . but flashes of this kind are fleeting indeed in this enormous amphigory.* Halfway through, the text goes off at a tangent and turns into a sort of contemporary historical novel focused on events in Poland and Russia, in which Europe was keenly interested. Faublas meets a great Polish aristocrat in exile, who tells him a tale in which the heroine was his own wife, Lodoiska, who died of exhaustion in the deep forest in which the last rebels were fleeing the troops of Catherine II and hoping to join forces with the great Cossack insurgent, Pugachev.†

A further misfortune: Count Lovzinski, the Pole, had a daughter by Lodoiska, a child endowed with every grace and virtue—little Dorliska, who disappeared in the upheaval; tears streaming down his face, the Count shows the young man a miniature of her.

Faublas cries out, "What a lovely face! She looks just like my Sophie!"[10]

You guessed it, although it takes another hundred pages for everybody else in the book to perceive that Sophie and the young Polish girl are one. Faublas marries her in the last line of the book. Louvet has already started calling Madame Cholet "Lodoiska."

---

*Littré defines the word in French as "a piece of farcical writing filled with gibberish." [Webster defines the word in English as "a rigmarole with apparent meaning which proves to be meaningless."—*Trans.*]

†On the Pugachev uprising and its aftermath in 1774, see Volume I.

10

MARCH—APRIL 1787

This Infamous Bankrupt

For all his too-apparent cunning, Calonne is naive. Having raised the alarm and set the Notables to work in their seven rooms, each committee or group presided over and, he hopes and trusts, kept in check by a prince of the blood, he feels confirmed in his mission and in his office; especially as the King still seems to trust him.

And yet, almost at once—at the beginning of March—people start exchanging ominous rumors about him. For example, we read in the March 9 issue of Lescure's *Correspondance secrète,* the confidential newsletter addressed to the rich and powerful of enlightened Europe:

"The Assembly of Notables is the mountain that will give birth to a mouse or . . . to a new comptroller general.* It was not anticipated that the mountain would display so much patriotism or energy. Among its most active members, and those who deserve the qualification, to borrow a phrase from the English, of 'leaders of the opposition,' is the archbishop of Toulouse [Loménie de Brienne], now making up for the scant success he has had hitherto."[1]

In the same issue, the reporter considers the other side of the question:

"For his part, M. de Calonne has completely taken over the mind of the King. We are assured that he said to His Majesty, 'I have performed the duties of a zealous and faithful minister; but I fear that in making my speech I have signed my dismissal, and will be sacrificed as M. Turgot was.'

" 'Fear nothing,' replied the King; 'I was a child then, now I am a man.' "[2]

"Calonne's term as a member of the government offers a striking example

---

*It will become clear from what follows that Lescure, himself a wealthy man if not actually a Notable, is not on Calonne's side. But as an astute journalist he knows how to "frame" the historical debate that is taking shape between Calonne and Brienne.

of the inability of a minister of finance to obtain effective results when his technical decisions, however excellent they may be, do not form part of an overall policy."[3]*

Turgot had one, and so did Necker. Calonne-the-pragmatist is finally emerging from a long euphoria and, just when he is seriously becoming minister of finance, and just when the kingdom is on the verge of bankruptcy, all he can do is patch and glue one day at a time, his present precipitancy made all the more pathetic by his past stagnation. His friend Talleyrand is greatly distressed and will defend him to the last;† he here learns one of his first lessons in applied history: "Delay, in matters of great moment, is a reproach that displeases no one. It gives the person making the reproach a sense of superiority, and the person to which it is addressed a sense of prudence. M. de Calonne was right, but his haste made him look as though he was wrong."[4]

His is a lonely haste, with no competent team to provide either a harmonious background or a use for it. Calonne may have the bit between his teeth, but things drag on as before. The speech he made on February 22 was potentially of interest to a large audience, but for ten days or more the only people to know about it are the 150 souls who heard it spoken; by the time it is published (that is, between March 2 and 13), in two or three Parisian gazettes, and, soon afterward, more widely circulated by peddlers in a twenty-four-sou pamphlet, it's too late.

Somewhere in the distance, a horn is blowing the mort.

Would Vergennes really have backed him? The question is no longer relevant.

What matters is that none of the present ministers are backing him, and several are openly against him. In particular, Baron Louis-Auguste Le Tonnelier de Breteuil, minister of the King's Household, has a grudge against him because of the obstacles Calonne put in his way when Breteuil was trying to promote one of the two famous schemes for the irrigation of Paris by a new water company. Breteuil wanted to exploit the resources of the Yvette; Calonne argued "that one stream was already flowing through the center of Paris [the Seine] and there was no need of another one."[5]

That in itself wouldn't have been so bad, but Breteuil is one of the men the Queen trusts, and she, acting through ministers devoted to her personally, is now stepping onto the political scene. This is new; it's also natural. After the Affair of the Necklace, in which she was wrongly accused by so many

*According to Robert Lacour-Gayet.
†On Charles-Maurice de Talleyrand-Périgord, see index to previous volumes.

people, Marie Antoinette could either retire or do battle. And as Louis XVI is leaving the field increasingly open, she is looking for support in the Council.

At first she counted on Calonne, whose only error in dealing with her was a lack of firmness. The Queen was expecting great docility from him, and he undoubtedly promised too much at the start; but he was also courageous enough to refuse more than people later admit.

Their quarrel took place in 1782, over the purchase of the St. Cloud estate.* In the end Calonne gave way to her colossal caprice, but so unwillingly that the Queen has hated him ever since. Then, too, the King's aunts are backing their protégé, Foulon, for the position of comptroller general. The Comte de Mercy-Argenteau, ambassador from Vienna and the Queen's mentor, writes to his sovereign, Joseph II: "When the Royal Treasury is being devoured by waste and profusion, a cry of poverty and terror goes up."[6] So he, too, is against Calonne, who is finding himself lost and alone in the no-man's-land that every "reformist" minister must try to navigate, between tradition and change. He might, for the latter purpose, have formed an alliance with others; but he has chosen to fight alone. "It was a blunder on M. de Calonne's part† to attack M. Necker and set all the fanatics against him for nothing. Their numbers were large, even in the Assembly of Notables, and, what is more, they were being urged on by several women [sic]."[7]

Swords are crossed. In the opening days of March 1787 Calonne submits a few very modest proposals to the seven groups, or committees, into which the Notables have been divided. He finds himself facing two brick walls, the nobility and the clergy.

The tout-Paris, meanwhile, is finding these groups, and their "presidents," highly diverting:

> Monsieur's is the best-behaved,
> Monseigneur le Comte d'Artois's, the jolliest,
> M. le Duc d'Orléans's, the maddest,
> M. le Prince de Condé's, the falsest,
> M. le Duc de Bourbon's, the most silent,
> M. le Prince de Conti's, the dreariest,
> M. le Duc de Penthièvre's, the silliest.[8]

The vehemence, and the intolerance, of the spokesmen for the higher clergy are like a wall of fire opposing Calonne. Boisgelin, the archbishop of Aix, for example, says to a friend of his, the Comtesse de Gramont, "Our views will save the Nation. But this infamous bankrupt is wearing the green

*See Volume IV.
†According to Besenval's Mémoires.

bonnet* and yet dares to tell us that we shall be responsible for his bankruptcy. Take a good look at him, right in the eyes. Remember every feature of his face. It is not yet written that the man will not be hanged by decree. . . ."[9]

But at this point all we're talking about is the organization of provincial assemblies with a view to a more equitable allocation of taxes. The vehemence is no accident, however: it is the expression of sheer panic at the very thought of fiscal justice. Calonne has his back to the wall and tries to wriggle free by publishing a pamphlet entitled *Avertissement,* which he commissioned the famous advocate Gerbier to write. It soon becomes known as the Gerbier Warning:

> Rumors and suppositions have arisen such as are likely to mislead the people; it is therefore necessary to inform them of the King's true intentions. It is time to tell them of the good that His Majesty wishes to do them and to dispel the fears that some have sought to instill in them. There has been talk of tax increases, as though fresh taxes were to be levied; of that there is no question. It is solely by means of a reform of abuses, a more exact levying of the present taxes, that the King seeks to increase his income to the level required by the needs of State and, insofar as circumstances will allow him, to relieve his subjects.[10]

And so on, for almost a hundred pages. This appeal to the people is a mistake, especially coming when it does. Calonne has put a match to the powder keg as Necker did in 1781 with the publication of his *Account Rendered.*

LA FAYETTE

II

MARCH–APRIL 1787

Come, the Danger Is Not So Great

March 2, 1787. Under pressure from some of the Notables who've been upset by his pamphlet, Calonne is forced into a sort of "hearing." This takes

---

*Littré says that the expression "to wear the green bonnet" was formerly used to mean "assigning one's property to one's creditors in order to avoid prosecution for bankruptcy"; it was also used because the person assigning the property was required to wear a green bonnet.

place in front of Monsieur, who is in charge of the first group. In a large, square room the comptroller general faces the seven "group president" princes. In reality, he is on trial. Hennin and Dupont de Nemours, the two Secretaries of the Assembly, are lurking in a window recess. A smattering of notables, selected from the most distinguished of their numbers, are seated on stools on either side, with little tables in front of them. The princes and "people of quality" are in "ordinary" dress, the councillors of state in short gowns, the prelates in their "long purple" attire and the magistrates in their official robes.[1]

"Throughout the sitting, which lasted nearly five hours,* M. de Calonne was exposed to everything that ill will, bad temper and even offensiveness could possibly contrive."[2]

The temperature begins to soar about halfway through, when the "opposition man"† interrupts Calonne's presentation of the general financial position: "The Archbishop of Toulouse said, 'It would seem, sir, in the present circumstances of the State, and as you have pronounced impracticable those means which the King found congruent with his own views, for the relief of his peoples . . . that it would befit your zeal to point out such means as you deem preferable.' "[3]

The Calonne-Brienne duel takes up the whole of the second part of this "conference of March 2nd," which marks the turning point of the Assembly of Notables. Some of the others try to put in a word or two—against Calonne—but are forced to give way to Brienne, who tends by nature to fill all the space available.

Calonne: "The chief thing is not to delay the resolution which must bring an end to the disproportion between the receipts of the State and its needful expenditure. To delay this resolution is to risk losing everything, to endanger the safety of the State."

Brienne: "O, come, the danger is not so great!"

Calonne: "You believe, sir, that I seek to exaggerate? Is that in my interest? And when I have the courage to give warning, can I be suspected of any motive other than my own conviction? I have announced the deficit; not to act at once to repair it would mean losing all the resources of credit."

Brienne: "All that is at issue is the choice of means; to change the form in which taxes are levied would be fraught with difficulties, especially as, in the words of the Comptroller General himself, we do not yet know the respective strengths of the individual provinces."

Calonne: "I pray you all to remember that it is nevertheless necessary, and

*According to Besenval.
†Loménie de Brienne, of course.

without delay, to come to some resolution, and that the need of the State cries out."

Brienne: "Something should have been done a year ago, before the need cried out."[4]

Calonne emerges from this meeting on March 2 punch-drunk, as a later generation would say of certain boxers. But he gets up off the mat. He will go on submitting his plans to the Notables for another month, although the ground beneath his feet is increasingly mined.

On April 3, when one of the Notables he was still counting on savages him, without warning and without mercy, he has no alternative but to see that the worm has turned. And this is no less a person than the Marquis de La Fayette, a member of the group of the Comte d'Artois, which prince (who would believe it?) has actually been whistling a mildly "liberal" tune of late. But La Fayette is about to yield to his "foible,"* his "canine appetite for popularity and fame."[5] Maybe he's also trying to get on the right side of the Queen.

In regard to the membership of the future provincial assemblies, La Fayette had calmly stated, back on February 27, that "the system of a monarchy should not be popular only, and the first nation of the world, which has subsisted so gloriously for so many centuries, should not lightly interfere with the principles of its Constitution [?]. But although these distinctions between citizens are needful to the dignity of royalty, to the order of the State and even to public freedom, it is not right to allow them to weigh too much upon our deliberations. I therefore subscribe to the general view, which is that the proportion of one-third ecclesiastics or nobles is the most reasonable that can be adopted in setting up the assemblies."[6]

March sees him steering his ship closer and closer to that of Brienne, and actually mooring himself to it. He sees the Archbishop of Toulouse as the man of the "bloodless revolution" of which he has been dreaming ever since America.[7]

But on April 3, when he moves into the front lines to sign, alone of the members of his group, a memorandum denouncing the real estate speculation, in Brittany and Berri in particular, with which Calonne's name has been linked by public rumor, he will be risking a quarrel with the Comte d'Artois.†

"Monseigneur le Comte d'Artois,‡ upon picking up the memorandum signed by La Fayette, told him very dryly that it was fine, that he did not in

---

*According to a letter from Jefferson to James Madison, dated January 10, 1787.

†A quarrel that lasts nearly half a century, up to the revolution of 1830; but that's another story.

‡According to the Duc de Laval.

the least believe all the allegations set out in it but that he would nevertheless hand it to the King."[8]

They're making too much fuss about nothing. Calonne's fate is played out offstage, this same first week of April—Easter week—under cover of a cat-and-dog spat between himself and the keeper of the seals. Miromesnil, too much of a cipher to have been anything but neutral thus far, decides it is a good idea to brandish his short-lived devotion to Necker. Calonne's nerves must be very much on edge; in any event, Miromesnil and he insult each other in front of Louis XVI, who hates nothing so much as to be called upon to arbitrate. The King says nothing, shuts himself up in his room, and lets the Queen take advantage of the opportunity to force some final decisions.

"On Holy Saturday, and again on Easter Day, the King refused to see M. de Calonne. This is how this last day went: M. de Calonne, worried by the refusal of the day before, sent to enquire of M. de Septeuil, the King's *valet de chambre,* whether he could see His Majesty. M. de Septeuil went to take the King's orders, which were that he did not wish to see him and that if he came, he was not to be admitted, and that the King did not want to hear his name. M. de Calonne, impatient, arrived *infiochi** with his customary suite. He asked to be let in; he was refused. He asked again, he was refused again; he said he had something urgent to say to the King, and was told that the King had positively stated that he did not wish to see him. He presented a letter. He was told that it could not be received. Had he awaited the reply to his first message, he would have avoided this mortification, which was very patent; judge, then, whether he should have been amazed that evening to learn of his dismissal."[9]

Calonne gets the sack on April 8; Miromesnil on the ninth. Lamoignon takes over the seals and Brienne "the presidency of the Council of Finance" . . . to begin with.

"A dastardly intrigue,† fostered by the person who ought most to have protected my rights, and who had promised me protection, upset my hopes and opened the way for the universal upheaval. The King, who had assured me a hundred times that he would support me with unshakable firmness, abandoned me, and I succumbed."[10]

Infiochi (Italian), "with full pomp and ceremony."
†According to a text written by Calonne for Bonaparte, when he was First Consul in 1802.

12

APRIL 1787

As a Prime Minister

Exit Calonne.

"The privileged classes* had still too much credit to be attacked successfully by M. de Calonne; the man himself could be seen as a compilation of all the abuses he hoped to reform. So vast a scheme, albeit skillfully conceived, must needs come to grief in the hands of a man who did not enjoy the esteem and confidence of the public."[1]

So, to take his place—*who?* The Court's hundred voices were all hailing Brienne, but Louis XVI, following the precedent he has set on the occasion of other disgraces, spends a few days sitting on the fence, if only to affirm his authority against that of the Queen.

She has been promoting Brienne for nearly three years, on the advice of the Abbé de Vermond, who is ostensibly her "reader" but is in reality her supervisor-guardian, put in place by her mother and Mercy-Argenteau before the young Dauphine ever got to France. Turn and turn about is fair play: when the Court of Vienna was looking for a young phoenix in the French clergy, it was Brienne himself who suggested Vermond. But Louis XVI doesn't like Brienne. The King's rudimentary faith has taught him to loathe clergymen who don't believe in God. From his father the Dauphin, Louis XV's son, it came to him as a first principle, arising out of the sinister memory left by the government of Cardinal de Fleury,† that everything went much more smoothly when the ship of state was not being steered by a prelate. However, the King is now being subjected to the combined pressures of

---

*According to Malouet.

†Cardinal de Fleury (1653–1743) was young Louis XV's tutor, gained his confidence and became principal minister in 1726, remaining in the post until his death. Although his administration of the royal finances was fairly sound, he allowed the country to embark upon the ruinous War of the Austrian Succession.

most of his ministers, old and new, and to those of the Queen—although many people are also hesitating between Brienne and Necker, who is calmly awaiting his second hour and has just been expelled from his estate at Saint-Ouen by Calonne in a fit of pique.*

Président Lamoignon, the Baron de Breteuil and the Marquis de Montmorin "agreed, all three, that the man in charge of finance had to be a person of consequence and capable of taking command. Knowing the King's aversion to M. Necker; also, possibly reluctant to have in the ministry a man who was both obstinate and vain;† and lastly, not unaware of the Queen's wishes in the matter, they settled the question in favor of the Archbishop of Toulouse, and went up to the King at once to submit their choice to him. Whether because the King was already predisposed in that direction by the Queen or whether it was circumstance that decided him, he accepted, although making no attempt to hide from the gentlemen his very strong disinclination to the Archbishop."[3]

By April 23, a decisive meeting between Brienne and, for the first time, *both* sovereigns has become imperative. The two of them together—as though Marie Antoinette were acting as a sort of co-regent—ask the Archbishop to state the principal conditions on which he will agree to assume "the guidance of affairs." It is a long time before anyone knows that he stipulates two: first, that Necker should be associated with him; and second, that the Estates General should be convened at once. The King's reaction is so violent that Brienne can hardly believe it. "What! Then you believe we are lost? The Estates General? Oh! You can overthrow state and royalty, do whatever you like, except those two things! Reforms, reduction of expenditure, the Queen and I are willing and ready; but for pity's sake, do not insist upon either Monsieur Necker or the Estates General."[4]

Brienne understands. He says no more. And yet he would like to carry out a policy of reform. But who is he, and whence does he come, Étienne-Charles de Loménie de Brienne?

The Loménies are "old nobility, and have produced great men,"[5] some in Picardy and some in Limousin, and latterly in Champagne, where they became seigneurs of Brienne at the beginning of the eighteenth century. Étienne-Charles was born in Paris in 1727. As a younger son he was, as a matter of course, destined for the Church. But unlike some others, he seems to have taken a fancy to it, because he continued his religious studies after his older brother was killed in the wars, and let his youngest brother become a man-of-arms and head of the family in his stead.

It was not for want of overweening ambition; only, he invested his

*Because Necker had published a book (another one) of self-justification.
†The style is typical of Besenval; here his testimony is confirmed by Weber.[2]

ambition in the assets of the Church, in politics and in books. His youth? The Sorbonne. His friends? D'Alembert, Turgot and a few other captains of the *"encyclopédiste* movement," with which, however, he never became more involved than was good for him. By 1760, when he gained favor with Jarente, the bishop of Orléans, whom Louis XV had made responsible for the "register of benefices"—meaning the allocation of titles among the higher clergy—he was already known for his intelligence and argumentative skill. He begins as bishop of Condom, becomes archbishop of Toulouse in 1763, and drives his career thereafter at a smart pace: abbé des Prémontrés of Bassefontaine near Troyes, abbé de Moissace in the same diocese, abbé de Moreilles south of La Rochelle, abbé de Saint-Wandrolle in the Rouen region; and he has long since begun a series of complex maneuvers aimed at securing the archbishopric of Sens, which was then the most important in the kingdom.* Meanwhile, he presides annually over the Estates of Languedoc, not without promoting some useful public works. In 1755 his reputation is already so glowing that Choiseul, then Louis XV's all-powerful minister, makes him the head of a "Regulars Commission," with instructions to produce an honest and explicit report on the position of the contemplative monks and nuns, whose vast holdings had long been regarded by the Crown, the nobility, and even the higher clergy themselves, as unjustified and parasitic.

Brienne detested monks. He had a field day. According to him, "almost all the religious bodies have lost the spirit of fervor that formerly inspired them. The religious are more or less dominated by the same passions that agitate other men, except that in their case those passions have an added quality of ruthlessness not commonly found in the passions of people living in the world. The superiors are always ready to sacrifice everything to their desire to command. Their subordinates, on the contrary, groan beneath a scepter of iron."[6]

You'd think you were reading Diderot. This quarrel is not ideological, however: as in the case of the confiscation of the property of the Jansenists, or the Quietists, or, of course, the Protestants, at the end of the reign of Louis XIV; and as in the case of the dissolution and expulsion of the Jesuits under Louis XV, the monarchy's main objective here is to appropriate those same vast holdings. As far as the "regulars"† are concerned, Brienne's commission has carried out, in the last twenty years, a stringent purge. When Brienne took on the job, there were 26,674 monks in France. By 1789 there

---

*Readers are reminded that under the Ancien Régime the holder of the position of abbé received the major share of the abbey's annual income but hardly ever set foot within the monastic walls.

†"Regular" monks and nuns belong to the contemplative orders, as distinct from "secular" priests, who comprised the main body of the active Church.

are only 16,235 left. The population of Cluny fell from 671 monks to 301; of Citeaux, from 1,873 to 1,624;* of Saint-Maur, from 1,971 to 1,652; of the Carthusians, from 1,004 to 821; of the Franciscans, from 2,395 to 1,558; of the Capuchins, from 4,397 to 2,674; of the Recollects, from 2,534 to 1,558; of the Dominicans, from 1,441 to 1,001; of the canonici of St. Geneviève, from 662 to 567, etc.[7] In twelve years, a number of major contemplative orders simply disappeared, including Grandmont, the Servites, the Celestines, the Benedictines, the order of the Holy Spirit of Montpellier, the monks of St. Bridget, the Holy Cross of La Bretonnerie, Saint-Ruff, Saint-Antoine. Of a total of 2,966 houses, 366 were liquidated.[8]

Having earned, through this harsh program of pruning and shearing, a reputation as an iron man, Brienne is being perceived in Versailles, by the end of April, as the chief candidate for the position of "principal minister," which has been empty since the death of Vergennes and which Calonne was never able to fill. A significant rumor follows him up the great staircase of the château as he mounts, most elegant in his purple robes topped by an open countenance, with a long aquiline nose and a broad forehead; about these features, everyone is in agreement.

But beyond them, the choir becomes polyvocal. "His gaze, when appearing to observe you, was in reality spying you out;† there was something unsettling even in his good humor, and some overshrewd quality in his physiognomy that disposed one to mistrust."[9]

On the other hand, and especially now, there are many who find his "outward appearance mild, simple, approachable; his conversation lively, with a natural gaiety, a kind of nonchalance, an ease when at work."[10]

"This man, who is devious with everyone, has a cold, noble, courteous mien, a determined manner, an incisive tone, but in the most laconic way possible; he never becomes involved in a discussion; he decides, imperiously, with a word, and then is silent."[11] Judge for yourself. . . .

But what's this? How is it, on this ascension toward the highest honor of all, the one he's been dreaming of since childhood, that he is having to be helped up the stairs? Ironically, just when the kingdom has greatest need of his abilities, Brienne is a very sick man. His persistent cough sounds almost

---

*These were Trappists who had been reformed a century before by Rancé, whose virtue was above suspicion. The figures are interesting, because they indicate that the initiative in dismantling the religious orders did not originate with the Constituent Assembly of 1790.

†According to those who were not overfond of him or knew him only slightly, as is the case, here, of Marmontel.

tubercular; he has lost his voice, he's feverish, the slightest effort exhausts him; sometimes his skin looks as dry as a leper's.[12]

The Court couldn't care less. It sees itself being saved by him from both deficit and reforms. All it wants now is to get rid of those killjoy Notables, convened—a hundred years ago, it feels like—by that master killjoy Calonne, who, under the threat of arrest, is compelled to hurry across the Channel and seek refuge in England; his accounts have not yet been rendered. . . .

On many previous occasions, La Fayette has acted as a sort of loudspeaker for public opinion. He was, with some reason, feeling shoved onto the sidelines of the Assembly of Notables, but now he sees himself as one of the main forces responsible for driving out Calonne and bringing in Brienne, whom he views as a sort of Messiah. In a letter dated May 5, he hastens to tell Daddy Washington all about it.

"And now we have got the Arch Bishop [*sic*] of Toulouse at the head of affairs. A man of the most upright honesty and shining abilities. . . . We may consider the Arch Bishop as a prime minister."[13]

He's all aflutter. At the beginning of May many of the Notables, far from expecting to be thanked for their services and sent home, imagine that Brienne is about to transform their Assembly into a great council that will, discreetly, govern the King. On May 21 La Fayette, who has been so shivery under Calonne—but then, he, too, was ill at the time!—hurls himself to the fore by making a memorable scene in his group. In an inspired piece of oratory he paints an idyllic portrait of the reforms that Brienne, with the Assembly's support, has undertaken to carry out in the next five years. After which:

"It seems to me that the time is at hand, and we must beseech His Majesty to determine it now, to assemble under one head the accounts of all the different transactions and consolidate forever their favorable outcome, by convening a truly national assembly."[14]

The chairman of his group reacts instantly; he's the Comte d'Artois, and as we have just seen, La Fayette and he, after starting out hand in glove, have recently had something of a cooling off. Here comes the big break:

"Artois: 'What do I hear, sir! You are asking for the convening of the Estates General!'

"La Fayette: 'Yes, sir, and even more than that.'

"Artois: 'So you want me to write down, and take to the King, *M. de La Fayette moved that the Estates General be convened?*'

"La Fayette: 'Yes, sir.'

"The only name the Prince had to write was La Fayette's. There was complete silence."[15]

La Fayette has burned his boats again. Now what has he dared utter?

Brienne, who has been pretending to treat him with great consideration, backs up as fast as he can. "M. de Brienne had at first been quite intimately associated with a very bold plan of La Fayette's,* which was to compel the King, even at this early date, to adopt a truly representative government. When he saw his former fellow Notable coming out so strongly for the convening of a national assembly, he hastened to point him out to the Council as the most dangerous man alive because, he said, he never thinks save to act."[16]

Brienne, meanwhile, presses ahead with the first of the tasks for which he has been appointed. Fully convinced that neither Queen nor King will ever accept a national assembly with any real decision-making powers, he prepares to send the Notables home again. They had continued to think they were half masters of the monarchy; on May 26 they are disabused by the announcement of their dismissal.

"They will each return to his home, leaving matters more or less as they were before, save that the whole universe is now informed of the dilapidated state of our finances and our pitiful distress."[17]

The *parlements* are standing fast, ready to oppose any new taxes. The higher clergy have not budged. The Court nobility are packed around the King in serried ranks. Mirabeau—like Calonne!—is exiled to England. Life goes on.

But everything is going to be all right, of course it will, now that Brienne's here. . . .

MIRANDA

13

FEBRUARY–APRIL 1787

A Citizen of the World

On February 18, 1787, Catherine II, empress of all the Russias, sends a letter, from Kiev, to her old friend Grimm:

---

*According to the original text of La Fayette's *Correspondance,* which attempts by this means to justify his chopping and changing throughout the Assembly of Notables: a little for Calonne, a lot for Brienne, but the most substantial amount for himself.

"I reached this place in good health, in twenty degrees of frost. Half of Poland is here.* The Prince of Nassau, a Spanish grandee, has come with a Spaniard named Miranda. When all these people leave, they will say it wasn't worth the trip."[1]

It must have been the cold and fatigue of the journey that put the Tsarina in a bad mood that day; but she's soon bestowing a goodly share of her attention and sympathy upon Miranda.

Where does he come from? What's he doing in Kiev, this subject of the King of Spain who has been running all over the world for the last few years and who, three years ago, was recommended to the private secretary of the British prime minister by a member of the American Congress?

"By nature and by upbringing Francisco de Miranda was a citizen of the world, which he traveled with a view to increasing his already far from negligible store of knowledge; so it was not surprising that he should have decided to visit England, a country long regarded by cultivated foreigners as a nation of philosophers, or that he should have wished to become acquainted with the great figures living there."[2]

And now here's the same blighter in the Russian marches, being presented to the "enlightened" autocrat who, after being praised by Voltaire and entertaining Diderot,† is still fascinating so many fine minds. Miranda is about to add himself to her collection, but not because of speculation or intellectual curiosity. He has come to Kiev for the same purpose as he went to the United States in 1780, and he will seek from Catherine II what he wanted from Washington. First and foremost, this sharp-witted, cultivated connoisseur of beautiful books and women is a "politico-military" man who aspires to become the *libertador* of Spanish America. He is a man with a grand design. The king to whom he supposedly owes allegiance is the King of Spain, simply because he has to come from somewhere. But Miranda no longer has anything to do with Madrid. His country is a continent of the future. He's a "citizen of the world" who has cut the umbilical cord. He would like to step straight out of the Age of Enlightenment into a revolution—his own. Any country that will further that end is welcome: the United States, Russia, England, Germany, France—all of them, except, precisely, Spain.

"To his misfortune [says his letter of accreditation to Lord North], he met his destiny, which is often the lot of men endowed with talent and

*What she means, of course, is "half of those who matter in Poland": the courtiers, chamberlains, ministers etc., who are there because Catherine has an appointment to meet Stanislaw Poniatowski, king of Poland, in Kiev.

†On Diderot's trip to St. Petersburg and his frequent and sometimes stormy meetings with Catherine II, see Volume I.

qualities, in his dealings with arbitrary governments; that is to say, he has been persecuted by fanatical and intriguing persons."

Or in still other words, the Inquisition has been after him for years.

While the Notables of France are learning of the nation's deficit and a "changing of the guard" is taking place among most of the sovereigns of old Europe, the year 1787 has introduced something new to two vast expanses which have not yet played much of a part in world affairs. It's as though both of them, West and East, are stretching their monstrous young wings before lifting the planet a little higher. English-speaking America is drafting a constitution, while an awakened Russia is observing the greatest domestic voyage ever embarked upon by her monarch. Catherine II seems to be moving the focus of her empire southward. St. Petersburg to Kiev, what an expedition in midwinter! But she's not doing it for fun; she is about to take possession of the Crimea, which she has just wrested from the Turks, and the old temptation to reconquer Constantinople is making Slavic Christianity's mouth water again.

Thousands of leagues from both frontiers of the French monarchy, still petrified in its ancient ways, everything here is motion, shift and change. Russia and America are not going to sink back into the void yet awhile; so maybe Francisco de Miranda's dreams of a new destiny for South America are not so farfetched after all.

He was born thirty-seven years ago in Caracas, soon to become the capital of Venezuela but at that time only the headquarters of the Vice-Royalty of New Granada.[3]*

Miranda's family are very well-off, although they've only been there since the boyhood of his father, who had consolidated his cloth merchant's fortune during a long stay in the Canaries before moving into the splendid house in which Francisco was born, on Divine Dawn Street near the main square of the town, all of whose place-names refer more or less directly to the Virgin. It was a typical colonial palace, roofed in red tiles; a swarm of servants fussed about in the drawing rooms, refreshing patios and endless corridors. Francisco de Miranda ate his white bread young and never knew need; he was honored like a little lord in his own home. In due course, a military life followed by exile will teach him enough about privation and hardship.

*Miranda becomes famous in France in 1792, when he takes part in the victory at Valmy as a general under Kellerman. A bronze statue of him stands today on the historic hill where he fought. His name is engraved on the fourth column of the northwest pilaster of the Arch of Triumph, near those of Grouchy and Carnot. In 1812, when he attempts to liberate Venezuela, he is given to the Spanish and dies in prison in Cádiz in 1816.

The only shadow in the landscape was that his father Sebastian was not a true Creole, nor was he one of those proud "peninsular" hidalgos who dominated the Spanish colonies as if by right. Coming from the Canaries, or in other words from nowhere, the Mirandas were not quite the genuine article, in the eyes of the titled Spanish. The local aristos disputed his father's right to command a militia unit in Caracas, although it was composed of immigrants from—the Canaries; and his son was not allowed to enter the royal cadet corps. At the age of twenty, Miranda was compelled to leave this congealed society, cross the Atlantic and go to Madrid, in order to obtain a traditional military training, with the result that he nurses a lasting grudge against his peers and is naturally disposed to challenge all privilege.

In 1772 he is made captain of an infantry battalion, thanks to a patent purchased by his family, and begins to keep a diary of his discoveries and travels. He pays his first visit, heading a list of hundreds embracing famous sites all over the world, to the Escorial. The first supplement to his already extensive learning is the eager exploration of French, then the language of universal communication. His first serious indiscretion, in a Spain confined within a cultural straitjacket, is the clandestine purchase of "philosophical" works—French, as it happens—the presence of which on his bookshelves is denounced by paid informers. While he is watching bullfights, attending masked balls and commencing a long career of amorous fluttering, a few quiet men are assembling the fundamentals of a file of which he knows nothing and which thickens year by year as the servants' reports come in: the Holy Office has stuck him with a Sumaria.*

Still carefree, he sets off to ply his trade: war. In Africa, the Moroccans are besieging the Spanish town of Melilla. Bravery, intelligence, a cool head; at most, he can be reproached for one or two quite unremarkable acts of rashness. But no one can deny he is ingenious, especially on the occasion of a general saber-assault upon the enemy batteries. Naturally, his superior officers are not enamored of this budding general, who has a slight tendency to show off his knowledge.[4] He applies for a promotion to Algeria, where a sporadic war is being waged between Spain and "Barbary." After letting him stew for a few months, they send him to Málaga instead, and then to Cádiz, where he is bored. No doubt about it, somewhere in the Court of Spain somebody's got it in for him. But who? And why? He doesn't learn until long afterward. In Seville, an ecclesiastical court institutes proceedings against him, the accused supplying the rope to hang himself with by buying

---

*Later ages will say "a confidential file," or "secret report." It consisted of all the evidence pointing to a person's heresy or atheism, of which the accused never heard a word until the moment of trial. The compilation of such a record could last a lifetime; the Inquisition was seldom in a hurry.

the Koran and making friends with liberal Englishmen during a visit to Gibraltar. He is even seen keeping company with Freemasons!

From Cádiz he bombards his superiors with pleas. He is so ill-suited to garrison life that he gets sent to the guardhouse twice for quarreling with senior officers. It looks as though there may be a war over the United States, between England and Spain, which is loosely allied to France. Now will they let him breathe a bit? These are the days when all Europe has been stirred up by the Inquisition's condemnation of the famous Pablo de Olavide, intendant of Seville and tamer of the Sierra Morena: a man of progress if ever there was one, who spends eight years in prison and is proclaimed "a heretical, infamous and rotten limb of religion" for the rest of his life, during which he is allowed to wear no color but yellow.*

Miranda can't believe it. On the road between Cádiz and Madrid, he has seen and appreciated Olavide's work: "This extraordinary man, imbued with far-reaching ideas, has brought a whole region under cultivation, building roads and founding villages. He is a good patriot who has successfully transformed the fallow land of the Sierra Morena, cradle of every thief and bandit in the kingdom, into the most comfortable place on the whole route."[5]

1780: Release? Miranda is sent to the Antilles, where he becomes an aide-de-camp to the good General Cagigal, the only high-ranking officer who consistently defends him;[6] at last, a command worthy of his abilities! He is put in charge of the Anglo-American volunteers, who, with Spanish and French assistance, capture the town of Pensacola in western Florida. In the decisive battles of 1781, the spring swallow of Pensacola (which capitulated on March 9) heralds the Indian summer of September that is to blossom in the Chesapeake and at Yorktown. He may be suspected of heresy, but he is nevertheless made a lieutenant colonel and can taste the fruits of his own little victory in Havana, still with his General Cagigal.

He then spends three months in Jamaica, negotiating an exchange of prisoners with the commander of the English troops. That's a lot of time to give to a humanitarian mission, although he takes advantage of it to acquire some sixty English works ranging from Shakespeare to Adam Smith's latest opus.† Jamaica is an open book to him by the time he goes back to Havana to learn of the victory at Yorktown. From Miranda to Cagigal on December 13: "I have just come into port with three ships carrying one hundred thirty Spanish subjects. I also bring you exact particulars of the enemy fleet in the island, expected reinforcements and troop numbers. Further, I have some

---

*On the Olavide case, see Volume I. Diderot wrote a *Précis historique* about it.

†Adam Smith (1723–1790), Scottish economist and philosopher, author of the celebrated *Enquiry into the Nature and Causes of the Wealth of Nations*.

topographical plans and other things which I must not send in writing."[7]

He is assuming this will earn him fresh rewards, or at least a kind word. Get off your cloud, laddie! The customs officials of the "Spanish Indies" want to search his baggage before he can show Cagigal his confidential documents. He refuses and, despite protests from his general, is duly accused of carrying contraband goods. In Havana he makes things worse for himself by inviting and entertaining the English General Campbell, whom he defeated at Pensacola and who is an honor prisoner. A long winter ensues, lasting the six months it takes communications to make the round trip from the colonies to the home country and back, and ending with a killing blow from the "minister for the Indies," which reaches Miranda in the Bahamas, where he has just conquered Nassau, the capital, still under Cagigal's orders. The General is recalled to Madrid, and Miranda is interned in the fortress at Cap Français.*

Cagigal manages to earn a measure of reprieve for his young aide-de-camp in the form of a sort of house arrest between Havana and Cap Français, but then he has to hurry away and look after his own skin at Court. The war is over now, so there will be no further opportunity for the accused to "rehabilitate" himself by some brilliant action; but in April 1783, after two days of spiritual agonizing between the four whitewashed walls of a colonial house in the little Cuban port of Regla where the waves had flung him up the strand, Miranda makes his critical decision. He is thirty. For him, Spain has definitively assumed the shape of the great impasse in which he has floundered away his youth. That page has got to be turned. He will go, wherever chance may take him. His choice is simple, after all; it's the guardhouse or the world. Farewell, Spain!

From Miranda to Cagigal: "I am going to the United States, leaving you to defend my honor before the King. I must tell you that my decision has been prompted not only by the necessity to avoid the penalty that has been imposed upon me but also by my desire to travel abroad. It is to this end that I have long been increasing my proficiency in the principal European languages, for a man gains much experience and solid knowledge by consulting the great book of the Universe at first hand and with his wits about him.

"The wise and virtuous societies comprising it, their laws, governments, agriculture, commerce, military arts, navigation, sciences and fine arts are alone capable of ripening the fruit, completing the immense task of forming a solid man who is looking to the future.

---

*The procedure brought against him by Spain for smuggling and treason arising out of his relations with General Campbell went on so long that the decision acquitting him was not pronounced until 1799, by the Indies Council in Madrid. Cap Français is now called Cap Haïtien.

"I should like to spend four years traveling through England, Holland, France, Germany, Italy, etc."[8]

He begins with the United States. In those days he had not even dreamed of the Tsarina's great Russian voyage; but here he is, four years later, being presented to her after leaving another empire, of which he was also certainly not dreaming back in the Windward Isles: in April 1787, Francisco de Miranda has just been to Constantinople.

CATHERINE II

14

FEBRUARY—APRIL 1787

The Europe Café

"What is the weather like in Venezuela?"[1]

On February 14, this is the Empress's first question to the person she calls "Count Miranda," just to be on the safe side, when he is presented to her by Prince Bezborodko, her minister of foreign affairs. Taking their cue from their sovereign, the rest of the Russians also call him "Count," although he has no right to the title and despite the protests of the Court of Spain. This form of opening gambit belongs to the realm of worldly show, at which Catherine has become a past master. But the man interests her, and she soon lets him know it. If Bezborodko presents Miranda to her, it's because Potemkin asked him to, and Potemkin is still a sort of unofficial prince consort, the most powerful man in the empire, even if he no longer shares the Tsarina's bed.

Francisco had done his homework, and knew that Potemkin was the key to the door of the "Semiramis of the North."*

So here, face-to-face, are the absolute sovereign of Russia and the man, for the moment without any mandate or backers, who is aspiring to become the first president of some vast future republic of South America.

She's fifty-eight, he's thirty-seven.

---

*Semiramis: legendary queen of Assyria, where she is supposed to have built the Hanging Gardens of Babylon. It was Voltaire who gave Catherine II that sobriquet twenty years before.

One could see she had been beautiful, rather than pretty; the majesty of her brow was tempered by pleasant eyes and a pleasant smile, but the brow said it all.* . . . The breadth of that brow bespoke a full complement of memory and imagination. . . . Her chin was slightly pointed but not absolutely prominent. . . . She must have had a fine complexion and a lovely bosom, although the latter only at the expense of her waist, which had once been slender unto breaking, but the Russians have a tendency to stoutness. She was clean, and would have been much better to look at had she not pulled her hair back so tightly; it should rather have fallen a little lower, to form a companion to her face. One did not notice how small she was. She told me, slowly, that she had used to be extremely quick, a thing that was quite inconceivable now. . . . The Empress had all the good aspects, that is, all the greatness, of Louis XIV.[2]

"Don François de Miranda, Spanish subject, is about thirty years old;† of average height, well set-up, a round face with regular features, a determined air, dark skin, white teeth, black hair. He expresses himself with vivacity in both French and English, which he speaks quite fluently."[3] He's the kind you don't forget, even if you've only met him once. His nutcracker chin denotes an iron will: "He walks with a very deliberate step, as though attacking with a fencing foil. The velvet glow of his eyes wins him friends among the women, his aloofness impresses the men."[4]

Even in the frosty spring of a country so cold that it is a true ordeal to him, in which he often has to hold a huge handkerchief over his large nose to keep it from freezing, "he knows how to use his rather low and supple voice most wonderfully."

A young American saw him three years earlier, already the man he is now, the man Catherine II is about to find so attractive, and wrote: "Miranda seemed to me a remarkable man, endowed with formidable energy. His favorite subject of conversation was the possibility of making a revolution in the provinces of Spanish America. He would speak on this subject with great passion, severely denouncing the causes [sic], striding across the room and punctuating his sentences with great gesticulations. In my young imagination he represented a new model of exceptional human elevation. I believe him capable of placing himself at the head of a people impatient to have their own government."[5]

Noon. Her Majesty graciously extracts one hand from her fur muff and bestows it to be kissed by the new "presentee." Will that be all? By no means.

*According to a description by the Prince de Ligne, written during this same trip. It was he who made the Empress so happy by calling her Catherine the Great.

†According to the passport-type description that the Comte de Vergennes had circulated in France a year earlier.

He has managed to get himself noticed, and to raise hopes of bright and novel conversation. Miranda is invited forthwith to the dinner for sixty that the sovereign is giving in the great hall. Catherine takes care to see that he is given second helpings of her favorite dishes, chosen by her for him from among the profusion of fruit from Astrakhan, sturgeon from the Volga and meat from Arkhangelsk, all of which melt in the mouth when accompanied by iced Constanza wine served in silver goblets.

Traditionally, this "offering the dish" is the sign of a courtier's acceptance. That very evening of February 14, which he remembers for the rest of his life, Miranda is invited to the Empress's reception and gaming-table, and she begins talking to him openly and with curiosity. At the whist table Count Cobentzl, the ambassador from Vienna, is an attentive observer and he notes, for transmission to Joseph II, the appearance of this new asteroid in the Imperial Court: "He [Miranda] is a man of wide knowledge, proud, speaking very freely on every subject but more particularly against the Inquisition, against the Spanish government, the King and the Prince of the Asturias,* and proffering many injurious allusions on the subject of Spanish ignorance."[6]

Catherine likes nothing better than to see herself treated as a *philosophe* by a distinguished visitor from the other end of the earth. So she talks to him indignantly about the misfortunes of Olavide and utters many sharp words about the monks and Jesuits, whom she nevertheless shelters, discreetly, in Russia; she boasts of entrusting the education of her grandsons to La Harpe, a "Republican Swiss," and trots out her charm act, which has so often left her audience gaping:

"I have valued philosophy because my soul has always been singularly republican. I concede that this spiritual predilection may be something of a phenomenon, when combined with the limitless power of my position, but, too, there is no one in Russia who will say I have taken advantage of it."[7]

In a few short hours, a friendship has been born between Catherine and Miranda. Or at least, what passes for a friendship in a Court—and what a Court! One of the most ostentatious of the day.

The great theater in which this encounter between Spanish America and Russia takes place is worthy of it: Kiev, the empire's oldest city, could easily look upon Moscow as its inferior and has often done so. When you first see it in the sun, especially in winter when the snow reflects earth light back into

*Who, like the Prince of Wales in the United Kingdom, is the traditional heir to the throne of Spain. In this instance, he is the future Charles IV, whom Napoleon dethrones. Cobentzl later becomes one of the chief Austrian ministers and a signatory, along with General Bonaparte, to the Treaty of Campoformia.

the sky, you might almost believe it a city in fairyland, with its green-roofed pink houses and the gold or silver domes of its hundreds of churches, its red palaces, hanging terraces and gardens. A fairyland image, but amended by the travelers of the day, to whom Kiev appeared as a great and venerable beauty now gone to seed. "It still occupied a vast territory, offering to our gaze a strange medley of majestic ruins, wretched hovels, gilded convents and churches and many buildings in stone that had been begun only to be abandoned."[8] The uncertainty of a great city caught between future and past.

Catherine and the tiny ruling class of Russia are meeting their mother-town for the first time. What a scene for master tourist Miranda! In the center, the broad flow of the Dniepr, which everybody in these parts still calls the Borysthenes, separating the three towns on their three hills—in this immeasurable flatland of theirs, the Russians build every time they see a hump. There's the "new town," a hundred years young; the religious town, a great clutter of monasteries; and the industrial and commercial town, also called "the Jewish district."

If, like Miranda and other privileged travelers, you can make your way to some choice belvedere, you overlook a forest of marble and gold, its hundreds of trees formed by cupolas and steeples.[9]

Kiev is all aflutter, like a sleeping princess kissed awake by history, as the Russia of today, and perhaps of tomorrow, arouses the Russia of days gone by. "Our Little Mother Empress" is bringing the friendly greetings of autocracy to the town that gave it birth a thousand years before. Since Peter the Great and the tsars' removal way up there to St. Petersburg, real Russians haven't known where to look for the master of all the Russias.

Here he is. Here *she* is. What an expedition: she left St. Petersburg on January 18, in the depths of winter,* with a suite of fourteen carriages, one hundred twenty-four sledges, and a supply and security train of forty vehicles.

Five hundred sixty horses awaited us at every stage.† The frost rose [*sic*] to 17 degrees, the use of wooden runners speeded us along; our coaches, mounted on high skates, seemed to fly.

To protect us from the cold, we were all enveloped in great bearskins, which we wore on top of finer and more precious furs; we wore sable caps on our heads. With these precautions, we never noticed the cold at all, even when it went up to twenty or twenty-five degrees. In the houses in which we were lodged, the stoves gave us reason to fear overheating rather than chill.

At that season, the shortest days of the year, the sun did not begin to give

*Historians are always astonished by the indifference to wind and weather shown in those days by travelers with means. Nine years earlier, Voltaire left Ferney to go to Paris, and die, at just the same season.

†According to the Comte de Ségur.

any light until very late, and after six or seven hours it set again, making way for deepest night. But the opulence of the East, determined to drive away the gloom, would not let us lack for brightness: at very short intervals, on both sides of the road, huge piles of faggots had been made, of firs, cypress, birch and pine, and set alight, so that we traveled along a road of fire, brighter than daylight; that was how the proud autocratess [sic] of the North desired and commanded, in the deepest darkness, that there be light.[10]

Every night the little gilded army is lodged in houses commandeered or bought and furnished for the occasion. However deep the frost without, when the travelers descend from their "sliding miniature houses," they are waited upon by swarms of servants carrying hot dishes in new china and setting them down on new tablecloths.[11]

This royal tour provides a perfect picture of the confrontation between the greatest opulence imaginable and the greatest poverty imaginable. Even a rich man like Ségur is mildly discomfited:

> Twice a day we would stop in villages and towns that would then, to their own great surprise, become the temporary residence of a Court and all its pomp. The poor, primitive inhabitants, assembled in crowds despite the fierce cold, stood patiently, their beards needled with frost, around the little palace built among their walls by a sort of enchantment, within which the Empress's joyful cortege, seated before a sumptuous table or on the cushions of capacious and comfortable divans, were aware of neither the harshness of the climate nor the poverty of the country, finding everywhere a pleasant warmth, delicious wines, rare fruit and elaborate food,* escaping even ennui, that elderly offspring of uniformity, by means of all the varied pleasures which an amiable woman knows how to give a large circle of people, though she be queen and despot as well.[12]

So proceeds the encounter of sovereign, Court and people. In Russia there are about twenty million "people," sixty thousand nobles, one hundred thousand monks and four hundred thousand soldiers. But these figures refer only to the population covered by the census and do not allow for probably another two million serfs, so untaught and so bereft of status that nobody even thinks of summoning them to witness the Tsarina's passage. Does one issue invitations to livestock?

One important reason for the 1787 journey is the recent conquest, by

---

*It was these resting-places that gave substance to the legend of the "Potemkin villages." According to it, the Empress and her suite moved through a series of stage settings, built as for an operetta, on Potemkin's initiative. That wasn't necessary: behind perfectly three-dimensional facades, primped and scoured for the occasion, the poor people were simply rounded up and stood in their places.

Russia, of half a million souls in the Crimea, plus approximately two million more in Poland.[13]

It is because of these new acquisitions that Catherine has decided to make her great progress, not (as was given out officially) for the fun of celebrating the twenty-fifth anniversary of her ascension to the throne, thanks to the deposing and subsequent assassination of her husband; and not for the pleasure of hearing herself acclaimed by a people who seem to have stopped murmuring since the Pugachev uprising.* The country itself is putting on weight. Its appetite in the west has subsided since the first partition of Poland in 1772, and in the south it is beginning to digest the Crimea (which Catherine would like to call by its ancient name of Tauridus), the strategic peninsula on the Black Sea to which the Sultan of Constantinople, who would seem to be losing momentum, has just restored independence following the latest Russo-Turkish war but which has in reality become a territory under Russian protectorate. Otherwise, why would she go all that way? No tsar has ever come so far south.

Dear old Potemkin, supreme commander of the Russian forces in the region, who has been credited with the great victory, is organizing the tour, but in fact this is only an incident, not a consecration. The Turks are still wide awake and capable of flaring up again. Now, if there were to be another war, why not try to capture the Christian provinces of Moldavia and Wallachia† which they are occupying, along with Greece and the rest of the Balkans? If this were to happen, the effort, and the spoils, would have to be shared with that other Christian emperor, Joseph II, for whom Catherine feels a curious mixture of mistrust and sympathy. So these two sovereigns are to meet a little later, a little farther south, at Kherson. But Russia wants a free hand in other lands, too, particularly Poland, and that is why the Tsarina has also planned a meeting with King Stanislaw Poniatowski.

So although the trip may look like an outing, it is really no such thing.

Heavens above! What a crowd! What a din! What diamonds and gold, medals and ribbons, not to mention the Holy Spirit! What chains and rosettes, turbans and redcaps, fur-lined or peaked! The peaked ones belong to little pygmies, who nod their heads like the porcelain grotesques on your mantelpiece and whose noses and eyes come from China. They're called Lesghis and there are a whole deputation of them who have traveled, with a number of other subjects,

*See Volume I.
†Out of which modern Romania was born.

from the frontiers of the great wall of the Chinese Empire and the other one
in Persia and Byzantium. There are people to suit every taste here, and every
style and type: politics small and great; intrigues great and small.[14]

These words are written to Madame de Coigny, his mistress, by Prince
Joseph de Ligne, whose arrival in Kiev adds just that touch of whimsy that
had been lacking in the cosmopolitan society comprising Catherine II's closest
associates. "One might have called it the Europe Café, it was never empty,"[15]
said the Comte de Ségur, the young ambassador from France who is here
getting his first taste of diplomacy, gallantry and drawing-room witticisms.*
But in Kiev there are also Cobentzl and Fitz-Herbert, the English ambassador;
and the Comte de Dillon, a newly promoted French colonel and engaging
playmate of Marie Antoinette; and Alexandre de Lameth, another American
veteran; and Beaumarchais's curious friend the Prince of Nassau-Siegen, who
is waiting for Catherine to put him in command of a fleet so he can wage
war against the Turks; and Comte Roger de Damas, who would dearly like
a little relief from twenty years of boredom, in the form of some action
somewhere around here, and who is of the opinion that Nassau "has more
flair and talent than knowledge, but his excessive bravura, his enterprising
character and tireless busyness make him capable of the greatest things."[16]
And who is that fierce-looking fellow often seen with Nassau, but only for
quarrels? It's the famous Scottish corsair John Paul Jones,† the ephemeral
"American commodore," also in search of a respectable job but "as incapable
of commanding a squadron as he was distinguished when captain of a frigate."[17]

I say, are there any Russians in this itinerant Russian Court? A few. The
most European of them, the ones for whom French, and sometimes German,
is the principal means of communication. The ministers, such as Bezborodko
and Naryshkin; Dmitri Mamonov, the "favorite" of the moment, who has a
pretty little cherub's mug and a pair of langorous eyes. Miranda, far from
treating him with contempt, speaks highly of his conversation and culture,
acquired—from the Jesuits.

Miranda himself is rumored to be, momentarily, the Empress's lover,
but his daily jottings are enough to refute that. He's a great lover of women,
yes, but he likes them young and pretty, and is not a man to seek advancement
through the boudoir. In this "Europe Café" he sits at a separate table. There

*Ségur was one of La Fayette's companions in America and will continue to be one of the
better memoirists of the day. After various other incarnations, he becomes one of the most
important aristocrats to join Napoleon, who appoints him First Master of Ceremonies—Chief
of Protocol, we would say.

†See Volume II. He was responsible for the only incident during which the American
war touched English soil.

is humor in his observation of his fellow patrons: "I do believe that the Russians and Poles alone possess more ribbons and medals than the rest of Europe combined. A few wear but two or three decorations while others have thirteen or fourteen on display, each accompanied by its star and diamond bar. More than sixty foreigners of note seem to have made appointments with one another in Kiev, not to mention ten or so single women." Of these, he singles out Princess Lubomyrska, "the loveliest woman in the whole Court."[18]

No, no, there's no danger that Miranda will try to oust Mamonov and take on Catherine II. Besides, she wouldn't have encouraged it. Supreme queen of her train of cosmopolitans, she is herself the most cosmopolitan of them all, a little German princess who has made her way, with the help of circumstances and an iron will, to one of the greatest thrones in the world. She's fond of listening to them all gossip and tell their jokes, but if one of them should hazard a presumptuous word, he is smartly put in his place. Perhaps the most original feature of Catherine's cosmopolitanism is that in her intense but "planned" sexuality she has chosen only Russians.

And the most russifying Russian of them all, the one who brings her her "candidates for the private rooms"—but only those whom he knows will not be a threat to himself—is Prince Gregor Alexandrovich Potemkin, the man she has loved best. These triumphal days, he is offering everyone who enters his palaces one of the most dazzling spectacles that ever was, built on a foundation of the bottomless despair of those who are said to be "blessed by the gods."

Francisco de Miranda is the sort who can understand this, and he never says a word against Potemkin, who, after all, never tries to get too close to anyone, not even the Empress.

"Whether from natural indolence or an affected hauteur which he thought useful and diplomatic, this man, Catherine's powerful and capricious favorite, after appearing a few times in full marshal's uniform, covered with diamond decorations, weighted down with embroideries and laces, curled and powdered like the most antiquated of our courtiers, could be seen most often in a pelisse over an open-necked blouse, his legs half naked, his feet in wide slippers, his hair flat and uncombed. He would stretch lazily on a big divan, surrounded by a press of officers and senior officials of the Empire, seldom asking any of them to sit and almost always pretending to be too engrossed in his chess game to notice the Russians or people from other countries who were continually streaming through his drawing room."[19]

Potemkin is undoubtedly the man who has spoiled Catherine least, as far as affection and attention are concerned, if not love. "As I do not yet understand the ins and outs of you, I am no more able to guess the meaning

of your silence.* Even so, I am filled with tenderness for you, my *giaour*,†
Muscovite, Cossack, Pugachev [*sic*], golden cockerel, peacock, cat, pheasant,
golden tiger, lion in the jungle."[20]

MIRANDA

15

APRIL 1787

Young, Enterprising, and Muddleheaded

On April 22, 1787, Francisco de Miranda takes his leave of Catherine II,
declining her magnificent offer of an important position in the Russian army
and sets out for St. Petersburg, while she, with all her court, embarks on the
finally unfrozen Dniepr to discover the Crimea—sorry, Tauridus.

Still sore from his bullying at the hands of the Spanish authorities, he
doesn't seem eager to take on another military post. The great traveler is
not prepared to give up his travels, nor to live in a twilight world as part
high-class secret agent, part army chief in the service of some power or other.
His conversations in Kiev with Catherine, Potemkin and even the favorite,
Mamonov, have helped him to get his priorities straight, and they are, precisely, to have no priority at all, just now. His horizon is still the great
revolution of Spanish America. Until such time as that becomes feasible, he
unfolds before the eyes of his Russian hosts the travel warrant of a Man of
Liberty, undoubtedly the one who has seen most and thought most deeply
about the world of those years. A few essential milestones will enable us to
see why he enjoyed so much prestige when he went places where people
knew how to listen.

1783, we were saying. Having just escaped arrest in Cuba, he reaches
North Carolina sometime in June, no longer regarding himself as a subject

---

*From one of Catherine's letters to Potemkin, undated but written in 1777, ten years
before.

†An insult of Turkish origin, meaning "infidel." Note, too, the curious connotations
attached to "Muscovite" = a brute; and "Pugachev" = vanquished rebel.

of the King of Spain. He spends eighteen months in the United States, which has just signed the peace with England. He travels the length and breadth of the new republic. From Charleston he goes up the coast by ship to Philadelphia and on to New York. This inaugurates the "Grand Tour" technique, which he will apply for the next five years: visits to notable sites and monuments, especially the private artistic and scientific collections that are the "museums" of the time, although people are beginning to imagine the public kind; visits to important people; close and attentive attendance upon the young and pretty women at the top of the ladder but without ever attaching himself to them; detailed writing in his diary, almost every evening. The treadmill of a world-discoverer.

In Philadelphia he meets Samuel Adams, Alexander Hamilton and the two Morrises, Robert and Gouverneur, who are playing a growing part in politics,* and has an audience with Washington, who no longer holds any official position but whose moral authority is unchallenged.

Miranda doesn't take to Washington, perhaps because he is such an extrovert and the other man so much the opposite.[1] Also, the triumphal receptions organized for the "General" in one town after another offend the traveler's egalitarian senses. "Men, women and children are ecstatic with joy and contentment, as though they were witnessing the Redeemer's entrance into Jerusalem. . . . It is rather curious to see that among the many illustrious figures in America who have contributed, by their virtues and abilities, to the success of the grandiose and complex labor of independence, he alone should have obtained this popularity and these unanimous expressions of praise. Just as, in physics, the concentrated foci of the sun's rays reflected in a burning-mirror produce a most admirable effect, so the acts and deeds of the many citizens of America are reflected in independence, with their foci concentrated in Washington. It is a usurpation, as unjust as it is capricious."

Nor does La Fayette, of whom he catches a glimpse in Boston, find favor in his eyes: "I had occasion to spend time with him and he seemed to me a rather mediocre character, of Gallic agitation and constant mobility."

Miranda's tracks are closely watched by Spanish diplomats and merchants, with whom he behaves very rashly and who do not fail to add more ballast to his files at the Court of Spain. On January 12, 1784, a man named Quintana writes to the minister of the Indies in Madrid, "I have met Miranda, whose dealings in Havana are known to you, and sufficient they were to try

---

*Gouverneur Morris, a conservative-minded man who succeeds Jefferson as United States ambassador to Paris in 1792–1794, will be increasingly appalled by the vicissitudes of the French Revolution. He had a leg amputated following a nasty fall from a horse, but everybody takes him for a war casualty. According to Miranda, "He shows all the outward marks of a man of spirit but I think there is more ostentation, audacity and tinsel than true value in him."

Your Excellency's moderation and natural mildness. He told me that from here he means to go to London, where he will submit a scheme for the capture of a few sites on our western American coasts."

The Spanish informers are assisted in their task by some Frenchmen, too, such as the Marquis de Barbé-Marbois,* Louis XVI's consul general at the American Congress, who hastens to tell the Comte de Vergennes of the arrival in Philadelphia of "Miranda, a Creole from Caracas, young, enterprising and muddleheaded, who said to me, 'It will not be long before our American kingdoms go through a revolution similar to the one you are witnessing here.'"

When Miranda leaves America in 1784, he does not know that the jaws of two of the greatest countries of Europe, Spain and France, are ready to snap shut upon him. He begins his travels in England, not before expressing some slight disappointment with the great new republic which is so courageous but also so tedious to this quintessential libertine who had been hoping to find the Promised Land in it. However, he managed to put up with many things while there—except the Puritans. One Sunday in Newbury Port he was compelled to endure a sermon, in the local Presbyterian church, by one Reverend Murray, the fashionable preacher of the day: "He began in a bombastic tone, praying God to devastate and eliminate from the face of the earth all pagans, Moslems, Antichrist [the pope], heretics and their acolytes. In this manner the whole of the universe, save his own flock, found itself excluded from divine protection in a few seconds. What a fanatical brute!"

1785. London, on the other hand, is love at first sight. Miranda inhales an air of freedom he wasn't expecting, and it ravels the last tatters of his vision of America as ideal. The aesthete in him appreciates the comforts of the Royal Hotel in fashionable Pall Mall. "I am dazzled by all the wealth, the culture and splendor in this country. What a vast quantity of shipping! I am sure that there is more navigation and commerce on the Thames than on all the other rivers of the world." Marveling, he attends debates in the House of Commons, "that sublime political and legislative school"; he becomes acquainted with the leading figures of the day, both Tory and Whig: Pitt, Fox, Sheridan, Burke, Shelburne . . .

Come to think of it, what does Miranda live on? How does he finance the great expense of travel in those days, his two servants, his carriage and horse, his coachman? How can he keep an open table and select such hand-

---

*Barbé-Marbois (1745–1837) is a senior civil servant during the Revolution and Empire, mainly in Santo Domingo. He is elected to the Council of Five Hundred, but after the coup d'état of 18 Fructidor, Barras orders him and a few other Notables to be deported without trial to French Guiana, for the crime of moderation. He serves, then betrays, Napoleon, and dies, laden with honors, under Louis-Philippe.

some gifts for the conquests he makes in every town and for the people who invite him? How does he pay for the rare and sometimes clandestine editions he buys so avidly and freely?

When he left Havana, he had a fair amount of money in hand saved from his colonel's pay, and it seems that his family in Caracas provided him with several generous letters of credit on American and English banks. Credit breeding credit, he begins to borrow, and ends up living from one debt to the next, performing the kind of financial acrobatics habitual to the majority of the people of his class. When a high lord commits himself to some expenditure anywhere in Europe, it would be tantamount to an insult to ask him for security, let alone a down payment. Most of the public figures and princes with whom Miranda associates, including Pitt and Fox, will die insolvent in the midst of luxury. Which is one of the reasons why he feels so much at home from London to St. Petersburg. All these folks are living on their debts. And it is also, no doubt, one reason why he felt a little cramped in America, where every penny is counted.

A little irresponsible, to be sure, but not daft, he knows that in this respect he is walking on the razor's edge. From now on, part of his essential activity, like that of a Beaumarchais or a Mirabeau, consists in the search for an enlightened protector; in other words, a minor god who subscribes to his way of thinking and will agree to pay off his past debts and provide him with a substantial income, earned or unearned. Since he is "barred" from the kingdoms of the family pact (Spain and France) and since the Americans are ragged pioneers with nothing in the bank, his thoughts turn to a few of the crowned Ali Babas in whose direction his wind is blowing him: Joseph II, Frederick the Great, or Catherine, who "treated herself" to Diderot. Provided always that he remain what he is—which, in passing, only enhances his value; for what intelligent angel would refuse a limited risk on a potential president of South America?

August 1785. Duped by the ruses of the Spanish diplomats in London, he is still hoping, or pretending to hope, that his position in Madrid will eventually be put right. But he also keeps his back turned to that country and sets off on a Grand Tour of Europe, leaving from Harwich and going directly to Holland—thereby eliminating the risks of a passage through France, where some "very special agents" are lying in wait to abduct him, in Calais and Boulogne. He quickly crosses Holland from west to east, hurrying to join the sphere of influence of Frederick, whom he, like others before him, would very much like to subjugate and seduce. He proceeds methodically across the mosaic of German lands, so chopped up that no traveler can tell if the ground underfoot belongs to the Emperor (in Vienna) or the King of Prussia; not to mention the claim of the Elector of Hanover, cradle of the present English dynasty and still a piece of its property. There's Brunswick, too, where the duke, who is related to the King of Prussia, might be classified for future reference as an enlightened despot;* there's Magdeburg, fortified like a porcupine, a "city of arms"—here he is definitely in "Prussianizing Prussia," whose ruthless king has devised a very simple solution to the massive problem of poverty, namely the drafting of every able-bodied insolvent male into the army. This is the kingdom of march-or-die, where the "guard on duty, who wears sweeping plumes in his headgear and is ready to perform any number of heroic deeds on an empty stomach, holds out his hand to you for alms. If he is caught, he will be severely punished. But soldiers do not beg in the same way as common beggars."

Faster, faster! Frederick is ailing, sinking. Brandenburg, another fortified town, on August 29. "We visited the cathedral and listened to old and fantastic tales of superstition and ignorance." Potsdam at last, Berlin's Versailles and Frederick's capital, on which a great crowd of visitors is converging on the eve of the splendid maneuvers that have become a model for all the armies of the earth. Miranda sees the sovereign only from afar, two days in September, when the soldier king, almost on his deathbed, sits straight as a ramrod on his horse and presides with critical and all-seeing eye over the movements of thousands of troops. His last public appearance.†

Yet another contemporary great whom Miranda does not adore: "The King combines the mentality of a *philosophe* with the heart and feelings of a tyrant. Performing deeds that only a lofty soul could conceive, he ruins them with his utter pettiness and matchless avarice."

Let him go; on to Austria, to see what's going on in the Empire. What if Joseph II were to prove less of a disappointment? By way of Saxony (Leipzig and Dresden), Prague, "where the famous Jan Hus undermined the foundations of the Christian religion," and so to Vienna, "the best-constructed city in Europe, with surroundings of great beauty." The traveler is overwhelmed by the Imperial Library, the richest in Europe; three hundred thousand volumes under an immense wood-paneled ceiling, typical of the Viennese baroque style. He does his duty conscientiously: visits to the Hofburg (Imperial palace), Prater gardens and, of course, Schönbrunn. But he does not seem to have been tempted to try to obtain an audience with the Emperor, whom he sees at no closer quarters than he did Frederick, probably for want of the proper letters of introduction and perhaps out of some instinctive aversion. Miranda observes Joseph II from a distance, at the opera, "wearing the simple green and red uniform of his regiment." "He is spoken

*We shall meet him again at Valmy, opposing Miranda.
†On the final illness and death of Frederick II and Mirabeau's almost eyewitness account, see Volume IV.

of as a prince of very little culture, never seen with a book in his hand. And although he wishes for his people's happiness, his despotic conviction that he is always in the right causes him to make many mistakes, which are attributed to the obduracy of his limited judgment."

Apparently, all that is left is for him to go back to England. But the Grand Tour itch is still upon him. He decides to push on farther, all the way to that other empire, so mysterious and so ominous, which even the most learned Europeans know only by hearsay: Turkey. In late October 1785 he leaves Vienna by coach for Trieste, where he hopes to find a ship bound for Constantinople.

Partly because he has no choice, and partly because he can't resist a temptation, but in the first instance because there is no ship available at Trieste he makes a devil of a detour to get there—right around Italy, in fact: Venice, Mantua, Parma, Modena, Bologna, Florence, Pisa, Livorno, Rome. . . . Knowing him as we do, we are not surprised to learn that he is not enraptured by the mass of Pope Pius VI: "This spectacle truly deserves to be seen and considered from a rational point of view. Such splendor, combined with such absurdity! How is it possible that peoples should have venerated and believed in so ridiculous a mishmash? I defy all the dervishes there are, whirling or howling or what, to equal it in extravagance. . . . When His Holiness says mass, the host is brought to his seat so that he can consume it at his leisure. He drinks the blood through a golden straw, just as the young women in Lima drink their maté. . . . I saw him come into the basilica through the St. Martha Gate, in a white surplice that looked like a dressing gown, with red slippers on his feet, powdered like some Parisian dandy."

Miranda-Sade? There's a little of that in some of his reactions. . . .*

February 26, 1786. He really can't miss Naples.† March 16: after a difficult crossing of the Apennines he reaches Barletta, a little port on the east coast, "to board a ship bound for Ragusa, whence I can continue my journey to Constantinople." There's no ship in port, so he waits another ten days, whiling away the time reading Baron von Todt's *Mémoires sur les Turcs et les Tartares*. Miranda's diary reflects a constant shifting back and forth, between his actual travels and his literary escapades.

April 2. Ragusa.‡ A microscopic Adriatic republic under Turkish influence. He is well received, thanks to the letters of introduction he has gleaned here and there on his travels, from everybody except the Spanish and French

---

*On Sade's impressions of Rome, see Volume I.

†One year to the day before the arrival of another escaping soul, Johann Wolfgang Goethe; see chapter 7 above.

‡Now Dubrovnik.

authorities. Even so, a health quarantine is imposed. More time wasted—reading. He disembarks in Greece on May 16, at Patras, bristling with the historical memories on which his learning is founded. This was Morea in the Peloponnesus of old, where the Turks put down a Greek uprising fifteen years before. He makes his way through one of the oldest areas of the civilized world, Christian for centuries and now chafing more and more under the yoke of a decadent Turkey.

Corinth, Piraeus, Athens. He reflects, suffers, treads the soil of his ancient history. Marathon. . . . On July 3, 1786, a little ship deposits him at Smyrna, a Greek town on the flank of the Turkish Empire. Miranda first sets his foot in Asia. July 12: another ship carries him to Constantinople, in a crowd of passengers that include "thirty young Negroes wearing hardly more than a shirt, to be sold in the Turkish capital, where they are reckoned to be worth five hundred rupees apiece." Eighteen days asea. On the morning of July 30, Constantinople rises into view.

He spends nearly two months there, in the shadow of the castle of the Seven Towers, where the grand vizier incarcerates the ambassadors of countries with which he is at war. Francisco sees this living god from an even greater distance than he saw Frederick and Joseph. He has few illusions. The merest glimpse is all he catches, during a caïque* excursion, of the Sultan Abdul Hamid I, seated on a silver sofa before his prostrate courtiers in one of the pavilions of the imperial gardens. It's enough to infuriate the Man of Liberty, who is incapable of acknowledging any potentate as "the man of god and divinity upon earth."

It is somewhere around this time that Miranda decides to head north to Russia, meet Catherine II and try his luck again in northern Europe. Despite covert assistance from France and England, Abdul Hamid I has just lost a war with Russia; the peace treaty of Küçük Kaynarca takes "Tauridus" away from Turkey, along with some southern Russian steppes and the port of Azov, plus freedom of navigation on the Black Sea, and limits the rights of Turkish protectorates over the Christian communities of Wallachia and Moldavia.

If he was ever really tempted to put himself in Catherine's hands, it was then. Especially as Turkey is grinding its jaws, cheating on the treaty and refusing, specifically in the occupied Balkans, to give way. The Divan is not cooperating† and this peace with Russia is more like a truce; which is why the two great Christian emperors, from Russia and Austria, are shortly to

---

*Caïque: light skiff used on the Bosporus.

†Divan: the Turkish privy council, presided over by the sultan, which met in a room containing cushions on which the participants could lounge. By extension, the Ottoman Empire.

meet in these parts. Miranda might almost believe the meeting had been arranged for him.

He sees many things in Constantinople and meets many people, mainly in diplomatic circles, where the only people who avoid him, of course, are those in the embassies of Spain and France. The Dutch, English, Prussians and Russians, on the other hand, vie with one another to help him. That is how Bulgakov, the Tsarina's ambassador, gets him the papers he needs to be received in Kherson and Kiev, where, it is now learned, Prince Potemkin is organizing an extravagant welcome for the sovereign on her greatest journey.

In the meantime Miranda knocks on many doors, listens to many people talking and, some say later, does a lot of spying—but cautiously: in Turkey it's an everyday occurrence for people who are suspected of excessive curiosity to be subjected to tortures of rare cruelty.

On September 9, 1786, he boards a little sailing ship bound for Kherson. Then comes another winter of waiting at the mouth of the Dniepr, following a period of "quarantine" employed, God be thanked, in reading Restif de la Bretonne's *Pornographe.* Kherson is a brand-new town but it already has forty thousand inhabitants; Potemkin has made it his private capital and arrives there in person in January 1787, with a royal train: three hundred horses and a bodyguard of two hundred men, "Germans, Greeks, Hebrews [*sic*], Armenians, along with Cossacks, Tartars, Kalmuks, and Georgians." Miranda is always awed and reticent when confronted with the external manifestations of power and has half a mind to run away, but he is pushed forward into Potemkin's presence at just the right moment, when his Supreme Highness, in excellent spirits, is preparing a "brandied fricassee" for his guests with his own hands.

The traveler has one trump card to play with the omnipotent master of southern Russia, in that he has just been to Constantinople and everybody knows there's going to have to be another war with the Turks.

"Did you say Constantinople?" From that moment on, Miranda is taken as a sort of friendly hostage by Potemkin, who gives him preferential treatment, never lets him out of his sight, and won't release him until he has presented him to the Empress. This period of waiting is spent indulging in what must be the highest privilege for an explorer: a three-month tour of "Tauridus" in preparation for Catherine's visit to the region.

Exhausted and suffering from a bad cold, Miranda just makes it to Kiev at the beginning of February 1787.

What happens next we have already seen: he's introduced to the Tsarina, takes her fancy, is offered a tempting position in the Russian army but decides to go back north instead, as she turns southward. Will-o'-the-wisp Miranda!

He still has Moscow to do, and St. Petersburg, and then, the day after tomorrow, Sweden, Denmark, and England again.

But on the horizon, unforgotten, there is always the image of his home-land to be "revolutionized."

BEAUMARCHAIS

16

JUNE 8, 1787

This Triumph Was Somewhat Soured

Will this make three in a row for Beaumarchais? After *The Barber of Seville* and *The Marriage of Figaro,** will he produce another brilliant work of art to set a seal upon his genius? He's going to risk it, anyway. After the Comédie-Française, first on the Right Bank (with *Barber*) and then on the Left (with *Marriage*), he is now tackling a new genre, not only for himself but also for most of the authors of his time: an opera libretto.

June 8, 1787: the attention of "informed circles," having no more Assembly of Notables to feed upon, focuses on Beaumarchais. The Paris Opéra is giving the first performance of *Tarare,* to music by the Italian composer Salieri. It looks as though this opening night is going to be as much of an event as that of *Marriage* three years before. Grimm informs his correspondents accordingly, not without a touch of acidity because he can't stand Beaumarchais:

"Never have any of our theaters witnessed such a crowd as came pouring down all the avenues leading to the Opéra on the day of the first performance of *Tarare;* barriers were set up for the occasion and defended by guards four hundred strong† but even they were scarcely able to contain it."[1]

The site is the huge hall, separated from the Palais-Royal by the rue Saint-Honoré, which the Parisians are calling "the new Opéra." The previous one, where Marie Antoinette met Fersen one evening at a ball, went up in

---

*For the first night of *Barber* on February 23, 1775, see Volume I; for the opening of *Marriage* on April 27, 1784, see Volume III.

†Of the French Guards.

flames in 1781, and the King's Household, under pressure from the Baron de Breteuil, has hastily erected a great hulk of a structure that can hold several thousand spectators and is equipped with all the latest gadgets. Paris could go without many things, but not, for long, an Opéra. To hear the Russian traveler Karamsin tell it, this was a sort of European religion: "Anyone who goes to Paris without seeing the Opéra is like a person going to Rome without seeing the Pope."[2] To the German Storch: "Almost everything I saw in Paris did not live up to the enthusiastic descriptions I had read, but the Opéra exceeded my expectations. Everything there is on a scale befitting the importance of the capital; the settings are admirably handsome and verisimilitudinous and the costumes of the three hundred artistes and chorus members do not have their equal anywhere."[3]

Beaumarchais and his intimates are enthroned in the best seats, in one of the boxes in the second tier, surrounded by an astonishingly novel decorative display. Farewell the fleurs-de-lis and heavy crowns of old. On this side, we see sheaves of pikes; across the way, beplumed golden helmets; and eagles of imperial mien and Gallic cocks. A murmur runs around the house as the curtain opens. Will the opera be as original as the house with its multiform decor, still baroque and at the same time already romantic?

Beaumarchais has aged a lot since his humiliating incarceration at Saint-Lazare,* his sharp exchange of polemics with Mirabeau about the water company—in which *Le Tout-Paris* asserts that he lost face. And lastly he has gotten married, after a long liaison, on February 26, 1786, to Marie-Thérèse de Willer-Mawlaz, who doesn't have much to offer except her excellent housekeeping, and peace and quiet, in which he can devote himself to their daughter Eugénie, already nine years old; he absolutely dotes upon her. Court people, and not only those of France, are eager to see him knocked down a peg or three. It took them two or three years of reading and watching to understand the danger of *Marriage of Figaro,* but now they've got the picture and they're waiting for him to make a slip.

Grimm mentions the fact, in his review of *Tarare:* "This triumph, so fresh and therefore so pleasing to the author's self-respect, was, however, somewhat soured. The audience made free to express, by marks of very acute displeasure, the reproaches it believed it was entitled to level at the work, especially in the fifth act.

"This work, one of the most singular designs I have ever encountered in the theater, was listened to most attentively, but only feebly applauded.† Subsequent performances were attended by equally large audiences but were not more applauded than the first. This form of success is yet another of

*See Volume IV.

†Supreme admission: When an audience *listens,* it does not applaud.

the singularities that seem to typify everything Monsieur de Beaumarchais does."[4]

The opening resounds with a violent noise in the atmosphere, an awful clashing of all the elements. The curtain rises upon nothing but clouds, rolling, rending, showing glimpses of unbridled gales; whirling, they form most violently agitated dances.

La Nature comes forward in their midst with a wand in hand, adorned with all the attributes characteristic of her, and imperiously tells them:

You've given the universe sufficient pains,
Wild winds, and have enough thunderbolts hurled.

Cease! Now resume your chains,
Let Zephyr alone rule the world!

(Overture, sound and movement continue.)
Chorus of furious winds:

No more torment the universe! . . .

(They rush off to the lower clouds. Zephyr rises into the air. The overture and noise gradually subside; the clouds scatter; all becomes harmonious and calm. A superb country landscape is seen and the Spirit of Fire descends on the eastern side, in a shining cloud.)[5]

And off we go, in the selfsame vein, for five acts. They tell a tale, in doggerel, of a palace revolution mounted against the dreadful tyrant Atar by his own troops, who want the best of officers, the good and just Tarare, to take his place. To add a little spice to the plot, Tarare is in love with a totally inert woman named Astasie, whose voice is heard on six occasions and no more. But all's well that end's well when the curtain falls. The wicked Atar, seeing his men rise up against him, stabs himself, and the men force Tarare to don the crown of the fairy-tale kingdom of Ormus.

Here and there, in this perfectly appalling libretto, are a few passages expressing a social concern, and by these it is occasionally possible to identify the author of *Barber* and *Marriage*. The characters call upon Brahma, but that really means the Supreme Being inherited from Rousseau. This only adds fuel to their resentment of the great and powerful, however; because this is, in spite of everything, a sort of minirevolution, and Beaumarchais dares to make it plain in the last four lines: they are sung by *La Nature* and *Le Génie du Feu*, whose words are painted on the clouds in letters of fire, while trumpets sound and the thunder resumes:

Mortal, whomsoever thou beest,
Prince or Brahman* or of sol-
    dier kind,
Whether on earth thou art
    greatest or least

By thy estate is in no way de-
    fined;
By thy character alone is it
    signed.[6]

"Thus, human dignity is the moral issue which I wanted to explore, the theme I chose."[7]

Pierre-Augustin de Beaumarchais defends his *Tarare* in a preface entitled *Aux abonnés de l'Opéra, qui voudraient aimer l'opéra,* with this argument: "I have learned a secret that I must pass on to you. I have discovered the real reason why people understand nothing at the Opéra. Shall I tell you, gentlemen? It is that they don't listen."[8]

For him this is not so much a new opera as a new way of interesting people in opera. "I thought one ought to strike a middle way between the magical and the historical. It also seemed to me that highly civilized customs were too methodical [*sic*] to be dramatic; Oriental ways, which are heterogeneous and less familiar, give freer rein to the mind."[9]

The preface to *Tarare* is the best thing about *Tarare;* in it, at times, Beaumarchais shows his old scope of vision: "The spirit of the nation appears to be undergoing a felicitous crisis: a bright and far-reaching light is giving us a sense that things can be better than they are."[10]

All those good intentions, ending in five solid acts of teeming bombast!

To the warrior bold who my life
    saves
This palace I offer, I freely give.
'Twas built by ten thousand
    Malay slaves
Of purest ebon and ivory rare;
This palace whose smiling aspect
    reigns
Over the broad and fertile
    plains

And on to the Eastern sea so
    fair.
There, one hundred women are
    kept apart—
Circassians, alluring yet most se-
    date [*sic*]—
Awaiting the orders that spring
    from your heart
To the treasures of Asia you
    t'initiate.[11]

What on earth has happened to the real Beaumarchais?

At the end, amid the tumult of whistles and bravos, part of the audience calls for the authors to come on stage and take their bows alongside the actors. Offended, Beaumarchais refuses.

---

*By this term Beaumarchais means the clergy, in reference to Brahma's Hindu disciples.

"This being unprecedented in the lyric theater, no one was prepared for the incident. The actors were quarreling over who would, or rather would not, speak to the audience; meanwhile the tumult continued, even the people in the boxes kept their seats. While this was going on, the actresses laid hold of M. Salieri, bore him away like some sacred body and brought him onto the stage. This ceremony peformed, the audience were still not content and called for the author of the text, but M. de Beaumarchais was inexorable. As the shouting did not cease, the lights in the theater were extinguished as the only means of putting an end to it."[12]

This is Paris's first meeting with Antonio Salieri, an attractive, black-eyed, dark-skinned little chap who dresses with great care. He's a very well-known music teacher in Vienna, where he aspires to embody the Italian tradition; in fact, an anti-Mozart! He has composed a number of celebrated operas, in particular *Les Danaïdes** and *Les Horaces*. He was born in Venezia thirty-seven years ago. Beaumarchais was not so eager to get him when he had finished writing his libretto; naturally, he wanted Gluck, who has been the dominant figure in the music world since the production of his *Alceste* and the *Iphigénies*.† That would have been a point in his favor, as far as the Queen's patronage was concerned, because she was loyal to the memory of her old music master. But Gluck was wary, and possibly put off by the "avant-garde" subject matter of *The Marriage of Figaro,* so he courteously declined, and sent Salieri to Paris instead.

For the deputy this is a great moment, despite the audience's reservations, justified by the insignificance of a score that is all recitatives and monotony. For the rest of his life, he will be convinced that he has just taken part in the creation of a masterpiece.

The Beaumarchaises have made him feel so welcome these last few months! Pierre-Augustin is incapable of entertaining anybody in his home without making him one of the family. "They treated me with such consideration and kindness!"[13] In the afternoon they would play four-hand piano sonatas for Eugénie, the little queen of the household.

"At two o'clock, M. or Mme. de Beaumarchais would come into the room and say, 'Come and dine, children.'

"We dined; afterward I would walk a little, read the gazettes at the Palais-Royal or go to some theater. I would come back early. When M. de Beaumarchais was not home, I would go up to my rooms on the second

---

*The music of which was composed almost entirely by his master, Gluck, who gave him a great deal of help. Needless to add, the fairy story that springs up five years later accusing him of having poisoned Mozart is outrageous.

†In this connection see Volume I (the opening of *Iphigénie en Aulide* and the quarrel with Piccini).

floor; sometimes, I would put my drunken German servant to bed; I would go to bed myself in a room in which, from my bed where I worked every day, I could see the sun rise with heavenly pleasure. Around ten, M. de Beaumarchais would come in; I would sing him what I had made of our great opera, he would applaud, encourage me, teach me like a father."[14]

Yes, but it is now June 8, and on April 17 a tract against Beaumarchais came out in Paris. Several thousand copies of it have been printed and sold. A shadow has been hanging over the rehearsals and opening night of *Tarare* that has nothing to do with the lighting in the theater. Most of the people calling Beaumarchais to come on stage tonight want to see him partly because of his opera but even more because of the Kornman affair, and the way he is defending himself in it.

BERGASSE

17

JUNE 1787

The Blood Went to My Head

In the feverish months leading to the production of *Tarare,* people often remarked upon the presence, among Beaumarchais's intimates, of a splendid young woman and an odd-looking man, the Prince and Princess of Nassau-Siegen. It was they who, with the best intentions, got him entangled in the Kornman affair, which has been brewing for a long while but only bursts now, like an abscess.[1]

The reverberations of this incident have been among the most unforeseen of his entire career. The Kornman affair is gnawing at him, demolishing him, even taking away his pleasure in *Tarare.* Maybe that's why so many people have come tonight. They're craning their necks to catch a glimpse of his face, to see how he's reacting. For the last two months he has been dragged through the mud, on the grounds that he got a pregnant young woman out of prison—in 1781! He's not the man he was on the first night of *Marriage;* he's not smiling, he doesn't laugh, he's not enjoying his meal. He's been hit.

Nassau-Siegen is a minor Rhenish prince, deprived of his principality by a family quarrel. In this year of *Tarare* he is forty-two, but looks younger.

Wherever gunpowder was being lit, he has distinguished himself as a soldier; so, is he German, French, Spanish or what? Between the ages of fifteen and twenty, when Louix XV made him a colonel and presumably more French than anything else, people sometimes also wondered whether he was a man or a woman, as they are still doing about the Chevalier d'Éon, now growing old in England dressed in women's clothes.*

Nassau-Siegen is still remarkable for his fragile, timid, effeminate looks and behavior. He comes into his own only in the presence of danger, and he has sought it everywhere. It's made him famous. He went around the world with Bougainville and fought tigers bare-handed somewhere. He became friendly with Beaumarchais at the time of the American war, when he was looking for yet another battlefield. He was almost burned alive at Gibraltar during the famous siege of 1782, when the Marquis d'Arçon tried out the first armored ships in history (although they were built of wood). Every one of those redoubtable *prasmes* blew up, and Nassau-Siegen was plucked out of the water by the Spanish, whose king conferred a "grandeeship" upon him. That did not make him any wealthier (he is covered in debt) but it did add to his recklessness. Shortly after the siege of Gibraltar, Otton de Nassau-Siegen stirred up all the noise he could by marrying a young and beautiful Pole named Princess Sangusko, who had just divorced her husband in her own country. At first, nobody in France wanted to know them, including the Archbishop of Paris. It is really not done, marrying a divorced woman. . . .

Nobody except Beaumarchais.

Pierre-Augustin, swept away as only he can be by the warmth of his friendship, overheated in this instance by a tinge of snobbery, set himself up as the couple's protector. He paid their servants and creditors and doled out a sort of allowance to them. By some miracle, he obtained permission from Louis XVI, otherwise such a stickler for the rules, for them to marry in France, on the pretext that the young woman's first marriage did not really exist, having been celebrated in Poland. True, that was at a time when the King could not easily refuse him such a favor, after the flaming insult of his imprisonment in Saint-Lazare.

Thereafter, the Nassau-Siegens formed part of the "Beaumarchais set." Which hasn't prevented the Prince from continuing his escapades; this very spring, 1787, he has gone all the way to the Court of Catherine II in Russia.

In late February the paper vendors distributed ten thousand copies, in Paris, of a *Mémoire sur une question d'adultère, de séduction et de diffamation pour le sieur Kornman, contre la dame Kornman son épouse; le sieur Daudet de*

*On the Chevalier d'Éon, see the index to Volumes I and II. The report of the autopsy performed on him in 1810 will ascertain that, physiologically at least, he was a man.

Jossan; le sieur Pierre-Augustin Caron de Beaumarchais; et M. Lenoir, conseiller d'État et ancien lieutenant général de police.[2]

The tract is signed Kornman but the writing betrays a lawyer's hand, one who has suddenly rolled across Beaumarchais's path without knowing him except by name and without having ever met him. He is Nicolas Bergasse, a thirty-seven-year-old advocate whose assault has hit Pierre-Augustin like a sniper's. He's completely at a loss. Why this new foe, all of a sudden? Why this "abduction of a life" inflicted upon him by the publication of Bergasse's pamphlet on the eve of the third great creative effort of his existence? Such violence in this accusation, which the "anonymous" author has painstakingly sent to all the top people at Court, members of the academies, *Parlement,* etc., while hundreds of copies of it are being sold in the shops!

Beaumarchais finds himself described in the text as, *inter alia,* a man

whose entire life has been one long assault upon decency and probity; a man who has immersed himself in every commerce and undertaking in order to take advantage of it for his own profit; a man who has never known any other resource, for the increase and perpetuation of his fortune, than intrigue, espionage, informing, bad faith; base, when it is in his interest to crawl; bold, when he has contrived matters so that he has nothing to fear; insulting to authority when he can be so without risk; selling himself to authority when he can hope to win favors; a man who, to mention one too well-known fact in a political context of importance to us, had himself made responsible for the supplies needed by English America at the time when we were helping it to break free from its chains and who, surrounded by the highest interests but intent upon nothing but his personal gain, inundated the countries of the New World with spoiled goods and thereby dealt a fell blow, beyond the seas, to the national commerce and to the reputation of the name of France. . . . A man, in a word, who all his life has done nothing but scurry around in a hotbed of corruption and imposture and whose sacrilegious existence proves with such shaming éclat the depths of depravity to which we have sunk.[3]

He even gets himself talked to with the familiar form *tu,* like a servant: "I know your whole life, it is execrable. . . . Ambitious for success in any form, finding in yourself, in the natural consciousness of your strength, no resource with which to achieve it; but bold, and vain, and heedless of the means you had to employ, because you know nothing of pity and the profound feelings of justice it engenders; intrigue, indignity, lies, calumny, attacks, one after another; you have employed every possible means to raise yourself to the level of renown, riches and power to which you have ascended and from which you now must needs descend."[4]

Conclusion: "Wretch, you reek of crime!"[5]

Gracious! What's going on here, in this life that has already known so much agitation? Kornman, Bergasse: who are these lice, swelling so monstrously in Beaumarchais's hair?

Kornman? A big Alsatian banker who keeps a somewhat political salon. He has been closely associated with a Lyons firm, that of the two Bergasse brothers. Nicolas Bergasse, the elder, a young, almost out-of-work lawyer, has helped Kornman to build up his little socialite society in Paris, in which such well-known figures as La Fayette, d'Eprémesnil, Brissot and Clavière can be seen along with a number of—at this point—unknowns, like Pétion, Gorsas, Carra.[6]

Since 1779, Kornman has been married to a pretty woman, and it is this woman whom the Prince and Princess of Nassau-Siegen asked Beaumarchais to defend, one evening when they were dining with him in October 1781.

He tried to wriggle out of it: "They insisted, I resisted, alleging (what is perfectly true) that I had never performed a praiseworthy and generous act without getting into trouble for it."[7]

"I am a bad man, but I beg it may be granted at least that of all bad men I am the best.*

" 'But suspicion attaches itself so readily to you: everywhere you have been taxed with loving women!'

"And why should I blush for having loved them? I love them still. Of old I loved them for myself, today I love them for themselves, in a just gratitude. A few dreadful men have caused me great trouble in my life, and a few good women's hearts have given it all the delight it has known. And should I be so ungrateful, in my old age, as to refuse my assistance to the beloved sex which made my youth happy? Never does a woman weep without my heart contracting. They are, alas, so ill-treated by law and men! I am pouring out my heart upon the paper here."[8]

In this business, the biographer is compelled to shuttle constantly back and forth between 1781 and 1787. A long stretch, and quite in keeping with the outlandishness of the rest of Beaumarchais's life.

So, back in 1781, Beaumarchais let his heartstrings be tugged by the tale of a pregnant young woman in prison.

Kornman did his banking in Strasbourg as in Paris, and in Strasbourg, a still young man named Daudet de Jossan had been appointed as the King's syndic in the town;† while there, he had known both the Nassau-Siegens, some of whose interests he looked after; and he had also known Kornman,

---

*From Beaumarchais's *Mémoire*, replying to the defamations of Bergasse and Kornman.

†In the jungle of functions under the Ancien Régime, a syndic sometimes acted as mayor, at other times as provost of shopkeepers; he worked closely under the orders of the intendant.

of whom he saw so much that, with his implicit consent, he had seduced his wife.

It was all the way of the world, in those days, for rich people. But since then, Daudet de Jossan has lost his position, Kornman's eyes were suddenly opened, and the magnificent cuckold decided that the best thing would be to have his wife convicted of adultery; whereupon the Nassau-Siegens, put in the picture by Daudet de Jossan, found Beaumarchais's weak spot.

He didn't know her. It happened just as he was regaining some credit at Court. The Nassau-Siegens showed him letters written by the indulgent husband to Daudet de Jossan, in which an understanding between the two men was patent.

> One of the zealous defenders [of Madame Kornman] gave me a packet of letters written by the lady's husband to the man he was accusing of corrupting her. I went out onto a terrace, where I read them eagerly. The blood went to my head. After I finished reading them, I went back in and said, deeply moved:
>
> "Gentlemen, I am at your service; and yours, Princess; I am ready to go with you to see M. Lenoir, to plead everywhere and energetically the cause of the unfortunate woman who is being punished for someone else's crime. Dispose of me as you see fit. All I know of the husband is the disorder of his affairs. . . . I have never seen his unfortunate wife; but after what I have just read I should think myself as cowardly as the author of those letters if I did not contribute all my energy to the generous deed you wish to perform."
>
> My friends embraced me and I went, with the Princesse de Nassau, to M. Lenoir, where I pleaded for our prisoner at length. I have no fear that I shall offend anyone by thus calling her "ours." Each one of us had adopted her! From there I set off for Versailles and would not rest easy until I had a promise from the ministers that the unfortunate woman would not give birth, would not perish, in the house of detention into which she had been thrust by intrigue.[9]

She did not give birth in prison. M. Lenoir, smiling broadly, said to her improvised champion, "The people you care for, Monsieur de Beaumarchais, are certain of being well-served,"[10] as he handed him the King's order to transfer Madame Kornman from her cell to a midwife's home.

Pierre-Augustin then experienced one of the joys he was born for. He went in person to give the notification of release to this victim whom he had never met:

> Picture to yourselves a young woman, in prison in December, her only clothing a thin summer bedcover, pale, distraught, pregnant and beautiful! Ah, above all, pregnant, and about to give birth! I do not know by what other men

may be affected; but I myself have never seen a young woman pregnant, wearing that air, so gentle and suffering, that renders her so interesting, without feeling an impulse that hurls my soul forth to meet her.[11]

1781–1787 . . . They had seen little of one another since then. She called him "my dear papa"; he found advisers for her in her long battle with her husband to reclaim her property. The whole process was quietly pursuing its course until the beginning of 1787, when Kornman, having exhausted all other resources, found an unexpected supporter in a sinister paid ruffian of morality—

—Nicolas Bergasse. Born in 1750 into a family that originally came from the county of Foix and is now firmly entrenched in the higher commercial and administrative echelons of Lyons. Poor health, from childhood on. Four brothers, a dreaded father named Joachim Bergasse, who took himself for Abraham. His first schooling was with the Jesuits, replaced, upon their eviction, by the Josephites and Oratorians. Favorite childhood reading: Pascal, Bossuet, the Bible. At twenty, taught philosophy at the Oratorians' school in Nantes, then Soissons, then Condom, then Auch. He's small, chubby, has large, scared eyes and a mass of well-cared-for hair. He finally went back to Lyons to take his "degrees in law." At that point he started practicing his literary scales in the service of the established order: a *Discours sur l'Honneur,* another *Discours sur l'Humanité des juges,* already swimming against the stream of Enlightenment.[12]

He is noticed in Lyons and manages to "go up" to Paris, where he arrives in the heat of the infatuation with Mesmer and his animal magnetism treatments using wooden tubs.* He publishes *Considérations sur le magnétisme animal.*[13] He meets Kornman and finds, at last, the blessed opportunity to get himself taken up by "the right people," by giving voice to the lust for revenge that so many abusive husbands and shameful seigneurs have been nursing for three years, against Tarare's claim that:

Fie! The abuse of supreme power	The evil man who makes all quake
Brings its ruin in its wake.	Tomorrow will be seen to cower.[14]

The opening night of *Tarare* decidedly does not show us a happy Beaumarchais. Whatever the libretto and music may be worth, he knows, he feels,

*On Mesmer and his connection with Bergasse and Kornman, see Volume III.

that people's minds are on other things. His too. He has just brought a libel suit in the Paris *Parlement* against the authors of that infamous pamphlet.*

DANTON

18

JUNE 1787

Our Dear and Beloved Danton

"Louis, by the grace of God King of France and Navarre, to all who shall these present [letters] see, Greetings!"[1]

With these "letters of provision" dated June 12, 1787, Louis XVI ensures Danton's professional career. Now twenty-eight years old, Danton is becoming an advocate in Council.† The text follows the form that has been used for centuries, and there is nothing original in it relating to the person it concerns; looked at with hindsight, however, a few of its terms are piquant enough.

"Be it known that for the full and entire trust we have in the person of our dear and beloved [*sic*] Georges-Jacques Danton, his sufficiency, loyalty, probity, ability and experience, fealty and affection to our service, for these and other causes, endorsing and confirming the nomination of his person made to us by our very dear and loyal *Sieur* de Lamoignon, keeper of the seals of France, we have given and granted and do hereby give and grant the office of advocate in our Councils formerly held and filled by *Sieur* Charles-Nicolas Huet de Paizy, latest incumbent." And so on, for two pages of fastidiously penned calligraphy, ending with the "order to *Sieur* de Lamoignon, having recognized the proper and decent way of life, competent age, conversation and Apostolic Roman Catholic faith of the said *Sieur* Danton, and after receiving the necessary oath, to accept, entrust to and institute him by Us in the said office."

---

*Beaumarchais wins his suit on April 2, 1789, by which time the public mind is preoccupied by very different matters.

†He was born at Arcis-sur-Aube on October 26, 1759.

This must not be understood to mean that Louis XVI has the remotest idea who Danton is. Forms of this type rolled past for the sovereign's signature thirteen to the dozen every week, and not only in the legal professions. The same jargon was used in every branch of the administration. But they gave sacred confirmation to those receiving them, and to their years of ambition. Danton now has a foot in the stirrup.

Notwithstanding their resounding titles, these particular councillors are in no position to advise the King. They move in planets remote from Versailles, called *parlements,* and may be found primarily inside the Palais de Justice in Paris, where they are entitled to plead the briefs of clients—most of them wealthy—involved in all manner of litigation except criminal cases. They have plenty to do: in this government everything—inheritance, contested functions, claimed titles of nobility, etc.—can become a procedural jungle. The relative stamp of authority conferred upon them by the royal approval gives them some weight with the magistrates.

Their office can be purchased, of course (there are about seventy of them in the kingdom), and can also be transferred by private contract provided that the transaction has the approval of the keeper of the seals. This is why, on the threshold of his maturity, Georges-Jacques Danton is at once promoted and in debt, having just bought his office from Huet de Paizy for a total of seventy-eight thousand livres. In the same week he gets married, and the two events are not unconnected. He has come a long way since the last years of his teens, spent at school in the Richard *pension* and with the Oratorians of Troyes.

It did look, in those days, as though he was heading for a constricted life of pettifogging and boredom in the provinces. Apart from his escapade in Rheims in 1775 on the occasion of the King's coronation, his youth has flowed past like some rural stream, its waters filtering slowly through the mill of study that destined him for a career in law. Like our friend Beugnot, another hardworking youth from Champagne, his prospects boiled down to the unending contemplation of dusty briefs,* especially as he has even fewer resources than Beugnot. Not that he lacks the essentials, or even the bonus of self-confidence supplied by loving parents. And as he is both physically and intellectually robust, he is already making a name for himself. But he has had to hoist himself up by his own bootstraps in order to keep out of the way of all those brother and sister Dantons and Recordains.

The book-learning side of his youth meant those long years in Troyes, starting at five-thirty in the morning and ending at eight at night. Not a

*On the future Comte Beugnot, adviser to Napoleon and gifted memoirist, and the part he played in the Necklace Affair when still a young man living in Bar-sur-Aube, see Volume IV.

failure, not a great success: just average, with respectable results in rhetoric, ancient history and Latin. For a little refreshment, there were frequent trips home to his mother in the gentle green town of Arcis on the banks of the Aube, population one thousand, all a little lost in their "wooden houses, only the handsomest being whitewashed to give an illusion of stone, which was scarce in this chalky region."[2] The mail coach from Paris comes once a week, on Sundays, but there Georges-Jacques knew, and remembers forever, the enchantment of nature, the jets of water splashing up when the kids went swimming in the river. Childhood, reaching back and back to the bottom of memory.

At twenty, he felt that a decision had to be made: will it be Champagne forever or the great leap? If his kindly grandfather Jean Recordain, who owned the cotton mill, had taken him on as a junior partner, maybe . . . But he was considered too young, and the hosiery trade, the only other local industry, was doing badly. So, like Brissot, like Restif, like so many others, he yields to the pull of Paris, ever stronger at the end of this century. Possibly with a sigh of relief, his parents provide transport and some means of subsistence for the beginning of his migration.

His first home is the Black Horse Inn, kept by friend Layron on the rue Geoffroy-l'Asnier behind the St. Gervais church, especially for people from Champagne. By cheek and by bluff, he gets a job as a clerk in the firm of attorney Vinot; then begins the hunt for clients, every morning in the great hall of the Palais de Justice, and the slow building of connections, occasionally developing into friendships, with men, some of them well known, in the legal professions. Now and then, somebody takes notice of the energetic young student who is so "keen." His parents are not the only ones to help him. He also manages to make that convenient round-trip to the Faculty of Rheims, in the wake of many another young lawyer of his day (including Brissot and Roland), to get some instant diplomas. By 1784, he is proudly adding the words "graduate in law" after his signature.

However, he has been vegetating as a "trainee" advocate for almost seven years, and at the beginning of 1787 he still is.[3]

Attorney Vinot is a decent fellow; he not only employs him, he also gives him a room next to his office, for all the long time Georges-Jacques is prowling the great hall stalking cases to plead. His solid self-confidence enables him to make do with the humble life-style of a *petit bourgeois,* hardly a notch above his student's life in the provinces. The little nest egg of fees gleaned here and there pays the rent on a furnished room on the rue des Mauvaises Paroles, his meals at the Hôtel de la Modestie, and two or three forays a year to the Théâtre-Français, where he applauds a young tragic actor who is shattering the box office and introducing a sort of new classical style to the boards—François-Joseph Talma—with his renditions of Cinna and Brutus. On special days, he treats some visiting Champagne friend to the limits of his purse, impressing him with the Parisian and already politically slanted tone of long evenings made glamorous by the presence of a few guests of a "higher" level, a few Freemasons from the famous Nine Sisters' Lodge that met on the rue Pot-de-Fer near St. Sulpice. Danton is not an initiate, but this "spectacular" type of lodge, which Voltaire attended a few weeks before his death, allowed nonmember fellow travelers to enter its salons, where they could rub elbows with Condorcet or Mirabeau, Laclos, even the Duc d'Orléans.

In another area of his life, he has, uncomplicatedly and naturally, frequented the women toward whom his temperament has always inclined him. In particular, he has a close relationship with Françoise-Julie Duhautoir. She comes from Troyes and lives on the rue de la Tissanderie, just next to attorney Vinot's offices. She may be "easy" but is certainly not a "bad-living" woman; she has a little income and can take care of herself, and she's chosen Paris as the place to find something more interesting than the provinces. She's a bit older than he, but quickly responds to the rough-and-ready appeal of the handsome lad whom many people call ugly. The network of scars stitched around his twisted mouth does not interfere with his captivating voice or his improvisational eloquence that goes straight to the point, even straighter in the presence of a pretty woman than in front of a judge. Now fully adult, Danton has turned into a broad-shouldered stalwart who likes physical exercise and is capable of laughing and making others laugh.

Throughout 1786 Françoise-Julie cherishes her dream of a higher style of life, thanks to the possible backing of the Loménie de Brienne brothers, the Archbishop and the officer who are the principal nobles of Champagne and who might give her man a push. But at the beginning of 1787, Calonne still seems to be in first place facing the Notables, and the Danton-Duhautoir liaison is drawing quietly to a close. Is he going to start going around in circles again?

What saves him is his instinct for discovering new things; one day, upon leaving the Palais de Justice, he walks across the Seine on the Pont-Neuf and finds, when he reaches the Right Bank, the warm haven of the Café du Parnasse.*

Danton likes and always will like the Parisian cafés that have a touch of class—half-salon and half-cabaret. In them one can savor a beverage that is still something of a novelty: coffee from the Isles, a rarity in the depths of Champagne. People meet and interact there without too much formality,

---

*It stood almost at the corner of the Pont-Neuf and the quai, on the site now occupied by the Samaritaine department store.

neither in their solemn Sunday best nor in the 1780s equivalent of jeans and T-shirts, and play endless games of dominos, the society game that has become all the rage and costs nothing. Cafés like this one are so many crucibles of ideas and friendships for the middle class, which aspires to higher things.

The Café du Parnasse has been run for the past fifteen years by a perfect embodiment of this new class named François-Jérôme Charpentier, a tavern keeper by trade but prosperous enough to have been able to buy some shares in the Contrôle Général des Fermes, or in other words, the profits on tax collection. He's become Somebody in the Palais district, many of the habitués of which associate with him and appreciate the wholly natural grin that widens beneath his round wig. He wears a muslin cravat, a red vest and a blue coat. He has other people to serve the drinks and spends his time moving from table to table, more like a host than a proprietor. Danton soon finds a favorite corner near the till, at which Madame Charpentier, who hails from Italy, officiates along with her twenty-five-year-old daughter Antoinette-Gabrielle, who owes to her mother a certain lustiness in her dark good looks, her black eyes and pure oval face, her energy, her sturdy good health. Well built, well mannered, it seems as though fate has put her there on purpose for the young lawyer.

Danton knows how to play this kind of game even better than dominos. They get engaged in record time, but Gabrielle is not the kind of girl for whom bed comes before the wedding mass. Danton, too, neither too much nor too little in love, is more than willing to do things according to the rules. Apart from her "expectations," the young woman's dowry could instantly provide the comfort he has always lacked. Jérôme Charpentier is a good man and a good father and, like many others even in those early days, is well aware of Danton's sweep and dash, so he has nothing against the marriage, but grumbles a bit over his prospective son-in-law's precarious financial situation. If only he could snare a position as advocate in Council . . .

Well, if that's all you're worried about! Danton rams his way into this narrow breach without too many scruples.* He is still on good terms with his former girlfriend, Françoise-Julie Duhautoir, now the mistress of a Council advocate named Huet de Paizy, who is trying to sell off his office. She good-naturedly undertakes to persuade today's lover to do business with yesterday's; but it still looks as though there may be a problem over the asking price of 78,000 livres, because there is nothing of the philanthropist about Huet de Paizy.

Danton proceeds to find the money, however. If he turns his pockets inside out, he can muster—5,000 livres. He borrows 15,000 more from old

---

*The arrangements he makes to borrow the necessary sum and soften up the seller of the office constitute the first in a series of money dealings by which his memory is besmirched. Beginning with Mathiez, his detractors all place this transaction firmly at the top of their lists.

man Charpentier, without a murmur, because the jolly old fellow is convinced that any Council advocate must soon get his hands on the big money. But that leaves him a long way from the total. So Julie Duhautoir lends him 36,000. She also talks Huet de Paizy (by whom she has had two children)* into giving credit for the remaining 22,000, to be paid in four years. The family in Arcis allow their land to stand as security for the loans.

Abracadabra. Danton turns up, poor as Job, for a marriage to which his spouse is also contributing 20,000 livres in cash and which has been made possible by his former mistress.

Two days after the King signs his appointment, the newly made advocate emerges, radiant, from the Church of St. Germain-l'Auxerrois, the one-time parish church of the kings of France (standing just across from the Louvre); its bells are pealing for a marriage that is, when all is said and done, a happy one, without infatuation or reticence on either side. The wedding is attended by an intimate little horde of Dantons from Arcis and Troyes, Gabrielle's two brothers and, of course, her parents, and an ample sprinkling of good middle-class professionals from the legal, administrative and commercial spheres who will, thanks to old man Charpentier, duly drink to the new-lyweds' establishment in a fine apartment on the Left Bank, Cour de Commerce, with some of its windows overlooking the rue des Cordeliers. Danton at home.

From now on he signs himself "d'Anton," his title costing him no more than the price of the plate engraved in the stone of his entryway.[4]

HAMILTON

19

JUNE 1787

The Assembly of Demigods

If we can accept a somewhat facile transition from the foregoing, we might say that at the beginning of this same month of June 1787, a great people

---

*The first of whom is alleged, without any proof, to have been Danton's.

tries to consolidate its own marriage with history. The thirteen recently liberated United Provinces of America are holding a convention, which should give birth to their definitive structure. At the moment, in fact, there are only twelve of them, because the tiny state of Rhode Island, the bit of coast sticking out in the Atlantic between Boston and New York, is having a fit of the sulks. In spite of Yorktown and the peace of 1783,* the new nation is still lacking any slightest degree of unity. Already huge as far as the extent of its territory is concerned—and the value of its three to four million inhabitants—America could disintegrate at any moment.

So here are those tall gentlemen, dressed in black and solemn of mien, back in Philadelphia, which, for want of the new town that is still a utopian concept, remains the de facto capital for historic meetings. They are gathering, as though for the second act of a play, in the austere setting of the State House, where Jefferson, John Adams and Franklin ushered in a new era nine years before by introducing into the Declaration of Independence the three words "pursuit of happiness." Then they were all risking their lives, but matters were simpler even so, or exactly so: it was defeat England or die. This time it's the double-or-nothing that often follows a victorious war: winning isn't everything, you've got to consolidate the victory, and before that, win a few victories over yourselves.

The states' representatives, summoned for May 25, have crept up in twos and threes at a Merovingian pace, owing to the ordeal of travel, and it isn't until June 15 that about fifty of them are actually assembled. Pennsylvania's capital, which has been growing since the War of Independence, now has a population of over twenty-five thousand and almost five thousand two-story houses, all built of brick as are the sidewalks and gutters, so elegantly laid out that European visitors gape at them in wonder. Efforts are being made to embellish facades by painting trompe-l'oeil white stones around the casements. But the town has kept its "Quaker feeling." Guests are made warmly welcome amid furniture that is handsome but rudimentary, in rooms without hangings, paintings or mirrors.[1] They are stuffed to the gills because the Quakers, having no other besetting sins, cultivate good eating. In the three-hundred-pillar covered market, also brick-paved, meat "sawn into round and appetizing shapes"† is covered with moist cloths, and one can also find "fish, fruit, vegetables, seeds, ironmongery, buckets and pails, paper, shoes [not sold at markets in the Old World, one has to buy them from the

---

*On the American insurrection and the Declaration of Independence see Volume I; Volume II, *The Wind from America,* follows events up to Yorktown; see Volume III for the signing of the peace between France, America and England in 1783.

†According to Moreau de Saint-Méry; the next quote is by Brissot. They both "did America" around this time.

cobbler] and delightful little baskets. One hears no carters' quarrels; everything is cheap." The summer heat is already here: three months of damp swelter in Philadelphia.

A large majority of the delegates come from the less well-off regions or from those still suffering the aftermath of the war. They know they have precious little time in which to save what is still most commonly called the "Confederation of the thirteen United Provinces."

United? Don't make me laugh. Each of them has jealously withdrawn within its frontiers and is interested solely in its own trade, which makes just so many mini–civil wars in the offing. And as there is no central government and no supreme court of justice, there's nobody to arbitrate among them. The federal army has been disbanded. There is still a roving Congress here and there, but the federal coins it is timidly minting are virtually unusable. Each state has its own money, gold or silver, made from old European coins, clipped or not. Wartime creditors have not been paid. Last year more than ten thousand of them, stirred up by a veteran named Daniel Shays, ran riot in Massachusetts until the local militia got control over them. And yet the ground is rich everywhere, the people hardworking, and substantial amounts of capital are lying about in often improvised banks. To the west, between the Alleghenies and the Mississippi, lies endless virgin territory, tenuously held by Spanish or Indians and offering a seemingly inexhaustible potential. But precisely because there is no unity and no overall plan, some of the states are snarling and snapping over it.

Pessimists in both worlds are already prophesying that America will be stillborn.

The last chance has come from that small class of "cultivated, liberal notables to which the radical masses had given the necessary support during the War of Independence; but in many cases the leaders were afraid of the regular soldiers."[2] Now those leaders want a return to order, they want unity, and they want proportional representation instead of revolutionary élan. Ten years earlier, the primitive impulse rising from the bowels of the American people was indispensable, but now, reduced to the service of the individual states' shortsighted nationalism, it has become meaningless. "There had to be a central government . . . a few men tried to create one. . . . They belonged to that breed of moderate reformers who inspire revolutions, and who begin them, but, more often than not, do not end them. In America, they were about to try to end the revolution in its opening phase. The strange thing is that they succeeded in doing so and that in the United States it was the moderates who made the republic."[3]

Foremost among them, since bidding a Cincinnatus*-style farewell to

*Semilegendary figure (5th century B.C.), peasant-soldier and ephemeral statesman. He

the army and returning to his Virginia estate of Mount Vernon, stands the irreproachable Washington. His untainted prestige has earned him mountains of pleas to step in, particularly at the time of the trouble in Massachusetts. Some fellow citizens have even written urging him to accept—a crown. But his mind has long been made up, since the days when he nearly lost the war for want of sufficient authority:

"You speak to me, my good sir, of using my influence to calm the present disorders in Massachusetts. . . . Influence is not government. We must have one by means of which our lives, liberties and properties will be safeguarded."[4]

At the other end of the spectrum stands another giant of the American Revolution, who could, had he possessed the same clout, have provided a radical contradiction, laying down for centuries to come the foundations of the unending debate between order and change. But Thomas Jefferson, whose role as governor of Virginia during the war was challenged, and his stature thereby diminished,* is now ambassador to France—honored, but at a distance. His startling attitude toward the Massachusetts uprising will not be known until long afterward, through his private correspondence: "God forbid we should ever be twenty years without such a rebellion! . . . I hold it, that a little rebellion, now and then, is a good thing, and as necessary in the political world as storms in the physical. . . . The tree of liberty must be refreshed from time to time with the blood of patriots and tyrants."[5]

So Jefferson is very much absent from Philadelphia, but when he hears what is happening there, his congenital instability will lead him, whatever he may believe, to vibrate in sudden harmony with this "assembly of demigods," as he calls it.[6]

This is high praise indeed from someone who is not one of them, any more than another potential "demigod" and friendly enemy of his, John Adams, who has been similarly hamstrung in a post as ambassador to London. Both men will maintain a position of admiring disagreement in regard to the Convention,† which is typical of one form of the Anglo-Saxon character.

For the opening ceremony, thus, the 1787 Constitutional Convention foregathers around the little table, raised only one short step above the rest, of its president, the good Doctor Benjamin Franklin, benevolent and warmhearted as always but weakened by age.‡ He is flanked by two of the rising men who are to play decisive parts in the proceedings of this assembly, called

---

was called upon by the Romans to win a few decisive battles before voluntarily going back to his plow.

*See Volume II.

†And, of course, will follow Washington as presidents of the United States.

‡In 1787 Franklin is eighty-one.

a "Convention" after that of the second English revolution, the one in 1688,* and implying that final agreement would be reached, between the people and those in power, upon an official text.

The leaders of the Constitutional Convention will be Hamilton and Madison.

MADISON

20

JUNE 1787

The Important Question

No one knows better than Hamilton how to rank the Constitutional Convention in world history: as foremost among the foremost of assemblies.

"After full experience of the unsufficiency of the existing Federal Government, you are invited to deliberate upon a new Constitution for the United States of America.† The subject speaks its own importance; comprehending in its consequences . . . the fate of an empire, in many respects, the most interesting in the world. It seems to have been reserved to the people of this country, to decide by their conduct and example, the important question, whether societies of men are really capable or not, of establishing good government out of reflection and choice, or whether they are forever destined to depend, for their political constitutions, on accident and force. . . . A wrong election of the part we shall act, may . . . deserve to be considered as a general misfortune of mankind."[1]

The man who was capable of writing this capital text is barely thirty. But unlike William Pitt or Bonaparte, there were no good fairies bending over his crib. Hamilton has a hard destiny to assume, and he sometimes confronts it aggressively. His diminutive size, "almost no larger than a child,"

*When the Stuart dynasty was replaced by the House of Hanover.

†From the preface to *The Federalist Papers*, a "combat book" published "hot" in late 1787 and containing papers written as the Convention progressed, by John Jay, Madison and especially Hamilton—who personally wrote fifty-one of them, out of a total of eighty-five.

is no help, any more than his origins, which are considered exotic by the New Yorkers who, beguiled by his intellectual qualities and fighting spirit into overlooking these drawbacks, have sent him to represent them at the Convention.

He was born on Nevis Island, one of the more pleasant of the English Antilles, on January 22, 1757, into a family of Scottish colonists who formed a remote twig on the tree of one of Britain's great families. His mother was named Faucette and was the daughter of French Huguenots driven out of France by the revocation of the Edict of Nantes. She died young but left her mark on him: he speaks French fluently and worships her memory.

Would she have prevented Hamilton senior from ruining himself? In any event, by the time Alexander was twelve, the thing was done. A rare fate for a colonist's son: when still a child he began clerking in a countinghouse on the island of St. Croix, but was already champing at the bit. "I contemn the groveling condition of a clerk or the like, to which my fortunes etc. condemn me, and would willingly risk my life . . . to exalt my station. . . . I wish there was a war."[2]

He would get his wish. When he was fifteen, he went to study in the colleges in New Jersey, and later in New York,* where his instinctive radicalism was shaped and given consciousness. He had a vague idea of embracing medicine, but with the American Revolution he embraced politics instead, like a monk taking orders. He was still only eighteen in 1775 when the rebels won their first victory at Lexington,† and he immediately organized a company of volunteers that were baptized the "Hearts of Oak." He dressed them in green with leather headgear and gave them a motto, "Liberty or Death." No less.

Captain in the artillery at nineteen, colonel at twenty after the battles of Trenton and Princeton, one of Washington's aides-de-camp before quarreling with him over a "question of honor" in 1781,‡ he took part in a bayonet charge at Yorktown, where he made friends with La Fayette and also was reconciled with Washington, but as an equal. After the war, as an attorney and representative of New York to the Congress, he made a good marriage§ and settled in that town. His reputation as a legislator and specialist in financial matters has been growing steadily since then, so that he has become one of the most authoritative spokesmen for the views of his friends in their dealings

---

*At King's College, now Columbia.
†See Volume I.
‡See Volume II.
§"To the daughter of General Schuyler, of Dutch origin, a respectable [*sic*] woman who was to outlive him by over fifty years."[3]

with the almost fiercely retired Washington.* And a good thing that was, too, because he has now managed to twist the great symbol's arm.

Perhaps it's gone to his head a little. From the opening days of the Convention, his uncompromising opinions and uncompromising manners lead him to adopt without qualification positions held by others to be "aristocratic." His patriotic extremism, bruised by the muddle of the last few years, has made him a sort of premature leveler: everything for a strong and permanent central power, as little as possible for individual states. "The voice of the people has been said to be the voice of God; and however generally this maxim has been quoted and believed, it is not true in fact. The people are turbulent and changing; they seldom judge or determine right. . . . We must do away with the distinctions between States."[4]

The organizer of the Hearts of Oak has come a long way—far enough to be dreaming of a sort of American monarchy, and daring to propose that it be entrusted to Our Father Washington, who once again sweeps the temptation away with an irritated flick of the wrist.† That's enough, in the eyes of the Convention, to turn Hamilton into the "Federalist" of all time—the term, in those days, being applied to the partisans of a strong central power as opposed to the centrifugal forces of the individual states.‡

James Madison is six years older than Hamilton and although he is by no means a champion of states' privileges, the mildness of his character, his disinclination to extremism and his refusal of categorical opinions distinguish him sharply from the younger man.§ All they have in common is their small stature and their problems with speechmaking, offset in both cases by a gift for writing. Despite his pallor, retiring airs and frequently blushing bashfulness, Madison's erudition will impose itself upon his hearers (he's unbeatable on ancient Greece), along with his patriotic fervor and intellectual curiosity, the latter being his chief qualification as the irreplaceable chronicler of the Convention. His advantage over Hamilton is that he is a delegate from Virginia (which produced Washington, Jefferson, Patrick Henry, etc.), that cradle of founding fathers, while New York, which sent Hamilton, is regarded

*Hamilton is Washington's secretary of the treasury when the general becomes the United States' first president in 1789. Young as he was, it was in the cards that he would have held that office, too, one day, if he had not been killed in 1804 in a stupid duel with an unscrupulous politician, Aaron Burr.

†Thereby saving the American republic from the sort of fall that lands the French republic squarely at Bonaparte's feet twelve years later.

‡The city of Washington is always commonly known as "the Federal capital" of the United States, and a special district is tailor-made for it so that it will never belong to any state.

§After Washington, John Adams and Jefferson, Madison became the fourth president of the United States (1809–1817).

by many Americans as a vague seaport that used to be called Neuwe-Amsterdam, tainted by long English occupation during the war.

Madison tackles the Convention with an ogre's appetite. He has chosen his technique and does not change it.

> The curiosity I had felt during my researches into the History of the most distinguished Confederacies, particularly those of antiquity . . . , determined me to preserve as far as I could an exact account of what might pass in the Convention whilst executing its trust, with the magnitude of which I was duly impressed, as I was of the gratification promised to future curiosity by an authentic exhibition of the objects, opinions & reasonings from which the new system of government was to receive its peculiar structure & organisation. Nor was I unaware of the value of such a contribution to the fund of materials for the History of a Constitution on which would be staked the happiness of a people great even in its infancy, and possibly the cause of Liberty throughout the world.
>
> In pursuance of the task I had assumed I chose a seat in front of the presiding member, with the other members on my right & left hands. In this favorable position for hearing all that passed, I noted in legible terms & in abreviations [sic] & marks intelligible to myself what was read from the chair or spoken by the members; and losing not a moment unnecessarily between the adjournment & reassembling of the Convention, I was enabled to write out my daily notes during the session or within a few finishing days after its close, in the extent and form preserved in my own hand on my files.
>
> In the labor & correctness of doing this, I was not a little aided by practice* & by a familiarity with the style and the train of observation & reasoning which characterised the principal speakers. It happened also that I was not absent a single day, nor more than a cassual [sic] fraction of an hour on any day, so that I could not have lost a single speech, unless a very short one.[5]

Madison had an obsession: "He felt that a great experiment was there taking place, to determine whether a republic were possible in such a vast expanse of land. There had been no precedent in the whole of history. When Rome tried to become a great republic it became an empire, at the mercy of its own military."[6] The one or two republics in existence at the end of the eighteenth century are small states, such as Holland (but is that really a republic?) and Switzerland. Madison's originality, in rejecting the monarchical temptation of Hamilton and a few others of that ilk, is that he is seeking "to organize in the best possible way the national power so that a republic can be formed."[7] A lasting republic.

---

*First as a lawyer, then as a representative, for the last ten years, to the Virginia Assembly. This "verbatim" account of the Constitutional Convention takes up 559 pages of vol. II of *The Papers of James Madison,* printed in Washington in 1840.

ABBÉ DE MABLY

21

JUNE 1787

A Key to All This History

The Americans in Philadelphia find themselves faced with the enormous problem of improvising, virtually overnight, the foundations of a huge republic with balanced powers; whereas in Europe a few of the protagonists of the century of Enlightenment have been applying their minds to it for years.

For one, there is Abbé Gabriel Bonnot de Mably, a relatively obscure member of the company of *philosophes* of his time.

He gave up the ghost, universally unmourned, in 1785, just as he was dispatching to the United States the essence of his search for a rational way to construct human happiness.

He had started it long before: "Never have I read, in the writings of any traveler, the description of some desert isle with untroubled skies and pure-flowing water, without at once desiring to go there and set up a republic* in which, all equal, all rich, all poor, all free, all brothers, the first law of us all would be to have nothing we call our own."[1]

That was the "raw" Mably of the 1750s, back in the reign of Louis XV when he was getting ready to write *Des droits et des devoirs du citoyen;* but he had gone on since then for more than thirty years, holding his puny lantern before him and groping his way clumsily through a dense forest of a work cluttered with reminiscences of antiquity. As he neared the end, his old heart beat faster when he thought he was catching a glimpse of the "desert isle" at the end of his era. Would America be capable of giving flesh and blood to the hopes of the Enlightened? The result is a precious exchange of letters between Mably and John Adams that throws some light on the concrete bases of the Philadelphia deliberations.

---

*Passages like this, of which there are very few, it is true, in the fifteen volumes of Mably's *Oeuvres,* have led some to see him as one of the philosophical precursors of utopian communism.

Mably was born in Grenoble on March 14, 1709, into the Bonnot family, which belonged to the "nobility of the gown" and was already relatively wealthy. His father, the attorney Gabriel Bonnot, had bought the seigneurial property [we might call it an estate, divided into various farms and buildings, worked partly by the owner himself and partly by tenants] of Mably near Roanne. Gabriel is the second son and inherits the estate. The firstborn, Jean, perpetuates the family tradition by becoming *grand prévôt* [a type of judge] in Lyons.* The third son, Étienne, is given a smaller property at Condillac. The younger boys had to let the eldest have the career, so they were forced into the ecclesiastical estate, but not to the extent of becoming priests. Both Bonnot abbés proved singularly gifted at intellectual speculation, however; and both were significant philosophers. Condillac, the founder of sensationalism,† died in 1780, and his older brother Mably has labored diligently for the publication of Condillac's works during the few years that are left to him. Meanwhile, he himself has written and published steadily, managing not to get into too much trouble with the royal censors, although, via the tangent of history, he has constantly hovered on the verge of politics.

His small readership, a scant few hundred copies scattered throughout Enlightened Europe, and his inability to make the tiniest dent upon the systems of his time by force of thought alone, have sustained a degree of bitterness in him which can be seen in the vertical wrinkles of his long, sad head. "There was a coldness about him that gave him an air of great dignity,"[2] but he let slip an occasional lamentation:

"My ideas are far removed from the current politics. I am told that many people pity me; I expected that. To speak the truth is to make a terrible satire upon the things of this base world."[3]

"I am in my seventy-third year, and death will come before I am able to witness all the misfortunes I fear for posterity. . . .[4] In the end, one grows weary of speaking to the deaf."

But at the very last moment, he is able to believe in a joyful surprise. Where did he get the idea that the Americans were about to ask him for the Tables of the Law, as the Corsicans did Rousseau yesterday? In any event, a rumor that such a thing was about to happen arose somewhere in the salons,

---

*Jean-Jacques Rousseau is a tutor in the family in 1740–1741; whence his contacts with its two *philosophes.*

†Theory derived from his famous *Traité des sensations,* in which he contends that all of our ideas and faculties are nothing but "transformed sensations"; it has been seen as a forerunner of positivism.

and is amplified by the inevitable loudspeaker Grimm: "A great scandal for philosophy and the *philosophes!** M. l'Abbé de Mably has just received the most glorious homage to which any man of letters could pretend. MM. Franklin and Adams have requested him, in the name of the United States Congress, to draft a Constitution for the new republic."[5]

Not true. "Hype," we might call it, to which the Abbé lent himself with the ingenuousness of an overgrown child with a long-frustrated expectation of seeing a dream catch hold in reality. Without waiting for confirmation, he set to work on his *Observations sur le gouvernement et les lois des États-Unis,*† beginning with a sermon, dated July 24, 1783, to John Adams, who was then in Holland on his way to London. For once, Mably showed some sparks of optimism: "I want to remind you, sir, of all that can contribute to the happiness of America. You have gained your independence before you knew ambition, and surely you will not imitate the nations of Europe, which have depopulated and weakened themselves by establishing their colonies by armed force. You know too well the rights of people and nations to allow cruel errors, the work of fiefs and chivalry, to mislead you as they have misled the Spanish, the Portuguese, the English and French."[6]

He was definitely not trying to sell integral democracy: "The multitude, degraded by needs and occupations that condemn it to ignorance and to thoughts that are base and vile, has neither the means nor the time to raise itself by its meditations to the principles of wise policy."[7]

His optimism, we see, is tempered by visceral misgivings about human nature. Mably is no Rousseau. He does not imagine that the Americans are going to turn spontaneously toward the good and, in the philosophical retreat in which he lived surrounded by books in the Hôtel d'Auvergne on the rue Saint-Honoré,[8] he forms one of that placid cohort of thinkers who innocently encourage massacres: "I have often said to one or another of your compatriots that I was too concerned about their fortune not to wish them a war that would last long enough to correct them of their prejudices and give them all the qualities that a free people ought to have."[9]

There, the poor fellow was going much too far, for so serious-minded a democrat as John Adams, who answers with a sharp rebuttal: "The foreign gazettes and journals have announced to the world that the abbé de Mably was applied to by the United States of America for his advice and assistance in the formation of a code of laws. It is unnecessary to say anything to this, only that it is a part of a million volumes of lies, according to the best computation, which are to be imposed upon posterity, relative to American affairs."[10]

---

*Grimm abhorred Mably, who had made a vigorous attack upon Voltaire in *De la manière d'écrire l'Histoire.*

†Twenty pages, published in full in vol. VIII of his *Oeuvres complètes* in 1784.

Having said this, John Adams allows his good manners to prevail in regard to the old gentleman who seemed to want to see himself as the Moses of the U.S.A. His consideration extends to the point of not publishing his denial, or the text below, until 1787, when the Constitutional Convention opens. Everybody understands that John Adams, in his Aventine exile in London, is actually speaking to the new generation of Americans. The sights of his *Defense of the Constitutions of Government of the United States of America and of the necessity for a balance in the powers of a free government** are set far beyond Mably's ashes, self-preoccupied France and deliquescent old Europe; it is addressed to his own people. It is the manifesto that one of the founding fathers would like to see read in Philadelphia. An American talking to Americans about America.†

John Adams finishes clearing the ground from which his preamble has virtually evicted Mably:

> But I hope, sir, you will not accuse me of presumption, affectation, or singularity, if I venture to express my opinion, that it is yet too soon to undertake a complete history of that great event [the American Revolution], and that there is no man, either in America or Europe, at this date, capable of performing it. . . .
>
> The whole of a long life, to begin at the age of twenty years, will be necessary to assemble, from all nations, and from all parts of the world in which they are deposited, the documents proper to form a complete history of the American Revolution, because it is, indeed, the history of mankind during that epoch. The histories of France, Spain, Holland, England and the neutral powers must be united with that of America.

There's a first-rate history lesson for a historian. After this invitation to strict humility, John Adams continues with a striking résumé of American sociology:

> Permit me, sir, before I finish this letter, to point at a key to all this history. There is a general analogy in the governments and characters of all the thirteen states; but it was not till the debates and the war began in Massachusetts Bay, the principal province of New England, that their primitive institutions produced their first effect. Four of these institutions ought to be amply investigated and maturely considered by any person who wishes to write with correct information upon this subject; for they have produced a decisive effect, not only in the first

*Translated in France in 1792.
†Two hundred years later the fabric of "inner" America can still be seen in it; this text by John Adams is a sort of grid that can help to decode the secrets of a great people too often grossly oversimplified.

determinations of the controversies in writing, and the first debates in council, and the first resolutions to resist in arms, but also by the influence they had on the minds of the other colonies, by giving them an example to adopt more or less the same institutions and similar measures. The four institutions intended are:—

1. The towns or districts,   3. The schools,
2. The congregations,   4. The militia.

The towns are certain extents of country, or districts of territory, into which Massachusetts Bay, Connecticut, New Hampshire and Rhode Island, are divided. These towns contain upon an average, say, six miles or two leagues square. The inhabitants who live within these limits are formed by law into corporations, or bodies politic, and are invested with certain powers and privileges, as, for example, to repair the great roads or highways, to support the poor, to choose their selectmen. . . .

The consequences of these institutions have been, that the inhabitants, having acquired from their infancy the habit of discussing, of deliberating, and of judging of public affairs, it was in these assemblies of towns or districts that the sentiments of the people were formed in the first place and their resolutions were taken from the beginning to the end of the disputes and the war with Great Britain.

2. The congregations are religious societies, which comprehend the whole people. Every district contains a parish or religious congregation. . . .

Each parish has a temple for public worship, and a minister, maintained at the public expense. The constitutions of these congregations are extremely popular, and the clergy have little influence or authority beyond that which their own piety, virtues, and talents naturally give them. They are chosen by the people of their parishes, and receive their ordinations from the neighboring clergy. They are all married, have families, and live with their parishioners in an intimate and perfect friendship. . . . Their sentiments are generally conformable to those of their people, and they are jealous friends of liberty.

3. There are schools in every town, established by an express law of the colony. Every town containing sixty families, is obliged, under a penalty, to maintain constantly a school and a schoolmaster, who shall teach his scholars reading, writing, arithmetic, and the rudiments of the Latin and Greek languages. All the children of the inhabitants, the rich as well as the poor, have a right to go to these public schools. There, are formed the candidates for admission as students into the colleges at Cambridge, New Haven, Princeton, and Dartmouth. In these colleges are educated future masters for these schools, future ministers for these congregations, doctors of law and medicine, and magistrates and officers for the government of the country.

4. The militia comprehends the whole people. By virtue of the laws of the country, every male inhabitant between sixteen and sixty years of age, is enrolled in a company, and a regiment of militia completely organized with all its officers.

He is enjoined to keep always in his house, and at his own expense, a firelock in good order, a powder horn, a pound of powder, twelve flints, four-and-twenty balls of lead, a cartridge box, and a knapsack; so that the whole country is ready to march for its own defence upon the first signal of alarm. . . .

Behold, sir, a little sketch of the four principal resources of that prudence in council and that military valor and ability, which have produced the American Revolution.

Out of the whole lot of these inhabitants, George Washington is the only elected representative to be universally approved. Wrenched almost by force from his premature retirement at Mount Vernon, he finally yields to the exhortations of the rest and sets off for Philadelphia, as though he were mounting the scaffold. But perhaps all this reluctance is just his little game—Washington does like to be implored.

He arrives to the ringing of every bell in town.[11] The very first evening he is invited to stay with Ben Franklin, relieved to be able to relinquish the chair of this assembly, however symbolically he may have occupied it. The Two Worlds have asked too much of Benjamin Franklin for over half a century, and if they could, they would ask more. Last year, there were some pioneers in Tennessee who wanted to found an ephemeral state that they simply called "Franklin State," in which taxes could be paid in deerhide, beaver or otter skins, smoked pork, fat, whisky or peach liqueur.[12]

Franklin goes back to sit in peace in the front row, where his dense, living silence will balance the majestic stillness to which Washington's presidential functions have reduced him, there on his raised platform. Between the silences of these two great sages, the other delegates are about to quarrel so noisily that the sages will ask, from the very outset, that their deliberations be held in private, as though for the election of a pope.

See you in September for the next installment.*

---

*The text of the Constitution, that is. Out of respect, Madison will ask that his notes not be published until his death.

22

JUNE–JULY 1787

My Mother Feudality

On June 3, 1787, François-Noël Babeuf tells Ferdinand Dubois de Fosseux, secretary of the Academy of Arras, about his "great plan for a little book" that will at last enable him, if it is published, to hold up his head in his province of Picardy and probably in front of his own mirror as well.

Here is its title:

Outline of a plan for a *perpetual land register* [or cadastre]* demonstrating principally a form of procedure whereby it will be possible:

1. To preserve all possible knowledge, and particulars which are at all times up-to-date, relating to ownership and the most detailed topography of every part of the landed property of the Kingdom;

2. To establish the most equitable apportionment for the levying of land tax;

3. To employ a system of taxation so simple that for a district of two hundred parishes a single chief officer assisted by no more than three clerks will be able, annually and within a period of one month, and without the help of a single collector and without creating any disturbance as regards the King, to carry it out.[1]

This is Babeuf's entrance into history, through the narrow gate of a private correspondence with a Notable of his region. He is twenty-seven years old.† He lives and works at Roye, a short distance from Amiens.

A few weeks before, he was bombarding the same correspondent with anxious queries on this same matter of property ownership: "In view of the vast sum of knowledge that has now been amassed, what would be the

---

*Cadastre = an official register of the quantity, value, and ownership of real estate used in apportioning taxes (Webster's Third International).

†Born at Saint-Quentin on November 24, 1760.

condition of a people whose social institutions were such that in each of its individual members there reigned, without distinction, the most perfect equality; that the land he lived upon belonged to no one but to all; that, finally, everything were held in common, even to the products of all the types of industry; would such institutions be authorized by natural Law . . . ? You will judge, sir, that all this has not come out of my imagination."[2]

If one were to hazard a geographical paradox, one might say that the lowly Picardy of Babeuf stands halfway between America and Russia, which we have just seen emerging from the foam. Is that any reason why a hayseed from Roye should spend his life staring at his own clod of dirt? With the very first stammerings of speech, François-Noël shows himself no less capable of thinking in terms of the whole world than Washington or Catherine II. On June 5 he writes Dubois de Fosseux again, sending him a leaflet that has been circulating in the public libraries and that has come to his knowledge because its author, Nicolas Henrion de Pansey, from Lorraine, was a "feudist" like himself: *Mémoire pour un nègre qui réclame sa liberté.*[3] After reading it, Babeuf is unable to restrain the indignation that becomes one of the major components of his personality: "It is we alone who have transmitted to another hemisphere the horrible vices that were degrading our own, and it seems that we can be brought to abjure one or two of them and banish them from among us only on the strange condition that we can employ them to infect a land that had hitherto preserved, with its extreme simplicity, all the candor and purity of the earliest of days."[4]

He is not, to be sure, the literary heir of Voltaire or Diderot. With every step he takes down the page he drags his heavy style behind him. But already in 1787, Babeuf is a sort of application of one individual's destiny to the dream of happiness of the whole race. In this latter end of the century, where writing is oozing from under every stone, these are the opening words of a man who would like to relieve the world's evils.

He is, thus, a "feudist." What does that mean? There is an etymological link between "feudal" and "feudist"* as witness a letter he received in 1781: "To Monsieur Babeuf, *féodiste* of M. Lamérie, canon of Roye in Picardy."[5] Here we find him in painful contradiction between his job and his mind. We have just learned, reading him, that he would like to see economic and property restraints abolished; and we find him employed in an occupation that compels him to serve and specify the rights of lords who are still feudal,

---

*See Webster's Third International, "feud 3. ML *feodum, feudum* etc.: an estate in land held of a lord or superior by a tenant or vassal on condition he render certain services to the lord or superior." This would seem to be as close as English can come to what Manceron is getting at.—*Trans.*

even when their estates, as is sometimes the case, are no larger than your handkerchief.

"In my youth I did not reason . . . Until then, I felt great respect for my mother feudality."[6]

His "mother," Picardian society as it then was, has enabled François-Noël to achieve the envied position of "commissioner for landowners," *commissaire à terriers.* The word has nothing to do with breeds of dog, a *"terrier* being a compilation of statements, enumerations, declarations and acknowledgments by the tenants of a holding, with exact indication of the services and payments required of them. It was of capital importance for lords to have well-made *terriers* and to be kept informed of all changes occurring among those holding land of them."[7]

To earn a living in the rare occupation of *archiviste-terriste* Babeuf has had, for years, to offer his services to most of the landowners in his part of Picardy, "near Roye, Montdidier, Noyon and Roye again": "You see, sir, that I have been familiar with your boundaries and that in engaging myself to keep your plan, I know the land well enough that I shall not be likely to be taken unawares."[8]

A feudist is no official, no senior civil servant—far from it. He is a superior servant of seigneurial rights; he is paid by a seigneur for whatever period of time it takes him to disentangle and specify those rights. He has to beg for his itinerant work from one seigneur after another; and that is just what François-Noël has been doing, since he emerged from his downtrodden childhood.

"I was born in the mire. I use the word to indicate very strongly that life was given to me on the harsh steps of grinding poverty."[9]

Despite a great deal of research, there is little to say about this childhood and youth condemned to hard work and committed to harshness. A peasant grandfather from Monchy-Lagache, a parish near Saint-Quentin. A father, Claude Babeuf, born in 1716, enlisted in a cavalry regiment, deserted, amnestied, and finally employed, and underpaid, first in the offices of the salt tax, then as a guard for the *ferme générale,* or collection agency for certain taxes, then as a laborer on the fortifications of Saint-Quentin, then as a salt-tax agent again, then on shipwrecks. His eldest son, born of a woman thirty years his junior who worked in a linen mill, is François-Noël Babeuf.

In his teens, François-Noël was already a day laborer on the Saint-Quentin canal at Cambrai, which connects the Oise and Somme rivers and has a subterranean passage, an object of widespread admiration. But the "exceeding harshness of the digger's work" drove him to seek some less arduous means of "providing for his sustenance."[10] He seems to remember his father only as a stern but worthy man (he died in 1780), the stranger in the family whom the child would have liked to love. A first glimmer of salvation, perhaps, comes from his beautiful script, which he learned from a little parish priest. It's enough to lean him in the seigneurs' direction: around 1780, confronted by the rising tide of protest, they need to have all their rights verified by an army of commissioners for landowners. "I tried to put my hand to a pen [although he had virtually written nothing in the preceding five years], it seemed to me that after a few sessions of practice I should manage to recapture the knack of it; I applied myself and succeeded beyond what I had hoped."[11]

The young laborer becomes a young clerk; he is taken on by the notary Hullin at Flixecourt, a town of some thousand souls on the road from Abbeville to Amiens. For two or three years he trains himself to master a trade well suited to his meticulous nature, in which he learns the finer points of the hard life of a rural population (already becoming industrialized by the first textile mills), and which teaches him to feel the sharp contrast between the oppression of the feudal rights he is so scrupulously cataloguing and the right of the wretched to some semblance of happiness. It gets him out of a hole, but leaves him in a state of perpetual internal conflict.

Only one portrait of him exists, undoubtedly posthumous, painted after he became famous; it has been reproduced in thousands upon thousands of prints and has endured for two hundred years.[12] It shows a round head, an aquiline nose, large searching eyes, and a humorless gaze. His dress is as impeccable as that of Robespierre, even to the carefully knotted cravat-ascot, and the whole is crowned by a big broad-brimmed felt hat. A few of the inhabitants of Flixecourt and Roye will remember meeting him between his home and his various places of work, "short, thin, his legs most commonly wrapped in tight leather gaiters, his hair lying flat, combed anyhow, his face rather common but enlivened by a fiery gaze."[13]

To this can be added the particulars of a passport issued in 1794, which mentions his height as five feet, six inches,* and a complexion qualified as "slightly colored."

"The impression one receives is of a bony man with an emaciated face; his energy completely at odds with the dreamer's disposition one can guess at from his wide-open eyes."*

The notary was only eighteen years older than he was; his wife would seem to have played something of the "little mother," in the Rousseau tradition, to their young apprentice; "she was fond of tying up the waves of his ash blond hair with bows and ribbons."[14] His employers' loving-kindness did not go so far as to pay him a wage, however, at least not right away: only after March 22, 1779, does François-Noël receive a pittance of three livres a month. Well, but doesn't he have his room and board? Yes, but how is he

French inches are longer than English (American)

*According to Jean Bruhat.

supposed to cover his nakedness when his lowly commoner's job requires him to spend all his time in châteaux and estates surveying, measuring, marking, chain in hand, in front of often taunting household servants? So, also in 1779, he swallows his pride and writes to his father, asking for help in order to buy himself a new pair of breeches:

"I am ashamed of those I have; they're no longer good for anything, they're torn all over; and yet I am in and about the châteaux all the time; one ought rightly to be very clean. . . . With the clothes I have, my coat and jacket, if I had some breeches too, I should be fine for working days, but I ought to have a clean outfit for holidays and Sundays." His ambition extends even to gaiters, "for there are many storms," and two shirts so as to have a change, or at least cloth to make them with, because Madame Hullin does the washing every six weeks, "a soap wash" too.[15]

In 1780 when his father dies, François-Noël, just turned twenty, becomes the head of the family, responsible for his mother and brothers and sisters. Is that all? No, because in 1782 he marries Marie-Anne-Victorine Lenglet, the daughter of an ironmonger in Amiens who is chambermaid to the Comtesse de Braquemont, in whose home he has duly measured and surveyed. A marriage of love? Almost. A young man with many dependents and a time-consuming job has an urgent need of a servant in the home; this one hardly knows how to write her name, but she is robust and has plenty of energy. Like him, she has a feeling for the things of life. In his effusive moments, her husband will compare her to Rousseau's famous companion Thérèse. So he loves her; but from above, or almost.*

Soon after his marriage Babeuf changes his home base. He and the family move to Roye in the little Santerre region around Péronne, in the heart of rural Picardy; one hundred square leagues, in which the peasants are particularly badly off and follow relatively archaic methods, thereby making matters worse. The innovations of the physiocrats, for instance, those that La Rochefoucault-Liancourt is trying out a little farther south, have not made their way into this backwoods, where the poor are squeezed between the great landowners and the prosperous farmers of Île-de-France, Artois and the Amiénois. "The climate is temperate in Santerre, but colder rather than warm. The ground, watered by the Somme and other less considerable streams, is fertile for wheat, fruit and hemp. There is grazing and some woods; the game is good [but available only to the nobility of course]. A bit of wine is grown in the southern part, of very mediocre quality. The best trade is done in wheat, woolen goods and linen."[16]

In Roye, around 1780, Babeuf starts to make his way, going into business

*In the passage in which the historian Jean Bruhat mentions these details he adds, with unintentional humor, that "from this date on Brabeuf was in favor of women's equality."

for himself, opening his own office of *commissaires à terriers* and employing as many as a dozen clerks whom he trains as he himself was trained at Flixecourt, and pays by the week.

He doesn't spend much time in his office. He is still trekking back and forth through Santerre, partly visiting the owners and securing increasingly important commissions from them, partly "in the field," in the scores of villages and hamlets where his relations with the peasants are growing more and more ambivalent. He is paid to keep them in their places and make them behave; but he is feeling ever closer to them. Picardy is seeping into his blood:

"Ah, if the people only knew, as I do, the history of the great possessions and great possessors of this world!"[17]

"The place where I first penetrated the hideous mysteries of the usurpations of the noble caste was in the dust of seigneurial archives."[18]

In 1787 he reaches the breaking point. The more money his work for the elite brings in, the more he rebels against them and the harder he tries to help the poor to resist.

To resist the Prior of Saint-Taurin, for instance, who was reigning over a Rabelaisian community near Roye, composed "of opulent men of God. . . . Swollen with pride and hyperbolically greedy, he tried to absorb everything, leaving the already hardly used inhabitants nothing but their eyes to weep with."[19] Speaking of himself in the third person, Babeuf finally confesses that "he would groan incessantly at the sight, the result of the perpetuation of sanctified abuses; sloth, slackness and debauchery living in ease on what they extracted in a thousand different forms from the sweat of the unhappy inhabitants of the countryside. . . . Unable to make over a world he had found already made, flung into the realm of injustice by idiotically respected traditions, he confined himself to observing, as strictly as possible, what was absolutely compulsory, until such time as a revolution should strike all usurpations dead in the name of equity."

Babeuf in 1787: a fatalistic and scrupulous integrity embedded in indignation.

23

JUNE–JULY 1787

Prelude to the Change of the Whole World

Having reached this level of tension, Babeuf might well have gone smash, abandoned his business, run away, decamped—or gotten himself thrown into prison. Instead, during this crucial summer of 1787, his correspondence with the Academy of Arras helps him to relieve his immediate discomfort and transcend his social complex.

By holding out a hand, or rather a pen, to him, Dubois de Fosseux convinces him that he is no longer just a "feudist caught in a crossfire" but is becoming a *"philosophe."* Speculation about the human race will keep him from going under.

The Academy of Arras *is* Ferdinand Dubois de Fosseux,[1] its "secretary" who runs a sort of letter-writing exchange, gradually spreading a spiderweb of learning all over France.* "It may be said without overstatement that Dubois de Fosseux was the creator of an institute of public opinion at a time when governments showed very little concern for it. . . . A country gentleman and secretary of a modest provincial academy, he may have been, between 1786 and 1792, the best-informed Frenchman of all."[2]

By him Babeuf is translated to a higher plane. It never occurs to the *feudiste* that the letters, so painstakingly penned by clerks, which he receives from Arras without postage because they're sent by the Intendance of Artois, which has a franking privilege, are no more than circulars, dispatched the same week in the same form to the far corners of the kingdom and vaguely "personalized" by a few lines from Dubois de Fosseux at the bottom of the page. He imagines that he is an object of special attention to the great

---

*Among his correspondents, though there were many more, we find Beaumarchais, but also Condorcet, Carnot, Robespierre (a native of Arras, and so obviously of the number), Monge, Roland, Lacépède, Rabaut Saint-Étienne, etc.

gentleman somewhere out there in Flanders, who in his eyes is the embodiment of all knowledge and the expert on all current events. When, beginning on June 8, the Academy secretary's letters issue a volley of information worthy of a Thomas More or Cyrano de Bergerac, concerning a strange book supposedly in the process of being composed, François-Noël feels that he is being initiated into the secrets of the gods.

Dubois de Fosseux was something of a jester, a whimsical devil, and he cultivated this aspect of his personality, which contrasted with the solemnity habitually attributed to academicians; it is discernible in the excellent portrait of him by Boilly.[3] Between two grave dissertations on the best methods of land cultivation or commercial treaties between nations, he would unsmilingly tell his correspondents about "the most remarkable and most original pamphlet in the world. . . . It is entitled *L'Avant-coureur du changement du monde entier par l'aisance, la bonne éducation et la prospérité générale de tous les hommes, ou prospectus d'un mémoire patriotique* sur les causes de la grande misère qui existe partout et sur les moyens de l'extirper radicalement."[4]

In the vein of a Diderot on one of his funnier days, the honorable Dubois de Fosseux adds, "This is all highly serious in appearance and yet gives rise to laughter. Another time, perhaps, I shall give you a more detailed outline of this work."

But nobody will ever see a page of it, and in this respect Babeuf's entrance to Utopia is a little like a Mother Goose story. The *Avant-coureur du changement du monde entier* is never published, and without this exchange between Babeuf and Dubois de Fosseux in 1786–1787, concerning a handout intended to lure potential subscribers, enable the author to complete his work and find a printer, we should never even have heard of the scheme.[5]

Who is this hypothetical author? An advocate, Claude-Boniface Collignon, residing in Dieuze in Lorraine, "member of the Academies of Science of Naples, Lisbon, Munich and several other places." Despite strenuous effort, we shall learn little more, except that the advocate from Lorraine had previously published a few opuscules, less ambitious than the *Avant-coureur* and apparently all of reformist bent, along with an *Essai de bien public* in 1776, in which he called for the confiscation of fallow land.

Nothing more natural than that Babeuf would be overjoyed by this prospectus. But what is amusing is to see the tranquil Dubois de Fosseux virtually inflamed by the text for several months, during which he, the Notable, the academician, continually bombards the humble *feudiste* with information.

On March 19, 1787, from Dubois de Fosseux to Babeuf:

*Before the Revolution, *patriotique* meant "relating to the author's own country."

Here is the outline of the work *Changement du monde entier,* of which I was telling you a short while ago.

It will be divided into six parts:

The first will give a detailed picture of all the extremes of wretchedness by which human society is afflicted today; and of the abuses, disorders, calamities, arbitrary prerogatives, injustices, bankruptcies, subjects of despair, piracies, thefts, assassinations, crimes and horrors of many kinds that occur.

The second will give the causes of these misfortunes.

The third, a few elementary notions and principles.

The fourth will set out clearly the expedients, resources and regulations whereby all needy citizens or those with the least means, and their wives and children, will in future be able to be very well fed, clothed, housed, heated and lit; to be perfectly educated and, in return for honest work, each according to his or her strength, abilities, sex, age, talents, estate and profession, to enjoy far greater comfort, liberty, justice, facilities and advantages than in our day.

The fifth will describe how it is possible to acquire a substantial amount of money immediately, without taxing the people.

The sixth will contain the replies to all possible objections.

On April 5, from the same to the same:

Here, according to the author of the *Changement du monde entier,* is the manner in which all individuals in society, of both sexes, are to be fed, if his plan is adopted. Every day of their lives without fail, they are to receive, for the midday meal:

Men: one-fourth of a bottle of wine from Champagne, Burgundy, Bordeaux, Languedoc, Tokay, Málaga or other superior vineyards of Europe or of the state in which they live. In addition, they will receive one half-loaf of the best and finest wheaten bread, with a piece of cheese, butter, melon, pâté, turnips, carrots, apples, pears and other similar products, all according to the season.

Women will get one half-bottle of coffee, tea, chocolate or whatever other beverage they please, according to the season and bodily disposition, with a half-pound of bread.

Women will have the right to opt for the men's meal and men to opt for the women's; all they need do is give notice beforehand.

I leave you, sir, to digest this meal and will tell you of the evening meal on another occasion.

From the same to the same again, on June 8:

I promised you the dinner of our world-reformer; prepare for a cracking good meal.

On meat days, every individual in society will be given, free, every day, the following: men and women, four dishes consisting of: 1. A good fat soup, well presented; 2. An ample piece of boiled meat with vegetables; 3. An entrée—stew or the like; 4. Dessert, which will be more or less the same fruits etc. as at midday. And on meatless days: 1. A well-seasoned soup; 2. A dish of lentils, peas, beans, vegetables, eggs, rice, turnips, cauliflowers or other similar products according to season; 3. A dish of river or pond fish, cod, herring, salmon or other. 4. Dessert.

You can infer the supper from the dinner-menu; only add a half-bottle of wine at each meal, for men, and a quarter-bottle for women. The wine measure will be doubled on feast days. On Sundays, a dish of game, fowl or fish and on very great occasions, as for example the author's birthday, the finest dishes will be served, and pastry at dessert. There is our reformer's first dream.*

June 12: Dubois de Fosseux, imperturbable in his hilarious solemnity, moves on to the catalog of clothing intended by the reformer for "all women in society," not forgetting six pairs of hose, three of silk, one pair of garters and a pair of embroidered mules.

June 16: what about housing?

Every married couple will receive, free, a very handsome house of two stories in addition to the ground floor, equivalent to one thousand louis in present-day value for the building alone. It will consist, on the ground floor giving onto the street, of a fine drive lined with freestone paving, a fine heated sitting-room and study next to it and, behind, overlooking the garden, a bedroom and kitchen. There will be no cellar, as cellars will be public. . . .

Every married couple will also be given, free, furnishings to the value of 4,000 louis including two twin beds with silk hangings, each comprising a good bedstead, pallet, feather cover, mattress, three pillows, two silk-lined blankets, a canopy, headboard, silk bedcurtains and railing etc., six pairs of sheets, twelve pillow-slips, six straw-seated chairs, two fine armchairs and a sofa covered in silk, two tables, a desk, a clothes-press and two handsome candelabra with prisms.

Beginning on June 18, the reformer's utopian ecstasy soars to heights that Dubois de Fosseux complacently and resolutely passes on, never dreaming that his youthful correspondent, who, as we know, has never been able to afford the luxury of humor, is taking them all for gospel truth. Now who's the stately scholar having a laugh at, Collignon or Babeuf?

The delightful thing is that everybody will be obliged to be curled and powdered every day. To that end there will be a wigmaker for men and a dresser

---

*Who'd have thought it possible? Here is a correspondence of academicians being metamorphosed into a little treatise on gastronomy. Adding together all the reformer's alimentary designs, as distilled by Dubois de Fosseux, we see laid before our eyes the table of the average eighteenth-century bourgeois household.

for women, and these, with their assistants, will have to curl and powder every member of society every day. Let us not forget that in France, within a period of fifty years . . . , there will be built one thousand towns with a circumference of two leagues, one hundred apprentices' schools for the arts and trades, sixteen thousand villages and three hundred and thirty thousand farms. All existing towns, burgs, villages etc. will be razed to the ground or burned. . . .

What a pleasure it will be, sir, to live fifty years longer so as to be able to see those thousand new towns!

On June 21, Dubois de Fosseux abandons the reformer and his elucubrations, but not before observing that all children will go to school, free, between the ages of four and twenty; that criminal justice will be abolished because there will be no more crime; and that, as far as religion is concerned, freedom of conscience will prevail, but every town will have a temple costing five million livres.

I shall say no more to you, sir, about this singular work; but what I can tell you is that I have searched with the utmost attention for one word that might betray the author's intention to amuse himself or indulge in jest, and it was impossible for me to find it.

These epistolary high jinks last almost a year, and it would seem that in the end it is Babeuf who wearies of them first. The final excerpts from the *Avant-coureur* elicit nothing more than polite acknowledgment from him; maybe he's a bit shocked to see so grand a person wasting time and ink sending him fragments of a utopia that the adamantine seriousness of his character, but also his profound good sense, are less and less able to relish.

He would prefer the Academy of Arras and its secretary to concern themselves more with what is really going on these days. Travelers from Paris and Versailles are bringing strange tidings to Picardy, and there's a run on the gazettes as the post delivers them to Roye. France is moving. Brienne, who's thought to be one step away from supreme power, has just dissolved the Assembly of Notables. The King's coffers are empty. The *parlements* will not let Louis XVI levy fresh taxes to fill them. In his letter of June 25 Dubois de Fosseux drops a few octaves and sounds a little shaken, even he, by the coming storm. The King has given the seals to Chrétien-François de Lamoignon, who's related to Malesherbes, who has himself been recalled to the Council. The two of them have been ordered to draft a code of justice that should, at last, be unified, and in preparing it they will surely be seeking advice from *Président* du Paty:

If Monsieur de Lamoignon succeeds, one of my correspondents tells me, in preventing the judges from receiving too much spice, the clerks' secretaries from receiving anything at all, and attorneys from writing superfluous documents, I should say that Monsieur de Lamoignon is more than mortal man; he is a demigod.

Ah, my dear colleague, what a great day it will be, when the nation is given a uniform code, abrogating, annihilating that chaos of absurd, ridiculous, contradictory customs that consecrate in one province what is forbidden in another; as though there were no demonstrable morality, as though men had several different consciences, as though the nature that forbids a firstborn in Picardy from despoiling his brothers and sisters would allow him to do it in Normandy!

At the beginning of July, it's Babeuf's turn to change gears. Until then he has been respectful, almost servile. He was writing to Dubois de Fosseux as to a teacher. But under pressure of events in the kingdom, and because he has just collided painfully with some big landowners, and because he is beginning to feel more self-confident, butterfly Babeuf is edging out of his chrysalis. On July 8 he dares point out to his distinguished correspondent that differences in matters of justice are primarily the result of inequality in possessions:

What could a new code be, that contained no greater change than to eliminate the discrepancy whereby what is forbidden in one province is legitimate in another? A mighty small palliative for a mighty great wrong. It would not prevent my children from being born poor and dispossessed whereas those of my millionaire neighbor open their eyes to the light of day with too much of everything. It would not prevent my neighbor, bloated by his vast fortune, from treating me with utter contempt solely because I should be only a wretch bending under the weight of my poverty. It would not prevent the feudal heir of this haughty man from being a very great seigneur, while his younger brother, by comparison, would be only a rather meager person, nor, to further increase the elder's share, his sister, whose tender heart might feel anything but the profoundest distaste for the nuptial knot, from being buried alive in a cloister. It would not prevent etc. etc. etc. and many more.

We have just witnessed the birth of babouvism, by spontaneous generation. Involuntary midwives: Dubois de Fosseux and somebody named Collignon.

24

AUGUST 1787

Renewed Energy and Life

Between the firing of Calonne (April 8) and the present, what a waltz the government of France has been dancing! Louis XVI has been bobbing about like a cork on the waves, stirred up by the convening of the Notables followed by their hesitations and conflicts with Alexandre de Calonne; first he supported him, then he dumped him, according to a process that has become the one constant factor in his reign. It was exactly the same with Turgot and then with Necker. The moment a comptroller general of finance (the appointment of a prime minister apparently being out of the question, the comptroller is the key man in the government) tries to impose any comprehensive plan of improvement, Louis XVI feels very relieved for a few days, promises full support and then, however much he might like to resist the pressure of the privileged, starting with the Queen and his brothers, gives way to a kind of blinkered jealousy of his own, which is enough in itself to push the "reformer" off the cliff.

In other words, Louis XVI has always wanted to be saved without a savior. Woe unto the competent man who truly desires to help him; that the King never forgives. And if he spared Maurepas until the end, it was because the old man never lifted a finger.

Once Calonne had been thanked and disposed of, a little court ballet was danced around the abyss of the deficit for a few weeks.* The King knows he is not going to survive without some "providential person," which Calonne did not manage to be. A large portion of his intimates are urging him to recall Necker, but Louis has always found him so antipathetic that at this point he wouldn't dream of it. Besides, there is a tradition in the monarchy that the King never recalls a minister who has fallen from grace. For want of anyone better, and despite his growing irritability over the political role

*See Chapter 12 above, for the conditions of Brienne's appointment.

being played by the Queen, he is beginning to yield to outside suggestions, some of which are ten years old; so he summons Loménie de Brienne, the archbishop of Toulouse who barely believes in God but whom one segment of public opinion is treating as the Messiah.

But not for the comptrollership of finance. Not yet for the essential job. In this, the King has a good argument: a prelate cannot possibly be a director of administration; the age of Mazarin is dead and gone. For that job, the sovereign has flopped about as though caught in a net, making overtures to three men, one after the other, each of whose sole claim to fame is his nullity; first, Chaumont de la Millière, who loyally wriggles out; then Bouvard de Fourqueux, who resigns on May 1 and is replaced by Laurent de Villedeuil. Brienne, meanwhile, must content himself with the dignity in which Vergennes was draped before him—head of the Royal Council of Finance.

Fine. But all those financial problems that are so urgent and that Calonne thought to solve by convening the Notables at Christmas are still there, and growing worse. The only thing in the coffers is dust. The kingdom is on the verge of bankruptcy. Irritated by the—very mild—stirrings of the Notables, Louis XVI expects Brienne to act hereafter without those superfluous dignitaries, even if all he does is use the expedients proposed by Calonne without saying so. There is just one formality to go through: the dignitaries must be dispatched with all due pomp and ceremony. It would seem that their sole function has been to broadcast the enormity of the deficit and remove from office the man who confessed it.

The King can't stand to have these people perched a few steps from his château a moment longer. What he would like is to revert to the good old tradition of "As the King wills, so wills the Law." The necessary measures will be adopted by the Council and, maybe, ratified by some microassemblies of Notables meeting here and there in the provinces at the whim of his gracious pleasure. But please, leave the poor King master of his hunts and building schemes! One last ritual, and he can bid farewell to the Notables, as a national body, on Friday, May 25.

It was their sixth and final plenary sitting. A monument to almost liturgical hypocrisy that might have been staged by Beaumarchais. The same short walk from the hall of the Menus Plaisirs and the same ceremony as on the previous occasions.* A festival of kneeling, bowing, and starchy speeches. The supporting cast has changed a little, but not the King and princes. The keeper of the seals who "approaches the throne making three deep bows"[1] is no longer Miromesnil, it's Lamoignon. After a few words by the King, his only memorable phrase being that "in order to establish and maintain order

*See the end of Volume IV for proceedings at the opening sitting.

it is necessary to balance income and expenditure,"² Lamoignon, with his matchless experience of rhetoric, soaps the plank on which those present are being made to walk back to their homesteads:

> The table of state income and expenditure has been disclosed before your eyes; and the contributions of the Assembly's various committees have given form to the solemn [*sic*] expression of public opinion.
>
> In this way, gentlemen, you have counseled your King and prepared and facilitated the most desirable revolution, with no other authority than that of trust. . . .
>
> You have sought the remedy for a disorder, the sudden disclosure of which has grieved but not discouraged you; and, as the King foresaw, you have found it, in the form of savings, reductions, and increase in tribute.*
>
> In carrying out reforms so worthy of his heart, the King will be gloriously seconded by his august family.
>
> The Queen, whose good heart seeks so ardently all means of contributing to the public weal, has commanded that the picture of the assistance and sacrifices she can offer should be presented to her at once.
>
> His Majesty's august brothers, who have just set such great examples of zeal and patriotism, are preparing for the public treasury all the relief that can be anticipated from the reductions of their households and their love of the people. . . .†
>
> The King has solemnly promised that this disorder in his finances will not recur and His Majesty is going to take the most effective steps to fulfill this sacred undertaking, of which you are the trustees.⁴

In the next hour, it's Brienne's turn, radiating the confidence newly invested in him, to display a certain degree of boldness, albeit prudently, by announcing the future convening of provincial assemblies. He's finding himself for the first time with the eyes of all France upon him:

> The King has not the slightest desire, gentlemen, to interfere with the forms and privileges of the first two orders [clergy and nobility]. He knows that in a monarchy there are distinctions that it is important to preserve; that absolute equality is proper only for purely republican or purely despotic states; that an equal contribution does not imply a confusion of ranks and conditions; that the ancient forms are the safeguard of the Constitution.⁵

Imagining himself safe, he then suggests that the third estate might possibly have twice as many representatives in the future provincial assem-

---

*Euphemism announcing a tax increase.

†Before convening the Notables, Calonne got the Treasury to pay seventeen million livres of debt incurred by the King's two brothers. Each of them is to receive another ten million in the next five years, to subsidize their household expenses.³

blies as each of the other two orders and that these bodies might adopt the principle of one-man-one-vote; he even ventures to make a lively attack upon the *corvée* [peasant's obligation to do unpaid labor on the roads] as "a terrible imposition"; "national works programs will no longer be watered by the tears of the poor and unfortunate."[6] He gives a promise, which is at the same time the first official criticism of Calonne, to publish without delay the exact amount of the deficit, estimated by the new minister at something in the neighborhood of 140 million. "The greatest service you have rendered to the state has been almost wholly to dissipate the clouds that made it impossible to have an exact knowledge of the financial position."[7]

He ends on a high note: "Such, gentlemen, are the assurances you are going to be able to take back to your fellow citizens, and if a few of them were to ask you anxiously what has come of this long and famous assembly, you will tell them, confidently, that through it the nation has received renewed energy and life from its sovereign."[8]

A little compliment, on behalf of the peers, from Monsieur. Anxious not to jeopardize the relative popularity he has gained in the last few months by keeping absolutely still, the Comte de Provence takes care not to utter the slightest word in favor of Brienne.

The Archbishop of Narbonne, oldest of the prelates present, mumbles a few words, followed by some from the chief magistrates of Paris and the provinces and even the provost of the merchants [head of municipal government in the capital].

Whereupon, everybody goes off to dine at four in the afternoon.

"The Assembly of Notables had hardly been dissolved when the public began awaiting most impatiently the results of the Council's deliberations that were to be the consequence of it."[9]

The public apparently got its wish. First, Brienne gets the King to approve the freedom of circulation of cereals (which takes us back to the great debates of the beginning of his reign);* then, in June, he gets the *Parlement* to register the setting up of provincial assemblies; and with the same sweep of his broom he gets the *corvée* converted to a cash payment; and lastly he writes a royal edict replacing the "two twentieths and four sous" tax that was raising such lamentations among the rich, by a territorial subsidy to be equitably apportioned throughout the kingdom.

Most of these ideas came from Calonne, but Calonne has just been hurled from favor. Brienne, temporarily in good odor, at least with the Queen, thinks he's got a free hand, now that the Notables have been courteously dumped, and is about to walk straight into the good old machine

---

*For Turgot's reforms, see Volume I.

that was built to resist change and progress in any form, the machine many kings have tried to ignore, or circumnavigate, or smash, but never succeeded: the *parlements*.

The *parlements*, especially the one in Paris, are the only powers capable of offsetting that of the monarch, to a point. Not because they are elected, since their offices are inherited or bought, but because it is an age-old tradition that no law becomes truly effective until the *parlements* have endorsed or registered it.

The issue here is not the question of a national assembly; the *parlements* have no desire to see such a thing in competition with themselves. The issue is centuries of pettifoggery.

A *parlement*'s opposition to a king takes the form of remonstrances, sometimes extremely insolent ones, which have no force of law. All a *parlement* can do is refuse to register the king's laws and decrees, which means they can't be transmitted to the rest of the kingdom and therefore can't be enforced, at least not for some time. But when the king in person orders them to accept his decisions, they have to give way.

August 6, 1787. Louis XVI does. In the midsummer swelter, the members of the Paris *Parlement* pile into sixty conveyances early in the morning and, after a long drive, reach the palace at Versailles where the King is holding his bed of justice in the great hall of the Life Guards. Color everywhere: six tapestries depicting biblical subjects surround the princes and magistrates, some of whom look quite comical wearing their mortarboards. Way at the back, a few high-ranking ladies and, in one corner, the King, seated on a throne beneath a gorgeous canopy, on a platform raised several steps and covered with a fleur-de-lis carpet. At his feet, on one of the steps, you can see a little creature in some weird sort of headgear, called the grand chamberlain.

"The King having seated himself and donned his hat, the keeper of the seals said, by his order, that His Majesty ordered those attending to be seated; after which the King, having removed and replaced his hat, said:

" 'Gentlemen, it does not behoove my *Parlement* to doubt my power nor that which I have invested in it.

" 'It is always painful to me to resolve to make use of my full authority and depart from the ordinary usages; but my *Parlement* compels me to do so today and the safety of the state makes it my duty.

" 'My keeper of the seals will now inform you of my intentions.' "[10]

Poor Lamoignon! In the stifling hall, where it feels as though that year's whole torrid Île-de-France summer has come to rest, this heir to a great dynasty of the nobility of the gown, after making the regulation genuflexions, has to open his speech by announcing "the King's determination to levy additional taxes in order to restore order to his finances."[11]

Essentially this is to be a "stamp tax," to be levied on every transaction and agreement carried out between citizens, whether relating to the purchase of goods, a marriage, or the issuing of a passport. In addition, a "territorial subsidy" is gradually to replace the automatic levy of one twentieth of the income on certain fortunes.

His audience is not with him. The King has been out on a little hunt and had a good lunch, while the magistrates have had nothing to eat. He's falling asleep, and actually snores stertorously while the history of the kingdom pursues its course. His decline, both literal and figurative, is much remarked upon.[12] "The body is thickening [as Mercy-Argenteau writes to Joseph II] and the returns from the hunt are followed by repasts so immoderate that they provoke periods of irrationality alternating with a sort of abrupt unconcern, which are most trying for those who have to endure them."[13]

After his speech, "the keeper of the seals said to the First *Président* [of the *Parlement*] that he could speak. Thereupon, the First *Président* and other gentlemen having knelt, the keeper of the seals said, 'The King commands you to rise.' "[14]

War is declared. The First *Président* protests:

"Sire, it is a source of much distress to your *Parlement* that in the last twelve years it has been required to endorse such an accumulation of taxes that the present proposals, if approved, would carry the total to an increase of more than two hundred millions since Your Majesty's accession to the throne. It does not believe its powers adequate to ensure the enforcement of the edicts among your people, whose love and zeal know no bounds, but who observe with terror the unfortunate consequences of an administration which has wreaked such extraordinary depredations, that they are not even able to credit them."[15]

So much for Calonne, "that administrator who has contrived to misrepresent your *Parlement* to Your Majesty and retreat behind the throne to cover his extravagance."[16]

In concluding, it was for *Président* d'Aligre to give public voice to what La Fayette and a few others had suggested in one or another of the Notables' committee rooms:

"Your *Parlement* finding itself unable, Sire, to vote for such oppressive taxes, it can only repeat its most lively exhortations, imploring that, for the preservation of Your Majesty's authority, the glory of your reign, and the recovery of your finances, you may be pleased to allow the convening of the Estates General."[17]

Back in Paris that evening, the members of the *Parlement* are applauded for having endorsed the stamp tax only under duress. Bookseller Hardy, who writes in his diary every day with manic regularity, attests that "the people were gathered around the vehicles in the courtyards of the château [of Versailles] and as the members of the *Parlement* were leaving, the people are said to have called out to them, 'Surely you will put right all the wrong that has just been done to us here.' "[18]

However that may be, the wrong has been done. The bed of justice of August 6 ends according to ritual. Once more the keeper of the seals pretends, on bended knee, to receive the King's orders, and then "to go, for opinion, to Monsieur, the Comte d'Artois, the princes of the blood, the lay peers, the grand écuyer and the grand chamberlain, and to pass in front of the King again,"[19] not without making a final bow.

After a further series of calisthenics performed in all four corners of the hall, poor Lamoignon has surely earned the right to sit down, put on his hat, and declaim:

"The King, sitting in his bed of justice, has commanded and hereby commands that the declaration just read out be registered at the registry of his *Parlement*. . . . He requires his attorney general to have the contents thereof sent, in copies which have been certified as true copies of the original, to the different bailliages and senechalsies, there to be similarly read, published and registered."

"The King then said:

" 'You have heard my will, I trust that you will comply with it.'

"After which, the King rose and left, in the same order as he had entered."

DUPORT

25

AUGUST 1787

The Most Ungovernable of the Magistrates

The *Parlement* does not comply with the royal will. It balks.

On August 7, the very next day, meeting among themselves and in their own precincts again, the magistrates do as their predecessors have occasionally done before them—when facing Mazarin, for instance, or, even before that, the Valois kings: they turn refusal into insurrection. They had not gone so far since that famous day, at the beginning of his reign, when Louis XIV strode in wearing his hunting gear, riding crop in hand, and told them, *"L'État, c'est moi."* They'd dearly like to prove now that Louis XVI is not Louis XIV.

History turns a new page in France today. Its name is not yet known; but the kick of the *Parlement* mule is incarnated in one Adrien-Jean-François Duport, councillor at the Paris *Parlement.*

He's not quite the person "informed" opinion was expecting. The chief seats in the opposition seem to have been assigned already, depending on your hopes and coteries, to Monsieur or the Duc d'Orléans, if you were remaining strictly absolutist; to Mirabeau if you were a dreamer; and to La Fayette if you wanted to go American.

But the princes are prudently sitting still, while Mirabeau has imprudently jumped onto a merry-go-round of polemics that is leading him on yet another chase around Europe. As for La Fayette, it's touch and go. Even now, it wouldn't take much. Some are seeing him as a sort of "lieutenant-general of the kingdom," but he lacks political experience and character, if not honesty; and he also lacks a party. His one recommendation remains his good behavior in America. In France, his aristocratic roots commit him to a lost land, Auvergne, and as for the Court—well, the King can't stand him, and the Queen, who was briefly friendly, is no longer noticing him. Besides, he's not the sort to curry favor. But what about support from the army? He's still nothing more than the colonel of a second-rate regiment and as a member of the upper nobility of the sword he has none of the qualities of the *Parlement* men. And it happens to be the *Parlement*'s turn.

They have thought of him, though. A few of the more liberal and progressive of the magistrates were considering, only a short while ago, how they could get him appointed "honorary councillor to the *Parlement* of Paris." They even made some overtures to him, arguing that there had been precedents in the past. But rightly or wrongly, he refused, and so informs Washington, "There is little of the *Parlement* about me, as you know, and whatever the arrangement made, the magistracy is going to have to go through the crucible of the Estates General."[1]

So the only force left in the kingdom, to set against the King and ministers, is the *parlements,* and the most visible man in the Paris *Parlement* just now is Duport.

He was born in Paris on February 24, 1759, the son of Mathieu Duport, councillor in the *Parlement,* and Marie-Magdeleine de Cabanel.*

---

*The father, himself a Parisian of long standing, came from an ancient family of nobles

If anybody belongs to a *"Parlement* aristocracy," it's Adrien Duport: one grandfather, one uncle, a cousin have all been or still are advocates or councillors. He has never known what it is to want or worry; the only slight shadow over his childhood was poor health. "Above average height, his face was thin, pale and pockmarked; he had small gray eyes, a high forehead."*

He could have been taught by tutors in the magnificent mansion formed by joining together three houses at the corner of rue Neuve-Saint-Pierre and rue Saint-Gilles. There would have been no shortage of men for the job. But in his circle it was assumed that one would spend one's school years in some reputable institution. So between the ages of ten and sixteen Adrien Duport learned his "humanities" at Juilly, southeast of Paris, with the best Oratorians of France. No visible problems. He was admitted to the bar and then, under a special dispensation (since by rights he should have been at least twenty-five), became a councillor in the Third Chamber of Inquest at the age of eighteen.[2]

How quickly everything has gone for him! A councillor before his time, he married Élisabeth de Blanzat,† seventeen, in 1782. His life looked to be all wrapped up and tied with a bow, if not actually over. But perhaps he suffered from too much success and the relative condescension of his peers. "Although very young, there was nothing youthful about him."[3] Hence, despite his aloofness, and some difficulty in communicating, it was impossible for him to remain circumscribed by the rigorous routine of investigations at the Palais de Justice, the fine town house which his father gave him on the rue du Grand-Chantier, and a scattering of country homes.‡

The only unique feature of Duport's early years was his meeting with the famous Mesmer. Was he a true believer in the "great man" and did he experiment with Mesmer's tubs because he was already aware of some weakness in his constitution? It's possible; but when Duport became vice president of the "Lodge of Universal Harmony," it was February 1784, the high point of an almost universal infatuation in this society that had been bored since the end of the American war and fell for the phenomena of animal magnetism in a big way through the contagion of snobbery. It gave the fine ladies and gentlemen the illusion of being part of something new, turning their backs on the Church, of course, and on devotion to the King; but also, or so they

---

from Champagne. He is guillotined on April 20, 1794, along with other members of the *parlements* who are sentenced as a group, partly, in his case, as a victim of his son's celebrity.

*According to a laissez-passer issued by the municipality of Melun in 1792. He dies of tuberculosis at thirty-nine, after emigrating.

†By whom he has three children.

‡He also owned three more houses, which he rented out, in Paris. The Duports had a considerable fortune.

imagine, going even further than the *encyclopédistes*. That was the year Diderot died; Voltaire and Rousseau were long since underground. Illuminism, recently born in Germany, provided a pretext for the relationships that the younger generation were cultivating in Mesmer's rooms. It was there that Duport became friendly not only with La Fayette but also with the Duc d'Orléans, Lauzun, Ségur, Bergasse and the banker Kornman, and a publicist whose name is becoming increasingly well known, Jacques-Pierre Brissot. It is no coincidence that they are almost all trying to demolish Beaumarchais now; he's had a bit too much of a laugh at their expense.

Mesmer has gone back to Vienna. Magnetism is becoming a thing of the very dead past. But the friendships remain, enhanced by the spice of secrecy, almost of conspiracy, which Mesmer sprinkled over a small group of young men who would like to shake the pillars of the temple.

In their name, beginning on August 7, the tall, slightly stooped silhouette of Adrien Duport gradually begins to rise. Brienne, who is not lacking in psychological acumen, has already classified him as "the most ungovernable of the magistrates," and the Minister will soon have an opportunity to verify his suspicions.

Prelude: "On Tuesday August 7.*

"Today, between ten and eleven in the morning, at the Palais [in Paris], the thirteenth sitting of the *Parlement* is being held, all chambers assembled, but with only twelve or thirteen dukes and peers,† including the Duc de Charost, the Duc de Luxembourg, the Archbishop of Paris [Leclerc de Juigne] and the Bishop of Beauvais [de La Rochefoucauld]."[4]

This is the rough draft of an insurrection of the high nobility of the gown. The nobility of the sword, which might have joined the movement at this point, steps quietly aside in a body, which is why Hardy lists, on the field of honor of resistance, the rare braves who were exposing themselves to peril by taking part in the sitting. Under Henri IV and Richelieu, the King's authority had cut off nobles' heads and razed their castles to the ground for less.

"Their Royal Highnesses, Monsieur and Monseigneur Comte d'Artois, and the other princes, were not there, although they were invited. But His Royal Highness Monsieur did send the *Parlement* a respectable letter regarding his involuntary absence."[5]

A growing crowd, gathered around the building, learns the incredible truth by word of mouth: at the close of an eight-hour sitting, the *Parlement*

---

*Continuation of Hardy's journal.

†The dukes and peers were part of the Paris *Parlement,* where they sat *ex officio* on grand occasions but without actually forming a separate Chamber of Peers [or House of Lords] as existed in England and as will exist later in France.

adopts a decision stating that the registration of the stamp tax and territorial subsidy, which took place the day before, is purely and simply illegal. According to Hardy, this "sacrilegious" resolution is adopted "by a plurality of sixty-three votes to fifty or fifty-two." He adds that "a great crowd, filling the halls, stairs and courtyards, rashly gave voice to redoubled shouts of bravo, bravo! and many and noisy clappings of hands, to such a pitch that no one could recall having ever seen so stupefying a scene at the Palais. . . .

"Many people apprehended that the Court would try to treat this extraordinary applause for such courageous resistance as a fault committed by the *Parlement,* and that the outcome would be the issuing of *lettres de cachet* against a number of magistrates. M. d'Eprémesnil,* councillor in the Second Chamber of Inquests, who is suffering from a bilious attack for which he has been urged to undergo treatment, is said to have given this hot-blooded reply: 'I know how to die when needs must.' He was forced to slip out of the Palais secretly, and very incognito, in order to avoid the uncontrolled manifestations of public enthusiasm."[6]

So it's back to square one. On one side the King, legislating in his Council; on the other, the *Parlement,* deliberately deaf to the new laws and refusing to register them. For a few days, a sort of peddlers' war is waged in Paris among the men who sell the five-sou pamphlets. Some of them represent the opposition, but most, subsidized and supplied with large printings by the Royal Press, set forth the position of the Court; that is, for the moment, of Brienne. Their cries jangle together at the crossroads:

"News! News!"

But the lack of any real direction in the government enables Duport, on August 10, to make a red-letter speech.

That day the *Parlement* holds another plenary sitting, deep in the Palais de Justice, at the behest of those who want to take action rather than submit to the royal will, or willfulness. They are no longer prepared to be summoned to Versailles like lackeys and have the desires of a snoring sovereign imposed upon them. Although the fundamental laws of the monarchy are unwritten, they do not allow *parlements* to challenge the ruler in person, or even the ministers in office. But if a scapegoat is needed, who better than Calonne-the-dismissed, the failed and soon to be called the false? Duport knows the rules of billiards: by shooting down a minister who was all-powerful the day before yesterday, some of his fire will surely hit ministers who are still in their seats today, may touch the Queen, and even singe the image of the King.

At first, the speech of August 10 is known only to a few; its author does

*See in this connection his role in the *parlements'* recall after the death of Louis XV, Volume I. In August 1787, he really is having a violent attack of jaundice.

not publish it at once. It produces a real spasm in "informed circles," however, reaching well beyond the members of the Paris *Parlement.* Its impact is reflected in the *Gazette de Leyde,* which is printed in Holland and purveys news of every description to a dozen countries:

"When, on August 10, M. Duport denounced the administration of M. de Calonne, he made a speech that, by the force of its thoughts and the terms in which they are expressed, has created a great sensation."[7]

In his introduction, he attacks the abuses for which he blames the former minister. This part of the speech is divided in two: an almost inquisitorial inquiry into the causes of the present disorder "in order to calm the terrifying uncertainty of the nation," followed by a far-reaching philosophical elaboration "on the tendency of all governments to become arbitrary."

In other words, the *Parlement* is perfectly justified when it demands "firmly and wisely, to know the nation's principles in the matter of taxation; a demand that no act by those in power can nullify."

There follows a heavy indictment of evils that are for the first time being attributed to the highest level of the state, although we've seen them denounced for years in underground books. Here Duport thunders against "arbitrary power," "despotism," and something even worse, which he calls a "vizierate":

"It is frightening to compare the weakness of an individual with the boundless power of a minister. Upon taking up his duties, he soon learns the resources of events and natures. He has many offices at his disposal, and this brings all who are motivated by ambition to his feet. *Lettres de cachet,* that ultimate abuse of authority, are his security against any who might feel injustice too keenly. Thus it is that all individuals, checked by the powerful forces of hope and fear, have no choice but to conform to the path he wishes them to take. Further, the press, an agency unknown to legislations of old, wins over the indifferent to his side."[8]

Conclusion: a demand that Calonne be indicted as a simple malefactor, for having hidden the true state of the nation's finances from the King and for having actually caused all the trouble himself—even to exaggerating the amount of the notorious deficit in order to camouflage his own misdealings, which chiefly involved the unjustified purchase of property.

From London, to which he has prudently withdrawn, Calonne objects energetically. He points out, quite rightly, that Duport and the other people accusing him are overlooking the financial pit dug by the American war; for that he was not responsible, and he has had to fill it in as best he could.

But tonight, Duport wins at the trial of history. The *Parlement,* "all chambers combined," issues a decision instituting proceedings against Calonne and summoning him to appear before the bar. Duport has become "the ideal exponent of the years 1787–1791."[9]

On August 14 the King's Council annuls this decision and repeats the order to *Parlement* to register Brienne's tax measures. The *Parlement* remains deaf. This is turning into a game of tit for tat. Duport is down on *lettres de cachet,* is he? Let's see what he has to say to *these;* and let's be quick about it. According to Breteuil, the Queen and Artois, the Palais de Justice is being transformed by this unprecedented agitation into a spawning ground for troublemakers, exacerbated by the hot weather. Louix XVI is made to believe that the great procession of the Vow of Louis XIII, which is to take place on Assumption Day, could turn into a mob riot around the insurgent magistrates. So much the better; we'll show 'em what our King is made of.

"On this feast of the Holy Virgin [Wednesday, August 15], it was learned that between midnight and four or five in the morning a *lettre de cachet* was delivered to every one of the *Parlement* magistrates, expressed in these terms:

" 'I hereby inform you that you are to remain at home, to leave Paris within twenty-four hours and to be at Troyes within four days, where I shall apprise you of my further intentions.

" 'I pray God to keep you in his holy and worthy care.

" 'Versailles, August 14, 1787.'

"The letters were delivered by officers of the French Guards accompanied by six fusiliers and followed by a police observer who was to guide them on their route and point out the magistrates' homes to them."[10]

A curious feast-day eve, with torches and a general mobilization for a scant hundred Notables, who will be permitted, if they have learned their lesson, to sit sulkily in the former palace of the counts of Champagne and find lodgings as best they can, in the inns or with friends.

Apparently, might is still right. The Court is going to try to find a way around the chastised *Parlement*'s refusal to endorse the tax measures. On August 17 one of the two first princes of the blood (Provence, with that put-upon sanctity he has adopted) goes to the Audit Court, while the other (Artois, in a saber-rattling mode) visits the Cour des Aides [the court dealing with disputes concerning certain taxes], there to reiterate the King's desires to these lesser magistrates, whose role, in the absence of their tutors and mentors, is suddenly glorified.

Even then, the risk is great. Provence comes off not too badly, but the Comte d'Artois is fiercely berated on his way into and out of the courtrooms, by a feverish little host of "lawmen" who are feeling not only outraged but orphaned as well. The Prince's bodyguard have to unsheathe their swords and are within an inch of ordering their men to fire, to clear him a passage. The moment he gets back to Versailles, Artois, white as a sheet, takes straight to his bed.

The kingdom is at a standstill. Some means of getting it moving, other than sending horsemen to bang on magistrates' doors in the middle of the night, is going to have to be found. Wearied by all this agitation, and also, undoubtedly, displeased at having resorted to violence, Louis XVI grudgingly makes up his mind, on August 26, to do what he has never wanted to do since he came to the throne: he appoints a "First Minister," or head of government, what we would call a prime minister, to whom his colleagues will be required to submit their files and their findings.

The country hasn't had one since Cardinal de Fleury, and the poor King is finding himself compelled to turn to the person he would least like to see in the job, Étienne-Charles de Loménie de Brienne, who has not involved himself too deeply in the chastising of the *parlements*. He'll just have to figure out some way, in the next few weeks, to make peace between the executive and judiciary.

LA FAYETTE AND WASHINGTON

26

SEPTEMBER 17, 1787

A Rising Sun

After a summer so oppressive that the weather alone would have been enough to drive the delegates of the twelve states to kill each other, mid-September brings milder days to Philadelphia. All honor to Franklin, Washington and the others, who decreed on May 19 that their deliberations must be closed to the public. Things were near the breaking point a dozen times, but on September 17 the last diehards can rise from the last sitting. There are only forty-two of them left, and three of those refuse to sign; so the foundations of the American republic are laid down by thirty-nine representatives of the prosperous middle class.

This will be known as "the miracle in Philadelphia."[1]

But that is yet to come. At the moment, after four months of fierce oratorical jousting, they don't quite know what they have. Never in history have so few men labored for so many.

And still nothing is settled, because the Constitutional Convention is not empowered to impose its conclusions on individual states. Each of them receives the text resulting from the compromise agreement and must, in the coming months, make a decision, in its own particular assembly, on the Constitution, which they have the right to amend. Thus begins one of the broadest political discussions of the modern era.

There may be two or three among the drafters of the Constitution of the United States of America who sense, on September 17, that their efforts will have a bearing on the centuries to come. Washington, with unfailing courtesy, has restored Franklin to the little presidential platform on which the old gentleman sat when the meeting opened. The dignified delegates file up to the desk for the final signature—because that's the way it is done for the Constitution, as it was for the Declaration of Independence, in this same building, eleven years earlier:* no solemn vote by show of hands or secret ballot, but a name written by each delegate at the bottom of the final draft of the document. Franklin looks as though he's asleep, in his aged glory and newborn worries. He is not in agreement with the pages he has to sign. He had been fighting for more than fifty years for a democracy that would be truly "of the people," one that expresses what he believes to be the wishes of laborers, craftsmen and tenant farmers, as distinct from the clergy, rich bourgeois, army chiefs and wealthy tradesmen.[2] Since the beginning of the American Revolution, Franklin has been hoping that the New World would be the promised land of a true republic, and here he is compelled, by the famous compromise by which they all are bound, to consecrate the birth of a new parliamentary aristocracy. One last time, he follows the advice Cotton Mather gave him when, as a young printer in Boston, he had to stoop to get through the door of the preacher's house:

"Bend! Bend!"†

But when the last men at the end of the line have finished signing, they see him point to an unremarkable painting of a landscape with a sun in it that hangs behind the president's chair, and hear him mutter, "I have often and often in the course of the session, and the vicissitudes of my hopes and fears as to its issue, looked at that behind the president without being able to tell whether it was rising or setting. But now at length I have the happiness to know that it is a rising and not a setting sun."[3]

Washington is little more enthusiastic than the rest but he knows how to make the best of things, having had to do so several times already in his life. He writes a sort of circular to the presidents of the individual state conventions, to be sent out with the draft Constitution:

"Sir, we have the honor to submit to the consideration of the United States in Congress assembled, that Constitution which has appeared to us the most advisable. . . .

*See Volume I.
†See Volume I.

"In all deliberations on this subject we kept steadily in our view, that which appears to us the greatest interest of every true American, in which is involved prosperity, felicity, safety, perhaps our national existence. This important consideration . . . led each state in the Convention to be less rigid on points of inferior magnitude. . . . And thus the Constitution, which we now present, is the result of a spirit of amity, and of that mutual deference and concession which the peculiarity of our political situation rendered indispensable."[4]

In a less "noble father" and more forthright style, Washington writes to La Fayette as well, almost the same day:

"Our new constitution is the result of four months of deliberation. It is now a child of fortune, to be fostered by some and buffeted by others. What will be the general opinion on, or the reception of it, is not for me to decide, nor shall I say anything for or against it. If it be good, I suppose it will work its way good. If bad, it will recoil on the framers."[5]

In reality, the Constitution is, above all, the outcome of a confrontation among the fifty-odd delegates, whose disinclination to agree with one another has been intensified by their allegiance to large but different economic—essentially landowning—interests. Among their number, there was not one of those thousands of small farmers who formed the seedbed of the future Union, not one laborer, not even an engineer from the infant industries of the larger towns.[6] Forty of these big landowners are owed money by Congress. Fifteen of them, including Washington, own slaves, and fourteen, also including him, have invested large fortunes in land. Such similarities might have been thought to create a relative degree of class solidarity among them, but the apparently incoercible opposition between the small states and the larger ones, between New York and Virginia, between the more go-getting North (Boston, Philadelphia) and the broad acres of the South, where Virginia was determined to preserve its supremacy, frustrated such thoughts.

Yet the main objective of their meeting was to work out proceedings for arbitration and coordination among themselves. And what saved them from disaster, in the form of unregulated pushes and shoves from public opinion, was the law of secrecy they imposed upon their debates from the start, combined with a respectful mistrust of any of their number whose age or intemperance seemed likely to loosen his tongue. Every evening, for example, two delegates discreetly accompanied Benjamin Franklin to his dwelling, and sentries stood guard at the doors of their meeting room.

Especially in the first two months it seemed as if there could be no way to settle the dispute over the powers of a hypothetical president, the establishment of a permanent Congress and whether it should have two chambers or one, the levying of taxes by individual states, and the extra "representation"—purely fictitious—to be credited to slave-rich states. The slave problem alone looked as though it might ruin everything. Not that slave states were proposing anything so mad as giving slaves the vote (any more than to illiterate farmers, or to people who paid no taxes); but the slaveholders wanted a higher proportional representation than the others.

One northern delegate bitterly observed, "Are slaves men? Then make them citizens and give them the vote. Are they property? Then why not give the vote to other forms of property? Why should the houses of Philadelphia and sailing ships of Boston not have the right to vote?"[7]

Only one chamber? The small states dig in their heels and resist, knowing they'd be swamped. Whereas to the big ones, a senate with two representatives per state, irrespective of the size of the state, seems silly and likely to slow things up. A few of the "smalls" go so far as to threaten to appeal for help from foreign countries. "So that's your idea," sneer the delegates from the "bigs." "Why not just go back to the English?"

And on and on, about anything and everything, including states' rights to conclude commercial treaties with the outside world. Having finally staggered to an agreement on a two-chamber legislature, they start quarreling over the length of members' terms of office. And this president—the result of another wearisome compromise—how long is his term of office to be? There are one or two suggestions that he be elected for life, and even that he be called "His Majesty the President." In the end, one more compromise gives him a term of four years, renewable indefinitely.

Pushing and shoving this way and that, giving way out of ennui but also, often, out of patriotism, on this September 17 they finally propose, for ratification by the thirteen states, the Constitution which is to govern the United States of America. It begins with a few almost musical lines, like a great symphony of freedom:

"We the people of the United States, in order to form a more perfect Union, establish justice, insure domestic tranquility, provide for the common defence, promote the general welfare, and secure the blessings of liberty to ourselves and our posterity, do ordain and establish this Constitution."[8]

All legislative power is vested in an elected Congress, composed of a Senate (two representatives for each state) and a House of Representatives, its size being in proportion to the size of constituent populations. Executive power is vested in a president, who is also supreme commander of the armed forces, replaced if need be by a vice president. He cannot dissolve Congress, and Congress cannot impeach him except on grounds of treason, bribery, or other high crimes and misdemeanors.

"VII. The ratification of the conventions of nine States, shall be sufficient for the establishment of this Constitution. . . .

"Done in Convention, by the unanimous consent of the States present, the seventeenth day of September in the year of our Lord one thousand seven hundred and eighty-seven, and of the independence of the United States of America, the twelfth.

"In witness whereof, we have hereunto subscribed our Names."

The first of the thirty-nine, it goes without saying, is George Washington, "President [of the Convention] and Deputy from Virginia" as though already marked by fate, but everybody else is already beginning to think of him, too, as the midwife to a stabilized peace, after being conqueror in the war.

Two days later, congealed in his perpetual, funereal solemnity, he sets out home to Mount Vernon.

That morose air suits him and inspires confidence, more than other personality styles might, among the large number of his fellow citizens who would be suspicious of a more jovial mien.

FOUCHÉ

27

SEPTEMBER 26, 1787

You Have Never Seen Me So Thin

At twenty-eight, Joseph Fouché reaches an enviable rung on the academic ladder: on September 26, 1787, he is appointed "supplementary for studies" at the Oratorians' college at Juilly.[1]

"What matter that I am the son of the commander of a privateer and that I was initially intended to study navigation; what matter that I was brought up by the Oratorians, that I was an Oratorian myself, that I worked as a teacher and that the Revolution found me headmaster in the school in Nantes;* it follows, at least, that I was neither ignorant nor an idiot."[2]

He's wrong to feel such contempt for his youth, because it paves the way for him by sculpting the particular type of behavior that will secure his entry into history.

---

*First falsehood in the *Mémoires* more or less "derived from" Fouché; the authenticity of the whole work is open to question, but some of its details do come from him. As we shall see later, the Revolution does not find him in Nantes, which he reaches only in 1790. In 1789 he'll be teaching in Arras, but he is not eager to linger over this period in his reminiscences, as he was then a friend of Robespierre and Carnot.

Joseph Fouché was born in Pellerin, "a large bourg of twenty-three and three-quarter households [say one hundred or so people] standing on the left bank of the Loire four leagues below Nantes and five leagues above Paimboeuf. There is a port and a roadstead. Quite sizable vessels can go up that far, but those of deeper draft stop at Paimboeuf."[3] Here "naval captain" Fouché, another Joseph—the same Christian name has been given to the firstborn in the family for generations—dropped anchor at the side of his wife, née Françoise Croizet, at the end of his long hauls between Brittany and the Isles. In this little lost world at the back of the French beyond, he was a person of importance, a "Monsieur." With the profits from their plantations in Santo Domingo, the Fouchés have bought land locally, including a piece of property called Rouzerolles, by means of which our little Joseph can gentrify himself upon entering the school in which he styles himself Fouché de Rouzerolles—until 1790.

He will never say a word about his parents, except that they were respectable. From the very first years of his life, he is a secret, closed-in, silent person. The Loire is his second mother and will play a large part in his behavior. He's a child of the river that was so animated in those days, and at the same time so calm, its silting-up only just starting to impede the movements of the ships of all descriptions that travel up it, sometimes into the very heart of the kingdom. That's where he gets his taciturnity and his kind of sobriety, which he keeps.

Unlike his father, who went down to the sea, he is more the type to head upstream, inland. The sea does not appeal to him. The family decided when he was a child that he, too, would be a "naval captain," but how were they supposed to make anything of such a pale, sickly, frail creature as he? By the time he is twenty-six, both his parents are dead, however, and his occasional letters to his sister contain some quite humble admissions—he doesn't take himself for a corsair.

"As soon as I can, I shall look into the means of conveying my body, or rather my dim lantern, to Pellerin. You have never seen me so thin, my bones will shortly be sticking through my whole wardrobe; I need two months to fill out again. Do please tell my aunt that I trust to her fervor to clothe my shanks."[4]

By chance, he came upon his true vocation through the Oratorians of Nantes, where his parents sent him when he was nine in hopes that he might still turn into a strong lad some day and head out to sea. If ever he took after his father, he'd need a firm grounding in physics and mathematics, because officers in the great sailing ships needed to be full-fledged engineers of wind and tide. And even before the Jesuits were expelled, the Oratorians were the best teachers of those subjects, which Fouché liked much better than grammar and pretty writing anyway. They realize that the young man is cut out to teach, not to sail. And they need him; they have what amounts to a monopoly over the education of the rising generations and in the last twenty years, since the expulsion of their chief competitors left the field wide open to them, they've been suffering from an acute shortage of teachers. Father Durif, the headmaster in Nantes, shunts Fouché toward the vast Oratorian network before he is twelve years old; its activities are so vigorous and multiple, especially in the provinces, that nobody is really sticking to the rule that future teachers must be priests as well. It's enough for them to take "the minor orders," that is, to be tonsured subdeacons. They have to wear a cassock and comply with the easygoing rules of the communities in which they lodge, but they remain free to throw their cassock over the windmill and marry the day they take a fancy to it. Nobody would ever call them "Father"? Big deal. These class-B Oratorians are simply "brothers," earning little but also having no expenses, as long as they respect the terms of the contract. It's something like a vast educational gendarmerie, which Brother Joseph Fouché enters as a duck takes to water.

Having completed his "humanities," he is sent from the school in Nantes to the Oratory's illustrious seminary on the rue Saint-Honoré in Paris, in December 1781. People from all over France talk about the "Saint-Honoré house." The order's founder, the glorious Cardinal de Bérulle, had worked side by side with his disciples to build the church in which Fouché attended mass, on the site of the former town house of the Bouchage family. At twenty-two, his arrival there means an irreversible choice of profession and a very big step up.

The Congregation of the Oratory of Jesus has been in existence less than two hundred years. In addition to the "Saint-Honoré house" it has three institutions, two centers for advanced study, six seminaries, thirty secondary schools and thirty retreat centers.[5] It also perpetuates the worship of Bérulle and Condren, its two founders, and nobody doubts that they will be canonized any minute now, unless the Jesuits and their hidden supporters should suddenly revive (inconceivable at this point).

Like all the great religious movements of Europe in this age, the Oratory is a landscape of spiritual history facing in two directions: its spiritual originality lies in a fresh approach to Christian devotion, in which a certain sensualism confers a novel aspect of inner pleasure—some will even say sensual delight—to the orison. Prayer is no longer a mere duty, it's a kind of hygiene of the spirit. Fouché is marked by it. "When I was with my superior, I felt generous ideas moving within me; I experienced religious sensations.... Years that were fertile in strong and sweet emotions."[6]

The other, political direction had been the attempt to create, in the France that was mourning Henri IV and about to become Richelieu's— around 1620, that is—a great religious order that would also be a great teaching order, pure Gallic, a successful rival of the Ultramontanes, who were rigorously controlled by the popes.

The result was a strong form of devotion, broad and inclined to tolerance, arising straight out of the Edict of Nantes—more than enough to motivate the moral education of a child of the Loire, even if his commitment to theology is gradually replaced by a fondness for the exact sciences.

And then, feeling relatively isolated by his parents' death and his lack of wealth, ambition begins to throb in the soul of Joseph Fouché. To it we can add the happiness he feels when teaching pupils who are almost his own age yet who respond to the magnetism in the gaze of his blinking "eyes of soap," despite his thin voice and rounded shoulders.

Like many other ambitious people, Fouché has the gift of seducing his superiors. At the seminary in Paris he chooses Father Mérault de Bissy, head of the house, as his confessor, and through him obtains access to the ordinarily prohibited "profane" writings of . . . Euclid and Tacitus![7] Also through him, fighting the pure anti-Jesuit war, he learns to keep Pascal and Nicole* as his bedside books.

1782. As long as he remains tractable and available, he will have no more problems about his career.

Under the direction of the Oratorian authorities, he is "like the stick in the blind man's hand." They send him all over the place; that's how young "brothers" of humble origin are trained. First, he's given the twelve-year-olds in Niort.

October 1783. At Saumur, in the Loire Valley, he teaches fourteen-year-olds, for barely a year.

October 1784. Sixteen-year-olds and the Royal Military School of Vendôme. He's given an official title, "professor of logic." Is this to be a permanent resting place? No, now the young teacher is ordered to leave Vendôme for Juilly, where he will be a sort of supplementary teacher.[8]

Juilly, the "best" school, is in the far northeastern corner of Île-de-France, on the Brie plateau, eight leagues from Paris and three from Meaux. The name probably derives from *Julius* Caesar, who must have had a camp somewhere around there.[9] Lovely countryside. A large medieval village with a castle, and even a church, falling into ruins (on the estate of the Marquis de Nantouillet);[10] the only life left in it is in the sprawling buildings of the

---

*Pierre Nicole (1625–1695) was one of the best-known theorists of Port Royal Jansenism, who shifted his allegiance to Louis XIV shortly before the revocation of the Edict of Nantes. He was a great writer and is undeservedly neglected today.

school, still occasionally called "abbey." Back in the days of Henri IV, when some people were hoping to make a sort of French Vatican out of it, the Nantouillets gave it to the Oratorians. Bérulle and Condren are buried there, and around the tenth year of the reign of Louis XVI a teaching élite is being trained there. "Brother" Fouché rubs elbows with "Father" Lebon, "Brother" Daunou, and just misses "Brother" Billaud de Varenne, who left Juilly shortly before his arrival.*

The buildings are vast, and so are the meticulously-cared-for gardens; the Reverend Fathers Bérulle and Condren are everywhere,† in statues, inscribed quotes and, during services, in lengthy readings from their homilies.

Youngsters who, like Fouché, come by great good fortune from a relatively modest background into this new temple of Catholicism may well imagine themselves on the threshold of a great career. The enigmatic title "supplementary for studies" that has been given to Fouché means that, on request, he is to give Juilly pupils free lessons in mathematics and physics. His pupils will be assiduous and attentive and he will never need to punish them. So he may have thought he was primed to become a great teacher. In theory, that was true; but he is also relatively poor and unconnected, and in these days, when teachers are so badly needed for the new sciences, his learning and ability condemn him to an itinerary as incoherent and unpredictable as that of an infantry recruit.

Before six months have passed, "Brother" Fouché is sent on to the school in Arras.

---

*Lebon, the only ordained priest among them, is one of those who orchestrate the Terror in Arras (in his case, as a member of the National Convention seconded to the town). For Daunou and Billaud, see Volume IV.

†Despite the hopes of the Church of France, the Vatican finally refuses their canonization. They were both too opposed to the Ultramontanes. Abbé Bremond has written some beautiful pages on the two of them in his *Histoire littéraire du sentiment religieux en France*.

28

OCTOBER 10, 1787

The Dutch Were a Free People

Jan Potocki's destiny might have been like Miranda's. He was born with the same silver spoon in his mouth, except that it was in the "Polish" Ukraine instead of Caracas. And Miranda had to earn his heritage by fighting for his king, whereas Potocki had nothing more strenuous to do than try to relieve his tedium by traveling wherever the breeze blew him. They are of the same generation.

Count Jan Potocki was born in Podolia in 1761, the heir to vast tracts of land producing an income that he could spend as he pleased, without having, like Miranda, to fear arousing the suspicions of the Grand Inquisition. It was a stroke of luck, for a millionaire, to be born into the sphere of influence of Catherine the Liberal, or rather that of Stanislaw August Poniatowski, her vassal and King of Poland. Provided, of course, that one took care not to cross them.

Thus, the gilded youth travels, accumulating knowledge, on the subject of ancient history in particular, and cultivating a growing interest in Islamic civilization and especially that of the Maghreb [northwest Africa]. For years he longs to create a Byzantine piece of writing called *Le manuscrit trouvé à Saragosse.*[1] He's a more creative type than Francisco de Miranda, but never displays the other man's determination. Politics bores him.

Nevertheless, on his leisurely way back from Morocco to England after a long ramble around Italy, Jan Potocki, on a side trip to Holland for a few days in 1787, stumbles into a powerful popular and military shake-up. In the Europe of the latest fashionable salons, where the East has eyes and ears only for Catherine II's grand tour and where France, still buzzing from Calonne's dismissal and the failure of the Notables, has no attention to spare save, fleetingly, for the founding of the United States of America, people like Jan Potocki can only rub their eyes and gape when they discover a microrevolution taking place before them, some hundred-odd leagues north of Paris. It looks for all the world like an instant caricature, a burlesque telescoping, of what has just happened across the ocean and what some people think is about to happen in the Old World.*

"A traveler is never so much a foreigner as in a country in time of revolution. He sees a great surge of movement but is ignorant of its goal and causes," Potocki complains, on September 20 in Amsterdam, even though he has made a point of finding out for himself at first hand. "I thought a civil war would be a spectacle worth stopping for and made my way to Holland. Faithful to my plan of having no plan, I want to tour the theaters of events and be as close to the stage as anyone in the audience can be."[2]

"The people he is told to ask know nothing, in many cases, and those who do know are too busy to explain things to him. What knowledge he may pick up as to the organization of a country serves only to mislead him further, because he seeks authority where it no longer is and finds people who give orders but do not govern. He seeks the law and the reason, and all he finds are inconsistency and animosity. He sees people running and does not know why they are running; he sees people assembling in crowds and does not know why they are assembling."

Whence these shots being fired from rooftops and out of casement windows? Why this explosion of orange on all these chests and housefronts? Only a few leagues from the hubbub, the tourist can revel in the infinite calm of a flat country in which the principal means of transport is the canal, and this makes the fuss all the more disconcerting. "Every tack brought us to the foot of some pretty farm or up against the pavilion of some well-tended garden. Everywhere, tea was being drunk, in total silence." A few days before he was in the neighborhood of Dordrecht, "such a tangle of streets and canals, houses, trees and ships that it would be very hard to give any idea of it at all to someone who had not seen any other Dutch towns."

Potocki also stops in Rotterdam, which he considers a larger and more active port than Marseilles, before reaching the vast metropolis of Amsterdam, the city of myriad canals, one of the ports around which the Europe of his time grew up and took form, and there he finds himself in the midst of a small apocalypse. Civil war. Ordinary war, too. In a few strides, Potocki passes from utter peace to armed conflict, as often happened in those days. Before that, he had time to appreciate the charms of the Low Countries, one might better say Holland, since that province is so much more important

---

*The historian of the prerevolutionary years is astonished at the detour most researchers seem to make to avoid confronting the events in Holland. There's a sort of blackout here, between Washington and La Fayette, between Yorktown and the storming of the Bastille. Perhaps somebody could take time to replace a fuse?

than the others. The sea never far away, the wind ever close at hand, the wind that turns thousands of windmills and provides the basic energy of the "United Provinces," which is the proper name for the collection of regions of "Lower Germany" abandoned by the Spaniards under the Treaty of Utrecht,* in the aftermath of the fierce onslaught of Louis XIV's troops.

So, what's going on in this region of hard work and placidity? The only country in the world that proclaims itself "governed by *gueux* [= ragpickers]." Don't be misled: the name was adopted by the Lowlands aristocrats, who decided to remain loyal to the King of Spain in preference to that of France or of England, provided they were allowed to retain their basic freedoms. *Gueux* actually refers to a symbolic pouch worn over the shoulder.

The United Provinces might have become a Switzerland of northwest Europe, except that they, unlike the Swiss Confederation, which is somewhat isolated from conflict by its mountains, lie at the literal and figurative junction of several large rivers. Whoever occupies the mouths of the Rhine, Escaut and Meuse will always be a hostage to strategy. And they also lie at the junction of the wars between France, the German empire and Great Britain. It is not easy for them to exist alone.

Whence the curious and uneasy equilibrium between the great burghers, awesome in business, boring and bored at home, the men with the big pipes and heavy wigs who want to be called "patriots"; and the stathouder,† a demisovereign whose job it is to command their armies and who has no other official power.

We can leave out the people, the fishermen and farmers; here as everywhere else, they are kept poor and ignorant. The 1787 conflict erupts between the great burghers, who control the economy (by keeping the people down in fact), and the stathouder, whose pretensions to the hereditary office, in the last generation or two, have further embittered the dispute arising out of his unstable position. Mirabeau has already had a rant on the subject: "Are we now to see the Netherlands armies commanded by a little girl of three?"[3]

In 1787, the stathouder is William V of Orange-Nassau. He has long since lost any connection with the blessed old town of the Lower Rhone, although his family and followers still wear its color like a talisman. Like many of the other princes reigning here and there, William comes from

---

*After various scores were settled between the larger countries on the issue of the Spanish succession, Holland and the other United Provinces (which had formerly been Spanish possessions) were granted a relative independence.

†Etymologically, lieutenant-general. Formerly, the stathouder was in charge of the Spanish troops in the Netherlands. After the Treaty of Utrecht, his functions became less clear; he's head of the armed forces but he keeps trying to horn in on the burghers' government.

Orange the way they come from Burgundy or Champagne, or Florence. All that remains of the connection is this elementary heritage, the color, unique in Europe. His clan is called the House of Orange.

His mother is Princess Anne of England, herself a descendant of the Hanoverian dynasty, which replaced the Stuarts on the throne of Great Britain. He married Princess Wilhelmina of Prussia, a niece of Frederick the Great and, since last year, sister of the newly crowned king in Berlin. He himself is insignificant; she has plenty of personality. In this Anglo-German couple, the symbol of an embryonic alliance between London and Berlin, she wears the pants. Contemporary painters and travelers describe her without undue enthusiasm, but she clearly intrigues them: "There is grandeur in her commanding and dignified features, but more of authority and obstinacy can be sensed in them than of sweetness of temper or goodness of heart." The painter Tischbein portrays her thus, gazing with some contempt upon a portrait of her husband, who has "an upturned nose, round, protruding eyes, fat cheeks, thick lips and a sullen air."[4]

This does not prevent him from also having a lofty idea of himself, which expresses itself in an obsessive insistence upon compliance with etiquette in his little Court. Wherever they hail from, the diplomats sent to him are unanimous in their lamentations: "Dissimulation and falseness are the foundations of his character." "He appears to have resolved to let slip no opportunity to destroy every shred of esteem and confidence." "The Stathouder will be undone by his stubbornness, his truly inconceivable decisions, his hauteur, his imbecility, insanity and irrationality."* "It is impossible to witness, without being stricken to prostration, the Prince's spinelessness and mental inertia; such a man can win at no game. If someone does not give him a sleeping potion, ruin is inevitable." "I am astonished at William's mulishness and imbecility. His wife herself never utters his name otherwise than with a semblance of respect, but she trusts him no more than he trusts her."[5]

The Stathouder does have excuses.† His father having died when he was three, he was brought up by Anne of England, hence exposed to British influence, and then abandoned to Louis, duke of Brunswick, who virtually ran the United Provinces, but in accordance with the ideas of the United Kingdom. Long after William V came of age, old Brunswick was still governing his ward's Court behind the scenes and had continued to do so until

---

*From reports sent home by Vérac, Berenger, and Rayneval, diplomats from France; the next two opinions are by the ambassador of England [retranslated from French] and the King of Prussia himself—the Stathouder's brother-in-law.

†It is the son of this lamentable pair who becomes the first king of the Netherlands (Holland and Belgium combined, until 1830) in 1815, after Waterloo; he is called William I.

recently, when he went gaga and retired to his estates. Wilhelmina of Prussia aims to become William's tutor as well as his wife.

The one objective they have in common is their desire to become full-fledged, officially crowned monarchs.

Facing them, and opposing them, are the heads of so many little grand-bourgeois dynasties, coopted rather than elected by their peers in the various states of which they hold the economic reins, often by heredity, and control the local forces, including the militia. Foremost among these men are a group called the Pensioners; they have no plans or ideas and are cut off from the outside world by indifference, and their sole desire is to reign in peace in the shadow of their windmills. Posterity will not record most of their names: Van Bleiswikj, Van Berckel, Gijselaar, Zeeberg, Temminck, Abbema, Van de Marsch, Capellen, Visscher . . . Feudal squires in a modern age, captains of commerce, fishing, industry. But they have the advantage of embodying an ostensibly republican form of provincial government, by comparison with the Stathouder and his monarchical ambitions.

From Holland to Zeeland, Amsterdam to Dordrecht, they are putting up a stubborn resistance to any change in their status.

The Stathouder, meanwhile, has an autonomous armed force, partly composed of mercenaries and amply subsidized by England. These are the two opposing camps in the summer of 1787. Between them stands an unpredictable, elusive arbitrator: the townspeople. They have no rights and are ignorant and crude but nurse a latent messianism in regard to the Stathouder as a potential savior capable of redressing the abuses they suffer daily at the hands of the Pensioners—because William and his wife are virtually invisible inside their palace in The Hague.

It cannot go on. The temperature has been going up, there's been a rumble of thunder in every province, a fitful agitation giving rise to conflicts and actual violence, still involving only a few people but each month a little more intense. Some overall solution is becoming imperative and the leaders on both sides are well aware of it.

Neither the Stathouder nor the "Pensioner/Patriots" have enough men to overcome their opponent. The fate of this hostage territory is going to depend yet again upon the three powers that treat it like a square on a chessboard—England, Prussia, France.

England and Prussia are Protestant states, which is a point in their favor for a large portion of the inhabitants, since most of the Dutch mistrust Roman Catholics, and therefore France.

Also, after her American debacle, England has a return match to play around here somewhere; she is represented in The Hague by James Harris, an inspired and voluntary emissary. Prussia, Protestant or not, is hesitating, despite its King's kinship with Wilhelmina. Owing to the marquetry of the European tabletop, the only military base it has between the lands attached to the Catholic Joseph II and the republic to be brought to heel is a microscopic strip of terrain; just in case, however, Frederick William II masses as many troops as he can on the border.

France could, and many are saying should, do the same thing on the southern frontier, where a base camp has been planned at Givet in the Ardennes. Encouraged by a dynamic ambassador named Vérac, many of the Dutch Patriots, Calvinist though they be, are putting all their hopes in the French. A strong French threat in that area would undoubtedly be enough to dissuade the Prussians from making a move.

But in 1785–1787 France is suffering from aphasia, and has also been unable to digest the cost of her victory in America. Vergennes is about to die, he's dying, he's dead; besides, even if he were alive, could he have brought his King's mind sufficiently to bear on happenings in Holland? More recently, the financial and political crisis of 1787 has filled all the available space, and Loménie de Brienne is not a man to push for intervention in Holland. Vergennes's successor, Montmorin, is spineless and uninformed. He remains passive.

That leaves the Patriots and Stathouder face-to-face. In September 1786, the former managed to impose their militia in the region around The Hague, even though the Prince of Orange was legally in command there. He withdrew from the capital despite the objections of his wife, who was in favor of immediate resistance but who followed him, with set jaw, into the eastern provinces of Friesland and Guelders, firmly resolved to prepare a stinging comeback.

At first, it is only skirmishing between minor teams—Friesland, Guelders and Zeeland against Groningen, Overyssel and Holland. North Brabant is not taking sides. "As a result, this patchwork image* does not readily lend itself to a clear-cut historical account. . . . In each province, also, the individual towns retained their specific personalities. At the provincial level, hence, there was nothing but a partial synthesis of innumerable municipal conflicts, each proceeding according to its own laws and particular circumstances.† . . . There was no center of action where all forces came together and capital decisions could be taken."[6]

---

*According to Pieter Geyl, the historian of *La Révolution batave*. It may help to explain that the militia were small bodies of prosperous burghers capable of paying for their own uniforms and weapons. They had no regular training and their notions of the military art were often very sketchy.

†Herein lies the essential difference between the Dutch and the American and French revolutions.

While awaiting the inevitable intervention from without, the United Provinces reach boiling point. In Utrecht, the "National Union of Patriot Regents" seizes power, but that makes the Orangemen and some of the nobles feel cornered, so they conclude an alliance. The example of Utrecht spreads slowly until June 1787, when the entire United Provinces are in a state of endemic civil war. Something has to happen. So, on June 29 the Princess of Orange tries to make it happen, in despite of her husband's desires, by attempting to return to The Hague from Nijmegen in imposing array, and without him. Her declared objective: to propose mediation to the Estates General; her actual objective: to mobilize the Orangemen, from the capital, against the Patriots. However, she is misinformed as to their resources. They are more or less dug in in the west and can count on a solid base in Amsterdam, the holy city of their hopes.

Wilhelmina is intercepted by some *corps-francs** when she has gone about halfway and is stopped near Gouda, with all due honors. Wrapping herself in her dignity, she retraces her steps, while the news of this offense causes a scattering of riots throughout the country. Almost three hundred houses are looted in The Hague (by Orangemen); few dead, but much vexation. It might seem as though the Princess of Orange were playing at loser wins, and the English foreign minister makes no mistake: "The incident can be good. If the King of Prussia is not the most foul and abysmal of kings, he will feel the affront, whatever the cost. I expressed the idea to his ambassador that a body of troops would no doubt receive orders to set forward, on hearing news of the arrest. That is what the monarch will do, if he has not been sold to France."[7]

For a while, nothing happens. Frederick William II of Prussia is no firebreather, he's delighted that his sister has been defeated and is—needlessly—afraid of a riposte by the French army. In the end, it is pressure from his entourage, his ministers, and England that compels him to step in, sending his troops across the frontier on September 13 after a vain attempt to obtain excuses and concessions from the Dutch. The Hohenzollerns' military monarchy now displays the capacity for swift mobilization and action that has given it its reputation of invincibility. The supreme commander of the invading forces is the reigning Duke of Brunswick, nephew of the Stathouder's ex-guardian and mascot of Enlightened Europe, whom Mirabeau, for one, was praising to the skies a few months before.† Mirabeau accordingly changes his tune: "I am grateful for the very distinguished consideration shown me by the Duke. I acknowledge his talents, I respect his administration of his state, of which he is truly the very enlightened father. But to refrain, like a

---

*That is, especially well-off burghers, the elite of the militias.

†See Volume IV for the previous contacts between Mirabeau and the Duke of Brunswick.

craven, from speaking the truth for his sake, is a horse of a very different color! I cared so much for this prince, it is true, that it was impossible for me to foresee his conduct in Holland."[8] As often, Mirabeau is going a little too far; Brunswick is no Duke of Alba.

Never mind, the Prussian machine swings into action, as though on maneuvers. "The Duke, one of the last to remain in Wesel, crossed the Rhine in the evening on a boat-bridge, and advanced toward Cleves. He had a large number of officers from England, Russia, Mecklenburg, serving as volunteers on his staff. The reigning princes of Saxe-Weimar and Anhalt had been given permission to accompany him. On the thirteenth, the province of Guelders was invaded; the occupying army proclaimed itself a friend and said it was coming to restore order, save the Netherlands from anarchy, and restore the Stathouder's rightful privileges. The Princess of Orange, followed by her ladies-in-waiting and escort, came out from Nijmegen to welcome her liberators and greet the valiant knight who was so gallantly defending her cause. The Prussian officers thoughtfully wore orange ribbons in their hats and were welcomed by the crowd to shouts of *Vive Orange!* William of Nassau's old refrain was heard on every side; the weather was glorious, the victory certain."[9]

With these twenty thousand veterans in front of them, the provinces, taken unawares, could only try to save their honor. Those on the east let themselves be punctured like an eiderdown, the Patriots pinning their last hopes on the resistance of the stronghold of Utrecht and, above all, Amsterdam, once the Prussians had advanced to that ultimate goal. But they had no qualified man of war capable of taking overall command, to oppose Brunswick; especially as the Stathouder's mercenaries were allied with the Prussians.

Some people, in Holland, in France, were apparently thinking of La Fayette for the job. Following the dispersal of the Notables, he's back in Auvergne again, yawning. Actually it would be more accurate to say he thought of himself. A few days later he admits as much to Washington: "In the mean while there was something going on in Holland, much to my wishes and advantage. . . . The Dutch had long ago thought of introducing me into their affairs, and it was lately much agitated to put me at the head of twenty thousand embodied volunteers, in case they did agree to meet, a measure which the interest of the cause, and the opinion of the most sensible among them called for very earnestly. I could also, and would no doubt as soon as affairs grew serious, have been placed at the head of the whole military forces in the Republican provinces."[10]

Yes, but there isn't the shadow of a central organization among the local Patriot militias, no authority has really appealed to La Fayette, and it'll be so much the better for his reputation. When anybody in Louis XVI's Council mentions Holland, he puts in his earplugs. Not to be dishonored, however, France has sent the Amsterdam Patriots a few cannons and advisers by sea. The only military leader, unofficially supported by France but about to make a very poor showing against Brunswick, is one of the many nobles of fortune of the Nassau-Siegen or Miranda stripe who are nosing about Europe in search of something to command: the Rhinegrave of Salm.

A scion of one of those microscopic Rhenish principalities, one throw of his dice landed this abundantly endowed young man in the French Court for a time. He made a sort of name for himself in Versailles and Paris by fighting a few duels and throwing a few extravagant parties. The favor of the French sovereigns enables him to become, at forty, colonel and owner of the regiment of Saxe-Gotha, but nobody knows exactly to whom it feels any allegiance—the regiment is recruited and paid by its colonel, and hires itself out to the highest bidder. So, at its leader's whim it could serve France or Holland or, why not, Prussia or the Emperor. Undoubtedly degenerate, possibly neurotic, Salm is "a talkative and braggart warrior with mysterious ways and outlandish costumes. Wearing a broadbrim hat, thigh boots, a self-assured air, elegant and persuasive in speech, he believed, and got other people to believe, in all the fantastical imaginings of his mind."[11] He obtains permission from the French to enlist his skeletal regiment in the service of the Dutch Patriots, but without the slightest sense of loyalty. "I'm not so fond of lemons that I can't manage just as well with oranges."

The Rhinegrave will never be given either a plenary mission from France or a unified command approved by the Patriots; which is just as well, since he is incompetent. He flaps vainly about between Amsterdam and Utrecht, one of the most powerful fortresses of the Netherlands, where the Patriots are in the majority. Its bastions and artillery, its supplies of ammunition and food, could put up a good show of resistance to the invader, even without the help of artificial floods produced by opening the dikes.

But there would have to be a man of iron to give substance to it all, and this the Rhinegrave of Salm is not.

His main second-in-command, the Comte de Portes, a Swiss gentleman serving France first, then Holland, bears witness to the collapse of all hope of defending Utrecht at two in the morning of September 15: "I went to the Rhinegrave. He was in bed. . . . My companions and I were thunderstruck when we heard that Utrecht was to be evacuated at once, that the frontier of Holland could no longer be defended, and that the only resource left for the common cause was to retreat to Amsterdam, where support would be available until the arrival of the French, who would surely come forthwith."[12]

The poor Comte de Portes seems doomed to embody the downfall of the Dutch, who are compelled to submit, within a few days, by the Rhinegrave's unmotivated retreat, the abstention of the French and the determination of the Prussians.

He, too, might be called a soldier of fortune, but that was a natural condition for many Swiss gentlemen who had no (more or less) distinguished origins to boast of. He was born in 1750 into a family of Languedoc Protestants who had taken refuge in Switzerland after the revocation of the Edict of Nantes. His parents and himself, disconsolate because they could no longer call themselves French, enlisted their swords in the service of the kingdom of Piedmont, and from there he proceeded to "buy a company" in the regiment of Saxe-Gotha. Under the orders of his disheartening colonel, he feels hardly better treated in the choice of men he is given to command—the scum of northern Europe. "It is hard to conceive how disorderly this march is, how undisciplined and insolent the soldiers. . . . My troop was a doleful heap of ill-equipped recruits."

However, the Comte de Portes has a sense of humor and a zest for life, which enable him to come through it all with a smile. A picturesque tableau: "While I soar in the higher spheres of politics, my brother [who had gone to serve the German empire with a battalion of French origin and is paying him a visit] was busy making an omelet. Two of his men beat the eggs and stirred up the fire; my mouth began to water. They were cheerful and merry, and cooked delightfully. I heard the sizzle of frying butter, one giving orders to blow on the fire, the other calling for the cheese. 'I've burned myself!' exclaimed the second; 'Let me do it,' said the first. Then my brother capped it all with 'You haven't put enough butter in the pan!' "

The Comte de Portes, swept along in the debacle, leaves notes that enable us to understand why the Dutch collapse is so rapid. He has only 250 men and seven cannons left with which to defend one of the outposts of the republican Mecca, the allegedly impregnable town of Amsterdam. Its defenders display a touch of heroism now and then, de Portes along with the rest, enough to keep a clear conscience despite the deflation on every side. They're inventive enough: "The Prussian light infantry posted themselves in the peat retrenchment behind the haystacks, and soon contrived to bring up their howitzers and place them near the peat. We were fortunately able to dislodge them by setting fire to the hay and peat with red-hot balls, which we heated on the frying pan at the blacksmith's. . . . My men bore themselves bravely, the dead and injured were transported in good order."

Despite such burlesque incidents, the fight for Amsterdam between Prussians and Patriots is dogged and violent for the better part of two days, even though one can't really call it a "battle of Amsterdam." The assailants outnumber the defenders twenty to one and are strictly organized. The outcome is not a total carnage. One hundred-odd dead among the defenders, two or three times that number among the invaders. The Duke of Brunswick, anxious to keep his good reputation, gives the municipality of Amsterdam several days before signing the capitulation. He and his troops do not move in and take over; all that's required is that the Stathouder and his wife be able to go back to The Hague in triumph, and that the leaders of the resistance remove themselves from the country en masse.

This is one war that ends in teacups, for the Comte de Portes anyway, who is received and elaborately complimented by Brunswick.

At the top, among people of good company, that is, it is all settled amicably: but as we descend the social ladder, the revenge of the lesser Orangemen grows more onerous and ramified. Almost forty thousand Patriot burghers leave for Belgium and France, mainly around Saint-Omer and Dunkirk, and those are the ones who can afford to go, even if the Court of France hides its brief shame by giving them what help it can. These emigrants from an impossible republic then hang around, waiting for the change Mirabeau has promised:

> The political system of Europe will change; but you are beneath our glacis, whereas those who have just so unwisely proclaimed themselves your oppressors will have to fight their way from the Weser to the Danube. In those awesome battles, surely the day of the Dutch Patriots can return. Why should they imagine themselves permanently destroyed? Their party bears with the eternal nature of things. You were always poorly organized but you were never slaves, and you shall not be. Even the coalition of the aristocrats and the Stathouder will not be so fatal to you as might be thought. In every country it is hatred of the aristocracy that causes the people to side with one man only. The House of Orange will soon be encompassed within that hatred if it allies itself with the aristocracy. . . . The Dutch peasant is piling up vengeance in his heart.[13]

On October 10 Potocki, who is on the spot, is less optimistic. He observes,

> This morning loud shouts brought me to the window. I saw the populace stirring in our street and the shopkeepers taking down their wares, but what was at first taken for sedition proved to be joy, and everybody was reassured. It had just been proclaimed that the color orange could be worn or not, as people desired, and that any person insulting any other person on that account would incur the death penalty. The people responded to the proclamation with wild rejoicing. The fishwives left their shops to form quadrilles in the streets.
>
> The Jews, doubly happy to see the triumph of the side they were secretly supporting, and to sell their bits of ribbon for a high price, were shouting deafeningly, and the street-porters, ship's carpenters, sailors and others of that ilk gave back as best they could, while the armed Patriots stared mournfully at the orange banner floating over the entrance to the town hall.

We dined in a house across from that of Burgomaster Booft. It was guarded by a company of burghers who had already been forced to fire on the populace three times. It happened before we assembled, but while we were at table, someone came to tell one of the guests that a man from his company had been killed by men from the company of another guest. The killers arrived a moment later, to justify themselves and prove that the man killed was completely in the wrong. There were several other deaths in different districts, and it is thought by all that the night will be stormy.

Sadly, he returns to his Poland, where things are not much better: "This diary, which I thought would be concerned with the construction of liberty, has turned out to be nothing but an account of its dying moments, and it has now disappeared from the face of the earth. The Dutch were a free people, and there are none left today."[14]

BABEUF

29

NOVEMBER 22, 1787

O, My Bowels!

As we have seen, the hot correspondence between Babeuf and Dubois de Fosseux has been cooling since July. They have dutifully gone on exchanging news items about methods of treatment or fertilizers for the Picardian countryside, or magnetism or the latest advances in inoculation, but there has been no follow-up and, since Babeuf's pronouncements on the social question, no real sincerity either. It looks as though Babeuf is trying to provoke the secretary of the Arras Academy, which only makes him more stiff-necked. On August 20, for example, about a work on agriculture in Roman times:

> The only thing I can wholeheartedly subscribe to in his ideas is the ridiculous light in which he shows the agricultural practices of the foremost citizens of Rome. To me, his stalwart, well-trained carters are in most cases no better than machines that, if they are not to break down, must perpetually be guided by skilled artists. And how can there be any such artists if the citizens of the higher classes, putting all their trust in their machines, do not stoop to turn a hand to

the job? Theory can only be improved by practice. Furthermore, it would assuredly be desirable that all those among us who might be equated with the Roman consuls, all those heroes ending in -us,* should have occasion, now and then, to put their often oppressive and almost always useless hands (what a blessing it would be if they were never worse than that) to the plow; it would teach them to have more respect for the rights of the wretched workingman.[1]

Dubois de Fosseux is finding this type of remark less and less to his taste, and a little gust of sour disapproval wafts from each of his latest letters. There are only eight more of them, over a period of seven months. He is the first notable to be scared by Babeuf. We can see it at the end of November, when François-Noël, lashed by misfortune, cries out to him from Roye, as spontaneously as he would have done a year before, when their friendship was at its apogee. He's twenty-six and has just lost the elder of his two children, Sophie, aged four and a half:

> Perhaps, sir, you will care to listen with some interest to the mournful tale of the most painful blow which I have just suffered. From my knowledge of your rare humanitarian feelings, and the expressions of special affection you have been good enough to lavish so continually upon me, I feel sure I can count on your readiness to do so.[2]

In the past, Babeuf's letters have been kept carefully within the confines of conventional "academy" style, if only so that he could look as though he were on a level with his correspondent. He has almost never spoken of his family life, even of the work he did on other people's estates. But his mourning, his loss, like a dike overrun, throws Babeuf's other side into sharp relief— an almost neurotic sensitivity, etched deeper by long study of Rousseau. No more theories or scientific palaver now; here the wounded soul is stripped naked before the great man, who becomes once more, for the duration of a letter, the surrogate father of whom he expected so much. He's deluding himself: Dubois de Fosseux is shocked by what seems to him like exhibitionism. Be that as it may, this soul-searching epistle completes our picture of Babeuf:

> Feeling, almost from the moment when my intellectual and physical strength first began to develop, an attraction to the sweet path of paternity, I spent a good share of my youth learning about the duties attaching to that condition. My studies in this field led me to a decided taste, an absolute determination, for whatever could bring me to that cherished position. I therefore entered very

---

*Babeuf takes the name "Gracchus" in 1793.

young, that is, five years ago (when I was only twenty-one), into the state of marriage. My union was crowned by the appearance of two children, a girl and a boy. Heaven seemed pleased to satisfy my ardent desires. At birth, my daughter aroused admiration in every eye. Her face, her whole conformation, compelled everyone who saw her to acknowledge this, and say, "There is a true masterpiece of nature!". . .

You will not question, sir, my affectionate and unblemished delight, nor my diligence in taking every pain with the cultivation of so rare a production [*sic*]. All my thoughts, all my time, all my attention were transferred to the dear object that enchanted my soul. Nothing could distract me from it. . . .

Whatever else might have been, my efforts were most happily requited and, at the end of four years, my pupil seemed made to charm in every respect.* On the physical side, Nature had yet further substantially embellished her work, heavenly features, grace, strength, agility, weight, everything combined. The mental and emotional sides corresponded. An extraordinarily excellent heart, even temper, right mind, straightforward ideas limited to the knowledge that was precisely and simply necessary for her age. In a word, my Sophie (that was her name), although not an exact replica of the Sophie of Jean-Jacques which he was bringing up for his Émile, nevertheless shared many of her happy qualities and on the whole I can make bold to say that she was very much her equal. . . . But alas! Sir, a burning fever assailed the idol of my heart, the next day I called to her side the ignorant and murderous physician who, heedlessly and through the crudest quid pro quo, called her affliction a superabundance of blood and humors (the child was fatter than she should have been), decided that the first thing to do was clear out the stomach, which he claimed was overfull of undigested food, administered an emetic to that end, as being the thing there would be least difficulty in getting her to swallow; the thing was done, my unhappy child fell instantly into strange convulsions and, four hours later, O woe! was taken from me.[3]

Medicine, especially for the poor and especially in the country, was still almost in the state of approximation so vigorously damned by Molière. What actually happened to Sophie Babeuf? It seems that she had fallen "into the fire while playing and burned both hips in July 1787."[4] Had she been more or less ailing since then, and susceptible to infection? For want of accurate texts it is impossible to have a clear idea of the statistics of infant mortality in the eighteenth century. All that is known is that at least one child in two died before puberty and that the local doctors, who were often profoundly untutored if not actually fakes, were content to alternate purges with blood-

---

*Throughout this whole long letter, as a result of the hypertrophy of paternal lyricism that was then in vogue among Rousseau's disciples, Babeuf fails to make a single mention of his wife, although he is a good husband and although she has just been as bereaved as himself.

lettings, to which they now added, with no rhyme or reason, appalling quantities of emetics, that is, substances that induced uncontrollable vomiting. Their diagnoses changed with their scientific pretensions.

"Catarrhal fevers, putrid and malignant peripneumonias, intermittent and remittent putrid and malignant fevers with exanthema,* spotted fevers, smallpox and measles, putrid and malignant diarrheas and dysenteries are, roughly speaking, the epidemic diseases prevalent in the countryside."[5]

In this instance, the choice is wide. Babeuf's daughter was copiously fed and well cared for, so, whatever she died of, it was not a physiological deficiency. What killed her and so many more was undoubtedly a twofold ignorance, that of her environment in regard to hygiene combined with that of the "murderous physician."

> Oh, sir! You would have to be me to feel the violence of a pain such as that which this event has caused me to experience! O, my bowels! Forever, oh, yes, forever, you will feel the effect of the cruel wrench you have endured in this dying moment! There is no need, sir, for me to dilate further upon my thoughts, for you to conceive all those that have risen up in me during these moments of horror.[6]

On December 11 Dubois de Fosseux sends François-Noël the consolation for which he was yearning in the form of two sentences of chilly condolence. A pallid funereal courtesy. Was it timidity, or embarrassment in the face of such lack of restraint in this long lamentation? Or is he simply put out by a disturbance in his routine?

> Sir, I am in every possible way concerned by your recent loss and I conceive of the extent of your sorrow, both through the feelings of my own heart and through the virtues of the child for whom you are grieving. However, you must accept this misfortune and try to resume the normal course of your occupations; this will be the quickest means of healing the wound in your heart, although it will bleed a long time yet.[7]

Then he shifts into four or five pages of news concerning the opening of the Estates of Picardy, one of the new provincial assemblies that Brienne is trying to set up. Farewell, Dubois de Fosseux!†

---

*Skin rash.

†One local historian of the nineteenth century, whose hatred of Babeuf seems to have precipitated him into a kind of delirium, calmly affirmed that, "having lost his six-year-old [sic] daughter, of whom he was very fond, he opened up her cadaver, removed her heart, ate half of it, in order, he said, that that part of his child might return to its origins, hung the other half about his neck, and wore it so for a long time thereafter."[8]

30

NOVEMBER 1787

The Great Affair

In the early days of November 1787 Chrétien-Guillaume de Lamoignon de Malesherbes, having made sure that no indiscreet ears are listening, including those of the servants, momentarily abandons his visceral, innate reserve and makes a rare present to a privileged audience of one, Jean-Paul Rabaut Saint-Étienne, who is waiting for it: he reads aloud to him a few sheets of paper covered with his illegible scribble.

The draft of the Edict of Toleration for Protestants is ready at last, and Malesherbes intends to submit it to the King to sign in the Council meeting on November 19:*

"We have noted that the Protestants, deprived of legal existence, have been placed in the inevitable position of having either to profane the sacraments by undergoing a simulated conversion or to jeopardize the condition of their children by contracting marriages that are declared null and void *a priori* by the laws of the realm."[1] The narrow limits of this "toleration" are carefully established; for the moment, we're talking about nothing more than civil status. We'll see about the rest later. Malesherbes always proceeds a step at a time; but this step is a biggish one and might lead to others.

Pastor Rabaut, called "Saint-Étienne," is not a very outgoing man either. His Cévennes origins, his Swiss education and long practice of semi-clandestinity among the Protestants of France have forged a man of self-restraint. That day, however, he does not hide the profound joy that he will shortly communicate to his friends and relatives, anxiously awaiting the news back there in the south and southwest. This embryo of the revocation of the Edict of Nantes is the reward of their hopes and struggles, carried on from

---

*On Malesherbes and the important role he played in Turgot's experiment, but also in his downfall in 1776, see Volume I. The man who has now replaced Miromesnil as Keeper of the Seals, Chrétien-François de Lamoignon, is his first cousin, fourteen years his junior.

father to son for a century; and for Jean-Paul Rabaut, it is the culmination of his first life.

Since La Fayette, the Don Quixote addicted to difficult causes, first introduced the youthful pastor to the aging great magistrate, the relationship between them has gradually grown closer and deeper. For the last two years Rabaut has held the risky and still unofficial position of representative of the Protestant churches in Paris, where, tolerated by the royal police, his expenses are paid "by the four consistories* of Montpellier, Marseilles, Bordeaux and Nîmes,"[2] that is, his fellow Protestants. But the mistrust of the still-all-powerful Roman Catholics is so great that for months he has had to plead the search for documentation for a book he is writing about ancient Greece as justification for his presence at Court.

Since June 1787, when Malesherbes, emerging from what was presumed to be a permanent retirement, made his second entrance to the King's Council, giving, in his capacity as a ghost of the Turgot experiment, a sort of stamp of approval to Brienne, Rabaut has felt a little less cramped. Even the Baron de Breteuil, the minister of the King's Household, responsible for both the Paris police and the surveillance of the Protestants throughout the kingdom (Protestants being looked upon as potential delinquents), even Breteuil, arch-conservative though he is, is helping Rabaut's mission, because the time is nigh when, as Malesherbes rightly says, "the great affair" will have to be brought to a conclusion: the status of the French RPRs [members of the *Religion Prétendue Réformée* = Protestants] has become unacceptable to everybody except a few fanatical clergymen.

After months of groping, the situation has finally been resolved, as so often in historical stalemates, by an agreement between two competent and qualified persons, in this instance the Pastor, who has had to soften some of the prophetic harshness of the Wilderness, and the government Sage, who is at once a skeptic and a largehearted man.

They usually met alone and always in Malesherbes's quarters, both before and since his return to the Council, sometimes at his large and lovely estate with its forests and pastureland, near Pithiviers on the edge of the Beauce, and sometimes in his apartment on the rue des Martyrs at the foot of Montmartre in Paris. Saint-Étienne conscientiously reports back to those who sent him: "I would see [Malesherbes] and dine at his home once or twice a week and on days when he came to Paris . . . I would send him memoranda and notes; he allowed me the freedom to combat him, and I had much recourse to that freedom because our principles differed. I had agreed upon mine with

---

*The consistory was the body responsible for the administration and management of local Protestant communities. It was made up of a small number of the more prosperous "elders" and all ministers/pastors were *ex officio* members of it.

M. le Marquis de La Fayette, and we each upheld the other. They could be reduced to these simple ideas: that there should not be two peoples within one people, if one does not want two parties; that dissident subjects should be accorded the same treatment as other subjects; that the separating wall should be knocked down, not replastered and kept up; and that a state religion is a creature of reason, because the state is not a religious entity."[3]

Physically, they bear small resemblance to each other; age and inactivity have added more layers to Malesherbes's thick body and round face beneath his outmoded wig. His eyes, however, are still lively enough; he is sixty-six. Rabaut is forty-four; his own already graying hair is carefully rolled on either side of a wide-awake face with a well-defined nose beneath heavy brown brows, an expression of benevolent curiosity, a large mouth, not very sensual but as though sculpted for preaching; and not an ounce of fat on him.

Listening to the Minister's preliminary draft, which he knows that the supreme Council is going to pore over, nitpicking and watering down, followed, no doubt, by the King himself, and in due course by the *parlements,* on which not one Protestant sits, he purses his lips at Malesherbes's euphemisms. In his view the man is being singularly unassertive; but in the end, the Minister persuades him to adopt, and to have adopted by his fellows, this prudent overture.

The elementary trick of the Edict of Toleration is to get the authorities to concede the same civil status to the Calvinists as to everybody else without compelling them to abjure their faith, and, at the same time, keep them in an inferior social condition. The author shows his adroitness by making it very clear that not only is the King remaining faithful to the wishes of Louis XIV, but he is actually carrying his predecessor's efforts on behalf of the "E.C.A. and R." (Apostolic Roman Catholic Church) one step further:*

"It may not be within our power to prevent the existence of different sects in our states, but we shall never tolerate their existence becoming a source of disharmony among our subjects. . . . The Catholic religion, which it is our happiness to profess, will alone enjoy the rights and honors of public worship in our kingdom, whereas our other non-Catholic subjects, deprived of all influence upon the established order in our states, proclaimed *a priori* and forever incapable of forming a body in our kingdom, subject to control by the ordinary police as regards the observation of holy days, will receive from the law only what natural law will not permit them to be refused by us, namely, the certification of their births, marriages and deaths; so that, like all our other subjects, they may benefit from the civil effects consequent upon those acts."[4]

---

*In the final stages of the drafting, Malesherbes worked with Target, one of the best Parisian advocates.

Poor Rabaut! It pains him to see "the survival of this frightening specter of the shadow of Louis XIV" but he makes the best of it, since "the specter is still worshipped in the vicinity of the throne and, whether the reason be religion or habit or mental laziness or national conceit or prejudice, it would have been impossible to overturn the colossus and establish a simple law based on the immutable principles of natural right."[5]

Before helping to institute tolerance in the kingdom, thus, Saint-Étienne had first to convince his own brethren, whose memories are still stinging from the gash made in the skin of France in October 1685 by the fell pen of Louis XIV when he revoked the Edict of Nantes:

"Louis, by the grace of God King of France and Navarre, to all present and to come, greetings . . ."

After a broad doff of the hat to Henri IV "for his edict given at Nantes in the month of April 1598" and another to Louis XIII, "our most honored lord and father of glorious memory," for the series of edicts that their heir pretends are simply so many attempts to return the strayed lambs to the fold of the Catholic Church, Louis XIV jubilantly announces: Protestants? What Protestants? Why, there are no more Protestants in France. . . .

We now see, with the just gratitude we owe to God, that our efforts have produced the end that we desired to attain, since the better and larger part of our subjects in the so-called reformed religion have embraced the Catholic; and since by this means the enforcement of the said Edict of Nantes and everything that has been ordained in favor of the said so-called reformed religion has been pointless, we have deemed that we could do no better, in order wholly to eradicate the memory of the disturbance, confusion and evils caused in our kingdom by the growth of that false religion . . . , than to revoke entirely the said Edict of Nantes and the particular articles enacted in consequence of it, and all that has been done subsequently on behalf of the said religion. . . .

Consequently, it is our will and pleasure that all the temples of the so-called reformed religion situated in our kingdom, lands, estates and the territories owing obeisance to us, shall be demolished immediately.

We forbid our said subjects of the so-called reformed religion to assemble for the practice of the said religion in any place or private dwelling, upon any pretext whatsoever. . . .

We enjoin all ministers of the so-called reformed religion who do not want to convert and embrace the Apostolic Roman Catholic religion to leave our kingdom and the lands of our allegiance fifteen days after the publication of this our present edict, without permission to remain beyond that time nor, during that time, to engage in any preaching, exhortation or other function, under pain of transport to the galleys. . . .

As regards the children who will be born to those of the said so-called reformed religion, we wish them henceforth to be baptized by the parish priests; we enjoin their mothers and fathers to send them to the churches for that purpose, under pain of a fine of five hundred livres and more if need be; and the said children shall thereafter be brought up in the Apostolic Roman Catholic religion; and this we expressly order the judges of the different places to ensure. . . .

We very expressly and repeatedly forbid all our subjects of the so-called reformed religion to withdraw, themselves and their wives and children, from our said kingdom, lands and territories under our allegiance, or to remove their goods and chattels, under pain, for the men, of transport to the galleys, and, for the women, of the confiscation of their persons and goods.

We wish and intend that all declarations lodged against relapsed persons should be enforced according to their form and purport.[6]*

This text, countersigned by Colbert, removed the Protestants of France to a place that was something like Pharaoh's Egypt, the mythical empire in the Bible they all knew by heart. They had become aliens in their own land, and their pride incited them to feel like honorary Hebrews, but that was the one and only consolation left them. In the last hundred years, they have virtually ceased to be French.

Like the Hebrews, they, too, underwent an exodus, but in slow motion, spreading over decades; also, it was selective, depending upon their possibilities and resources. Only those with money were able to obtain a special authorization to settle abroad, in countries of their own faith, where some of them put down roots.† Most of these were nobles, and some took their servants along. But the farmers, tradespeople, craftsmen, paralegals, were all condemned to vegetate where they were, exiled within the kingdom, suspended between abjuration and persecution. Those who stayed behind and remained faithful to their creed had an even greater need of moral support, meaning pastors, who necessarily officiated in secret and would certainly be martyred if caught.

That is what Rabaut Saint-Étienne's fate looked like when he was born; his entire youth was spent shuttling back and forth between the Promised Land of the Calvinists and the kingdom of Pharaoh.

---

*Which, in this case, implied the ordeal of the wheel.

†In the twentieth century many families with obviously French names can be found in Switzerland, Germany, England, the Netherlands, and even Sweden, where they have been since the revocation.

31

NOVEMBER 1787

My New Name Is Saint-Étienne

"On the twenty-first of November 1743 I baptized, in the name of the Father, the Son and the Holy Ghost, Jean-Paul Rabaut, my son,* whom I had of my wife Magdeleine Gaidan. Born the fourteenth of the above-mentioned month and presented by Jean Béchard and Gabrielle Rouvairol, wife of Pierre Paulhan, of the town of Nîmes."[1]

The record of baptism and birth, thus, was penned by his famous father Paul Rabaut, whom Protestants, but also *philosophes,* call "the great pastor of the Wilderness." It must have been a happy day for him: married at twenty, he had seen his first three children die in infancy. Jean-Paul and those who come after him, and who also survive, inherit their father's sinewy looks. His travels and the life of hiding have made him thin as a rail. "About five foot four inches tall,† uniform features in a long, thin face, complexion rather dark, black hair . . . nose long and pointed, slightly aquiline, eyes black, quite large, body bent slightly to the right, legs very thin, the right one turned inward."[2]

By sheer spiritual power, fervor, and "zeal for religion," Paul Rabaut soon became an outstanding figure among the little class of young pastors who were succeeding the exiled or executed older generation and who leaped into action the moment they finished their accelerated theological training. He was born in 1718 at Bédarieux in Lower Languedoc, of Protestant parents who had remained faithful but, being cloth merchants, had limited means of expression. Paul would speak for them. His offended adolescence turned him toward his church. When Jean-Paul was born, his father had recently

---

*This phrase reveals one of the particularities of the "reformed" religion: a married clergyman baptizes his own child.

†This is the description written at the order of the Intendant of Languedoc when Paul Rabaut becomes a full-fledged citizen.

completed a hurried course of training in Lausanne, where he was noticed by Antoine Court, the incoercible beacon and energy giver of Protestantism after the revocation. Like old Simeon prophesying on the head of Jesus, this weary old lion of resistance prophesied over young Paul.

Paul Rabaut risked a return to France, where his brothers in Nîmes and the surrounding region greeted him as a godsend. But oh, it was a hard place for them, and harder yet for their preachers, the France of the middle of Louis XV's reign, when the King's fits of devoutness served to absolve his debauchery. This king did not practice the icy cruelty of Louis XIV, and there was nothing Maintenon-like about Madame de Pompadour, but it was no less strictly forbidden than before to be a Protestant, and between dogbites and pats on the head, they didn't know which way to turn. In 1724 their situation was made even worse by the terrible edict of the Cardinal de Fleury, signed by the little King when he was fourteen. Legally they remained zombies, since the kingdom was still insisting that they had disappeared. Around Nîmes, where there were still thousands of them, one would have had to be pretty nearsighted to believe that. Who in Versailles could care, though? On the day he was baptizing his oldest son, "a price had been put on Paul Rabaut's head;* his wife had to go into hiding to escape the Constance Tower,† and if little Jean-Paul had not been hidden from the people who were looking for him in the first years of his life, he would have been taken from his parents and placed in one ecclesiastical institution or another as ordained by the laws of those barbaric times, in order to be taught the basic principles of the Catholic religion in the name of which his family was proscribed."[3]

"Upon reaching adulthood, Jean-Paul never forgets the years of his nomadic, unstable early childhood, when he did not know in the morning where he would be taken to sleep that night."

First images: a father at once admirable and remote, fleeing, like Moses; a nonexistent mother; friends glimpsed rather than seen. He seems to have no memories of the Languedoc of those days; he was barely six when his parents snatched him out of reach of immediate danger and tried to make sure of an education for him by sending him to Switzerland, in the care of a man named Paul Bosc,‡ an apprentice-pastor, or "proposant" as they were called, from Antic in Auvergne.

---

*According to the *Notice sur Rabaut-Saint-Étienne* written during the Directoire by Boissy d'Anglas, a moderate member of the Convention who was also a Protestant and also from Nîmes, and whom we shall meet again later.

†In Aigues-Mortes; the persecutors' favorite place of incarceration for middle-class Protestants who refused to abjure their faith.

‡Who abandons his religious career to become a doctor and physicist. He is one of Madame Roland's best friends (see Volumes II and IV) and plays an important part in the last moments of her life.

Stage two: Lausanne, and the hospitality of the venerable Court family
in the country-town/lake-town where four to five thousand Calvinists live up
and down the vineyard slopes, their tranquility deepened by the more or
less total absence of Roman Catholics. Morality, piety, tedium, a secret nostalgia for his native south of France where, even in the state of anxiety in
which he had lived, Jean-Paul had breathed more freely. But he did what he
was told; he ingurgitated the predominantly biblical religious education dispensed by Paul Bosc for two years, under the supreme authority of Antoine
Court. Jean-Paul never complains of the "gifted child's" education he was
given, thanks to which, in 1757, he was able to adopt a slightly superior
attitude toward his two younger brothers, Antoine and Pierre, when their
father, still living "underground," decided to send more of the family to
Lausanne rather than accept a comfortable job as pastor in Holland that
would have taken him away from his flock in Languedoc.

His eldest boy was already able to elucidate the Gospels of St. John
and St. Matthew in Greek, translate Cicero's speeches and read the *Aeneid*
fluently with a new teacher, no less a person than the great Antoine's own
son, the pastor (naturally) Court de Gébelin, who was put in charge of all
three boys.

Now, thirty years later when we are making his acquaintance, Jean-Paul
Rabaut solemnly attests to the qualities and formidable erudition of the man
who taught him when he was ten, writing about Court de Gébelin after his
death in the midst of his work on the *Histoire naturelle de la parole, ou précis
de l'origine du langage et de la grammaire universelle,* of which he had time to
compose a mere nine volumes: "His soul was always in a state of calm, and
at peace, as was his heart. . . . The simplicity of his life and ways was that of
his character, which he preserved as candid and good as he had received it
from nature. . . . His father was pleased to see that so strong a mind was
capable of conceiving and embracing everything; he wanted his son to be
ignorant of no aspect of human study."[4]*

"I speak here as an eyewitness, and I still remember in amazement how
one and the same man used to give lessons on seven or eight different subjects
every day, with the same ease and the same success." His childhood had not
been so easy, though, presumably on account of his father's personality: "It
will come as a surprise to some, that the man who wrote so well about speech
had not begun to speak himself at the age of seven, and that the scholar who

---

*Court de Gébelin was born in Nîmes in 1725; after Switzerland, he goes to Paris, where
he gives up his pastoral activities to specialize in ancient history, and is accordingly more easily
tolerated. He keeps up enough contacts and authority with his religious past, however, to precede
his former pupil (Rabaut) as unofficial representative of the southern French Protestants.

studied a very great number of languages so profoundly had a most treacherous memory."

This sweeping bow to a distinguished man at his death did not cover the unease that the Rabaut children felt in their dealings with what the eldest boy calls "the meditative taciturnity" of Court de Gébelin. They worshiped him, he bored them.

It lasted just two years, from February 1753 to April 1755. Neither the host family nor the three children lodged and taught by it ever confide much about a state of discomfort that was acute enough to bring about a further migration of the little Rabauts, this time to the Chiron family, who were also friends of their father, in Geneva. It would seem to have been a step down from the royal way of the Courts, to continue their education with these less illustrious folks. But maybe the Court de Gébelin family had other irons in the fire, or scolded them too often, and its severity drove them into bashfulness.

Their father had kept an eye on them and guessed that something was amiss. He took his friend Chiron into his confidence: "When my children left here, I can say they were admired for their vivaciousness, their little quips and comments, their talent and precocity, which seemed to indicate that they would go far in little time. I cannot conceive through what fatality they have remained so backward and become so timid. Almost a year and a half ago the eldest was ready to do his rhetoric. If I am not mistaken, he should now be able to do his philosophy course. The others were also making good progress, and especially the second. They have not had teachers, as appears in the accounts remitted to me of their expenses. Hence, it is not surprising that they have not been brought on. I say this just between the two of us. . . . While they were with us, good reasons did more to amend their ways than punishment."[5]

Lausanne to Geneva; the "three myrmidons" were still in Switzerland. Still the same lake, the same lessons, the same discipline, albeit somewhat tempered by the easygoing atmosphere at the Chirons'. There they were given their secret nicknames, which were necessary because Geneva was so close to a still possessively Catholic France.* Jean-Paul, before his twelfth birthday, wrote an impeccably courteous farewell to Court de Gébelin in which he informed him, with some pride, of the new identity that the Rabauts of the future owed to their new hosts: "M. Chiron thought it proper to change our names: my new name is Saint-Étienne, Antoine is Pommier,† Pierre is Dupuy, and we are [fictitious] cousins."[6]

---

*See in this connection Volume III, for the account of the crushing of Genevan independence by the French armies in July 1782.

†The Rabaut known as Pommier [apple tree], because he was so merry and easy to get

Four years of steady progress ensued; Paul Rabaut could now be proud of his son Jean-Paul, and brought him back to France at last when he was sixteen for a few months of reacquaintance with his family and homeland after a ten-year separation. It was then that he really got to know Nîmes, its forty thousand inhabitants, Roman ruins, the surrounding garrigue in which ever more numerous Protestant "assemblies" were being held almost at the town gates, tolerated by an intelligent intendant and bishop. There, Saint-Étienne saw the stature his father had acquired: he had become the equal of Antoine Court and could bring the consolation of the Gospel to thousands of human hearts. From this time forth, Rabaut Saint-Étienne aspired to continue the work for which he felt himself prepared. What a great dream: the trinity of French Protestantism, embodied for all time in Antoine Court, Paul Rabaut and Rabaut Saint-Étienne. . . .

First, he would have to finish his studies, which meant another trip to Lausanne, in 1761, to the School of Theology where students could attend— or not—whatever courses, and take whatever degrees, they liked. One of his fellow students, André Jeanbon from Montauban, could never speak scornfully enough of the instruction he received there, and wrote about it to Rabaut Saint-Étienne.[7]

Paul Rabaut did not want to wait any longer; perhaps he was afraid that his children would be unable to resist the temptation to stay on in Switzerland and become "the civil servants of Reformation." The great man did not want them "to acquire too much of a taste for free countries and take it into their heads to leave France for more fortunate lands."[8]

November 11, 1764. Jean-Paul Rabaut, called Saint-Étienne, was ordained a pastor in Lausanne by the laying-on of hands, to the sound of Martin Luther's hymns. Ten days from his twenty-first birthday. He was going to follow the path of preaching, perhaps of persecution too.

Has there ever been a moment when he could choose his own life? Like his two younger brothers, he was born a pastor.

Officially accredited by his father, who appointed him as his assistant, he quietly married a woman named Boissière de Durfort, of good Protestant family, in 1768. "She was the most interesting person in the world, a model

---

along with, becomes a pastor in Nîmes and later in Montpellier, in the time of Louis XVI. Overshadowed by the fame of his father and older brother, he is remembered for a well-constructed defense of vaccination. He represents the Gard at the Convention and associates with the Girondins but escapes the fate of Saint-Étienne, because he is one of the seventy-three members of the Convention arrested in the course of a sitting who refuse to derogate from revolutionary law and are spared a trial by Robespierre. Returning to the Convention after Thermidor, Rabaut-Pommier is on the Council of Elders during the Directoire, allies himself with Bonaparte on 18 Brumaire and then with Louis XVIII in 1814. He dies on March 16, 1820.

of virtue, as of charm and beauty."[9] And that is absolutely all he will ever say about her.

He soon found his feet in the new Languedoc of the day, where men like himself were so greatly in demand. Coming in the wake of the great Protestant leaders, he found a special place prepared for him by a changing mentality. As officially banned as ever, but unofficially increasingly tolerated, he gave a heartfelt thanksgiving homily in 1770 on the occasion of the marriage of the Dauphin, soon to become Louis XVI; ten years later, he did as much in a funeral oration for Monseigneur de Becdelièvre, the bishop of Nîmes and protector of his fellow Protestants. Praise for the descendant of the persecuting kings, praise for the apostle of Babylon-Rome, which felt, he had been taught, nothing but hatred for his kind.

Does this mean life was all wine and roses? Far from it. Jean-Paul Rabaut's work was still subject to the gracious pleasure, not of an increasingly remote king, but of some local martinet. That was the only difference; the gracious pleasure had climbed down a few notches.

And when Rabaut Saint-Étienne comes to Paris to take over from Court de Gébelin, negotiate with Malesherbes and push through the Edict of Toleration, that lifelong indignation is still inside him. The Protestants are still living in abeyance. Legally, nothing has changed. In his suitcases, he brings along the most lively and truest product of his pen, *Le vieux Cévenol,* a sort of novel of edification; beginning in 1784, several editions are published and distributed by the peddlers, teaching the French about two things of which most of them were totally ignorant: the history of the Protestants in the previous century and the precarious position in which they still stand in the 1780s.

RABAUT SAINT-ÉTIENNE

32

NOVEMBER 1787

Le vieux Cévenol

"The London papers informed the universe of the death of Ambroise Borély, born in a little town in Languedoc on March 10, 1671, and died in London on September 14, 1774, consequently at the age of one hundred and three years, seven months and four days."[1]

Ambroise, the son of Hyacinthe Borély, was the eldest of seven children "of a gentleman of that country," Protestant and of little fortune. The course of his life promised to be uneventful. But then Louis XIV turned into the Sun King. "As everybody knows, this monarch's predilection for arriving instantly at his *ends* without taking the trouble to negotiate any *means,* * was taken advantage of in order to persuade him to revoke the famous Edict of Nantes, inflicting so deep a wound upon France that it is still bleeding today."

The Borély family witnesses the arrival, in its little town, of two battalions of armed missionaries. This was the beginning of the *dragonnades*. "These converters practiced the most unheard-of cruelties against the heretics. They were beaten without mercy, they were made to stand naked by fires, they were hung in wells, the women and girls were outraged, and the King believed that there was no resistance to his orders and that the grace of God was working efficaciously in the Protestants' minds."†

Thirty troopers were billeted on the Borélys; looting and violence. Ambroise's mother was close to her confinement; she was driven out into the road and nearly died on the cobblestones. Hyacinthe objected, was charged with being a *relaps* or false convert, and burned alive on the public square while his son looked on.

Whereupon the King's men withdrew, "highly pleased with their expedition, and went to carry the Catholic faith elsewhere. . . . Within two months the little town, formerly so populous, was reduced to one-third its size."

"Great hardship makes great souls." Ambroise's mother, assisted by the remaining members of the flock, struggled to manage what property was left her and look after her children, in a continual state of dread lest they be taken from her and deported to Roman Catholic schools.

At fifteen, Ambroise, already well read and full of good intentions, set out to learn a trade. Many of his ancestors had been advocates, but no chance there! The revocation has made that profession illegal for Protestants, along with those of attorney, notary public, even of clerk: " 'My friend, give up all thought of entering the Palais and donning the black gown; the laws do not permit you to be so much as a tipstaff, sergeant-at-arms, constable or process server's assistant.' "

---

*Rabaut's italics.

†At this point Rabaut adds one of his many footnotes, giving details of the places in which dragoonings took place, their dates, and the depredations committed, to fill in the plot of his docu-novel.

His optimism unscathed, he leaves the forbidden palace "laughing with all his might."

" 'Very well, then,' he said to himself, 'find a doctor; it is better to spend one's life healing people's ailments than meddling in their disputes.' "

The physician he happens upon is an old pedant who tranquilly informs him that "the more noble, the loftier our profession, the more such ignominious heretics must be kept out of it. . . . And therefore Père Lachaise* and Monseigneur de Louvois have ordained that in order to be a good physician, one must be a Catholic."

"Ambroise asked him if Aesculapius, Hippocrates and Galen had been such.

" 'No, they were pagans, and I do not know how God permitted them to be so skilled as they were; but that all happened in the age of miracles, and as miracles no longer occur in our day it is plain that only Catholics can be doctors.' "

Still able to produce a laugh, Ambroise decided to settle for a career as an apothecary.

" 'You can't mean it! Such people, having occasion to visit patients, might turn them aside from the true faith.' "

The young Cévenol begins to feel as though he's being driven mad. Well, what if he were to be a house-servant? Certainly not! "A declaration by the King forbids people of the so-called reformed religion to have any but Catholics as servants, and that is wisely done, for the others are all spies. . . . That is also why Protestant midwives are not allowed to practice their profession. It is true that in a number of places there are no others, and many women have died in childbirth for want of assistance, but their death is only temporal, which is no great evil for the state. As you see, there must be more than enough people in France, since such numbers of them can be killed and exiled."

"Shall I find some means of living in France without being a doctor, surgeon, obstetrician, apothecary, advocate, attorney, bailiff's man, tutor, inspector, auditor, clerk, guard, secretary, *feudiste*,† bookseller, printer, goldsmith, etc.?"

---

*Here he sets out to settle an old score between the Protestants and Père Lachaise (1624–1709), one of the most famous Jesuits of the end of the reign of Louis XIV, whose confessor he was for thirty years. Lachaise was devoted to Madame de Maintenon and has been attributed a major role in the religious quarrels of the day, against Fénelon, the Quietists and the Jansenists, and especially in the revocation of the Edict of Nantes. The cemetery in Paris that bears his name stands on the site of a piece of land given to him by the King.

†If Babeuf had been a Protestant, his occupation would have been closed to him.

Taking counsel of the night, Ambroise wakes the next morning determined to enlist in the army as a common soldier. His mother explodes: would he join his father's murderers? What acts might he not be ordered to perform against his own kind?

Having looked on every side, he finds the only niche left to Protestants, as to Jews: business. "He went to work for a shopkeeper as a sales clerk, and by hard work and good behavior endeared himself to his employer."

Brief respite. Then the odious informer Hypocris rats on his mother, her remaining property is confiscated, and her younger children are taken from her so that they can be compelled to abjure before the age of seven, leaving her alone, without resources and ailing.

The *vieux Cévenol*'s memoirs begin in a relatively clownish vein, but by the time Rabaut has related the mother's death, the torture of an uncle and the consignment of Ambroise himself to the galleys, from which he escapes by the skin of his teeth,* the tone has shifted to one of deep rancor.

On one occasion he is an eyewitness (as was St. Stephen [Étienne], the first martyr, whose name Rabaut takes for his alias) to the kind of atrocities that can erupt in a mob:

> The confused tumult of an excited, shouting and screaming rabble brought him out of his reflections. He drew closer to find out what the hubbub was about and saw, all straggling through the mud, archers, soldiers, priests and magistrates and, in their midst, the executioner, who was dragging a naked corpse through the mire, covered in filth and bruises. The cadaver's head had been completely disfigured by the blows of stones and clubs that were constantly raining down upon it. Ambroise had no need to ask what it was; insults were streaming from people's mouths against the Huguenots and shouts rose up on every side, "Well done! That's what should be done to the lot of them! Oh, if we could see them all hanged and burned!" He understood that this was a brother of his, who had refused the sacraments on his deathbed.

A Jesuit to whom Ambroise confides his horror tells him that this example "will edify and frighten the others. . . . We are certain that such spectacles, repeated from time to time, will keep alive in the people a hatred from which the most efficacious results may be expected."

When he and the rest of his convict gang are picked up by an English ship in the Mediterranean, they all sing out as one, "Praise be to God! We're not with the French anymore!"

And Ambroise adds, "We no longer have to fear the King's declarations."

*One scene described in the course of this downward progression shows very clearly the bloodied soil on which the violence of the Revolution grows and flourishes.

• • •

By publishing his book at the same time as he is engaging in his negotiations with the authorities, the author of *Le vieux Cévenol* adds to his
stature as the champion—rather than writing "of the Protestants" again, one
might better say, of a freedom of mentality that he has inhaled with the air
of his age; and also of a certain kind of anger: the rising kind.

SAINT-ANDRÉ

33

N O V E M B E R 1 7 8 7

The Fanaticism of Democracy

The backgrounds of André Jeanbon Saint-André* and Jean-Paul Rabaut
Saint-Étienne differ considerably, if only because of the distance from Nîmes
to Montauban. Two souths, two temperaments, two youths.

André Jeanbon is six years younger than Rabaut. He was born on February 25, 1749, in Montauban, the big town of the Guyenne region on the
banks of the Tarn, already a town of workers and beginning to be a town of
industries, with a climate and site that direct its citizens oceanward.[1] Nîmes,
on the other hand, definitely belongs to the Mediterranean, so when the
Rabauts need to escape, they head east.

The Jeanbons have been living in a Calvinist environment for at least a
century. They were part of a little class of prosperous bourgeois, most of
whom were involved in running the textile and dye works that had already
given the region a personality of its own. Around 1740 the Jeanbon family
married into the Molles family, who were fullers and flour millers. All of
them had to spin smooth and grind small, however, because of the Catholic
authorities. André Jeanbon, for example, was actually baptized by the parish

*Jeanbon Saint-André becomes a member of the Convention and of the Committee of
Public Safety in year II; in that capacity he is asked to reorganize the French navy, and fights
the English on board the *Montagne,* a ship of the Brest fleet. Joining Bonaparte, he becomes
prefect of the department of Mont-Tonnerre and dies in office in Mayence, in 1813.

priest of Saint Jacques. If they were prepared to pay this price, the "religionnaires" of Montauban were permitted to labor for their own prosperity and the town's.

To some extent, these were "the Jews of Languedoc." They went to mass with their Bible in their pocket. They were allowed to trade and manufacture, yes, but little André Jeanbon can recollect gatherings "on the Négrepelisse road" that scattered like flocks of starlings when the King's men drew near. He was twelve when François Rochette, pastor of the Montauban region, and the Grenier brothers, three gentlemen of his flock,[2] were executed at Caussade, just near his home, for the crime of heresy.

So his early childhood was a constant tension between dread, revolt and compromise. Because it was easier, or because they could not do otherwise, his parents sent him to the Jesuit school, where, like many of their pupils in the years immediately preceding the dissolution, he contracted a strong curiosity and a taste for humanism.

Why don't we turn him into one of us? The Jesuits were hoping that he, like most of the "good material" they had to teach, would join the Society.

Not so fast. André's father snatched him back in time; but when he got to be fifteen, he found himself cornered, like poor Ambroise Borély, between the law, which was closed to him by his parents' furtive Calvinism, and the commerce-and-industry world of his own people, which seems never to have had much appeal for him.

There was one way out: westward, down the Tarn.

The Montauban seafarers, whose religious background was not too fiercely scrutinized, often went, as though borne by the current, to work on the ships of the Bordeaux outfitters. André Jeanbon's Jesuitical childhood was followed by a deckhand's adolescence.* At sixteen he was taking lessons in piloting in Bordeaux and at seventeen he had already made a round-trip to the Antilles, specifically Martinique and Guadeloupe. At eighteen he was first mate in the merchant marine, and "master mariner" before he was twenty.[3] But in those days, if you held that rank, you had to invest in the goods you were carrying, just as highway carriers did. It was a deadly game of double-or-nothing, governed by storms and naval warfare. Three times he lost what little savings he had in a series of shipwrecks, and the last one, on a journey back from Santo Domingo, seems to have discouraged him for good.

Unlike Jean-Paul Rabaut, André Jeanbon lived many lives before he

---

*His family papers and private letters have been lost, so we cannot follow his course at sea; the four most eventful years of his life are missing. Nevertheless, his apprenticeship in navigation forms one permanent component of his personality.

finished growing up. He did not become a Jesuit, he did not remain a privateer on the high seas. When he finally returned to his birthplace, he discovered, to his parents' amazement and perhaps terror, a late-developing vocation for the Church. Leaving them a letter, he suddenly absconded to the theological seminary in Lausanne.

O blessed place! As we know, people didn't stay there very long. Jeanbon seems to have done what he had to do there in twenty-six months, January 1771 to April 1773. He was "consecrated" a pastor by the Consistory of the little town of Castres on May 28, 1773. Louis XV was about to die. Conditions for the Protestants were growing easier in fact, if not in law. But he needed a pseudonym anyway, in case a fresh retreat into clandestinity became necessary. He didn't take much trouble over it: his first name was André, so he would call himself Jeanbon Saint-André.[4]

It was a stroke of luck for him, no doubt, that he was not immediately sent to preach in Montauban, where, in that same year 1773, "hunger riots* showed how wild and bloodthirsty the people had remained."[5]

Things were much calmer, for a novice pastor, in Castres, a town with a population of eight or ten thousand, "lying at the foot of the Montagne Noire, an impression of which may be formed from the district along the banks of the Agoût, all crooked little houses."[6] The local Protestants, of whom there are many, are left in peace to spin and weave their woollens, which are sent mainly to Montauban: they are involved only by hearsay in the events of the bigger town. Here, with a salary of twelve hundred livres a year paid by his Consistory, Jeanbon lived a time of truce.

The transition was fragile, however, and his personality was such that he was unable to appreciate it. He had become too intense to enjoy his status as a sort of "canon of Calvinism." Jeanbon Saint-André was not an easy person. There was the conflict within the family, the ups and downs of his sailing years, the inadequacy of his theological training in Lausanne. Not that he rebelled against the authorities; on the contrary, he found, upon his appointment to Castres, that the Protestants were no longer living in the Wilderness of his childhood: "The peace and quiet enjoyed by our churches is as great as one could wish, in the present state of affairs."[7] In this part of Quercy they were tolerated long before the Edict of Toleration, even though it was an uneasy kind of toleration with no security behind it.

But the new generation of pastors is not like the great resisters of old. In this respect Rabaut Saint-Étienne and he have something in common when they begin their correspondence, after being appointed to their respective

---

*As remembered by Mathieu Dumas, then second lieutenant in the Médoc regiment (in Montauban), which put down an uprising caused by famine. A few of the rebels were killed on the spot and others hanged later.

congregations in Nîmes and Castres. They are no longer breathing prophetic fire, they no longer brandish the Bible in opposition to the catechism, they practice Rousseau and would readily claim kinship with the *Vicaire Savoyard*, but would just as readily plagiarize some purple passage from Bossuet.* In 1778 Jeanbon Saint-André gave, and printed, a sermon overflowing with compunction on the occasion of the birth of Madame Royale; two years later Rabaut Saint-Étienne adopts the same style in speaking of the Dauphin's birth. So much for the disputatious manner of old, and the allusions to Luther and Calvin. These men's preaching has been watered down to the level of the Supreme Being; even their master, Court de Gébelin, has given his approval to the Freemasons. "Ministers of the faith were known to have become little more than officers of morality."[8]

Nevertheless, the duties of a pastor, whether at Castres or in Montauban, have recently become those of community administrator as well and are tending toward a degree of involvement in local polities, which they share with the foremost members of the Consistory—especially as, unlike the Roman Catholic dioceses in which the organization of religion is still in the hands of the prelates, the Protestants have no bishop.

After "getting religion" and rushing off to Lausanne to get more of it, Jeanbon is gradually initiated, beginning in Castres, into a sort of elementary democracy that works against the grain of his religious bent, and things begin to go wrong. As his quality and energy grow, he becomes less and less able to swallow the contradictions he sees in his brethren, not only in Castres but also in the Upper Languedoc synod to which he is delegated by the Consistory.

After months of friction and dispute among the chief religious figures and himself, his peace of mind has diminished considerably. He is bogged down in daily quarrels and his position in Castres is growing more and more uncomfortable, while at the same time he is beginning to be recognized as one of the foremost pastors of the province.

Would he wriggle out "through the top" by being appointed pastor in Montauban, his town, his starting point? He is offered the job in 1778, but turns it down, "out of some remaining shreds of mistrust that past experience had led me to believe only too justified."[9]

The hostility he aroused is not universal, however, because only a little while later, at the age of thirty, he is asked to be nothing less than the third pastor of the town of Bordeaux. Sixty-eight notables from the big port had signed a petition in his favor. The scales might yet tip another way. It was

---

*In a sermon on the difficult birth of Louis XVI, Jeanbon quite openly paraphrases the famous *"Madame se meurt, Madame est morte."*

tempting enough for him to make the trip and take a closer look. But at the last minute other Bordeaux people, warned off him by those who have previously collided with his inflexibility, vote instead for—young Rabaut-Pommier, the happy-go-lucky and less flamboyant younger brother of the already celebrated Rabaut Saint-Étienne, who has no share in the decision. It must have been the work of another Bordeaux pastor, a man named Olivier Desmont: "The intriguing supporters of M. Saint-André* were somewhat taken aback by the determination of our Consistory. . . . The other person was not universally liked and, between you and me, his dogmatic and uncompromising ways were positively disliked."[10]

In the end, neither Rabaut-Pommier nor Saint-André goes to Bordeaux, and the feud between Consistories, synods and pastors throughout the southwest drags on for months.

Just as Protestantism is within reach of becoming legal again, a kind of explosion takes place within it, in the regions in which it had survived. Even former champions are saddened by this, such as the great Paul Rabaut, who laments the absence of hierarchical leaders to deal with "the mighty petty quarrels" that are producing an anarchy among the Protestant ranks that brings smiles to the lips of the Catholics:

"I find the most useful plans impeded, and I will not hide from you my strong dissatisfaction with our presbyterian government. The least of the elders imagines himself a person of importance, and the most undistinguished pastor throws out his chest like the highest of them all."[11]

One is almost tempted to say that they miss being persecuted. Is this the price of their relative prostration before the authorities? "As the Calvinist democracy† was no longer under the sway of great thoughts and great souls, small minds, impervious to every influence, attached themselves to small characters."[12]

Saint-André's aggressiveness toward his fellow Protestants grows in inverse proportion to the civil obedience he is supposed to be teaching them. "The conflict between Jeanbon and the Consistories of Montauban and Bordeaux shows that although church administration may give pastors a political education, it also sets many a snare for them when they chance to have energetic temperaments."[13]

In other words, the compliance of the Protestant ministers is smoothing the path for the attempt at legal recognition in which Saint-Étienne and Malesherbes are engaged, but the more successful it is, the more it stimulates

---

*According to a letter written by Desmont to Saint-Étienne, the unhappy arbitrator between his brother and the author of the letter. Rabaut-Pommier, always an accommodating sort of chap, was not pressing for the job.

†According to the historian Léon Lévy.

the latent grouchiness of those same Protestants, in which there is an element of guilty conscience. Thus, they are paying the first toll on the highway to spontaneous democracy.

Jeanbon, unprepared for this constant contradiction, finds the tension almost more than he can bear. Hurt by his failure in Bordeaux, he begins fighting with his flock in Castres and is constantly being caught between them and the Prince de Beauveau, who is the regional intendant, on the subject of possible sites for worship closer to the town. Jeanbon preaches docility toward the intendant, but with a harshness that seems to have become second nature to him. Rabaut in Nîmes gives him what support he can. Around 1780 one might have said they were two fingers of the same hand, except that Rabaut is mildness itself, whereas Jeanbon is already rubbed raw: "Your approval of me* was seen as an interference with the independence of the church of Castres devised by you and me, and the people, who are always the dupes of canting hypocrites, the people who are so easily put upon by gesticulations, believed it was so. Possibly half the Protestants in Castres are convinced that you and I are two scoundrels, the object of our iniquity being to force them to use their legs on Sunday. . . . After such goings-on as this, it will not amaze you to hear that I have lost all desire ever to meddle again in ecclesiastical matters."[14]

His inner tension prompts him to strike out for more space. Maybe if he could go down the Tarn again, return to the New World . . . First, he asks for a year's leave of absence, which the Castres Consistory gladly grants him and which he spends with his family in Montauban. In 1782 it was hard enough to go back at all, and it was made harder by the fact that the Protestant upper crust of Castres, led by a banker named Baudecourt, had become so locked in hostility toward him that he no longer dared receive letters openly from the Rabaut father and son, although Jeanbon himself still manages to send a few significant wails to his friends in Nîmes, accusing Baudecourt of bad faith and calling him an upstart, intriguing poltroon. On April 13, 1782, he informs them of his "unshakable determination to resign his office as pastor." The men in Nîmes counsel patience. To which Saint-André replies, to Paul Rabaut, on April 24, 1782, "What you say against my decision, flattering and meant to encourage me as it is, will not make me change my mind. . . . As I am unable to keep order in the church, the futility of my efforts makes it imperative for me to think henceforth only of my retirement."[15]

At thirty-four.

On June 21, the Castres Consistory dryly endorses his departure: "Mon-

*Jeanbon, writing to Rabaut, on May 24, 1780.

sieur Saint-André, pastor, having announced that his health and other essential considerations private to himself had moved him to submit his resignation, it was duly accepted."[16]

Does that mean that his religious life is over? Not yet. He takes advantage of a five-year hiatus to write his *Considérations sur l'organisation civile des églises protestantes*.[17] Having come so far and fallen from so high, he wants to prepare the public to welcome the Edict of Toleration. Huddling in oblivion in his hometown, the provincial pastor awaits the fruit of the labors of the Parisian immigrant Rabaut.

Jeanbon Saint-André's *Considérations*, which remain his major work, show the point reached by religious minds, both Catholic and Protestant, shortly before the Estates General. No movements, no mysticism: pastors and parish priests alike were approaching absolute zero. No waves, no noise, no quarrels; just: how do we organize our parochial or pastoral communities to produce the best discipline? This implies leadership by notables. Let us eschew "elders chosen from among the dregs of the people in the days when there was no one else to be found, for they often led us to make rash mistakes."[18] "Consistories shall be composed of six individuals only, but care will be taken to choose men of mature years, established integrity, mildness of character and enlightened minds. . . . Married men will be given preference over bachelors. A wife and children create stronger ties to one's birthplace."[19]

The author actually argues that the Edict of Nantes had been too favorable to Protestants, whence the necessity for Louis XIII and Richelieu to cut them down to size at La Rochelle and elsewhere; whence the final (and, granted, excessive) revocation by Louis XIV. And whence the need for the Edict of Toleration, which everything seems to indicate will come under Louis XVI, provided the Protestants keep a profile low enough to deserve it. "A religion, be it proven false as to its dogma, is useful by virtue of its morality, to keep order in the state." Protestant worship will accordingly be tolerated, but "without allowing it any brilliance, any outward pomp to draw attention to its existence, and even in its obscurity it must be subject to a system for maintaining order that does not allow it to overstep the bounds."[20]

All the places in the sun will continue to be occupied by Catholics. Only a bit of shadow will be set aside for Protestants, as long as their ministers "live like ordinary persons and avoid all controversy." In this respect Rabaut Saint-Étienne sees eye-to-eye with him, having just written (early in 1787) that "their houses of prayer must bear no external adornment."[21]

They were right to maintain their low profile with such determination, because Malesherbes and Target both, with all the goodwill in the world, foresaw the wave of Catholic indignation that would swell up and roll, even before the Edict of Toleration was submitted to the King's Council and then to the *Parlement;* this explains the thousand and one precautions taken in drafting the new text, even though it leaves the dominant Church in sole possession of the right to public worship. "The Roman Apostolic Catholic religion alone shall continue to enjoy the right of public worship in our realm. The birth, marriage and death of those professing it can under no circumstances be observed otherwise than according to the rites and customs of the said religion."[22]

Humbly, almost slyly, the authors of the Edict, approved not only by Breteuil but by the King himself, who could not be suspected of harboring much sympathy for the Calvinists, confine themselves to granting "non-Catholics" the right "to practice their commerce, arts, trades, crafts and professions" on terms that are still very vague, and edging back the bolts that bar them from one or two offices and one or two administrative positions.[23]

Even that is too much.

A large number of prelates forgather in the home of the archbishop of Paris and compose an "entreating"—and insolent—text, which they submit to the King, asking him to defer proclamation of the Edict. Louis XV's "favorite" daughter, Madame Louise de France (about whom one anecdotal interpretation of history claims that she took religious orders out of sheer spite when her father elevated the Comtesse du Barry to the rank of a semiqueen), is grimly urging on the anti-Protestant faction. From the Maréchale de Noailles to the lowest abbés in Court, they're queueing up outside the Carmelite gates to make sure of her support; and Madame Louise finds some unexpected allies. Duval d'Eprémesnil, for example, the big man of *Parlement* opposition in the 1770s and also in the present, who has become so fanatical that he actually believes in some of the apparitions touted by one crank or another. Sitting in the *Parlement* one day, he points to a huge painting of Christ on the wall and yelps, "Do you want to crucify him a second time?"[24]

After becoming the mother superior of her convent, the poor grande dame departs this life around the age of fifty. To the end, her royal nephew remains deaf to her exhortations against the new civil status of the Protestants. Brienne has managed to convince Louis XVI that the Treasury can no longer survive without help from the great Protestant banks and capital, which might be forthcoming if ever Necker returns to power. Also, the King never really liked his aunts, especially the Carmelite one, when they preached at him. In this time of crisis, his "Mistress-Mary-quite-contrary" penchant is gaining force. Is that what finishes off Madame Louise; or is it something that comes via the extern sister, in a package containing an envelope on which somebody has written, "Relics of the Eternal Father"? Inside, there is a tuft of powder-sprinkled white hair. Madame Louise sniffs it, feels unwell, throws everything into the fire, takes to her bed, swells up, turns black and expires. But not before writing one last letter about the Protestants to the King.[25] "She is said to have taken this matter too much to heart and was killed by her fears for the salvation of her fellow citizens.* To this holy princess, the purity of the faith was being endangered by the Protestants' recall to France [*sic*], and she could not be persuaded that the damned deserved to be treated as human beings."[26]

We might indeed take the incident as no more than an anecdote, except that it shows the kind of delayed-action ideological warfare being waged against the grand design of Malesherbes and Rabaut. Baron de Staël, ambassador to Sweden and unemotional observer, informs Gustavus III, "Fanaticism is assuming every conceivable guise to prevent the registration of the King's edict giving non-Catholics the rights of citizenship. Last Friday, the Bishop of Dôle made a speech to the King on the matter, concluding with these words:

" 'Sire, you shall answer to God and men for the misfortunes that will follow the restoration of the Protestants. Madame Louise, in the heaven her virtues have earned her, sees your conduct, and disapproves it.' "[27]

There is a proliferation of this kind of statement, brochure, pamphlet, all bearing witness to a panic fear, not only of the authorities but also of thousands of Catholics, and making it easier to understand why Rabaut in Paris and Jeanbon in Montauban are advancing so cautiously, wriggling through the undergrowth on their stomachs. Another example is the *Lettre d'un magistrat dans laquelle on examine également ce que la justice du Roi doit aux protestants et ce que l'intérêt de son peuple ne lui permet pas de leur accorder,*[28] the author of which affirms that "Calvin violates the authority of kings, seeks to overturn monarchical constitutions and replace them with an aristocracy . . . , and the Protestants of old were zealous republicans; do we not see the fanaticism of democracy reigning almost everywhere today?"

This onslaught does not prevent the King from signing, on November 17, the timid and yet courageous text of the Edict of Toleration. As luck would have it, the Edict is scheduled for submission to the *Parlement,* to be endorsed, two days later, along with some other edicts by Brienne—which are to produce a veritable earthquake. So the Protestants are going to have to be patient yet awhile, even if the proclamation of the Edict brings some hope and consolation, especially to one whom we may still call the Pastor Jeanbon Saint-André, now surfacing again as third preacher in the church of Montauban, at last! after five years in retirement.

Meanwhile, he has married Marie Desuc in Castres.[29]

---

*According to Lescure's *Correspondance secrète.*

34

NOVEMBER 19–21, 1787

It Is Legal Because I Wish It!

The French Revolution begins on November 19, 1787, at a plenary sitting of the *Parlement,* which has just been recalled from its exile in Troyes. It might have been a stroke of luck for history: the government has consented to share a shred of power, but on condition that the *Parlement,* restored to its home and duties, also gives ground and endorses the reform bills that can wait no longer.

The sharp edge of the quarrel between Brienne and the magistrates concerns the heart of the matter, which is the immediate need to bring in the money the Treasury must have in order to avoid bankruptcy.

Throughout the summer and early autumn Brienne and his chief ministers have been working hard. Some provincial administrations and a few garrisons are already unable to make payments. Brienne, a product of the Assembly of Notables himself, called by some "a Notable in power," is trying to salvage something of what Calonne sought to achieve, too late and too optimistically, when he convoked those Notables.

He is failing and ill, but he has done his best in the few weeks destiny has allotted him, and it's all the more to his credit because the King, stricken himself with a sort of aphasia, is giving him scant support—perhaps because the Queen, on the other hand, is standing up for the "principal minister" with more conviction than she ever showed in regard to any of his predecessors.

Brienne has three men to rely on: Chrétien-François de Lamoignon, fifty-two, who is to reform the system of justice and in particular abolish the remaining forms of torture; Le Tonnelier de Breteuil, fifty-seven, who is to reform the Households of King and princes;* and Armand de Montmorin, Vergennes's successor for foreign affairs.

*One historians' tradition, based on the important role played by Breteuil as an émigré,

Two other ministers who have been in office for some time now—Ségur, for war, and Castries, for the navy, both of them marshals of France—find themselves unable to serve as "an archbishop's assistants,"[2] so the Archbishop replaces the former with his own brother, the Comte de Brienne, and the latter by the Comte de La Luzerne, another relative of Lamoignon and a man of honor and ability; but he has to be brought in a rush (that is, in three months) from the Leeward Islands, where he has been governor, and may well turn up after the battle is over. Two living monuments, both academicians and both embodiments of the spirit of Enlightenment, are also members of this Council, with the title of minister of state, and add to its credibility: the Duc de Nivernais and Malesherbes. "Would one summon such witnesses as these* if one meant to deceive a nation?"[3]

The "Brienne administration" is the most coherent of the reign.

During their brief months of "grace," the ministers do some mild pruning of the plethoric budgets of the Households of the King, Queen and princes. One or two medieval services are made redundant in the administration of the royal hunts: falconry, the wolf hunt, the boar hounds. They set up a Council of War, which undertakes to reform the army under the direction of the Comte de Guibert, a prominent theoretician since the publication of his *Essai général de tactique,* which is becoming a staple in the military diet of all young officers, including Bonaparte.† The Life Guards' numbers are reduced, farewell, Musketeers, ta-ta, Light Horse . . . Henceforth, instead of eighteen camp marshals there will be only twelve, and only half the former number of generals. The soldiers' pay is increased by a blushing two or three sols a day, but the Prussian disciplinary veneer (for instance, punishment by blows with the flat side of a sword) imposed ten years before by the Comte de Saint-Germain is preserved, and commoners are still ineligible for promotion.

Brienne has tried to muddle together some provincial assemblies, comprised of local notables, of course, whose duty it will be to accept the taxes requested by the King and decide how they are to be apportioned. This is

---

shows him as a dyed-in-the-wool conservative; but his support of the Edict of Toleration and other relatively progressive measures, as indicated in the memoirs of Bailly and Barras, reveals, according to Jean Egret, his "feelings of humanity and sense of the necessary sacrifices which the monarchy must accept in order to survive."[1]

*According to the Comte de Virieu.

†In 1787 Guibert is forty-three; he was precocious enough to be elected to the Académie Française in February 1786, although the first edition of his *Essai* came out in 1770. He is known chiefly to historical anecdote as one of the lovers of Julie de Lespinasse (see Volume I) but in fact he was a major French military theorist.

the first approach to "decentralization" in French tradition since Richelieu pulled all power into a single hand, and this is the framework into which Malesherbes was hoping to tiptoe with his Edict of Toleration.

"The month of November having arrived, all arrangements for the services in 1787 were coming to a close, without any possibility of making provision for those in 1788. . . . All people with money were refusing to give it, in whatever form they were solicited. Payments at the Hôtel de Ville, a clear indicator of the state of the Royal Treasury, bore witness to the acute discomfort in which it stood, and which could only grow worse instead of better. Terror was writ large on every face."[4]

Which is why, swashbucklers notwithstanding, Brienne has not been able to send so much as one regiment out to Holland. Some polemicists are counseling a *politique du pire,* saying that all payments should be suspended and the kingdom declared bankrupt. Linguet is one of them, the advocate stricken from the bar in 1775 who became the publicist of the *Annales politiques* and has spent the last few years either in the Bastille or in London, and who is now said to be in Brienne's employ. With his fondness for paradox and the financial knowledge he boasts, Linguet may be testing the wind for the Minister when he says that "this violent tremor would crush very few of the twenty-four million souls by which France is populated, and would restore the full play of its immense forces to the fair kingdom."[5]

Suggestions like that give nightmares to men as different as Brissot[6] and Mirabeau. Our hero has just returned to France, no longer having cause to fear Calonne's persecutions but hardly more cheerful for all that: "We are here in such a turmoil that it is impossible for me to open myself to you in writing.* From a state of tranquil chaos, the country has now progressed to a state of distracted chaos. Out of it can and must come some creature. Will it be embryo or man? I do not know, but it is impossible for us to remain as we are and we can go no lower."[7] It may well be that the gravity of the situation has hastened some secret negotiations between Brienne and the bigger fish in the Paris *Parlement,* among whom we find—who'd have believed it?—the hyperactive d'Eprémesnil.

The magistrates' resistance is still simmering and spreading from Paris to the provinces, helped along by their "deportation" to Troyes; but it is still no more than resistance, although it's becoming bolder in Bordeaux, Brittany and the Dauphiné. But there is no open revolt, no declaration of war. Brienne was not trying to precipitate a trial of strength, and that is one reason why he sent the magistrates to Troyes, near his own home base at Brienne, and not to Sens as was initially proposed. During those four months there were

*Letter dated November 3, 1787, to Major Mauvillon, his friend from Brunswick.

frequent contacts between Brienne and Troyes; visits and receptions were smoothing things out a little. Many of the magistrates were beginning to fear being overrun by demands from below, from the populace.

Throughout this entire period, of course, the tax edicts could not come into force; but more than that, the elementary processes of justice had become impossible in Paris, where the law's underlings stood twiddling their thumbs in the Palais de Justice: nearly six hundred advocates, eight hundred attorneys and five hundred tipstaffs were like to waste away, not to mention their clerks and secretaries.[8]

By the end of August a deal was beginning to take shape. A compromise peace was being envisaged that would save the *Parlement*'s face: there would be a royal promise to convene the Estates General (in 1792!), in return for which the *parlements* would concede the "compulsory loans" Brienne had to have for the Treasury.

November 17: the King's Council endorses the "bursal edicts," meaning the loan and tax provisions to be spread over a period of five years. The King, making a calculated concession, agrees to appear in person in the Palais de Justice on November 19 before the assembled magistrates, who, he has been told, are now meek as lambs and almost repentant. Therefore the sitting on November 19 should end the resistance, culminate in a great royal pardon, put the finances back on an even keel and seal the reconciliation between the nobilities of gown and sword.

It nearly does.

The government imagines it has set the scene perfectly, employing a mixture of prudence and cunning that should produce what Calonne failed to achieve with the Notables and what Brienne failed to achieve last spring. This time the *Parlement* is convened at eight in the morning of the nineteenth, too early for the Parisians to gather in force outside the Palais, which is surrounded by large numbers of French, Life, and Swiss Guards. A final briefing was held in Versailles on the evening of the eighteenth, to work out the fine points of this strange ceremony that is to be called, not a "bed of justice" but a "royal sitting."

The magistrates (some of whom will be absent because the summons doesn't reach them in time), dukes and peers, and princes of the blood are arrayed beneath the paneling of the Great Chamber, the King has come from Versailles in "hunting coaches," and his armchair is uncanopied. Partisans of a compromise might believe themselves on the threshold of a change in the embodiment of French law, an improvised parliamentarianism in the English manner, when they are informed, upon arrival, that the King will hear the views, oral and not written, of anyone wishing to give them.

Eyewash. What they don't know is that despite Malesherbes's reservations, what the Council decided the previous evening was to "hear" but not to "record" any such views: "Would you have the King a mere councillor to the *Parlement?*"[9]

There is a reading of the Edict, "establishing a series of graded loans over five years," after which Louis XVI gives them a grating sermon: "I come to hold this session in order to remind my *Parlement* of the principles from which it must not deviate. . . .

"I shall never consent to be questioned indiscreetly as to what is to be expected of my wisdom and love for my peoples. . . .

"They are of the essence of the monarchy and I shall not permit them to be disregarded or adulterated. . . .

"My *parlements* must rely upon my trust and my affection, but they must deserve them by not exceeding the duties entrusted to them by the kings, my predecessors, taking care not to depart from them, never to refuse them, and, above all, setting for my subjects an example of loyalty and submission."[10]

Except for the last battalion of sourpusses, the audience gapes. What, not one word from the heart? Louis XVI proceeds to inform them that "my keeper of the seals will give you fuller particulars of my intentions."

Lamoignon's pedantic harangue makes matters worse, although it starts off promisingly enough: "Before instructing you as to the result of his measures of economy and explaining to you the purpose of the Edict, the King has ordered me, firstly, to reply explicitly to the wish you have put before him, to hold an assembly of the Estates General of the realm."

In any less starchy room one could imagine a shiver of relief. But it doesn't last long.

"His Majesty, rightly displeased by a request that you were basing on an alleged failing in the powers you hold from him, and that seemed to be in the nature of a demand, a thing rejected and reproved by the sacred rights of his authority, has not thus far seen fit to consider the matter. . . .

"He owes to the nation, to his descendants, he owes to himself, never to permit the authority that God has placed in his hands to be diluted in any way."

The keeper of the seals scolds the magistrates for two solid hours, reminding them, for instance, "that to the King alone appertains the sovereign power of his realm.

"That he is accountable to God alone for the exercise of supreme power.

"That the bond uniting the King and the nation is indissoluble by nature.

"That it is in the nation's interest that the rights of its leader should suffer no adulteration.

"That the King is sovereign leader of the nation, and it and he form a single entity.

"Lastly, that legislative power lies unconditionally and wholly in the sovereign's person."

Therefore, the King will not envisage any Estates General, and will set no date for any, unless they be held "as great days celebrating the love of all French for their sovereign."

At the very most, the minister feels he can tell them that *if* the *parlements* behave themselves and *if* the five loans produce the desired results, "it will be at a meeting of the Estates General that His Majesty, surrounded by his faithful subjects, will confidently present to them the comforting image of order restored."

"This speech was followed by the reading of the first Edict, providing for a series of graded loans, for a total of 420 millions, for the years 1788, 1789, 1790, 1791, 1792.

"When the reading was finished, the First *Président* called for opinions in the customary manner. These opinions were based on lengthy argumentation and lasted seven hours. MM. Robert, Fréteau and Duval d'Eprémesnil in particular were remarked upon for their eloquence, as persuasive as it was respectful."[11]

Seven hours . . .

The King's patience is sorely tried.

And he gets an earful. . . . Most of the councillors give opinions favorable to the edicts, but the real event of the day, the only one that sticks in the public mind, arises out of the statements made by one or two diehards.

Sabathier de Cabre, his words wrapped in respectful formulae,[12] opposes endorsement. He agrees to the first loan only, for one year, and asks the King to convene the Estates General in the near future.

Fréteau de Saint-Just, speaking with diffidence but firmness and clarity, his forty years glinting with youth in this setting of ancient rites and medieval language, reiterates the arguments put forward by Sabathier. His comely face with its forthright gaze below a high brow framed by rolls of powdered hair on either side impresses the whole *Parlement*. For several years now the King's advisers have been looking upon him as "a dangerous *philosophe*."

The prize for home-truth-telling that day, however, goes to a sort of Wild Man of the *Parlement*, Robert de Saint-Vincent, whose straight-talking, Jansenist convictions and utter indifference to any potential punishment make him a sort of St. John Golden-Mouth.* He certainly doesn't mince words. "A plan is formed for five years! But since Your Majesty first came to the throne, has a single policy ever directed the administration of finances for five successive years?" And, speaking directly to the Comptroller General

---

*St. John Golden-Mouth = an eloquent and/or unbridled orator, by allusion to St. John Chrysostom (from the Greek *chrysos,* "gold," and *stoma,* "mouth").—*Trans.*

(who was absent by protocol, but listening in a nearby room), "Can you fail to know, sir, that every minister, upon entering office, throws out his predecessor's system and puts the one he has invented in its place? Do you flatter yourself that you will have time to make yours a reality? Do you hope that the favor that has raised you to the ministry can keep you there so long? You are the fourth minister of finance to be appointed within eight months; and you put forward a plan that cannot be carried out in less than five years!"

Coming back to the King: "Sire, the remedy for the state's wounds has been named by your *Parlement:* it is the convening of the Estates General. To be salutary, this must happen promptly. Why the delay? The truth is this: your ministers wish to avoid the Estates General, whose vigilant eye they apprehend. But their hope is vain; the needs of the state will compel you to assemble them within two years. . . . The views of those who say you must wait cannot be honest. If they want time, it is in order that they may intrigue and put together some Estates General of courtiers prepared to applaud them, or of turbulent men who would disrupt them and make them unfruitful and possibly prejudicial. God preserve the kingdom from such misfortune! But there is reason to fear it, for past experience has taught clearly enough that there are men who would risk the fate of their fatherland for the pleasure of being able to say afterward, You see, the *Parlement* was wrong, the Estates General ought not have been called."[13]

Like everybody else, Louis XVI has been waiting for d'Eprémesnil, the hotheaded magistrate of his youth, to speak. The King has been promised that he's much calmer now. But when his shrill voice pipes up in the middle of the afternoon, a hush falls.

D'Eprémesnil is a temperamental man, who acts on impulse rather than reason, and just now he's fuming, simply because his carriage lost a contest with that of the Comte d'Artois for a parking space in the courtyard outside. His fury lowers the credibility of the appeal that he had prepared most carefully for the King's ear, hoping to produce a sort of *coup de théâtre.* For almost an hour he publicly urges the compromise which he has more or less fathered and negotiated himself: the *Parlement* should endorse the first two loans, for 1788 and 1789, at which point the King would convene the Estates General. Then he turns to Louis XVI and makes a public appeal:

"Sire, with one word you are going to satisfy our every hope. In the twinkling of an eye, a universal enthusiasm will reach out from this room to the capital and from the capital throughout the realm. I am assured of this by a presentiment that will not deceive me; I read it in Your Majesty's gaze; the intention is in your heart, the word is on your lips: pronounce it, Sire, grant it to the love of all the French."[14]

Some people, in the brief moment of silence that follows, observe a slight clouding of the King's gaze. They imagine him giving his consent, the Assembly transfigured by enthusiasm, one sentence spoken to the magistrates transforming, at last, the character of this government.*

But d'Eprémesnil has not found the right tone. Louis XVI can't shed his abulia in two minutes. The angel has passed over.

Time is passing too. They have all said their pieces in front of the King. The first *Président* is waiting, pen in hand, for Louis XVI's command to count the votes for and against his edicts. Despite a few body blows dealt here and there, it is probable that the majority will vote in favor of them.

And the keeper of the seals goes up to receive His Majesty's orders, and the scales tip back into the ancient mode. This authorized release of *Parlement* repressions has achieved exactly nothing.

Without calling for a count, Lamoignon announces that the King has just said to him as follows:

"After hearing your opinions, I find that it is necessary to institute the loans described in my Edict. I have promised the Estates General before 1792; you must be satisfied with my word. I command that my Edict be endorsed."[15]

The thunderbolt.

According to the *Archives Parlementaires,* "at that instant, the sitting was transformed into a bed of justice. Returning to his place, the keeper of the seals proclaimed the endorsement without any summing up of opinions or counting of votes."[16]

So, what was the point? Most of the men attending this strange ceremony feel as though they've been watching a play. So much hope for so little. Yes, they have been heard, but not listened to.

The King has risen and is about to leave the chamber, when an unforeseen but qualified troublemaker makes his move. On either side of the sovereign, the princes of the blood—his brothers and cousins—are standing in their opulent array. And, suddenly, without being asked, Philippe d'Orléans speaks.

"Speaks" may not be quite the word. Philippe has never known how to open his mouth in public, any more than Louis XVI himself, if he has to improvise, although he can declaim a written speech well enough. Pulling himself together, the Duc d'Orléans asks whether this sitting is a bed of justice or a royal sitting.†

---

*The next day, Louis XVI admits to the Archbishop of Paris that he was within an ace of forgetting his Council's resolutions and interrupting the speech to grant the request (according to Pasquier's *Mémoires*).

†That night at Court people say his interruption was planned at home, by his followers and himself; this is not certain.

Unheard of. For the first time in history since the Fronde, the King is being addressed directly in a public gathering. He goggles, but has to reply: "A royal sitting!"

"It is illegal," says the Duke. "I demand that it be stipulated that the endorsement has been performed at His Majesty's very express command."[17]

"We must refer to the ideas then prevailing in France,* the principles of authority in force there, in order to grasp the effect that must have been produced by this first instance of a prince of the blood making a protest inside the *Parlement,* and contesting, in the presence of the King himself, the orders he had just given.

"There had been nothing comparable in the entire history of the monarchy. Princes of the blood had been seen resisting the King's power sword in hand; they had never been seen trying to set constitutional limits upon his authority."[18]

It's stammer versus stammer. Louis XVI mumbles a few words: "I don't care. . . . You're certainly playing the master. . . . Yes, it is! . . . It is legal because I wish it."[19]

Whereupon he flees, purple with anger, followed by his family. But most of the magistrates stay put, and a few of them try to turn the Prince's protest into a viable text, with the following result:

"Sire, I entreat Your Majesty to permit me to lay at your feet, and in the Court, the declaration that I regard this endorsement as illegal, and that it would be needful, in order to relieve the persons who are presumed to have deliberated upon it from responsibility, to add that it has been performed at the express command of the King."

The writers charitably record the King as replying, "The endorsement is legal, since I have heard the opinions of all."[20]

What a day! It marks the failure of the attempt to carry out a "royal revolution" initiated by Brienne. It reveals the Duc d'Orléans to the public as the incarnation, unintentionally or by design, of royal opposition. In the past, it was Monsieur, the King's first brother, who took a few sly stabs in that direction, and was rewarded with a small popularity. But he has never stood up to his brother in public. From now on, there is open conflict between the King and the Duc d'Orléans, which is why, on this same evening of November 19, a *lettre de cachet* "exiles" Philippe d'Orléans to his estate at Villers-Cotterêts, north of Paris, while Sabathier de Cabre and Fréteau de Saint-Just are arrested in their homes and removed, the former to Mont-Saint-Michel and the latter to Doullens.

On November 21, the King summons a delegation from the Paris *Parle-*

*According to Talleyrand's *Mémoires.*

ment to Versailles and orders it, without further ado, to endorse the measures so lengthily debated two days before.

35

NOVEMBER 22, 1787

A Person Has to Live

After November 19, the conversational bees in the gardens of the Palais-Royal buzz even more loudly than before because Prince Philippe, wearing a martyr's crown, has been driven from these haunts of which the Orléans branch are the lords and masters.

On Thursday, November 22, Second Lieutenant Napoleone de Buonaparte emerges from the Théâtre des Italiens and goes for a stroll, "striding down the paths of the Palais-Royal,"[1] the only link between the two events being the young man's curiosity about what might be going on in these parts.* He is about to have an adventure and writes an account of it almost immediately afterward.

He is eighteen. "Small, beardless, pale, excessively thin, he is totally unprepossessing. His narrow shoulders inside his uniform" of royal blue, with scarlet lapels and facings, black wool breeches and hose and gilded epaulets, "his neck wrapped in a high cravat, his temples covered by long locks of hair worn flat to his head, hollow-cheeked, his eyes quick and his gaze searching, his voice hollow, muted in timbre, seldom heard: in every respect he appeared a thoughtful, concentrated, bashful young man."[2]

He is living in the Hôtel de Cherbourg on the rue du Four Saint-Honoré,† where he ordinarily limits himself to one meal a day. He's just back from Corsica, having spent a six-month furlough with his family "after an absence of seven years and nine months."[3]

His mind is in a whirl, he spends all his time reading. Recently (on May

---

*See Volumes III and IV for Napoleon's childhood in Corsica and school years in France.

†The street no longer exists; it was close to St. Eustache and owed its name to a public oven situated on it.

9) he has written a *Réfutation de Roustan** for his eyes alone, in which he berates an obscure author who has dared to criticize his god, Jean-Jacques Rousseau. In pretending to defend Christianity, Second Lieutenant Buonaparte actually makes an all-out assault upon it, even though (or precisely because) it has dominated his whole youth:

> Your empire is of the other world, and yet you disrupt this one! That is how Christianity has broken the unity of the state, that is how it has caused wars that have torn apart nearly every kingdom of Europe. . . .
>
> You triumphantly enquire why Protestant Switzerland and the French and Piedmontese Calvinists have not been troubled by civil dissension. Why? Because they had a common foe, the Papist. As long as the Christians were being persecuted and repressed by pagans, they were meek and good.
>
> . . . Rousseau was right to say that it was the doctrine of Jesus that has engendered the internal divisions that have never ceased to agitate the Christian world. . . . Consider whether paganism has ever done the like. It matters not to me whether or no churches have conducted themselves in a Christian manner, only that these wars have been a consequence of the institution of Christianity; that is all I require.[4]

This is his philosophy now, on his return from Corsica, as he lets himself slip into the stream of Paris.

To a young man as reserved and inhibited as Napoleon, the Palais-Royal and its gardens and surprises are what the "hot" parts of towns have often been—a breath of air.

He steps onto a building site. The little craftsmen whose shops used to stand around the rectangle are being expropriated. In the middle, the Duc d'Orléans is building what is called a "circus" or "manège," half buried in the ground. It will virtually never be used.[5]

The uglier the place becomes, the more it draws people. Among other things, it harbors the highest density of prostitutes. And here comes Buonaparte, whose only contact with love has been a few vague triflings, who is just emerging from a barren youth, and who has certainly not had time for any flings in Corsica, where customs are fiercely repressive. He has been spending every day helping his older brother, Joseph, manage the family's vineyards and olive orchards.

• • •

*And it is perhaps in mocking memory of this that General Bonaparte, returning from Egypt twelve years later, gives the name Roustan to a Mameluke prisoner and faithful manservant of his—as though he were a dog.

He's back, he's got the evening off, he is about to give a few moments' freedom to his curiosity, as much as to his sexuality:

My spirit, stirred by the vigorous sensations characteristic of it, enabled me to bear the cold with indifference, but once my imagination had cooled, I felt the rigors of the season and stepped into the galleries. I was just outside the iron gates when my gaze fell upon a person of the opposite sex. The time of day, her figure, and her extreme youth assured me that she was a tart. I watched her; she stopped, not with the brazen air the others have but in a manner that perfectly suited her outward appearance. I was struck by this harmony. Her timidity gave me courage and I spoke to her. . . . But her pallor, her physical weakness, her low voice did not leave me a moment in doubt. Either, I said to myself, this is a person who will be useful for the performance of that which I wish to do, or she is only an idiot.

"You must be awfully cold," I told her. "How can you brave these pathways?"

"Oh, sir, hope keeps me going. I must finish my evening."

She spoke the words so indifferently, her reply was so unemotional, that I was touched, and moved alongside her.

"You don't look at all strong. I'm surprised you have not wearied of your trade."

"Ah, well, sir, I have to do something."

"That may be, but is there no trade that would be better for your health?"

"No, sir, a person has to live."

I was delighted, I saw that at least she was answering me, and not all the other attempts I had made had been so successful.

"You must be from some northern region, because you dare to come out in this cold!"

"I'm from Nantes in Brittany."

"I have never been there. . . . Mademoiselle, you must do me the pleasure of telling me how you lost your virginity."

"It was an officer."

"And are you sorry?"

"Indeed I am!" Her voice took on a timbre and softness I hadn't noticed before. "I promise you I am sorry. My sister has a good situation now. Why should not I as well?"

"How did you get to Paris?"

"The officer who ruined me, and whom I hate, abandoned me. I had to run away from my mother, who was wild with indignation. Another man came along, brought me to Paris and abandoned me, and he was followed by a third, with whom I have been living for three years. But even though he is French, he had to go to London for his business, and now he's there. Let's go to your place."

"But what will we do there?"

"Oh, come now; we'll get warm and you will have your pleasure."

I had no intention of making difficulties; only, to prevent her from running away when pressed, I had needled her with the questions I was putting to her, feigning a disinterestedness, an innocence that I meant to prove to her I did not possess.[6]

This was two days after the King banished the Duc d'Orléans from the Palais-Royal.

MERLIN

36

FEBRUARY 5, 1788

The Pretty Girls at Valmunster

On February 5, 1788, Antoine Merlin marries Anne Blaise in Thionville. He's twenty-six, she's thirty-two—an unusual gap in those days, when the tendency was for girls to be married in their teens to men in their middle years. He comes from a line of increasingly prosperous "tradespeople"; his father, Christophe, has just been made a tipstaff and will become an attorney. She is the daughter of the "charitable director of the bourgeois hospital of this town."

She is also blind,[1] having lost her sight recently after a bout of smallpox. She is no stranger to him; they were childhood friends. He loves her, and will love her far beyond the twelve years their marriage will last. Shortly before his own death he speaks of her as though it were only yesterday:[*] "She was well taught and clever. Her voice was quite unusual and cultivated; she sang and accompanied herself very nicely on the guitar and was not

---

*Two Merlins became known during the Revolution. This one is Merlin de Thionville (later a member of the Legislative Assembly, then the Convention and the Five Hundred; also a member of the Committee of General Security and leader of the defense of his hometown in the year II). The other one is Merlin de Douai, far more moderate in his views; after sitting in the Constituent Assembly, the Convention, the Elders, and the Directoire, he becomes a Comte d'Empire. He is known primarily as a jurist. Merlin de Thionville never becomes a follower of Bonaparte.

without ability on the piano. She was tall and graceful, with easy manners, although her sense of her infirmity gave her a somewhat timid quality and she seemed to radiate melancholy. . . . Esteemed and sought after by all, who would not have loved her? The whole town applauded our marriage."

Which puts a full stop to the stormy youth of Antoine Merlin.

He was born on September 13, 1762, in Thionville, the little stronghold on the banks of the Moselle that has been fought over at length by Germans, Spanish and French but was finally won for the latter, a century ago, by the Prince de Condé. During that time the name of Antoine's ancestors was gradually Frenchified. First it was Merlinger, then Merling, and now Merlin.

Antoine is proud of his father, who "did very well in his studies with the Jesuits in Luxembourg; he spoke Latin and German as readily as French." His offspring couldn't wait to follow in his footsteps. "Almost as soon as I could walk, I attended the classes given by a master of arts and secondary school tutor named Manisse, our neighbor on the rue de la Tour." He went to Manisse's school at twelve, and stayed five years. His parents wanted him to join the clergy. In 1779 he entered the Lazarist seminary of Sainte-Anne in Metz. Before he was twenty, he was a "master of arts" in philosophy, at the University of Nancy. The Bishop of Metz, who was the Duc de Montmorency-Laval, thought highly of him; but it was the favor of this prelate that led, quite by accident, to the revulsion that pulls him from the priesthood.

I had just been named to the bishop's choir, and in that capacity I rode in Monseigneur's carriages to Thionville, where he was called to visit a portion of his diocese. We stopped at the château of the Comtesse d'Hunolstein at Hombourg, a village three leagues from Thionville, and thence continued from château to château, visiting almost all the religious houses of both sexes and all the parish priests. This trip did not strengthen my determination to take orders. . . .

After this tour, during the same holiday, I was invited to various village festivities by the parish priests and, among others, attended one at the home of M. Francon of Koenigsmaker; he was the finest-looking man in the county, which has since caused him to be made constitutional bishop of Metz. I went to another organized by Dom Colignon in Valmunster; he was the seigneur who administered both high justice and property, he was the representative of the Abbey of Metlach, he was tithe taker and parish priest. Some mendicant monks and nuns from the convent of Richstroff near Sierk, who were, like me, invited to the Koenigsmaker festival, did not give me a very high idea of monastic piety when I saw them drinking too much, dancing and making merry in the home of the good parish priest, who was a great huntsman, talked very loudly, drank like a German himself and permitted all these orgies. Although I was very much affected by the praise given me for my modest behavior and my learning, these scenes, repeated before my eyes, inflamed my imagination and turned me aside from the path of grace. At Dom Colignon's home in Valmunster, propriety and decency prevailed; I there saw for the first time the Abbé Grégoire, a young parish priest who has since become a bishop and member of the Constituent Assembly and Convention. . . .

I stayed on alone with him [Dom Colignon]. Then his conversation became serious, interesting, even friendly, and above all, novel for me. He looked upon religion as the best law for peoples and kings, because its basis was charity and fraternity its maxim; but he made a distinction between religion and ritual, ceremony and hierarchy, something he saw as needful to keep the people occupied and in their places. The order he wanted was that established by the early missionaries, who had brought the first seeds of civilization to fruition among the Gauls; he held nothing higher or better, for himself as for everyone else. But he did not believe one word of the necessity for a priest to submit inwardly to what is demanded of him as an example to the people in public, because for him the only sins were injustice, want of charity and scandal. He avoided the latter insofar as possible, and was extremely fair and humane in his behavior.

Remaining alone with me, as I have just said, he resumed his customary ways. Two handsome peasant girls, about eighteen or twenty years old, one dark and the other fair, whom I had not noticed before, came to sit at the master's table in the evening. Dom Colignon's teachings had prepared me for this scene, and he did not seem to be aware of the state of my emotions. Full of faith, and yet finding nothing to say to my reason, which had declared itself on the priest's side, I was in an extraordinary state by the time we left for Thionville. Dom Colignon stayed there a few days; my father kept staring at me; he seemed to be wanting me to confide in him. . . . I told him the scandalous scenes of the Capuchin fathers and the sisters from Richstroff; I expressed my indignation to him on that account, but said not a word of the pretty girls at Valmunster.

When Antoine got back to the seminary, he brought with him, "in his head, the tempest that the world outside had aroused in it."

The foundations were laid; all that was needed now was the influence of Henequin, the great childhood friend, the one who leaves a lifelong mark.

No science or art was an obstacle to him. When only seventeen, he had already completed his studies in logic and physics at the professed house of Saint-Lazare in Paris; he had a superb *basso cantante* voice, and although he could not read a single note at first, after three months of lessons he had learned to sight-read. . . . Teachers, superiors, grand vicars, everybody was delighted with him, they forgave him everything, and unfortunately he took advantage of the fact. There were, in the convent of the congregation, two very young sisters, both extremely pretty and witty as well. Victims of necessity, which had despoiled them in order to support their family and military brother, both had taken orders. Henequin, like myself, was in the choir and sometimes, when the bishop came to officiate, he would meet Sister Sainte-Marie alone on his way to fetch some fire. That was enough.

There followed a liaison between Henequin and Madame Sainte-Marie, which lasted nearly a year; she would slip through a cellar window to pass from her cell into the street to meet her lover. They were, inevitably, caught in the act, and an ecclesiastical trial of the two lovers ensued. "She was sentenced to one year of prison on bread and water, and her lover was barred forever from the seminary.*

There was not much chance that Antoine would still want to be a priest now. His features are formed, in a full and rather wrathful face with large eyes, a devil of a mustache framed by a mass of not very neatly arranged black hair.[2]

He would like nothing better than to set his course by poor Henequin's star. "The niece of the parish priest of Manom near Thionville was a boarder in the nearby Madeleines' house, and the good priest had entrusted me with a letter for her. . . . I left the monastery in transports, I could hardly contain my leaping heart; a young lady of seventeen, lovely, witty, and possessed no doubt of every gift and every virtue, had seemed to find me worthy of attention."

Leading to an amorous correspondence "worthy of Héloise's letters to Saint-Preux" . . . and naturally discovered one fine day by the superiors, who sent Merlin to Paris—Saint-Lazare, of course. But he was not the kind to knuckle under. He ran away. He remembered that he had a jolly Carthusian uncle named Dom Effinger, who was the administrator of a monastery at Val Saint-Pierre in Thiérache, a brave, harsh little region on the fringe of Picardy. A solution: neither committal to the Lazarists nor the wild spree in Paris that had momentarily tempted him and would have led him, like Saint-Just at the same period, to jail. He took refuge with the monks under the wing of his kindhearted uncle, who, "after petting and spoiling me to my heart's content, gave me rooms and a servant, with orders that I should want for nothing and be obeyed in everything."

There he spent several months of peace, but also boredom, in a little earthly paradise—for a single person, that is—like hundreds of others that were flourishing in those days. He observed everything and wrote down

---

*Henequin becomes an actor in Nantes, and is assassinated there on his way out of a lively supper party. "Madame de Sainte-Marie" tries to burn herself to death in her cell, and is not released until the Revolution.

quite a lot, including a description of his meals in the refectory, where he was accorded "the signal favor of being allowed to eat with them. In front of each Carthusian was a pewter pint jug full of beer, another of the same size containing ordinary Champagne wine and a sealed bottle of old wine; each was served a slice of sturgeon weighing a good pound, the same amount of river fish, a six-egg omelet, as much fresh bread as he could eat, cheese, and the finest fruit. Each monk, shrouded in his hood, ate in deepest silence without looking at his neighbor. I could not conceive how a man, and especially an inactive one, could consume so much food; yet every monk ate all that he was given."

Merlin was not about to be seduced by the monastic fattening-up process he encountered in that monastery. Especially as he also encountered there a man of quality, the prior Dom Le Noble, who opened his eyes with a few hair-raising confidences:

"Even though, as prior, I can push my freedom to considerable limits, travel comfortably and give orders, until my dying day I shall regret entering into an estate that is fit only for brutes. . . . You will despair when you see yourself mewed up forever within these walls, without books, without conversation, without friends, surrounded by envious and spiteful imbeciles whose sole object will be to keep you from setting foot outside the cloister. . . . So take care you do not become a Carthusian; and if you do not know how to feign, do not even become a priest, because your studies will enlighten you, and then, woe unto you if you are seen to doubt!"

At the end of this sort of truce, he finally reached Paris, in 1781, "in good health, well dressed in a lavender coat, black waistcoat and breeches, my trunk well filled, twenty louis in my pocket, and carrying a small box of toothpicks." Thanks to recommendations from the Carthusians, he was taken in by some Augustinians, but again without nibbling at their bait. He found some temporary jobs as a tutor. One night when his spirits were high, he heartily concurred in the sentiments of an *agent provocateur* at the porte Saint-Martin, and for this he nearly got himself jugged in the Bastille. A policeman was dispatched to take him there in a carriage and he had to make a proper brigand's escape, administering "a vigorous blow between the eyes" to his escort and jumping out the door.

After finding out what it was like to be lonely in Paris, he tried a little touch of the prodigal son. Well-intentioned go-betweens secured him a pardon and a welcome from his father, with whom he made a deal: they would not force him to take orders, but he would become a tipstaff, like Christophe Merlin, and one day, they were sure, an advocate. All was in readiness for his marriage and installation in the Third Estate of Thionville.

DAVID

37

FEBRUARY 1788

I've Lost My Emulation

At the beginning of 1788 David experiences one of those radical contradictions that can deflect a life's trajectory.* Just as he is becoming the most
famous painter in France, a letter reaches him in Paris telling him that Drouais
has died of smallpox in Rome.

Despite his aggressive mien, David has always been vulnerable, and he
tends to dramatize things. In this instance, however, no deeper grief could
come to him. Drouais dies at twenty-three, David is going on forty, and may
well have thought he had only begun a long partnership with his favorite
pupil. There's nothing hollow in the cry he utters when he hears the news:
"I've lost my emulation."[1]

Jacques-Louis David was born on August 30, 1748, in the home of his
parents, "mercer-tradesmen" on the quai de la Mégisserie in Paris.† In those
days a "mercer" was many things: Maurice David, his father, is principally a
wholesale dealer in "construction iron," which is delivered to his doorstep
by the Seine boats. The new fashion for antiquity in building style meant
that architects needed such iron for the columns they were dotting about the
place in new houses, as well as for the strong rafters to hold them together.

He was a painter in his mother's womb. His early life was a straight line,
despite his relative impecuniousness and a few incidents that would have
stopped many another in their tracks, such as his father's death in a duel

---

*David is influential as an artist, of course, but he is also an important member of the
Robespierre and Marat circles at the height of the Revolution. As a member of the Convention,
he sits with the "Mountain." He organizes several great festivals in Paris, in particular the Festival
of the Supreme Being. He has a close call during the Thermidor purge but survives and joins
Bonaparte early enough to be appointed "First Painter" under the Empire.

†He is one of the very few "Parisians from Paris" among the leading figures of the
Revolution.

when Jacques-Louis was only nine. This fortified the rumor that "the Davids are all hotheads."

A shopkeeper fighting a duel? No shopkeeper he; Maurice David had just bought himself an office in the tax administration. It must have involved some trouble over a woman. Before he died, in any event, he had time to give his approval to his son's choice of career. His mother, swathed in her widow's weeds, bears no grudges against fate or the memory of a husband who died too soon, and especially not against Jacques-Louis. In the 1780s, when the crowds are elbowing each other in front of his enormous canvases at the Salon, they find a woman sitting on the floor beneath them, smiling sweetly. His in-laws are also behind him—the master-mason Buron, Desmaisons the architect. The worries of Jacques-Louis as child and boy were not material ones; the only angst he suffered he invented for himself.

As a boarder with the Picpus Fathers he did not care for Latin but got along in it, always being near the top of his class. After his father's death, his uncles put him in the Beauvais school in Paris and then in the very superior Collège des Quatre Nations.* He sat dutifully through his rhetoric classes there but was bored and spent every moment he could sketching. His teacher was an understanding type: "I can plainly see that you will be a better painter than orator."[2]

The ember-eyed youngster with the penetrating intensity of expression could not (and never will be able to) communicate in writing or indeed in speech. His elocution, like his father's, is impeded by thunderously rolling *r*s, and to make matters worse, he has a bony excrescence† that enlarges one cheek and slightly deforms the lower part of his face.

He's not too bothered by it, because he's sure he can say all he wants to with his pencil and brush. There he makes up for everything else. Can his kinship with François Boucher account for his artistic fire?[3] Because of this distant cousinship, the master is able to give him a few helpful nudges at decisive moments, although the two never meet. There are forty years between them, and after Madame de Pompadour's death, Boucher becomes something of a misanthrope. He suffers from his ambivalent situation: he is a decorator of genius who is not given space enough for the great, the real compositions he never manages to produce. He is caught between the age of the painters of Louis XV—so sweet, but so cloying—and the new generation of big, hulking lads who work for museums rather than private dwell-

---

*The Institut has its home there now; the school was founded by Mazarin to provide an inexpensive education for gifted pupils from the "four Nations," or provinces newly conquered by France: Alsace, Roussillon, Flanders, and the *"territoire de Pignerol."*

†Caused by a nasty wound received during practice in a fencing hall.

ings and who mean to paint history and heroism, not shepherdesses and gallantries.

When David was allowed to earn his living doing what he loved, a page was turned in French painting: *exeunt* Watteau, Chardin and Boucher. With the new wave, which one might call back-to-antiquity, beginners were encouraged to dip their brushes in the springs of a history strictly shackled to the tracks of the Roman roads, as described by their teachers: Seneca, Pliny, Livy and the ruins of Pompeii, and don't try to tell us any different. It was high time for Boucher to die.

But he was still top man when he got his little cousin the recommendations that started him on his way. He even asked for, and obtained, a favor for him, thanks to d'Angiviller (brother-in-law of the Marquise de Pompadour), who was director of the royal buildings: an apartment in the Louvre, which the kings had given over to approved artists in the last few decades, and which the artists had transformed into a caravanserai in the heart of Paris,* displaying their paintings in disheveled rows all the way up to the vaults.

David finally found his way into the class of the indispensable mentor: Joseph-Marie Vien, this one was called; no great genius except as a teacher, where his even-tempered kindliness made him the best.

Under him Jacques-Louis undergoes a rough ten-year apprenticeship. The "French manner" and the "Antique manner" were fighting it out inside him. For a long time, he thought he was on Boucher's side. Vien, meanwhile, was exhorting his students to follow the Roman muse, whom David found too chilly: "The Antique style will not attract me, it lacks spirit, it doesn't stir."[4]

For ten long years the two traded punches inside him, and his nerves showed the strain beneath his outward appearance as a strongly built young man with short hair. At an early age he had everything he needed for success with the ladies except a voice, but he didn't seem to worry about them. Vien's influence kept him away from the *Escarpolette* or the *Verrou tiré* and led him instead, unwillingly, toward *Le combat de Mars et Minerve lorsque Vénus vient au secours de son amant†* or *Diane et Apollon perçant de leurs flèches les enfants de Niobé.* He'd have preferred to honor the young beauties of his day but was being forced to fill vast acres of canvas with enraged old men, draped and moaning women with eyes raised heavenward, and only one consolation—a major one, it is true, for his temperament—which was to give pride of place to the third component of his painting: beautiful, fierce, undraped

---

*The future Madame Roland went to visit Greuze there; see Volume II.

†First topic assigned to David for a prize, or at least a medal, at the competition of Rome to which beginners submitted their canvases. In 1987 the painting is in the Louvre.

young men with sword or spear in hand, painted from "the naked model,"
an innovation in artists' ateliers. Beginning in the 1770s, this "naked model"
proclaims the revenge of the mature, often brutal male over the little masters
and effeminate shepherds of the past. Commissions were for war, no longer
for pleasure. One could hear a rumble of chariot wheels in the background
of these highly posed, and composed, confrontations and solemnities. All
the up-and-coming painters were beginning to fancy themselves military
stategists.

Perhaps these great, elaborate machines had little appeal for David, or
perhaps he simply didn't have enough experience; in any event, his early
paintings swim before an almost sepulchral black background, and sometimes
he gets the proportions wrong. At twenty-two he fancied himself on the road
to the big prizes, but Vien was careful not to give him too much encour-
agement, and although there was a risk that he might despair in the present,
it was doing him a favor for the future. At first, all David won was trinkets,
and he swung pendulumlike from the exaltation of having mastered his trade
to the thwarted self-conceit of a budding prizewinner. At one point he nearly
came unstuck:

"I was excited by the challenge,* so I made superhuman and, alas! vain
efforts to succeed. The time had not yet come. I became acquainted early,
to my cost, with the face of human injustice. . . . I painted my picture [based
on a passage from Ovid's *Metamorphoses*]. . . . I was not fully satisfied by
anything I did, so I would start again, not thinking that a fresh color, when
laid on top of paint that has not had time to dry, could change. This is what
happened during the months before the works were judged."[5]

And this explains the funereal obscurity of his canvas, which costs him
the prize. He heard the news at his uncle's, in Paris, and managed to keep
his chin up during dinner; but afterward . . .

I retired, still with the outward appearance of the most tranquil indifference,
but when I was free at last and alone with myself, I made ready to carry out my
plan of letting myself die of hunger. [More an appeal than a suicide, thus,
especially in a robust youth of twenty-one.] As will readily be believed, I had
quite lost my appetite, which made it all the easier for me, and so it was the
next day too. The following day I began to weaken; two and a half days had
passed when, hearing my sighs, some people who lived in the same house went
to alert M. Sedaine, our landlord.† He knocked at the door, no answer, knocked

---

*According to the *Notes* found among David's papers in Brussels at his death, in 1825,
on which he may have based his *Mémoires*. With the passing years, they have acquired a patina
of humor, in which their author was singularly wanting at the time he wrote them.

†This was pending his move into the Louvre. Michel-Jean Sedaine (1719–1797) was a
generation older than David; he started out life apprenticed to a stonecutter and, after a detour

again, still less answer [*sic*], although he was told that I was certainly within.

What did this good and delicate man do then? [Sedaine was a kindhearted fellow and prided himself on being a sort of second father to the overgrown baby lost on the frontiers of his art.] He went to fetch the painter Doyen, his friend and one of the judges,* and told him what had happened and what he feared.

Doyen, who was then working on his ceiling in the Invalides, quickly left his scaffolding. They both came to knock at my door again, but as I did not answer:

"What's this!" said Doyen loudly. "Sedaine has been telling me about your state; you're not making sense, my friend. When a man paints a picture like yours, he ought to consider himself happier than those who won the prizes. They'd be only too glad to change places with you."

Jacques-Louis needed words like that more than a glass of rum.

Those comforting words, spoken by a man whose ability I respected, a man who was my judge, made me drag myself to the door and open it. Then it was good to see them. That is an image that will never leave my head; one of them holding me under the arms as I sat on a chair, while the other put on one of my hose, then the other. In the end they got me completely dressed and made me eat and drink, a little at a time, until they finally took me away with them to dispel my morbid thoughts. Just imagine the neighbor women, when I was restored to life!

He won his coveted first prize in 1774, when the new king was just twenty, for *Antiochus, fils de Seleucus, roi de Syrie, malade de l'amour qu'il avait conçu pour Stratonice, sa belle-mère; Erasistrate† découvre la cause de son mal.*

"Ah, my friends! For the first time in four years, I can breathe."[6]

Nevertheless, he continued to hesitate between the two "manners." What he needed, having never breathed any air but that of the Seine, was a long period of initiation in Italy. Vien was appointed director of the French Academy in Rome and took David and a few other pupils along, to discover that "Antique" painting was more than theatrical scenes set in conventional landscapes. The beauty of Rome in those days was wonderful, and ephemeral;

---

via architecture, helped on a bit by David's uncles, ended up a man of letters. He wrote *Le Philosophe sans le savoir* [in English, *The Duel*] and established a new dramatic genre, the "bourgeois" prose play, in which his friend Denis Diderot far excelled him. He also worked on a *Richard, Coeur de Lion* for which another friend of theirs, the composer Grétry, wrote a tune that quickly became a hit, *"Ô Richard, ô mon roi, l'univers t'abandonne."* This subsequently became a sort of Royalists' *"Marseillaise."*

*Who had wanted to give David the prize.

†A famous physician of antiquity, grandson of Aristotle.

it was the Rome of Piranesi's engravings, where Hubert Robert, Soufflot, the Vernet brothers and other masters of tomorrow found a new inspiration, as David did, in an almost dreamlike blend of greenery and ruins; cows were grazing under the crumbling walls of the Colosseum.

The definite shift from one "manner" to the other took place still farther south, in Naples, thanks to a scholar named Vivant-Denon, who was the French consul there and was himself making a transition from diplomacy to art.

There David also met Quatremère, a rich antique dealer and former sculptor in Pigalle's studio who subsequently turned archaeologist and became a disciple of the German Winckelmann.* "In Naples, Quatremère rubbed the sand from my eyes"; when he returned to Rome, David said he had been "operated upon for cataract."[7]

After 1780, David was in full possession of his style, his expanded spaces, his pictorial doctrine, and the pupil proved greater than his master. At the same time, as a sideline to his huge and elaborate "machines," he started painting some of the most expressive portraits of the age. At the crossroads of his art in Naples, he also crossed the path of Count Stanislaw Potocki, the gilded young Pole on his "Grand Tour."† David immortalized him sitting firmly astride a snorting steed, one muscular leg sheathed in the fine cloth of his pale breeches beneath a wide-sleeved, flaring blouse, hair curled, keen-eyed and wide-awake, with a little of the La Fayette air about him that was being aped by young aristocrats just then.

Potocki's portrait gives many other gentlemen a desire to have their pictures painted by David. But that means putting up with his whims and his unavailability, for he will never be satisfied with a career as portrait painter, and always sacrifices that side of his work to the event of the moment.

More intrigued by the creative mission he has just invented for himself, David still needs the opening years of the decade to establish his reputation as the "still-life stage director" of the Graeco-Roman world.

Further travels; he returns from Rome before his time is up, having had more than his fill of Italy and needing to feel himself back in the midst of

*Winckelmann died in 1768, after serving as the prophet of neoclassical aesthetics. Some of his disciples carried on from him in Europe. The close association between Antoine-Chrysostome Quatremère de Quincy (1755–1849) and David was a great help in launching the painter, but does not withstand the heat of the Revolution. Their paths diverge; Quatremère is a member of the Legislative Assembly, but on the Royalist benches, and is imprisoned during the Terror. They come together again later, though, as supporters of the Empire.

†Shortly before Potocki's adventures in Holland at the time of the Prussian invasion, which has been reconstructed in chap. 28 above. David's portrait of him is in the Warsaw museum.

things, which means Paris. There, although no longer a believer, he turns out a flawless life-size crucifixion and a *Saint Roch priant la Vierge de guérir les pestiférés.**

In 1782, he moves into the Louvre for good, officially opens his teaching atelier under the auspices of the Academy of Painting, and contracts an arranged marriage with the daughter of some sound Parisian burghers, Marguerite-Charlotte Pécoul (he is thirty-three and she seventeen), by whom he has two boys, in 1783 and 1784, apparently without taking much notice of them. His wife's parents, on the other hand, are relatively immortalized by him in a pair of portraits painted in 1784. "M. Pécoul,† his shoulders weighed down by a life of hard work, smiles benignly out at the son-in-law he has won. The fleshy hands are carefully observed and the brush grows bolder only when drawing the ripple of the edge of the waistcoat. Madame Pécoul may have had a thousand good points but distinction had not fallen to her lot; from under her diamond drop earrings, her pearl choker, her big satin bow, her lace mobcap and fichu and her Valenciennes ruffles, emerge hands accustomed to performing household chores."[8]

Far more important, in David's eyes, is another trip to Rome in 1784, like a last, refreshing pause before achieving glory. The moment he turns his back on the city, he wants to return, but this time it is almost a regal procession, far different from his student pilgrimage. He has just been accepted into the Academy of Painting, he is a master, like Vien ten years before, he is traveling with a little group of his very own pupils, among whom he has singled out a shy, willful, moody lad, a mirror image of his own youth, and so much his imitator that his influence, in the *Marius à Minturnae* that Jean-Germain Drouais has just completed, will surely inaugurate an unending series, as everybody supposes, of scenes "in the manner of —"; one might call it the first copy of the new school. At Minturnae the aged but redoubtable Marius, toppled from power by the wicked Roman rebels, is visited by a soldier, sword in hand, with orders to execute him; but the great loser, almost naked among the folds of his toga, so intimidates his executioner that he covers his face and cannot perform the deed.

In Drouais's new-fledged brushes David thought he saw fate granting him an even closer heir than his own children. For two years, his strongest

---

*Commissioned by the aldermen of Marseilles for the Lazaret chapel to commemorate the famous plague of 1720, during which the long-observed worship of the legendary Saint Roch, miraculous sufferer from the plague in the fourteenth century, very noticeably declined. David nearly caused a scandal when he used a splendid male nude as the model for his Christ.

†According to d'Angiviller, "one of the most honest and intelligent contractors in His Majesty's Buildings"; Pécoul furnished David's rooms in the Louvre.

emotional bond has been with Drouais, even though he leaves him in Rome for this last trip to Paris, after reaping his rewards for the three most important works of his maturity: early in 1788, David receives every praise and prize imaginable for his *Belisarius,* his *Socrates* and his *Horatii.* No one tells better than Drouais himself the shiver that goes through his pupils, his little brothers, *his* own. "M. David completed his painting a fortnight ago. No expression can equal its beauty; to my mind, it can be given no higher praise than to say that it equals the three great, capital masters;* it has been acclaimed and pointed out by everyone in Rome. Italians, English, Germans, Russians, Swedes, who knows what else; every nation envies the good fortune of France in possessing such a man."[9]

David's troubled soul has no time to savor these panegyrics. For two years Drouais has been writing to him from Rome, dutifully submitting his every effort for approval and reminding him of the faithfulness of a more than filial affection. "Whenever it will please you, think to write to me [on August 10, 1787]. Make me cross; spur and brand me beneath the belly."[10]

Just as David is finishing his *Socrates,* a letter, dated February 6, 1788, comes from Ménageot, the director of the school in Rome, informing him that Drouais has smallpox:

> His illness began with a putrid fever and the delirium of the first stages. He was bled twice in the arm and once in the foot, which quieted his mind and relieved him greatly. The next day, which was a Monday, the eruption began and is continuing abundantly. Thus far the pox, which is confluent, has shown no signs of producing complications. He is in as good a state as his condition can permit; his head is very clear and the delirium has ceased entirely.
>
> The doctor considers it most fortunate that he was able to bleed him at the outset of his illness. He says the fever was such that it would never have been possible to gain control of it otherwise and forestall inflammation in the subsequent stages of the disease.
>
> Although there have been no complications thus far, and our doctor, who seems to be a wise man, is not worried, I have decided upon a further consultation and shall do my best to get M. Salcetti, the Pope's first physician and most renowned doctor in Italy, to come and see him.

But on February 13, 1788, Drouais dies. David, his sensibility pierced to the core, is left forever after as though orphaned by that child.

To take the edge off his despair, there is the prospect of other study trips. Soon he will hurry off to Flanders on the trail of the great painters there, and he will find another distraction in the rumble that is beginning to shake its way through the kingdom, even into its artists' ateliers.

---

*Raphael, Michelangelo, Poussin.

38

FEBRUARY 1788

He Took the Whole Habitable Globe for His Fatherland

The year 1788 is a leap year. Jacques-Pierre Brissot marks his February 29 with a seemingly modest deed, the aftermath of which can be foreseen by no one at the time.

"On February 29, 1788, I founded the Société des Amis des Noirs."[1] It happens in a commonplace salon on the Right Bank, on the rue Française between the porte Saint-Denis and the rue Montorgueil. Here, Brissot has temporarily laid down his publicist's pack, between three trips to London, two months in the Bastille, a quick jaunt to Holland at the time of the uprising, and a few short runs to Boulogne to collect the saving pennies of his dear mother-in-law, Madame Dupont.*

Perhaps a pause is in order; and he may have tried to take one by doing some odd jobs for the Duc d'Orléans, in whose home his wife serves as governess to the little princesses; but Brissot is soon bored with a vague role as "secretary in the chancellery"; he doesn't have the right temperament for service, either to this great lord or any other. What this son of the sausage maker of Chartres wants, this scribbler who has Anglicized the name of his native hamlet, transforming himself from Jacques-Pierre Brissot of Ouarville, as they called it in Beauce, into Brissot de Warville, is action.

Until February 1788 he's never been more than a hack, a pen for hire. Founding the Amis des Noirs moves him one step up toward politics.

It's not much, and it might have been nothing at all, in France anyway, where the condition of the Negroes in America and the mechanisms of their

---

*In the last volume we left Brissot in the throes of his already complex travels and writing the inspired text in which he defended, not without peril to himself, the Wallachians of Transylvania, who were being persecuted by the Hungarian lords with the blessing of Emperor Joseph II. This pioneer championing of the underdog earned him the ill will of Marie Antoinette. The rue Française still exists, the name being a deformation of that of François I, who had it cut near the Cour des Miracles.

"trade," meaning their deportation from Africa, remain unknown, not only to the public at large but to most of the more enlightened minds as well. A vast genocide has been going on for decades, to the benefit of ever more numerous French, bringing them the poor man's sugar and coffee as well as the sumptuous fabrics and pet pickaninnies of their fair ladies.

The readers of Volume XI of the *Encyclopédie*,[2] for instance, were informed that "the excessive heat in the torrid zone, the difference of diet, and the white man's low resistance and minimal endurance make it impossible for him to perform hard work in these climates and survive, so the lands in America occupied by Europeans would be lying fallow today without the help of the Negroes who are brought there from almost every part of Guinea [the generic term for the whole coast of West Africa]. These Black men, born vigorous and used to crude eating, find more clement conditions in America, making their physical existence much easier there than in their original countries. . . .

"Masters who have acquired large numbers of slaves are obliged to have them taught the Catholic religion. It was for this reason that Louis XIII decided to permit the trade in human flesh."*

People learned to put up with it. Thus sanctified, their rising fortunes justify it all. "Negroes are the chief asset of the inhabitants of the Isles. Whoever has a dozen of them may consider himself rich. As they multiply freely in hot countries, their masters, provided they treat them gently, gradually see the increase in these families, in which slavery is hereditary." The writer conceals all but a glint of nostalgia for the good old days when this compulsory manpower was less costly. "An Indian Negro unit (as they are called) between the ages of seventeen or eighteen and thirty, used to cost no more than thirty or thirty-two livres' worth of goods from the purchasing countries, namely liquor, iron, cloth, paper etc.;† but since the Europeans have been outbidding one another, so to speak, these barbarians [the African slave merchants] have made the most of their jealousies, and good Negroes can seldom be found nowadays for sixty livres, some Companies having paid as much as one hundred livres apiece."

This is the type of situation, like that of the Wallachians in Transylvania or the Natifs in Geneva,‡ that fires the tinder of Brissot's indignation. He's

---

*The author of the *Encyclopédie* entry seems a little uneasy here. Never mind. The practice of "the ebony trade" among the three worlds has been described in the passage on the *Zong* scandal in Volume II; this, in 1782, was the starting point for the great antislavery movement begun by a handful of English.

†Slaves were seldom paid for in cash; barter was the basis of the trade.

‡See Volume III for the quelling of the Geneva revolt by Vergennes and the French troops; Brissot was an eyewitness.

thirty-four now, his brow is rising under his black hair and over the big and often flashing eyes on either side of his aquiline nose. He is still the spontaneous advocate of lost causes. He met and wedded that of the Negroes in London, through his contacts with a few hotheaded young men of fiery eloquence, Englishmen, Whigs—even Tories, some of them—the followers of William Pitt, Wilberforce or Priestley, who, by virtue of their Bible-based religious feeling, are a good generation ahead of the French. They've infected Brissot with their antislavery virus and he has brought it over the Channel, a germ of one of the many epidemics being sown in France by Anglophilia.

In the shop of a progressive bookseller on Lombard Street, Jacques-Pierre made friends with a young pastor, Thomas Clarkson,* who has recently won a prize at Cambridge for an essay entitled "Is it just to make men slaves against their will?"[3] Thanks to it, the author became known in both worlds within months.

Clarkson is one of the leading abolitionists and devotes the rest of his life to the struggle. His keen gaze produces a lively picture of Jacques-Pierre at the time when Brissot is beginning to lead the efforts on behalf of the blacks in his own country:

"Brissot was a man of common and modest appearance. In his family he set an amiable example as father and as husband. On all occasions he has been a faithful friend. He was particularly attentive to his private life. Because of the simplicity of his dress and severity of his morals he was known as 'the Quaker' in the circles he frequented. He was charitable to the poor, within the limits of his meager income. But his benevolence extended beyond the ordinary bounds. He was not a patriot in the accepted sense of the word. He took the whole habitable globe for his fatherland, and wished to regard every stranger as a brother."[4]

On March 19, after founding, with a few of his cronies, the French Société as a branch of the English one, Brissot, in high spirits over this new adventure, gives an account of it to James Philips, the bookseller friend who introduced him to Clarkson:†

I have already had the honor to send you the particulars of our first assembly.[5] . . . The committee meets regularly every week and keeps a record of its

---

*Thomas Clarkson outlives the turbulence of the century and all the other pioneer abolitionists as well. On June 16, 1840, on the eve of abolitionist victory, the great Convention of London gives the old fighter a triumphant reception.

†The statutes of the French Société, vague enough to avoid charges of subversiveness, are a catalog of good intentions rather than concrete measures. Based on those of its English counterpart, they were deposited in the archives of the Institut, where they are to this day, along with a list of 107 members, representing the high point of its existence.

transactions. We thought we ought first to elaborate upon the object of our assembly. This point was necessary for the edification of the public; we did so in a speech that has been printed in a publication entitled *Analyse des papiers anglais.** . . .

We have no doubt that there are in France, in the highest nobility as well as among the clergy, men who will hasten to subscribe to the object of this Société; but we did not consider it fitting to inform them of it before we had tested the ground on which we trod, and foreseen the way in which the Société's foundation would be viewed by the government.

We did think, however, that we might depart from this circumspection in regard to three persons, who are distinguished either by their reputation, their position or their birth. The Marquis de La Fayette is one of them. As soon as the project to found the Société was formed, I personally hastened, in the company of M. Clavière, to apprise him of it. . . . M. de La Fayette answered us, expressing his satisfaction and confidence in our success. . . . At an appointment he gave me today, he told M. Clavière and myself that he considered himself one of our Société's members and spoke to us of the measures he had taken and would take, either in connection with the government or other persons of repute, to encourage them to join us; judging by his undertakings, we must trust that our Société will grow steadily stronger, through the accession of distinguished persons.

During this year of abeyance, La Fayette is promising a lot to those who seek his patronage; owing to his ostracism from the Court, they're less numerous.

In passing, but not otherwise, because there will never be any real intimacy between Brissot the commoner and the great aristocrat from Auvergne, La Fayette becomes one of the most illustrious of the members who meet, irregularly, on the rue Française or in the home of Clavière, the Swiss financier who was exiled after the Geneva uprising and the liberality of whose ideas, and patronage as well, is equaled only by the size of his fortune.†

Having failed to found a minirepublic for the Geneva outcasts in Ireland, he has settled temporarily in Paris and is suffering from a shortage of noble causes to defend. The abolition of the slave trade is right up his alley, and he and Brissot are its protagonists. After La Fayette, there will be Mirabeau, on the lookout for opportunities to show himself; then Talleyrand, but from a distance; Lubersac, the bishop of Chartres, and his grand vicar Sieyès; a young lawyer, also from Chartres, named Pétion; two of the four Lameth

---

*The periodical was launched in London by Mirabeau, who, like Brissot, has been writing for it often in recent months—both of them anonymously.

†Brissot does not forget his friends: during his brief period of influence, he gets Clavière appointed minister of finance in the last moments of the reign of Louis XVI and the opening days of the Republic. Both are brought down in the fall of the Girondins.

brothers; and Jean-Louis Carra, a pamphleteer of republican leanings and an eventful destiny—shuttling from a very poor childhood in Burgundy to the hospodar in Moldavia and then to the service of the Cardinal de Rohan, then to another prelate, Brienne, who has just found him a job in the King's Library in return for a few articles against Calonne.*

Carra has a knack for writing, especially writing with a political slant, and has just translated Clarkson's text for the Société, shamelessly amputating at least forty pages in the process because his somewhat aggressive atheism is discommoded by the author's Christian allusions. Brissot, forced to put up with his companion's moods but not approving his methods, observes that "what remained [of the essay] was enough for the Negroes' cause and the author's reputation."[6] This is not the first time, nor will it be the last, however, that the ebullient Carra has made complications for Brissot. For example, he causes the premature departure of Mirabeau, "who was loyal to us so long as we were useful to him [according to Brissot] and even resigned himself . . . to spending time in the company of people he did not like and listening to arguments and rebuttals that his superiority caused him to endure with scant patience. There was one person above all who seemed to make it a duty to provoke him, and that was Carra; I remember a very sharp note Mirabeau wrote to me against him one day, when I had entreated him to vote for Carra to replace me as secretary of the Société."[7]

Because in March Brissot begins to make preparations to accomplish one of his dreams—a trip to America—and although he was the ideal person to give birth to the Société, he is not the type to tie himself to any administrative job for very long. Failing Carra, he is now in search of somebody else to take his place, and Mirabeau suggests Valady.

"Through his father, Jacques-Godefroy-Charles-Sébastien-François-Xavier-Jean-Joseph d'Yzarn de Freissinet, Marquis de Valady, belonged to one of the oldest families of Rouergue, praiseworthy also for its services and alliances, which, toward the end of the eighteenth century, combined the prestige of high birth with the advantage of great fortune. His mother was of the house of Jurquet de Monjesieu, firmly rooted on the frontier of Rouergue and Gévaudan. The infant's cradle† would seem to have been laden with rich privilege and lasting hopes"[8] (according to one of his biographers, who, like so many others writing about so many others, has succumbed to the temptation of hagiography).

---

*We will meet Pétion again as mayor of Paris in 1792, and Carra among the rioters on August 10; and both of them among the Girondins.

†He goes by the name of Xavier. Born September 23, 1766, in the diocese of Mende, he is a delegate to the Convention, votes against the King's death, is proscribed with the Girondin leaders and executed at Périgueux in December 1793.

Valady may have been blessed by the fairies, but he was soon scratching at the walls of an invasive family and a "good" marriage (to a girl named Vaudreuil) contracted so precociously that the newlyweds (aged sixteen and eleven) were separated the day after the ceremony to await a deferred consummation of their union. Shunted into the traditional military career of eldest sons, he became an officer in the French Guards and deserted at twenty to go on a wild spree in London, where some friends barely managed to prevent him from sailing for America and, with some difficulty, contrived to make his peace with the military authorities in the form of a series of furloughs, ostensibly granted for ill health. A fresh escape followed, this time to Geneva, where he became an ardent disciple of Rousseau and whence he returned a fervent vegetarian. "I would gladly sacrifice my life on this abandoned planet rather than taint myself by feeding on the flesh of animals that have been removed from earth, air or water."[9]

People were both troubled and fascinated by this kind of waywardness, which indicated some degree of psychological disturbance in his case. His penchant for defiance drove him to the Amis des Noirs because, "under cover of the emancipation of colored people, the group's real aim was a revision of the entire social structure."[10] Early in 1788 he writes to Brissot, making fun of his own noble title: "Xavier d'Izarn otherwise known, by usage and vanity, as the Marquis de Valady."[11]

By the time he is twenty-two, he has acquired a few fans. One of them, Aubert de Vitry, expresses his bedazzlement thus: "One cannot imagine how prodigious, how truly magical was his speech. . . . Never had we experienced the enchantment, the astonishment he awoke in us. It really was a divine gift. Whenever he improvised, and the flow of his emotions incited him to do so often, ideas, facts, images, all clothed in the most splendid and at the same time most elegant elocution, poured out with equal volubility. . . . After listening to him one day, Bernardin de Saint-Pierre, who was very fond of him, exclaimed, 'You are Orpheus come back to life, to inspire people by the charm of words.' "[12]

His gift of eloquence won him Mirabeau's affection, but Brissot is not so blind as to imagine he possesses the qualities of a good secretary: "Valady was not enough in the habit of writing, and there was an air of inconsequentiality about him that made it impossible to give him this office."[13]

For instance, he has just fluffed badly by trying to forcibly co-opt as a member Bernardin de Saint-Pierre—the man who published *Paul et Virginie* a few months ago and who, thanks to its roaring success, is becoming a lion at fifty.

Jacques-Henri Bernardin de Saint-Pierre has been a traveler, by land and by sea, in Poland, Russia, the islands of the Indian Ocean, and Île-de-

France* in particular, and his ability as a writer has long been apparent, especially in his descriptions of tropical settings. Inclined to misanthropy, an uncomfortable companion, he had affinities with Rousseau and became attached to him in the last years of Rousseau's life. In addition to his series *Les éloges de la nature,* he has now composed a little novel, melodious of prose and sickly sweet of sentiment, in which he conceives the character of an author who is the exact opposite to himself. In 1788, *Paul et Virginie* brings him instant celebrity. Fresh editions are coming out as fast as the presses can produce them, people are plagiarizing him, operas are soon to be inspired by this eclogue on the exotic and absurdly chaste love of young Paul and his Virginie, who prefers to die in a shipwreck a few arms' lengths from shore under her beloved's eyes rather than remove the wet clothing that is dragging her under and expose her naked self. Many readers find in this tale a teary counterpart to their own libertine morals. *Paul et Virginie* is the conscience cleanser of the practitioners of *Les Liaisons dangereuses* and the amateurs of Restif de la Bretonne. And it's all money in the pocket of Bernardin de Saint-Pierre, himself amazed by his good fortune, who is circumspectly setting out to husband the product of his notoriety.† There is precious little chance of him becoming a member of the Amis des Noirs.

From Bernardin de Saint-Pierre to Brissot, in late April: "M. de Valady proposed me, against my will, for membership in the Société for the abolition of the slave trade. It is impossible for me to accept this honor for several reasons, some of which I explained to him. Chief among them are my distance from the center of Paris,‡ my predilection for solitude, and above all my poor health, which does not permit of my attendance at any gathering in a closed place. I am a member of the human race, which includes among its interests those of the Negroes and many others; I want no more; nonetheless, I shall wish very particularly for the success of your Société, to which I contributed in writing some time ago."[14]

Bernardin de Saint-Pierre has already paid his dues, thank you very much.

Another refusal comes from Marie-Jean Hérault de Séchelles, who, still under thirty, has been one of the three "King's advocates" in the Paris *Parlement* since 1785; this is one of the most important offices in the magistrature.§ Brissot suspects him of declining out of cowardice and a fear of

*Which became Mauritius in 1815.
†He dies in 1814, rich and as widely read as ever.
‡He lived on the rue de la Reine Blanche, which still exists, near the Gobelins.
§We met him visiting Buffon in October 1784, in Volume IV.

endangering his eminence. The result is a skirmish between the two that ruins their relationship forever:

> Hérault de Séchelles, who was heart and soul in the *Parlement* at that time, refused to become a member [of the Société.]. He told me he was infinitely touched by my proposing it to him and that it would be a happy occasion for him to hear the eternal rights of mankind discussed in an assembly that honors it, by men noted for their genius and attainments. But he confessed with genuine regret that his position would scarcely allow him to join associations that the *Parlement* had not yet authorized. Moreover, he added, seeking to justify his reluctance, if a case of this type should arise, he would find himself ineligible to defend in public that very liberty at which he should too hastily have conspired. Hérault, thus, wished only to keep abreast of our work from afar.
>
> All I told him in reply was that the *Parlement* could not prevent any of its members from taking part in a Société commanded by natural law, the work of which was dictated by humanity.[15]

Less richly endowed than Hérault, but better known to the general public through his writing and his recent polemics against Beaumarchais, Nicolas Bergasse is hardly more cooperative: "He promised his energy and efforts but . . . withdrew soon after joining. As haughty as Mirabeau, with pretensions no less ambitious, and fancying himself as much an eagle, they could not long agree. They quarreled, and Bergasse, foolishly vexed, left first."[16]

Among the disappointments, two other celebrities dash Brissot's hopes: Jefferson and Brienne.

From the outset he tried to enlist the most glorious of the Founding Fathers of the young American republic, who had taken over from Franklin as its ambassador to France. The Parisians supposed that Jefferson had more influence in both worlds than he actually did at the time. It was natural that Brissot would approach him as a possible member, but he should have remembered that a "reserved position" was an obligation for the ambassador of a nation in which slavery was so widely practiced.

From Jefferson to Brissot, undated but written early in 1788:

> Sir, I am very sensible of the honor you propose to me of becoming a member of the society for the abolition of the slave trade. You know that nobody wishes more ardently to see not only the abolition of trade but of the condition of slavery; and certainly nobody will be more willing to encounter every sacrifice for that object. But the influence and information of the friends to this proposition in France will be far above the need of my association. I am here as a public servant; and those whom I serve having never yet been able to give their voices against this practice, it is decent for me to avoid too public a demonstration

of my wishes to see it abolished. Without serving the cause here, it might render me less capable to serve it beyond the water. I trust you will be sensible of the prudence of those motives, therefore, that govern my conduct on this occasion, and be assured of my wishes for the success of your undertaking and the sentiments of esteem and respect with which I have the honor [etc.].[17]

Brienne's reaction to a premature approach from La Fayette is more serious, because it condemns the Société, as was predictable, to remain unsupported, on high, in France. Like Valady in his dealings with Bernardin de Saint-Pierre, La Fayette had imagined that his backing at the close of the Assembly of Notables, when the Archbishop was about to take Calonne's place, would be worth a favorable response. He asked for a hearing, but Brienne turned him down flat. This did not come as a surprise to Brissot:

La Fayette saw the minister and informed him of the founding of the Société, its membership, its purpose [which was primarily] to publish English works printed on the subject; he told him that the subscription about to commence was intended to cover the necessary expenses. Brienne pretended, in his presence, to be pained by the slave trade and Negro slavery; he desired more than anyone, he said, that it might be possible to find a means of abolishing both without damaging the interests of the planters; a Société that should be formed with a view to finding such means must be able to count upon the protection of the government, but care must be taken to establish that it is in the interest of both planters and tax office to replace slave work by free work and, in general, the Société must be most prudent and circumspect in its meetings, approaches and writings. . . . All of this was pure Court talk, and La Fayette knew it as well as I.[18]

The King's minister would appear to have been more severe than his king, if we are to believe a remark attributed a little later to Louis XVI, in response to a courtier who had interests in the Isles and was complaining to him about the Amis des Noirs: "So those poor Negroes have friends in France? I am very glad for them."[19]

Solace comes, month by month, in the form of a handful of new members who are not to be sneezed at: the authors Sébastien Mercier, Volney, Raynal;* the physician Lanthenas and his friend Bosc d'Antic, both regular

---

*The philosopher Volney (1757–1820) became known in 1787 through the publication of his *Voyage en Égypte et en Syrie.* Later, as a member of the Constituent Assembly, and then with the Idéologues in opposition to Napoleon, he achieves some literary notoriety with a work containing antireligious overtones, *Les Ruines.* Abbé Raynal is a "lip-service" member;[20] after seven years of self-imposed banishment following the publication and condemnation of his *Histoire des Deux Indes,* he is not anxious to jeopardize his imminent return to France.

correspondents of a couple of notables living outside Lyons: Inspector of Manufactures Jean-Marie Roland and his wife, who's feeling a trifle bored out there, despite the pleasing novelty, for a true-born Parisian, of life in the country. From Manon Roland to Lanthenas and Bosc,* in November 1788: "What is happening with the Société for the emancipation of the Negroes?"[21]

More important, Condorcet joins, and his membership is likely to smooth over a number of difficulties. In him Brissot finds the "president-secretary" he has been looking for, a man whose prestige and commitment will enable Brissot to set out for the United States in peace.†

Installed in the Mint by Turgot, whose *La vie* he has recently published, Condorcet has not awaited the Société to support the cause of the Negroes; back in 1781, writing under the Germanic pseudonym of Joachim Schwartz [= "black" in German] and using Neufchâtel, Switzerland, as the fictitious place of publication, he issued some *Réflexions sur l'esclavage des nègres,* a revised edition of which is about to be published in Paris, in 1788, again under a pseudonym.[22] The powerful boost from this inspired if somewhat ponderous pen adds life to the Société's first productions. Without it, for all Brissot's good intentions, there was a definite lack of style.

Turgot's memory is invoked in a voluminous note more than four pages long, in which Condorcet attributes abolitionist aspirations to him "when death had not yet deprived France, Europe and the world of the one man, perhaps, of whom it could be said that his life was necessary to mankind."

Not without repetition and circumlocution, nearly two-thirds of the essay is taken up with meticulous plans relating to "the means of doing away with Negro servitude" and, until that becomes a reality, "the means of rendering their slavery less harsh." These are the titles of chapters in which the author attempts to propose transitional measures and not look like a daydreamer agitating to burn down an established system, thereby imperiling the economic balance of the colonies. Another chapter in the work, tending to the same end, is called "Farming After the Destruction of Slavery," and there is also a long "Reply to Some Arguments Put Forward by Its Adherents."§

*She sometimes wrote to both young men together. I looked at Madame Roland's youth in Volume I and described her problematic marriage in Volume II.

†See the passage on Condorcet's marriage above.

§At the end of the reign of Louis XVI an attempt is made, by some members of the Constituent Assembly, to enact the first abolition laws. There is a fierce battle with the proslavery faction, and Condorcet's arguments provide the basis for their opponents' position.

Condorcet—or Joachim Schwartz at least—does, however, venture to shoot some of polemics' sharpest arrows at the slavers:

> The interests of power and national wealth must give way before the rights of a single human being; otherwise, there is no difference between a regulated society and a band of thieves.

> The arguments of politicals who believe that Negro slaves are necessary all come down, in the end, to saying, *Whites are greedy, drunken and ignoble; therefore Negroes must be slaves.*

> Inquire of any tyrant; they will always give, as excuse for their crimes, the vices of those they are oppressing, even though those vices be, in every instance, the fruit of their own efforts.

> It is the incontinence, avarice and cruelty of the Europeans that are depopulating habitations; as when Negresses are prostituted so that what they have earned may then be stolen from them; when they are compelled, by dint of barbarous treatment, to give themselves to their master or to his lackeys; when the Blacks they are suspected of preferring to their tyrants are torn apart before their eyes; when greed overloads the Negroes with work and blows, and the necessities are refused them; when they see their comrades put to the question or burned alive in ovens in order to hide the traces of their murder, then they desert or take poison; the women abort themselves. . . . It is so untrue that the Negro population is unable to recruit itself on its own that the traces of runaway Negroes can be found who sustain themselves in forests and surrounded by boulders, although their masters amuse themselves by chasing them like wild animals and boast of having killed a runaway Negro, as in Europe they swell with pride at having killed a fallow deer or roe deer from behind.

> There can be left, to a man who engages in the Negro slave trade, no scrap of feeling, nor any virtue, nor even any honesty.

Brissot can depart for the Americas on May 10 with his mind at ease. He is leaving his newborn Société in the hands of a lion.

39

APRIL 24, 1788

Laudable Courage Displayed Facing the Enemy

Joseph Poniatowski was born on May 7, 1763, in his parents' palace in Vienna.* He was a child of the imperial capital, where he spent the years of his youth before returning to his roots in Poland, and what roots! His father, Andrey Poniatowski, was starost of Ryki, that is, a nobleman who owned an estate in Poland given him by the Crown, which crown his older brother, Stanislaw August, was to receive, by virtue of a fictitious vote of the Diet, through the favor of Catherine II.

Joseph is a very model of the great Central European aristocrats, an ethnic tangle of heredities. He is part Lithuanian, through his paternal grandmother, a Czartoryska; and from his mother, née Rofranco, he inherited a mixture of Czech and Italian blood. His father had enlisted his sword in the services of Frederick, Catherine, and, latterly, Maria Theresa, all of whom heaped promotions upon him—colonel, inspector of infantry, prince of the Holy Empire—before his death, still a young man, of pneumonia.

Having lost his father when he was ten, the son was brought up by a rather trying mother. "An embittered valetudinarian, fleeing society, tender and morose by turns, she would smother her only child in fervent caresses and overwhelm him with affection."[1] Like many persons of high lineage, Andrey Poniatowski's widow was intimately acquainted with money problems, her assets being far inferior to her titles; but the uncle, who was king of Poland, proved a good surrogate father. He engaged three tutors at once, a German, a Frenchman and an Englishman, for "his dear little Pepi," as he

---

*Most of his biographers mistakenly have him born in Warsaw because of his Polish ancestry and destiny. He is first in the employ of Austria, then of Napoleon's Poland, rebaptized Grand Duchy of Warsaw, and even becomes minister of war of that half-nation before entering the service of France. When he is drowned on October 19, 1813, trying to cross the Elster on horseback at the end of the battle of Leipzig, Napoleon had just made him a marshal of the Empire. One of Paris's belt roads, known as the marshals' boulevards, is named for him.

called his nephew, and signed over the income from huge tracts of land in Poland to him. Since Stanislaw August himself was growing old without glory, humiliated by his impossible role as lifeguard to a Poland that, as a sort of prefect crowned by Catherine the Great, he ruled but did not govern, he transferred the dreams and ideals of his youth to his nephew Joseph.

Upon emerging from his bicephalous childhood, divided between Austria and Poland, the young man found himself, at fourteen, in the service of the Hapsburgs. In 1777 he was presented to the future Joseph II while on maneuvers in Bohemia.* There was no shortage of good fairies protecting his early years.

His military career? A shooting star. In February 1780 he was second lieutenant in the second regiment of heavy cavalry under the "honorary" command of Grand Duke Francis, Maria Theresa's grandson, who was even younger than himself.† That same year Joseph, then seventeen, represented his uncle, the King, at the Empress's funeral.

1781: deputy major; January 1782: major, before his twentieth birthday, of two cavalry squadrons.‡ September 1784: regimental adjutant, in other words, the first officer to be called upon to assist or replace a regiment's colonel, and very often its effective chief while in barracks.

January 1785: lieutenant colonel, second in command of a regiment of light horse comprising three or four hundred uhlans, most of them recruited in Galicia. Poles, at last! February 1786: lieutenant colonel of the same, but this time first in command, or in other words a colonel in everything except name. He was given the same rank and post again, in October 1786, but in the most envied unit of Europe, as lieutenant colonel of light horse in the regiment that belonged to Joseph II himself. He had become "the Emperor's military projection."

Does this mean that in 1788 Poniatowski is essentially a military creature? By no means. A fatherless adolescence, punctuated by irregular contacts with a difficult mother, had injected a large dose of Polish melancholy into his personality, which is visible enough in his manners to make him highly interesting to noble young ladies. What more moving sight, for them, than a soldier who is "admirably built, sanguine, quick, frank in his ways, and often exuberant in his mood" but who is also, at bottom, "sensitive and nervous. His excessively impressionable character, tending to complicate

---

*For the "two-headed" monarchy of Maria Theresa and her son Joseph II, see Volume I.

†This nephew of Marie Antoinette becomes emperor of Austria from 1792 to 1835, under the name of Francis II.

‡The squadron is the basic cavalry unit, like the infantry battalion. There were about one hundred mounted men in each squadron.

things and see only their darker side, made him a frequent prey to moral depressions."[2]

Slender, keen, in that beautiful white uniform that adds so much to the stature of the Austrian officers, he soon became the pet of Viennese high society, where he was operating on a different field of maneuvers, one in which a Vienna liberated by the death of Maria Theresa was beginning to look like Paris during the Regency. He founded a circle of friends, the "Indissolubles," of which the Prince de Ligne, that pan-European Belgian, seems to have been the other chief instigator. As in certain island tribes, the Indissolubles consisted essentially of one man surrounded by many females, but what females! Princess Jablonowska, Princess von Lichtenstein, Countess Lichnowsky, Princess Kinsky, Countess Kinsky-Dietrichstein . . . At the opening of this ball of love and war, in which the young warriors of the new generation were unable to distinguish between comedy, tragedy and buffoonery, Joseph met a child-woman named Caroline de Thun, six years his junior, and she became the object of his first passion, which marked him all the more deeply in that the relationship was purely platonic.

"People said he danced well and read even better";[3] sometimes, what he reads is Shakespeare, and he's also starting to sing Mozart. "He had quite a gift for music and played the harpsichord very nicely, usually selecting pieces that were easy, agreeable and not at all sophisticated." His high rank entitles him to a tent of his own, and on his very first campaign he has a spinet installed, which follows him to every one of his battlefields.[4]

Music doesn't always soothe his savage breast. He had to fight two or three "courtesy duels" with his playmates. These "formalities of honor" were carefully stage-managed by seconds and blood was seldom drawn, not even by the traditional slash on the face; such events commonly terminated in a supper party. But Poniatowski had to win his honorary first-class swordsman's stripes.

What else, before 1788? His first peril, on maneuvers, when he made a foolish bet that he could cross the Elbe in state on a heavily laden horse. He survived. According to subsequent accounts, a Gypsy woman was passing by; but there's no way of knowing whether the prediction she is said to have muttered belongs to the realm of myth or reality: *"Der Elbe Herr bist du geworden, doch eine Elster wird dich morden."*[5]*

His first wound: a nasty fracture of the leg, falling off a horse during a practice charge. Three months in his room, not long enough to keep him from joining his uncle, the King, in Warsaw in February 1787. Great and mysterious things were toward in the East, where there was to be a meeting

*"Of Elbe you're now the master proud, in Elster shall you find your shroud."

of sovereigns.* Catherine and Joseph II were to meet in Kiev, in the course of the Tsarina's great progress. The energies of Austria and Russia were being gathered together for grandiose objectives: the Emperor's was the conquest of the Balkans; that of the Empress, Constantinople.

The two supersovereigns had condescendingly invited Poland to the proceedings, as one might ask the local squire in for dessert. Stanislaw August did not want to turn up too soon in Kiev and have to sit there twiddling his thumbs, so he sent his nephew on before him, and the nephew reeled from his first contact with the luxurious society of the Ségurs, Nassaus, Lignes, Damases and other titled cosmopolites who formed Catherine's personal rainbow. She gave him her blessing without further ado:

"Why, he's absolutely delightful, this young prince, he reminds me of his uncle the King"—as she turned to Cobentzl, the Austrian ambassador—"but as he was when I first knew him, all of twenty years ago."[6]

All of twenty-eight years ago, if the truth were told; and the current meeting of the two old lovers was lugubrious. She had become the stout babushka of Russia; Stanislaw August bore all the stigmata of age, dissipation and foundered ambition. He had hoped for at least one hour alone with her to discuss Poland's most urgent problems; she never saw him unattended, and forced him to suffer the constant presence of her favorite of the moment, the dainty Mamonov.

Then war, too; one of the bitterest of the age for the men floundering through the mud, swept away in the rivers and seas; it wrenches Poniatowski out of the whirlwind of Court life. Sultan Abdul Hamid, driven to fear and then to wrath by the increasing military pressure and Austro-Russian demonstrations on his frontiers, resigns himself to a fresh bout of fighting, all the more readily as the Turks have failed to digest the Russian occupation of the Crimea four years before. He imagines that his revenge is ripe; and his two great foes have done all they could to keep him imagining so.

And yet the outcome is not a foregone conclusion for Austria and Russia. Both have been weakened by famine and sporadic revolts and by conflicts of nationalities at home. They cannot count on anyone except themselves: England and Prussia are backing Turkey, although only with words, because neither can do any more, one being prevented by the aftermath of the war in America and the other by the reconquest of Holland. Most Christian France is traditionally friendly to the Moslems of Asia, but the utmost extent of her support of Constantinople is the dispatch of military advisers and engineers. As for Sweden in the north, Gustavus III would like nothing

---

*See the description of Catherine's trip in the chapters on Miranda in this volume.

better than an excuse to attack Petersburg with an eye to the acquisition of Finland, for which Stockholm still has a hankering. Abdul Hamid issues an ultimatum at the end of 1787, commanding Russia to restore the Tauridus to him. Bulgakov, the ambassador, flatly refuses. To punish him, and as a symbol of his declaration of war, the Sultan shuts him up in the Castle of the Seven Towers. Catherine II and Joseph II have gone too far to go back. The die is cast, the eastern side of Europe is about to boil.

Throughout the winter of 1787 and spring of 1788, the war machinery rolls ponderously into place on two widely separated squares of the board: in Russia, north of the Black Sea, where Catherine, long since returned to St. Petersburg, gives her beloved Potemkin a free rein and plenty of soldiers, but no equipment, to face the Turks, who are excellent fighters but hardly better equipped with arms and supplies; while in the Balkans, to the west of the Black Sea, the Austrian empire musters its heterogeneous armies, hoping to compel the enemy to relinquish the Carpathians and Serbia (then still known as Servia, the land of slaves), followed by the Moslem protectorates of Christian Wallachia and Moldavia.* Bucharest: what a morsel that would be for the Hapsburgs! To make the dream come true, they're going to have to overrun seventy inhospitable leagues of mountains and plains. And before that, seize Belgrade, the capital of Serbia on the Danube. But a dozen leagues still farther west, on the Sava, stands the stronghold of Sabac, its thick walls and enormous cannons making it look like a medieval fortress; and this outpost is defended by a corps of the military elite, Aga Mehemed's janissaries. The kind to stand and be killed on the spot.†

The troops from Vienna lay siege to it for several weeks, and Joseph II sends one of his own aides-de-camp along to pep them up; somehow, the lock has to be blown off that door. This newly promoted aide-de-camp is Joseph Poniatowski, whose career has just been crowned by another step up in the month of his twenty-fifth birthday. He might have taken the easy way out and hung around in the background at the imperial headquarters, but he insists on commanding an assault column against the citadel on the morning of April 24. Not a tea party. Heavy fire from the assailants, who succeed in occupying the lines of the first enceinte; furious defense from Turkish artillery case-shot. Several eyewitnesses notice, and some of them disapprovingly, "the mad bravura" of the young prince. He crosses the trench; followed by a handful of men, he reaches the foot of the parapet, and there receives a

---

*In 1859, these two provinces are united to form the bulk of modern Romania. In Volume IV we saw, in conjunction with Brissot's pamphlet, that Wallachia was in a state of larval insurrection against the aristocrats.

†The janissaries were part of the sultan's guard, and the *agas* were its officers.

fragment of shell in the thigh. He falls from his horse; a violent hemorrhage; for a few moments he and everybody else thinks he's a goner.

A common soldier, a Croatian named Koerner, hoists him onto his back and carries him to shelter.* He is laid on a makeshift stretcher and transferred to the hospital at Semlin; his friend the Prince de Ligne, protean in war as in peace, comes running and makes sure that the surgeons do not cut off his leg. It is months before he can walk at all and he limps forever after.

In November 1788 Joseph II names him colonel and proprietor of his own light horse, "in recognition of services rendered to Us and Our House, in reward for the laudable courage displayed facing the enemy."[7]

MOZART

40

APRIL–MAY 1788

Viva la libertà!

Like a cloud from afar, the war drifts over the Vienna sky and floats lazily away again.

The Viennese have never been bellicose and have paid scant heed to the clash of arms, especially as they had not been directly threatened by them since that time the Turks surged against their city walls and were beaten back by Jan Sobieski's Poles almost a thousand years after Poitiers.†

In January 1788 Mozart, whose fame has solidified since the success of *The Marriage of Figaro*,‡ composes an *allegro contredanse* for two violins, cello, two clarinets, bassoon and trumpet entitled *The Battle*. How pretty it makes the war, what a lilting air! When the *Journal de Vienne* speaks of the piece, it calls it *The Siege of Belgrade*. The last section is a "Turkish March" ending with a snappy drum roll.

---

*Poniatowski takes Koerner on as his batman for the rest of his life.

†In 1683. That was the beginning of the Turkish decline in eastern Europe, which has continued ever since.

‡In Vienna, April–May 1786. See Volume IV.

Two months later his *German War Song* reaches a graver register, as though the news of increasingly arduous fighting were darkening the cloud over Vienna. In this piece violins, flute, oboe, bassoon, horns, cymbals and even a bass drum accompany a short patriotic text by Gleim, interpreted by a fashionable singer named Frederick Baumann. On March 19, the same *Journal de Vienne* announces the "new *War Song of a German Soldier* by Kapellmeister Mozart, in the service of HM the Emperor, on sale from Lausch, Kartnerstrasse, in Vienna."[1]

Trifles, in an ever-richer opus, now that he is setting to work on his three greatest symphonies and composing, as if for fun, his *B minor Adagio* for pianoforte (dated March 19), "which shows Mozart's very temperament in the raw, one might say."[2]

He's now thirty. His wife and he are back in Vienna after a series of trips to Prague, where *Marriage* was so well received that the Opera of the great Bohemian city commissioned another lyric work, which has also just been premiered there.

Those trips to Prague in 1787 are Mozart's last happy travels. Surrounded by friends, adulated by a musical public different from the Viennese, Mozart hears "the music of *Figaro* arranged into goodly contredanses. . . . Because here, *Figaro* is all anybody talks about. People play, hum, sing and whistle nothing but the arias from *Figaro*. The only opera that draws the crowds is *Figaro* and *Figaro* again. This is assuredly a great honor for me."[3]

He later says that he composed *Don Giovanni* for the people of Prague and one or two other friends.[4]

Even though he doesn't speak their language and is not of their culture, the Czechs love this man, this composer-hireling of the Emperor and those German princes who are taking up their positions, and filling every position, in Bohemia as in all the other lands of the empire these years, to the detriment of the native populations. With the advent of Joseph II, the country's Germanization had become systematic. Resisting in the only area possible, namely culture, Counts Nostitz and Rineck, a couple of Czech aristocrats who are also fervent nationalists, have just built an exquisite blue and gold theater in Prague. They're also notorious Freemasons, whose Lodge communicates regularly with the Lodge of La Bienfaisance in Vienna, with which Mozart is affiliated.[5]

The Mozart family is not having an easy time of it. Even the performances of *Figaro* and *Don Giovanni* have not been able to plug more than two or three holes in the leaky bucket of his debts. What good has it done him to be given, on December 7, 1787, the title of "Composer to the Imperial and Royal Chamber"? Until then it had been held by the great Christoph Gluck, but he died on November 15, to the sorrow of his former pupil Marie

Antoinette in Versailles.* Gluck was being paid two thousand florins in emoluments; Mozart will get only eight hundred. "Too much for the services I render, too little for those I am capable of rendering."[6]

His only other resources come from a small percentage on the sale of tickets to his operas, as most of the box office take goes to the cast, musicians and staff; and he also works "on commission" for any nobles who, with the Emperor's permission, care to ask him to compose occasional pieces for their entertainments. The purse strings are tightly drawn in the modest dwelling that Constance and Wolfgang Amadeus have just rented on the Landstrasse.[7]

Here, torn by the conflicting pressures of his creative power and his nagging financial worries, a preoccupied Mozart is visited by a sixteen-year-old musician named Ludwig van Beethoven, second organist to the prince-archbishop of Cologne, who has come to express his ardent admiration. Emerging from an unhappy childhood dominated by an alcoholic father and a tubercular mother,† Beethoven has none of the attributes of the young prodigy that Mozart was at his age. He's attempting to complete his musical education so that he can develop the gifts that some of his protectors in his hometown of Bonn think they see in him.

It is hard to imagine those exchanges between the two men in April 1787. An intimidated Beethoven plays a few of his pieces on the piano. Mozart has no recollection of the occasion in later years; Beethoven does, but remembers it as a disappointment,[8] and it remains a lasting sorrow that his god played nothing for him.

On May 28, 1787, Leopold Mozart dies in Salzburg after a month of illness. Notified the next day, Wolfgang Amadeus writes to a friend, "Coming home today, I received the sad news of the death of my excellent father. You can picture the state I am in."[9] This event wipes out ten years of misunderstanding resulting from Leopold's cantankerous old age and the inevitable jealousy of a respectable musician confronted with a son whom he has turned into a genius only to see him wriggle out of his grasp.

In the radiant days of his early blossoming, Mozart used to dream of putting his father in a glass jar, the better to preserve him: "First after God comes Papa!" Then, after his mother's death in Paris and his rejection by Aloysia Weber,‡ there had been a seesaw of quarrels and reconciliations, especially at the time of the son's "consolation" marriage to the sister of the faithless Aloysia. Leopold had made it possible for Wolfgang Amadeus to move to Salzburg and prosper there, despite the arrogance and inconsistency

---

*Almost as soon as she mounted the throne, she had called Gluck to Paris to promote his three best-known operas, *Orphée aux Enfers* and the two *Iphigenias*. See Volume I.

†She dies on July 17, 1787, soon after this disappointing encounter.

‡See Volumes II and IV.

of his "protector," the Prince-Archbishop Colloredo. The last row between the two Mozarts dated from the son's break with this petty tyrant, which Leopold had not understood; he wanted his son to give way, as he had done himself throughout his life. The success of *Marriage* had patched things up, however. The dead man's earthly goods and chattels are shared without acrimony, by exchange of letters, between Wolfgang and his sister Nannerl, whom he never sees again.

One Mozart dies, another is born, in late December 1787—little Theresa.

But Mozart's true offspring, that winter, is *Don Giovanni, or The Libertine Punished.*

He knew he had one more great opera buffa to write; and despite his strong resolve to compose in German, he was still seduced by the fluency in which the Italian language clothed his musical intuitions. There were passages in *The Marriage of Figaro*, two years before, that were already hovering on the verge of tragedy, but the peculiarly Italian relationship to life and death that Da Ponte expressed so well enabled the characters in that opera—even Cherubin—to cling to the edge of the abyss without falling off.

Also, the choice of Italian as the language of the libretto was more than a mark of respect for a convention of the European lyric theater; using Italian meant "siding with and supporting the Czech nationalists; it meant refusing German, which was the compulsory language of administration and instruction. . . . Mozart and Da Ponte were thus joining forces in a sort of passive resistance.* . . .

"In the autumn of 1787, three words in Da Ponte's libretto did not fall on deaf ears. They were *Viva la libertà,* and they are heard six times in Act I, Scene 5, while the dancers and masks are circling on stage."[10]

And then, as though he were incorporating a secret signature into a coded message, Mozart introduces a certain instrument into the orchestra, to accompany the peasant Zerlina's aria *Batti, batti, o bel Masetto!*—an instrument enthusiastically listened to by the music lovers of Prague but little used elsewhere: the violin.[11]

To strike another great blow in the Empire's fairest theaters, Mozart chooses a subject that is much in the minds of his contemporaries because of the intimate mingling of libertinism and war that is creeping over Enlightened Europe; although the idea may actually have first been mentioned by Lorenzo Da Ponte.

The sprightly Abbé needs no introduction; everybody is chasing after his libretti and not just because of *Figaro:* his swift wit and easy pen have won universal attention.

*According to Philippe Olivier.

In 1787 he is being inundated by proposals from composers of every description; and the Emperor in person, who finds his company diverting, tells him which to accept:

> "Da Ponte, you must write for Mozart, Martini* and Salieri." . . . The three masters gave me the opportunity to do just that, by coming to ask me for a libretto all at the same time. I was equally fond of all three of them and esteemed them equally as well. . . . I asked myself whether it would be possible to satisfy them all, to write three stories at once. Salieri was not asking for something original. In Paris, he had written the music for *Tarare* and wanted Italian words fitted to it. . . . Mozart and Martini, on the other hand, left the choice of subject to me. I decided that *Don Giovanni* should go to the former, who was delighted with the idea, and the *Tree of Diana†* to Martini, as a mythological subject befitting his talents. . . .
>
> I sat down at my table and remained there for twelve hours on end, with a bottle of excellent Tokay wine on my right, my writing desk in front of me and a pouch filled with tobacco from Seville on my left. A young and lovely creature of sixteen lived with her mother in my house; whenever I rang, she would come into my room to perform whatever little domestic tasks I required. . . . I should have preferred to love her only as a daughter, but . . . And so, for two months, I worked away for twelve solid hours a day, interrupted only by a few brief distractions.[12]

Da Ponte's distractions aren't as brief as all that: "This girl, who breathed softly, smiled graciously and occasionally seemed ready to melt into tears, was my Calliope for all three operas and, in fact, for all the verse I wrote over a period of six years."[13]

The fact that Da Ponte unashamedly loots another *Don Juan* (by Bertati), which had been produced a little earlier in Rome and had been such a success that Goethe went out of his way to see it on his Italian tour, makes it all the easier for him to finish his libretto at top speed. Goethe said, about the version plagiarized by Da Ponte, "the craze was such that the whole city, down to the most modest shopkeepers' families, parents and children alike, had taken over the lower-level seats and balconies, unable to live another day without seeing Don Juan burning in hell and the Commandant's soul wafted heavenward."[14]

What of it? Mozart uses the raw material cobbled together by Da Ponte to reach, in two months, "the exact point of incandescence that would leave a mark upon his age."[15] Through the voices of Don Juan the cynic, the

---

*Vicente Martin y Soler, aka Martini (1754–1806). They were the three composers most in vogue in Vienna at that time.

†Despite a brief moment of success, the text of the *Tree of Diana,* based on a fable by Tasso, is lacking Da Ponte's usual humor.

trembling valet Leporello, one or two initially charmed and subsequently enraged women, the father of one of the women (the Commandant) and the fiancé of the other, this comedy of love tears apart like a net curtain to reveal the seducer's implacable hunt, leading, after the Commandant is killed by Don Juan in a duel, into a whirlwind of vengeance from beyond the grave that sucks the seducer into eternal damnation.

La ci darem la mano . . . Viva la libertà . . . Love, libertinism and death intertwine until the final punishment of a character who is guilty of a liberty that has no goal but to slake his own pride. But Mozart's Don Juan, developing the little foretaste given in the *Dom Juan* of Molière* (who was made to pay so dearly for it by hypocrites and Jesuits), eschews the supreme punishment of repentance. He falls into the abyss with a fearful shriek, but shards of laughter cling to it like strips of flesh. God and the devil, the Commandant's ghost, the outraged women and jealous lovers may inflict death and martyrdom upon him, but the culprit will have none of his guilt. He will not collude with his judges or executioners by denying himself, even if he is no longer boasting. Don Juan is his own man, to the end.

Somewhere between Prague and Vienna, between 1787 and 1788, a new breed is born: the Provocateur.

Leporello, at the end of Act I:

But there's no want of guts in
    him,
No confusion, no hesitation;
Earth can quake, sky can fall,
Nothing frightens him at all.

"The hand that kills Don Juan is not made of stone.† I can readily believe in the legendary bravado, the mad laughter of a healthy man defying a god who does not exist. But I believe even more that on that evening when Don Juan was waiting in Anna's house, the Commandant did not come, and that, once midnight had struck, what the unbeliever must have felt is the galling bitterness of those who are right."[16]

The inspired, innocent and cunning author of a work as insolent as this is not expecting to be covered in flowers and flattery once he leaves his beloved fans in Prague. But *Don Giovanni* has to be shown to Vienna some-

---

*DOM JUAN: I believe that two and two make four, Sganarelle, and that four and four make eight.

    SGANARELLE: And a fine credo that is! If I understand you aright, then, arithmetic is your religion? [Molière, *Dom Juan*, III, i.]

    †According to Albert Camus.

day; and it is, on May 7, 1788, in the National Theater. A few of the roles are taken by the same people who sang in *Marriage,* and Mozart himself conducts; but Joseph II is not there, having gone to do battle with the Turks, and undoubtedly feeling relieved not to have to give an immediate opinion of such a very unconventional work:

"The Emperor sent for me and, with all manner of kind expressions and praise, made me a present of one hundred zecchinos and told me [Da Ponte, that is] he could not wait to see *Don Giovanni.*"[17]

He adds, "The work was duly produced and, must I say it, I did not like *Don Giovanni* in the least! Everybody except Mozart felt there was something lacking in it."[18]

There are ten more performances, spread over a year, and Joseph II attends one of the last of them; he is dubious, and none of the performances is a success.

" 'This is no dish for the teeth of my Viennese,' he said, after some words of mild praise. When the imperial *mot* was repeated to Mozart, the composer retorted, unruffled, 'We must give them time to chew it.' "[19]

In any event, "with those performances of *Don Juan* in Vienna, the mask of the artist accursed, cast out of society, was permanently affixed to Mozart's face."[20]

But on May 9, after the second performance, Joseph Haydn, the top arbiter of German music, who is now at the height of his glory, speaks up loud and clear in Prince Razumovsky's salon, in front of a large audience:

"I cannot settle the point one way or the other; all I know is that Mozart is the greatest composer in the world today."[21]

ARREST OF GOISLARD
AND D'EPRÉMESNIL

41

MAY 3–5, 1788

An Aristocracy of Magistrates

On November 19, 1787, at the end of the royal session, the Duc d'Orléans had dared to defy Louis XVI in public. The King's swift and decisive reaction, the very next day, seemed to score a point for the government in power. The Prince's (relative) exile to his Villers-Cotterêts estate, the arrest of Sabathier de Cabre and Fréteau de Saint-Just, and the compulsory endorsement, on November 21, of the edicts that had been disputed two days earlier left public opinion in a state of shock. The Treasury's five-year plan could get under way; the Edict of Toleration of "non-Catholics" was to be promulgated at last. For a few days, many people thought France was calming down.

But time was pressing. In December, a game of puss-in-the-corner began between Court, government, the *parlements* and the "Orléans party."

The King, proud of having put his foot down, went back to hunting and swilling. As far as work was concerned, he continued to trust Brienne and the ministers, convinced that things would now go as they should. His immediate circle, purged of the disruptive cousin, was coming out with ever more conservative opinions. Marie Antoinette's ideas were no longer a secret. "What distresses me greatly," she wrote to Joseph II on November 23, 1787, "is that the King has announced that he will hold the Estates General within five years. There is on this matter so widespread an effervescence that it was thought the King must forestall any direct demands, and that by making himself master of time he could prevent the calamities of these assemblies." She had contributed greatly to the punishments meted out on November 20: "I am sorry that a show of strength has been necessary. Unfortunately, it was so, and I hope it will have full effect."[1]

For the court, thus, order is restored; not even the Comte de Provence is heard to utter discordant noises.

Orléans? At first, the Prince did no more than bemoan his isolation and the restrictions imposed upon his visitors by the government. To him, the beautiful forest of Villers-Cotterêts, where he could hunt to his heart's content and display his customary physical courage by rescuing a groom who had fallen into the water, was a sort of Siberia. But he seemed to have given up all thought of public opposition.

The government? It had time to catch its breath. The first of the five loans ordered in November was fully subscribed in a few days and brought the Treasury 120 million livres.[2] One or two men of letters, as influential and dissimilar as the Abbé Morellet and Condorcet, had given Brienne their support.* The Abbé was even indulging in a spot of mudslinging: "We begin to see our way around the abyss into which the imprudence and unbelievable irresponsibility of M. de Calonne had cast us,"[3] while Condorcet was preparing to publish two pamphlets, in the summer of 1788, in support of an

---

*Even though, as we saw at the beginning of this volume, Condorcet had ties with Fréteau; for Abbé Morellet, see *inter alia* Volume I.

idea that he saw as a development of some of Turgot's intentions: *Lettres d'un citoyen des États-Unis à un Français sur les affaires présentes* and *Sentiments d'un républicain sur les Assemblées provinciales et les États Généraux.*[4] But this republican, possibly the only man in France who dared to call himself by that name at the time, publishes his writings anonymously.

As soon as they recover from the November trauma, the *parlements,* on the other hand, gradually reopen hostilities.

In December, some signs of "*parlement* anarchy" are visible in the provinces, where the courts of justice, siding with the one in Paris, are defying not only royal authority but other established powers as well. In Toulouse they refuse to register the taxes requested by the Estates of Languedoc; in Rennes they refuse the taxes in Brittany; and in Metz they refuse those for the entire region of the Three Bishoprics. In many parts of the country, the setting up of provincial and municipal assemblies is being impeded by the *parlements'* perversity:

> Several provinces continued without the benefits of a provincial assembly because a court of justice had forbidden them to have one and because a gift from the King to the people had been intercepted by their judges. *Parlements* wrote to one another to embolden their resistance; some wrote to the sovereign to say they would not obey him and to insist that he convene the Estates General at once. They would agree among themselves on one point and contradict each other on another. A commanding officer representing the King would enter one of the courts to have an edict endorsed and the membership would disappear in a body, leaving the officer alone with the registrar and first *président.* Once the law was registered and the officer gone, the members would hurry back to declare the endorsement null and void. The roads were covered with large deputations from the *parlements* on their way to Versailles to see their decisions struck out by the King's hand. They would then go back to their towns and fill a fresh page with a new decision yet more defiant than the one that had just been annulled.[5]

December 8: the Paris *Parlement* sends four delegates to the King bearing their *Représentations* on behalf of the men who had been punished:

"We make bold to demand that M. le Duc d'Orléans and the two banished councillors, who have been imprisoned by undeliberate* orders contrary to Your Majesty's feelings and interests alike, should either be tried and sentenced or released."[6]

Louis XVI tells the delegates to go fly a kite: "I shall inform my *Parlement* of my intentions."[7]

---

*In keeping with the conventional language of understatement, this should be read "orders extorted from a good king by bad ministers."

And in his own good time. On December 27 the royal response, written by Lamoignon, blends hauteur and goodwill. On one hand, "my *Parlement* must not solicit from my justice what it must expect only from my benevolence," but on the other, the "benevolence" will be forthcoming only if his *Parlement* behaves itself.[8] The results of the first loan having been satisfactory, it looks as though the quarrel might be patched up fairly easily, under pressure from the people dealing in finances. D'Eprémesnil is on the conciliating swing of his mood cycle and would be glad to lend a hand. But Brienne, increasingly unwell,[9] is keeping to his room and devoting what little strength he has left to a study of the assets of the very rich archbishopric of Sens, which he has just offered himself upon the death of its previous incumbent, and doesn't spare a backward glance for Toulouse, where he hasn't set foot for ages.

The group known as "the American faction" in the *Parlement* have not abandoned the fight, and show their teeth on January 4, 1788.

That day Duport makes another assault upon the breach. He speaks eloquently in support of a motion against *lettres des cachet,* proposing that they be declared nothing less than "invalid, illegal and contrary to public and natural law." While they're at it, the members of the *Parlement* calmly vote "that the monarchy is degenerating into despotism, so true it is that the ministers, misusing the King's authority, have been disposing of persons by means of *lettres de cachet.*"[10]

Another tantrum from Louis XVI. Another summons of a group of magistrates to Versailles, with their record books, in which the sovereign has the impertinent vote struck out. The delegation withdraws, angry but still obedient, walking backward according to custom. Old Séguier gives one of his colleagues an opening for a *bon mot:*

"The King's response is not so harsh as one might have feared," he says beneath his breath, before being scandalized by a snort of laughter and resounding comment from Hérault de Séchelles, parodying the medieval fabliaux:

"Oh, good Lord, Yes! Long live our good King Louis!"[11]

Spring is coming, but the system that Brienne hoped to set up is still snowbound. Louis XVI's provincial assemblies are to remain in the memory of France as the embryo of a reasonable but insufficient first step, although some of the best men of the day tried to help them along, hoping to use them as a springboard to national prominence for themselves.

For instance: Talleyrand at Châlons-sur-Marne, the Lameth brothers in Picardy, the Comte de Noailles and Intendant Bertier de Sauvigny in Paris, Sieyès, Rochambeau and Lavoisier in Orléans, La Fayette and Advocate Cothon* in Auvergne, the Duc de Coigny in Caen, the Marquis de Custine

---

*In the year II Cothon is, along with Saint-Just, one of Robespierre's closest companions.

in Nancy, forge-master Dietrich in Strasbourg, the Comte de Narbonne in Besançon, the advocates Barnave and Mounier and Claude Perier the industrialist in Grenoble, the Maréchal de Castries in Languedoc, the writer Chamfort in Burgundy, the jurist Merlin (de Douai) in Flanders, and the inevitable Mirabeau in Aix-en-Provence.[12] Things are starting to move in France, but only behind the *parlements'* barrier.

The government's inconsequentiality is met by an opposing thrust from the "avant-garde" nobles and men of power in the middle class. A series of skirmishes heats the Court's temper to flashpoint.

March 11: The Paris *Parlement,* reverting to the dispute of the previous winter, serves up its remonstrations once again: "Several quite flagrant occurrences prove that the nation, more enlightened as to its true interests, even in the least elevated classes, is disposed to receive the greatest good a king can give his subjects, liberty."[13]

Rejected by the King on March 16.

April 11: The *Parlement* tries again, even scratching the Queen, for the first time, by indirect allusion: "Such means are not in Your Majesty's heart. Such examples are not in your principles; they come from another source."

April 27: Louis XVI manages to get a little hotter under the collar: "If the totality of my courts [of justice] were to force my will, the monarchy would become nothing but an aristocracy of magistrates, contrary to the nation's rights and interests no less than to those of the sovereignty."[14]

April 29: the *Parlement* lashes out impulsively: "No, Sire, no aristocracy in France, but no despotism either."[15] A twenty-seven-year-old councillor in the Chamber of Appeals takes advantage of the occasion to suggest a means whereby landowners could oppose payment of the "second twentieth" tax. He convinces his colleagues that "any landowner is entitled to grant subsidies, either in his own person or through his representatives." Goislard de Montsabert wins the popularity contest in Paris that day.

Brienne's mind is made up: the magistrates' fit of the sulks has to be brought to an end by something more decisive than banishment; for instance, by replacing all the *parlements* in the kingdom with a plenary court of registration copied after the one Maupeou installed in the last years of Louis XV.

All the officers representing the King and all the provincial intendants were ordered to betake themselves to their several places, there to await instructions that all would receive the same day, and to carry them out without deviating by one hairsbreadth. In Versailles, sentries were seen stationed at the door and by every window of the royal presses. None of the workers employed within were allowed to leave; they slept in the workshop and their food was brought in to them from outside. A bed of justice was announced for the very near future, and as being very high and solemn. There was talk of redeeming both royal authority and the people's interest, of cutting off the root of all these insurrections among the *parlements* at one blow. Uncertainty and anxiety were rife among the foremost classes of society and were felt most keenly by the magistrates.[16]

Meanwhile, partly as a propitiatory gesture and partly out of lassitude, the two magistrates arrested on November 20 are released from prison and the Duc d'Orléans is allowed to return to Paris to resume his habitual daily, and nightly, routine. D'Eprémesnil, alarmed by the preparations going forward at Court, bribes a printer's wife and then the printer himself, who throws the texts of the new edicts out the printshop window, hidden in a lump of clay.[17]

May 3: the instant the edicts are in his hands, d'Eprémesnil hurries to the First *Président* to demand an immediate meeting of the *Parlement* and denounce the coup being organized against it.

Duval d'Eprémesnil is forty-two. Short, chubby, sharp-witted, bilious in complexion and disposition, irritable, "with expressive features, a wrinkled brow, intense eyes, a high voice and given to dramatic gestures . . . , ever ready to take the floor and capable of speaking for hours without tiring,"[18] he now confirms the reputation as an orator that he has earned from his colleagues, notwithstanding the serpentine course he has pursued and the ragbag of his contradictions. There's no consistency in his ideas. At twenty, as an advocate at the Châtelet, he became noted for his defense of the India Company, in which his uncle, Duval de Leyrit, the governor of Pondicherry, and his father, who was the son-in-law of Dupleix and governor of Madras, had substantial interests. This was the origin of his opposition to the touching efforts of the young Lally-Tollendal* to seek, and finally obtain, in 1778, rehabilitation for his father, whom Louis XV had beheaded for allegedly losing the East Indies to the English. The execution aroused the indignation of Voltaire—whom d'Eprémesnil detests.[19] First and foremost, he is a magistrate. After meeting him at Kornman's, Brissot observes that "his only object in debourbonizing France, as he put it, was to set the *Parlement* to reign in their stead."[20]

D'Eprémesnil reveals, document in hand, what he has just learned of the Minister's plans, in particular the workings and possible membership of the plenary court, which would relegate all the *parlements* of France to the status of mere tribunals with no control over the laws of the realm. In doing

---

*Gerard de Lally-Tollendal (1715–1830) is a representative of the nobility to the Estates General. Initially a supporter of reform, he quickly shifts to the monarchists' camp and emigrates at the end of 1789.

so, he proposes an oath "whereby all members would bind themselves[21] to permit no innovation whatsoever."*

On the evening of May 4 the King's Council quashes the *Parlement*'s inflammatory ruling, forbids it to adopt any more like it thereafter, and gives orders to arrest the two new instigators. So, in the night of May 4–5 armed officers duly set out to apprehend the two councillors, d'Eprémesnil and Montsabert, the new leaders of the resistance who have taken over from Sabathier and Fréteau.

They may have been warned by Thierry de Crosne, a member of the government who was chief of police but also a magistrate himself. In any event, when, about one in the morning of May 5, "three individuals wearing the uniform of the *prévôté de l'Hôtel*"[22] [an office having jurisdiction over cases arising within the Royal Household] knock "in the King's name" at d'Eprémesnil's door on the rue Bertin-Poirée, they are ushered out by the door-keeper, who calmly informs them that he is unable to let them in or even awaken his master because he would need to go through five or six doors, for which he does not possess the keys, in order to reach him. Duly intimidated, the minions of the law depart. Their colleagues do the same, having met with an identical response a little further on from Montsabert's door-keeper on the rue Plumet near the Abbey of Saint-Germain.

After having their orders confirmed, but too late to avoid a ruckus, the police return at dawn, this time in coaches, to the two culprits' residences . . . to be informed that the culprits are no longer within. Both of them have just reached the Palais de Justice, where they are sitting among their assembled colleagues.

The days of May 5 and 6 are pure farce, good enough to have been invented by Beaumarchais himself.

At the heart of the huge Palais de Justice is the Great Chamber, repeatedly rebuilt after repeated fires—the most recent of which disturbed the sleep of Manon Phlipon one night†—and that imposing setting now houses a good hundred magistrates in full regalia, a few of them wearing the large rectangular pies of their mortarboards.‡ The outer areas of the building are beginning to fill with several hundred legal underlings, clerks, tipstaffs, bailiffs, etc., with reinforcements from the craftsmen and burghers of central Paris. In this explosive atmosphere, d'Eprémesnil and Montsabert tell the tale of their aborted arrest:

*Weber sees this oath "as a prelude to that of the Palm Court, which was to follow eleven months later."

†In the apartment of her father, the place Dauphine engraver, in 1775; see Volume I. She became Madame Roland in February 1780.

‡They are joined by nine peers, including the Duc de La Rochefoucauld.

"The court, deliberating upon this account, considers that the ministers, instead of reverting to the principles of the monarchy, are on the contrary endeavoring solely to deploy all the resources of the despotism that they seek to establish in place of the laws. . . .

"The court places MM. Duval, Goislard and all other magistrates and citizens under the protection of the King and the law.

"It decrees that the First *Président,* two other *présidents* and four councillors shall convey themselves to Versailles at once, for the purpose of representing to the King the dire misfortunes hanging over the nation. . . .

"Without rising, the court shall await the return of the First *Président* and other delegates."

It'll wait longer than it thought. The *Parlement* has just violated established procedure; the King never gives anybody an audience until the request has gone through the channels of protocol.

The gap between Paris and Versailles is widening. The *Parlement*'s one concern is this quarrel, whereas the King is still feeling all puffed up from the grand review of his military Household, which he has just attended on the Sablons plains not far from the village of Auteuil, where the terrain, dried to dust by the warm weather, is well suited to troop deployments.

Almost one hundred thousand men, including the glorious regiments of the French and Swiss Guards—the latter in their carefully starched blue and white uniforms led by the Comte d'Artois, their major general—marching to the rhythm of fife and drum, paraded past the King, who sat heavily but well in his saddle, wearing his red parade costume. There is quite a throng of spectators. One of them, an advocate named Bertrand Barère de Vieuzac,[*] who had come up from his valley in the Pyrenees to plead an inheritance lawsuit, compared the crowd "to the flight of the inhabitants of a town under siege."[23]

Coming from the other end of the country, Barère was happy to see such a magnificent spectacle, but his spirits fell when he became aware of the true aspect of a King whom he was looking forward to seeing "with pleasure, because I feel that all Frenchmen love their Prince; that is our form of patriotism." Brought close to him by the eddies of the crowd, he saw his ruler as "common and massive, as to his physical conformation, with a pallid face, bluish eyes devoid of all expression, a loud, coarse laugh with an imbecilic ring to it."

---

[*]For references to Barère, who will be one of the chief members of the Committee of Public Safety in the year II, see Volume IV. As *Président* of the Convention during the trial of Louis XVI, he conducts part of the interrogation himself.

. . .

The afternoon of May 5 languishes at Versailles, where the solemn delegation from the *Parlement* has to endure the ordeal of the antechamber, its only consolation being to refuse the supper that the keeper of the seals invites the gentlemen to partake of in his mansion facing the château on the other side of the place d'Armes.[24] They feel they are being patronized. And yet their First *Président,* Étienne-François d'Aligre, has given so many proofs of submissiveness in the course of his long career! He possesses "none of the qualities needed to make a great magistrate."[25] "A stout, rich, miserly man, the recipient of every mark of favor, he had been able to maneuver his company skillfully while the waters remained calm, but the personal disagreements that placed him in opposition to Calonne and Lamoignon" had been too much for him.[26] The junior officials accompanying him have likewise displayed little hostility to the authorities thus far, but the treatment they are now receiving tips them into the faction of protest—especially Michel Lepeletier de Saint-Fargeau,* twenty-seven years old, who "despite his outstanding gifts as an orator, preserved a great restraint in those days,"[27] and is chiefly conspicuous for his nose, sniffing the wind as keenly as any Cyrano de Bergerac.

Time languishes even more in Paris, where the *Parlement* is waiting for its delegates to come back and is unsure which way to turn. As the night wears on, the Great Hall is half-emptied of its magistrates, who have gone off to tend to their more basic needs. A miscellaneous crowd of people, who have previously been kept in check outside, takes advantage of their absence to slip into the inner sanctum and compromise its sacred dignity.

Around eleven o'clock, a sudden noise and stir. The Palais is invaded by two hundred French and Swiss Guards, "bayonets fixed to the end of their guns,"[28] who have made a forced march up from Sablons. A clatter of hoofs and clank of weaponry are heard outside. A cavalry detachment. So—force of arms is about to tackle force of law.

An uncertain pause, almost a panic, ensues in the Great Chamber, while the members who had been carousing in the corridors pour back inside and the motley intruders are hastily shoved out through a little door leading to the bar. The soldiers then station themselves in front of the other exits.

Even Duval d'Eprémesnil and Goislard de Montsabert don't quite know what to do. At first they try to replace the disguises they had worn that morning to escape from their homes, but it's too late. "They had no choice

---

*Lepeletier de Saint-Fargeau goes down in revolutionary memory as a martyr, because he is murdered in Paris on the evening when the death sentence is passed on Louis XVI, although he voted in favor of it in the Convention.

but to resume their gowns and return to their places. Soon avenues, corridors, chambers, everything was occupied except the Great Chamber, at the entrance to which the commanding officer of the French Guards presented himself, with some sappers, threatening to break down the doors if those inside refused to open them."[29] The sappers have already brought out their great pliers, pincers, axes and levers. M. de Gourgue, the acting First *Président*, composedly orders one of the doors opened; the troops enter the Great Chamber four by four and place themselves in the best order they can around their commanding officer, on the level space in the middle.

Poor Marquis d'Agoult! He deserved better than this mission. A scion of old Provençal nobility, "imbued with the idea of his ancestry, he was far more likely to exceed the principles of honor than to forget them for one second."[30] Why, he actually fought a duel with the Prince de Condé, from whom he had imagined some offense. And here he is changed into "a base tool of ministerial despotism." Redfaced, he looks far more troubled than on any battlefield "by the imposing spectacle of one hundred and fifty magistrates and seventeen peers of France who face him, without a sound, displaying on their faces only pain and indignation."

But orders are orders, and d'Agoult knows how to obey. With frosty courtesy, the *Président* asks him to be seated, between the last two councillors in the row, and requests if he might know the motive for this act of violence. The poor fellow pulls a piece of parchment from his pocket and reads out the fatal order:

"I hereby order Monsieur d'Agoult, captain of my French Guards, to go to the Palais at the head of six companies, occupy all the approaches to it, and arrest, in the Great Chamber of my *Parlement,* MM. Duval and Goislard, councillors, thereafter to be given into the hands of the officers of the police.

"Signed, Louis."[31]

Having read his piece, d'Agoult rises and commands the *Président* to turn the two men over to him.

De Gourgue replies that the court would have to deliberate upon this order secure from any foreign ears, and that "this had been the custom of the assembly from time immemorial and in all circumstances."

D'Agoult's answer:

"Gentlemen, I am not familiar with your procedures. My orders command me to arrest MM. Duval and Goislard without further ado; you will therefore kindly point them out to me."

Thereupon a dozen hands are held up, and the objection is made that the words "without further ado" are not in the order he read out and that he has added them out of his own head, in the heat of the moment.

"Therefore, we can deliberate."

He replies that "his verbal orders implied that such was the King's intention." He needs only one more jab to finish him off, and it is provided by the Duc de Luynes, who, having been commander-in-chief of more than one army in his day, points out, as though speaking to some junior officer, "the irregularity of his dress, seeing that he is wearing no gorget."[32]*

Humiliated in front of his men, d'Agoult sheepishly extracts the aforementioned gorget from his pocket and displays it. But the Duc de Praslin has already picked up the rebound:

"Monsieur d'Agoult, when one undertakes to carry out orders such as this, one must have them made explicit enough so that one does not become entangled in their execution. . . . You could not imagine that we should hand over two members of the court to you; if you do not know who they are, do not look to us to point them out to you."[33]

Pandemonium breaks loose. Like schoolboys at recess, the venerable members of the *Parlement* all begin to shout as one man:

"We're all MM. Duval and Goislard; if you mean to capture them, capture all of us!"

At the end of his tether, d'Agoult almost implores the *Président* to sign a refusal to hand the two councillors over to the military. The only result of this is to raise the pitch of noise still higher. The magistrates, now out of control, shout that since all of them refuse, they will all sign his paper.

Hell and damnation! Where are they going to find a piece of parchment big enough for over one hundred and fifty signatures? The Marquis d'Agoult has lost this skirmish. All that is left to him is the eternal last resort of the military. He announces "that he will withdraw to make a report to his superior [the Maréchal de Biron in this instance] concerning what has transpired."

It is now half past two in the morning.

*According to Webster's Third, a gorget "is a small ornamental plate worn on a chain about the neck by officers in full uniform in some armies."—*Trans.*

42

MAY 6–12, 1788

The Restoration That My Love Has Prepared

One hour passes; two hours. Changing of the guard: a handful of exhausted magistrates trail into the Great Chamber, which the military have just vacated. Behind *Président* d'Aligre comes the little group sent to Versailles to see the King, who have drunk the cup of insult to its dregs.

Gloom prevails. "The King announced that he would not see the delegation from his *Parlement,* for the reason that he had not been notified of its visit in accordance with the usual formalities."[1]

Sticklers for formality themselves, the members of the *Parlement* acknowledge that they have been out of line. They mean to try again, though, but this time in compliance with all the rules and regulations. "Following a brief deliberation it was decided that the King's people should withdraw to Versailles at once, with a view to ascertaining the day, hour and place in which the King would be pleased to receive his *Parlement*'s petition, and that the *Parlement* would await their return, and future events, in silence."[2]

This step is blocked by barred doors. The army let the delegates returning from Versailles into the net, but will not allow anyone to leave the Palais.

Nine o'clock. Skin smudgy, eyes reddened, voices hoarse, they continue their "captive sitting," as it will come to be known. A few servants make their way into the Great Chamber, still under the one-way ruling, and hand their masters *lettres de cachet,* dated the previous day, ordering them not to sit in the Palais anymore. And d'Agoult sends word that he has been instructed to allow them to leave the chamber as soon as they agree to end their sitting.

No way. Here they are and here they stay.

Eleven o'clock. The Marquis d'Agoult, his gorget fixed in its proper position, requests admission. "The First *Président* and his venerable colleagues, the peers of France and all the members of the court were on the fleurs-de-lis.* The deepest silence reigned throughout the assembly, pain and consternation were depicted on every face. . . .

"Monsieur d'Agoult entered the Great Chamber; he walked forward almost to the middle of this floor that only princes of the blood and *présidents* are entitled to cross; he read out the order to arrest MM. Duval and Goislard once again. He charged the two magistrates to follow him; no one uttered a sound. He repeated his injunction three times; still there was no sound."[3]

D'Agoult thinks he's found a new weapon. He has just sent for Monsieur Larcher, a legal adjutant, and orders him to enter and "tell me, in the King's name, whether MM. Duval and Goislard are present here, and point them out to me."[4]

Poor Larcher, a sort of mixed-breed, part gendarme and part man of the law, is caught in a crossfire. He looks "quite undone, and white as his own shirt";[5] "his face was visibly affected; his eyes uncertain and troubled; Captain d'Agoult watched his every move most closely."[6]

It's certainly a tight spot. If he points to the two councillors, he'll be reviled by the *Parlement,* and if he doesn't, he may well find himself in the Châtelet prison. He does his best to wriggle out, swears he's very bad at remembering faces and, borne up by the universal consensus around him, says he doesn't see the two men anywhere.

D'Agoult is not a bad fellow; he tells Larcher to get out and go to the devil. At his wits' end, he turns to the First *Président* once more:

"For the last time, I call upon the court to point out MM. Duval and Goislard to me."

For that last time, silence.

"Since no one answers, I shall withdraw and report your refusal."

The bells ring noon. They have been sitting for thirty hours straight. They can abandon the field without dishonor.

To the relief of all, the two "wanted" men ask for the floor. D'Eprémesnil, imagining himself on the Mount of Olives, speaks with the sort of sincere bombast that is his hallmark. To keep poor Larcher from becoming "a third victim immolated to despotism,"[7] Goislard and he have decided to give themselves up, and ask the *Président* to call back the Marquis d'Agoult.

He comes in alone. The two accused men take their time, d'Eprémesnil with an actor's poise, Montsabert "with the proud and timid modesty befitting his youth."[8]

"Monsieur d'Agoult having come to the bar in the courtroom, M. Duval,

---

*The fleur-de-lis-covered carpet which it was their privilege to tread when they were in session.

who was wearing his hat and had remained seated in the upper rows toward the middle of the left tier, spoke to him thus:

" 'I am one of the magistrates you seek; . . . I feel that the time has finally come to complete the sacrifice of my person, which I have sworn to perform at the feet of the sacred altars. I therefore require you to tell me if, should I refuse to follow you of my own free will, you have orders to remove me by force from the place I occupy at this moment.'

"D'Agoult: 'Yes, sir, and I shall carry them out.'⁹

" 'Enough; rather than expose the court of peers, the temple of justice, the sanctuary of the laws to yet greater profanation, I yield to force.' "

Amidst a large number of moist embraces, but "without shedding a single tear" himself, Duval goes over to the officer and is conducted "between two rows of bayonets to a carriage that was waiting in the New Court."

". . . The court, still assembled, waited in silence and dismay for the second victim to be torn from its bosom. This painful situation was prolonged for an hour and a half, until the beginning of the afternoon."

D'Eprémesnil's carriage headed for the Sainte Marguerite Isles; Montsabert's took him to the fortress of Pierre-Encize.* The "abduction" takes place without much external agitation despite the efforts of a few of the law clerks, who go up to the French Guards asking if they would fire upon their fellow citizens and are brushed away like flies. Paris, that afternoon, has its attention fixed on the punishment, on the place de Grève, of "the so-called Comtesse de Morangiès, a bigamist who was put in the iron collar,"¹⁰ and is not ready to riot. Bookseller Hardy thinks the iron-collar incident could not have come at a better time, "as though to distract people from these sorrowful events [in the Palace] and afford a unique recreation to the crowd." It's not much of a spectacle, though, in comparison with the public executions, which are occasionally long and refined in their cruelty and bring together a great horde of people whose sole authorized collective diversions are punishments and processions.

Louise Fontaine, wife of François Fremain, otherwise known as Jacquin, is spared the worst—a few years earlier she'd have been burned to a crisp—for having married him without revealing an earlier wedding to Jean-François-Charles de Molette de Morangiès in Frankfort, in 1781. She is simply attached to the iron collar, more than half-naked, from noon until two in the afternoon, "having a sign placed before and behind her bearing the word 'Bigamist' . . . and two hats beside her, being subsequently branded with a hot iron in the form of a fleur-de-lis on the right shoulder, and then taken to the prison in the general hospital of La Salpêtrière, there to be detained for the rest of her days." Jacquin, her legal husband, is convicted of having

*See the note at the beginning of Volume IV for details of the King's prisons in France.

"ceded" his Louise to the Comte de Morangiès, and has skipped town, so he is sentenced *in absentia* to the galleys. The only one who is let off relatively lightly is Morangiès, a nobleman. All he gets is six months in jail.

On May 7 at nine in the morning, as soon as the magistrates have reassembled, the "King's men" who have ridden full tilt from Versailles inform the *Parlement* that the master of ceremonies "was in the tipstaves' offices."[11]

"Our beloved and feal men,* we have resolved to hold, on Thursday next, being the eighth day of this month, in our château of Versailles, our bed of justice in order to make known our will. We hereby give you notice of it; let each and every one of you be there at nine o'clock in the morning, to assemble there in a body as court, and in red gowns, and receive us, when we shall enter, with the honor due to us. . . .

"Fail not in this, for such is our pleasure."

The magistrates set out at dawn in forty or so carriages, heads lowered as to meet the storm. They go to this bed of justice like pupils being called to the principal's office.

The King lets them have it with both barrels from the start:

"There is no irregularity which my *Parlement* of Paris has failed to commit in the past year. . . .

"The provincial *parlements* have made bold to put forward the same pretensions, the same initiatives. The result has been that valuable and desired laws are not achieved, that credit has weakened, that the course of justice has been interrupted or suspended; that, lastly, the public peace might be shaken.

"I owe it to my people, I owe it to myself, I owe it to those who come after me, to put a stop to these irregularities. . . .

"I wish to transform a moment of crisis into an age that will be salutary for my subjects. . . .

"The order I intend to establish is not new; the *Parlement* was a single body when Philippe le Bel settled it permanently in Paris. For a great state, there must be a single king, a single law, a single endorsement of that law."[12]

Louis XVI concludes:

"Such is the restoration that my love for my subjects has prepared and is instituting today for their happiness. . . .

"My keeper of the seals will inform you more fully of my intentions."

Whereupon Lamoignon launches into a series of five speeches. His mark has already been recognized in the King's diatribe. Everybody gets lost in the ensuing rosary of reforms combined with judiciary or administrative

---

*[The French expression is *amés et féaux*.] A medieval formula used by Kings to start off their proclamations. Napoleon revives it under the Empire. "Feal" means "faithful."

backlash, which are presented with a sort of coarse finesse not unlike sheer cunning. For instance, it's a good thing to reduce the plethora of tribunals sprinkled across the realm, not to mention all the *ad hoc* courts, to forty-seven large *"bailliages"*;* but the common people will get no benefit from the measure, since all trials—including criminal ones—in which nobles, church dignitaries or even landowning bourgeois are involved are to be heard by that famous plenary court on which will sit, for life, such lofty officials as will be appointed by the King—his grand almoner, for example, or the grandmaster of his Household, etc.

"That same evening many people turned to whatever dictionaries they had to hand in search of an explanation for a word they had not understood, and all their dictionaries agreed, although Trévoux's gave the most details. It said, 'Plenary court: Are so called those magnificent assemblies that our kings of old convened at Christmas and Easter or on the occasion of a marriage or other subject of special rejoicing; sometimes in their palaces, sometimes in some large town, at other times in the countryside, but always in a place where the great nobles might be comfortably accommodated.'

"In this practice lies the origin of the proverbial expression, 'he is holding plenary court,' when speaking of a man who invites many people to a party and serves them very fine fare."[13]

As for the convening of the Estates General, alluded to between two commas, no date is mentioned at all. Not even 1792.

The King, overcome by his depressing victory, rises at the close of this interminable flood of disappointment and drops a few last bombshells:

"You have now heard my will.

"The more moderate it is, the more firmly it shall be carried out."[14]

And out he goes, followed by his court, although not before adding, in a confusion that remains totally without effect because he would not have been obeyed in any case, that those of the audience who will be chosen to form the nucleus of the plenary court will receive orders to meet the following day; everybody else is to leave.

The doors of the chamber in which the bed of justice has taken place are flung aggressively open. The authorities are anxious to forestall any little schemes that the *Parlement* might be entertaining for digging itself in at

---

"Bailliage" and *"sénéchaussée"* both referred, the former largely north of the Loire and the latter in the southern part of the country, to judiciary circumscriptions, several hundred of which were interwoven and entangled in one another without the slightest respect for any logic, following the whims of local history. A *bailli* was always appointed by the King but was not necessarily a magistrate; he could also be a noble of the sword.

Versailles. *Président* d'Aligre scarcely has time to utter the protest agreed upon the day before: "Your *Parlement* declares that it cannot, and must not, and will not, give its opinion or take any part in what might be done. . . .

"Everything [said here today] points to a complete innovation in the structure of the monarchy."[15]

He's talking to empty air. A military escort assists the magistrates to withdraw, not without some pushing and shoving. In the court of honor they collide with the carriages that Breteuil has sent to await them, so that those not chosen for the plenary court on the morrow can be returned to Paris without a moment's delay. But not even Breteuil can pick the gentlemen up by their collars and hoist them bodily into the carriages. Having gone too far in their resistance to give way now, they march through the line of coaches and police and hold a meeting on the spot in the Bonne Auberge hotel, a place within walking distance that had been reserved beforehand just in case. A highly irregular sitting of the *Parlement* is about to commence under the King's nose, almost under his very windows, amid disorder made almost gleeful by the drinks and snacks being served. Impromptu remonstrances are hurriedly drafted and signed. A small crowd of Versaillese gathers outside the inn and cheers on the defiant magistrates, for there's a rumor going around, based on the fact that the police commissioners have "been ordered by a circular to remain in their homes and await the King's orders," that some of them are going to be put into the Bastille.[16]

In Paris, that same day, Barère writes in his diary that the "mere whim of the King has force of law. His words need no commentary. This is the style of the Oriental potentates."[17] Bookseller Hardy anxiously wonders whether he should put up his shutters. He records, appalled, that just near him "between two and three in the afternoon, the Marquis d'Agoult, who has been nicknamed 'Sewage' since his arrest of the two magistrates, was recognized at the entrance to the place Dauphine by a squad of young men, who began shouting, 'A cat! A cat!' and made to belabor him with sticks, but he escaped them and succeeded in taking refuge in a jeweler's backyard, where a brigade of the horse watch commanded by the Chevalier Dubois arrived just in time to rescue him."[18]

May 9, the date the King was hoping to hold the first sitting of his plenary court, sees an embarrassed Versailles. "The procedure, which ought to have been so imposing, turned to absurdity instead. The First Minister, who had promised such firmness, suddenly found himself unable to decide anything. The magistates kept in Versailles by the King's orders wandered the streets of the town or the apartments of the château but never went near the Chamber which had been made ready for their sitting. They had to be sent back to their homes, to give the authorities time to devise a policy. The poor plenary court, which died stillborn, was ridiculed and jeered at in song on all sides."[19]

Louis XVI and Brienne were anticipating a revival of authority and majesty in the style of the early Capetians; what they get is desertion by the government's most venerable institution. They find themselves as isolated as enraged children kicking vengefully at a molehill, in the form of the deserted Palais de Justice, where the French Guards arrive on May 10 to seize the keys and post themselves outside the doors.

This gives the Parisians an opportunity to indulge in their favorite pastime, namely, watching the downfall of a minister. Dithering, the Baron de Breteuil, alarmed by the attack on the Marquis d'Agoult, imprudently sends out the watch to patrol the capital but forbids them to use their weapons, which only makes matters worse. The result is a series of scuffles and punchups between the sergeants of the watch and people of the Cité. When news of this reaches the Council meeting on the eleventh, Brienne is unable to restrain a snarl at Breteuil for having gone too far. This is not the moment to touch off an explosion in Paris!

"The next day [according to Besenval], the Baron [de Breteuil] went to Brienne to demand an explanation for the scene he had made. The Archbishop tried to smooth things over, but the Baron said that the other man was apparently coveting his office, and the Archbishop lost his temper again and said that if he had wanted it, he would have had it long since.

" 'I understand the meaning of that,' returned the Baron, and immediately tendered his resignation to the King.

"The King accepted it."[20]

LAPÉROUSE

43

MAY 1788

The Old Spirit of Discovery

On the first day of August 1785 the "brigadier of the naval armies," Jean-François Galoup de Lapérouse, hoisted the sails on his frigate *La Boussole* in the Brest roads; his friend and associate Captain Fleuriot de Langle followed suit on board *L'Astrolabe,* twin of the other ship. The two vessels were setting forth on a "scientific voyage" around the world that promised, in Louis XVI's own words, to be the expedition of the reign. Their orders were to return to Brest, having completed their tour, in July 1789.

Lapérouse was realizing the guiding dream of a lifetime of reasonable adventuring: to revive "the old spirit of discovery [which] seemed to have become utterly extinct"[1] since the Anglo-French conflict had turned all exploring navigators into warriors.

He was forty-four.* A portrait shows him as a self-possessed man, with that firm stance habitual to seamen, a head round as a ball, intelligent, with fine blue eyes and powdered hair. His gaze is keen and far-reaching, his large, straight mouth beneath an aquiline nose shows decisiveness and a sense of command.

He was born in the town of Albi in Languedoc, but his true mother is the sea. He began serving her at fifteen, starting with an apprenticeship in the naval guards in Brest. Twenty-two ships, nine commands, twenty-five years of navigation, a wound in November 1759 during the last-but-one Franco-English war, followed by two years' imprisonment in Portsmouth, then the campaigns off the coasts of America and then India. He never found time to get married until 1783, to a Mademoiselle Éléonore Broudou, who doesn't see much of him.

In the great frozen waste of Hudson Bay, Lapérouse was as humane as a man can be to an enemy when he captured and destroyed a forty-gun fort but sent supplies to the defeated men who were hiding in the forest. Fleuriot de Langle was already his companion on that expedition.

Perhaps it was this trait of his that led the King to put him in charge of the grand tour. Louis XVI did not care for needless violence and had sent word to him that "His Majesty would regard the conclusion of the [Hudson Bay] expedition without costing the life of a single man as one of its finest achievements."[2]

The King himself wanted to outline the itinerary for this new voyage, the details of which were to be worked out by the Maréchal de Castries, his minister of the navy, with the assistance, for the writing side, of an academician, the Marquis de Condorcet.

The King also wanted the geography master of his youth to have a share in planning the expedition: Philippe Buache de Neuville, who was honored

*Unlike most people of that day, he never divides his family name in two and always writes Lapérouse as one word, although the name comes from a small estate called La Peyrouse. See index to Volume II for other references.

with his gracious favor for having introduced him to "mathematical and astronomical geography."[3]

The trip was to have three objectives: to improve the mapping of large tracts of ocean that were still little known, to learn more about the natives of America and the Pacific, including the Tartars and Mongols at the far end of Siberia, and to survey the prospects for commercial exchanges of hides, plants, ore, spices, diamonds and pearls, etc.

"At first,* a very precise itinerary was drawn: Lapérouse was to cross the Atlantic, leaving Brest and sailing down the coast of Spain and Africa, then set his course for the southern part of America and rounding it beyond Tierra del Fuego. After entering the Pacific, he was to sail northward as far as Easter Island and set a course for Tahiti, where his actual explorations would begin. He would sail along the virtually unknown coasts of North America and try to find if there were not some narrow waterway through which Hudson Bay might be reached. He would then continue up to the Bering Strait to southern Kamchatka. Then he was asked to sail down the Kuril Islands, Japan, Formosa, Macao and the Philippines and to reconnoiter the more scattered isles in that region before setting sail for the Indies and thence back to Europe."[4]

The works of the great "discoverers" are Lapérouse's missal. He had on board the *Journal of the Last Voyage of Captain Cook,* published in London in 1781, two years after Cook was slain in a squabble with natives in the Sandwich Islands. Cook is the idol of all sea explorers, and Lapérouse says he himself is "filled with admiration and respect for the memory of this great man; in my eyes he will always be foremost among navigators, the man who determined the exact position of the islands, explored their coasts, made known the inhabitants' ways, customs and religion, and paid with his blood for all the knowledge we have today of those peoples; this man, I say, is the true Christopher Columbus of this country, of the coast of Alaska, and of almost all the islands of the southern seas."

He has also studied the *Voyage autour du monde* of Louis-Antoine de Bougainville, who, twenty years before, gave the King a handful of islands lost in the Atlantic off the coast of Patagonia, which he baptized the Malouines in honor of the port of Saint-Malo [today the Falklands]. His account, published in 1771 and in a large number of editions since then, gave support to the *philosophes'* ideal of the Noble Savage.[5]

Lapérouse's two frigates were in reality a pair of sailing barges transformed in the shipyards at Brest, rather ponderous craft built to carry heavy loads and withstand heavy seas. They were not easy to sail, weighted down

*According to Evelyn Lever in her recent and very comprehensive biography of Louis XVI.

as they were by livestock, which was "divided into two categories: animals intended for consumption by the crew and animals to be given to peoples who had none." Also, "to gain the savages' goodwill, a very miscellaneous portage was massed on board: iron, nails, which are said to be highly valued in the isles, two thousand hatchets, six hundred mirrors, colored glass beads, fifty-two dragoons' helmets and twelve scarlet outfits,"[6] not to mention the hundreds of barrels of water and wine.

Among the passengers were two professors of mathematics, botanists, geologists, naturalists and even "a gardener from the King's Gardens to cultivate on board ship and preserve the plants and seeds of various species that we would be able to bring back to Europe." Also on board *La Boussole* was M. Duché de Vancy, who had been instructed "to take ship in order to paint the costumes, landscapes and in general all the things that are often impossible to describe.... In short, our frigates contained an incredible number of things."

From August 1785 to December 1787, Lapérouse piloted his ships through two oceans. He personally supervised the hygiene and recreation of his crews, and made them dance on deck to a musical accompaniment every evening when the weather was fine. He tried never to make the men work more than six hours at a stretch, despite the sort of tranquil haste that was nibbling at his mind, driving him to keep as close as possible to the King's schedule.

Three times, letters were sent from one continent to the other, whenever an opportunity arose, even though it meant turning some of the companions into couriers. They brought news of the voyage to France and were to constitute its sole, unfinished chronicle.

Madeira, La Praya, Cape Horn, the coast of Chile, Easter Island, the coast of North America up to San Francisco, Kamchatka; then turn southwest, Manila, Macao ... Everything went well for nearly three years. But fate was lying in wait for the poor fellows and dealt them two crushing blows, one just before and the other just after the coast of New Holland.*

Before, Fleuriot de Langle and ten of his men were massacred on the shore "by the savages of Maouna Island, on December 11, 1787," within sight of their companions who had remained on board the two frigates.

After, both ships were wrecked on the reefs of Vanikoro Island, where most of the voyagers died; the few survivors were later killed off by the natives. The exact date of "Lapérouse's disaster" will never be known, but it undoubtedly took place toward the end of May 1788.

As *La Boussole* and *L'Astrolabe* were scudding downwind toward their

*Later called Australia.

ultimate encounters, Lapérouse's notes began to show something like a pre-sentiment. His morale is low, and his last anthropological observations are totally at odds with those of Bougainville and with the rosy conclusions drawn from them by Diderot in a few sparkling pages that are being handed secretly around France, the *Supplément au Voyage de Bougainville, ou Dialogue entre A et B sur l'inconvénient d'attacher des idées morales à certaines actions physiques qui n'en comportent pas.*[7] The second part of the title is enough to show why the text remained confidential. Diderot went a long way toward imagining complete sexual freedom, excluding neither adultery nor even incest, on the basis of Bougainville's accounts. But by now, Lapérouse is sick and tired of "*philosophes* who travel in their libraries, while sailors go over the seas and see things as they are." He doesn't want to hear another word about Noble Savages. His mind is made up for good about the disposition of the island dwellers in the "Navigators' Archipelago." "The ferocity of their features constantly expresses either amazement or anger; the smallest disagreement between them leads to blows of their sticks, clubs or paddles and the op-ponents often lose their lives in the fight. They are almost all covered with scars that can only be the consequences of these private quarrels." As for the women: "Before their springtime is over, they lose that soft expression and elegant outline, whose mold nature has not broken among these barbarian peoples. . . . Of the very large number of women I have had occasion to see, I have perceived but three who were pretty. All the others had such coarsely shameless airs, indecent motions, and made such revolting offers of their favors, that they were exactly the right mothers and wives for the fierce beings surrounding us."

He wrote these lines shortly after Fleuriot de Langle was killed.

Despite his grief, Lapérouse openly lays the blame on the attitude of his closest friend, who continued to trust the natives and was destroyed by his credulity, whereas his commanding officer had adopted a different course:

"These reflections had altered our ways of behaving toward the Indians [*sic*]. We punished the most trivial thefts and injustices by force. We showed them, by the effects of our weapons, that flight would not save them from our rancor. We refused to allow them on board ship and threatened to kill any who should dare to come in spite of us. This behavior was a hundred times preferable to our former moderation, and if we have anything to regret, it is that we first came to these peoples bearing principles of mildness and patience."

By the end of his life Lapérouse has forged for himself the mentality of a colonist; but that doesn't save him either.

On December 11, Fleuriot wanted to "water," that is, to take on board a supply of fresh water and fruit for *L'Astrolabe,* and he goes ashore into a throng of natives who, already made uneasy by the sight of the two large vessels anchored three-quarters of a league offshore, look upon the two longboats and two dinghies coming toward them, with sixty-odd white men on board, as predators. Hoping to pacify them, Fleuriot only drives them into a frenzy by presenting "a few bumpers to some sort of chiefs they had; we were certain, however, that their leadership was only pretense,* and if those alleged chiefs had any authority at all, it was over only a very small number of men. The gifts distributed among five or six of them aroused the displeasure of all the rest; a din rose up on all sides, and we were no longer able to control them."[8]

The French, now aware of the danger, turn tail and just make it back to their boats, but the boats have thrown grappling anchors overboard, into the rocky bottom. The two dinghies manage to cut loose but the longboats' lines are thicker and the attackers get hold of them and begin hauling the craft toward shore. The French had to walk through water when they first went ashore and almost all the soldiers' guns are wet. "Soon a hail of stones was falling on us, hurled with equal speed and strength. Fighting started on both sides and became general." Almost six hundred natives "went on with their stoning, which was most frightening and deadly. . . . Whenever someone was hit and fell on the savages' side, he was instantly finished off with blows of paddles or clubs.

"Monsieur de Langle was the barbarians' first victim, who had done them nothing but good. At the very start of the attack he was overturned, all bloody, in his longboat, and fell into the water, with the chief officers and master carpenter. The islanders went after him so furiously that the other two were spared, and managed, like myself, to get to the dinghies."

The dinghies row back to the ships at top speed while, "in less than four minutes, the islanders mastered the two longboats and my heart bled to see our hapless companions massacred without my being able to lift a hand to help them."

At last the dinghies draw alongside *La Boussole,* "bearing a large number of dangerously wounded men who lay stretched on the seats and prevented the oars from doing their work."

Forty-nine survive, out of sixty. "It is impossible to express the emotion that this dire event caused on board the two frigates." Lapérouse tacks back and forth off the deadly shore for two days, wanting to punish the murderers with cannon fire. But he would have had to come in too close and risk running aground on the reefs, so in the end, brooding on his convictions, he gives the order to set sail for "New Holland."

*According to the account by M. de Vaujuas, one of the officers who went ashore with Fleuriot de Langle.

"I am a thousand times more out of patience with the *philosophes* who glorify the savages than with the savages themselves. Poor Lamanon,* whom they massacred, was telling me on the eve of his death that those men were worth more than ourselves."

Lapérouse's last pages seem as though written in the shadow of death. "Every island we glimpsed reminded us of some instance of treachery by the islanders; Roggewein's crew had been attacked and stoned in the Recreation Islands, in the eastern Navigators; Schouten's were attacked at Traitors' Island, south of Maouna Island, where we ourselves were so atrociously assassinated."†

He decides to abandon the detailed exploration of the dust of islands through which he is sailing. "Having lost the longboats, and seeing the state of fermentation of the crews, I determined not to drop anchor until Botany Bay in New Holland, where I proposed to build a fresh longboat with material I had on board. . . . I gladly leave to others the task of writing the most uninteresting history of these barbarian peoples."

In December 1787, he's sailing along the east coast of New Holland, that land so vast that no one has yet decided whether it is an island or a continent. His frigates anchor in Botany Bay, where he is greatly relieved to be able to recoup the expedition's forces in the shelter of a safe anchorage and the beginnings of a civilization, which is being built by a population of convicts deported from England in convoys over the last decade or two, all of whom seem delighted, whatever their misdeeds may have been, to escape the close confinement of the London jails. "We had a sight that was quite new to us since our departure from Manila: an English fleet anchored in Botany Bay. We could make out its pennants and flags. At this remove from their countries, all Europeans are fellow citizens."

The French exchange visits with the officers of the English fleet of Commodore Phillip, who has been ordered by the British Crown to explore everything he can in those parts and set up other settlements. Among others, the Commodore has just baptized the site of what would become a great city, to the north of an inlet where there is a beautiful spring and ships can sail right up to shore. He calls it Sydney, after an English secretary of state.[9]

Lapérouse gives Phillip the last letter written on his trip, in which he relates the tragedy of Fleuriot de Langle, and asks him to deliver it to the

---

*Physicist and naturalist, who had been so happy to go on this voyage.

†Schouten (died 1625) and Roggewein (died 1733) were two Dutch navigators who were famous in their time for discovering many islands in the South Pacific. The Navigators' Archipelago was so baptized by Bougainville because the inhabitants did all their traveling by pirogue and "never went on foot from one village to the next."

Maréchal de Castries, whom he supposes still to be in office. Phillip remembers saluting the two French frigates as they sail away, bound for New Caledonia, on May 10, 1788.[10] No European sees them again. They enter into a mystery for eternity.

What happened at Vanikoro?

Here, for relics of Lapérouse's catastrophe, the historian has to be content with the meager scraps of information and one or two objects scratched together by other navigators setting out later in search of him. Did he, after sailing north and crossing the Tropic of Capricorn, call at the Tonga Islands as he had planned to do? There is no proof. Perhaps, with an eye to his timetable, he merely made a superficial exploration of New Caledonia, to the north of New Holland but closer. He is heard of off the little island of Vanikoro, somewhere between the Solomons and the Hebrides.* Nobody knows the date of his passage too close to this mountainous, heavily wooded place inhabited by a "small and wretched people that would not appear to amount to more than fifteen hundred souls† . . . , fierce and mistrustful like all the savages of the Black Oceanic race."[11]

One thing is certain: both ships were wrecked, violently and simultaneously, or almost. They broke up, possibly during the night, on the girdle of reefs surrounding Vanikoro, which did not appear on any of the maps Lapérouse was using. It is not known whether they were driven against them by a cyclone or were trying to find a passage. *La Boussole* is thought to have been the first to go onto the reef, whereupon Captain de Clonard, whom Lapérouse had just appointed to take the place of Fleuriot de Langle, clumsily tried to come to the rescue and led *L'Astrolabe* to the same fate. Of the first frigate nothing remained, whereas the second could be identified long afterward, lying in fifteen or twenty fathoms of water. According to the stories teased out of some aged natives, a few French from *L'Astrolabe* came ashore on the island in a dinghy, but the entire crew of *La Boussole,* including Lapérouse, was drowned. After gaining some sort of control over the natives, the handful of survivors from *L'Astrolabe* may have built a longboat in which they tried to reach some other place but either were shipwrecked in turn or perished at the hands of unidentified natives.

It is most unlikely that any of the members of the expedition succeeded

---

*In 1989, the Solomon Islands are administered jointly by Great Britain and Australia.

†According to Dumont d'Urville, the first French officer to land there, on March 17, 1826, searching for the truth of the death of Lapérouse, whose opinion of the natives he shared. An English ship got there a few months before Dumont d'Urville and its captain, Peter Dillon, gleaned the first few details by means of which it became possible to assign an approximate date to the event. Before that, in 1791, the Constituent Assembly asked d'Entrecasteaux to carry out a mission, but he died of illness before reaching Vanikoro. Dumont d'Urville's surmises were not confirmed until 1964, by research carried out by Admiral de Brossard.

in establishing themselves or founding families in the Pacific. The bodies of a few French washed ashore at Vanikoro were buried by the inhabitants, who called the place of burial the Tomb of the Maras, from a word meaning, more or less, devils, evil spirits . . . "bad men."[12]

BERNADOTTE

44

JUNE 7, 1788

First Blood

Henri Beyle, round all over from his fair head to his thickset little body, is leaning out the second-story window of his grandfather's house this morning, June 7,* trying to make sense of the indescribable racket coming up from the place Grenette (the old grain market, that is), where all he ordinarily hears is "the sound of the pump when the serving-women were pumping at mist-fall with a big iron bar."[1] But where have the serving-women gone? The child is in a fever, as though the mounting revolt of the people were an answer to his own inner revolt. Since January 23, he's been five years old.

Dr. Gagnon's house is the best placed on the whole square, facing full south on the corner of the Grand-Rue, which is the only street wide enough to let two small vehicles edge past each other. The "grand'rues" in most old towns are like that, by comparison with the twisting intestines of their midsections, which can be traveled only on foot, in a sedan chair or on horseback. They are "grand" in the way that the Pont-Neuf ("New Bridge") is "new," two hundred years after being built.

Henri classifies this day as the third noteworthy memory of his early childhood.

"The first thing I remember is biting my cousin, Madame Pison du Galland, on the cheek or forehead. . . . I see her now,† a woman of twenty-

*It takes almost a century for him to achieve posthumous celebrity under the pseudonym of Stendhal, which is the name he uses when writing his books. He takes it from the little German town of Stendal in Prussian Saxony, which he visits in 1807 as a senior official in Napoleon's armies.

†As he writes his embryonic autobiography, *Vie d' Henri Brulard,* in 1835.

five, rather stout and wearing a good deal of rouge. It was apparently the rouge that provoked me. She was sitting in the middle of the meadow known as the Glacis de la Porte de Bonne, and her cheek was exactly my height.

"She wanted to make me embrace her, as they call it in that part of the world, that is, give her a kiss. I didn't want to, she was cross, I bit hard. . . . I was instantly treated as though I had committed a crime, and people were forever on at me about it."

"The second character trait was far more dire." The poor little lad had dropped a kitchen knife he was playing with out that same window, narrowly missing the head of one Madame Chenevas, "the nastiest woman in the whole town." His Aunt Séraphie, the hobgoblin of his toddling years, accused him of nothing less than attempted murder. "I rebelled; I must have been about four years old."

"My horror of religion dates from that time. . . ." Aunt Séraphie "was filled with the vinegar of a pious woman unable to find a husband."

Ten o'clock . . . Soon. The weather is stifling, as it sometimes is in this twice-cramped town, hemmed in near at hand by its ramparts and farther off by an ineffable circle of lofty mountains with snow-covered peaks. Insurrection weather, people say later. And yet the day seems to begin with the collective resignation of the lawmen. The Dauphiné *parlement,* sitting in the home of Bérulle, its First *Président,* because the Palais de Justice has been closed by the soldiers, has been debating whether or not to obey the order to disperse that it has just received from the government. In the past month the provincial magistrates have caught the plague from those just quelled in Paris, sending back echoes of the same protests, the same calls for the convening of the Estates General, and the same refusals to register the May edicts. In the first three weeks of May alone, the *parlements* of Pau, Rouen, Rennes and Nancy have rebelled.

Now, today, June 7, the Grenoble gentlemen cannot bring themselves to commit an act of *lèse-majesté* and have agreed to disband. But "the advocates and attorneys assembled and came, in mourning clothes, to pay their respects to the First *Président.* At the same time, all the law clerks and underlings scattered throughout the squares, streets and homes. . . . Everybody was saying that if the town's *parlement* were shut down, the town would lose all its wealth. . . . All the church bells in Grenoble sounded the alarm, the common people divided into various groups. Some went to the gates [in the ramparts], shut them and took the keys. . . . Others went to the First *Président* and other magistrates to confiscate their trunks and carriages and, proffering threats, . . . forbade the exiles to depart."[2]

· · ·

The magistrates themselves may still, just, be reluctantly obedient and unwilling to assume the consequences of their verbal expostulations, but the local people want to force them to take the next step. This is Saturday, market day. The streets are packed. The modest folk who earn their livings from the presence of the *parlement* in this town, the tradesmen, caterers, judiciary secretaries and clerks, valets and hemp hacklers, can't bear the thought of their gentlemen going off to some unknown destination, no more than can the peasants from the surrounding countryside, who've been hauled into town by the alarm, rung under the priests' noses—or by the priests themselves. They've grabbed up whatever weapons they could lay their hands on, axes, pickaxes, pitchforks, clubs, carving knives, scythes and old flintlocks, and come running. It's the people who're going to start acting out. Acting.

By noon, all the shops are shut. A sizable crowd has gathered around the First *Président*'s carriage and unharnessed his horses.

Other rumbles and roars, near and far and on every side, respond to the din on the place Saint-André, the noise of little mobs that have made doubly certain that none of their magistrates would be leaving by closing the town gates, nailing them shut with great clamor, and putting the guards out of commission even though their numbers had been doubled—thirty men for each gate. Here's the Gratianopolis of old* transformed into a boiling caldron under a leaden sun, and within the precincts of Lesdiguières, anger is turning into revolt.

How many people are out there shouting? The population of Grenoble and its "election," comprising some hundred and fifty nearby villages and hamlets, is over a hundred thousand.[3] Most of them are still in their homes, but a few thousand of the more resolute are out in the streets, women as well as men, and the females are among the most irate of the lot, especially "the market vendors, who assembled in clumps. . . . They threw themselves on the magistrates' coaches, cut the harness and waved the keys to the gates aloft."[4]

Inside the majestic residence of the military government, the Duc de Clermont-Tonnerre,† garrison commander and lieutenant general for Dauphiné, has no choice but to crack down. He doesn't like it. He's an old man and abhors spur-of-the-moment decisions. "Nature, in giving him a mild and peaceful temperament, withheld all the energy and resources needed to

---

*From the name of the Roman Emperor Gratian, who subjugated the town when it was still the capital of the Allobroges, or "Gauls from the Mountain."

†Sixty-eight this year, commanding in Grenoble since 1765, guillotined during the Terror. A cousin of Stanislas de Clermont-Tonnerre, who plays a part in the early days of the Revolution, first in Auvergne and then in the Constituent Assembly.

devise fitting remedies for heated and overwrought heads," according to one of his subordinates, the Chevalier de Mautort, a captain in the Austrasie regiment.[5] But now the Duc must, willy-nilly, order a hundred grenadiers from the Royal-la-Marine regiment to issue forth and restore order. They advance by butting their way, without much conviction, and are immediately overwhelmed by the crowd, but their efforts are enough to create a shock wave that gradually moves along the rue Neuve and on to the place Grenette.*

"The detachments of the Royal-la-Marine regiment fired upon the people and charged with bayonets and sabers.

"A few persons were killed and several injured. The people took up the paving-stones in several parts of the streets to use as weapons, climbed up on the roofs and hurled tiles and stones to clear the troops away."[6]

Considering that some of the hollow tiles that covered most of the roofs in town in those days weighed as much as four pounds, and that the rioters were supplementing their ammunition with the big slabs laid on top of the tiles to keep them from sliding off in the wind, it's surprising there were not more casualties.

Around two in the afternoon the soldiers retreat to the residence inside which Clermont-Tonnerre is trapped. The mob starts to stone his walls and shatter his windows. Is he going to let himself be massacred, or will he have to order his guards, whose morale is shaky and numbers insufficient, to fire at will, causing general havoc and not necessarily producing a victory?

Anything can happen.

In his catalog of early memories, Henri Beyle speaks of this: "M. de Clermont-Tonnerre, the commander in Dauphiné, who lived in the governor's residence, standing by itself and giving onto the ramparts (with a wonderful view of the Eybens hills, a tranquil and beautiful view worthy of Claude Lorrain), and having an entrance through a fine courtyard on the rue Neuve near the rue des Mûriers. He, it seems to me, wanted to disperse the gathering. He had two regiments, against which the people defended themselves by hurling tiles from the housetops; whence the name, *The Day of the Tiles*.† . . .

"But this is all History; related, it is true, by eyewitnesses but not seen by myself. I want to tell . . . only what *I saw*."

. . . Through the window the family can hardly tear him away from. He hangs on for dear life and keeps returning again and again. "The fact is that

---

*According to a report written that evening by the First *Président* of the *parlement* and six other magistrates.

†Stendhal's italics throughout.

my parents, who were *rightminded* people and greatly put out by anything
that deviated from *order* . . . did not want me to be affected by these indi-
cations of the people's rage or strength. I, even at that age, was already of
the opposite persuasion.

"That day I saw flow the first blood shed by the French Revolution.* It
was that of a poor hatter's assistant, killed by a bayonet thrust into his lower
back. . . .

"My parents having left the table before the end of the meal, and myself
being alone at the window . . . , I saw an old woman holding her old shoes
in her hand and shouting at the top of her lungs, 'I revort! I revort!' [*sic*].

"She was going from the place Grenette to the Grand-Rue. . . . I was
much affected by the absurdity of this revolt. One old woman against a
regiment!"

As for the hatter's assistant, "he walked with great difficulty, supported
by two men who had passed his arms over their shoulders. He had no coat
on, his shirt and white trousers were full of blood, I can see it still, the wound
from which the blood was pouring was in the lower part of his back, about
level with his navel.

"As is natural, this is the sharpest memory that has stayed with me from
that time."

At the very moment the child named Beyle is inscribing this image
forever, the Day of the Tiles is turning into a great popular insurrection.
Part of the "naval troops,† which had fired on an old man in the rue Saint-
Jacques, fled down a narrow alleyway and under the Jesuits' vault to reach
the reserve quarters."[7]

Assaulted from the rooftops as they go, the soldiers take shelter in a
poor woman's house, which is almost demolished by the mob.

"About half-past three there came a request to capitulate. The colonel
of the Austrasie regiment and its major, the latter with a head injury, went
to the Duc [Clermont-Tonnerre] and gave notice that if he did not order
the troops to withdraw, they intended to leave town at the head of their
regiment, in order to save their men and officers from the risk of being
massacred."[8]

In fact, what the governor is facing is a sort of military insurrection that
doesn't dare to speak its name.‡

*Here Stendhal unknowingly uses an expression employed also by Barnave in the first
volume of his works, p. 97. "It was on the Day of the Tiles that flowed the first blood shed for
the Revolution." This is pure coincidence, neither man having read what the other had written.

†According to an anonymous informer of Brienne's, an eyewitness who sent this account
to the Minister the following day.

‡Which is why the Day of the Tiles makes such a stir at Court—can't we even count on
the army anymore?

"The Duc ordered the troops to withdraw, except for the guards"; which is the last thing he should have done, since it puts him at the mercy of the rioters. "The people came in a throng to M. le Duc, who was dining. Many, entering the guardroom, took up guns, cartridge pouches, etc., and ran through the house until they came to M. le Duc in his room. A citizen who had received a bayonet prick in the arm threatened him with an ax he had in his hand. . . . Then M. le Duc told all these people not to take his life, that he was carrying out the King's orders and would leave them to do as they pleased."[9]

Meanwhile, the women who have swarmed into the main courtyard are screaming at the soldiers, "Will you fire on your brothers?"[10] And a group of armed peasants who managed to float their way into town on the Isère on boats and rafts of wooden logs are taking advantage of a breach in the crumbling ramparts near the governor's residence to slither into the cellars and work their way up to the main rooms.[11]

The shattered Clermont-Tonnerre writes a letter to First *Président* Bérulle and has it taken to him along with the keys to the Palais de Justice. The Duc implores the magistrate to return to the Palais, with his colleagues, as soon as he can. Armed force surrenders to law, but law was defended by people's force.

"While this was going on in the residence of M. le Duc, part of the populace were breaking the windows of its rooms and smashing chairs and other furniture, tearing up the curtains to make flags, invading the kitchens and eating everything that was cooked there, throwing the silver dishes out the windows. . . . They carried away the barrels of Spanish wine and took all the bottles of foreign wine and all the strong spirits, and broke the porcelain.

"This day is said to have cost M. le Duc de Clermont more than 50,000 livres."[12]

The officers are no less amazed than the men of the *parlement*. Has something happened to "the Dauphinois temperament [which] has a tenacity, a depth, a keenness and subtlety one would look for in vain in the civilizations of its Provençal and Burgundian neighbors. Where the man of Provence breathes deadly insults, the Dauphinese ponders and takes counsel with his heart."[13]

This must not have been the day . . .

One battalion of the Austrasie regiment that is still reliable and has come rushing in from its barracks in the suburbs provides last-minute reinforcements and saves the Lieutenant General's life, but can do nothing to stop the looting.

"One of the junior officers in these regiments was Bernadotte."[14]

Sergeant Major Jean Bernadotte, promoted less than a month ago to this rank in Captain de Belcastel's company in the Royal-la-Marine regiment, plays no particular part in the skirmishes of June 7.[15] He's there, obeying orders, smothered like his comrades in the agitation of the crowd. He may have commanded a few salvos, but that was what he was told to do, and he wasn't the only one.

A handsome man in his grenadier's uniform, with red epaulets lined in white and a round scarlet wool tassel on his hat, on top of the white cockade.* He's twenty-five, slender, very straight and seems taller than his five feet nine inches. The first thing people notice about him is his big curved nose, almost an eagle's beak, under thick, curly black hair and tufted eyebrows surmounting keen eyes.[16]

He's a typical incarnation of the Béarn, an old region of stockbreeding and crop farming at the bottom of great Gascony, a land of contrasting plains and pastures and rugged mountains. To the west, the Labour (French Basque country); to the east, the Bigorre where Bertrand Barère, his "neighbor from the Pyrenees," has just made his debut as an advocate. Pau, Béarn's proud capital, is Bernadotte's womb, cradle and school. From his homeland he has acquired his swarthy complexion, fluent and image-rich speech and swift repartee.[17]

His forebears? A long line of Bernards, Bertrands, Bertrandots, eased by usage into Bernadottes. You can find their traces in the sixteenth century, when they'd already been around awhile, working at safe and increasingly "honorable" trades: weavers, tailors, "legal practitioners," notary's clerks, advocates. The father, Jean-Baptiste Bernadotte, was an attorney in the seneschalsy of Pau on January 26, 1763, when his son Jean was baptized, the last of the five children he had with Jeanne de Saint-Jean, also of a good Béarnese family.† The eldest was born nine years before, another Jean but attached to the Evangelist, whereas this one, like his father, was dedicated to the Baptist.

His childhood? Turbulent, they say, and in view of his disposition it's likely. Perhaps it was because his health was oddly fragile, conflicting with his strong, husky frame; perhaps because he was born prematurely. Sometimes he spit blood, and he had "dizzy spells." The Bernadotte children were brought up by a conscientious but undemonstrative mother and a father who was usually away working. The family lived in an unpretentious house on the rue Tran, running from a big empty field to the Cordeliers' church. It

---

*Bernadotte becomes a general during the Revolution and a marshal of the Empire. As governor of North Germany he wins favor with the Swedes, who offer him their vacant throne. In 1812 he allies himself with the Tsar against Napoleon, and as a result reigns over Sweden until his death in 1844, with the name Charles XIV John. The dynasty of the kings of Sweden descends directly from him.

†Claire and Arnaud die in infancy, Marie in 1795.

had four stories and was tall and narrow, overlooking a little tributary to the Gave de Pau from wooden balconies.*

School? Following the linear progression of his ancestors, his education ought to have ended in some legal position giving access to the lesser nobility of the gown. After learning his abc's at home, Jean was sent to the Collège Royal in Pau, rather badly run by an obscure congregation of Saint-Denis before being taken over and more successfully operated by the Benedictines of Saint-Maur.[18] When he was fifteen, his father found him a position as a junior clerk with a fellow attorney at the *parlement* of Navarre. He started attending lectures in the university law school, which gave Pau a claim to be the equal of Lyons or Montpellier.

Almost from the start, however, there was a sort of hitch in the well-oiled gears of this youth. Jean Bernadotte seems to have been bored, not out of any lack of intellectual ability, because he had an inquiring mind, but rather out of lack of interest in the law and a need for physical activity. He had been allowed to earn a few pennies at the post house on the rue Tran, where he liked to saddle horses and shift luggage, and was spending more and more of his time there instead of at his studies. Was that the origin of the two scars on his forehead? He says they came from fights with local kids.

On March 31, 1780, his father dies, and on September 3 of that year Bernadotte enlists as an ordinary private in the Royal-la-Marine regiment.

The link between these two events of his eighteenth year is one of cause and effect: his father had been the one adamantine rock keeping him in the legal profession. Neither his mother nor his elder brother had enough influence to deafen his ears to the call of adventure, which grew louder after he began meeting various local lads at the post house who had already enlisted in the same regiment. Its recruits came chiefly from the Franche Comté, but there were also quite a few from Béarn and Gascony, and its colonel, the Marquis de Lons, was born in Pau in 1738.† Like most other higher-ranking officers, however, he moved in circles far removed from his regiment. It was one of his junior officers, Captain de Lassus, also from Pau, who knew the Bernadottes and grew close enough to Jean to understand him and encourage this good element, with more learning than the average soldier, to join his company.

Lassus helped with the formalities, which were not a foregone conclusion for a boy who was under age and had a reluctant family. A statement by the

---

*The people of Pau, proud to have given a king to Sweden when they had already given Henri IV to France, have preserved it well; today it is the Musée Bernadotte and has kept all its eighteenth-century charm, forming a pretty concerto in wood and slate.

†And returns there to die under the Restoration, as governor of the château.

subdelegate of the regional intendant was needed as a certificate of identity, but Lassus asked the farmer-mayor of the nearby village of Billères to provide it instead; and Bernadotte's destiny shifted from law to war.

What attracted him most was the idea of travel, and the Royal-la-Marine was basically a naval unit that had recently been on several campaigns in the Indies. But though Bernadotte joined during the American war, he went nowhere more exotic than Corsica.

Two uneventful years passed, between Ajaccio and Bastia, then a year and a half of sick leave in Pau because of his poor health. While there, he read a lot, especially lives of the great military leaders. Paradoxically, the less he was compelled to study, the more he felt like doing it. Back to Corsica in January 1784, a year of here-today-gone-tomorrow for the increasingly unnaval regiment, which was sent, for no discernible reason, to Toulon, then to Briançon and finally to Grenoble, where it still is four years later.

So Bernadotte's career had been stagnating for five years, but as the time drew near for him to reenlist (soldiers had to sign on again every eight years), things began looking up for him. He was serious and careful, cheerful and popular with his friends, able to make his superiors believe that he could deliver what his relatively high degree of learning had promised. Noncommissioned officers were the very marrow of the army, first in barracks and then in war, when a unit's zeal depended on the daily contact between the men and their leaders. In June 1785, young Bernadotte began climbing the ladder: corporal, sergeant and quartermaster sergeant in one year. On March 9, 1786, he wrote to his brother:*

> I have had several offers. . . . In the meantime I shall follow your advice, and shall accordingly fling myself body and soul upon the promises that keep being made to me, but shall wait for a more stable rank before making a final choice of the [military] career, for I confess that it has many vicissitudes. The truth is that one can endure the rest for the sake of the few moments one can snatch from the preoccupations demanded by the service. I came back a week ago from Avignon, where I had been sent on the trail of a young man of good family who had deserted the regiment. I arrested him alone, in the presence of nine soldiers of the navy. . . . I was praised by the major and all the other officers. I was even given to hope that I should get some reward at the review, which I have surely deserved because that makes three men I have arrested in the last three months. . . .
>
> If I am made sergeant major, as I am led to hope, I shall have a base pay of at least thirty-two sols daily.[19]

*This is from the first autobiographical text we have by him.

And he is and he has, by the time of the Day of the Tiles. He has decided to sign up again. There was no danger he would ever become one of the "unreliable" elements in his regiment.

Grenoble: the sun is dipping toward the horizon. Even in midsummer it disappears sooner here than elsewhere, behind the towering mountains.

A precarious quiet blankets the town, through which news of the military commander's capitulation has quickly spread. Will the mob's excitement fade before night? Rather, it changes direction, from anger to rejoicing.

In the note that the Duc de Clermont-Tonnerre wrote calling on M. de Bérulle for help, which has been repeated all over town because a dozen of the rioters were reading over his shoulder while he wrote it, the Duc sounds like a shamefaced puppy dog:

"I beg you to take all the precautions your prudence may suggest to you, and in particular, to go to the Palais in your gowns with as many gentlemen of your company as you can assemble and, in the name of King and *Parlement*, impose order upon the people."[20]

The magistrates do their best, but they've had a bad scare and it takes time to drag them out of their lairs. "The gentlemen of the *Parlement* were unable to assemble before six in the evening, at the home of the First *Président*. There were more than eight hundred people in the street. Four coaches had been brought up, and were to be drawn by twenty-five persons each [in place of horses]. When the First *Président* came out of his house with his company, he was presented with a crown of roses, but would not take it and threw it away behind him. They tried to force him to get into the coaches with the other men, but he refused and told the people they would go on foot. All the people went with them as far as the Palais, with loud and repeated cries of *'Vive le Parlement!'* . . . A bonfire was lit when they arrived, and the bells of Saint-André were rung for over two hours."[21]

The magistrates find their Palais de Justice in a sorry state. The crowd, getting hold of the keys before them, has invaded the chambers ordinarily devoted to serious thought and argument. It has tried to break down the registry doors and seize the books, in order to destroy the texts of the royal edicts. The *Président* and his men begin their meeting, not without difficulty. They finally impose silence and set out to prevent the worst. "As soon as he felt he had control of the audience, the First *Président* rose and spoke, from his high seat, as follows:

" 'You must all believe that the King wants his people's happiness and that we shall not cease from pursuing his justice. But the surest means of accelerating the return of his goodwill is to await it in peace and quiet. All of you go now to your separate homes.' "[22]

The gentlemen have hardly sat down when they have to get up again, to move through the groups and cajole them into obedience. Some, fearing a fresh eruption, patrol the streets and squares until nightfall.

They are soon complimented for their courageous conduct, so different from the shilly-shallying of the military. At the time, though, few people are sharp enough to see that the magistrates' courage changed direction in the course of the day. At first they were opposing the King; a few hours later they are opposing the people, who have become their unexpected but cumbersome ally. The nobility of the gown want a more flexible government, but for their own sake, and among honorable people. Their hotheaded ally has just scared them almost as badly as it scares the aristocracy. In Versailles, the Baron de Besenval is chagrined to learn that the Grenoble *parlement* was within an ace of joining forces with "an order other than what were known as people of society."[23]

He shouldn't get too worked up about it. From the morning after the Day of the Tiles, the Grenoble magistrates have only two concerns: first, to keep the people quiet, and then, as soon as possible, to get away from them. But soon the thunderclap of June 7 will be raising strange echoes among the people of other big towns, although the Dauphiné, their point of origin, remains the hottest spot of the summer of 1788.

BARNAVE

45

JUNE 8–JULY 18, 1788

A New Light

Less than two months after the Day of the Tiles, the government gets another jolt. An immense innovation, an open provocation: instead of waiting for somebody else to convene the Estates General, which had been promised to the Paris *Parlement* in May but without any mention of a date, the clergy, nobility and third estate of Dauphiné organize an Estates General of their own at Vizille, without asking anything of anybody.

The four instigators of the event are the two advocates Barnave and Didier, a "royal judge" named Mounier, and Perier, a rich industrialist. They were the ones who had the original idea and they also direct the whole operation from start to finish, in an opulent setting provided by Perier. The "Vizille Estates."

Barnave sets the ball rolling on the very evening of the Day of the Tiles.* While the hot breath of insurrection is cooling, the street police trot up to their superior bearing copies of an anonymous pamphlet, stacks of which have been deposited all over town, at booksellers' but also inside and around the churches. The attorney general, the intendant, and the wretched military commander, whose day this decidedly isn't, glance through the inflammatory text, entitled *L'Esprit des Édits enregistrés militairement au Parlement de Grenoble le 10 mai 1788.* It is clear from the first sentence that this is good and careful writing, that the arguments are those of a man of law, and that this is a torch that might well revive the fire just brought under control.[1]

Which provocateur wrote the thing? Did its distribution coincide with the uprising by chance? Or was it the second act of a vast conspiracy?

The author was not acting deliberately. His text was already printed at the beginning of June and the men who distribute it were hired on the sixth.

Nor is the unforeseen pamphleteer trying to hide and everybody soon learns that he is one of the most up-and-coming young men in the third estate, the advocate Antoine Barnave, attorney Pierre Barnave's boy.

It's a very short piece, twelve or fifteen pages, depending on the edition (and there are a series of them, making a total of six or eight thousand copies, which is a lot for those days, especially for a regional publication). It is a reasoned appeal that can be summed up in a few short arguments, and it is tossed from hand to hand. It contains a ferocious indictment of the decrees the government tried to have registered by force in May; attacks upon their authors, Brienne and Lamoignon, mentioning them by name; a denunciation of their unkept promises; a warning against their efforts to win people over; a defense of the *parlements* as the last bastion against despotism until the Estates General can meet; a series of appeals aimed at rallying all classes, all threatened interests and all provinces, "for I consider the prejudices dividing us to be a great evil and I believe that a Frenchman's fatherland must be the whole of France." . . . And Barnave ends with the ritual prayer to Louis XVI: "And Thou, open thy eyes at last, good and feeling King!"[2]

In the eyes of the "good and feeling" King's representatives in Grenoble the publication is tantamount to a crime of *lèse-majesté*. What can they do to stop it from spraying all over the country and giving birth to a whole batch

---

*See in Volume III the chapter on his background and youth, the incident in 1770 when he and his mother were removed from a box in the Grenoble theater and the already "advanced" maiden speech he made in August 1783, at the closing of a session of the *parlement.* He was then twenty-three.

of Days of the Tiles? Within a week it would be read out in every *parlement*.[3] To put a stop to it, they'd have to perform a ritual auto-da-fé and have its author thrown in the Fort Barraux, Grenoble's Bastille, which is what they would have done a few months ago. But Clermont-Tonnerre is not the man to jail the Barnave boy, so the authorities do nothing and *L'Esprit des Édits* becomes the manifesto of the boldest faction of the Dauphiné third estate, those who don't want to lose a minute in following up the Day of the Tiles.

Barnave is not alone. On June 9, one vociferator who signs himself "Anonymous is my name" puts up a poster on the town walls addressed "to the noble burghers of this town." He claims that a messenger from the King will soon arrive bringing bad news, and that the government is getting ready to crack down for sure.

"I exhort you to take up your arms again.* . . . Go out to Pique-Pierre bridge, take your guns, and arrest the messenger, take his parcel from him. Go to someone who knows about things and force him to unseal it and read what is written in it about that ugly mug of a Tonnerre [*sic*]. . . .

"Don't lose heart; don't be afraid of the six cannons they've armed at the arsenal. They're meant to intimidate you. If you have no gunpowder, send to Lyons for some; rise up and rebel! Force the Royal-la-Marine regiment that fired upon you to go away. Kill the first man you see who belongs to it. If you can find its colonel, ax him, so to speak. . . .

"Call up the Savoyards and Briançonnese to help you. . . . They have said they would come with eight thousand men in arms. . . . Keep watch, and don't let a single man from the *parlement* leave town."[4]

So within three short days, the leaders of the Day of the Tiles are already beginning to suspect that their *parlement* would like to give in. The domestics and clerks have told them that something is afoot. On the eleventh or twelfth, another piece of "people's writing" is going around town, a sort of follow-up to the swarm of women who came out and joined the riot. This is an extraordinary piece of scurrility signed, and why not, "Mme. la C. de l.R." and entitled *Représentation des femmes du Dauphiné au Roi:*

"Sire, So you imagine that at your whim you can overthrow, overturn, exile, change the form of everything, leave the nation but the bare ghost of its former constitution!† And after reducing the defending class [*sic*] to silence, you make game of the weaker sex, who are supposed always to be content as long as they have their gewgaws and pleasures and flirtations for

*As we have seen, it wasn't the "burghers" who took them up in the first place, it was the people. But the appeal to them is a practical move, implicating the third estate by treating it as though it had been to the party after the party was over.

†Another clever ploy. There is no constitution in France and everybody knows it, but poor Louis XVI is being put forward as its destroyer.

homage! Sire, you are mistaken. Our party most often becomes the one most to be feared. . . . Your soldiers, your bayonets, your bombs and your cannons will not drive us back one step; beneath the light costume of a helmet of gauze we shall oppose them with the brow of courage. . . .

"We remain Your Majesty's very humble, very faithful, but very intrepid female subjects, all the united women of your province of Dauphiné."[5]

The effect of these outbursts is rather the opposite of what was intended. The men of the Grenoble *parlement,* increasingly frightened by the courage being attributed to them, are not about to take on a rebellion that in their eyes goes too far. They have found a way to leave town almost secretly, as soon as the King orders them to do so again.

Versailles has understood that there is little time to lose. If it was only Grenoble . . . But "*parlement* anarchy," which has already been impeding the processes of justice and administration, is breaking out in explosions of collective bad temper all over France, and in some cases becoming positively seditious. Events more or less comparable to the Day of the Tiles have occurred in Pau (where Bernadotte, if he had stuck to the law, would have been playing a very different role) and in Rennes—two towns in which the uprisings follow the same scenario. The *Parlements* refuse to register the May edicts; the local governors, acting on orders from the King, dissolve them; a "committed" portion of the third estate, supported or preceded by "people's groups," comes out into the streets to back them up. In Brittany, where the local nobility demonstrates its resentment of the Court nobility by taking command of the movement, the situation is almost as bad as in Dauphiné. So when people hear what is happening there, look out!

"Great news from all sides;* France is for Dauphiné. The Estates of Béarn are fraternizing with it. Gentlemen from Lyons, Toulouse and Provence are subscribing to its resolutions and want to act in unison. Guyenne is going to follow suit. The same resistances are breaking out from one end of the realm to the other, in Pau, Amiens, Arras. In Pau a gibbet has been erected to hang [in effigy] the commander. In Arras the *bailliage* has been pursued and thrashed, everything has been sacked and smashed. The Rouen *Parlement* is still sitting, and has laid charges against the minister."[6]

Grenoble's punishment is not long in coming. As predicted by the anonymous proclamation, a messenger from Court brings notice of a relatively moderate measure. His Majesty will forgive, but "the *parlement* must set an example of obedience,"[7] that is, must disperse, as ordered in the *lettres de cachet.*

---

*According to Michelet, to whom I seldom refer because it is too easy to make his great voice do all the work. But in this instance his summary is too good to omit.

Within a few days, troops of the line and artillery converge upon the town, where batteries (such as the six cannons mentioned by "Anonymous" on June 9) are placed very visibly on the heights.

The common people are no longer keeping a close watch on the magistrates' doors. The "bourgeois guard," itself a respectful enough body, has been replaced by royal troops. The Grenoble *Parlement* is about to jump ship. After a final consultation, its members almost sneak out of town during the nights of June 12 or 13, bound for their country homes or the destinations assigned by the government.

But it's too late. On the fourteenth, the notables left in town begin to react. If the *Parlement* is eluding its implicit job of embodying the opposition, then they'll do without it, but this time in an orderly fashion and without any rioting in the streets. A few nobles who meet annually as a "standing commission" with unspecified duties consider themselves qualified to convene the gentry of the surrounding countryside, the municipal administrators, the two consuls responsible for the smooth running of local affairs and a number of people from the third estate, arbitrarily selected, it must be said, "from among their most distinguished members."[8]

All these fine fellows meet "on Saturday, June 14, 1788, in the town hall of Grenoble, at ten o'clock in the morning," according to the record of proceedings of the "Grand Town Council."[9]

They have no right to do it. Nobody can meet to deliberate except on the King's order. But there are over a hundred of them, and they are the people who run things in the town and region, and they are surrounded by a ring of flames of the commoners. Their chairman is the highly respected Baron des Adrets. The commanding military officer of the town turns up and timidly points out that they are acting illegally. He is courteously shown the door. After fourteen hours of debate, this "peaceful uprising" ends in a decision that replaces the power of the King with the power of the three estates. Since the King has failed to take the initiative he should have taken, the impromptu assembly will take upon itself to convene the Dauphiné estates. Barnave later writes that this act marks the effective entrance of the third estate into the history of France.[10] That of Grenoble has stepped in between monarchy and people. Your turn to play. Barnave did give a helping hand, true, but the real leader of the discussion on June 14—and a masterly job he does of it—is Jean-Joseph Mounier.

Thirty years old. Not much to look at. A scrawny body with narrow, rounded shoulders and a long and impassive face that directs upon the world a gaze weakened by frequently blinking eyes. He is uncommunicative in ordinary conversation although he can work up plenty of steam on the platform when he's talking to everybody, that is, to nobody in particular. People who have no love for him say he is "censorious, unfeeling in his ways, reserved, cold, and sometimes curt in his responses."[11] At school his fellow pupils nicknamed him Cato. A German woman who loathes him says, "He looks as though he feels nothing but contempt for everything around him."[12] True, he's stiffened with the Dauphiné shellac; but there are other portraits of him that indicate a genuineness and depth of thought capable of inspiring confidence.

He was born in Grenoble on November 12, 1758, in the home of his father, François Mounier, a cloth merchant.* His mother's maiden name was Priez. Part of his moral inelasticity comes from his relatively modest, unexceptional family, respected by friends and clients. Dr. Gagnon, Henri Beyle's grandfather, told how a lady named Borel came to the Mounier shop one day to buy some cloth. By chance it was Jean-Joseph himself, who sometimes helped out in the shop, who waited on her. He unrolled the bolt:

" 'The price of this cloth is twenty-seven livres an ell.'

" 'Well, sir, I'll give you twenty-five for it.'

"Whereupon M. Mounier rolled it back onto the bolt and coldly replaced it on the shelf.

" 'But, sir, I'll go to twenty-five livres and ten sols.'

" 'Madame, an honest man has but one word.' "[13]

Jean-Joseph has six brothers and sisters and is on good terms with them. He learned his three Rs from a maternal uncle, the parish priest of Rives, whose native severity was apparently intensified by a certain Jansenism, producing in young Mounier an even greater timidity. After that, he followed the traditional educational route. At eight, he entered the Royal-Dauphin school in Grenoble. This was the "in" school, run, after the Jesuits' departure, by a nondenominational group of churchmen. The boy rubbed elbows with high society there, the curriculum was varied and the environment comfortable. He was an average pupil and made progress in most subjects, except philosophy, which, at the end of two years, became a stumbling block[14] following an argument with a teacher, who found some comments in his metaphysics notebooks that left little doubt as to his lack of religious fervor. He remained a tranquil agnostic, his skepticism fortified by a congenial as-

---

*At number 6 Grand-Rue, where there is a plaque giving him the title of *"Président* of the National Assembly," a position he occupies during the October Days of 1789. Mounier is one of the chief orators in the early months of the Constituent but he is also a dyed-in-the-wool royalist who views La Fayette and Mirabeau as extremists, so he emigrates in 1790. Joining Bonaparte in 1801, he returns to France and becomes prefect of Ille-et-Vilaine and later councillor of state. Dies in 1806.

sociation with the "good Doctor Gagnon," who gave him free access to his library, which was filled with works that were classified as "subversive" from a religious point of view.[15]

Was he expelled? It was more like an amicable parting of the ways, especially as his father wanted to take him on as clerk before making him a partner in his business. But François Mounier soon realized that his son had little heart for the work and could aspire to higher things. This being the case, he should go into law, which he studied at home, taking lessons from private tutors. At eighteen, he virtually bought, as did so many others, his first degree (at the University of Orange). At twenty-one he was admitted to the bar of the Grenoble *Parlement* and became assistant to Anglès, one of the top barristers in town.* He was immediately marked out for his wide knowledge and precocious maturity, and was entrusted with a few thorny (civil) cases, which he pled successfully.[16] But he remained an advocate for only seven years. With his weak constitution and puny voice, pleading was an ordeal. A higher but less demanding office would take him another step up. The position of royal judge for the town fell vacant in 1783; however, it, too, had to be bought. That might have put it out of his reach, despite his parents' relative prosperity, because the asking price was twenty-three thousand livres, which was too much for them. As with Danton when he becomes King's Councillor in 1787, however, the difficulty was circumvented by the simple expedient of a good marriage. For several months, Jean-Joseph has been sighing after sweet Marie-Philippe, the sister of Achille Borel de Champvallon, one of his best friends and son of an attorney—and of the lady for whom he refused to knock down the price of his father's cloth. That's probably not the reason why the Borels asked him to wait. Their daughter was too young, not yet eighteen. By 1783, however, all's well that ends well, with a beautiful marriage of love and money making possible the purchase, a few weeks later, of the coveted office, which also conferred upon its holder "nobility in a personal capacity." The royal judge sat in even years; odd years were for the episcopal judge.†

Mounier can now indulge his taste for reading, and his preferences become increasingly political. A meeting with a young English traveler named William Byng‡ leads him into the stream of Anglomania that flows through Grenoble after 1785 and surfaces in every issue of the local gazette, *Les*

---

*During the Restoration Anglès is First *Président* of the royal court in Grenoble and doyen of the Chambre des Deputés [House of Representatives] in Paris.

†The Mouniers have three children, two girls and a boy; the son, following in his father's footsteps, plays a part under Louis-Philippe.

‡Who becomes a much respected Whig parliamentarian in his own country.

*Affiches du Dauphiné.** Byng sends him the works of two authors in vogue in London, Blackstone and Delolme, the first of whom is the top law professor at Oxford, the "English Montesquieu," and the second a refugee from Geneva who has just defined the basic principles of constitutional monarchy. Thereafter Mounier is also a full-fledged Whig. In his eyes, a parliamentary monarchy is the solution to every problem.[17]

When he goes to the town hall at sunrise on June 14, 1788, he becomes the man of his own ideas. Inside, he finds a herd of comrades who are brave enough, for the most part, but irresolute. They need a mobilizer.

"Then appeared a man who had hitherto been almost unknown.† He amazed every mind with the profundity of his knowledge of law, whether public or political, by the sagacity and clarity of his discussion, by the force and soundness of his reasoning. In a word, he lit a new light in every eye."[18]

There they are, perplexed and defiant at once, and with courage enough to meet in the town hall: nine churchmen, thirty-three gentlemen and fifty-nine members of the third estate, all of them involved in some way with the law. But to what end? Twelve or fourteen hours of uneasy discussion ensue. Would it have led to anything if the royal judge of Grenoble hadn't imposed their final decision less by the power of his vocal cords than by his "gravity, severity, clarity and conciseness"?[19] Mounier, that day, is "exact as a professor of mathematics and vigorous as a Roman censor whose every sentence is a judgment."[20] Barnave speaks before him, with his customary sharpness, energetically defending what people are soon going to call "doubling the third," meaning that the number of representatives of the third estate elected to all Estates General, regional and national alike, should be equal to the total number of representatives of the first two estates: nobility and clergy. But the faint-hearted are put off by his aggressiveness. Mounier defends the same idea, but more moderately and thereby wins them all to his cause.‡ He is instructed to write an open letter to the King, respectful but firm, announcing the forthcoming meeting of the Dauphiné Estates.

When? How? And where? The Notables disperse, leaving all these questions unanswered. They are expecting some strong reactions. Not until July 7, at another restricted meeting, do they choose July 21 as a possible date. Meanwhile, the intendant and governor issue numerous plaintive and

---

*In this case Anglomania was not a form of snobbery, as at Court, but rather an ideological and political penchant.

†According to Berriat Saint-Prix.

‡First sign of incompatibility between the personalities of the two main leaders of the Grenoble movement.

ineffectual appeals. From Intendant Caze de la Bove (on July 4): "Most of the minds in this town have fallen prey to the vertigo, they wish to escape from all authority whatsoever. . . . Were it not for the danger of giving rise to some fresh uprising, I should not have hesitated to ask the duc [de Clermont-Tonnerre] to send a garrison of dragoons to the town hall."[21] The poor duke has been worried by the tokens of support for "Mounier's manifesto" that have been pouring in from all over Dauphiné. "The whole province has no interest in anything except the invitations being issued by the town hall. Emissaries are going everywhere, inciting people to hold assemblies and carrying ready-made draft deliberations hither and thither. Thus far, very few towns have refused."[22]

You can say that again . . . Between June 17 and June 26 the "conspirators" receive statements of agreement from places as far-flung and dissimilar as Vif, Briançon, Crest, L'Albenc, Die, Saint-Marcellin, Voiron, La Mure, Corps, Embrun, Vienne, Vizille.

On July 6, according to the intendant, "excitement is running so high that people are going out in the streets wearing the colors of Humbert II, the last Dauphin."[23] And in fact, people are beginning to be harried in Grenoble if they are seen *without* the famous colors, "a saffron yellow and sky-blue ribbon," on their hats, walking sticks, lapels or watch chains. Everyone is reminding everyone, even among the illiterates, that in 1343 the illustrious Humbert II would not accept the province's incorporation into France until he was given assurance that it would be allowed to retain its former exemptions and rights.

As usual, the Court's reaction comes too late and is irrelevant. On July 12 the townspeople learn that the King has relieved Clermont-Tonnerre of his command and appointed the Maréchal de Vaux as commander-in-chief of their province. Presumably, everyone in Versailles thought that would give the rubes a jolt, because there's no more hardened trooper in France than this tough, rough old man. He is renowned for his style in the conquest of Corsica, when he used to boast that his eye was so sure, he could tell at a glance how many rebels could be hanged at the same time from the branches of a single tree. The instructions the government has given him for Grenoble sound as though they're meant for that earlier campaign:

"The agitation is apparently as great as before, an assembly is said to be planned for July 21, and, judging by the accounts we have received from the Bishop of Grenoble, it is feared that this assembly will meet as a united state, under the banner of Dauphin Humbert. . . .

"The Maréchal is to know that the seat of the disturbance is in Grenoble. . . . It is essential that he attempt to identify the authors of the revolt of June 7. . . .

"The King will very shortly take steps to convene the estates of the province, but he will not tolerate illicit assemblies, still less recourse to revolt and sedition.

"Wherefore, if the assembly announced for the twenty-first is formed, the Maréchal will not permit it to take place, at Grenoble or elsewhere."[24]

De Vaux turns up on the fifteenth with a military apparatus that he trusts will intimidate, only to find himself the next day in the same position, if one may so call it, as your common Clermont-Tonnerre. His blustering sinks into the sands. The people, the bourgeois, nobles and most of the clergy, far from running away or locking themselves in, give his soldiers an ironic and in some cases cordial welcome, more calculated to demoralize them than open hostility. He is soon forced to negotiate and begin parleying with those he has come to chasten. The nobles, summoned to appear at the town hall and ordered not to proceed with their schemes, answer that since "they had given their word to assemble, they must keep their promise in whatever place it might be in spite of all obstacles and dangers, even in the cannon's mouth."[25]

The cannon's mouth . . . The Maréchal is the type to be tempted by such a challenge. He's got the artillery and the ammunition, but will his soldiers obey? And where the devil is he to use his cannons? The Notables have decided that the estates will not meet in Grenoble, but on July 17 the royal authorities still don't know the name of the place they have chosen. For two more days everybody plays cat and mouse.

Until the nineteenth, when the news runs through town like wildfire: the estates will meet in two days, at Vizille, in one of the finest châteaux in the region. The Perier brothers have gotten into the act.

THE MEETING AT VIZILLE

46

JULY 19 – 22, 1788

Powder Does Not Explode More Quickly

Like the Montgolfiers, the Wendels or the Réveillons, the Periers belong to the first generation of the new breed of great industrialists. It was Claude

Perier, head of the family, who bought, just seven years ago, the big château built at Vizille in the sixteenth century by the dreaded Connétable de Lesdiguières. They call him "the richest man in Dauphiné," and he undoubtedly is.

The Periers have not wasted their time since coming down from the hamlet that gave them their name in the high mountains of Trièves near Mens, south of Grenoble. As farmers and livestock breeders, they laid the foundations of a great rural fortune up there.[1] The founder of the dynasty of the commercial Periers, the agent of mutation and industrial prosperity, was a Jacques Perier, born about 1700, who was the first to move down to Grenoble, where he converted a cloth merchant's business into a factory and virtually monopolized the hemp industry. At his death he controlled the whole of the "manufacture of Voiron linen,* the most valuable that we have and the one I love like a child, the one I took as a nursling and reared for almost forty years."[2] When he died in 1780, leaving at least six hundred thousand livres to his heirs, he was the little king of the Dauphiné hemp hacklers, owned two houses in Grenoble and shares in several large European banks. He brought up the eldest of his six children to succeed, and in fact exceed him, for by 1788 Claude is already being nicknamed "Milord Perier" on account of his connections with English high finance and industry. But people also speak of "the Perier brothers" because there is a younger brother, Augustin, whose aversion to the "manufacture" propelled him toward the Indies Company, of which he is now the director.†

On this July 21, Claude Perier is forty-six. He's got business in his blood. He's a hard boss, his portraits have an uncompromising, bulldog look. Stingy and imperious, "accustomed to make great demands upon himself and others,"[3] he's not a man to lose sleep over his employees' working conditions, even if "the weavers' shops, all below ground level, almost all damp and unwholesome, contribute to the poor health of the people who make linen cloth.‡ After a certain number of years at work they become pale and livid of complexion, with swollen or ulcerated legs."[4] So if Claude Perier is offering the estates his château at Vizille, a town in which he has already set up a wallpaper and cotton factory,§ it's not out of concern for the welfare of the workers who are dependent upon him. Besides, he's only the host, and also

---

*This did not mean ownership of one factory but rather control over a number of small rural shops.

†Augustin commits suicide in 1794 when the revolutionary government abolishes the Indies Company. A few of the brothers' descendants have political careers in the nineteenth century. The great-great-grandson of the eldest, Jean Casimir-Perier, becomes president of the Republic in 1894 (but only for six months, because of his impossible disposition).

‡According to an industrial enquiry made in 1788.

§Employing sixty-nine workers in 1788, with an annual output of twelve thousand units.

the financial backer, of the Dauphiné Notables on this occasion, and no word from his mouth is recorded in the minutes of the meeting. But he's a man who can feel which way the wind is blowing, and his go-getting spirit is incensed by the obstructionism and inertia of the present government.

Bright and early in the midsummer sun, trains of carriages converge upon Vizille; the largest, of course, come from Grenoble, traveling under the eyes of the Maréchal de Vaux's assembled troops, who stand with their guns by their sides, plainly unable to disperse, let alone arrest, the actors on this great day. Some people even wonder if the soldiers are not there, in a sense, as an honor guard.*

The mass of the château looms over the poor houses in the little town below, which is built on a narrow band of level ground squeezed between towering mountains at the confluence of the Drac and the Romanche; the latter stream crosses the town, and a little bridge over it leads to a mule track that scrambles two leagues up to the lakes of Laffrey. A plain often insulted by snow; the houses too low, the mountains too high. In places like this, you might think geology copies society. Unless it's the other way around.

The minutes of the Vizille Assembly are written from start to finish by Mounier, all twelve long-drawn-out pages of them, and are followed by another, similarly interminable letter to the King. They begin with the solemnity of a trumpet fanfare, to tell the tale of the Estates' twenty hours of existence:

"On July 21, 1788, at eight o'clock in the morning, in a room in the château of Vizille where the assembly was held, owing to the impossibility of it taking place in Grenoble, the gentlemen of the clergy, nobility and third estate gathered without concern as to rank or precedence as between the persons of each order, or between the towns, villages and communities they represented."[5]

They hasten along in a sort of grave and merry jostle, not unlike the sittings of the American Constitutional Convention, and in sharp contrast to the hierarchical usages of France. The employees of Claude Perier and some townspeople from Vizille who have been hired for the occasion lead them to the tennis court,† a structure on the edge of the château itself, bare and bright between high, undressed stone walls, containing nothing but a rug-

---

*Perhaps sheer frustration is the cause a few weeks later of the Maréchal's death. Little Henri Beyle is impressed by the pomp and ceremony of his funeral. The Court, overtaken by events and having nothing better to offer, simply recalls Clermont-Tonnerre and sends him back to Grenoble.

†Destroyed by fire in 1825, rebuilt and destroyed definitively by another fire, in 1865, which also ruined one wing of the château.

covered platform four steps up from the floor, for the long table where the chairman and secretary are to sit.

Grouped around it, most of them on their feet except for the sick and the very old, 50 canons and parish priests (not a single bishop), 165 nobles, and 276 representatives of the third estate (187 of them from Grenoble) choose the Comte de Morges, nominated by the nobility, as their chairman, and Jean-Joseph Mounier as their secretary. Meaning that the bulk of the work has been done before they start. Mounier has spent the previous days writing the first draft of the two texts which are approved by acclamation. Thanks to him, they know where they're going, and they proceed there in a straight line even though, out of respect for the assembly, many of those present are given a chance to speak their pieces about the individual paragraphs as they are read out. Depending on their inclinations, some of the speakers want the text watered down, while others, on the contrary, say it needs punching up. The "watering-down" faction are mostly men from the third estate, perhaps because they are well aware that in the event of a crackdown it is they who will be punished first and worst. But there is another fraction of the third, led by Barnave, that is distinctly more aggressive. On this day, however, even Barnave is overtaken by a thirty-six-year-old advocate named Paul Didier, one of the rare speakers whom the chairman finds it necessary to call to order.*

While the speakers are taking their turns, a committee of fifty representatives puts the finishing touches to Mounier's drafts, which does not prevent all of them from sitting down in the afternoon to a superb snack offered by the Perier brothers. Many of those present know the château only from hearsay, so they take advantage of the break to stroll through "the vast gardens,† magnificent terraces, beautiful avenues of huge poplars planted two centuries before, handsome walled garden, a mall, and in general all the things that go to embellish the days of a very grand lord, which had been assembled by M. de Lesdiguières."[6]

---

*This day makes Didier's name in Dauphiné. His is a curious and fluctuating fate. At first an ultrarevolutionary, he turns coat in year II, enough to play a part in the Lyons insurrection against the Convention. He manages to escape and becomes a secret agent of the Comte de Provence in Germany. From the Directoire to the Hundred Days and after, he wavers between Bonaparte and the Bourbons. At last, pro-Bonaparte at the wrong moment, he foments a plot, shortly after Waterloo, in Grenoble, on behalf of the king of Rome. Denounced and promptly sentenced in 1816, he and twenty of his companions are executed in one of the legal massacres of the White Terror.

†The Vizille château became an occasional residence of the presidents of France during the Third and Fourth Republics, before being given to the Conseil Général of Isère, which, on the initiative of its president Louis Mermaz, transformed it, in 1980, into a national Museum of the French Revolution.

By the middle of the night it's all finished, the participants can get back into their carriages and leave Vizille, crossing the cordons of the Maréchal de Vaux's useless troops. The last lines have been written:

"Done in the château of Vizille at three o'clock in the morning on July twenty-second, one thousand seven hundred eighty-eight.

"Le Comte de Morges, Chairman; Mounier, Secretary."[7]

In these two hodgepodge texts a few phrases stand out, like the first drops of the downpour of words that is soon to become a flood:

> Whereas it is one of the most precious privileges of the inhabitants of Dauphiné to meet and deliberate upon public matters . . .
>
> Whereas it is a fundamental law, as ancient as the kingdom itself, that the French may not be taxed without their consent . . .
>
> Whereas, lastly, governments were established in order to protect the freedom of individuals; and *lettres de cachet* can be regarded only as acts of violence . . . ,
>
> [We have] resolved that the three orders of the province, eager to set an example to the whole of France, of union and attachment to the monarchy, will not grant the taxes until their representatives shall have deliberated in the Estates General of the kingdom. . . .
>
> Further resolved that, in the states of the province, the representatives of the third estate shall be equal in number to the total of those of the first two orders; and that all members of the assembly shall be elected . . .
>
> Further resolved that the three orders of Dauphiné shall never part cause with the other provinces and that in upholding their particular rights they shall not abandon those of the nation.

Even in the respectful packaging concocted by Mounier, five or six ideas that would have been positively scandalous only a few months before can be glimpsed peeking through these lines:

French citizens are deciding that they have "the privilege" to meet when they please, without asking anybody's permission.

Lettres de cachet must be abolished.

A sort of tax strike is declared upon taxes that have not been accepted by the taxpayers.

The "doubling of the third" is permanently established for Dauphiné, hence proposed as a model to all the other provinces.

At the same time, the "Dauphiné movement" refuses to be treated as unique; it allies itself with all demands for justice and liberty arising in all the other provinces of the realm—no, the *nation!* The word has been spoken, and will travel.

And thus end the "Estates of Vizille." In themselves, almost nothing—a peaceful party and a few speeches. Thanks to the determination and tenacity of a handful of men, everything was done *before,* beginning with the people's uprising and despite the *parlement*'s hesitations. And everything is going to come *after,* since, as Barnave says, this meeting lays down "the initial foundations for a democratic revolution."[8] "Powder does not explode more quickly* than did the resolution of Vizille, in public opinion."[9]

MALESHERBES

47

JULY–AUGUST 1788

I See a Storm Gathering

But what does it mean, the "nation"? In July 1788 Malesherbes delivers a definition of the word to Louis XVI, in a sentence that might have been taken from the *Encyclopédie:* "The Nation is composed of all the King's subjects and all the individuals who are established and have their fortunes in France, whose persons and assets are governed by the laws of France."[1] In these seemingly innocuous words lies the beginning of the end of the fateful division of the French into three orders.

And Malesherbes sternly adds, as though he were speaking not to his sovereign but to a dishearteningly unpromising pupil: "The time is past when one can try to deceive the Nation. . . . Let us speak plainly. What the Nation is asking for is a new constitution, something that has never existed in France. Not only is this what the Nation wants, it is also what the King has committed himself to in all his acts in the past year and a half.† . . . The Nation, seeing itself ruined because this constitution has not existed in past reigns, is entitled to ask for it, and the King is obliged to grant it."[2]

Sounds like one of those rabble-rousing tracts by Barnave or the anonymous posters in Grenoble; but what it is, is a carefully thought-out text by Chrétien-Guillaume Lamoignon de Malesherbes, sixty-seven this year, minister without portfolio in Brienne's government, "the great Malesherbes" as

---

*According to Bertrand de Molleville, who was then intendant of Brittany and will become a minister under Louis XVI.

†By convening the Notables and announcing that reforms were to be made.

he's called by all and sundry. The Wise Man par excellence. Yet there's nothing of the thunderbolt about him, his long statesman's career looks more like a series of curves, zigzags and dotted lines, some of them pointing backward. In 1776, for instance, he began by supporting Turgot, then sabotaged his experiment. And more recently, working with Rabaut Saint-Étienne, he has imposed the Edict of Toleration for "non-Catholics," but oh! so cautiously, almost sneakily. We know he is by no means a coward, but as he sees it, in this antique monarchy, every twist and turn of which he knows so well, such precautions are the only way to be sure of getting results.

So, what's happening now? Has Malesherbes undergone another change of heart? The truth is that, paragon of patience though he may be, he's too angry to take any more. There's a taste of ashes in his mouth, and it's about those very "non-Catholics." What's the point of getting the King to sign the Edict of Toleration if this wrangle between authorities and *parlements* is going to prevent it from being applied? A sober look at himself leads to bitter clarity: "The position of minister is not suited to those who have distinguished themselves by opposing other ministers on behalf of the people's rights.*. . . It is therefore unreasonable to want to keep in the Council a man whose way of thinking is diametrically opposed to what is being done there." He wrote that in a memorandum he gave Louis XVI before a Council meeting, entitled "Reasons for the Request [to resign] that I Submitted to the King in June 1788."[3]

He points out that thirteen years before, he became a minister "out of pure obedience," in order to help Turgot. This time he was willing to do so again, at Brienne's behest, but he feels useless sitting on the Conseil des Dépêches, which deals only with the domestic affairs of the realm, and he's not allowed to sit on the Conseil d'En Haut, which directs foreign policy and declares war and peace. He's a methodical person and is irritated by the pace of the Conseil des Dépêches, "where reports on twenty matters take two hours. I do not have the gift to understand matters on the run."[4]

He complains of having swallowed too many bitter pills. He wasn't happy even when they exiled the *Parlement* to Troyes, and from then on he has wanted to leave. He became all the more determined to go after the conflicts in November and May, and especially after the last royal session, the one that turned into a bed of justice, which he was "pained to attend" without even having been allowed to give an opinion beforehand, since it had all been arranged in a secret meeting between his cousin Lamoignon, Brienne and the King before it was ever mentioned to the Council.

"The King can surely not condemn me forever to the grief and humiliation of remaining an idle spectator at events that must, in every respect,

---

*Allusion to the Cour des Aides' sharp remonstrations to Louis XV.

pain me to the core."[5] When will they ever understand that Malesherbes is
first and foremost a *parlement* man, even if he doesn't always approve of his
colleagues?

He's been wanting to tell Louis XVI all this to his face for a long time,
and he's been asking for a private audience for a long time. But they have
eluded him, and thereby sickened him. "Since I was called to the Council I
have not been allowed to speak to the King privately even once. I always
had to make my request through other ministers, and I was always put off.

"Some while after the bed of justice relating to the plenary court, I
said this must cease and that I absolutely desired to speak to the King
himself."[6]

He had resigned himself to hanging about Versailles, and even Marly,
all spring, with his mournful air, his big swelling nose and his large-bellied
ponderousness, bedeviled by "that accursed sword that gets tangled in my
legs."[7]

"The audience that was granted me transpired thus. The King, coming
into the Council, called me up and, in the presence of the Archbishop of
Sens [Brienne], said to me with a most benevolent air that he knew I absolutely desired to leave him and that he was sorry to hear it but that he
required me to remain a little longer. . . . After these few words, the King
turned away in great haste, leaving me no time to reply. I had only time to
tell him that I should make bold to send him the reasons for my resignation
in writing.

"From that day forth I have considered myself on the Council in the
same way as one is in the Bastille: as the result of a *lettre de cachet*."[8]

All right, if they won't listen to him, he'll write. At first, he imagines it
is solely in order to explain his hypothetical resignation, but what he submits
to the King is in fact the voice of Cassandra. Maybe it's better to do it in
writing, at that. His elocution is subject to entanglements, and he feels that
the warnings he bears within himself are so grave that he'd be likely to stutter
if he were to speak them out loud. "I see a storm gathering that all the royal
power will not be able to dispel, and faults of negligence and delay that in
other circumstances would be looked upon as only minor wrongs can today
become irreparable, and will plunge the King's entire life into bitterness and
hurl his kingdom into troubles of which no one can see the end. . . .

"The old ministers of young kings have often been criticized for showing
a culpable indifference to future calamities that they will not be there to see.
That is a reproach I do not want to deserve."[9]

Spoken to his face, these prophecies would have been intolerable to
Louis XVI, who has always found it difficult to put up with "M. de Males-

herbes's downright ways."* But the King probably never even reads them, because when his "captive minister" gives him the paper on June 15 or 16,† "he took it with a smile, put it in his pocket, and has never mentioned it to me since."[10]

Nevertheless, Malesherbes spends over a month on a second text while he's at it, his *Mémoire sur la situation présente des affaires.* In this, he speaks his mind with the force and serenity of a man who is burning his boats. "Confined in total solitude"[11] in his house on the rue des Martyrs in Paris, he chooses to endure the stifling heat and summer stench of the big town on the unhealthy slopes surmounted by the mills of Montmartre, rather than retire to the greenery of his estate at Malesherbes, where he could abandon himself, surrounded by his family, to his growing passion for botany. He doesn't want anybody to know how far he's going.

Here, he pays the price of his destiny. Malesherbes sincerely believes that he is the man of the last chance. His whole life of reckless prudence culminates in these few pages, which he has the good fortune, despite all the barriers, to succeed in placing in the hands of the other man of the last chance, his sovereign, who might still, if he could hear, if he could make up his mind . . . Isn't he the living god of twenty-five million "subjects"?

According to him, the King can still save the day. This conviction Malesherbes unwittingly shares with another man of the law, the Mounier who has suddenly leaped into the limelight out there in Dauphiné by opposing abuses, a man who, like himself, still has rooted in him, by his whole upbringing, the certainty that the King is a good king badly counseled, and that once he knows, thanks to them, he will understand and act.

Thanks to me, Chrétien de Malesherbes. "I see a storm gathering . . ." Nowadays the word "revolution" is current all over the country. The old man, schooled in a knowledge of the deeper levels of what he has never been heard to call the "populace," sees from most palpable signs that in France this revolution is likely to exceed by far anyone's expectations.

Well, then, carry it out yourself, Sire. And all will be well. Malesherbes's memorandum to the King is an outcry. The last that could have made itself heard before the meeting of the Estates General.‡

He's not talking about France alone. "There has spread over the whole surface of the earth, or at least all those nations that communicate their

---

*The expression is by the young Chateaubriand, whose family had recently become connected by marriage to the Rosanbos, the "Wise Man's" direct descendants.

†Not before distributing copies, for form's sake, to Brienne and Lamoignon, "for it is a principle of mine to attack no person secretly."

‡This text remains unknown to everyone, including the historians, until Pierre Grosclaude discovers it in 1950, in the Rosanbo archives.

feelings by reading, a spirit of independence unknown to our ancestors. For forty years now people have constantly been debating the respective rights of sovereigns and peoples, and there is no individual who is not questioning the conditions in which obedience is required of him."[12]

Now Malesherbes comes to his justification as councillor, his *raison d'être:* he submits his proposals for salvation.

The Estates General must be convened in 1789.

The King must not convene them just from time to time; his object will be to set up a *perpetual relationship between himself and his people.**

The King will give the nation a constitution in order to control abuses and put an end to privilege.

The King will authorize the printing of all works relevant to the issues raised by the Estates General (except those opposed to religion or morality, or those that contain personal attacks).

After setting out sound reasons why the voices of the representatives of the third estate should be heard individually—in other words, why future assemblies should vote by name and no longer by order—Malesherbes concludes, "The time is past when people could be persuaded that the work of their legislators was the work of the gods and, like the gods, immutable. . . . Other assemblies will perfect what will be accomplished by the one of 1789 and, so long as the two orders that comprise only a tiny portion of the nation are not allowed to perpetuate their right to vote for the whole of the nation, time and the progress of reason will do the rest."[13]

There is but one way out: "The King must proclaim, in terms leaving no room for doubt, his intentions regarding the nation's happiness. He must open his heart in the nation's presence, as he has done more than once to his ministers."[14]

At the beginning of August, Malesherbes is again granted a condescending permission to hand this final memorandum to Louis XVI,† who says no more about it to him than he did about the first.[15] It has the ring of a testament. It is his testament.

His resignation has now been accepted, but he is asked to keep it a secret for the time being. He does not know that his fate as minister is tied to Brienne's, as it was before to that of Turgot.

On August 21 Mirabeau writes to his friend Major de Mauvillon, "I do not share the *parlements'* fanaticism and I have not written a single line for the opposition party. Nor, to tell the truth, have I written for the other side. I have always believed that between King and *parlement* there was a poor,

---

*Malesherbes's italics.

†Some historians have claimed, without evidence, that the text was not read by the King until four years later, before his execution.

obscure little party called the nation, to which people of sense and sincerity must belong."[16]

Malesherbes is about to go away, then, once again without having been able to accomplish anything, but in his heart he carries the words he will say to the King a few weeks later, when he is just another privileged private person attending the Sunday levée, "You read widely, Sire, and know more than people think you do. But reading is nothing unless it be accompanied by reflection. . . . Charles I was a gentle prince, virtuous and attached to the laws; he was never harsh, never aggressive; he was just and bountiful, and yet he perished on a scaffold."[17]

ABBÉ GRÉGOIRE

48

AUGUST 1788

Tear Up the Gospels, or Conform to Their Morality

There could be no plainer proof of the reputation achieved by Malesherbes in the different classes of society and different parts of the realm than the long letter he receives, in late August 1788, from a little Lorraine religious, the Abbé Henri Grégoire, parish priest of Embermesnil.* The two have not met. Grégoire has never even "gone up" to Paris, much less to Versailles. But when he wants to publish a piece of writing of which he is very proud,

---

*This little priest becomes a very big man in the Revolution. Henri Grégoire is sent to the Estates General by his parishioners and immediately allies himself with the "grassroots clergy," who lead the order of the clergy to join forces with the third estate. During the Constituent he is always one of the first to do battle for new ideas, readily takes the oath on the civil status of the clergy, and is elected constitutional bishop of Blois. Sent to the Convention by his diocese, he invariably sits with the Mountain [ultraliberals] but remains no less loyal to his faith and religious commitments. After the Concordat he resigns from his bishopric and becomes an ordinary priest again, but later becomes a senator and Comte d'Empire, despite his lack of enthusiasm for the service of Napoleon. Under the Restoration he lives in a sort of inner exile, writing many books in which he always defends the same causes. His funeral in Paris, on May 31, 1831, is the occasion for a great demonstration by the liberals.

the fruit of years of research and reflection, where should he turn but to the minister who has done his utmost, for thirty years now, to foster writers with something new to say?

Listen to the tone of his request—respectful, to be sure, but almost as between equals: "I possess the pride of virtue and should scorn the protection of the Minister of State, did I not also venerate, in Malesherbes, the enlightened philosopher, true friend of men.*

"I present my petition to you with confidence, Monseigneur; may you find it in yourself to approve it, if only to spare your heart the pain of a refusal."[1]

The subject? The situation of the Jews in France.

Malesherbes is the ideal person to approach on this matter for two reasons: his reputation, of course, but also a decision taken by the King a few months previously. From Grégoire: "The periodical sheets have announced that the King desired a memorandum on what could be done about the Jews, of whom there are some forty thousand in France. I have been conducting research into this matter, Monseigneur, for ten years, and the Academy of Metz has just awarded prizes to three works relating to the question, mine at the head."[2] And so it was; the decision of the "Royal Society of Sciences and Arts of Metz" is dated August 23 and is mentioned in the preface to the *Essai sur la régéneration physique, morale et politique des juifs,* by Monsieur Grégoire, parish priest in the diocese of Metz, now member of the same Society.[3]

On November 17, 1787, when Malesherbes got Louis XVI to sign the Edict on the status of the Protestants, the King made a curious remark, pure product of his coarse sense of malice: "Monsieur de Malesherbes, you have made yourself a Protestant; I hereby make you a Jew; do something for them."[4]

A praiseworthy intention on the part of a kindhearted sovereign troubled by the downtrodden condition of a group of his subjects? No doubt. Also a welcome opportunity to divert Malesherbes's zeal into another humanitarian channel. As long as this eternal champion of forgotten causes is busy taking care of the Jews, he might keep his nose out of matters of high policy.†

Abbé Grégoire is thirty-eight. Average height, broad-shouldered, with regular features framed by thick brown hair. His nose has a slight hook at

---

*Could this be an unconscious allusion to the famous nickname of Mirabeau's father?

†On the eve of the Revolution, thus, Malesherbes, the last great enlightened mind of the monarchy, is collaborating with the two most famous religious figures among its leaders—the Protestant Rabaut Saint-Étienne and the Catholic Grégoire.

the top, then drops straight down over thin, tight lips. His customary expression is one of determination, tempered by the mildness of his big dark eyes. There's something a little vague in his gaze, the result of a slight strabismus; his detractors say he's cross-eyed.[5]

He was born in Vého, a very small village in Lorraine—we would call it, despite the piquant observation with which he begins his *Mémoires.*[6] "The hamlet of Vého, where I was born, was in the province of the Three Bishoprics, which, with Lorraine, formed a sort of complex political marquetry. The localities belonging to these two provinces were so intermingled that a number of towns and villages were themselves divided by different jurisdictions; this, no doubt, is the origin of the error, or rather ineptitude, of certain geographers who write *Metz in Lorraine,* as others say *Monaco in Provence;* it would be tantamount to saying *Nancy in the Three Bishoprics. . . .* To return to our Lorraine: its sufferings under Louis XIV were unheard of; the acts of ferocity committed there by the satellites of this tyrant left almost no trace in history; nobody dared to make them public so long as the Bourbons reigned. . . . Ancient wars between Lorraine and the Metz country . . . gave rise on both sides to a hatred that became more intense after the latter was attached to France. . . . I have known French travelers who would never consent to eat a meal prepared in a hostelry called the Croix de Lorraine."

Priest though he be, then, and a sincere priest too, Grégoire has a caustic wit and quick repartee. His parents were small farmers (even if his father did rise to the status of "garment cutter"). He's proud of it: "Born plebeian, my plebeianism goes back to Adam, and I will not separate my affections and interests from those of the people. . . . The more importance one attaches to birth and wealth, the less one has to spare for virtue. . . . Out of one hundred men traveling by coach, ninety-five think themselves better than the wretches going on foot and forget that one day they must leave their carriage for a hearse."[7]

Henri was an only child and a happy one, but not spoiled. He speaks of the "authors of his days" with "inexpressible tenderness. We were never happier than when we were together."[8] His childhood was unruffled: first lessons from the priest of Vého;* then the Jesuits in Nancy, "where I encountered nothing but good examples and useful lessons. Childhood is the antechamber to life, memories from those years have a delicious charm. . . . For a schoolmaster I had, among others, Père Beauregard, a famous preacher."[9] Perhaps it was from him that Grégoire learned the catchy, lively

---

*Looking for traces of his early years in that village, which can't have grown much since, we find it twelve miles from Lunéville. The steamroller of World War I passed over it, but it is touching to see a plaque giving his date of birth on a house built where that of his parents stood.

style, so unlike the usual tepid piety of his fellows, that strikes the ear from the very beginning of his essay on the Jews. In any event, "I shall preserve until my dying day a respectful attachment to my teachers."

Never does Abbé Grégoire utter one word of regret about his ordination. In Vého he was born to be a priest. A priest he is, a priest he will remain.

He took orders in 1775, early in the King's reign. For a while, he taught theology at Pont-à-Mousson, then he was made vicar at Miramont-le-Haut. In 1782 he was parish priest in Embermesnil,[10] three leagues from Lunéville, that mini-Versailles of the dukes of Lorraine where Stanislas Leczinsky, ex-king of Poland and father of Louis XV's wife, ended his days in clover before the quiet absorption of Lorraine into France.

If there is no revolution in France, Grégoire will stay where he is now. As a country priest he has led the life, at once unglamorous and protected, of so many other microscopic clerical chiefs woven into the fabric of France. Day by day, he is first among his thousand parishioners, even if some local squire might occasionally preside on the churchwardens' pew at high mass and receive the homage of incense and consecrated bread. But the village priest is permanently in the field and on the spot, where he wants for nothing except the superfluous, about which Grégoire couldn't care less. Through the confessional, he knows all about the private lives of everyone. He marries people, sometimes a little forcibly; he baptizes, teaches, buries. Every Sunday, during the announcements that follow the reading of the Gospel, he transmits the news of the realm and desiderata of the authorities. Henri Grégoire is one of the thousands of compulsory wires through which the current passes from top to bottom. There is every reason to believe he performs his duties well. His parishioners swear to it, at any rate.

He does more. Open to the spirit of Enlightenment, he assembles, at his own expense, an educational library in his presbytery, in which works on hygiene, agriculture and the "mechanical arts" stand next to religious works.

Such has been the soil of his life, in which a luxuriant autodidact's crop has grown from his wide reading, fertilized by an idiosyncratic sense of humor. When the natural good spirits of a man at ease with himself turn to consider the plight of his fellow creatures, the priest of Embermesnil moves into a loftier mode.

He was about thirty years old when he was first confronted with the problem of the Jews in Lorraine, and Metz in particular, where the aftermath of the Middle Ages circumscribed them with a weird medley of restrictions combined with privileges doled out with an eyedropper.

In the whole of France there are about forty thousand Jews, living in small autonomous communities in places where they are tolerated. "Their status and living conditions varied from one region to the next. . . . But in no place did they have equal rights, and almost all were poor and had little education. The Jews of the eastern provinces, also called *German Jews* to distinguish them from the Jews of the south who came originally either from the Iberian Peninsula or from the Papal States, were by far the most numerous and the most unfortunate, especially in Alsace."[11]

Living on the border between Lorraine and the Three Bishoprics, Grégoire met them every day, these people condemned as usurers because they were condemned to the practice of usury. Forbidden to engage in any occupation but trade, forbidden to farm, to serve in the army, to be civil servants, all that was left them was their skill at trading and their obstinate religion, in which they awaited the Messiah and stuck together.

"In one of our towns of France a Jew is arrested for practicing a trade; he is hailed before the judge: 'I have,' he says, 'six children lying in filth, dying of hunger and cold; my brother is about to be hanged for a theft he committed in despair. I ask to be allowed to share his fate, before becoming a criminal myself.'*

". . . It is we who compel the Jews to become perverse. If we are entitled to be surprised by anything, it is only that they are not more so. . . . When shall we restore to mankind this people who have been outraged by our prejudices and relegated by our hatred to a position halfway between us and brute animals?"[12]

His pen shakes so, one would think he's undergoing a sort of second ordination: "Pity those who stray, pray for them, love them, serve them, fraternize with them. . . . A priest congratulates himself when, insofar as it is in him to do so, he can perform so sweet a duty as this. . . . How could I anticipate that people would be shocked by my intimacy with Protestants, Quakers, Jews, etc. The Gospel says we must spare the weak; but must we be sparing to the wicked and to fools? Oh jaundiced humans, will the world always look yellow to you?"[13]

Wrapped in a title that is not only cautious but, with its allusion to "regeneration," almost demeaning to the Jewish community, Abbé Grégoire's tract provides a table of contents that might be the perfect anti-Semite's vade mecum, covering the divers vices of the Jews, their usury, their prejudices. And then he drops his mask:

"Let us remember that the Jews are scarcely beginning to breathe; that from the capture of Jerusalem to the sixteenth century there are few countries from which they have not been driven, only to be called back again and then

---

*There are many such outpourings in the notes that comprise almost half of Grégoire's book. In them he lets himself go, indulging in strokes of burlesque erudition in which, while pretending to make fun of Judaic superstitions, he shows scant mercy for those of the Roman Catholics.

driven out once more, plundered, massacred or burned; and their sufferings have indeed continued to the present day. A rabid universe has worried at the cadaver of this nation; their best has almost always been to shed nothing worse than tears. . . . We all speak with horror of the St. Bartholomew massacre; but the Jews have been victims of more tragic scenes a hundred times; and who were the murderers?!"[14]

"For seventeen centuries they have been struggling and supporting each other through persecution and carnage. All the nations have truly united to annihilate a people who exist in every nation and yet are unlike any other, who identify with none. . . . In a word the Jews, everywhere hated and persecuted, exist everywhere. They are, as it were, a tree that has no more trunk but only scattered twigs and yet continues to produce a robust vegetation."[15]

There he is, Grégoire, perpetrating these extraordinary statements from the height of the pulpit of his little church in Lorraine. He's not bothered about it. He has made his peace with himself, and keeps it. "The Savior was careful not to impart to his religion an aspect of violence that would have made it loathsome. . . . *Charity** is the word of the Gospels, and when I see persecutors who call themselves Christians, I am tempted to think they have not read them. Tear up the Gospels, or conform to their morality."[16]

"All too often we see men of iron who profane the name of mercy. Their hearts go out to people two thousand years or two thousand leagues away, their hearts swell for helots and Hottentots, whereas the poor wretch they pass in the road merits at most a pitying glance. And here at our door are the scions of this ancient people, abandoned brothers who for fifteen centuries have not seen the glow of happiness upon their heads. . . .

"Children of the Gospel . . . , you ignore your obligation to posterity. . . . You have only just been born, and very soon the worm will crawl across your monuments. Are your cadavers all that you will leave to the men of the future? Let them learn what you have been to the Jews. . . . Hasten to pay this debt, lest you depart insolvent."[17]

This piece of dynamite lands on Malesherbes's desk too late for him to give any immediate response to it. But during the summer months of 1788, alongside his last-ditch effort to make the King understand that he can even now be the initiator of the great reform, Chrétien-Guillaume works with a small group of friends to compile a survey of the situation of the Jews in France and try to improve their status. He has frequent contacts with Cerf

*Grégoire's italics.

Beer, an important businessman in Strasbourg who has made a name for himself there, despite his race, as an active and sagacious person. He also consults, on many occasions, two Pierre-Louis: the first is Pierre-Louis de Lacretelle, one of the best advocates in Nancy and a defender of the Protestants and Jews in Lorraine; the other is Pierre-Louis Roederer, a councillor in the Nancy *Parlement* who makes no secret of his political ambitions.*

Malesherbes also takes note of the views of Mirabeau, who has just brought out a book in Berlin, *Sur Moses Mendelsohn et sur la réforme politique des juifs*. Once again, the man ruined by love and debt has put his finger on one of the real problems of the day. If Malesherbes had kept his place in the government, it would have been easier for him to bring about a change in the status of the Jews than it was in that of the Protestants because all that is involved here is the tolerance and integration into the national fabric of small autonomous groups who practice a "marginal" religion with beliefs and practices that could not interfere with those of the Catholics or lead to possible heresies.

The publication of Abbé Grégoire's text would have come at just the right moment to guide public opinion. What could be better than a priest pleading on behalf of the Jews? So the priest of Embermesnil is perfectly justified in hoping for a wide readership and government support. Under ordinary circumstances, his book could have been one of the events of the coming year.

But Grégoire and the Jews will have to wait awhile. In early September Malesherbes replies, saying he can do nothing for Grégoire:

"Sir, I am no longer in a position to obtain from the government the facilities you wish for the publication of your work.

"As a private person, I can tell you that I greatly desire the work to appear.

"In this matter and in almost every other pertaining to legislation, I have always thought it necessary to begin by educating the public, before publishing laws."[18]

This is a bitter disappointment for Grégoire, but cannot deprive him of the essential satisfaction of a job well done. Its being awarded a prize by the Academy of Metz makes it possible for him to issue a series of small editions, aimed at societies of thinkers and reading centers throughout France. If, in a few months, he becomes a delegate to the Estates General in the ranks of the lower clergy, as he fully expects to be, at least he won't be a complete unknown.

---

*As *procureur-syndic* of the municipality of Paris (we would say prefect of the department of Seine), Roederer plays a principal role on August 10, 1792 [when the monarchy is finally overthrown]. Later, on the Council of State, he is one of the men Bonaparte listens to most.

49

AUGUST 1788

The Nation Has Stepped Forward a Century

On August 8, 1788, the King's Council announces that the Estates General of the Realm are to meet on May 1 of the following year.

No doubt few citizens have the perseverance to read all the way through the decision, which fills over six pages in the "records of the Council of State" (that is, the supreme government body, consisting of a few ministers and the sovereign). Ponderous, slow and dreary, the text weaves back and forth from the announcement of the much-desired assembly to a funeral oration for the plenary court that was stillborn in May. A few disingenuous allusions even imply that the defunct court may meet soon after the Estates General.[1]

Who cares? And who cares that there is no mention of the venue? The news itself explodes its wrapping. One or two people know what it means: "From this day forth, there was no human cause that could prevent the meeting of the Estates General, save perhaps a foreign war."[2] Mirabeau bubbles over with joy: "The nation has stepped forward a century in twenty-four hours. Ah, my friend,* you will see what a nation this will be on the day it is established, the day when talent will also be a power. I hope that when that time comes, you will hear your friend well spoken of."[3]

A few days after this first outpouring his enthusiasm is dampened by second thoughts. The essential man in him, the man of order, has doubts about the stampede that will soon be on all over France, in the direction of the great forum: "What has happened to the government is what I so often have told them would happen: If you don't want them on foot, they'll come on horseback. By trying to push them back, they've brought them on sooner instead, and there will be a rush; it will be felt, all right. What will they

*He's writing to Major de Mauvillon.

accomplish? A great deal of nonsense, no doubt. . . . The first Estates General will be tumultuous, perhaps they'll go too far. The second will ensure their permanence. The third will ensure the Constitution."[4]

But Brienne was called to power precisely in order to forestall the Estates General, even though he had to promise to hold them in 1792, but still vaguely. . . . The Court, and especially the coterie of Marie Antoinette's advisers, was betting on the new government's ability to straighten out the financial situation within a few years and establish, by dint of authority and skill, a structure for the state that would at last be workable. And in that case, what would be the point of any Estates General? Everybody'd have forgotten all about them!

But the floor has slipped out from under Brienne's feet. The *parlements* are on strike. The army is softening. The bourgeoisie of gown and commerce has joined the opposition. From Brittany to Dauphiné, Normandy to Béarn, the people are grumbling.

He thought everything might still be all right if his own people would give him the help he absolutely required. His own people, meaning the clergy, his peers, those of his own class and background, even if many of them possessed no more spiritual vocation than himself.

The clergy is the first order of France, even richer, in land and money, than the nobility. The bishops, all of whom, in the past century, have come from the nobility, as well as the powerful abbots of the great monasteries, hold almost half the real estate of France. This property is presumed to be the product of accumulated centuries of endowments and is regarded as sacred, untouchable by any form of taxation. Every year, thanks to the tithe system from which no layman—except for the great noble families—is exempt, it grows. More than the most wasteful extravagance of the princely households, more than the abyss of the expenditure of the American war, this paralyzing immobilization of the wealth of France is what has brought about the collapse of the national treasury.

But since *some* money must nevertheless move from Church to state, a general Assembly of the Clergy agrees that every five years it will make a "free gift" to the King, who has no say in the amount involved—that would have been a sort of sacrilege, an insult to the Ark of Alliance. One of the hidden reasons for Necker's fall in 1781 was that he dared to point out this monstrosity in the French financial system. But what could one expect from a Protestant? . . .

Now, on the other hand, we have Monseigneur, archbishop of Toulouse yesterday and Sens today, as first minister. He thought the return of a prelate to the supreme office would encourage his colleagues to be princely to their Prince. If the Assembly of the Clergy of 1788 had voted a "free gift" on a substantially larger scale than its previous efforts, it would have created a draft in the Treasury, the banks would have followed suit, and not even the obstruction of the *parlements* could have prevented the situation from righting itself.

No luck. Brienne can hardly recognize his own clergy.[5] Not content with refusing to add one jot or tittle to its "free gift," the Assembly produces a set of Remonstrances to the King that go well beyond even the boldest pretensions of most of the *parlements:* "The evils are great but their remedies are even greater, for the grandeur of Your Majesty is to be, not King of France, but King of the French, and your subjects' hearts are the most beautiful of all your estates."[6]

Off with the head of the plenary court, shoulder-to-shoulder with the *parlements,* and even . . . on with the Estates General!* As for an increase in the "free gift," in its Remonstrance of June 15 the Assembly of the Clergy smugly snaps its purse shut under the King's nose: "We make bold to say, to a master whose magnificence is equal to his power, that our conscience and our honor do not permit us to agree that what can only be the offering of our love should be changed into a compulsory tribute."[7]

In the offices of the Assembly, of which he was one of the standing secretaries, Abbé Charles-Maurice de Talleyrand-Périgord must have enjoyed rolling that sentence off his tongue.†

By the beginning of August 1788, the King has spent his last penny. This has happened before in the history of France, but adroit ministers had always contrived, by means of taxes and loans, to find last-minute resources. On the eighth, Brienne announces the convening of the Estates because this time his back is to the wall and he's down to his last card:

"I am by nature mild and accommodating but I did not believe the King should give way. I rejected all proposals that demanded sacrifices that I believed to be unreasonable.‡ And it was my opinion . . . that the sacrifices must be made to the nation, and not to bodies that I have always regarded as the nation's foes, usurpers of its rights, concerned solely to safeguard their own interests, and the true bane of a good government. I accordingly made up my mind and told myself that this must be stopped, there must be no

*True, the clergy assumed that voting would be by order and not by name, so that it would be able to defend its privileges.

†Two years later he gets the Constituent Assembly to vote the nationalization of Church assets.

‡According to Brienne, even the Comte d'Artois was asking for the "factious *parlements*" to be recalled. The Archbishop adds that his idea was to convene the Estates in Rheims, far from Paris, and to choose their members, by means of a secondary vote, from among the members of the provincial assemblies.

further thought of delaying the Estates General. Perhaps this announcement will calm the universal infatuation with the *parlements*."[8]

But he keeps going around in circles, he mixes up the wording of the preliminary decision of July 5 with that of the second one on August 8, and all over the country people start reaching for documents on the membership of the last Estates General—held in 1614. He has opened Pandora's box. How can he fail to see that while pretending to conduct historical research each group, whichever order it belongs to, will be thinking and acting solely in terms of its own immediate future? The traditionalists never forgive him. "It would have been hard to conceive of an evil of any kind, of which such a measure would not become the principle. The indefinite promise was met with suspicion; the positive invitation was swallowed wholesale. . . . At a time when people should have been calmed and contained, every passion was exacerbated and a limitless field opened to unbridled liberty."[9]

Did he imagine he could count on the support of the progressives, a few of whom had been generous with their approval? Too late again, Brienne! "Neither enlightened enough to be a *philosophe*** nor firm enough to be a despot,"[10] the "principal minister" fails, despite his decision to convene the Estates, to create any belief in the conversion to liberalism of a government that has been trying for several months to impose a Maupeou-style absolutist rule. "The Archbishop of Sens stirred up the third estate to gain its support against the privileged classes. Whereupon the third estate made it known that it would take its place in the Estates General; but it did not wish to owe that place to a minister who reverted to liberal ideas only after attempting and failing to impose the most despotic institutions."

It's the eternal parable again, of the new wine that can't be poured into old bottles. It's also Marie Antoinette's first serious political setback. Louis XVI's inertia has led the Queen to do what her mother always advised against: take over the running of France through the agency of other people—all those bishops and abbés who were placed around her long before, all those Véris, Vermonds and Briennes whom she had arranged as a protective screen against the return of the "virtuous," the "censor," Necker. If only to avoid seeing him in power again, she would gladly have let Brienne convene and run the Estates General; but that's one plan gone wrong.

Bad news has come pouring in in gusts and floods, drowning whatever positive impact the convening of the Estates General might have had. Grenoble, Vizille, Pau, Rennes, Besançon . . . then the negative response of the Assembly of the Clergy. The heavens have done their part, too, with a frightful storm on July 13, followed by a whole series of storms that ruin

---

*In the words of Germaine de Staël, who is the author of the following quote as well.

the summer and rot the crops. Devastation in Maine, Vexin, Beauce, Normandy, Picardy, Boulonnais, Calaisis, Angoumois, Poitou, Touraine. The Academy of Sciences has calculated that 650 square leagues have been laid waste by hail, for a total loss of 24,962,693 livres.[11] Thousands of small farmers have been reduced not just to penury but to starvation. The government would help them, but it has no resources; so it floats a loan for 12,000 livres, in the form of a lottery, but the loan isn't even subscribed and Brienne is later accused of dipping into the money raised for that purpose to meet other debts *in extremis*. He is lurching from one abyss to the next.

August 16. The criers trot through Paris and Versailles announcing a fresh decision by the Council regarding the *order and form of payments*. The financial world and other people in the know are not long misled by this euphemism, which is in reality a notification of the state's partial bankruptcy.* In fact, the Treasury's coffers contain, at this moment, the sum of four hundred thousand livres—that is, "the funds required for state expenditure for one or two days," according to Dupont de Nemours, the former secretary of the Assembly of Notables and Talleyrand's adviser on financial affairs, who has some harsh things to say about Brienne: "The Archbishop of Sens had spent everything: the money requested as charity to build hospitals, the money intended to give help to the provinces damaged by hail, even such sacred deposits as these were not sacred to this prelate."[12]

For want of any better solution, Brienne still tries, by using the word *atermoiement* [renewal of a bill, arrangement with creditors for extension of time for payment—*Trans.*], to camouflage what anyone else would have called a cessation of payment. The result is widespread panic, in particular outside the offices of the Caisse d'Escompte, which are besieged by people holding short-term notes and demanding payment in specie, but having difficulty obtaining it. On the contrary, the King starts paying his civil servants, soldiers and pensioners in notes redeemable at an unspecified date in the future. And since it takes at least two weeks to get the notes printed, most of the Treasury transfers are delayed.

A letter from La Fayette informs one of his friends of the general state of disruption: "I enclose this new regulation for the form of payments. . . . I confess I can speak of it only with anger and distress.† I had led myself to

---

*The etymology of the word is intriguing; it comes from the Italian expression *banca rotta*, in the late fifteenth century, when the counter of a banker who could not meet payments was broken. When referring to a state, the meaning is extended and does not have fraudulent connotations; it means a partial or total cessation of payments owed by the public treasury.

†He had wanted to replace Calonne with Brienne and stood up for him to the last, which only adds to his bitterness. It is not known to whom this letter was addressed.

suppose that calm was about to be restored. . . . I was writing and telling my friends that now that the Estates General were on the horizon and the plenary court defunct, any kind of opposition that smelled of an *esprit de corps* must quickly be dropped. I have said and posted things that are going to be thrown in my face. . . . This damnable cessation undoes all the good of the decision to hold the Estates General. . . . Discontent will be revived and suspicion doubled. . . . This letter is a great deal about politics . . . , but I like to open my heart to you. Those who suppose it to be turbulent do not know it well, but those who believe it steady do justice to it. I should like to see you one more time before entering upon my thirty-second year, for although I am thought to be so young, come September 6 I shall have lived three hundred and seventy-two months.

"Paris is thunderstruck; the guards have been doubled and orders prepared."[13]

Within the walled world of Versailles, Brienne is going around and around like a squirrel in a cage. He still hasn't resigned himself to defeat, but he's surrounded by a tight little community of pets and favorites, all trying to hang on. His repudiation is not going to look like those of Louis XVI's previous "principal ministers": Turgot, Necker and Calonne were fired like kitchen maids, overnight. This time will be different. The Archbishop tries to stand fast in the storm and keeps hoping that the Queen will defend him to the end. Mercy-Argenteau, the Austrian ambassador, acts as the link between the two and is busily trying to save the furniture. Lacking any sign from the ever-inexistent King, Marie Antoinette and Brienne sigh and decide, on August 19, to send for Necker.

How badly they must have needed him! And the King himself is going to have to do what he has never done before—recall a disgraced minister, and a Protestant at that, and a liberal, and a Genevan . . . But all the financiers and businessmen are hailing him as the Messiah. And in fact, Brienne would have been glad to have Necker working beside him all this year. But isn't it too late? It is too late. In a letter that is terribly damning on the subject of her royal spouse, Marie Antoinette writes to Mercy, on August 20, "I greatly fear that the Archbishop will be obliged to leave altogether. And if so, what man can we take to place at the head of all the rest? For there must be one, especially with M. Necker. There has to be some curb. The person above me [that is, the King] is not capable, and I, whatever may be said and whatever may transpire, can never be anything but second, and despite the trust of the first, he often lets me know it."[14]

So who is running France during these five days? Where's the King, except out hunting? What's he doing, writing, saying? This change of government is about to be negotiated by the Queen, Mercy-Argenteau, Brienne and Necker, against a background of rumor issuing from the salons of Yolande de Polignac and the Comte d'Artois, "that whole set of favorites [according to Brienne] who looked upon the public Treasury as a spring that would never run dry, at which I had prevented them from drinking their fill."[15]

Squirrel-Brienne goes on banging against the bars of his cage. "I did not want M. Necker, with whose ambition and conceit I was well acquainted, to make conditions with the King, and I begged M. de Mercy to insist that he accept without imposing any. I was willing to go, but I did not want M. Necker to send me away." And on he flounders, in the course of his conversations with Mercy-Argenteau, who receives Necker on August 20, 23 and 24.

It sounds as if the government of France is in the hands of Joseph II's ambassador this week, doesn't it? In response, Necker writes to him, "I should be powerless and without resources if I were associated with a person who has lost all credit in public opinion."[16]

So there will not be a "Necker-Brienne government"; Marie Antoinette's mirage fades on August 25, when she explains to Brienne that, regretfully, she is going to have to abandon him. But she does not abandon the ground she has gained in the sovereignty of France. The moment Brienne tenders his resignation to the King, who can then make public that of Malesherbes at the same time, she writes to Mercy-Argenteau, "The Archbishop is gone. I cannot tell you, sir, how affected I have been by this day. I believe this course was necessary but I fear, at the same time, that it may lead to much misfortune. . . . I have just written a line to M. Necker, sending for him to come to me here tomorrow, at ten o'clock. There can be no more hesitation; if, tomorrow, he can set to work, so much the better. The work is very pressing. I tremble to think, forgive this weakness in me, that it is I who am bringing him back. It is my fate to convey misfortune."[17]

Brienne doesn't go without his table scraps. Having become, "after M. de Rohan, the most opulent of all the prelates, on August 24, 1788, as he was about to leave the ministry, he sent to the Treasury for the 20,000 livres representing his month's pay although it was not yet over, a proof of most noteworthy exactness on his part, especially as, not counting the appointments attaching to his office and the 6,000 livres of pension that came with his Blue Garter, he had 678,000 livres of income in Church livings and, only recently, the felling of trees in one of his abbeys had brought him a million."[18]

The King asks the Pope for a cardinal's hat for him, which he receives later in the year.

50

AUGUST–SEPTEMBER 1788

So Close to the Rocks

On Sunday, August 24, 1788, Germaine de Staël sends her husband a little note from the château of Courteil near Verneuil in Normandy, where she is staying with friends. He's in Paris, in his Swedish embassy, being required by the situation to keep close to the center of events, while she, like almost every other society lady, has fled the heat and stench of the capital for a rustic holiday in this "quite flat country . . . , where the garden is so well arranged and the stream [the Avre] so well mannered that the whole huge grounds are like a sort of country one sees all of at once."[1]

"Nothing can keep me from Versailles tomorrow, my friend. I shall tell you why."[2]

The Baron de Staël has a pretty good idea why. Jacques Necker is about to return to power, and "tomorrow" is the feast of St. Louis, when the whole Court is to fete the King. Germaine's beloved father, her living god, is coming back seven years after his fall from favor—a unique event in the history of the monarchy. With his wife and a large company of friends who have come galloping up to take part in the victory parade, he's in his château at Saint-Ouen, waiting for the summons to Versailles which Mercy-Argenteau told him two days ago would soon be coming. He already knows he's to have an audience with the Queen before being officially instated by the King. He is ready and willing, and has just let Marie Antoinette know that he will be "utterly abandoning his destiny" at her feet, now that there is no more talk of making him share power with Brienne. His daughter is beside herself with joy.* He himself, no doubt, is the least delighted of them all. He knows the

---

*In her remarkable commentary on Madame de Staël's *Correspondance*, Beatrice Jasinski observes, in connection with this note, "I do not believe there was another moment in her whole life when she could have desired more ardently to go to Versailles" (note 624).

state of the Treasury and is not expecting a cocktail party. But, too, he's been getting ready to take his revenge for years. Ponderously, patiently, he has constructed his doctrine, not only as an economist but also as an anti-*philosophe*, by publishing three fat tomes titled *L'administration des finances de la France*,[3] and, just recently, since he was about to step into an archbishop's shoes, a 550-page treatise, *De l'importance des opinions religieuses*,[4] with which he hoped to regain the good opinion of the King.

The program is simplicity itself: first, on the strength of a renewal of confidence, get advances from the money manipulators in order to meet immediate demands and pending the Estates General, which would be more of a gigantic ceremony than a political event. Then, immediately afterward, set up the provincial assemblies, which he had in the back of his mind as long ago as 1780 and which should, as he sees it, form the foundations of a moderately representative system under which taxes, shared equally by all, would be voted annually and paid to a monarch who remained as omnipotent as ever. Is Necker still so deluded? Perhaps a little less so, since he has just told several people how sorry he is not to have had "the Archbishop's fifteen months."[5] At times, a shiver of "too late" runs over him, but he still has his high cards, or at least he thinks he does: his unshakable confidence in himself and his strict honesty. And then, the unanimous chorus of third-estate voices is wafting up to his ears: Necker, Necker, Necker . . .

He's now fifty-six and, although thickened by a sedentary life and his majestic mien, he looks fighting fit in comparison to the debilitated Brienne. His daughter is still only twenty-two and her life is about to change radically with her father's return, which for her is a return to her father as well, after two years of a marriage that has never been easy. She's ready for the part of salon-mistress in a world where she outstrips her own mother in liveliness and dash, if not in beauty, and she's very sure she can assist the comeback in the social realm, where her father can hardly be said to shine. Beginning on this feast of St. Louis, where she intends to triumph, she's determined to help him wherever he may have need of her presence and her pen. Less and less the wife of the ambassador from Sweden, she means to become Jacques Necker's top public relations agent and opens her career with a letter to her number-one pen pal, Gustavus III in Stockholm, who awaits her monthly reports on the situation in France. To him she dares confess even her own doubts:

"Sire,

"In other circumstances I should have been pleased to inform Your Majesty of my father's appointment, but the ship is being placed in his hands so close to the rocks that even my boundless admiration is scarcely enough to give me confidence."[6]

This letter is dated September 4, which, of course, is ten days after the first gush of enthusiasm, when Necker is facing up to a Niagara of difficulties. She has moved in with him, at the Contrôle Général des Finances, leaving her husband to his embassy on the rue du Bac. The many letters between them are evidence that their marital crisis is advancing. They never really loved each other, although they have put up a loyal show.* He's not nasty. He's not ugly. But she has never had any illusions about him.

What she married was not a man, but one of the most honorable positions possible for a Protestant in France. And she's already accusing her husband of having mistresses, while she herself takes refuge in a series of intense little mental romances that are not much to his liking. Shortly before her father's return to power, she puts her position squarely to de Staël:

> I should very much like, my dear friend, for us not to torment each other. . . . Without giving any positive cause for jealousy, you have just put me through three days on earth of the Purgatory that is to come. You proffered the harshest and most insulting expressions, you are unable to control your temper and there is nothing you would not be capable of in a moment of violence.
>
> I have faults, surely. But do you imagine you have none that pain me? Do you suppose there are not a thousand strokes of jealousy that offend me? . . . My friend, heaven is not on earth. I, too, could be depressed, and when you treat me as you have done in the last three days, many bitter thoughts come to darken the gaiety of youth that is passing with every day. It may be that we are not perfectly suited to each other. But we are united. I am the mother of your daughter.† You have loved me very much, and those qualifications must continue to be mine. . . .
>
> I beg you, no more storms. A thunderbolt comes only once; but bad weather every day is almost worse.[7]

That week, condemned for life to be known as Madame de Staël, she becomes once more what she has never ceased, truly, to be, "the Necker girl." The other one, the husband, the pretext—let him keep his place as prince consort and live as he pleases. Germaine is about to abandon herself to her passion for politics.

Bookseller Hardy's diary, on Friday, August 29, 1788: "This day's *Gazette de France* baldly announced, under the heading Versailles, dated August 26, that M. de Brienne, archbishop of Sens, has tendered to the King his resignation as head of the Royal Council of Finance; that, upon the resignation

---

*For Germaine Necker's marriage to the Baron de Staël on January 14, 1786, after a long period of hesitation among various brilliant suitors including William Pitt, see Volume IV.

†Named Gustavine; born in July 1787, she dies in April 1789.

of M. Lambert from the office of comptroller general of finance,* the King has appointed M. Necker as director general of his finances with the rank of minister of state; and that His Majesty brought him into the Council in that capacity on August 27"[8]—the Council he was never permitted to enter during his first term as minister.

But Louis XVI lacks self-assurance in his decisions and is unwilling to make the clean sweep everyone is waiting for. "People were still uncertain what to expect in regard to the ministerial changes that had taken place the day before. And on all sides it was being said that M. de Lamoignon, keeper of the seals of France, was still in office."

So Lamoignon is hanging on, a result more of apathy than sympathy on the King's part, while his cousin Malesherbes has managed to tiptoe out almost unnoticed. Malesherbes is not unpopular, moreover, except among the bigots, whereas Lamoignon has made even more enemies than Brienne, if only because of his tactlessness and brutality in trying to put down the insubordinate *parlements*.

The first obstacle Necker meets, before even taking office, is the chill of the Court. His daughter is too sharp not to see this, on the great feast day to which she was looking forward so eagerly:

"I went to the Queen, according to custom, on St. Louis's day; the niece of the disgraced Archbishop was paying her court at the same time. The Queen made it very plain, by the way in which she received the two of us, that she much preferred the minister who was gone to the one who was taking his place. The courtiers were different, however, for never have so many people come forward to lead me back to my carriage."[9]

She's not blinded by a gaggle of grinning courtiers; she knows how fleeting their smiles are. The ostentatious cold shoulder of the King and Queen is more serious. It implies that their support of Necker will be like the rope's support of the hanged man. Necker himself has little time to savor his return to power and deflates Germaine's euphoria on the seventeenth with the warning that "for a minister's daughter there is only pleasure; she enjoys the reflected power of her father. But the power itself, especially nowadays, is a fearsome responsibility."[10]

Faced by the gaping coffers, Necker is immediately plunged into a morass of uncertainty, trapped as he is by the unfriendly gaze of the sovereigns, the lack of cooperation from the princes of the blood and other ministers, and the legal and administrative paralysis resulting from the *Parlement*'s exile. A

---

*The myth of a dyarchy at the head of the royal finance was maintained in order to preserve Brienne's ecclesiastical persona. But it was he who took all the decisions; Lambert de Villedeuil simply carried them out.

large part of France is expecting him to produce ducats out of a hat within the week. But the Dauphiné is more or less in a state of secession, preparing to confirm the Estates of Vizille by a full-scale assembly of the three orders in Romans. In Brittany things are even worse: the province has been on the verge of insurrection ever since a delegation of twelve nobles coming to demand justice in Versailles was thrown into the Bastille. And in the rest of the provinces the prevailing attitude is, at best, wait and see. How can he inject a little life into this lethargy-sapped country?

Paris looks like a more approachable ally; a few groups there have cheered the news of his recall. But although the capital might be ready enough to love Necker, it loathes Lamoignon, whom the King is stubbornly insisting on keeping as a special councillor, primarily with a view to entrusting him with the negotiations for some form of reconciliation with the *parlements* along good old-fashioned lines, with *lettres de cachet* announcing a bed of justice in Versailles on September 15—even if it means he has to listen to some more unpleasant things. La Fayette, still in Paris, is gasping.

"I think I can say with certainty . . . that the *Parlement* has been asked to return, provisionally, with the present keeper of the seals. . . . I cannot conceive that he will want to stay."[11] Neither can Necker, but there's nothing he can do about it; he is a long way from having full powers, all he's being asked to do is manufacture money out of thin air. So things might well take another turn for the worse, except that Paris itself is about to move, although not in the anticipated direction.

The contrary currents of rejoicing (for Necker) and irritation (with Lamoignon) produce a series of overheated swirls in the teapot in which a few hundred Parisians are swimming. They are the ones who have been stirred up by the impromptu orators in the gardens of the Palais-Royal and by the young law clerks, who have had nothing to do but hang around the streets since the closing of the Palais de Justice on the other side of the Seine. The Pont-Neuf is their meeting point. The place Dauphine opens onto the middle of it, with its placid pink brick and white stone houses, and provides the playing field on which clerks and craftsmen's apprentices join in what begins as a sort of carnival but turns into something else in the last days of August.

Enlightened Europe learns about this to-do in Paris from the *Gazette de Leyde:*

"The degree of excitement was such, at the resignation of the archbishop of Sens, that the people's joy at the appointment of the new minister could not be contained within the limits of order. For three days skyrockets and other fireworks were fired from the Palais-Royal and place Dauphine. People even forced the inhabitants of the district to illuminate their houses and, following the English fashion,* broke the windows of any that were not lit up."[12]

A curious effigy is made, said to look like Brienne, and burned at the feet of the statue of "Good King Henri IV" on horseback. When the atmosphere reaches fever pitch, some of the revelers even force passengers to get out of their coaches and kneel down in front of it. The party begins to get rough when the "rogues, mingling with this populace, started looting the shops; they extorted money from passersby, saying that it was to buy fireworks."

Another turn for the worse, between six and seven in the evening. The watch tries to close off the place Dauphine and quays to everyone except those who live there. Then "a frightful tumult began, set off by a sudden rush of young people followed by a large crowd, who made several attempts to force their way through the guards and seize the place Dauphine. . . . It was said the next day that on all sides, in the areas around the Palais, place Dauphine, Pont-Neuf and quays, the populace had waged a sort of war upon the watch, with stones and sticks, lasting a large part of the night."[13]

As the agitation goes on, Hardy phlegmatically notes at least three times, in a sort of parenthesis to his diary, "M. de Lamoignon is still in office."

On August 29 the whole center of Paris is violently offended by the methods employed by "the foot soldiers and horsemen of the watch," who actually do very little damage; but this is probably just a flare-up of the eternal tension between the population of any large city and its police.

Friday is comparatively quiet, because people don't want to lose a day's wages and because the watch, obeying prudent orders, keeps out of sight. If Lamoignon's departure had been announced, calm could in all likelihood have been restored; but he's still there, and so tonight it's his turn to be burned by Paris.

Around seven in the evening, "the turbulent young people, again followed by the populace . . ., began to collect on the Pont-Neuf and in the place Dauphine, inside which all the shops had to be shut up and the façades of all the houses illuminated." By nine o'clock the movement has spread far afield, "the populace of the Saint-Antoine and Saint-Marcel faubourgs having come to swell the ranks of the local urchins. . . . Instead of simply letting off rockets . . ., a very big fire was then set alight in the middle of the place Dauphine and fed with whatever could be found in the neighborhood, such as the sentry box of the Pont-Neuf guard and the board-and-wicker trays of the men who sell oranges, lemons and fowl on the quai de la Vallée, so that the nearby houses were in danger of taking fire. In this fire the effigy of M.

---

*Read: "copying the recent riots in London."

de Lamoignon was burned . . ., after being forced to make honorable reparation. The mutinous populace then turned upon the Pont-Neuf guardroom, razed it to the ground and set fire to it as well, after driving out the soldiers of the watch, taking away their clothes and weapons and throwing them into the fire, together with a gold watch and another of silver."

One poor corporal of the watch who tries to stay at his post goes through several uncomfortable minutes while the rioters debate whether to throw him into the river or the fire. "But in the end all they did was make him beg pardon in the middle of the place Dauphine, whereupon, as the man was feeling faint, they decided to let him go."

The riot spreads over a large part of Paris. In the dead of night six other guardrooms are destroyed, on the quai de l'École, rue Saint-Honoré, les Halles, the Marché Saint-Germain-des-Prés, the Marché Neuf and the Port au Blé. Doors and windows are torn off and furniture removed and "fed to the flames, along with the uniforms of the soldiers, who were stripped naked in some places."

Some of them defend themselves at first; at least fifty shots are fired and three persons killed, while two more are beaten to death where they stand.

"The tumult did not end until past three in the morning, and most of the brawlers did not go home until they had set fire to everything they could."

There is a clear distinction between the attitude of the unfortunate watchmen, trying to save their possessions and their skins, and that of the numerous patrols of French and Swiss Guards, who have no orders to act and simply roam around as though watching a circus, "in squadrons of ten, bayonets fixed, walking all about the quais and Palais without saying a word."

As evening draws in on August 30, the heart of Paris is covered by a great cloud of anxiety, because it seems as though "the populace had declared a sort of open war upon the whole watch, both foot and mounted." The authorities, having finally woken up to the danger, impose a superficial calm by quadrupling the number of regiments of French and Swiss Guards in the streets. A propitiating proclamation signed (for once) by the King is posted on the walls. Any battle will be unequal, because this evening there are no fewer than twelve hundred men from the royal forces ranged around the improvised battleground, although three or four hundred rioters almost succeed in breaking into the home of the Chevalier Dubois, commander of the watch, on the rue de Meslai.

The situation seems to be stabilized in Paris, but in an impossible state of equilibrium resembling so many of the one-legged solutions adopted by this unmoored monarchy. Are they going to ruin the "Necker effect" by imposing an unpopular keeper of the seals upon a capital in a virtual state of siege?

51

SEPTEMBER 1788

More Evils and Men

The country's going to have to hold its breath through almost two weeks of political uncertainty, which seriously compromises Necker's restoration efforts. In the end, he's not the one who gets rid of Lamoignon, because it is not in his power to do so. Nor does the minister leave as a result of the fuss being made by the Parisians. Once again, it's the men of the *Parlement,* stoking the stoves of their opposition to white heat. They have been wanting nothing better than to be called back, but not like that and not by that person. Summoned to meet on September 15, they hold a series of private preparatory meetings that are just so many little conspiracies, aimed at transforming this "bed of justice" into a spectacular public event. A majority of the mortarboard *présidents* resolve to have a resolution read out at the opening of the "recall session," in which the *Parlement* and Court of Peers proclaim their absolute refusal to deal with the keeper of the seals. This is unprecedented. By this resolution, a body of magistrates recalled to endorse laws and resume the administration of justice would virtually be setting themselves up as an English-style House of Commons and usurping a political role. Many of them see this step as not only a way for the judges to take over the powers of the minister of justice, but also as a first step toward blocking the attack upon *parlement* privileges that is almost sure to be made by the Estates General.

At Court, the King's circle is frightened by the prospect of this judiciary coup d'état, and even the most conservative princes, led by the Comte d'Artois, are urging Louis XVI to put a stop to anything that could transform that riffraff, those scruffy men in the *Parlement,* that source of all evil in the past two years, into some form of national assembly. Just recall them at once, throw Lamoignon to them like a bone, and get these Estates over with as soon as possible. Once they have no more political battles to wage, their popularity should sink back into the sands. The King will not appear before them, there will be no bed of justice, they will resume their ordinary occupations with honor and sinecures, often at the expense of the man in their legal streets. As for the reforms and new apportionment of taxes, why, that will be taken care of by an old dream of the monarchy, which the nobility and higher churchmen are dredging up again from the depths of their slumbers: a direct alliance between the people and their King. The trick could be turned by January. Meanwhile, it's Necker's play.

But finally, Lamoignon is treated no more harshly than Brienne. The days of the boot are decidedly over. There could be no better indication of Louis XVI's weakness than the airs and graces put on by Lamoignon during his few last days in possession of the seals. What others have not dared even to think of after twenty years in power, he demands and obtains after one year of calamitous administration. He's covered in debt, which has become almost *de rigueur* among the great of the realm, who are condemned to make a big show and entertain too much. Artois, who's right at home in this field, piles Pelion upon Ossa for him: in addition to his retirement pension, the King grants him 400,000 francs out of the public treasury. One small problem: since Necker hasn't yet been able to get down to work seriously, there are only 380,000 francs actually in it. Lamoignon magnanimously agrees to take only half now, provided he gets a promise that his eldest son will be made a duke and given a major embassy on reaching the age of twenty-five.[1]*

Now, having so richly dispensed with the services of Lamoignon, who do we put in his place? There was one name on many lips, *Président* du Paty, become the foremost defender of the underdog since the case of the "Three Men on the Wheel."† Doffing his magistrate's wig and donning his advocate's gown, du Paty obtained a "Decision by the King's Council on July 20, 1787" quashing and annulling both the first sentence of the Chaumont court on August 12, 1785, and the terrible ruling of the Paris *Parlement* that, on October 20 of the same year, after the *a minima* appeal lodged by the prosecuting attorney in Champagne, upgraded the original galleys sentence to the wheel. The Council also "referred and hereby refers the matter to the *bailliage* of Rouen."[2]

For a royal decision, this in itself was most unusual; but then, what of the ruling of the judges of Rouen, who, quickly setting a date for retrial on October 29, 1787, "dared to take an unprecedented initiative. . . . They allowed the accused to be assisted by their counsel for defense."[3] So this is

---

*He gets the rest in January but has little time to enjoy his loot, because he is found dead on May 23, 1789, with his hunting gun at his side, in the grounds of his château at Baville. Suicide? In the absence of any investigation, this is the commonly accepted hypothesis. As for his son, the events of 1789 ensure that the promises made are never honored.

†On du Paty, his close connection with the Condorcets and the case of the Three Men on the Wheel, see the first three chapters of this volume.

how small revolutions with great consequences occur—by surprise. Out of the blue, a provincial judicature has just introduced a radical novelty in criminal law. Until this moment, no advocate had ever been present before the judges at the same time as the accused.

The last act took place, with du Paty in attendance, in three hearings on October 29–31, followed by the final examination on November 5. The eleven magistrates of Rouen, in a decidedly charitable mood,* spared the three accused men the humiliation of the courtroom "stool." Then came sixteen hours of deliberation, more because this new procedure had to be improvised as they went along than because of any hesitation. The accused were declared innocent. The moment the decision was read out, du Paty rushed to the prison. A few of the last lines he left us sum up his whole life: "Open up their prison to me; where are they? Let me see them! Hurry, friends, you have been absolved; give me your hands. Bradier, embrace your child; child, embrace your father. Oh, my friends, take my joy into your hearts as I took your misfortune into mine."[4]

Hey, there, not so fast! We must not trifle with the majesty of the law. As though taken aback by its own clemency, the Rouen *parlement* dispatched the acquitted men to its courthouse lodge until such time as the King's attorney might care to enter another *a minima* appeal—with the *Parlement* of Paris! And the whole thing would start over again from the beginning. Du Paty, exhausted and ill, his nerves shot, did not restrain his indignation:

"More prisons, more courts, more sentences, more judges, that is, more evils and men? . . . Since this case came to me two years ago, and I have had it constantly in my head, in my heart, in my entrails, I must certainly be more inhabited by it than anyone else. That fatal wheel; I've written so much alongside it, trying to break it, that I can see it before me!"[5]

On December 18 he was allowed to plead against any further appeals in the Chambre de la Tournelle in Rouen, packed with people who were all on his side. Another precedent: "the unwonted sight of a mortar-*président* making the first great criminal defense."[6]

He gave his all, and a little more. That day, those close to him had the impression that the very substance of him was somehow diminished. It was all over that afternoon. "The Chambre de la Tournelle hereby orders Bradier, Simare and Lardoise to be released from the Court's prisons forthwith."[7]

"The Three Men on the Wheel were immediately released and led through the streets in triumph. We have been most reliably informed that the *président* of the *parlement* supped with them that same evening and gave

*Yet the Normandy *parlement* judges had a reputation for severity, and a few recent death sentences and galley convictions for minor offenses were being held against them. But the wind has changed, and du Paty's personality cast a spell on the court.

them various people of quality and little mistresses of Rouen for table companions."

So it's not surprising that everybody should be talking of du Paty as Lamoignon's successor. He had always been sparing in his criticisms of the keeper of the seals himself, looking with candid sympathy upon his flirtations with legal reform. Besides, the minister had asked him to sit on the committee he had just set up to produce a criminal code that would, at last, have some consistency to it. Du Paty might have ensured a smooth takeover and a transition to a more modern form of justice, alongside Necker, who would be doing the same thing for the administration. A very pleasant dream.

Only, on September 17—

"News has come of the death of Messire Charles-Marguerite Jean-Baptiste Mercier du Paty,* mortar-*président* of the Bordeaux *parlement,* in which he had previously served as advocate general."[8] Like Diderot, he is buried, the next day, in the church of St. Roch in Paris, "as he lived on the rue de Gaillon. A putrid fever carried him off, they say, in his early forties." In fact, he was forty-four; his constitution was always delicate, he had been unwell since the Rouen trial, and he died almost overnight.

"It was his misfortune to be at odds with his colleagues for many years. They never lost their unwillingness to have him among the number of their *présidents;* for that reason he resolved to move away from Bordeaux . . . and come to live in the capital, where he delivered himself, in various writings, of unduly harsh and unjustified statements against the *Parlement,* pretending all the while to act on behalf of the unfortunate accused, calling heatedly for a reform of our criminal jurisprudence, and being keenly ambitious to have chief responsibility for carrying it out, so that he could claim all the honor of it for himself . . . . He was even suspected of being in a sense one of the mainstays of the revolution that was being prepared in the magistracy, and may have thought that through it he could achieve an even higher degree of honor, gain and glory. He left several children."

But "in a will written a year earlier, when he was setting out for Rouen to defend the Three Men on the Wheel . . . , he ordered that all his papers were to be given to his niece, the Marquise de Condorcet."[9]

To Sophie, to "Grouchette," from her "little uncle."

Since he can't have du Paty—but would the King really have accepted him?—Louis XVI opts for Charles Louis François-de-Paule Honoré de Ba-

---

*According to Hardy's journal, which gives him a nicely packaged dose of venom in the guise of a funeral oration. The bookseller has no affection for men who are open to the suspicion of possessing progressive minds. Du Paty dies on the seventeenth and is buried on the eighteenth; Hardy's note is written on the nineteenth.

rentin, whom nobody expected and nobody wants, to replace Lamoignon. An insipid creature of fifty, former advocate general in the Paris *Parlement*, first *président* of the Cour des Aides since 1775, he aroused little public notice until the day in September when the King, handing him the seals, promotes him to the second position in Necker's government. The current of opinion supporting Necker assumed that he himself would be allowed to choose the chief ministers. Don't you believe it. Louis XVI is quite cross enough at having Necker forced upon him, so, faithful to his policy of checks, balances and bullying, he appoints Barentin without a word of warning, following the advice given long before by the dreary Miromesnil, the man who shipwrecked Turgot in 1776 and Calonne just the other day.[10] Here's a nice anti-Necker standing face-to-face with Necker.[11] All the latter's friends can hope is that the new keeper of the seals will be as much of a nonentity in the future as he has been in the past.

The Parisians have never heard of Barentin, and the mob is utterly unmoved by the little sigh of people in the know. The mere news of Lamoignon's resignation, at last! is enough to create an explosion of joy in the town. On Sunday evening, September 14, the weather is glorious; "a person came out of the Café du Caveau [in the Palais-Royal] and climbed upon a stool. He announced to the public in a loud, clear voice, 'Gentlemen, that good-for-nothing Lamoignon has been fired!' Thereupon a poster was hung from a tree on which was written in large print: *Today, Lamoignon goes down; tomorrow, the Abbé de Vermond*, who is reader to the Queen .... It is said that shortly after the news of Monsieur de Lamoignon's removal, these words, written in very large letters, were put up on the door to his mansion on the rue de Grenelle in the faubourg Saint-Germain: *Smoke your pipe, jackass.*"[12]

The uproar continues the next three nights, September 15, 16 and 17, and gets louder and more and more menacing, but there's some pleasure in this violence. For two days, the forces of law and order let the Pont-Neuf act as a safety valve for high spirits. Henri IV's statue becomes a sort of counterculture altar, and the "local coachmen, having been taught what they must say if they wanted to move ahead more quickly, were soon bawling out with all their might, and without prompting, 'Long live Henri IV! To the devil with that damned bastard Lamoignon!' "[13]

And off we go for another round of rockets, fireworks and skies streaked with Roman candles. During these few evenings, one slice of old Paris achieves a collective identity, before any of the others. Memoirists speak of the "youth of the place Dauphine and Palais area" as though it were a sort of social person; it sets the rest of the capital in motion, within a radius that spreads extensively during the night, as it did before at the end of August. Worse. On Tuesday the sixteenth, starting at six in the evening, the party gets rough, merrymaking turns to madness. The crowd makes another effigy of Lamoignon, but this time the craftsmen have outdone themselves in portraying the fallen minister.

"A kind of figure representing the keeper of the seals was carried around various places, dressed in a black gown and wearing a wig, clerical bands, a square hat, and decorated with a blue ribbon."[14] It was made by a master basketmaker, and gets burned at two in the morning on the place de Grève, "after several *amendes honorables* and a public reading of the death sentence." Hundreds of people dance around the stake, shouting that next day it will be the Abbé de Vermond's turn.*

On Wednesday, things get so bad that the police and their associates can no longer stand around and watch. Some of the rioters are too excited to wait until nightfall, and set up a proper little racket on the Pont-Neuf at eight in the morning. Every vehicle is stopped and everyone inside it is forced to pay a contribution to increasingly dubious gangs. Is this supposed to be for fireworks? Not likely.

"Four priests were forced by the populace to kneel down in front of the statue of Henri IV, and the same thing happened to four devout goodwives who charitably refused to wish Monsieur Lamoignon to the devil."[15] The wine must have been flowing by the riverful in the taverns, and the baser instincts begin to bubble. It's no longer a handful of youngsters working off excess energy on effigies. On the place Dauphine a girl, hit in the face by a firecracker, indignantly "slaps an urchin" and is immediately surrounded and maltreated by "a frenzied horde, who subject the poor creature to a thousand indignities." That evening, other human eruptions surge against the walls of the homes of Brienne and Lamoignon in the faubourg Saint-Germain and renew their attack on Chevalier Dubois's house near the porte Saint-Martin.

Between ten and eleven in the evening the soldiers and guards receive their awaited orders. Giving free vent to an irritation held too long in check, they react so violently that even the respectable townspeople are taken aback. They slash and smash the crowds ruthlessly, sending "a goodly number into the Hôtel-Dieu. . . . If the public rumors are to be believed, the number of killed, wounded and captured in this incident rose to a total of more than eighty persons." The Parisian military motor, unlike that of Grenoble, does not stall.

There's no way of proving that figure, but other testimony indicates that the toll was heavy. The riots of joy do more damage than the riots of impatience. It really was time for Lamoignon to go.

---

*Sometimes Hardy knew what he was talking about. He adds, "This abbé, the Queen's reader . . . , was sent to Vienna to give French lessons to the Austrian archduchess before her marriage. He is a scheming parvenu, now rejoicing in an income of sixty or eighty thousand livres from Church livings. He had a reputation for sticking his nose into many things at Court."

Dazed by the bludgeonings of the guards, threatened with further punishment by proclamations from the Châtelet, where a few of the rioters who
were arrested on the spot may well be hanged today or tomorrow,* Paris
gradually subsides, although not without some final tremors that go on until
late in the month. But September 22 brings relief and hopes of a golden
age.

On that day, the official reopening of the magistrates' sessions takes
place in their regular home in the Palais de Justice, with no other interference
from the Court than the reading, by a few emissaries from the King, of letters
written in the customary style convening their session. No bed of justice,
not even a sermon by the new keeper of the seals. They might be a hundred
leagues from Versailles; it's as though May 8 and everything that followed
never happened. The worst they get from Louis XVI is a declaration that
opens with a nice example of retreat masked by rhetoric:

"In Our unremitting desire to bring about the well-being of the state,
We adopted the plans submitted to Us with a view to simplifying the administration of justice. . . . Our only object in adopting these laws, on last May
8, was the perfection of order and the greater advantage of Our peoples. . . . Those same feelings have now brought Us to give Our full attention
to the various representations made to Us. . . . They served to make Us aware
of drawbacks that had not initially been clear to Us; and, since We have
brought forward the date of the Estates General . . . , We have seen fit to
defer the accomplishment of Our beneficent views until that imminent
time."[16]

Why, it's magic! The rest of the royal declaration convenes the Estates
General for the following January and orders "that all the officials of our
courts, without exception, shall continue to perform the duties of their offices
as before."[17]

The meeting ends at four-thirty, after a long paean of victory from
Advocate General Séguier, jumping up and down on the remains of his old
foe Lamoignon, and also Brienne, in front of a large and joyful audience that
fills the chamber and surrounding courtyards. There are gusts of bravos,
waves of applause. The Paris *Parlement* feels that it has reaped the fruits of
its "persecution"—which hasn't been so very harsh, after all. Its members
suppose they're at the top of the heap for a long time to come.

They'd better make the most of it; it's going to last exactly three days.

---

*In fact, at a discreet request from Necker, they are all quietly released at the end of the
month.

52

SEPTEMBER–NOVEMBER 1788

A True Peasant Child

Now, when everybody is expecting energetic decisions and swift change, begins the great, vague void of the closing months of 1788. Within days, the *Parlement* transits from the Capitol to the Tarpeian Rock; Grand High Wizard Necker doesn't know which alchemy to try next and hides his irresolution under a veil of silence; the Court returns to its distractions and futilities; the Notables are reconvened for no discernible reason—a month wasted, a blow struck in empty air. The embers of the people's fires are glowing beneath the ashes, in Paris and in ten or twelve provinces, but the only visible turbulence comes from a little bomb set off at the foot of the throne, from a place where nobody expected it—the princes of the blood. The chronology of that autumn and early winter records nothing but a long list of false moves and missed opportunities.

Councillor Duval d'Eprémesnil, released, thanks to Necker, from his prison on the Île Sainte-Marguerite, comes galloping back from Provence to Paris as fast as his horses can carry him, almost a conqueror, pausing only to grace the receptions and accept the compliments served up to him on the road. In the provinces he's being treated as the nation's protector; so he naturally anticipates a joyous return to the capital. What is his surprise, then, when he finds himself not only ignored but occasionally jeered at by the Parisians! Why these stones thrown at his carriage? Whence this sheet tossed into it on the short journey from his house to the Palais, and posted up on the walls? Some anonymous hero has written what purports to be a letter from the governor of Sainte-Marguerite demanding the arrest of a madman escaped from his fortress. The "May martyr" very quickly learns that the glory that he was flattering himself was his, and on which he was being congratulated a few leagues out of town, has soured to opprobrium like turning milk, and through the fault of his colleagues.[1]

On September 24, two days after the ovations hailing the *Parlement*'s return, it exposes itself to a wave of fury. This sudden swing of mood is a sign of continuing extreme tension in the capital. Imagining themselves secure in its affections, a large majority of the magistrates ask the King to convene the Estates General, now sure to be held soon, exactly as they were convened in 1614 and with an equal number of representatives for each of the three orders, thereby reducing the third estate to impotence. And if that weren't enough to keep the bourgeoisie in its place, their request serenely goes on to demand that the third estate be represented solely by men of the gown.

In two days, Paris becomes as enraged with its *Parlement* as it was adoring of it before. "Never did a revolution take place more swiftly in people's minds; never did enthusiasm give way more suddenly to execration."[2] D'Eprémesnil and Fréteau may just as well sit down again. The only man in the *Parlement* to emerge unscathed is Adrien Duport, chief adversary of the conformist majority, who vehemently opposes the holding of the Estates General in their antiquated form.

There's little chance that tears will be shed in Versailles over this change in the wind of opinion. All *parlements* be damned! Serves them right. The King is out hunting, eating, drinking and relying on Necker, just as, in the beginning, he had relied on Turgot, then on Necker his first time around, then on Calonne, then on Brienne. The Queen, still lamenting Necker's return, has withdrawn into the background of the political scene. Her private life, these days, is a mixture of sorrow and joy. Since the death of her last daughter, little Madame Sophie, aged less than a year, on June 18, 1788, of a "putrid fever," the Queen has become increasingly anxious about the ill health of the Dauphin. "I am quite worried by my oldest son.* He has always been weak and delicate, but I was not expecting anything so acute as this. His growth is somewhat awry, in that he has one hip higher than the other and his spine is a little twisted and unduly prominent. For some time now he has been running a temperature every day and is greatly weakened and reduced in weight. It is certain that his teeth are the chief cause of his sufferings . . . . The King was also very weak and sickly in childhood, and the air of Meudon was very good for him. We are going to settle my son there."[3] The ailing child is now seven years old.

On the other hand, she relishes the consolation of Axel Fersen's return to France. He has finished his reluctant term on the battlefields of Finland, served at the behest of his king, Gustavus III, who has dragged Sweden into an unplanned war against Russia, on the overoptimistic assumption that Cath-

---

*Letter from Marie Antoinette to Joseph II on February 22, 1788; since then, and despite his removal to Meudon, the child's condition has been growing steadily worse.

erine already has too much on her hands in Turkey.* Fersen never approved of this military excursion, which was badly begun and badly conducted by an army in a sorry state.

He's thirty-three, the same age as the Queen. Nowadays, despite his great discretion, her own irresponsible behavior has made it impossible for their relationship to remain a secret any longer. He has no more illusions about his own sovereign, if he ever had any. Perhaps he did, for a few months, sixteen years before, when Gustavus III's "royal coup d'état" enabled the young King of Sweden to regain absolute authority, immediately after his coronation, over the oligarchy of his decadent nobility. One of the most prominent of those decadent nobles was old Senator Fersen, Axel's father, whose ambitions were thwarted by the coup. As though seeking the old man's forgiveness, Gustavus III showed interest, even affection, for his son Axel, who was almost promoted to the rank of favorite in those early days. But the King's open homosexuality made people suspicious of his preferences, which tended too much in the direction of the young noblemen he gathered around him. And the Lord knows, Fersen was a handsome boy. But his cool, unfluttered good looks were for the ladies alone. He sidestepped the King's overabundant kindnesses and quickly chose, for himself, the life of a cosmopolite, divided among Sweden, France and England. For years his sword has been employed by the first two, under a six-monthly contract the terms of which are scrupulously applied by Gustavus III. If he could not be everything to the young man, he could at least be jealous.

Between wars, Fersen has been looking halfheartedly for the "good marriage," somewhere in Europe, that would befit his lofty estate; he nearly married Germaine de Staël, before stepping aside (it was understood he would) in favor of his friend Eric de Staël. When wars were on, he went to the American campaign as one of Rochambeau's staff officers, nursed disappointed hopes of the aborted conflict between Bavaria and Holland, and now, unwillingly, has taken part in this Swedish foray into Finland. As for love, he has, without making the slightest effort to fight for her, won the Queen of France.

He's had enough of Gustavus III for a while and has just proffered some harsh views of that contradictory character, whose face is all twisted to one side but whose gaze is so appealing, sometimes; intelligent but inconsistent, effeminate but courageous, passionately interested in literature and the arts but unbalanced. In the last analysis, he's a megalomaniac, and his retinue were rather alarmed by the things he said before setting out on his impossible assault of St. Petersburg:

"I view myself as the avenger of all these people on the shore [in

*On Marie Antoinette's relationship with Fersen see Volumes I, II, and IV.

Stockholm] watching me set out. . . . It is I who shall save the Ottoman Empire. . . . My name shall be known in Asia and Africa."[4] Catherine, in Petersburg, laughed at him: "He has donned the costume of Gustavus Adolphus and, in armor, brassards and cuisses, crossed my frontiers between the Finnish rocks. Thus far his exploits have been confined to the massacre of a good old officer with two men who, all unsuspecting, were conveying a boatload of wood."[5] And as Catherine's pen sets the tone for the rest of Europe . . .

Fersen, meanwhile, on campaign, and irremediably humorless, was not laughing: "The soldiers have neither cloaks nor blankets, and the prevailing tone of the army makes all good citizens tremble."[6] "All is over here. The King sees that he has been misled on every count; he is in despair; he has decided to finish it off as soon as possible, and if he does not do it himself, the entire army will desert him . . . . If this could make him cease his follies, it would be good for something, but I believe he is incorrigible."[7]

France looks so much healthier to him! The revolution he is dreading for the morrow will be in Sweden, as he sees it, not in Paris or Versailles: "The situation in this country is equally agitated, and in fact people here are wildly excited, but what a difference! This is a disease of a sound constitution in the full force of maturity, needing only a good physician; the problem is to find him. . . .

"Here, within a short span, the great heat subsides and calm reasoning returns. The important question dividing people's minds just now is whether the number of representatives of the third estate at the Estates General will be equal to that of nobility and clergy."[8]

That's not the only subject of his earnest conversation with the Queen, although politics are looming increasingly large in their private moments. But they are about to live the two best months of their whole relationship this winter, when "Fersen would ride his horse through the grounds,* near the Trianon, three or four times each week; the Queen . . . was doing the same, and their meetings were the source of public scandal, despite the favorite's modesty and restraint. He never let anything appear on the outside."[9]

When did they actually make it into bed? After the American war, no doubt, when Marie Antoinette's "leaning" grew more acute with every month of his absence. They were certainly lovers in 1784, in any event, when Axel accompanied Gustavus III on a frenzied round of parties in France. Beginning that year, a mysterious Joséphine appears as a regular recipient of letters in the meticulous record he keeps of all his correspondence. And he was beginning to let slip ecstatic expressions about a wonderful *She* in his letters

---

*According to the *Mémoires* of the minister Saint-Priest.

to his sister Sophie, the only person in whom he confides. Now, just after his return to France, he writes to her on November 6: "At this moment the cup of my happiness is full."[10] Two weeks later he adds, "It is eight in the evening, I must leave you now, I have been at Versailles since yesterday but don't say I am writing to you from here, for all my other letters are being dated from Paris."[11]

Now, for the only time in her life, Marie Antoinette's imprudence verges upon the defiant, like that of a woman who is in love and, however fleetingly, is satisfied and proud of the man she loves. Unconsciously she must feel that it is her right, after over fifteen years of an almost platonic marriage to a man for whom she is beginning to feel contempt—not just as a defaulting husband but as a sovereign as well, who has so grudgingly allowed her to acquire the compensatory influence she is determined to have upon "matters of state." She's the daughter of Maria Theresa, after all, a descendant of the Hapsburgs. Their beauty is perhaps a little fleshy, but that only adds to her radiance, and she has a strong potential for sensuality. And now, in spite of everything, she's making them all dance to her tune, that whole flock of Court butterflies who'd have liked nothing better than to have consoled her, back when she was hardly more than a girl. There was Artois, Orléans, Lauzun, Coigny, Esterhazy, Besenval, Rohan . . . what a graveyard of panting suitors! But in those years the only hold calumny could get upon her was her pronounced friendships for a few young women—Lamballe yesterday, Polignac today.* In the end, she produced the two sons for which they had dragged her from Vienna to Versailles. And as often happens after a long crisis of waiting, the man she wanted was the man who wasn't after her and who began by trying to avoid her—and Fersen is also the one she got.

The ideal backdrop for their romance has just been imagined in the spirit of the time, as the stage setting for a pastorale. In the last ten years, a fancy for living *à la paysanne* has become the supreme refinement of the great lords. White gowns, bare arms, hair unset and unpowdered, snacks of honey and milk fresh from the cow. But since the great and powerful cannot actually stoop to visiting the villeins in their villages, where they would have to see the pig cheek by jowl with the cow, manure instead of flowers and rags rather than white lawn, they took the expedient of building little rustic paradises hard by their own châteaux. "As a result, there came to be, on the grounds of our Île-de-France, a great many of these hamlets copied from Norman farms,† some inhabited by workers on the estates, others put there

---

*See Volume IV for the capital that Jeanne de la Motte managed to make of the rumors of the Queen's lesbian proclivities at the beginning of the Necklace Affair.

†According to Pierre de Nolhac, the most infatuated and knowledgeable lover of the estates of Versailles. Thanks to a restoration program carried out largely with the help of

simply for their picturesque value; Trianon is the best preserved of them all."[12]

The Condés were the first to have a toy village built on the grounds of Chantilly, followed by the Orléanses at Raincy and the Provences at Montreuil. The Queen's hamlet was built, beginning in 1785, near the Petit Trianon, under the supervision of a young painter who was then still an unknown, Hubert Robert, and, as it should be, it is the best of them all. To take her mind off that most distressing business of the necklace, Marie Antoinette had proudly resolved to put her mark on Versailles, a place where she could escape from the haunts of Madame de Pompadour or Madame du Barry and free herself from the corseting of "Madame l'Étiquette," a place with no invitation lists, as for the trips to Marly, nor even any foreordained dates for anything. Whomever she chooses comes, according to her preferences of the moment, and pretends to milk real cows and feed real carp in her tame stream. Her ladies-in-waiting learn to churn butter in real churns, and the King himself occasionally turns an unprotocoled hand to tinkering at an overlooked detail here or there, some little domestic job. But even he, like the rest, can come only when the Queen invites him. This is the one tiny space in France where she reigns uncontested, over the nine houses with their thatched roofs, wooden stairs, little leaded panes of glass and walls rendered to look like old brick with trompe-l'oeil cracks running down them. A variety of vegetables and fruit trees grows in borders and orchards connected by rose-bowered pathways. One would, however, have to look hard through the rest of France to find any other hamlet containing 1,232 flowerpots in white china from Lorraine, marked with the Queen's initials in blue.

At present, Fersen is the only permanent guest. The Queen, imagining that the people around her are true friends, goes off alone with him when the fancy takes her, to "the farm," "the dairy," or "the mill," and especially to the large two-story house called "the boudoir," while her playmates amuse themselves across the way in the "billiard house."

A stout little three-year-old bundle is often there with them, Marie Antoinette's familial consolation, the child whose health does not cause her concern: the little Duc de Normandie, bursting with energy. "In strength and health, he possesses exactly everything of which his brother has too little; he's a true peasant child, big, pink and fat."[13]

Really, "a peasant child"? A murmur is beginning to circulate about this little imp whose health is much too good for the envious. The malevolence will become increasingly tenacious, emanating from those same "true

---

American sponsors, what he wrote sixty-five years ago is true today. Marie Antoinette's hamlet at Trianon still gives the best available image of the mentality of the end of this reign.

friends." The little urchin's ruddy looks, his resilience, energy and wild spirits mark him out, indeed, as a child of a different substance from the lymphatic Madame Royale and the dying Dauphin. The search for some father other than Louis XVI for this third child sinks into a lip-smacking slough of anecdotes and historical gossip.* But nobody is trying to insinuate that he is some sort of "peasant child," that's for sure. His other putative father, the handsome man bursting with good health, is the Comte de Fersen. The more resolute scandalmongers have already started counting on their fingers. Now, little Louis-Charles was born on March 25, 1785. That was nine months to the day after a great bash of a party at Trianon, still spoken of by intimates as a high point in the Queen's pleasure. "The greatest freedom reigned; people went this way and that, with whomever they pleased."[14] Fersen was there. That's all that is known at the time. It's pretty much all that will ever be known.

DUPORT

53

NOVEMBER 1788

This Conspiracy of Decent People

Minister of state since the end of August, Necker sets to work with a will and a half, although on the day after his appointment the King manages to relieve himself, in front of a few close friends, of one last drop of poison:

"I have been made to bring Necker back. I did not want to do it, but it will not be long before we shall be sorry it was done. I shall do everything he tells me, and we'll see what comes of it."[1]

For better or worse, the "Necker government" is able to function. Even if, unlike Brienne, he does not hold the title of First Minister, nobody, at least in public, disputes the preeminence of the man in charge of money. His cabinet: Montmorin for Foreign Affairs; Puységur to replace the Comte

---

*A few lively imaginations had already tried to assign paternity for the first Dauphin to Coigny, but the similarity between his ailments and those of Louis XVI in the first years of his life scotched this calumny. The Duc de Normandie, of course, becomes history's Louis XVII.

de Brienne for War; La Luzerne for the Navy; Laurent de Villedeuil for the King's Household; Barentin for Justice. Three men in favor are ministers of state without any specific field of action: the Duc de Nivernais, the Comte de Saint-Priest and the ephemeral comptroller of finance, Bouvard de Four-queux.*

Absolute priority goes to filling in the financial breach that has been gaping ever since the disguised declaration of bankruptcy on August 16; in other words, to procuring what the state needs to meet essential payments before the Estates General can lay down the foundations for a new, coherent budget. A banker's job, thus, which Necker performs as well as anyone could, according to La Fayette, who is not one of his ardent supporters, "by dint of *tours de force,* sheer ability and the confidence of the public."[2] During these trying weeks, he accomplishes the bulk of what he has been asked to do.

"When I took the helm again . . . , every form of credit had been an-nihilated, and yet I saw that it would be necessary to find several millions at once in order to meet specific commitments or payments in regard to which the slightest delay would expose the state to terrifying dangers. I took some initial steps [by lending two million from his own pocket, interest-free, to start with], but difficulties kept arising to confront me because every form of levy had already been spent in advance."[3]

He works like a Trojan, tries every possible gimmick and contrivance. He invites the 113 notaries of Paris to his offices in order to borrow money from them, although the unseemly words are not actually spoken. Yield: seven million at 6 percent to be repaid . . . in thirty-seven years. He im-poses a sacrifice upon the farmers general, which is easy enough for these money-crammed men to make but which they have never been asked to make before—the postponement of their annual rake-off on the funds they collect, from which their own salaries are paid. Yield: three million. He renews and almost institutionalizes a measure introduced by Brienne a bare week before his downfall, by making the notes issued by the Caisse d'Escompte—the great regulator of commerce created by Turgot—count for cash in the following year. This means that not only can the Caisse resume payments at sight; it can also advance ten million a month to the Treasury.[4]

"Thus it was that by maneuvering, by recourse to every conceivable arrangement and resource circumscribed within a very small circle, I con-trived to conduct the frail ship of state without it breaking up or going on the rocks until the opening of the Estates General, the date that I looked upon as the first sighting of a safe port.

*Who dies six months later at the age of seventy-three.

"I maintained payments for a year, without any help from the *parlements* or Estates General;* by taking unheard-of precautions, I saved Paris and France from the horrors of famine. . . .

"The great crowd of onlookers below must have seen me constantly moving about a chariot that was swiftly descending from the crest of a high hill, and might have supposed that I was accelerating its pace when in reality, on the contrary, I was braking it with all my strength."[5]

Also, despite his innate complacency, Necker does all this almost silently, without speeches or publications, quite unlike his behavior during his first term in the government, when "I was continually in motion; I busied myself with everything, I acted upon everything, a major reform, a trivial savings, the reorganization of the finance companies . . . ; in short, I was active in some sense every day. Upon my return to the government in August 1788 I saw that I should be well advised to adopt an entirely different line, in the interests of the welfare of the state; this great objective imposed upon me an obligation to keep the administration of finance in a sort of darkness and silence."[6]

So that is what he does, not realizing that now he's going against the spirit of the times and that his unwonted discretion is going to damage him just as badly as all his trumpets and drums did in 1781 when he published his *Account Rendered*. The public is used to boasts of achievement, and this abstention from propaganda works against him. "He had a shy conceit,† based on his ability and his fame, and it was forever making him fearful of compromising himself with public opinion."[7] The shyness hasn't always been easy to see, but now it does begin to be visible . . . only, now is not the right time.

So Necker is out of step with both the financial and the political situation of the realm. Two or three years before, already dreading the uncontrollable disturbances that the Estates General might produce, he had a few ideas on the subject. He was not in favor of the Estates and would have preferred a more cautious system of municipal and provincial assemblies, but by the time he returns to power, Brienne has already set the other process in motion. Some people suggest that Necker call it off, or at least postpone it, on the basis of his popularity. But that can't be done.

"Would it be conceivable for a man such as M. Necker to propose that

---

*Because the "safe port" itself, overtaken by political events, postpones consideration of the financial crisis. Necker's financial expedients, for which he gets no thanks from anybody, enable the opening months of the Revolution to proceed without precipitating bankruptcy. In May 1789, the credit of the Royal Treasury stands at almost one hundred million livres, twenty times more than it had been a year before.

†According to Malouet.

Louis XVI take back his word?" expostulates his daughter. "He could have found no political advantage in the degradation this would have implied. When a thing is neither morally right nor useful, what kind of madman could recommend it?"[8]

However, some sort of statement is going to have to be made, at least in Council, on the question that is beginning to stir everybody up and has become a positive obsession since the *Parlement* made that faux pas when it reconvened: to double or not to double?

From the end of September on, at Court, in the streets, and wherever people understand that the reference to the 1614 Estates General boils down to two main issues, that's all people can talk about. Is the third estate to be represented by the same number of delegates as each of the other two or by a number equal to the total of the other two? And assuming some decision is reached on this question, will the nation's thousand representatives vote on taxes—and also, as everyone is now convinced it should, on reforms, and possibly a constitution—by head or by order? In other words, will the vote be six or seven hundred against three hundred, or two chambers against one?

"What a curious situation is that of France!" Mirabeau writes to Mauvillon. "The question at issue among us pertains to the least-known parts of our history, it pertains to the most important principles of the social order. It will determine the nature of the revolution that will take place among us, whether reason or prejudice is to prevail, the interest of all or private interest, whether our century is to move forward or back.... And this trial of the nation versus the nation must be prepared and judged in less than two months.

"On the other hand, should the 1614 Estates be followed, as the *parlements* are so insistently demanding, because their sole aim is that the Estates General should be seen to be futile, then we return to the condition of a feudal people. We shall be testing the recent achievements of enlightenment only to bury them under the obsolescence of our old prejudices."[9]

All other problems are trifles. How delegates are to be chosen—on the second or third ballot, by the electors in each order; and their qualification, and the formalities of convening, and the locations in which the successive ballots are to take place, and the drafting and discussion of the grievances to be produced by each *bailliage* or municipality: these are all matters that can be settled without difficulty. But until the two crucial questions are decided, nothing else can be done. And only the King can decide them. This is where, now that the Treasury is in better condition and the rioting has subsided, everybody is expecting Necker to take over a political role even though he is visibly avoiding it. Opinion assumes, more wrongly than rightly, that he has a decisive influence over the Council's choice.

One trouble is that Necker has only half made up his own mind. Far from soaring off into the prophetic trances of a Mirabeau, he is unsure, almost as hesitant as Louis XVI, and at times he seems himself to be ruled by "the obsolescence of our old prejudices." Elementary common sense inclines him to share the conviction of almost all the French, that the third estate should be doubled, but his fear of upheavals makes him doubtful as to the second part of the question. At bottom he's not far from favoring the old vote by order, as a check upon extreme proposals. He would like to reconcile the irreconcilable; his ambivalence is explained by a confidence he makes to *Président* d'Héricourt, a magistrate friend of his, one day in November: "We do not want individual participation any more than you do, but we think* that double representation of the third estate should be granted in order to calm people's minds and bring back those of good faith."[10]

In the beginning, he doesn't have the courage to impose even this half-baked compromise. He makes his first big mistake when he tries to have the basic choice made by another Assembly of Notables, something nobody was expecting.

On October 5, 1788, the King's Council emits a sort of muffled thunderclap that takes the kingdom by surprise. "Yielding solely to that love of the good that guides all the feelings of his heart, His Majesty has considered the wisest course to be the reconvening of the same notables who gathered on his orders in January 1787, to assist him with their counsel."[11]

La Fayette doesn't like it: "It has been decided that the former Notables are to be called back and made responsible for the convening of the Estates General. This is a plan of M. Necker's; I fear it may delay the truly curative assembly too long and postpone the elections until midwinter, which would make it impossible for some provinces to form proper elective assemblies because the snow would prevent them from meeting.... I do not think . . . the Notables have much skill at constitutional matters. We meet on November 3; some decision must be reached by the end of the month. The convening of the Estates will take place in December. In this Assembly of Notables there will be some very singular things seen."[12]

Another inconsistency in Necker's behavior: on one hand, he retreats, setting off, behind the screen of the Notables, a whole process of delays and indecisive behavior at a time when every minute counts. At the same time he authorizes the revival of dozens of fermenting little societies, which Breteuil outlawed in 1787 at the beginning of the *parlements'* unrest—all the clubs, "café gatherings," reading groups, Masonic lodges, philosophical so-

---

*This is not the royal "We"—or rather it is, in the sense that Necker thought he was giving the King's opinion as well as his own.

cieties, etc. So there will be, simultaneously, the majestic, official and useless meeting of a second Assembly of Notables whose discussions nobody will pay any attention to for the very good reason that they take place in exactly the same six committees as on the first occasion, and in secret; and the takeover of opinion by little groups of speakers and leaders who very quickly fill the gap left by the discrediting of the *Parlement.* It is the sayings and writings of this new wave of "notables" that are going to channel the rising pressure in people's minds. The beginning of the wildcat assemblies can be dated from this time.

On November 20 an anonymous correspondent writes to Gustavus III, "The famous salon near the Comédie-Italienne, frequented by all the most distinguished figures of Paris . . . , has just reopened, to the great satisfaction of its subscribers. . . . Another coterie meets in the home of M. Massé, who has a restaurant in the Palais-Royal; this is composed of military and magistrates . . . , who talk with unimaginable boldness and wildness. The King, they say, has called them the Enragés [= rabid], a jest that puts them in the same category as the postilions, who are similarly qualified and who drive us through the streets like madmen. . . . The agitation seen here and in the provinces has to do with the great issues that are to be decided by a national body. Everywhere, the third estate is trying to recover its rights and shake off the yoke of the other two orders. Nobles and priests are fighting every inch of the way. . . . In the end, they will have no choice but to yield."[13]

The most active of these societies, the one most subscribed to by people whose names are already known, combines the more sophisticated members of the *Parlement,* the world of high finance and banking, a few nobles disgusted with Court society, and a few "unclassifiables," such as Mirabeau. This is the Society of Thirty, which is led by *Parlement* Councillor Adrien Duport and meets in his home on the rue de Grand-Chantier in Paris. Its days are Tuesday, Wednesday and Sunday, and it soon numbers many more participants than the symbolic figure mentioned in its name. Beginning in late November, *Président* Lepeletier de Saint-Fargeau is to be seen there, along with Advocate General Hérault de Séchelles, Condorcet, Talleyrand, Mirabeau, La Fayette, two of the Lameth brothers, the advocate Target, Dupont de Nemours, the financiers Clavière and Panchaud, and the Duc de La Rochefoucauld. D'Eprémesnil and Fréteau* try to regain lost ground there; but Duport is committed, unwavering in his politics, and consistent in his thinking, and it is he who conducts the orchestra. He has invented a kind of New Man: the intellectual group leader. He knows what he wants and he knows where he's

*The names of these men of liberty will be found in the index to this and previous volumes, if any readers care to refresh their memories of their backgrounds. The time has now come for them to begin to act together.

going: toward a kind of monarchy *à la française* in which the executive power, which is naturally still the King's, will be tempered by a legislative power originating in an assembly in which all classes of the nation will be represented. So he's already trying to go one better than the English monarchy, in which there are two unequal chambers (the House of Lords having more power than the Commons), and the sovereign remains all-powerful. Duport is becoming one of the founders of what is starting to be known as "the national party," still shapeless, its policies unformulated, but soon to stand at the forefront of "enlightened" opinion.

In a unified France, with all internal barriers abolished, a great wind is about to rise, blown by men of differing social backgrounds, born in different regions, "having nothing in common but human reason,* beyond all corporate bias . . . and caste prejudice, the objective being, by bringing their ideas together, that the issues raised for debate should be settled solely according to the laws of justice and reason. By this method, all individual viewpoints would blend into a single national spirit."[14]

So many seeds are planted by the "Thirty"! The double representation of the third, naturally, but also the combining of all three orders into a single assembly with one man, one vote; the idea that the representatives of the *whole* nation should have virtually full powers to establish and defend "the rights of man," and the idea that no one, not even a minister, not even the King, can tell them what they should talk about or how they should talk about it. And since Necker's pointless convening of the Notables is going to add to the delay, the Thirty, acting in conjunction with other similar clubs, are determined not to waste their own time, at least. In November they start working out standard forms for the drawing up of the lists of grievances [*Cahiers de Doléances*].

Mirabeau, ready as always to take the bit between his teeth, is positively drunk with it all at first. On November 10 he tries to enlist his friend Lauzun: "Panchaud must have spoken to you again of our plan to form a constitutional club. We have already attached several men of merit to ourselves, and are gathering at six o'clock today, for the second time, in the home of M. Duport, Councillor at *Parlement,* on the rue de Grand-Chantier. Your presence is eagerly awaited and has been promised, and I believe you will not regret falling in with our wishes, for this conspiracy of decent people will go farther than anyone imagines."[15]

---

*According to Georges Michon, in his biography of Duport.

54

NOVEMBER–DECEMBER 1788

How Easy It Would Be to Do Without the Privileged!

Versailles. In the end, the Notables assemble on Thursday, November 6, 1788, a chilly, fog-shrouded day. The ceremony exudes massive boredom. The gestures, participants, settings are almost the same as on February 22, 1787,* when this body was convened for the first time. But then France was listening, ready to set its clocks by the Notables' time. People believed. They shivered in anticipation. Calonne seemed on the verge of greater glory, although Brienne, seated on one of the clergy's benches, was waiting for him to start making mistakes. The King hadn't begun to squander the capital of his popularity and had actually benefited indirectly from the Queen's discredit over the Necklace Affair. Even the worst of the pessimists were still hoping the monarchy would regenerate spontaneously. . . .

Today, the gorgeous blue, white and gold apparatus is in motion for the second time, and in motion to no purpose. Where have all the fine hopes gone, and in less than two years? They have shrunk into the eyes and burning words of a handful of men who were meeting last night in Duport's salon or a few rooms in the Palais-Royal cafés and some dozens of feverish printshops. But in the Salle des Menus Plaisirs, where the King will meet the Notables after hearing mass, there is nothing but lassitude and ennui.

The princes have climbed into the King's coach—his two brothers and three cousins, Orléans, Condé, Bourbon. "The King's cortege was the same as at the previous assembly," but the record of it, read out during the announcements in every church, mentions one change in the retinue, "a detachment of House Guards replaced the Light Horse, disbanded by order [of Brienne] on September 30, 1787."[1]

*See Volume IV.

One other innovation—a sixteen-year-old prince, the Duc d'Enghien,* last scion of the Condés, looking pretty enough to eat in his white silk outfit topped with a Renaissance toque, sits near the throne for the first time.

For the inaugural ritual, Lamoignon has been replaced by Barentin, who duly performs the genuflexions and grimaces and utters the orotund phrases of the welcoming speech. The only quiver of curiosity that momentarily arouses the Assembly occurs when it is the turn of the man who is both old and new—the greatly, perhaps too greatly, longed-for Necker, seated at the long table placed below the King's feet—to read out a speech that feebly points to a way out of the stale stalemate. Introduced simply as "Director General," the man without a handle to his name, the banker, the Genevan, the Protestant, swings into a panegyric of the third estate that makes it clear that now is now and relegates the Estates of 1614 to their drawer in the archives.

"You will see, gentlemen, how things have changed since the age of the last Estates General. The considerable increase in specie has introduced what might be regarded as a new kind of wealth, and the enormity of the public debt shows us a large class of citizens who are closely bound up with the prosperity of the state, by ties that were unknown in the olden days of the monarchy. Trade, manufacture and all manner of arts and crafts have reached a level that could not even be thought of before and are today vivifying the realm by all the means arising out of an active industry."

Some of his listeners suppose that Necker is setting out to analyze profound social change before proceeding to draw political conclusions. After glorifying the growth of commerce and industry, he moves on to sing hymns to the countryside in almost Rousseauist tones:

"Lastly, the increase in enlightenment and the gradual emancipation from a host of prejudices have brought us to the realization that we must honor those who peacefully pursue the fertile labors of agriculture in the countryside."

But this is not the day for Necker to raise himself to the heights of true ministerial innovation. His labored bow to the third estate is three sentences long, and that's it. After bestowing the barest lip-service recognition upon a few of the century's new words, new at any rate by comparison with the feudal manner of the Court, he hastily draws the curtain and, in the same paragraph, extends his most reassuring salutations "to the first two orders of the realm; for the King remains fully aware how much he particularly owes them." The clergy even hears itself attributed "the unique and precious merit of influencing moral order"; and Necker keeps the score even with a reference

---

*Shot on March 20, 1804, in the Vincennes trenches, on the orders of First Consul Bonaparte, after his abduction at Ettenheim, followed by a summary trial.

to "that generous nobility, united to France and her kings by many glorious services."

After that, perhaps he's earned the right to weary everyone with a long list of his proposals for the working methods of the six committees and a catalog of the provisions to be devised for elections to and procedure during the Estates General. But his words aren't getting across. Nobody listens, nobody is waiting for anything more to come from him. Besides, he never has been able to hold a large audience. From that angle the only one who doesn't fare too badly is Louis XVI, even when he's talking, in his well-modulated voice, to hear himself talk; he keeps it short and sweet.

On the evening of November 6 the curtain falls upon a wasted day. But many other curtains will fall in the coming months, upon the Notables' activity, or rather apathy. Full, heavy curtains, the deadly minutes of the proceedings of each of the six committees, in which scores of more or less urgent problems are raised, and then tabled, in relation to the convening of the Estates. The whole futile record piles up in the Court archives and threatens to drown the secretaries.* Hardly anyone notices when Monsieur slyly steps into the still-very-unassuming shoes of the champion of novelties—his committee being the only one to decide, by a weak majority, in favor of a possible doubling of the third. At this point, the Duc d'Orléans is leaving the role to the King's brothers to play. Scorched by his "exile" to Villers-Cotterêts the year before, he has adopted a policy of frequent absenteeism from his committee (the third), of which he isn't even, in fact, chairman, "for reasons of health." So it is that early in December the Notables are drifting toward a reapplication of the 1614 rules by a majority of five committees to one, and that one not what you could call do-or-die. A most Louis-XVI sort of drowsiness might be said to have fallen upon official circles, then, were it not for two opposing jolts that occur in December.

The first is in the direction of change, and it hits the *Parlement,* believe it or not, under the impetus of the Society of Thirty, for whom this is an opportunity to test their youthful influence. On December 5, the Paris magistrates issue a decision that is an attempt to compensate for their moral abdication on September 24. They adopt a motion petitioning the King to consider the possibility of doubling the third. The text was virtually copied from a draft written two days before at Duport's, and it is presented to the sitting by d'Eprémesnil, acting on the principle that it's never too late to do the right thing. This attempt to win the race by running the other way doesn't restore the *Parlement*'s lost popularity but it does show that general opinion

---

*When the first *Archives Parlementaires* are printed, 150 double-column pages are occupied by the minutes of the Notables' committees.

is still in there pushing, without regard for the Notables' scribbles. On the other hand, people react very strongly to the opposing jolt, administered through a violent memorial submitted to the King by five princes of the blood, who have placed themselves at the head of the opposition—before there's anything to oppose! Artois, Condé, Bourbon, Conti and Enghien sign and issue a sort of manifesto, which sweeps rapidly and at great expense through the kingdom.* The whole lengthy document, which was written by Robert Auget de Montyon,† the Comte d'Artois's chancellor, or head of secretariat, reeks of anger and fright. Scion of a family of Parisian magistrates, advocate at the Châtelet himself, then intendant in Auvergne, Provence, and Aunis before buying his Court office, Montyon is a fifty-year-old worldling with pretensions to membership in the Academy, supported by his recent institution of an annual prize for "virtue" bearing his name and intended to reward docile and right-minded "common" people, men and women alike, who perform some outstandingly virtuous deed. M. de Montyon's own virtue, however, is turning sour. We are not surprised by the acerbity of what soon comes to be known as the "princes' letter" when we learn, for instance, that this "do-gooding niggard's"‡ view of Necker is that the minister is "insanely ambitious and ignorant of history . . . ," that he "praised Colbert without knowing him, is scheming, shrewd and gross; a charlatan . . . incapable of any feeling other than vanity, in thrall to his wife and infatuated with his daughter, who is equally infatuated with him."[2]

The redressing of the financial situation and preparations for the Estates General might have been thought sufficient to calm people down. People maybe, but not princes, and not Montyon. Their text spits fire. Facing the energetic but still prudent remonstrations issuing from the *parlements,* as well as the thousand and one lists of grievances that are beginning to be drawn up, cap in hand, all over the country, this "princes' letter" is the first install-ment of combat propaganda from the one small caste that obstructs all the others: the upper nobility.

"In speaking for the nobility, the princes of your blood are speaking for themselves. They cannot forget that they form part of the nobility and must not be separated from it, that their first title is that of gentlemen."[3]

The most petulant of the group is the Prince de Conti. He sent up a

---

*It is undated, but must have been given to Louis XVI on December 9 or 10.

†Montyon emigrates in the footsteps of the Comte d'Artois very early, on July 23, 1789; after some hesitation, he does not join Bonaparte and does not return to France until the reign of Louis XVIII. He dies rich, in 1820. The Montyon prizes are awarded for another hundred years afterward.

‡The expression is Paul Morand's.

sort of trial balloon a few days earlier in Monsieur's committee. He had written a virulent letter to the King's brother, read it aloud in his presence, then published it immediately afterward.

"Pray, sir, impress upon the King how important it is, for the stability of his throne, for law and order, that all new systems should be eschewed forever, and that the constitution and old ways should be preserved in every particular."[4]

The Comte de Provence squirms a little and passes on this singular request to the King, who is not best pleased to see his brother being used as a middleman in this kind of approach and is not afraid to say so. But Conti was only out scouting; here comes the full charge of the princely army:

> Let the third estate desist from attacking the rights of the first two orders, rights that, being no less ancient than the monarchy, must be as inalterable as its own constitution; let it confine itself to petitioning for a reduction of taxes, where, perhaps, too much is being asked of it.
>
> Sire, the state is in grave danger . . . , a revolution in the principles of government is in the offing; it has been brought about by the fermentation in people's minds. . . .
>
> There is every evidence, every indication of a system of methodical insubordination. Every writer sets up as legislator. Eloquence, or the ability to write, even when supported by no study, knowledge or experience, appears to be sufficient qualification for its possessor to dictate the organization of empires. Whoever puts forward some extreme proposal, whoever proposes that the law be changed, is sure to find readers and followers. . . .
>
> Who can say where this rashness of opinion will end? . . . Soon the rights of property will be attacked; the inequality of fortunes will be presented as a goal of reform.

The princes' letter is more than a series of lamentations. The handful of men who sign it believe themselves to be the possessors of a formidable potential for repression. And judging from the plethora of châteaux, land, servants and financial resources in the hands of Artois, the Condés and the Contis, they can indeed see themselves, in December 1788, as the masters of no insignificant portion of France. Looking behind the balanced clauses of their manifesto, one sees a thinly veiled threat: "In a kingdom in which there has been no civil dissension for so long, the word 'secession' can be spoken only with regret: nevertheless, this must be the expected outcome if the rights of the first two orders were to be changed in any way."

"Secession"? Do they really spell it out so plainly?

One of the hundreds of men scribbling away this winter is quite tempted, when the princes' missive comes into his hands, to take it literally. Abbé Sieyès is writing a text into which, in addition to his thoughts, he is pouring his very life and those of all the poor people he has known, from Fréjus to Tréguier and Chartres. He's delighted by this talk of "secession." The princes "seem to be saying to the third estate . . . , therefore, you must leave the old way alone, in which you were nothing and we were everything, and it was easy for us to pay only what we liked."[5]

With their intention of disabling the Estates General before they convene by persuading the nobility to boycott them, the hereditary leaders of the absolutist party have just declared war. Sieyès, unlike the princes themselves, is not at all convinced of their might and looks upon them as stuffed shirts. They talk about seceding, they swear they'll go sulk in the corners if the third estate imposes a new pace and character upon future assemblies—all the better: let them do it! And they needn't wait for the third to come crawling, begging them to stay. The prostrate age is over.

"They dared to speak the word 'secession,' they threatened the King and people with it! Ah, God in Heaven, what a glad day it would be for the nation if their so desirable secession were to be consummated eternally! How easy it would be to do without the privileged! How hard it will be to turn them into citizens!"

Here Sieyès provides just one example of the protest aroused on all sides by the princes' letter. They wanted to produce an effect, and so they have, but exactly the opposite of the one they were hoping for. It's as though Their Highnesses were pouring boiling oil on the nation's wounds.

Monsieur and the Duc d'Orléans can congratulate themselves on not joining in the attempt. They diligently open the Luxembourg and Palais-Royal gardens to the public and find the status of their palaces as little poles of Parisian defiance considerably enhanced. The capital's streets are quiet. There are no more riots; but from Duport's home to the Café du Caveau, from the Batignolles taverns to the university departments on the Montagne Sainte-Geneviève, a great tidal wave is rising, of petitions, pamphlets, tracts and lampoons, while impromptu orators are making the most of every shaft of wintry sunlight to leap onto chairs, benches and tables, even into the crotches of trees. Nobody pays much attention to what they say; people applaud before they even open their mouths, because they know they're going to speak against the princes. Anybody crazy enough to utter a word in their favor would be torn to shreds.

Madame Necker notes, in the pages of her intermittent diary, that "the spectacle of Paris just now is indescribable: opinion is sweeping through every class, inspiring, impeding, saddening, casting into despair, assuming every conceivable form and speaking through every mouth.[6] . . . Women are talking about the constitution as heatedly as they used to do when analyzing sensibility at the Hôtel de Rambouillet."*

But the gulf between Versailles and Paris is growing so wide that on Friday, December 12, at the closing session of that Assembly of Notables-for-nothing, some people think the King is going to throw in his lot with the princes and their diatribe. It looks as though the doubling of the third may not happen after all, since the proposal has been rejected by five committees out of six. However, all the Notables can do is "advise and counsel." The final decision is referred to a forthcoming meeting of the King's Council. A whole month wasted, for that!

The relative interest shown in the Notables' closing moments has less to do with anything they may have achieved than with their value as entertainment, made picturesque by the arrival of an early cold spell. Is this the harbinger of a bad winter? There's so much snow and ice in Versailles that it is feared the carriages may come to grief on the short trip from the palace to the Hôtel des Menus Plaisirs. "His Majesty having taken cold, He decided to hold this session in the great guardroom of the château."[7]

The cold is so acute that it disrupts life inside the château itself, as there is no way to heat the place adequately, and it spoils the Notables' leavetaking of their sovereign. "To receive them, the King stood in front of the fire in his study. The princes entered and placed themselves on either side of His Majesty. The Notables walked past, one by one, in no order of rank, and bowed deeply to the King, entering from the parade room and leaving through His Majesty's bedroom, as the cold was too intense for them to go through the Hall of Mirrors."

But is anything ever going to get decided? A large part of France is champing at the bit, but Louis XVI will not consent to do more than make haste slowly, and another two weeks pass before he signs the decree convening the Estates General and announcing the number of delegates.

From December 12 to December 27, Necker bobs like a cork on the waves of turbulent opinion. Out of complicity with the princes? Oh, no; he knows they hate the sight of him. Out of fear, rather, of a universal uproar the shape of which he cannot yet discern, but he has a premonition that at least one of its victims will be himself: "I see the great wave advancing; will it engulf me?" he asks Lally-Tollendal.[8]

At home he is being urged every day by his wife, and even more by his daughter, seconded by his oldest friends, Dupont de Nemours, Abbé Morellet, Malouet and even Montmorin—the only minister capable of entertaining and giving support to progressive views—to proclaim the doubling

---

*In the days of the *"Précieuses."*

of the third. But Necker's constitution is such that some spirit of contradiction causes him to lend his other ear to the conservatives. Also, he is intimidated by the silence of the two persons on which everything still depends: the King and, now, the Queen.

The men in the greatest hurry try to shake him. What can he say to Morellet, when he tells him that it is "ridiculous to pretend that twenty-four million men in the third should have fewer representatives in a national assembly than one or two hundred thousand nobles in the two privileged orders, or that, a much more cogent argument . . . , these twenty-four million men wished it to be so, and it was true that they had successfully been made to wish it so . . . . How is it possible to resist this torrent?"[9] Whereupon a man as moderate as Lally-Tollendal chimes in and tells him of the many voices heard among the third estate who were saying "to everyone who approached them, that if you do not double the third it will multiply tenfold."[10]

Necker is a letter writer and a man of the study, and his final hesitations are overcome less by the pressure of salon conversation than by the letters he receives from the provincial intendants—all of them unanimous. For example, that from Marc-Antoine de Caumartin, intendant for the *généralité* of Besançon: "In the last five months people's minds have grown clear and informed, respective interests have been discussed, leagues have been formed. You have been allowed to remain in ignorance of the fact that in every category of the third estate excitement is at fever pitch and a spark would suffice to set the whole alight. If the King's decision is favorable to the first two orders, there will be a general insurrection all over the province, six hundred thousand men in arms, and all the horrors of the Jacquerie."[11]

In the last week of 1788 it becomes unthinkable, even for the King, to start the new year without reaching some decision. Having reverted to his position of the previous summer, namely that the third should have double representation but that the consequences of this should be offset by preserving the rule of voting by order and not by name, Necker joins forces with Montmorin to gain the King's approval, in spite of the barriers put up by Barentin to stop them, at the very door of Louis XVI's study. These are hard days for the keeper of the seals, who is conducting his delaying tactics frenetically and will repeatedly denounce the preliminary consultations between Montmorin, Necker and the King. But by his own admission,[12] the King insists upon holding a series of small committee meetings, each lasting at least four hours, at which he can hear the considered opinions of all his ministers and secretaries of state before the decisive Council on December 27.

In favor of doubling: Necker, Montmorin, Puységur, La Luzerne, Saint-

Priest, Nivernais and Fourqueux. Against: Barentin and Laurent de Ville-deuil, whose wits are so shaky that what he proposes is nothing less than the immediate scrapping of the whole idea of the Estates General.

All eyes turn to the sovereigns—for, to everyone's surprise, Marie Antoinette has been invited by her husband to attend, for the first time, a meeting of the Conseil des Dépêches. Not since Anne of Austria has a queen of France sat there. But "as the King wills, so wills the law" and the monarch is free to ask whomever he pleases to his Council. Well advised on that day, Marie Antoinette wants to be there so that she can be associated, if only by her presence, with a decision that will unleash wild enthusiasm and might restore some of her lost popularity.

"The King decided in favor of double representation. The Queen did not utter a word. Nevertheless, it was easy to ascertain that she did not disapprove of the doubling of the third."

MARAT

55

DECEMBER 1788

Cries of Freedom

In 1789, France is buried under an avalanche of intersecting verbiage. The convening of the Estates General heralds the age of the orators, but it is preluded by the age of the penny-a-liners. An ocean of pamphlets, lampoons and whatnots pours over the heads of everybody in France and Navarre who knows how to read. That means no more than one-fifth of the realm, roughly four million people, but it's enough to institute the practice of collective reading, at the end of centuries of great silence.

Now is the time for mass transmission of the Enlightenment, "the sparks of which had been struck for some time by a small number of *philosophes*."[1]

The embers had been languishing in the great libraries, where the idle filed but seldom opened their volumes of Voltaire, Diderot and Rousseau. The argument over the convening of the Estates and associated proceedings, however, is like a draft that fans the flames. Thousands upon thousands of writings, from the deadly dull to the glittering, open up issues that had long remained confidential. "The most crucial questions of public law were soon being debated by every mouth.... The Revolution then moved into the masses." France is learning to read out loud.

The roles are reversed: ostensibly, the Court shows no interest in this paraliterary explosion. In a sense, after all, it encouraged it, by encouraging Brienne in the death agony of his power and Necker in his hesitations. By abdicating from his job as sole interpreter of the people, the King has invited the people to din it into his ears. He has also abdicated from censorship, leaving that to the *Parlement,* which, in a paroxysm of ambiguity, has stopped claiming to represent the voice of protest and is beginning, on the contrary, to adopt its own delaying tactics by unmethodically confiscating or burning the publications that the police are still halfheartedly seizing in the book-sellers'. But for every bundle of printed pages destroyed, ten more are distributed the same day.[2]

Not that there's any shortage of public executioners or firewood for pyres; on the contrary, the trouble is that there would be too much to burn. One noteworthy example is the book that leads the way, printed under a prestigious name, widely distributed, first and best of the new wave of publishing, which has been lying dormant on the shelves these thirty years: Mably's *Des droits et des devoirs du citoyen,* which one of the executors of his will takes the risk of distributing, in an edition of two thousand copies in Versailles alone, "during the second Assembly of Notables. People on all sides were exclaiming that it was an incendiary book.... The keeper of the seals, alarmed by the tacit consent he had given to it, caused one thousand six hundred copies to be buried in the dungeons of the Bastille."[3] Why bother, because other editions are on the way? The executor insists: "It was not enough to enlighten the nation as to its age-old and unfortunate circumstances; it was also necessary to explain how it could move beyond them."

A resounding resurrection for the great Bonnot de Mably, who died three years before almost totally unmourned and in despair, at the end of his life, "by dint of speaking to the deaf."* The august godfatherly aegis of the Abbé (though so very unecclesiastical an abbé) is noted by Rabaut Saint-Étienne, whose hearing, sharpened by his youth in the Wilderness, enables him to detect the sound of quills beginning to scratch on all sides. The Protestant, the man of Holy Writ, exclaims that there has never been so much writing done in France: "The writings of Mably, the sage, in particular were being circulated; at a time when truth had taken refuge in the libraries of the learned, he had foreseen, predicted and, so to speak, ordained the Estates General. His book became the catechism of the French."[4]

*See above, Chapter 21.

Here begins the transition not only from *philosophes* to politicians but also from historians to men of action: "If history be not a school of morality and policy, it is good for nothing but to satisfy the curiosity of a child. It should present the people's rights; it should never turn aside from this first truth from which all others flow, namely, that a man is not made to obey the will of another man."*

Following the thread of eight dialogues between an imaginary English nobleman, Lord Stanhope, and Mably himself, both of whom are constantly comparing the institutions of an idealized England with those of a France sinking into despotism, the reader of these three hundred pages finally understands that the gist of the subject is the possibility of revolution, and the author does not shy away from the word itself. Is it the citizens' right and duty to make the revolution? What resources do they have for setting it in motion? Once they obtain their freedom, how can they make sure it endures? There certainly were grounds for burning the book, the opening pages of which are a meditation on the "admirable royal country taverns," meaning the exquisite little châteaux in the grounds at Marly, those symbols of Court luxury, which are contrasted with the poverty of the people. A crime that is virtually a matter of course: "To be born great is a reason to remain small one's whole life long. Corrupted in infancy by flattery and lies, drunk with pleasures and passions in youth, one finds oneself a man without having learned how to think, and vegetates in old age in the midst of pride, prejudice and courtiers. A few princes have been gifted, but none have known their duties or been worthy of their fortune." That was written twenty years before the death of Louis XV. Mably didn't confine his censure to France, though; he wanted to arouse the whole continent.

"What dismays me is the lethargy, the prostration, the stupidity, the solitude, the slow, far-reaching and relentless devastation produced by our European despotism. . . . A civil war might cause greater damage, but at least it would be short-lived and, by stirring up the soul, give it the courage it needs to endure that damage. . . .

" 'You get so carried away!' milord said to me, chaffingly. 'Here you are, a republican as arrogant and zealous as any I ever knew in England.' . . .

" 'When one sees things thus, milord, there can be no more hanging back; we must have revolution or slavery.' "

Behind this great captain of battles presumed lost because fought too soon pours a dense horde of invaders of the blank sheet of paper. They jostle and shove one another in a giddy melee.† Many of them copy each other;

---

*Mably's major works are found in Robespierre's library after 9 Thermidor.

†More than twenty-five hundred pamphlets dating from this time have been cataloged by the Bibliothèque Nationale.

many contradict themselves; a few give one another a leg up across boundaries still sacred the day before. It's like the second coming of Genghis Khan; there is no dearth of boldness, pomposity or repetition in the campaign, but a very great dearth of marching plans and battle orders.* Historians must work very hard to find their way among the texts, some of which are anonymous, others signed by names otherwise unknown, or forgotten, or relatively renowned or already creeping toward fame. All you can do in these swirling waters is cast your line and fish.

Between prisons, for debt in England and for sedition in the Bastille, Linguet surfaces momentarily with a treatise on *L'impôt territorial.* D'Eprémesnil misses no chance to run after his lost popularity with some *Réflexions impartiales sur la grande question qui partage les esprits, concernant les droits du Roi et de la Nation assemblée en États Généraux;* but then he spoils it all by obstinately concluding that it is "more useful to the interests of public affairs that voting should be by order rather than by name."[5] Some Parisians already esteem the good Dr. Joseph-Ignace Guillotin for his philanthropy, generosity to poor patients, and efforts to make the hospitals cleaner places; he will become even more popular with his *Pétition des citoyens domiciliés à Paris,* in which he calls for one-man-one-vote and for which he escapes condemnation by the *Parlement* only because of the eager crowd that accompanies him to his hearing. Similarly, the people of Provence turn advocate Pastoret into a minor celebrity after the publication of a monument of erudition called *Les Recherches sur les impôts mis dans les Gaules depuis César jusqu'à Clovis.*

A few socialites know the Marquis de Beauvau (*Avis au Tiers État*) and the turbulent Marquis de Lauraguais, who went to London with Beaumarchais in 1774 with orders to nobble the Chevalier d'Éon. Lauraguais emerges from his château with a *Recueil de pièces historiques sur la convocation des États Généraux.* He swims from Louis XI to Louis XIII and concludes his 116 pages with a lively defense of the word *cohue* [= mob], the hobgoblin of the killjoys who're afraid of overpopulating the Estates General. Faithful to the spirit of Beaumarchais, Lauraguais promises that a new fundamental order will emerge from this mob, as creation did from chaos before it:

"I absolutely insist upon the mob of the Estates General. Ah, may the clergy of this mob be composed of true pastors, imbued with the morality of the Gospel! May the third estate be represented by hardworking farmers convinced of the sacredness of their rights, and not by privileged oppressors who, noble and bourgeois by turns, and yet both together, would be no worse than eternally ridiculous were they not already so consistently odious."[6]

Other nobles who, like Lauraguais, aren't afraid to sign what they write, go just as far: the Marquis de Cazeaux, for instance, "of the Royal Society

---

*This demolishes Cochin's theory of a vast conspiracy fathered by the Freemasons.

of London and Society of Agriculture of Florence," who earns high praise from advanced circles for his pamphlet with the peculiar title *Différence de trois mois en 1788.* Cazeaux gets compliments from Mirabeau and a great but precarious celebrity for having produced some inflammatory apothegms:

"Government is made for people, not people for government.

"Reason alone should govern anyone capable of hearing it.

"Reason and law alone should rule human society. . . .

"Ministers of France, speak no more of opinion; today you are under the rule of truth."

From the south comes yet another marquis, Pierre-Antoine d'Antonelle, whose *Catéchisme du Tiers État, à l'usage de toutes les provinces de France, et spécialement de la Provence* speedily secures him respect on the regional level.* He's forty, and had a taste of command in the Bassigny regiment in Champagne before leaving the army in 1782. Arles is his town, where he attends meetings of the philosophical societies and has for several months been in touch with what are known as the Provençal patriots, whose dream is to bring Avignon and the Comtat Venaissin, still under the sway of the pope, back to France. That ordinarily wouldn't have been enough to make Antonelle a household name in Paris, but the age of pamphlets is the age of overnight notoriety, as though there were a storm of meteorites cascading down upon the booksellers' heads.

An Abbé Gouttes, a much lesser lord, voluptuously settles his score with his betters in some *Considérations sur l'injustice des prétentions du Clergé et de la noblesse, suivies d'un dialogue entre un noble et un évêque.* He refers his readers to the religion of the early Christians:

"When one considers the intentions of the sovereign legislator of Christianity, one cannot conceive upon what basis the clergy claims the immunities and worldly honors that were expressly forbidden to it.

"In instituting this holy religion, Jesus Christ makes no distinction of rank between his disciples, which he chose among the dregs of the people to show that the first virtue of Christianity was humility."

As swarms of peddlers are distributing these writings all over France, a few readers begin to feel a little sorry for the highly privileged, who will be going into the Estates General as though diving off a precipice into a world overturned. Already, before the first debate opens, they're being blamed for every sin of France.

A few new reputations are made among this variegated counterchoir.

---

*Antonelle is elected mayor of Arles at the first municipal elections. A member of the Legislative Assembly, he is responsible for several special missions during the Revolution and leads a fluctuating but increasingly republican political existence; he narrowly escapes being sentenced with Babeuf and the Égaux in 1796.

That of a Jesuit of Italian origin, for instance, Joseph-Antoine-Joachim Cerutti, "recycled" into literature and tutoring after the Society's dissolution.*
He seems to have abandoned his religious convictions when he abandoned
his Jesuit's garb and does not feel inhibited by the protection his abilities
have earned for him, first at the Court of Lorraine and then in Versailles.
The title of his pamphlet is *Le gouvernement sénati-clérico-aristocratique:* "What
remains, in the present state of affairs, for the third estate? Much pain,
seasoned by the revolting contempt of the other two orders." In passing, he
sets the record straight in regard to the nobility's chief ground of defense,
their tradition of shedding their blood for France. As Cerutti points out, in
reality the nobles form a very small proportion of the army: "How is it that
the soldiers who fall beside them are not counted? Is the people's blood
made of water?" Many career officers are soon repeating this *mot.*

A Norman magistrate named Charles-François Lebrun, still young—only
fifty, that is—who has been an administrator of estates since Turgot's ministry,
would seem an unlikely person to have a part in this libretto. In his early
days, he is said to have lent his youthful and fluent pen to Chancellor Maupeou; but Lebrun lets himself be swept away by the tide and publishes an
energetic *Voix du citoyen,* on the future allocation of taxes.†

If we wanted to mention here all the chatterboxes we have met before
as well, it would take several additional pages. There are Servan and Mounier
(from Grenoble), and Roederer, and Target, and Bergasse, and Rabaut Saint-
Étienne (still writing on behalf of the Protestants), and Dr. Marat, who is no
longer the physician of the Comte d'Artois's guards and is going through a
nasty unhealthy patch but who nevertheless produces an *Offrande à la patrie*
in which he proclaims himself the "people's friend" with a fury that has not
abated since his publication of *Chaînes de l'Esclavage.*‡ However, the first
person to bring the expression into fashion is a young advocate from Saines
and Bordeaux named Elysée Loustallot, when he publishes *Le véritable ami
du peuple, ouvrage paru par cahiers, en 1788 et 1789,* with a Virgilian epigraph:
"The snake is hidden in the grass."§

---

*Cerutti is a moderate member of the Legislative Assembly and becomes known for *La
feuille villageoise,* which, beginning in late 1790, tries to bring the ideas and events of the
Revolution within reach of the more advanced peasants. He dies of overwork in February 1792,
aged fifty-four.

†A member of the Constituent, then a moderate in the Five Hundred, he becomes one
of Bonaparte's advisers, Third Consul, archtreasurer of the Empire and Duc de Plaisance.

‡See Volume I.

§Loustallot was born at Saint-Jean-d'Angély in September 1761; after July 1789 he becomes one of the most committed publicists of the Revolution. He dies (of grief, they say)
upon learning of the Marquis de Bouillé's fierce repression of the uprising of the Swiss soldiers
in Nancy, in August 1790.

As for Marat . . . instead of bouncing back from the gloom into which he sank two or three years earlier after failing to get a position at the Court of Spain, he seems to have gone into a permanent depression. Perhaps he tried to go back to London; it's possible, but there is no evidence. He's past forty-five and has no ground beneath his feet. Gone is the distinguished clientele; finished, his affair with Madame de Laubespine; his reputation is compromised by misconceived and mismanaged scientific jousts,* and he's receiving no more emoluments from the Comte d'Artois's house-hold . . . nobody would bet one sou on his future. In the two rooms in which he has had to make his home for want of anything better, at 47 rue du Vieux-Colombier,[7] he himself admits that he has come to the end of his rope.

He has scraped a living by selling a few parascientific books, often dealing with electricity but also with rainbows and . . . the iridescence of soap bubbles. He has sold equipment for physics experiments, he has even sold the ointments touted by charlatans, such as "factitious antipulmonic water." As always with this great bundle of nerves, the collapse of confidence leads to the collapse of his whole organism, so it's not surprising that he has been imagining himself at death's door. In July 1788 he made his will, but the announcement of the coming Estates General and Brienne's call to this procession of little lights revives him. With the (unsigned) publication, in February 1789, of the *Offrande à la patrie,* the arena of Dr. Marat's destiny shifts definitively from science to politics.

The opening cries of joy in his text would seem to indicate a cure.† "It is done, prestige has been destroyed. So here they are at last, the impudent ministers, being cried down for their incompetence, debased by their dep-redations, abhorred for their excesses and outlawed by public indignation! Traitors to their master, traitors to their country, their wrongdoings have driven the state to the edge of the precipice. . . .

"Madmen! They did not know that patience has limits . . . , that moans of despair change to howls of fury, and that the cries of freedom are always ready to leap from the fires of sedition."[8]

Once the vehemence typical of Marat's opening pages has subsided, he reverts to his schoolmasterly vein; he wants to be not just the people's inspirer, but also its instructor. In connection with the representation of the third estate, *l'Offrande à la patrie* gives so comprehensive a definition of that order that future history textbooks might well make use of it:

"The French third estate is composed of the class of servants, mechanics, laborers, craftsmen, shopkeepers, commercial agents, merchants, farmers,

---

*See Volume III.

†Even though he writes, in 1793, that it was "a work by a dying man who did not want to leave this life without having done something for truth."

untitled landowners and stockholders, schoolmasters, artists, surgeons, physicians, men of letters, scholars, people of the law, magistrates of the lower courts, ministers of the altar, army and navy—a numberless, invincible legion containing within its breast both wisdom and talent, strength and virtue.

"At its head stand these gentlemen, magistrates, lords and prelates, these generous and magnanimous princes who are forgetting their prerogatives, espousing your cause, and asking no more than to be simple citizens."

At times, one can see in Marat the other face of his fury: a longing for the union of classes, like peace after war.

ABBÉ SIEYÈS

56

DECEMBER 1788

So There Is One Man Left in France!

Coming just then, Marat's pamphlet doesn't make much of a splash. Other bricks are being patted into shape in its vicinity that will give the senior magistrates and courtiers a sharper jolt when they come hurtling through their windows. Marat—the people's friend, no doubt, but still with bourgeois aspirations—has not moved beyond writing justifications of the third. But voices of unprecedented violence are already being heard, on behalf of "the last class of the people," the ones whose cause nobody yet has thought of defending. A man named Dufourny de Villiers, for one, is brandishing some *Cahiers du Quatrième Ordre, celui des pauvres journaliers, des infirmes, des indigents, etc.*, with the most eloquent subtitle, *Ordre sacré des infortunés*, in which he says that "the right of direct representation at the Estates, which is that of every Frenchman but to which this order is not yet entitled,"[1] must be made universal.

A "parish priest in the diocese of Auxerre," for another, has flung out, like a blazing torch into high mass, a *Gloria in excelsis du peuple, auquel on a joint l'Épître et l'Évangile du jour, avec la réflexion et la collecte, suivi des litanies du Tiers État;* it's a "work within reach of the people, containing bold truths and ingenious associations." Judging by the title of his next publication, the same priest—or the author(s) expressing himself (themselves) under that name—must have plenty of lung power: *Prône à l'usage de tous les Ordres, contenant le Magnificat du peuple, le Miserere de la noblesse, le De Profundis du clergé, le Nunc dimittis du Parlement, la passion, la mort et la résurrection du peuple, et le petit prône aux roturiers en attendant le grand sermon.* "The devil you say!" might well be the response of a few privileged persons upon hearing, from this singular improvised pulpit, the prayer that "the words of this Gospel may ensure the annihilation of our executioners, the magistrates and nobles, forever and ever. Amen!"

There's enough here to dislocate the jaws of the King's last censors with gaping, especially when they happen upon another distinctly unaristocratic marquis adding fuel to the fire of the distinctly un-Catholic priest and signing himself Vil——, representing the first three letters of his name (Villiers?). His lampoon is a *Protestation d'un serf du Mont-Jura, contre l'Assemblée des Notables, le mémoire des princes du sang, le clergé, la noblesse et le tiers état;* it describes the lot of two or three thousand serfs in that part of the country who have been abandoned there to the exactions of the "merciless grave-diggers who come every three years *on the King's order* to dig in the floors of the houses, down to three feet in depth . . . to get out the saltpeter," not before smashing the bedroom floor, dismantling the beds and the very hearth itself.

"We add that every year, boys and men from sixteen to forty years of age are decimated by the militia" and that "in the whole region it is impossible for a poor man to hire out his arms, to work, as they say, by the day. No navigable stream, no national product, no manufacture, no rich man, no service. . . ."

"On fine days in July, they go down in troops to the swampy plains of Bresse, skinny as death, hoary as time, scythe in hand. . . . There they spend a few weeks making hay; there they earn twelve sous a day, and a fever."[2]

The grand prize at this festival of shooting stars is awarded by informed circles to a member of the second order, a comte. "The most violent of all these writings, the one that did most to inflame people's minds, was the memorandum by the Comte d'Antraigues,"[3] whom few people outside his native Vivarais have ever heard of until now. "He left all the rest far behind, not only by virtue of his ability and eloquence but also because of the vehement heat, or rather, the inconceivable audacity that burst from every page."*

---

*According to the ultraroyalist author of Weber's *Mémoires,* whose indignation betrays a hint of scandalized jealousy in regard to the successful sales of this "traitor to his class"—who does not long remain one. D'Antraigues represents the Vivarais at the Constituent but soon forgets his furious notions, emigrates in February 1790, and becomes one of the most active secret agents in the spy ring of Louis XVIII and his allies. Some historians, in particular Albert

The definitive edition, signed with name and title, appears in January 1789: *Mémoire sur les États Généraux, leurs droits, et la manière de les convoquer.*[4] The first page bears an impertinent epigraph typical of the tone of the whole. It is a translation, from Spanish, of the oath that the high justice of Aragon made to his king in the name of the Cortes: "We, who are each of us worth as much as you and who, taken together, are more powerful than you, do promise to obey your government, if you preserve our rights and privileges; if not, not."

The text is in the same vein, embroidering a series of invectives, any one of which would have sent its author to the wheel ten years before, on a frame of world history that claims to proceed "from the primitive rights of man in the state of nature, through all the vicissitudes of the French government over a period of fourteen centuries, up to the present time."[5]

In it, republican systems are praised, the French people portrayed as a flock of slaves, the absolute monarchy accused of keeping the people in a state worse than the Turks, all courts seen as hotbeds of corruption, all courtiers as the natural enemies of the public, and the hereditary nobility as "the most appalling scourge that the wrath of heaven can visit upon a free nation," etc., etc.[6]

What a curious discrepancy there is, between these peremptory statements and the colorless personality of Louis Emmanuel Henri Alexandre de Launay, Comte d'Antraigues, born in Montpellier on December 26, 1753, son of a lesser nobleman, captain of the grenadiers, whose main claim to advancement has been the fact that he was the nephew of the Comte de Saint-Priest. Having failed to obtain "the honors of Court" from the genealogists, that is, the right to proximity to the King, and having no inclination for a barely outlined military life, he has amused himself traveling to the Orient and has been distantly connected to a few men of letters, including Rousseau.[7] He married a noted actress from the Opéra, Madame de Saint-Huberty, who appears to have kept him in thrall throughout his life. He seems to have done all this without much difficulty, thanks to the rigorous enforcement of his feudal rights in the Vivarais, and nobody understands the origin or reason for the explosion of resentment that causes him to say, toward the end of his pamphlet, that "there is no form of disorder that is not preferable to the funereal tranquillity arising out of absolute power."[8]

What can he know about it? The wind was pushing him. . . .

Ollivier in his *Saint-Just,* attach a great deal of importance—perhaps too much, because there seems little reason to credit the gossip of his money-mad mythomania—to the newsletters he sends to Russia, Austria and England during the Terror, Directoire and Consulate. On July 22, 1812, he and his wife are murdered in London, in mysterious circumstances. The spelling of his name has changed from time to time; I follow that adopted by Jacques Godechot in 1986: Antraigues, rather than Entraigues.

Three men of national stature also plunge into the torrent. The first two are famous already, Condorcet and Mirabeau; the third soon will be: Sieyès.

Nicolas de Condorcet, although kept on the sidelines of power and Court, is not actually gagged. Sitting forgotten in the splendid Hôtel de Monnaies, he scrupulously performs his duties as supreme overseer of the weight and metal content of every piece of gold, silver and alloy current in France. He tries to preserve the idyllic image of his marital bliss with Sophie, just-the-two-of-them; but he feels increasingly moved to play some role in laying the foundations of a new France.

Brienne's appeal to all opinions to express themselves set him off. It's just what he's been waiting for. Unable to do anything else, he has written, will write, and is writing now so hard that he's losing sleep over it. Of all these loquacious ones, he is probably the most long-winded.

Between November 1788 and February 1789 Condorcet brings out seven pamphlets, all of them dealing with the convening of and proceedings at the Estates. The spiteful say he thinks he's the French Ben Franklin, at the very moment when Franklin's pen, back there in the United States, is slipping from his aged hands.

First tract: *Sentiments d'un républicain sur les assemblées provinciales et les États Généraux.* The text is unsigned but he doesn't disown it. "Republican" is a word people are not yet using openly, in a France that is still royalist at heart. You could count on both hands the authors who would dare to admit that they were afflicted with that particular disease; so Condorcet finds it preferable to disguise what he has to say in the polite fiction of some *Lettres d'un citoyen des États-Unis.*

As follow-ups, he issues, one after the other: *Idées sur le despotisme, à l'usage de ceux qui prononcent ce mot sans l'entendre; Déclaration des Droits; Lettres d'un gentilhomme à Messieurs du Tiers État; Réflexions sur les pouvoirs et instructions à donner par les provinces à leurs députés aux États Généraux; Sur le forme des élections; Examen sur cette question: est-il utile de diviser une assemblée nationale en plusieurs chambres?*[29]

Assembled in one volume, these texts would form a book two-hundred-odd pages long, reeking of tedium. Even as units, they are full of repetitions and wearisome descriptions that make considerable demands upon his readers' patience and attention, however favorably they may be disposed by the great goodwill of this simultaneously naive and solemn doctrinarian. Condorcet's main failing as an author is that he is humorless. Everything he writes is honest, high-minded, logical and consistent, but he exhausts his readers by taking himself so unremittingly seriously. He doesn't put himself forward as a prophet, no; but as a mentor, oh, yes. In his first text, he relies on the accuracy of his ideological construction to gain approval of "the most important work of constitutional law to have been published in this age."[10]

He experiences occasional moments of anxiety at the thought of the poverty of the cultural soil on which the edifice must be built. Ah, if only Turgot had been allowed to act, France would not now be this desert, between a fringe of highly educated elite and a population still incapable of adulthood!

"A national assembly prepared by public education would have given grounds for every hope; it might have been, for the nation, an age of assured restoration rather than a crisis with an unknown outcome.

"Today we have but a few short months left in which to dispel this cloud of error established by the ignorance, habit and prejudice of several centuries."

The only thing this great warrior of the intellect fears is the history of France, the history that, to the monarchy and all its appurtenances, is on the contrary a source of pride, pride unto sanctification.

Condorcet's optimism does not lead him into demagogy. Some presentiment makes him write (in the second pamphlet) that it is "easier to free a nation from direct than from indirect despotism; people can see the former, but suffer from the latter without knowing it, and often look upon those who inflict it as their protectors."

He differs from a man like Marat in his mistrust of "the populace, which deprived Holland of liberty by restoring the stathouder's office in 1787. . . . But what is it that makes the populace of a great city dangerous? It is ease of assembly, and the people's ignorance of their own ferocity. The effects, thus, can be prevented by overcoming the causes."

His vision soon shifts back to the rosy. "The one means of preventing tyranny, that is, the violation of human rights, is to gather all those rights into one declaration, set them out clearly therein . . . , and bring the declaration before the public with all due solemnity."

Here, Condorcet joins Mably, by whom he was nourished, in fact. The panacea of the future will be that Declaration of the Rights of Man that many people are beginning to want proclaimed at the opening of the Estates General.

The kindly Condorcet also reassures any of his fellows who might fear the institution of a military dictatorship. "Modern Europeans have found the way to secure themselves against the despotism of the army, by dividing it into regiments, by distributing it among a great many garrisons, by not assigning permanent leaders to the divisions composed of several regiments. So, no army has disrupted the tranquillity of the state or practiced any kind of despotism."

No; he certainly is not a prophet.

Mirabeau, just now, is not living up to his potential. Bowing to the fashion, he publishes two or three occasional pieces, all except one anonymously, however, as he is still under the shadow of his *lettres de cachet*. Toward the end of November 1788 he brings out a bare hundred unsigned pages, *Sur la liberté de la presse*, which he claims for some peculiar reason is *imitated from the English of Milton*. It's a muddle with two main components: a restatement of his political Anglomania, and a total messianism in regard to the Estates General, which will repair everything, set everything to rights, build everything. "In England all that are needed are some corrections, whereas we must begin all over again. . . . What must we be, then, if the English are still no more than that?" Possibly aware of the flimsiness of his arguments, he ends with a lyrical hymn to the freedom of the press, which he sees as an all-powerful check upon any possible errors or abuses of the coming assembly:

"Let the first of your laws [he writes, to the future delegates] embody forever the freedom of the press, the most inviolable, the most unlimited freedom, the freedom without which no other freedom will ever be conquered, because it is through that one alone that peoples and kings can learn what they are entitled to obtain and what it is their interest to grant."[11]

This is poor-vintage Mirabeau, too complicated and wordy. The odd thing is that while he is writing this tract, streaks of fire are leaping out in his letters to Mauvillon, Lauzun-Biron and Levrault, the Strasbourg bookseller on whom he is half-counting to prepare his election as a representative of the third in Alsace, should he fail to get through the polls in Provence.

So, "let us eschew erudition, let us scorn what has been done, let us seek what must be done, and not undertake too much. The nation's consent to taxation and the loans, civil liberties, regular assemblies: those are the three capital points that must rest upon an exact declaration of rights. . . . War upon the privileged and upon privilege, that is my motto. . . . In faith, what would be a republic composed of the aristocrats who are gnawing at us! A breeding ground for the most active tyranny."[12]

This thought brings Mirabeau to make a significant confession as regards his own basic motivation: "I shall be a most zealous monarchist in the National Assembly, because I feel deeply how much we need to kill the despotism of ministers and raise up the royal authority. . . . Recourse to violent revolutions would be a barbarous regression of our age; education, thanks to printing, is enough to carry out all the revolutions that it befits the human race to make."[13]

The truth is that in the last few months the mill of his life has been grinding some dreary flour. He's clearheaded enough to see before anyone else that if a brilliant election does not renew his chances, he'll go under. He was not secretary to the Notables; after being rejected by Calonne, he failed to get any subsidies from Montmorin and won't ask Necker for any. Driven from the duchy of Brunswick by his own anger at the time of the unrest in Holland, unable to drum up anything but a few meager pittances in England, here he perches, at the end of 1788, like a migratory bird on the end of a limb in a little house in Passy, imagining himself forsaken by everyone. His father is mad at him again; those of his caste have thrown him off. To survive, he's reduced to publishing an enormous *Histoire de la monarchie prussienne,* which is primarily the fruit of the research and efforts of his last true friend, Major de Mauvillon. Mirabeau signs this book with his right hand, but with his left he perpetrates an unsigned *Histoire secrète de la monarchie prussienne,* which he knows full well is likely to get him into more trouble. His accelerating slide toward the depths has placed him in the power of a dubious couple, a bookseller named Lejay and his wife, who became his mistress so quickly, so invasively and in such a muddle of debauchery and money that even the all-forgiving Henriette de Nehra has had her fill of it. She leaves him forever at the end of the summer. There will be no more love in Mirabeau's life; at least, nothing that deserves to be called by that name.

Whence the bitterness oozing from his third and final pamphlet, published in early January 1789, this time under his own name: *Correspondance entre M. Cerutti et le comte de Mirabeau, sur le rapport de M. Necker et sur l'arrêt du conseil du 29 décembre 1788, qui continue pour six mois force de papier-monnaie au papier de la Caisse d'Escompte.* Here, Gabriel-Honoré is back in the saddle as a shock-polemicist, annihilating the poor Jesuit, who really doesn't deserve it. Through him, it's Necker he's really after, following on from his *Dénonciation de l'Agiotage,* which was the cause of his break with Calonne. This might be seen as a constant in the visceral mistrust felt by this scion of the greatly landed gentry for all financiers; it shows his courage, too, as he is one of the first to tackle a minister who is still so popular. But he is also trying to get himself noticed by the Queen, and even the King, whose aversion to Necker is no secret to anyone. It is true that the methods he employs here are rather unsavory, because he publishes Cerutti's letters without his permission; and so Cerutti brings out a plaintive denunciation in the *Journal de Paris* on January 21, 1789. Mirabeau also goes too far in making a personal attack upon a man (Necker) whose integrity is absolutely unimpeachable and who is beginning to drag the Treasury to its feet again. It is really unnecessary to berate him "for purchasing a life annuity with the principals and income of the monarchy."[14] One might say he's got hold of the wrong comptroller of finance.

His friend the writer Chamfort is annoyed by it and writes to him, on January 3, "I think that what you have written here does not befit your views. To make noise, to get oneself talked about, is too trivial a gain in the circumstances; . . . you should not strew your path with stones before you tread it."[15]

The path that Mirabeau takes on January 5 is toward Provence, since he has now made up his mind to take his chances in the election there.*

Abbé Sieyès, meanwhile, is counting heavily on his election to the order of the clergy. He has already started making preparations by setting up numerous contacts in Paris (why not?), on the off chance, and also in Chartres, where he's been grand vicar since 1780.

He trusts that his election is in the bag and that all he has to do, to be chosen by acclamation, is to stand up in front of a body of electors. He's relying on the enormous success of the last of the three essays he has just published, which has projected this nonconformist priest, great secret scholar and improvised expert on politics, into the glare of the footlights. He's well aware that he has already beaten them all with his pen, so why shouldn't he prevail at the polls?

Until now, however, he has done little to speak of. We left him on his way to Chartres in his bishop's team, after a conventional term of residence at Treguier in Brittany, where the pontiff and his deputy patiently earned the key to the see of Chartres, one of the most coveted in France. His thoughts have strayed farther and farther from his humble origins in Provence, and from his father, who is still vainly badgering him, in letters from Fréjus, to come to his family's rescue. Since his hopes of a chaplaincy at Court have been thwarted, Sieyès, unflaggingly courteous and ostensibly glad to form superficial relationships, has shut himself up in an elemental selfishness increasingly tinged with hauteur. Unable to get his hands on a bishopric, he has deliberately adopted a policy of oscillation between the two poles of his life, money and influence.

So he's jogged along, acting as administrator for his diocese and attracting notice, but also much criticism, for his role in the Orléans provincial assembly, where another delegate, the illustrious Lavoisier, opined that "several of his ideas are good, but might have been presented in more moderate terms";[16] he got himself appointed "chancellor to the bishop," in other words, mini-minister of finance, and took advantage of the position, skillfully but without lending himself to actual corruption, to pad out his little pile to the tune of twelve or thirteen thousand livres a year, a comfortable subsistence but still far from his aspirations. This period of more or less marking time has not been good for his disposition. Little affection is felt for him in Chartres,

*In this overview of the publications of the winter 1788–1789 I have deliberately omitted those of Camille Desmoulins, Robespierre, and Laclos for the Duc d'Orléans. They will be covered later, in the chapters on their authors. Also, I will talk about the publications appearing in Brittany, especially Volney's *La Sentinelle du peuple,* in conjunction with the riots in Rennes.

where he doesn't even get along very well with Monseigneur de Lubersac, and bows no lower to him than to any other of the great and powerful:

"Abbé Sieyès, could you ever have dreamed before of the income of ten thousand livres you now enjoy?"

"Monseigneur, you have one hundred thousand."[17]

At forty he is committed to a solitary life (women interest him less and less) and has contracted a solid hostility toward the privileged but is careful not to let it show too much. For the last two years he's been hanging around fashionable haunts: the Club de Valois, where he became distantly friendly with the Duc d'Orléans; the Society of Thirty, where he was not seen much more often than Mirabeau; a few Masonic lodges; the Amis des Noirs; even the salons of the Marquise de Condorcet, Madame Helvétius and Madame Necker, where Germaine de Staël's first glance at him was not an indulgent one: "The superiority of his mind cannot outweigh the misanthropy of his nature. He dislikes the human race and does not know how to handle it."[18]

But he's made many acquaintances among the little horde who are about to go into action, and they have been impressed by his all-knowing airs, his high, reserved brow and the rather somber light that burns in his large eyes. At the moment when he is becoming an overnight celebrity, Sieyès's inner life has made him almost handsome.

Coming one after the other between November 1788 and January 1789, his three essays, all signed, constitute both a conclusion to and a summary of the whole spate of unleashed opinion: *Vues sur les moyens d'exécution dont les représentants de la France pourront disposer en 1789; Essai sur les privilèges; Qu'est-ce que le Tiers État?*

The last-named, by virtue of its clarity, terseness and logic, is the only one to have remained a truly important work in the eyes of history.

This is easy to understand, when we read its opening sentences and see how unnecessary they make it to quote any subsequent ones, neatly wrapping up, as they do, the whole huge debate of the dawning Revolution:

"What is the third estate? Everything."

"What has it been until now, in the political order? Nothing."

"What is it asking? To become something."

On February 23 Mirabeau informs Sieyès that he has received his copy and thanks him for it in his inimitable manner: "So there is one man left in France!"[19]

57

JANUARY 1789

The Plot of Every Play Belongs to Me

Grimm does not miss the curtain raiser of 1789, and hastens to tell the noble recipients of his *Correspondance littéraire* all about it. It takes place, of course, at the Théâtre-Français, where the audiences of the rue de Richelieu have been edgy for months, expressing in their own way the simmering state of the capital.

"The fate of plays at the Théâtre-Français has been most unhappy for some time. The audience's impatience is such that it has become impossible not only to perform more than one or two acts at a time, but even to hiss them comfortably."[1]

No easy profession in those days, acting! Unless they are as fair as the gods and goddesses on Olympus, and therefore candidates for the refined suppers and bedchambers of the powerful, actors, even in the first company of France, still enjoy, if that is the word, the status of outcasts. They are excommunicated, ineligible for religious sacraments and burials, condemned to cliff-hanging existences by the uncertainty and precariousness of the box-office take, shunted back and forth between the King's sneers and the whims of the audience. But then, what is the status of their authors? They might almost believe that Molière had it good, by comparison.

For instance, Philippe François Nazaire Fabre, who chose to call himself Fabre d'Églantine one day in 1773, without having the smallest right to do so.*

The company is "unable to perform more than two acts of *Le Présomp-tueux, ou l'Heureux Imaginaire* by M. Fabre d'Églantine. . . . The play's fate was settled thus arbitrarily, or precipitously in any event, on Wednesday,

---

*He's thirty-nine. See Volume I for the story of his youth in Languedoc, his stage debut and his picaresque adventure with a very young girl in Namur in 1777, when he nearly got himself hanged high and short.

January 7. We cannot give so much as an outline of it, for although the audience allowed a little over two acts to be performed, it was really possible to hear only the opening scene. In this first scene the character of the *présomptueux* seemed fairly well defined; but in the second, the dialogue was found to drag on so tediously, there were so many boring and tasteless details, and the ill humor of the audience was expressed with such turbulence, that with the closest attention in the world it was impossible to make any reasonable judgment either of the play itself, or even of the author's intentions."[2]

Without investigating too closely, Grimm (or rather his associate Meister, who's holding their pen this year) lays the blame for the ruckus on a rumor that has been spread about, "not without some foundation," to the effect that *Le Présomptueux* is no more than a barefaced plagiarism of a piece by Collin d'Harleville, one of the rare authors who, despite—or perhaps because of—his manifest mediocrity, is in favor with the Parisians. Meister might have checked his sources a little more carefully, because Collin's play, *Les Châteaux en Espagne,* has not been either published or performed as yet. It would seem that the anti-Fabre clique was led by one of the men who are envious of his amorous achievements with an actress who has smiled upon him this winter. In any case, his play is choked before it hatches. He's used to this kind of setback. He doesn't know how to make an audience appreciate him personally and he doesn't know how to surround himself with friends or critics capable of defending him. Fabre d'Églantine has a positive genius for spawning animosity wherever he goes. The irascible temperament he was born with and has carried around since infancy from Carcassonne to Limoux, where the blood tends to heat quickly, has worsened as he has accumulated the punches and jabs of a roving actor's life, so unstable that he has never spent more than two years with the same company.[3]

His candid and increasing fatuousness, however, has put within his grasp a few brief affairs with women, momentarily seduced by his rather coarse allure. In fact, he positively asks to be swatted down, like some great ungainly moth bumbling through the entertainment-world nights. But he can stand up for himself, has a quick tongue, courage to spare, and sometimes a lively pen and ideas—and he's about to prove it.

Since being condemned to death for the abduction of a minor, and pardoned immediately thereafter by the governor-prince of the Lowlands, his life has been one long zigzag. He survived on poetry in Paris, then on small parts in plays in Languedoc, Avignon, Strasbourg . . . where he married, for once without misadventure, a young lady named Godin. He performed Regnard in Maëstricht and wrote his first play there, the libretto of an opera that was never printed and never performed. But an unknown violinist found time to set a few of his verses to music, and they put Fabre on the map, at last, at the high tide of the craze for pastorals:

Rain! Rain! my shepherdess,
Haste thy white sheep to the
    fold.
Home to the farm, my
    shepherdess,
Quickly, out of the cold.
Under the boughs I can hear

The roar of the storm pouring
    down,
The lightning's upon us, my
    dear,
The water will spoil thy new
    gown.*

On to Thionville, Sedan, Liège, where he composes and reads on stage a verse eulogy of Grétry, the local hero; Spa, where he does the same for the King of Sweden, who's taking the waters there; Arras, Douai, Cambrai, where he directs a few emaciated companies; Geneva, where he tries, unsuccessfully, to launch a follow-up to his shepherdess romance by imagining her parents wringing their hands over her loves:

Naught but a tinge of afterglow
    Lingers in the West,
And yet our girl, all for market
    dressed,
Is still not home, I know.

Tell me, wife; Marie, tell me
    And quiet my alarm:
How can our lass have come to
    harm
All out upon the lea?

In Lyons he meets another actor with a checkered past, Collot d'Herbois;† then Nîmes, Avignon again, trying to keep one jump ahead of his creditors; then back to Paris, Paris along with the rest of the world, Paris eternally. What a lot of traveling since he was twenty. No peddler can have covered more ground in those days than an actor.

He dropped anchor in the outlying districts on the rue du Foin-Saint-Jacques, at the Hôtel Chaumont, "which was not the hotel of opulence."[4] After being forced to tread the boards herself in order to survive, his wife came to join him. Then they settle, for a few months, in a small apartment

---

*Rendering *Il pleut, il pleut bergère* into English is like rendering "Ring Around the Rosy" into French—a task beyond all but the greatest translator. I would further point out a discrepancy between Manceron's text, which has *sur le feuillage,* and my French children's songbook, which has *sous le feuillage*—a substantial shift in meaning and implication, as will be obvious to any attentive student. When we observe the enigmas to be resolved in establishing a definitive text of so simple a thing as a nursery rhyme, we begin to understand what is at stake in trying to establish any kind of reading at all of the French Revolution.—*Trans.*

†See opening of Volume III.

near the Barrière Saint-Laurent. The only thing that keeps them alive is Fabre's engagement as secretary to a writer who is not only prolific and worthless but also well connected in Parisian salons, the Marquis de Ximinés. He pays badly but takes care of his protégés; which is how, a year ago, the Italians came to produce *Les gens de lettres, ou le Poète provincial à Paris,* five acts in verse, also well hissed and utterly demolished by Grimm, in which poor Fabre set a bunch of characters with such perilous names as Daily the journalist, Tearful the author, Fastidor the wit and Musophage the bookseller, against the Parisians, whose omnicompetence he was trying to challenge with a provincial riposte. The author spared neither authors nor critics, nor even the burghers of the capital; and his play was brutally rejected. Any other reaction would have been more than a surprise.

But the obstinacy of Fabre d'Églantine is unshakable. Less than a month later, Ximinés was recommending him to the Comédiens-Français, to whom he submitted *Augusta,* itself a rehash of *Vesta,* previously booed and actually driven off the stage in Lyons. Another five acts and another definitive uproar in the second act, in spite of a most audacious plot, which might have made it a hit in that atmosphere, dealing as it did with the trial and punishment of the Chevalier de La Barre—but unfortunately so sopped in Graeco-Roman sauce that no native of Abbeville could recognize in it the unfortunate young man of 1776. *Vesta* actually survives six performances before foundering for good. Fabre waits over a year before he tries again, with his *Présomptueux:* third try, third failure. But it'll take more than that to discourage him. In the end, the only real *présomptueux* is himself. He's already getting ready to produce his next play, *Le Collatéral, ou l'Amour et l'intérêt,* at the Théâtre de Monsieur.*

Immediately after the execution of his *Présomptueux,* he publishes a pamphlet containing a plea in his own defense that is both lively and self-assured. In this respect, he knows he'll never be better served than by himself. It's one more pamphlet in the universal inundation, but this straw floating on the waves is not like the others. Fabre seems to be quite ignorant of the thousands of pages exchanging interwoven arguments about the Estates General. He never once refers to them and might have written his text on another planet. It's easy to picture him scribbling furiously away at this long, grumpy saga, sitting alone in the twilight of some theater from which the audience has fled, his sheets of paper on his knees. The warmth and emotion of some of his pages make one sense that he is arguing about more than his poor flop of a play. It's a sort of appeal to his contemporaries to resist the critics' contempt that for nearly fifteen years now has been gnawing away at the

---

*It opens on May 30, 1789, and finally breaks through the anti-Fabre barrier, being performed occasionally throughout the year, with some success.

failed actor, scorned author, ex-gallows bird, skirt-chaser, who is beginning, thanks to this charge of plagiarism, to acquire yet another unsavory reputation, this time as liar and thief of ideas.

One or two passages are worth listening to; they're the cries of a man being flayed alive:

"I can only love, truly and tenderly love, the few good people I know, and quarrel frankly with any bad person I find crossing my path. When one doesn't know how to look as though he loves the whole world, he must expect to be loved by few people in return. I am not opposed to patrons, but I see what those who seek them must pay to obtain them. . . . Come what may; we'll pass our way without them."[5]

This is the stance taken up by the man of so many failures, firmly shouldered, with no attempt to find extenuating circumstances. What he wants is justice, not pity. "As for the public and the means of swaying its affections in my favor . . . , shall I go tell it about me and mine? What can there be in common between the public and my private affairs? What a paltry ploy, to force it to look upon such indignities! By way of complaints, may I not tell it whatever I please? . . . Let people do me the courtesy of listening to my plays and judging them, even, if they like, with severity. . . . I attempt to offer the fruit of fifteen years of work and observation of the human heart; if I am rejected, I am deeply sorry."

It isn't all in this vein. The dear liar gets a little confused in an overelaborate explanation about his famous *Châteaux en Espagne,* admitting that Collin d'Harleville did discuss the subject with him during a conversation in the home of a mutual friend.*

"My imagination was struck by the idea but I had no definite plan in mind. I read every evening in bed, especially Montaigne, at sight. The next day I opened the book to the chapter on Idleness. At that point I was struck very deeply, for the second time, by the idea of *Les Châteaux en Espagne,* but in a completely new way."

He swears that this is all the borrowing he did from Collin's ideas, and confesses to it with foxy sincerity.

And anyway, what if I did? "I will go so far as to say that every time anyone gives me such ideas, I shall seize upon them and take advantage of them without the slightest scruple. . . . My delicacy is frank, rather than persnickety. . . .

"And after all, the plot of every play belongs to me, without exception, in whosoever's head it may be lying in wait to be embroidered by my own.

*Collin d'Harleville, a naturally placid type, keeps out of the campaign against Fabre, which is conducted by third parties. Fabre remains hostile, but not excessively, and the quarrel goes no further.

"I should sooner die than do the opposite of this. I shall write plays with malice aforethought, that is, without subjugating my genius to any of the ridiculous, pedestrian or perverse conventions that the writers of the century are supposed to respect. I shall keep nature and Molière before my eyes at all times; I know no other masters."

So Fabre d'Églantine has not yielded to pressure or depression. Once again he stands fast in the storm and forces his way by sheer nerve right up to the King's Household, where the minister responsible for entertainments obtains for him, on February 22, 1789, the King's signature to a sort of counter-*lettre de cachet,* a breather, just as the pack of his creditors are about to move in for the kill:

"His Majesty, wishing to give Monsieur Fabre d'Églantine the means to carry on his business, hereby grants him a personal safe-conduct valid six months, during which His Majesty forbids his creditors to commit any act of coercion against him; also all bailiffs, sergeants or others, to arrest or molest him."[6]

Six months' grace? For him it's an eternity.

VOLNEY

58

JANUARY 21, 1789

God Preserve Atheism

On January 21, 1789, the priest of St. Roch parish records the death of Paul Thiry, Baron d'Holbach, lord of Heese and Leende, in his home in Paris, at the age of sixty-six. The death notice tactfully fails to mention whether the deceased received the holy sacraments. Having spared the dying man his ministrations, the writer prefers not to tell a lie. D'Holbach is the last of the century's great atheist monsters and, like Diderot five years before in the same parish, he contributed more than enough to charity while he was alive for the priests not to bother him on his deathbed and to spare his family the scandal of a nonreligious burial. Hence, his noble coffin is quietly packed away in the crypt of St. Roch, not far from that of the son of the Langres cutler.[1]

It would have been hard for so extraordinary a man to leave the world
with less ado. In the depths of this agitated winter, on the threshold of a
year that everybody senses is going to be more than eventful, d'Holbach's
death is a sort of nonevent. No one could speak of it better than his old
friend André Naigeon, that paragon of reserve and discretion, one of the
unknown hacks of the *Encyclopédie* who, like Boulanger and a few other
"noncommissioned officers," patiently built the foundations of the great work
in the light of the profound insights of Diderot, d'Alembert, Rousseau.* In
the first flush of grief Naigeon writes, in the *Journal de Paris,* that "no one
was more communicative than M. le Baron d'Holbach; no one took a keener
or more heartfelt interest in the progress of reason or undertook more
zealously and actively to hasten it. . . . He was not just one of the men who
had the most truths in his head, he was also one of those who had the fewest
errors; a very rare advantage, and specifically characteristic of him."

The somber intensity of Naigeon's sorrow is comprehensible. One could
count on one's fingers the number of authors as resolutely atheist and at the
same time as profoundly tolerant as d'Holbach. The only one to exceed him
on those counts was Diderot, whose universal indulgence occasionally made
him look like what in Provence are called *ravis.†* In his obituary letter Naigeon expresses equal affection for the two giants of materialistic philosophy
when he tells how d'Holbach couldn't keep himself from scolding Diderot:
" 'You are the happiest man I know. You have never seen a fool or a
scoundrel, and you have never read a bad book because you rewrite every
page as you read it.' "

Naigeon could have hit upon no illustration better befitting his desire
to endear the unrecognized giant to the public, even if that public was only
a handful of the happy few. "I have known no man of a more amiable, natural,
true cheerfulness, or one whose piquant jests and original turns of speech
resembled more closely what the English call *humor.‡*"

"One day when Madame Geoffrin was bitterly disputing with a man of
letters, and he was justifying himself with no less vivacity and warmth,
M. d'Holbach, who was listening to them in silence, came over and asked,
with a smile, 'Would you two by any chance be secretly married?' "

---

*In addition to his substantial contribution to the *Encyclopédie,* André Naigeon (1738–
1810) left a few tomes of solid scholarship, including a *Dictionnaire de philosophie ancienne et
moderne,* and he also wrote the *Mémoires sur Diderot,* which are the basis for biographical research
on the author.

†*Ravi* = "ravished, delighted"; as used here, "the ecstatic simpleton with his eyes full of
sky."—*Trans.*

‡In English in the original.

In the painful weeks of the summer of 1776, when Turgot's friends were trying to find the right words to console him for his downfall, humor was again the tack d'Holbach chose, when he told the disgraced minister, "You were an excellent coach driver and you drove your wagon most skillfully; but you forgot the little tin of lard to grease the axles."

There was more to d'Holbach's life, however, than such sparks of wit, which were only the spume flying from a perpetually alert mind. "He was unable to hate anybody. Nevertheless, it required effort for him to conceal his natural abhorrence of priests, of all the tools of despotism and superstition. When speaking of them, his mildness would begin to rankle in spite of himself, his camaraderie would often become bitter and provocative. One of the most violent passions of his entire life, but even more in his last years, was curiosity," writes Meister, in March.[2]

Humor and curiosity, so far; then, we can add to the escutcheon of Thiry d'Holbach the art of living and originality of thought.

He was born in 1723 into a rich family of the landed gentry in the Palatinate, at Edesheim, a Rhenish town of vineyards and cattle that he left in his youth to become a citizen of Île-de-France, predominantly Paris. There was soon nothing German left about him except his name; the first part of it came from a long line of Dietrichs that had passed through a series of prisms to produce Dirre, Dürhe, Thyre, Thierry, and Thiry. He had enough money not to need to earn any, and his natural inclinations led him to shun the army. When still a young man he became connected with a good Champagne family, distant relatives of his, called d'Aine, who had property in the Palatinate. For love, and after obtaining a papal dispensation, he married, in 1750, his "little cousin" Geneviève Suzanne d'Aine. Their happiness had no time to wear out: she died in 1754. It took him two years to get over her and marry again, this time to her sister, Charlotte Suzanne. No grand passion now, but a loyal union. She outlives him by many years. She gave him three sons, and he had had another by his first wife. He doesn't seem to have looked elsewhere for women; his close and chosen friendships, philosophical creation and a good and beautiful life in society had taken up all the room in his life. The only woman who counted for much or for long in his adult years was Madame d'Aine, his mother-in-law, a saucy baggage if ever there was one, even with her title. She turned life into a permanent carnival full of nooks and crannies and plain-speaking at their château de Grandval at Sucy near the Marne.

In it, d'Holbach regularly gave "two dinners weekly, on Sunday and Thursday. Then, and occasionally on other days, ten, twelve, or as many as fifteen or twenty men of letters and people of society or foreigners would assemble, all of whom were attached to and cultivated the arts of the mind. The food was good but not overrefined, there was excellent wine, excellent coffee, many discussions but never a quarrel. Manners were easy and simple, as becomes reasonable and educated people, but never degenerating into vulgarity; there was true merriment and high spirits, never becoming wild; in short, this was a genuinely attractive company, as could be seen by the simple fact that, having arrived at two o'clock, which was the custom in those days, we would often be there still, all of us, at seven or eight in the evening," [3] recalls Abbé Morellet.

At these literary and ludic repasts, over which Diderot presided as chief compère, d'Holbach had entertained, listened to and savored pretty much everything his day had to offer in the way of great minds. Helvétius, Rousseau, Abbé Raynal, Suard, Marmontel, d'Alembert, Condillac, Turgot, Buffon, Condorcet, Saint-Lambert, Chamfort, Cabanis, and many other seigneurs from the four corners of France rubbed elbows there with those from the rest of enlightened Europe—although they all spoke French, of course, which was then the universal language: Franklin, Hume, Adam Smith, Wilkes, Shelburne, Priestley, the great actor Garrick, the Italians Caraccioli and Abbé Galiani; Grimm and Dalberg,* the Germans, and even, when he had a moment and could just drop in, the Duke of Brunswick.

For years this improvised academy, no less distinguished than the official ones, had sat cheerfully at Baron d'Holbach's table and in his drawing room and strolled through his grounds, while he was investing it with his mixture of mournfulness and verve. Meister was "always struck by the relationship between M. d'Holbach's physiognomy and his mind. All his features were fairly regular and quite comely, yet he was not a handsome man. His brow was broad and high and, like Diderot's, bore the mark of a vast, extensive mind; but . . . it was less rounded and did not show the same warmth or energy. . . . His gaze did not reflect the mildness and habitual serenity of his soul."[4]

That reserve, that narrow margin between bitterness and companionableness within which d'Holbach maneuvered, had come with the passing years—for him as for Helvétius—from having written too soon and, in the end, opting for a comfortable life and a clandestine opus. In this he differed from Diderot, who did not always choose to avoid persecution. In his lifetime d'Holbach, whose bibliography totals over fifty titles, signed only a tiny proportion of them, and so he never saw the inside of the Bastille or Vincennes. But his silences were filled with the melancholy of the great writer stifled. He gave the *Encyclopédie* 375 articles spread over sixteen volumes; a few of them ventured to mention the authorship of "M. le B. d'H.," but there was no great danger in that when the subject of his dissertation was coal, fossils, gold, sulfur, or volcanos. Some things, on the other hand, could

*Who becomes one of the top Rhenish dignitaries of the Empire under Napoleon.

not be told (here, by Meister) until his death: "It is no longer an indiscretion to say that he is the author of the book that caused such a to-do eighteen or twenty years ago, the famous *Système de la Nature*.* All the fame derived from this book could not for one moment tempt his conceit, and although he was fortunate enough to be safe from suspicion, his own modesty served him even better in that respect than all the prudence of his friends."[5]

In 1789, when freedom of the pen has suddenly become almost total, Meister tries to forget that the modesty he mentions was gag-induced. In 1770 the universal response of Court and town, still dominated by clerical conformism, was a wave of outrage directed against "this highly proscribed treatise," as Bachaumont wrote, which "purports to justify atheism. . . . Religious persons groan to see how boldly and profusely abominable systems are being spread about today, which used to be confined to dusty manuscripts."[6]

One reason why d'Holbach found it particularly expedient to keep quiet is that in 1761 he had already published *Le Christianisme dévoilé,* and three years after his *Système de la Nature* he went even further with *Système social, ou Principes naturels de la morale et de la politique avec un examen de l'influence du gouvernement sur les moeurs,* and *Le Bon Sens, ou Idées naturelles opposées aux idées surnaturelles.* Grimm, however much a tablemate and in d'Holbach's debt, displayed his habitual ambivalence toward his friends in connection with the latter:† "This is the *Système de la Nature* divested of its abstract ideas; it is atheism brought within the grasp of chambermaids and wigmakers."[7]

As it stands, the *Système de la Nature* remains the backbone of Baron d'Holbach's copious oeuvre. Galiani, that curious unpriestly abbé and true friend, was appalled by it: "My heart leaps in terror at the thought of the clergy's vociferous uprising against the *Système de la Nature.* Those people have keen noses. Most assuredly they know or suspect its author; they will denounce him, he will be sacrificed. . . . May God preserve atheism from some pernicious persecution; but I tremble for it."[8]

It would have been one thing if the only people forcing d'Holbach to immure himself inside gilded towers for the rest of his days were the devout. But there was also a break between him and the deists. Voltaire and Rousseau had gone their ways. He had seen two of the greatest, who liked their idea of the world better than his, move away from him; he consoled himself by associating with lesser men, not so brilliant and not so famous but more honest with themselves. Naigeon had mended the hurt caused by Rousseau.

---

*Full title: *Système de la Nature, ou les Lois du monde physique et du monde moral.* The first edition came out in 1770, in two 400-page volumes.

†See Volume II for the drubbing Diderot gave Grimm when he behaved the same way about the *Histoire des Deux Indes.*

A few words of Diderot's were enough to show him that at least one great genius was fighting the same battle he was: "I love a clear, clean, frank philosophy, such as there is in the *Système de la Nature,* and still more in *Le Bon Sens.* . . . The author of the *Système de la Nature* is not an atheist on one page and a deist on the next; his philosophy is all of a piece."

In that book, d'Holbach sets out a radical philosophy for a revolution nobody was even talking about yet. The word began slipping onto people's lips at the very twilight of his life. His pen never wrote it. One wonders if he was concerned about the tumult preceding the Estates General. But it hardly matters. If any one thing set the Revolution in motion a generation ahead of itself, it was his *Système de la Nature.*

The inventory of his papers mentions a little *Essai sur l'art de ramper à l'usage des courtisans.* It is one of the last things he wrote and it's like a nose thumbed from the tomb at all the people execrated in his work.*

> The man of Court is indisputably the most singular production our human species has to show. . . .
>
> The most difficult of all arts is that of crawling. This sublime art may well be the most miraculous conquest of the human spirit. Nature has placed in the heart of every human being a self-conceit and pride that are the most daunting of all his inclinations to overcome. The soul rebels against whatsoever tends to depress it. . . . If the habit of fighting, containing, and crushing this powerful resource be not contracted early in life, it becomes impossible to master it thereafter. The courtier begins to practice this discipline in infancy. . . .
>
> Say no more of the abnegation of the devout before their Divinity; the true abnegation is that of a courtier before his master. Behold how he annihilates himself in his presence! He becomes pure machine, or rather, pure nothing. . . .
>
> There exist some mortals who have a stiffness of spirit, a want of suppleness in the spine, a lack of flexibility at the nape of the neck; these regrettable flaws of conformation make it impossible for them to perfect themselves in the art of crawling, and render them incapable of making progress at Court. Snakes and reptiles slither to the summits of mountains, whereas the most fiery steed can never clamber so high.[9]

D'Holbach is dead, long live Volney! D'Holbach departs on January 21. That same week Volney, one of his most ardent disciples, completes the process of emerging from the mass in the general movement that is translating enlightened ideas into action. That winter, after a breakthrough that did not

*Meister does not dare publish this "philosophical witticism" in his *Correspondance littéraire* until December 1790.

go unnoticed by opinion in Brittany, with the publication of five issues of *La Sentinelle du peuple,* Volney decides to stand for election to the Rennes delegation to the Estates General.

The torch is passing from the old philosopher to the "committed" youth. Constantin-François Chasseboeuf de La Giraudais, aka Volney, is one of the first examples of the *encyclopédistes'* word made flesh. He has very little of his life-master's genius and charm, true, and none of his fortune or surroundings; nevertheless, he is d'Holbach's true heir. At the school of medicine Cabanis, already famous, had noticed the young student from Anjou who was trying to make up his mind between science and literature, and introduced him to his best friends, including d'Holbach and Madame Helvétius.

At twenty, Constantin-François felt as though he had been transported to Olympus in the company of the gods. He was not a regular visitor to the d'Holbach salon and he never stayed in Paris long because of his lengthy voyages and trips back to his birthplace. But his extreme attentiveness had been remarked upon, as well as his ability to take in the most advanced theories. He spoke little; he was shy, affected, a little starched and not very good-looking: a long knife of a face, prematurely thinning hair, a rather dull gaze. He was plainly made for writing rather than talking, but the eagerness of his mind and strength of his convictions impressed people.

Introduced as Chasseboeuf in 1777, he became Volney in 1785, that being the pseudonym he used to sign his first account of his travels—probably the product of a rather ambitious amalgamation of Voltaire and Ferney. He's one of the few men of liberty to invent a nobility for himself out of a *nom de plume* instead of a piece of land.*

He'll soon have to start living up to his alias: he hasn't even learned of d'Holbach's death when he finds himself in the fray, hurled into action between Brittany and Val-de-Loire. On January 28 and 29, Rennes explodes.

*Hoping to win him over, Napoleon makes him a noble of the Empire, "Comte Volney."

59

JANUARY 26–FEBRUARY 4, 1789

The Youths Became Quite Frightening

No novelist could have made it up: the cradle of the Volney family lies near the Angevin town of Athée [= atheist, nonbeliever], 260 families; and also near Craon, a somewhat larger place a league farther north. In 1757, the year of Constantin-François's birth , you could find eight or ten Chasseboeufs between Craon and Athée, all of them "male collaterals."[1] In the course of two or three generations they followed the regular progress of farmers who have prospered, from sharecroppers to tipstaves to notaries and attorneys. Volney's grandfather was mayor of Craon in 1740. Jacques-René, his father, "advocate to the barony" of the region, increased his substance by acquiring quite a few smallholdings with melodious names—Bois-Gautier, L'Hommeau, La Marinière. The ascension was consecrated by a good marriage to a demoiselle Gigault de La Giraudais, offspring of an older bourgeoisie settled in the fair valley of Candé, near which Constantin-François's maternal grandparents had a small manor.

Candé is the good earth of Anjou, sweet and fertile, subtly lit and shadowed, whereas the Craon country, in which the young woman felt herself a deportee, suffered from the microclimate of "a muddle of boulders, forests, racing streams and brooks that power a great number of forges." The Chasseboeufs had had the good fortune to elevate themselves to positions of prominence in this damp, sad landscape,* where people lived half from farming and half from spinning hemp and flax in their cottages. Volney's childhood memories are marked by the poverty of the spinning peasants, vegetating in their hovels above the workroom-cellar.

He had little to do with his father, apparently a misanthrope who lived hidden away in his study, and still less with his mother, claimed by some to

---

*It has improved since.

have died of boredom two years after his birth. In early childhood he was looked after by grandparents and an uncle-priest. Constantin-François was not spoiled. At seven, he was dumped into a little boarding school at Ancenis—between Nantes and Angers on the Loire—run by a mediocre priest who taught him some rudiments of Latin.

He didn't get a chance to start developing until he was twelve or so and at school with the Oratorians in Angers, where he was finally able to study a "good humanities" course, but even then his hypersensitivity made life difficult for him. "I avoided my schoolmates and liked silence and reading better than games and noisy amusements. I can still recall how, when I entered the school at Angers, at the very first recreation period, when the other boys were playing in the garden, I retired into a corner to read the history of France, and how they teased me about it and nicknamed me the hermit."[2]

His fellow pupils weren't really cruel, though, especially the little group he met every day in bookseller Boutney's lodging house on chaussée Saint-Pierre, where he was given room and board, for 450 francs a year, with a pleasant family "consisting of the father, mother, two young ladies and a son who had just been tonsured before taking orders."[3]

Some of the boys, like Yves Besnard,* went on teasing him but also learned to respect him: "Volney was the only one in the house who took no active part in our games, although he was happy to remain a silent spectator for hours on end; he would come to any entertainment with us, he often accompanied us on the excursions we would make, on foot or horseback, into the countryside around Angers. . . . I remember that one day, riding to Pellouailles, he fell off his horse across from the château d'Écharbot, which sent us into fits of laughter before we even knew whether he had been injured in his fall, because we attributed it to his clumsiness, about which we had teased him before."

At this stage in his youth Chasseboeuf was already proudly calling himself a "student of philosophy," but his interest was more in languages and civilizations than in logic or rhetoric. Before he was eighteen he was looking for somebody in Angers who could give him lessons in Hebrew, because he wanted to be able to identify the mistakes that had crept into the various translations of the Bible. So he was very young when he took up a position at the crossroads of history and religion, where he finds the ever-widening field of his intellectual research.

---

*François-Yves Besnard, a mischievous little hunchback shoved by his parents into the priesthood; his *Souvenirs d'un nonagénaire* is among the most entertaining memoirs of the age. He is a conforming priest in 1790, quietly unfrocks himself at the Concordat, becomes a civil servant in the tax administration, then observes the Empire and subsequent reigns of the Bourbons and Louis-Philippe with a sagacious eye.

In 1774, the year when the King was twenty and himself only eighteen, he left his unrewarding youth as though he were abandoning a suitcase somewhere, and obtained his legal emancipation[4] from a family council, a most unusual step in those days. But his desire for independence was very strong, and if he had to live in solitude, he meant to fashion his solitude to suit himself. By providing him with an annual income of eleven hundred livres, an inheritance from his mother made this possible. The moment had come for him to escape to Paris by public transport, in what the west of France called the *carrosse,* drawn by eight horses, which took eight days to cover the road from Angers to the capital. In Paris he dabbled a little in law, then in medicine, but was put off by the lowly status of its practitioners.

The center of his life had already shifted from the search for a profession to the study of Eastern languages and advanced ideas. This explosive mixture propelled him, in less than ten years, from the Arabic lecture halls at the Collège de France to the banks of the Nile, by way of the salons of the Baron d'Holbach and Madame Helvétius, where he found his intellectual family.

He did not break all his ties with his own father and relatives in Anjou, though, and went back from time to time, a little absentmindedly, his head full of other things. Perhaps, if a "young and lovable cousin" named Charlotte had not been under sixteen, he might have settled there for good. She is the only hint of a youthful romance in the life of this boy who doesn't seem to have been much drawn to affairs of the heart.*

The time had come to make something of himself outside the libraries and salons, to go and practice, *in situ,* those ancient languages he had been studying as abstractions. His departure for the "Ottoman Empire" (the southern part of it) enabled Volney to begin developing, before he was thirty, his own very specific personality as a traveler-philosopher. His first book, published in 1787, is an account of his two-year tour through Egypt and Syria and immediately earns him a reputation as a writer who has something important to say. He spent several months in Cairo, then went up from the Dead Sea to Antioch and Aleppo along the east coast of the Mediterranean, with a little side trip to Cyprus by sail. Jerusalem, the Jordan, Jaffa, Acre, Damascus, Beirut, Tripoli. In the net of his meticulous observation he captures over five hundred leagues of settings, ethos and customs, scattered through the huge maritime territory of the remnants of the decomposing Turkish protectorates. He is one of the first to bring back to Europe a book of discovery that is not cluttered with romanticism and anecdote.

Le Voyage en Égypte et en Syrie is like its author: gray, sober, dense and

---

*He meets Charlotte Gigault de La Giraudais again in 1810, at Candé, widowed, and marries her at the end of that year. Between them there is never anything more than a courteous understanding. She is a royalist. He is Volney.

full. After 1788 no literate person in France can discourse upon the Near East without having it in his library.*

Volney laid his book on the table at d'Holbach's and Condorcet's, and at the feet of Madame Helvétius. He has become one of them. He makes friends with Jefferson, Sieyès, Mirabeau, Brissot. But he has not traveled all those miles and done all that work just to sink back into a walled-in world. He has a calling to go into politics as another man might go into the Church, and now is the time.

"Friends and citizens, you know that, having by the grace of God been endowed with a small and decent income, I am able to live as a good gentleman, that is, without working; but since every one of you works, I feel in conscience obliged to join your labors too. This is why, while one man plows my field and another bakes my bread, I have considered by what means I might make myself useful; and, thinking that there are people with evil intentions in the world today, I have taken as my trade that of sentinel, so that I can raise the hue and cry, and call out, Who goes there?"

These are the first lines of the first issue of *La Sentinelle du peuple,* "a periodical intended for people of all professions, sciences, arts, businesses and trades comprising the third estate in the province of Brittany, by a landowner of that province."[5]

The string of five pamphlets that Volney issues at the end of 1788 kneads Brittany like a batch of dough. Seldom has anything written for a special occasion produced such a commotion among a local elite; but that's what its author wanted. The traveler to the Levant is burning his boats; the man people thought would soon be joining the Academy becomes a sort of people's tribune instead. You can feel his delight as he unleashes all his repressed violence. In the first issue he says that all the arts useful and necessary to life are carried out by commoners and suggests that if they consider themselves insulted, they should refuse their services to their lords and make them cry mercy.

"That is when I shall pounce, and that is when you must be firm, because if you listen to them first, they will send you to sleep with their petting; those noblemen are so winning, when they need us! . . . and we commoners are so easily duped that when a nobleman doffs his hat to us, we immediately give him a lump of butter."

And so on, about the questions that have become so burning since the convening of the Estates General: equality in respect to taxation; opening of all ranks and offices to all; and, as a corollary, the reform of the ancient

---

*Marie-Joseph Chénier sees it as "the masterpiece of the genre." On his return from Egypt, Bonaparte congratulates Volney for the accuracy and truthfulness of his work and orders his compliments to the author published in the *Moniteur* in October 1799.

estates of Brittany, which had never ceased to meet but remained, under pretext of preserving some degree of independence for the province, largely under the control of the nobility. Volney even attacks the Rennes *parlement,* which, like the others, squared off to fight the nobility of Court the year before, but only in order to take its place, at the people's expense. And it is the people whom the *Sentinelle* wants to alert, proposing that the Bretons should stipulate in their grievances that "the new *parlement* of Brittany is to be made up one-quarter of ecclesiastics, one-quarter of nobles, and one-half of commoners; that offices shall no longer be hereditary but shall be obtained by competitive examination and that the office of *président* will be held for a term of one year, and shall be filled by each of the three orders in turn."

This initial bombshell secured for Volney the animosity of the *parlement,* followed by that of the nobility, which is much preoccupied by its wranglings with the King on the one hand and the *parlement* on the other, while both nobility and magistrates lean alternatively on the third estate, and even the "low people," in a specifically Breton hodgepodge. With the second issue of the *Sentinelle* Volney is forced to move partly underground. The magistrates in Rennes ban his paper, making it all the more eagerly sought after, and compelling him to take refuge in a dilapidated feudal manor house lent by friends in the countryside. There he prints the last three issues himself and from there the damp sheets are carried away in a milk vendor's baskets and taken to Vatar, the best bookseller in Rennes, where the gazette is snapped up by back-room purchasers, almost under the guards' noses. This might have become a profitable business, since there are no fewer than forty thousand people in Rennes, but Volney is no speculator, nor journalist either, in reality. To his mind, the *Sentinelle du peuple* was to be simply a sort of platform for his election to the Estates General. After Christmas, when the excitement in Rennes shifts from individual minds to local assemblies and then out into the streets, it becomes prudent for him to drop it. But this does not prevent him from publishing, and signing, three pamphlets heated by the same fire in January: *Petit Prône aux roturiers, Lettre d'un solitaire philanthrope,* and *Lettre de M. Chasseboeuf de Volney à M. le comte de Serrant.*

In the last he ventures to explain, in response to the nobleman who had publicly denounced him to the King's legal representative, that "*dead weight* is the weight of a peasant persecuted by a high justice who defends himself with arguments, while *live weight* is the weight of another peasant who, when pushed to the wall, takes up his gun."[6]

But why Rennes? Originally, Volney is 100 percent Angevin, then Parisian by adoption. Why do we see him first stretching his polemicist's wings in the big Breton town far to the west of his own roots, where he's never had an opportunity to affirm himself? Was he advised, oriented, possibly even subsidized in that direction by Necker, whom he met in the salons before and since the minister's return to power, and with whose daughter he maintains a relationship of the same order as with Madame Helvétius? He's very much a follower of Necker, and shares the general messianism about him. It is rumored, and will continue to be, that Volney is one of his penmen, just as people were saying five years before that he got money from Vergennes during his travels to the East, with orders to investigate at first hand the economic and political potential of the Turkish Empire, that dying ally that is beginning to weigh like a stone around France's neck.

By January 20 most of the towns of Brittany, even the minor ones, from Rennes to Nantes and all the way to Quimper, are in a state of ferment. There was that delegation of twelve gentlemen sent by the estates of Brittany to Versailles, who were thrown in the Bastille by Brienne and liberated by Necker, but who came home empty-handed; there were, as everywhere in France, meetings of the *parlement* that were almost rebellions, then a compulsory dispersal, then support from the people, then hanging back and uncertainty. To make things worse, there is, in the very seat of power, a prevailing feud between the governor, the Comte de Thiard, who is a military man of peaceful disposition, and Bertrand de Molleville, the intendant, who is a bellicose magistrate.* One of France's largest provinces is decomposing, against a background of two million penurious people in rags.†

Brittany is the very epitome of a poor country, where the yokels' distress is painted blacker by the contrast between the enormous acreages of the rich and their own minute rectangles that could provide no living for anyone. Those who manage to eat wheat consider themselves fortunate; the majority feed on buckwheat, rye or barley and drink only cider, which has become scarce after a series of poor years—leading also to a shortage of feed for the livestock, and hence to the slaughter of many animals. For years milk and butter have been available only to the gentry. But these inhabitants of a disaster area have now been ordered to pay a higher *fouage,* the name given around here to the annual tax levy.

The countryside is crisscrossed with epidemics; prisons and hospices are overrun. And then comes the terrible corset of cold from which the whole country is suffering. (On November 20 the Seine freezes so hard in Paris that people can walk across it, and the slow thaw does not begin until January 20.) Half the lambs are dead of the epizootics and neither hemp nor flax has been harvested this year, hence the rising unemployment among cottage-industry spinners, weavers and wool carders.

---

*A fervent royalist, Bertrand de Molleville is one of Louis XVI's last ministers and just manages to emigrate after the fall of the throne. He writes inflammatory memoirs.
†An approximate figure, given at the time by Lanjuinais.

Resistance among the "little people" is benumbed by indigence and illiteracy. Imprudently—and in this lies the uniqueness of events in Brittany—it is the nobles who prick the starvelings into action, trying to arouse them to protest against a hypothetical alliance between King and people, as a riposte to the rising bourgeoisie.

The third estate is already overheated, if only by the agitation of the "clubists," who are seething away in fifteen or twenty Breton bookshops, where enlightened bourgeois can connect with the more sophisticated of the "louts." That's where the *Sentinelle du peuple* and other publications have given consciousness to initially formless demands. Suddenly, the people in the street, previously ignored by all three orders, are being courted by each of them separately. Times change.

December 29. The estates of Brittany open, as every year, at four o'clock in the afternoon in the former convent of the Cordeliers near the ducal residence in Rennes. So far, everything happens as before, but for the last time, with the majesty of a wonderful machine perfected by centuries of protocol.

Gorgeous costumes, broad hangings of black-tipped ermine blazoned with gold fleurs-de-lis, ritual presidency of the Bishop of Rennes assisted by the Comte de Boisgelin, the Baron de La Roche-Bernard on behalf of the nobility, and a few other barons. On his right, the traditional seats of honor are occupied by 950 members of the order of nobility, many of them "newly made" and diligently recruited by their relatives to pack the house, having lurched up from the depths of the countryside with manners so rough (in some instances) that even in their costumes one might mistake them for their own peasants. These are "the swords of iron," in the sarcastic words of the 54 delegates of the third estate, huddled into the space reserved for the nonprivileged on the *président*'s left, like a bone thrown to a dog.[7]

But the bourgeois, although outnumbered ten to one amid all this pomp and ceremony, are perfectly aware that the true ratio is the other way around, as seen in the tumultuous support being given them on every side by a strange amalgam of well-dressed youths and poor devils almost in rags. This is the first manifestation of an osmosis that has taken place, mainly in the nearby cafés, between the Young Men's Society, meaning the university law students, and the "Young Citizens," meaning workers who are out of work and therefore available for whatever excitement might be going on and whom the students have been trying to assemble and organize for the last month. Together they're noisy and even insolent to the nobles, and loudly declare themselves to be *patriots,* that still indefinite but aggressive-sounding word that is beginning to be heard in France. Their chief leader, the one they often ask to speak for them, is Jean-Victor Moreau, provost of the law school, an office that conferred certain responsibilities. He is relatively mature and also has "patriotic" convictions,* and he's writing an *Arrêté des étudiants en droit et jeunes citoyens de la province de Bretagne réunis,* which he distributes to the representatives of the third estate around about now, with 278 signatures on it, confirming their active support.[8] And the third are going to need it, because on December 30 the beautiful protocol machine goes off the rails. Despite their numerical inferiority, the bourgeois representatives refuse to endorse the nobles' decision and are obstinately asking the King for double representation of the third, which is being demanded by almost the whole of France but seems absolutely shocking and unheard of in the medieval marches of Brittany. The trouble is that from time immemorial the decisions of the Estates of Brittany have been valid only if they are unanimous. After three days of bittersweet debate, the *président*-bishop can think of nothing better to do than adjourn the sitting, and the gentle Comte de Thiard, all of whose energy seems to be concentrated on the avoidance of bloodshed, rides off as hard as he can go to ask for instructions in Versailles.

His return on January 7, with an order from the King (actually Necker) extending the suspension of sittings and hinting that here as elsewhere the doubling of the third will ultimately be approved, simply confounds the confusion.

Twenty more days of it follow, in the big cold, gray town where there are fewer jobs to be found every day and the cold, but also the "trouble" is preventing supplies from reaching their destination, while both camps, instead of dispersing as the King has asked them to do, firmly stand their ground. Nobility and clergy on one side, protected, nonviolently, by the military; and representatives of the third and "Young Men" on the other, in the neighborhood of the town hall. The authorities were hoping they could hold out until the elections, but now it looks as though the Estates General will not be meeting until April or May. A confrontation has to come, sooner or later.

Monday, January 26. Early that morning, some unscheduled actors enter the scene. The Breton nobles hit upon the plan of giving their servants money and not only permitting but positively enjoining them to go out into the town to attack the "Young Men" near the Cordelier convent. A motley band

*Born in Morlaix in 1763, Moreau plays a part in the Breton federations in 1790, then enters the revolutionary army. A general by 1793, he is commander-in-chief of the armies of the north and east beginning in 1796. He wins major victories in Germany while Bonaparte is making himself conspicuous in Italy. In 1800 his victory at Hohenlinden combines with that at Rivoli to bring Austria to its knees. Resisting the omnipotence of the First Consul, Moreau becomes involved in the Cadoudal and Pichegru conspiracy, is sentenced to prison, exiled to the United States, and returns in 1813 as adviser to the army of the tsar. He is killed at his side by a French ball near Dresden, on September 2, 1813.

of lackeys, doormen and coachmen foregather on the Champ de Montmorin, the equivalent in Rennes to the Champ de Mars in Paris.* Armed mainly with cudgels, its ranks are swollen by various vagabonds aroused by repeated bellowings of some rather singular sentiments:

"We're for the nobles, we're going to fight for our money!"

"Hit 'em hard, there's six francs a man to earn."[9]

It may never happen again: the flood of riot unites the demands of abject poverty with devotion to the nobles. But in this instance the devotion is to the Breton gentry, whose manor houses are often actually joined to the barn. By contrast with them, the "Young Men," those brats of the wealthy bourgeois who get paid to study—that is, according to their detractors, to do nothing—look like the overprivileged. The youths who are fighting for the integrity of the great Estates General are seen rather as profaners and oppressors of the people, especially when a delegation of the rioting servants is received at the Cordeliers by the nobles, who shamelessly (and without the slightest ability to do anything about it) promise to lower the price of bread.

"A horde of half-drunk valets overran the squares, armed with logs and sticks and uttering screams of rage, in search of their designated victims; then they ran to the Union Café, the young people's customary meeting place. . . . Not only the youths, but married men too, fathers of families, anyone who . . . still had some look of youth about him, were beaten with sticks and pelted by a hail of stones with which the lackeys had filled their jacket pockets, and several were seriously wounded."

A few of the gentlemen, bolder than the rest, plunged into the melee to urge on their troops:

" 'That's the way to go,' said one. 'Things are beginning to shape up now.'

" 'Courage!' another called out.

Some of them grabbed the young men by the arms and held them while they were being thrashed by their valets.

No deaths so far, but many bruised and injured. Monday, the raid remains more in the tragicomic mode and quiet slowly descends in the evening, so that a few of the more valiant magistrates go in a body to call on the "Young Citizens" who are back "home" again, that is, in the law school classrooms and the Union Café.

Since, after all, the literal meaning of its name, and its age-old function, is "the talking place," the *parlement* dutifully initiates a move to lower the temperature. But the magistrates seem to be distinctly out of touch with the

---

*The Comte de Montmorin, governor of Brittany before becoming a minister, had ordered the space cleared for maneuvers and parades.

general interest of this town, and stubbornly plead the cause of the nobility, berating their listeners for attacking the good folks who were stoning them. They've got it backward, and they get themselves thrown out.

" 'The people? What people!' most of the young men shouted. 'Not on your life! Those were noblemen's servants and nobody else.' "

The rumbling wears on through a feverish night.

January 27. The storm gathers during the morning, while the deceptively quiet streets encourage the *parlement* men, after reading out a memorandum by the "nobility of church and sword," to institute legal proceedings against the leaders of the real people, not the noblemen's lackeys.

This raises the curtain on the second act. It opens in the Union Café, where thirty armed young men are permanently stationed. Around three o'clock their indignation is brought to the boil by the appearance "of a pale, bleeding man who had just been assassinated by the grooms of the nobility," but he's not dead, that's just the way people talked in those days; in town they are saying that "the honest craftsman was assassinated by grooms who saw him coming out of the law school. . . . The poor wretch fainted in the café and came to his senses only to burst into tears and implore mercy for his wife and children."[10]

This is just the little spark that was needed. "The youths became quite frightening; they marched to the door of the Cordeliers' cloister, where the nobility were meeting in the convent." The marshalsea tries to step in between the opposing groups. Who fires first? Each side says it was the other. In any event, a pitched battle ensues, with firearms but also swords and knives and a wide variety of projectiles. It spreads through the whole center of the town, shops close, the people barricade themselves inside the tall, stately houses rebuilt half a century ago after the fire of 1720, beautifully aligned under their somber slate roofs.

The muddled melee swirls through the two big new squares, around the statue of Louis XVI on horseback and that of Louis XV on foot—the latter seeming to gaze benignly upon two hefty unclothed females performing a theatrical gesture that is apparently meant to portray Brittany imploring the goddess of health. There is hand-to-hand fighting, and shooting continues, sometimes at close quarters, in the nearby walks, among the three rows of pollarded trees, and in the Benedictines' garden, which is "always open to decent folks, with a view reaching far into the countryside."[11]

Owing to the large number of pistols involved, not to mention the double-barreled guns "of which the nobles made most use," this day is as deadly as those in Grenoble, Pau and even Paris last August. It's true that at four o'clock the "Young Men" loot a gunsmith's shop, break into the King's weapons store and remove about 130 guns, but can only use the stocks as clubs because the hammers have been taken out. Swords and bayonets from the same storehouse make nasty wounds. Who is the first man killed? Is it the Comte de Boishue's eldest son, just twenty years old? Is it the anonymous butcher shot down in the middle of the street from a window in the nobility's reading room? How many people are injured by the pistol fire of two incensed ladies, one of whom is posted in the window of an attorney's house, screaming, "Kill all the nobles, leave not a one alive!" while the other, a "woman of position, stands fast at her windows with a pistol in either hand, shouting, 'Is that a student going past?' "[12]

On January 28, after an "appalling night" during which the virtually besieged nobles' only reinforcements come from a fresh contingent of armed domestics, many dressed as bourgeois in order to pass unnoticed, dawn rises on a day that promises to be bloody. But Thiard is relieved to see the arrival of four or five hundred grenadiers and infantry. Also, a curious assembly of "family fathers" from the lower classes is being held in the town hall, in a room near the one in which the youths stand ready for anything. This spontaneous move by the tradesmen and craftsmen of Rennes has two results: it pacifies the "Young Citizens," who no longer feel so desperate because they know their parents are behind them; and it intimidates the motley little army of the nobility and prevents it from making a sortie.

Excitement subsides as quickly as it rose. Both sides disperse and everybody goes home, at the behest of the municipal forces of law and order, who have some effect on this occasion.

But the news from Brittany makes a splash in Paris, where bookseller Hardy notes, on February 3, the appearance of a *"Relation de ce qui venait de se passer à Rennes,* eight printed pages in 8vo, wretchedly bound, although it unfortunately contains facts that were all too true."[13] In the next ten days two further *Relations* come out, one of which informs the Parisians that one of the representatives of the "Young Men" of Rennes bore the extraordinary name of Monsieur *Omnes Omnibus.* Everybody imagines it's a pseudonym for "Monsieur Everyman," but not at all: he's the son of the town's top engraver.

Volney shouldn't be too sorry to desert the ship of Rennes, which he boarded a trifle hastily. He was born to write, not to instigate crowd movements. His *Sentinelle du peuple* has served Necker's cause and enabled him to do his job as a polemicist. He doesn't have enough backers or resources in the big Breton town to get elected there without a fight, as he had hoped. And although his pugnacity is great, it is intellectual. Nobody can see the "new Voltaire" orating on street corners, cudgel in hand.

There are plenty of other constituencies he can try in order to get himself sent to the Estates General. What about Nantes? Brittany's other capital town is coming to the rescue of the first one: "The young Nantese, on whom the youth of Rennes had called for help, arrived in force on Saturday the thirtieth around eight in the evening; several detachments preceded them in the course of the afternoon; they announced their coming with the proclamation of a decision ablaze with that fire so proper to youth. *'Vive le Roi!' 'Vive le Comte de Thiard!'* were the rallying cries of these warmhearted compatriots . . . , who were welcomed with cheers by the inhabitants of Rennes."[14]

There were eddies in Caen and Angers as well. The whole youth of the west is on the move, for King and Necker. On February 4, the "Young Citizens" of Angers, "informed by the students of law and medicine, and the members of the legal professions, of the attacks made in Brittany upon the 'Young Citizens' by members of the nobility," proclaim that they are and always will be "ready to fly to the side of our unjustly oppressed brothers."[15]

And who would have believed, a few weeks before, in a town ordinarily so right-minded and placid as Angers, that the ladies there would also be giving tongue, announcing that "the intention of us all is not to depart from the respect and obedience we owe to the King but [that] we will sooner perish than abandon our lovers, husbands, sons and brothers, preferring the glory of sharing their dangers to the security of shameful inaction"?

Back home in Craon, Volney finds that this is his chosen land, and, having every likelihood of being chosen himself by the local third estate, prepares to glide into place as one of the four delegates sent to Versailles by the parish of Angers. Almost the moment he gets there, his seemingly inexhaustible fecundity engenders a *Lettre des bourgeois aux gens de la campagne, fermiers, métayers, et vassaux de certains seigneurs qui trompent le peuple.*[16]

The seigneurs he's referring to are beginning to take a very dim view of him and plan a few blows below the belt. His next publication is *La confession d'un pauvre roturier angevin,* for which he collects a full gamut of epithets, deserved or not, from his opponents in Anjou: "seditious, firebrand, emissary, upstart, jabberer, hypocrite, madman, vendor of incoherence, *philosophe,* rabid, atheist and fanatic."

As campaign mate, he finds a local friend, Louis-Marie Larevellière,* the owner of a little piece of land on the border between Anjou and Poitou, on the strength of which he can call himself Larevellière-Lépeaux; their close association continues on the benches of the new assembly. Sickly-looking,

---

*Born at Montaigu in 1753, dies in Paris in 1834; Larevellière-Lépeaux, republican by temperament and conviction but less so during the Terror, becomes a delegate to the Constituent but goes further than Volney, as he is also a member of the Convention. His tolerance nearly gets him killed by both Blues and Whites during the Vendéan rebellion. After Thermidor he becomes a member of the Committee of Public Safety, and is in the Directoire from 1795 to 1799. He does not accept Bonaparte's seizure of power on 18 Brumaire, never follows him and retires from public life forever.

timid as a deer and enormously gentle, this other confirmed atheist, whose affability stands out in sharp contrast to Volney's chill, observes in his *Mémoires* that "the boldness of our opinions struck all the Angevins, who were unanimous in their belief that they would never see us again and that we were destined to perish in the cells of the Bastille."[17]

MIRABEAU

60

FEBRUARY 4–MARCH 5, 1789

Between the Nobility and the Third Estate

Act I in Mirabeau's political life, Act nth and last in the long tragedy of himself and his father that has consumed his entire life. At the end of January 1789 he reaches Aix, in the same movement that took Volney to Rennes and many others to many other parts of France, trying to get themselves elected.

While Brittany is going through the commotion in Rennes, a process at once similar and different is getting under way in the largest city of Provence, swept by the icy howl of the mistral, which is bringing to Aix the curse of one of the worst winters of France. The fears expressed by La Fayette three months before, in his irritation at Necker's shilly-shallying, are being borne out all too fully. Almost everywhere, foul weather has impeded the activities of the electoral assemblies.

Mirabeau thinks he's traveling through Siberia: "One is tempted to say that the exterminating angel has struck the human race from one end of the realm to the other. Every scourge has been unleashed. Everywhere I have found men dead of cold and hunger, bread often at five sous a pound, never less than three sous and seven deniers. In fact, people are starving to death with wheat all around them, for want of flour. All the mills are frozen."[1]

People as poverty-stricken as this could not be visited by bad weather at a worse time. Virtually all the waterways are frozen solid, so that the log trains that supply the only form of energy for cooking and heat are unable to move, and the thousands of water-powered mills that transform grain into flour are also paralyzed. The bakers are beginning to denounce "hoarders," who are being blamed for every famine since the Flour War, but this is not fair, because the fullest loft is no use when the mill wheel cannot turn.

Mirabeau takes note of it all almost absentmindedly. Very soon, he thinks, will come the day when France, organized at last, will no longer be at the mercy of a cold spell. He has come to Aix to accomplish the political destiny that he believes is invested in him. Someone has followed his progress from far-off Argenteuil, where the eternal witness to his life has withdrawn into his destitution. Witness, but also author of his days, deadly and admiring foe, gigantic sneerer, unconquerable resenter, the Marquis de Mirabeau, Friend of Men and despiser of his son: at seventy-three and close to death, he still has strength enough to draw this bittersweet portrait of Gabriel-Honoré:

"They'll not have seen such a head as his in Provence for many a day. . . . In one or two conversations and communications between us I have glimpsed true genius. He works tirelessly . . . , he never has a doubt about anything, he has an inborn hauteur, and this, added to a great deal of what is called wit, have made him a figure in banking and printing and especially in the modern politics. He says openly that he will not suffer France to be demonarchized, and at the same time he is a friend to the leaders of the third . . . , and the populace of listeners . . . takes him for Podagrombo the Giant;* while his aristocratic ways, his elaborate dress, in this century of rag-and-tatter fashion, his double and triple secretaries and packed antechambers; his traits as an author who is respectful to the great . . . , and as a performer of gay and noble jests with women, and his dominant impetuosity in everything he undertakes, all make of him a sort of icon laden down with relics, that seem to cling to his very skin."[2]

So the Mirabeau train rattles on, father and son, two monsters of the age, both worn out, exhausted by the floggings they have been administering to each other all their lives, the father ruined by thirty lawsuits and the hatred of his wife, the son driven to the end of his tether by debauchery and wasted genius. Now he's going to have to get himself elected without any money and without the support of his father, which would automatically have given him an initial boost among the other feudal lords of Provence. Cursed as Cain from birth, cursed again after his failed reconciliation with the Marquis when he got out of prison at Vincennes, facing the fierce hatred of the local nobility fueled by the Marignane family, eminently disliked by the two most influential ministers, Necker and Montmorin, he has no choice but to wheedle votes from that third estate that is so uncongenial to his nature. By his ambition, his cynicism, his dream of the military life, even his libertinism,

*Character in a novel by Duclos.

Mirabeau is an aristocrat to his fingertips. But on January 26, when the brother of advocate Portalis, a young eyewitness with a good memory, describes him walking in the procession that precedes the opening of the estates of Provence (held in the great hall of the Collège Bourbon, the biggest chamber in Aix, its nave hung solid with damasks and tapestries), he'd be glad of a vote from Satan himself.

"He was walking, so to speak, between the nobility and the third estate, last in the line of the order of nobility. His sharp and inquisitive eye ran over the crowd of onlookers and seemed to probe the multitude with his provocative gaze. He carried his head high and tilted upward. His right hand rested upon the pommel of his sword . . . . Part of his thick hair, drawn up and curled over his broad brow, stopped at his ears in heavy curls. The rest, pulled to the back of his head, was gathered inside a large black taffeta bag that floated on his shoulders. There was something imposing in his ugliness, and his face, pitted by smallpox, expressed the energy of a strong will and a soul shaken by passions as changing as they were violent."[3]

He's landed himself in a fine kettle of fish. Two years before, after a solid century of silence imposed by Colbert, the Estates of Provence were authorized, as part of the decentralization process set in motion by Brienne, to meet annually again in order to vote their taxes. This might have looked like liberalization, except that the "enfeoffed nobles" and senior clergy of Aix put a stranglehold on the structure of the Estates by restricting the representation of the third and jealously contriving to protect their own tax exemption rights. The result is that in 1787 and 1788 the King's representatives, and in particular Caraman, the governor, paradoxically collected less tax than in the days of absolutism. In this respect, the position of Provence is "Breton" rather than "Dauphinois" or "Parisian." But here as everywhere else the third is grumbling and has actually held, alongside the hierarchical, closed sittings of the ancient Estates, a few noisy gatherings of its own, if only to prepare for the elections to the Estates General. In churches too small to hold them, there have been meetings of "thirty advocates, as many attorneys, several bourgeois . . . a great many craftsmen, tradespeople, farmers and housekeepers [sic], in all a little over a thousand men."[4]

Part of this little crowd goes to see Mirabeau on January 13 and makes a fuss over him for coming to Aix. He wasn't expecting them so soon and, anxious not to look as though he were trying to be a "people's tribune in spite of myself,"[5] has taken a seat among the nobles, in the "official" Estates, on the strength of a little fief fictitiously ceded to him by his kindly uncle the bailli, to compensate for his father's refusal. During the preliminary meetings of the order of nobility he even achieves a rare exploit, for him: he keeps his mouth shut for eight whole days. "I am going to the meetings, but shall not say a word. That way, they can poison my silence but not my speeches."

He is also in touch with the official representatives of the third estate, however, and two or three progressive nobles, including the mayor of Grasse. Together they get a "protest" document notarized against the first two orders' restrictions of the rights and representation of the third.

Within a few days he has regained his status as "our little mother Mirabeau" for the people of Aix, the nobleman who comes out to the people, the one who was cheered in the streets after losing his trial.* "My arrival has set off an explosion. The third is saying that I have come to be its advocate, crowds form, plans are laid for acclamations, petitions, nonsense, and I am being given the bleak, ephemeral and perilous honor of tribuneship . . . . Between ourselves, the nobility is really frightened,"[6] he can't help writing to his father in spite of everything, like an incurably boastful overgrown kid. But it would take more than the two or three contributions that Gabriel-Honoré makes at public meetings after January 30 to convert the Marquis to the primacy of the third estate.

The son's reasoning: "I ask whether it is just, even in the century in which we are living, that the two orders, which are not the nation, should dominate the whole nation. We can proclaim until we are hoarse that the power of the nation is invested in us; there are 600,000 voices to contradict us."

The father's sarcastic comeback: "From his principles, it follows that the only place in which a legal assembly could be held is the Valley of Jehoshaphat," where a parabiblical tradition convenes the whole of mankind for the Last Judgment.

It's too late for the last rounds of ammunition being fired by cornered nobles in Aix and elsewhere in the form of gibes and witticisms. Mirabeau the elder is a long way away and his day is done, but after January 30 Mirabeau the younger becomes, by virtue of his authority, his obstinacy, and his talent, the interpreter of the people's rights. And *he* is not being witty; he is expressing the anger that is still contained but rising and has begun to heat the streets and markets under the broad-shouldered budding plane trees between the town hall and the Collège Bourbon. Rowdy gatherings form every day to cheer him on, along with Mougins de Roquefort (the mayor of Grasse), and to yell insults at Governor Caraman and even Archbishop Boisgelin, the *président* of the Estates. Every one of Mirabeau's harangues affects the atmosphere in the town, calming and exciting it by turns, because he

---

*For the "Aix trial," in 1783, when Mirabeau was ordered to live apart from Émilie de Marignane and first gained the hearts of the people, see Volume III.

consistently stands at equal removes from demagogy and repression. Mirabeau is not a man to curry favor. He lets the crowd love him but only in order to keep control of it, and he refuses to encourage its intoxication.

In these first days of February, when he is being canonized as the folk hero of Provence, Mirabeau becomes what he has always dreamed of being, politically at least—the man of the middle way. In the past he has been known only for his excesses; now people are going to have to get used to a new image.

January 30. He reveals his arsenal with a speech of great eloquence, sonorous but solid, prepared with a little team of advocates combined with a few intelligent nobles, who are tending to gather around him and have no choice but to acknowledge the mark he is leaving on local events. "I have been, I am, I shall be until death the man of public freedom, the man of the constitution. Woe unto the privileged orders if that means being the man of the people rather than that of the nobles!"[7]

Statements like these are so much boiling oil poured upon the vast majority of the nobles. They get the picture. Too bad if they don't want him in Versailles, they're going to have him anyway—in spite of them, without them. On January 31 Archbishop Boisgelin prudently takes to his bed, to avoid whatever further stones might be cast. The Marquis de La Fare, consul of Aix, takes over the leadership of the hard-core conservatives, who are demanding that Mirabeau simply be expelled from the Estates, "for having, by his incendiary motion, incited the people to open conflict and professed principles that constitute an attack upon the King's authority."[8] Once again they try to treat him as an outcast, the black sheep of the nobility. The acting *président* tries to have him stopped at the door to the chamber in which Mirabeau wants to read out a protest against this renewed ostracism. "Their fright was such that they didn't dare listen to me again," he writes to Comps, his secretary back in Paris. "What have I done that is so culpable? I have desired that my order should be shrewd enough to give today what will infallibly be wrested from it tomorrow."

It would take more than that to keep him from publishing, also at the beginning of February, another undelivered speech, *Sur la représentation illégale de la nation provençale dans ses États actuels,* followed by a *Réponse aux protestations faites au nom des prélats et des possédants . . . contre le discours précédent.*

These essays quickly make the rounds of the larger gatherings, which began on Saturday, the thirty-first, not only in the big market of Aix but in ten other towns from Draguignan to Sisteron. This is a larval agitation, a kind of chronic low fever, rather than the strong periodic bursts that are threatening property and promises in other regions. It's not an uprising, more an attack of Provençal disobedience in which there is still some good humor and a mildly festive air. Beginning on February 1, for instance, groups of peasants, although doubly incapable of having read Mirabeau, firstly because they don't know how to read and secondly because he doesn't speak their language, gather under his windows and shout up to him, offering their services whenever he's there.[9]

Maybe it's this relative affability of the people that inspires one of the most ossified groups of nobles in the realm to attempt a last trial of force. Even though the man who, in less than a month, has become the incarnation of change and progress for Aix now looks like a "leader of the people," the nobles imagine that he is still vulnerable because he's so utterly broke. And it's true that in February Mirabeau's position is buoyed up by nothing firmer than the great wind of poverty—which is known, in Provence, to subside very quickly sometimes. This local conflict would seem to boil down to one apparently simple problem: if the privileged can only mow him down, their quarrels will be resolved more smoothly than elsewhere. It'll be just too bad about him; the powerful people who still hold all the money and offices will be top dogs again and can impose their will even on Necker, even on the King. That's what they think, anyway.

On February 3 Archbishop Boisgelin decides to adjourn the Estates; Monsieur de Caraman posts sentries at the doors of the main public buildings, theoretically to contain the people but actually as a direct threat to one man. Intendant La Tour writes to Necker on the sixth, "The meetings of the Estates would be disrupted by more serious confrontations in their later phases, and by the demands and protests of Monsieur le Comte de Mirabeau, and might be followed by even larger gatherings of people . . . . So we have decided to suspend the Estates."[10]

They go on holding what will later be called "informal meetings," however, in one another's homes, pending an endorsement from Necker, whose hostility toward Mirabeau is no secret to them. On February 8 they take advantage of the time gained to expel Mirabeau definitively from the order of nobility by demolishing the fragile legal basis that has enabled him to sit among them, thanks to his uncle's intermittent benevolence. The Marignanes make this possible, stepping in with a convenient copy of the marriage contract, from which it emerges that if Mirabeau is not officially possessed of his father's estates, he is nothing. So these people, at least, he will never represent. Rejected by his own class, he writes, on February 15, a fifty-six-page *Appel à la nation provençale,* in which he sums up the grounds for his condemnation as follows: "This man who does not hold the same opinions we do is not one of us."[11]

His friends in Aix think that all he has to do now is let things take their course and install himself as "king of the people" in opposition to the conspirators, who, by excluding him, have only consolidated his influence. Let the *Appel à la nation provençale* sink into people's minds and become a sort of manifesto of the province's essential demands: the right to universal suffrage, citizenship for all, equal taxation. As for his election to the Estates General as representative of the third, no other number being available to him, they can trust the government in Paris to impose, in due course, the same rules on the electors in Aix as on the rest of the French. Even if it goes against the grain, Necker is too fair and too committed to the whole operation to make an exception in favor of one local nobility, just to ruin Mirabeau. That a seigneur should be deprived of civic rights enjoyed by mere commoners—that would be the day!

So, patience? But in Mirabeau's life nothing ever happens the way it's supposed to. Around February 15, when the whole town is counting on him, he suddenly vanishes from Aix-en-Provence. His abrupt absence makes almost as big a hole as the hillock heaved up by his presence. Hundreds of people are asking where the devil that devil of a man has gone now. One or two who are close to the horse's mouth finally learn that he's on his way back to Paris as fast as his horses can gallop. But he only "came down" a month ago! Some people wonder if he hasn't been kidnapped, just to put a stop to his irresistible ascension.

No. He's gone under his own volition, to endure one final suspense in his lamentable private affairs that give him no peace until he dies. Once again, there's a sword hanging over his head, and through his own doing. He has to untangle a whole bag of worms he floundered into in Paris two months before; and things in Aix have happened so fast since then that the two poles of his life might as well be two hundred years and thousands of leagues apart.

The person who is cheered on every street corner in Aix has just been burned in Paris; well, if not exactly himself, his best book, the *Histoire secrète de la Cour de Berlin.*

Its publication by the Lejays—anonymously, of course—has raised such a tempest from Versailles to Berlin that Mirabeau finds it expedient not to show himself in Paris, and even less at Court. He hides out in a little country house in the hamlet of Polangis on the banks of the Marne across from the Saint-Maur bridge, with a few of his trustworthy cronies, Panchaud, Lauzun, Dupont de Nemours. One of them is missing, though—Talleyrand—and for good reason.

In itself, the book's publication should have been a good deal, especially for a man with the hounds at his heels who has to find money for his election campaign. The two volumes, in the form of "letters from one Frenchman to another," paint an unvarnished portrait of the last weeks of Frederick the

Great in the summer of 1786, and the first months of his nephew's reign.*

On the borderline between anecdote (occasionally spicy) and high politics, the book is full of gusto and vitality, and its author knows how to use imagery and handle thoughts. Nobody could fail to see that this is a world-class witness, on the outskirts of official diplomacy but used to rubbing elbows with the powerful. He oscillates, curiously, between outlining a plan for an alliance between Prussia and France that would balance the Austrian monopoly of influence and presenting a rather cruel vision of the Court and governors of that same Prussia. King Frederick Wilhelm is shown as narrow-minded, lazy and debauched; the morals of his uncle, Prince Heinrich, are as "particular" as were those of Frederick II; most of the ministers and senior officers are thick-skulled brutes and the French ambassador himself, the Comte d'Esterno, is not let off lightly, being presented as vain and pretentious (from this one detail people in the know recognize the pen of Mirabeau, who had so many run-ins with him). Everything combines to give the book a unique tone, pleasing to the light taste of the French, who have bought twenty thousand copies of it in one month, despite police prohibitions and the thunder of the *Parlement,* which has just symbolically consigned the book to the flames on its great staircase.

In Paris, where Prince Heinrich is visiting, and showing wit enough to shrug, Advocate General Séguier observes, in his usual style, that "today prohibition adds to an author's celebrity, accelerates the sales of his book, doubles its price and gives greater publicity to imposture and calumny."[12] In Versailles, His Excellency Montmorin makes apologies to the ambassador of Prussia. In Berlin, according to d'Esterno himself, "the chief of police sent for all the booksellers in town and notified them that any who should receive the book attributed to the Comte de Mirabeau and fail to turn it over to the authorities at once would be sent to the fortress of Spandau."[13] The King of Prussia himself "stamped his foot and said, 'So that is the kind of person they are, these French who come traveling through my states!'"[14] It looks as though prosecution will be in order for both author and printer, and some are already seeing Mirabeau on the receiving end of yet another *lettre de cachet,* or in the Bastille, or exiled, or worse, notwithstanding his insolent preface to the first edition:

"The letters in this collection were scattered among the miscellaneous papers of a traveler who died last year in an obscure village in the depths of Germany."[15]

But he's got them by the short hairs. How can they haul him into court when they know that these are minutes of the letters he was sending to

---

*For excerpts from these letters, see the description of Frederick II's final illness and death in Volume IV.

Calonne, via Talleyrand, during the two years of his mission in Prussia? Some of the mud would surely splatter the French monarchy. So, no effort is made either to denounce or otherwise harass him. The only damage he suffers is the permanent loss of Talleyrand's friendship. But his trip can't be said to be a total waste of time. The effect of the effort and expense of the long haul from Provence to Paris and back can be distilled into one door, slammed in his face by Montmorin when he requests a hearing in order to justify himself, and a few public or private texts he writes while lurking on the outskirts of Paris in an attempt to disown paternity of the book.

In these, Mirabeau raises cynicism to the dignity of an art. It will be hard to equal him in this field. He gets a superb denial published in the *Journal de Paris:* "I have no knowledge of the book in question. Could credit, cunning slander, the dexterity of perfidy have laid hands on some of the letters that I may and should have written to the ministers of the King? Could someone have thought it amusing, or deemed it useful, to mutilate and falsify them, poison them and make reprehensible additions to them? This book might make it seem that I am evil or insane."[16]

So much for the public denial, but as long as he's wallowing in falsehood, he might as well write to his friend Mauvillon: "You will have heard talk of a *Histoire secrète de la Cour de Berlin,* in which your duke [of Brunswick] is praised to the skies. Many Prussians receive harsh treatment in it. Here, the book has put everyone's head in a spin. The people who wanted to stir up trouble for me have not failed to attribute it to me . . . . For the rest, the book is said to be good. I have not yet read it."[17]

It becomes a little easier to understand why, in refusing to give Mirabeau an audience, Montmorin writes, "I was not aware that there had been any allusion to you in the gazette in connection with the *Histoire secrète de la Cour de Berlin* . . . . If the book is being attributed to you and you have had no share in it, I quite see how pained you must be by it."[18]

Never mind. Mirabeau seems to get a kick out of going too far. Before he leaves Paris, he writes to Mauvillon again: "The disclosure of the *Correspondance secrète,* containing perfidious omissions and scandalous and iniquitous interpolations, is one of the thousand and one tricks that have been played upon me to prevent me from being at my citizen's post."[19]

Then, to top it off, he turns mischief into pure virtue and writes to his secretary: "My dear Comps, how can you ask me to disown a book that I have not read and can hardly say the title of? You ought to have sent it to me, if my friends thought it so pressing for me to disown it. . . . Under the circumstances, I can do no more than authorize you to publish, under my signature and wherever you can, the denial of authorship of a book that I hold to be most certainly reprehensible because the people I most love and esteem condemn it and keenly regret that it should be ascribed to me. Get in touch with M. Panchaud about the drafting of this denial."[20]

And again: "You have no idea of the horrors uttered on the subject of these two books.* I am being called nothing less than a mad dog, the people of Provence must not dream of placing the smallest shred of trust in me. To those who have said this I replied, if I am a mad dog, what better reason to elect me, for then despotism and privilege will die of my bite. . . . I shall be found unworthy of the Estates General, because all my life I have been the proudest foe of every abuse of authority, every prevaricator, every enemy of equality. Patience, once more; time will give justice to all!"[21]

From one world to another, one life to another. Mirabeau returns to Aix even faster than he left it. But what a difference! In the little house at Polangis he was living underground. Here in Provence, in the first days of March, he is triumphant. Meanwhile, the government has unified election rights throughout France: a noble, and *a fortiori* a "degraded" one, can be elected to represent the third estate anywhere in the country. His disappearance has made the people want him more. Provence has been waiting for him as no other man was awaited that month. Mirabeau is the first great popular star in what everybody is now calling the *révolution*. He's almost more surprised than anybody else. The outcast, the sick man, the man burned in effigy in Pontarlier, abducted in Holland, imprisoned in Vincennes, spurned by the Court and ministers, the man who is drowning in debt, loveless, cursed by his father, will experience, on his native ground, that rare fusion produced by the encounter of an individual, a people and a set of circumstances.

Who gave them warning of his return? On March 5, at Lambesc, five leagues before Aix, he's cheered by thousands of people, who make a sort of Palm Sunday procession for him.

Bells ring, fireworks are set off. The local authorities come to greet him as a prince amid shouts of joy.

"*Vive le Comte de Mirabeau!* Long live the father of the fatherland!"[22]

At every stage the crowds rush to his coach, unharness the horses and start pulling it themselves. He's shocked. Not only was he not expecting this, he is also very much aware of the gulf between his real self, his wasted life, and the destiny that is about to be his. If a crowd can catch fire like this for a Mirabeau, before he has done anything to deserve it, how is it going to treat the others? Several witnesses testify that he burst into tears in the

---

*The *Correspondance secrète* and his *Correspondance avec Cerutti,* in which he again publishes letters that were private.

suburbs of Aix upon hearing the fipple flutes and tambourines. He expostulates angrily with people, to stop them harnessing themselves to his coach:

"Friends, men are not made to carry a man, and you are already carrying
too many of them! A people never owes gratitude, because one can never
give it enough! Hate oppression as much as you love your friends, and you
will never be oppressed."[23]

And to whom does he confide, in a mutter, when two hundred craftsmen
of Aix come to greet him as he enters the town, "I see how men became
slaves: by grafting tyranny onto gratitude"? To his friend the advocate Joubert, the only lawyer who would defend him at his separation trial, and who
is waiting to welcome him into his home on the place des Prêcheurs in the
center of town.

But they still have to get there, and the Provençal enthusiasm is almost
homicidal. After the last stage, at Saint-Cannat, the coach has to stop every
quarter of an hour to let him receive delegations of craftsmen, tradesmen,
peasants, all carrying crowns and wreaths of flowers. It's a beautiful day; the
sky is that pale blue it becomes after the mistral has scoured everything clean.
When the travelers reach the top of the Aix hill and the beginning of the
careful descent into town, "they saw floods of people emerging from the
city."[24]

Nobody counts too closely that day, and Mirabeau is complacently informed that there are more than ten thousand citizens on their way to meet
him. That's a fairly steep exaggeration, since the town's total population is
only twenty thousand, but the only thing that matters is that there are
hundreds and thousands of them, deafening him with cheers and bravos.
Some witnesses note that he is far more enthusiastically acclaimed than was
the King's brother, comte "de Provence" though he be, when he toured the
province fifteen years before upon taking possession of his fief. The town
within its stout belt of seventeenth-century ramparts looks like a boiling pot,
between the long chain of purple hills parallel to the Durance and, farther
east, the lofty limestone eminence of Sainte-Victoire, still snow-crowned.

Even before he is clear of the magnificent olive groves, badly damaged
by the recent frosts, and facing the entrance to the town, "which resembles
that of a splendid château formed by an elegant grill, with the Marseilles
road passing outside, which leads to the famous concourse composed of four
rows of trees and lined by two rows of houses, each more handsome than
the last,"[25] he is startled by the sound of those irregular explosions without
which no festivity ever takes place in Provence. They're coming from the
old town, still some distance away, but they're in honor of his servant, who
was sent on ahead.

The main body of the crowd is awaiting him there, at the entrance to the concourse* where they think he'll be staying: "It was lined with people and boxes; his horses went at their best pace to avoid the possible consequences, but all these flocks of people ran after him as fast as their legs would carry them.

"In a twinkling, all the boxes were carried to the place des Prêcheurs. . . . The square was covered with people, a hundred boxes of fireworks were set off, and he stepped down into the arms of the people, to whom the doors of the house had to be thrown open. . . . A harangue, interrupted by cheers, shouts of joy, embraces, all the intoxication of joy and confidence. . . . The director of the theater came to ask him to promise to attend the play that evening; two thousand souls were laying siege to the theater. He said it was impossible. 'Then give me your promise for tomorrow,' he said, 'or I cannot answer for the consequences.' Meanwhile, sixty-nine deliberations of different communities were brought to him, proclaiming their thanks."[26]

The day ends with a huge bonfire that nearly burns down the square.

For the first time in his life, Mirabeau can be said to have come home; he's sleeping with success. All the riots that have been shaking Paris and the provinces since the Day of the Tiles were *against* some person or persons; this is the first one that is *for* someone.

The anonymous author of the account of his return observes that "not one noble dared show his face; and a good thing too."

TALLEYRAND

61

MARCH 15 – APRIL 2, 1789

The Church of Autun, My Spouse

Sunday, March 15. The town of Autun is celebrating, to the peals of its parish churches and the tenor bell of the Cathedral of St. Lazar, all swinging

---

*Today, the cours Mirabeau.

to their fullest stretch. It's still cold as the grave here in the heart of Burgundy, where the fierce winter has hung on longer than in Provence, but a chilly sun beams down, a little after noon, when a solemn procession of cathedral canons, huddled inside their ceremonial robes, marches to the episcopal palace behind cross and holy water.

Flanked by his grand vicars, their new bishop awaits them in cape and rochet "at the upper door." This is his day of enthronement.

At last! Oh, how he has been waiting, and waiting, for this day! At thirty-five, Charles-Maurice de Talleyrand-Périgord officially takes possession, "by divine mercy and the grace of the apostolic Holy See," not only of the bishopric of Autun but of a host of attendant offices and honors as well. Here he is, "first suffragent of the see of Lyons and his provisional substitute if the seat falls vacant, perpetual *président* of the Estates of Burgundy, Comte de Saulieu, Baron d'Issy-l'Évêque, Lucenay, Grosme, Touillon and other places."[1]

As long as he's standing still, he looks splendid in the magnificent panoply of red and gold—the colors of the Holy Spirit—which has been taken out of the cathedral treasure for the occasion. His limp becomes visible only when he moves into his place in the procession. His air, kindly albeit a trifle haughty, the graciously impassive superiority of mien that generations of ancestors of the old nobility have bred into his blood, and the rosy flesh tones of maturity intensified by a long acquaintance with the finer things of life, make him look very much the right man for the part. The phrase "a prince of the church" would seem to have been coined for him, when he speaks the Latin oath:

"I swear on the Holy Gospel and I promise to observe unfailingly and to defend all the privileges, liberties, allowances, immunities, statutes, exemptions, rights and customs of the Church of Autun, my spouse."

The procession re-forms, this time with him in its midst, and leads him, to the chanting of the choirs of St. Lazar, through the steep streets of ancient Gaulish Bibracte, known as Augustodunum after the Roman conquest and finally, by contraction, as Autun, to his nearby cathedral. Ten thousand people crowd inside the old ramparts, among such a forest of sharply contrasting stone walls—from pagan ruins to Christian churches that are now themselves falling into ruin, lengths of wall of totally unknown ancestry or utility, temples of a succession of religions, a decadent Romanesque cathedral with early Gothic additions—that some travelers swear they never saw a muddle to equal it outside the Forum in Rome. Talleyrand may be bringing something a little more up-to-date to the crowd that leans toward him in respectful density as he passes, blessing it as he goes: churchmen, nobles, officers, Knights of St. Louis, magistrates, elders, advocates, doctors, craftsmen, urchins, even nurselings held aloft by their mothers. Because of all the chanting and praying he is not wildly acclaimed, but in their eyes he can read a friendly welcome and feels as though already enthroned by his diocesans before he takes his place, in the name of the good Lord, upon the episcopal throne, there to enter, as the record says, "into the real, actual, corporal and personal possession of the said bishopric, honors, prerogatives, fruits and income of the same." He can sing the *Te Deum* that follows with a sincere and glad heart, especially as his earnings, which he was finding a trifle meager in Paris, have just been supplemented by those of the Abbey of Celles in Poitou, twelve thousand livres a year awarded by the King's gracious pleasure, in addition to the twenty-two thousand a year he gets from Autun and the eighteen thousand he will continue to receive from the Abbey of St. Denis in Rheims; making a total of fifty-two thousand a year.

The service proceeds with the incomparable majesty of the Catholic liturgy, and although a few carping canons may note that Monseigneur is not letter-perfect in his words and gestures, despite the vigilance of a battalion of masters of ceremony who prompt him at every turn, nobody can dispute that his first performance is a success.

Not the triumph of Mirabeau in Aix a week before; but a different layer of France, that of the clergy and the devout, has pushed Talleyrand into the same slot. Already designated by divine right, all he has to do now is be invested by the people's right. And in Versailles they'll just have to make the best of it. At first sight these two men, products of exactly the same caste and harboring very similar failings, would seem to be the exact opposite of each other; but if we take a closer look, we see this is not so. Both of them, in fact, are leaning in the same direction, toward "moderatism."

On this day of his investiture Talleyrand can't have spared many thoughts for his old friend, and has not yet heard about his conquests in Provence. And if Mirabeau, who at least has no pretensions to faith or worship, were lurking behind a pillar in the cathedral, the pious public would surely have heard his loud bray of a laugh. His mind has been made up for the last two years about the "Abbé de Périgord"; he branded Talleyrand with one of his scathing judgments in the days when he was still feigning friendship for him and sending him those famous letters from Prussia:

"The chain of my misfortunes threw me into his hands, and I must still be circumspect in my dealings with his vile, greedy, base and intriguing person; what he needs is mud and money. . . . For money, he would sell his soul and be right to do so, because he would trade his own manure for gold."[2]

What he is expressing there is friendship embittered, which can sometimes be as vicious as embittered love. At bottom, Mirabeau and Talleyrand are made to agree. Neither of them believes in what he professes, namely, human rights for the former, God's rights for the latter. Both of them were miserable as children, Mirabeau because of the big head that caused his father to hate him and Talleyrand because of the clubfoot that made him an outcast in a family of soldiers and politicians. And for both of them there has always been only one absolute: money—Mirabeau because he has never had any, Talleyrand because he can never get enough. Again for both of them, money is primarily the means of satisfying a thirst for power rather than pleasure. They are fellows, comrades, in their love of being seen and noticed and their desire to exert influence. Their differences are of the kind that arise between brothers, but of course those are the worst of all.

On the surface their triumphs, in the month of March 1789, face in totally different directions. Mirabeau comes to the fore in a great spontaneous splash and flurry; Talleyrand, as the culmination of years of patience and a natural progression. Nobody these days could imagine His Grace the Bishop of Autun with a revolutionary heart. He is a name, a fortune, and, now, a function.

A few months later, a young writer named Antoine-Vincent Arnault draws a portrait of him:

"In June 1789, walking around the pond known as *'des Suisses'* at Versailles, I noticed a person lying under a tree who seemed to be deep in meditation, concerned with his own thoughts more than with those of others, although he held a book in his hand. I was struck less by the beauty of his features, although they were not without grace, than by their expression and a particular blend of unconcern and malignity that gave them a unique character, as of an angel's head inhabited by a demon's spirit. He was plainly a man of fashion, one more accustomed to being a center of interest for others than to taking an interest in others himself, a man already weary of the pleasures of this world despite his youth. I should have ascribed his features to some first page or colonel in favor if the hairstyle and bands had not told me they belonged to a churchman, and if the pectoral cross had not proved to me that the churchman was a prelate."[3]

Talleyrand should be able to take a well-earned rest at Versailles after doing his job in the manner of the high clergymen of the day. He performs his bishop's duties for three weeks, the only weeks he spends in Autun in his entire life. If he were not aiming to get elected by his order, there's no indication that he would ever have strayed into the wilds of Burgundy, so far from his pretty house in Bellechasse; probably, like many other titular bishops, he would have considered it sufficient to send a grand vicar to represent him in Burgundy while waiting for some higher position, one more worthy of his ambition: Lyons, or Chartres, and why not Paris? There's really only one subject that interests him, and has for years, and that is politics, at the top level, the politics that govern.*

*His *Mémoires* do not contain a single reference to his passage at Autun, but he does let

Autun may be a little off the main highway, but the appointment comes at the right time. The King, whose duties include the handing out of bishoprics, has been more than a little reluctant to perform them in the case of this man of lofty lineage who has been the agent general of the clergy for the last five years: Louis XVI is known to have a distaste for libertine priests, and Brienne has also been standoffish with Talleyrand, for making common cause with Calonne a little too openly. At the end of 1788 he was becoming the object of sneers and snickers among the Jansenists, and Father Émery, the abrupt and upright superior of the august house of Saint-Sulpice, will stand for no monkey business in matters of virtue. Talleyrand was then within an ace of the first major setback of his life. For a man like him, not to be a bishop at thirty-five was like not getting married for an heiress. But his lieutenant general of a father died in November, on his way back from a tour of inspection of the army, and it so happens that the head of the Talleyrand-Périgord family had been the *menin* [young nobleman attached as companion to a prince of the blood] of the Dauphin, Louis XVI's father— in other words, they played together as children. Fate gave him two days of sufficient clarity of mind to implore the King to appoint his son to Autun, whose former bishop, Marbeuf, had just been transferred to Lyons. Louis XVI is not tough enough to resist a dying man's last wishes, even when the dying man's wife, whose charitable bigotry has always made her son's flesh crawl and who has never forgiven that son for being a cripple, was exhorting the sovereign not to do him any such favor. Louis XVI prefers to err on the side of benevolence: "Madame, it will make him mend his ways!"[4]

So, on November 4, the very day of his father's death, Charles-Maurice became bishop of Autun. His family were less and less fond of him, and none of them came to the little Chapel of Solitude at Saint-Sulpice for the minimal, almost secret, ceremony of consecration. Perhaps Talleyrand thought that would be better than the gibes and smiles and stares he could not have avoided in Paris. Besides, he was a long way from the emotional upheaval of his ordination, which had kept him awake all night ten years before.* Since he has no choice but to be a churchman, then it'll be bishop today and cardinal tomorrow and no nonsense about it.

Even so, Father Émery, the vigilant censor of the ceremony, observes that the color suddenly drains from his former pupil's face as he is being anointed with holy oil, and that at the laying on of hands the new bishop nearly faints.

In Autun, nobody can point to the slightest want of piety or the least

---

fall a significant sentence about the moment he spent as a young Sulpician priest, pondering deeply in front of Richelieu's tomb in the Sorbonne.

*See Volume II.

suspicious association. He still makes one or two mistakes at the high mass on Annunciation Day, March 25, when he insists upon officiating pontifically, but he prudently abstains from performing any other ceremonies. He sticks to the rules of the game closely enough for his priests to think they are electing a good bishop and can make a good representative of him. In that respect, at least, he doesn't have to pretend: if he wants to be well thought of, a prince-bishop in this regime has to be a prince who is also a good administrator of his assets. And for a few days Talleyrand quite likes being the first person of the place, the object of consideration and respectful greeting, whereas he goes almost unnoticed among the throng at Versailles or in Paris. His lordly bearing does the rest. He gives audience to all his grand vicars; he makes appointments to vacant livings; he presides over his council every other day; he arbitrates between regular and secular clergy, he even shows himself in the churches, and in his garden, with a very visible breviary in his hand.

His table is open to all comers on a truly princely scale, and the renown of his cook, whom he brought down from Paris, soon spreads far and wide, in particular as regards one special dish, skate in a black butter sauce, which is greatly appreciated these Lenten days when the butchers are closed except on Sunday. He even plays at stewarding, by rerouting the Paris-Lyons mail coach through Autun so as to have fresh fish delivered three times a week. In reality, this is all part of his election campaign, which he has had carried out in a businesslike manner by a few young Sulpicians sent on from Paris ahead of him. Between November and March, these rather unusual publicity agents have called on most of the parish priests in the diocese, so that when the 209 ecclesiastical electors, representing the clergy of the bailliages of Autun, Montcenis, Semur and Bourbon-Lancy, gather in the little seminary at Autun to hold their meeting, with himself in the chair, the match is over before it begins.

He has plenty of ammunition for his campaign, too: on April 1 he reads them all a profession of faith, modestly entitled *Extrait du Cahier des délibérations du Clergé à Autun,* which is in reality his election platform.[5]

He worked at it over the winter, creaming off the best of what he found in the mass of pamphlets being published in Paris. The contrast between the medieval vocabulary of the ceremonies of his enthronement and the clear-cut style of this text is amusing and striking. There's very little indication in it that its author is a member of the high clergy, but there is some Montesquieu, and some Sieyès too. To hell with his religion! He neither attacks nor defends it; it doesn't concern him. His text is an enumeration of aspirations or, as they will come to be called, grievances, covering every aspect of society. At the meetings, the only use he makes of his religious position is to speak with authority, and he takes full advantage of it to shelve, without even a vote on their publication, a series of other writings produced by a few over-wrought priests of the *philosophe* persuasion who are thundering against the "tyranny" of the arrogant nobility and "the domination of the invasive clergy," roundly damning all sumptuary laws, wanting to send the prelates back to the fields, demanding the sharing out of land, inviting the canons to abandon their prebends to aged and infirm priests, claiming that country priests should be justices of the peace and that abbey treasures should be distributed to the poor, and on and on.

Mirabeau would certainly be the first to be amazed, upon reading Talleyrand's text, to learn how firmly he places himself, like Mirabeau, exactly in the middle of the road. He calls for a freely voted constitution (Talleyrand actually writes "charter"), absolute freedom outside the precincts ruled by law, adoption of the principle of *habeas corpus,* trial by jury, and the reform of criminal procedure. The end of his text is of special value in that it proposes a rigorous and reasonable plan for new taxes to finance the reforms.

On April 2, the day after he reads out his manifesto, Talleyrand is chosen to represent the clergy "by a very large majority and to a general round of applause."[6] Will he celebrate the Easter high mass in his own cathedral, at least? You must be joking. He's elected. On April 12, the very morning of the holy day, he leaves Autun forever.

CARNOT

62

APRIL 3, 1789

He Deserves the Scaffold

On the edge of this late springtime, one of chronology's little tricks brings us a most unlikely encounter with one of the last victims of a *lettre de cachet,* the abolition of which is being called for in so many lists of grievances. For once, it isn't Mirabeau, although he's just had a close shave. Nor is it another of the great *parlement* objectors, or even the princely ones like d'Orléans; their new fame and regional backing has put them out of reach. It's a man whose name is known only to one or two Burgundian Notables and three or four offices in the Ministry of War. It's Carnot.

Who would know, who would believe, that Royal Engineers Captain Lazare-Nicolas-Marguerite Carnot, eighth of the eighteen children (but only the second to survive) of Claude Carnot, notary at Nolay, was about to spend several weeks in prison in Béthune and will have to watch the opening of the long-awaited drama from behind iron bars?

Politics has nothing to do with this; Carnot's life is being sabotaged by a morals charge. It's preposterous. There could be no way of foreseeing such an incident in the quiet existence of a military engineer of modest origins, the only noteworthy feature of whose life thus far has been the award of a prize, on August 2, 1784, by the Academy of Dijon, for his *Éloge de Vauban*.*

Since that day, his existence has been wholly provincial, spent in barracks towns in the north and along the English Channel, with long furloughs in his native Burgundy. There's nothing he doesn't know about counterscarps, bastions and trenches. His one attempt to escape the dreary round of garrisons was the application he made in 1786, on the strength of his brief flash of renown after writing the *Éloge de Vauban,* for transfer to the Engineer Corps in the Windward Islands. And of course, if the all-powerful Prince de Condé, tutelary governor of Burgundy, had been willing to lift a finger—but Lazare Carnot is much too insignificant a person to deserve more than a glance and a compliment from a great seigneur. He does not go to the Windward Islands. The round continues: Cherbourg, Béthune, Arras for a little longer, where he associated with some people of "quality," made up a few songs and met, but did not become intimate with, the two Robespierre brothers and their sister Charlotte. They used to gather at the Société des Rosati, for sessions of tranquil group tedium. The young advocate Maximilien de Robespierre and Captain Lazare Carnot have one thing in common: they both stand out from their surroundings and get themselves noticed, the first for two or three resounding courtroom speeches against privileges and in favor of the poor, and for his defense of the rights of bastards; and the second because of the mildly heretical accents of his *Éloge de Vauban*. The glorious marshal's reputation was not dear to the fans of Louis XIV, and their resentments have been perpetuated from generation to generation.

Robespierre and Carnot showed similar tendencies to criticize established authority, although with a leavening of courtesy and even good humor. They disconcerted the good people of Arras, who couldn't quite figure out what to make of them. Both are aware—one in the world of law and the other in his new concept of warfare, with the accent shifting from standing to mobile artillery—that they have something to say to an audience larger than their immediate circle; but how are they to set about it?

---

*On Carnot's youth and education, his life as a military engineer and the relative success of his *Éloge de Vauban,* see Volume III. In 1789 he is thirty-six.

Carnot has an idea. One of the few oases in the desert of the last five years of his life is a well-reasoned essay called *"Sur la fortification perpendiculaire,"* the object of which is nothing less than to emancipate the kingdom from the policy of motionless firing power; in opposition to other military writers, such as Laclos, Guilbert, even Fourcroy (his own superior officer in Paris), he is introducing the prospect of a great migration of cannons all over the face of Europe.[1]

So Carnot hasn't been bored for nothing during this long period of inactivity and withdrawal into himself, which he has shared with the rest of France since the end of the American war. He has been forging a doctrine of war to fit his own experience. But his adversaries are wrong to imagine that he is an all-out champion of mobile warfare. He will always be convinced, if only out of *esprit de corps,* that France cannot dispense with the fortresses from which fire power leaps like lightning. But fewer soldiers would be mobilized in peacetime, 100,000 instead of twice that number, and there would be a transfer between army and agriculture. "Warfare is the art of preservation *par excellence*; the art of destruction is its abuse. . . . The essence of fortresses is to preserve, not destroy."[2] That also is Carnot. He gets on their nerves, especially Fourcroy's, who is the paragon of artillery conservatives. He is forcing them to think.

Lazare might have gone on theorizing until the end of time, between the shadows of Vauban and Frederick the Great. But year by year, something in the air has made the breach between his qualities, his intelligence, and the seemingly immutable order blanketing France too wide to bridge.

Something in his life had to give.

He's not made of stone. Attractive, pleasant although shy, he has remained a bachelor without wanting to. An officer's career does not entail vows of chastity. But he's not a butterfly either. Almost every year he has gone back to Dijon or Nolay to see a family of friends, the Bouillets, respectable small folks who pretend to more nobility than they possess and whose chief has himself called "chevalier." This Carnot from the land of great wines and old stones, whose destiny is being circumscribed by retrenchments, is a stalwart, tenacious, faithful fellow. In 1789, he has been "walking out" with Ursule de Bouillet* for eight years, waiting for her hand to be given to him. The girl's mother, Anne Calon, daughter of a Dijon advocate, died a while back, and Lazare's own mother died on May 13, 1788. But the rest of her family, starting with the "chevalier," are continuing to inflict a humiliating purgatory upon a man who is fully mature. Ursule herself, having no mind of her own, has helped to impose these eight years of maybe-yes-maybe-no,

*Born October 25, 1761.

and his pride, more than his passion, is beginning to be fed up with it. The Bouillets would be content to try Lazare's patience for another eight or ten years. For them he is neither poor and worthless enough to be sent packing, nor rich and high-ranking enough to be accepted. His life heretofore has been shaped like a waiting room, and this winter, during his latest furlough, he knocks its walls down.

Her mother's death, the growing freedom given to Ursule and her older sister Thérèse, an accomplice and active abettor, and those long evenings in the provinces during which people mistakenly suppose that nothing ever happens, all helped them to cross the last barrier some time ago, and almost openly. Since Christmas 1788 they have been lovers, to the satisfaction, Lazare later affirms, of Ursule, whom he calls by the pet name Nanette. For Carnot this is a minor victory but also a promise of better things to come, and thus far life has not been overgenerous to him in this respect. Last winter it also seemed to him that "chevalier" de Bouillet was behaving more indulgently and that "by paying so little heed to his daughter's supervision, he was transferring responsibility for her to Carnot; the behavior of Mademoiselle Calon [Thérèse] was the same."[3]

So, wedding bells any day now? Some lively village nuptials in Nolay?

Oh, no. An earthquake. Tragicomedy, or just plain comedy?

On February 14 Lazare is sitting peacefully at home with his family in Nolay when he learns, almost incidentally, that Ursule is about to celebrate her marriage to—another chevalier, real or fictitious, named Morel de Duesme, a captain in the Beauvaisis regiment. His heart gives a leap and he races off to Dijon as feverishly as all calm people do when they lose their grip. It's high time. According to Bouillet *père,* "the marriage contract was signed on February fourteenth, the banns posted on the fifteenth, the dispensations* granted by the Bishop of Dijon, who was to give the nuptial blessing on the twenty-third, and all the necessary expenses put in hand."[4]

That same Chevalier de Bouillet is about to see his pleasing edifice shattered by Carnot's blows.

Nobody can say he was expecting it, although the Bouillets' rush to conclude this other, unexpected marriage seems likely to have been prompted by occurrences that winter. If they don't want Lazare and Ursule to get married, then it's time they separated them for good.

But their plan misfires badly. All Burgundy is filled with the lamentations of the Chevalier de Bouillet and Advocate de Calon, Ursule's maternal uncle:

"Everything was broken off and changed, and the most heartrending despair followed the sweet, pure joy that had reigned in every heart. Ma-

---

*Meaning the customary waiving of a waiting period, often granted to notables upon payment of alms. Once these people make up their minds to marry, they're in a terrible hurry.

demoiselle de Bouillet,* shrouded in the deepest grief, is in such a condition that her very life is in danger.

"In short, this is the result of the crime of perfidy that Monsieur Carnot has shamelessly committed."

So what has he done, this fiend? Again, according to Calon, on "Thursday, February 19, he set out from Nolay, where his father is notary; the next day at seven in the morning, upon reaching Dijon, he went to the Chevalier de Duesme . . . , and, his eyes glittering with anger, and his hand upon the hilt of his sword, said to him, 'I have learned, sir, that you have pretensions to the hand of Mademoiselle de Bouillet, I have come to tell you that I have more pretensions than you,' and thereupon gave him twelve or fifteen letters written by the young woman. 'Should you persist in wishing to marry her even so, it will be your life or mine. That is the price.' Then he made the Chevalier de Duesme promise, upon that very sword that should hear naught but oaths of honor, that he would return the letters after reading them. Carnot's rage next took him to the door of the Chevalier de Bouillet, where he handed in a paper addressed to Ursule, in which he told her, 'I have just learned of your marriage; the only means I had of preventing it was your letters, and I am using them to ruin you.' "[5]

A nice mess. Carnot almost never talks about those hours,† which he can't have been too proud of once his blood pressure is back to normal. He was acting with the reflexes of an injured animal, not as a man of honor. However, although he doesn't get Ursule for himself, he makes sure nobody else gets her either. Morel de Duesme has virtually fled, incensed at having been betrothed in such a rush to a young woman whose virtue was so flimsily guaranteed. That's one marriage that will not take place. Morel de Duesme must have been in a hurry himself, however, because hardly a month after the scandal breaks he marries another local heiress named Barbuat de Palaiseau.‡

Meanwhile, the hilly little district between Dijon and Nolay, where the Chevalier de Bouillet is hugging the walls and not daring to show his face in broad daylight, has been thoroughly shaken up by these juicy scandals. He sticks to the forced separation of his daughter and Lazare, and neither of them, in all likelihood, asks him to change his mind. They don't try to

---

*That's how the uncle speaks of his own niece, in his letter complaining to the Minister of War.

†His first biographer was his son Hippolyte, who doesn't dwell on them either. As we shall see, Lazare gave only one full explanation of his conduct, in a letter to his family.

‡Ursule de Bouillet, poor thing, floats some time longer on the stagnant waters of spinsterdom and doesn't marry until 1790—to a Monsieur de Malherbe—whereas Carnot, duly scalded, weds a northern girl, not a Burgundian, named Sophie Dupont, the daughter of an army paymaster, in May 1791 while he's stationed at Saint-Omer.

meet again. But the Bouillets and Calons institute punitive proceedings against the ill-bred boor, partly out of anger, partly seeking revenge and the restoration of their prestige in the region, and even more for reasons of security. Because in the course of his altercations with Morel de Duesme and the elder Bouillet, on February 19 and 20, Carnot hints that he has other letters written by the young woman and will make them public if the Duesme wedding plans are not canceled at once. This is pure blackmail, but he has gone too far to withdraw. Ursule must have had a pretty hot pen, too, since her family is purple with anguish at the thought of her letters passing from hand to hand in Dijon next month, when the bulk of the Burgundian nobles gather, as they are doing all over France, for the assemblies from which delegates to the Estates General are being elected. Outraged and outrageous, Lazare's got them under his thumb. The only way to make him let go is to get his supreme superior, the Minister of War, to take action.

There follow two plaintive and declamatory appeals to Monsieur de Puységur (on February 28 and March 2) from Calon, "cloak bearer to the King,* brother-in-law of the Chevalier de Bouillet and uncle of Mademoiselle de Bouillet . . . , authorized by them and by his own family to demand justice from the minister against Monsieur Carnot."[6]

To get some action in these proceedings and prevent them from sinking to the bottom of the piles of paper mounting up around a government that has a great deal else on its desk just then, Calon goes up to his Paris residence in the Marais and sends his complaints to Versailles by special messenger.

Ordinarily, Puységur is not too hard on officers with good records, especially as trivial morals offenses are as common as spurs in garrison towns. But this is no time for even a minister to incur the ill will of an advocate who carries weight in the Dijon Estates and is simultaneously and relentlessly firing off rounds of vociferous charges, not only at himself but at six camp marshals and the heads of the main departments of his ministry, against a mere captain in the engineers, the son of a country notary, a "traitor who, without a qualm, went to the extremity of blindest fury to plunge his dagger into the breast of the victim of his deceit and then debase her by the most scandalous outburst."

Between Calon and Puységur, the little lord and the great, the caste network functions, even on the eve of the Estates General, in this kingdom in which it is not good for a commoner to get himself accused of trying to

---

*In the old monarchy, this literally meant the equerry who carried some of the King's clothes in processions; by extension, it became something like the "captaincies of hunts" or honorary secretaryships—an ennobling title that was often purchased from a distance. Calon becomes a representative of the nobility at the Estates General.

force his way into a noble family. The whole shaky scaffolding of the charge against the "monster," described as having "an eye glittering with wrath, foaming at the mouth in rage, laying his hand upon the hilt of his sword and using the tones of a hired assassin," rests upon the allegation that he meant to seduce Ursule and then marry her, after breaking into the house as it were. Advocate or no, Calon actually tells the minister that he "deserves the scaffold." Also that he is "degraded by his misdeeds, debased in his own eyes, unworthy to wear uniform . . . , incapable of serving King and Fatherland."

He winds up his diatribe with "we therefore trust, Monseigneur, that you will order this person, on behalf of the King, to restore whatever letters he may have to Mademoiselle de Bouillet, in a sealed packet."

A few years earlier, and depending on the mood of the minister or King, such an attack upon a man with no better defense than his ability and skills could have meant, at best, the end of his career and expulsion from the army, at worst, years in prison. It doesn't go that far now, but Carnot, who is already starting to feel the backlash of his punitive expedition to Dijon, is nevertheless stunned by the severity of the penalty inflicted upon him.

He speaks his mind on the matter a few months later, when he has recovered his breath and taste for life.* He was expecting his superiors to let him off the hook, especially as he had quietly returned the letters to Ursule the first time he was asked to do so, through the agency of the Marquis de La Tour du Pin, the commanding officer in Burgundy. His persecutors mistakenly suspect him of keeping a few of them back, however, and one or two of the minister's advisers, who are a little jealous of his *Éloge de Vauban,* manage to blacken his name in Versailles—what an excellent opportunity to put that fool of an engineer who thinks too much in his place.

"In Dijon I was ordered to return to my garrison [at Béthune] immediately, and I left. On my way through Paris I learned that the minister, having received letters from Calon, had called together the generals of the Engineer Corps and asked them to settle the matter. I was at daggers drawn with the most important of those officers [Fourcroy in particular], respecting our attitudes toward our profession. The council wanted to break me . . . ; so that it was almost a sort of pardon, made at the behest of Monsieur de La Tour du Pin . . . , when the minister only issued a *lettre de cachet* against me, whereby I was to remain for two months in the military prisons of Béthune."[7]

Once again, Carnot proves that resigned repentance is not his strong point. Informed of the decision by "the camp marshal commanding the Engineer Corps in Flanders," who finally tells him exactly what he is accused

---

*In a letter to a female cousin, November 28, 1789.

of, he flies off the handle again. The year 1789 certainly seems to be the springtime of his wrath. The Flanders tantrum echoes the one in Burgundy, and at first he's quite proud of it too:

"As he was awaiting my humble thanks, I replied with these shattering words: 'How is it, sir, that among so many generals honored by the minister's confidence there should not have been one who thought to point out that people are not convicted without first being heard? The paper on which you have based your irregular decision is a tissue of impostures. You are guilty of failing to verify your facts. Furthermore, this is a purely civil matter and no concern of yours.' "

His feelings relieved by this outburst, he goes to Béthune, where the Comte de Beaulincourt, commanding officer of the garrison, gives him what might be called the honors of war: a dinner and a supper "in high society" and the best rooms in the fortress in which he is to remain under arrest, on his own word and with no supervision, for the term of his punishment—two months, during which he "savors the satisfaction of seeing how keenly everyone was interested in my case." He takes advantage of his arrest to bombard the authorities with a series of memorials protesting his innocence, using arguments far more cogent and solid than any the Bouillets and Calons could produce.

With tranquil fury Carnot plows the field of his defense. No, he showed Ursule's letters to nobody except Morel de Duesme, and it was Duesme who, shocked and angry, had passages from them read out in the town; no, Ursule is not a minor, and she had promised to marry him as soon as she was legally of age; the other letters from her that he was keeping were not indecent but reiterated that promise "a million times, in the least equivocal and most innocent manner." By compelling him to hand them over to his superiors they had deprived him of documents on which he might have based a lawsuit for the damage he suffered as a result of the broken promise.

He is probably bluffing a little. His comrades do stand by him, though, and his popularity is firmly established in Béthune and thereabouts from the day of his "incarceration," to such a degree that some people swear he could have been a candidate for election to the Estates General for the third estate if this persecution had taken place a month earlier; but Lazare Carnot is still a very medium-sized fish in a very small pond, a hero of persecution by the great and powerful, who, he believes, can still decide the fate of a military man. Will they really give up the idea of running him out of the army once the Estates General are over? Throughout the country, plans are already being laid to settle scores when that moment comes, and he feels so unsure of the future that he writes to the minister of the navy, just in case, asking if he might be transferred to that branch of the forces. Carnot's two wounds, one to his heart and the other to his pride, bleed for a long time to come, and with the signature of a *lettre de cachet* on April 3, by the King, he finds himself dissociated from human society:

"In the King's name, His Majesty hereby orders Monsieur Lazare-Nicolas-Marguerite Carnot, captain in the Royal Engineer Corps, to go, upon taking cognizance of this order, to the military prison of Béthune, where he will be admitted pursuant to the letter that His Majesty has written to the officer commanding in that place, most expressly forbidding him to leave it until further orders shall come from His Majesty, under pain of disobedience.

"Done at Versailles, April 3, 1789.

"Louis."[8]

Two months of patience awaiting his release that, he finally understands from the scraps he gleans through the grapevine, will end with his pardon by his superiors. But a rumble inside him continues. "So it will not be until next winter that I can show those curs that I have not been thrown out. . . .

"There, dear cousin, is a summary of my tale. I thank you for your kind offer of lodgings [in Dijon]. I shall take advantage of it to show these mad dogs that I have not been expelled."[9]

Curs? Mad dogs? For the time being, an angry Carnot is not thinking any further than the Bouillets and the Calons.

MIRABEAU

63

APRIL 6, 1789

I Was Obeyed Like a Beloved Father

Paris–Aix, Aix–Marseilles, Marseilles–Aix, Aix–Marseilles, Marseilles–Aix, Aix–Paris . . . At the end of March and beginning of April 1789 Mirabeau's life looks like that of a marathon runner in training. One wonders if he isn't sleeping on horseback at times; and the man turning in this performance is undermined and vitiated, his nerves are frazzled, and he's not even doing it deliberately; but he emerges the winner.

The tumult of his welcome back to Aix has settled into a steady fizz around the home of his friend Joubert. Deputations of every description file past, all wanting him to bear witness to their rising exasperation: there is the urban "little third estate," angered by the alliance between the "big third estate" and the privileged; but also, beyond the whole of the middle class, there are the corporations of craftsmen. In this region of perpetual invention and creation, stimulated by constant competition from producers in Venice and Naples, Barcelona and Palermo, even Turkey, whose cargoes are piling up on the wharves of Marseilles, there are many of them: hatmakers and painters, sculptors and gilders, tinsmiths and coopers, mirrormakers and coachmakers, sailmakers and potters, tailors and fishmongers, butchers and carpenters. They total more than 300,000 people, all of whom feel they can endure no more. The problem is the same for the peasants, who can no longer sell their wine except when they're forced to sell it at a loss, and for the stockbreeders, who have to pay a fee for every sheep, ewe, lamb, goat and kid at every tollhouse before they enter the towns, in which the purchasing power is so low that they aren't sure to sell their stock.

On top of all that, the millers and bakers of Provence are subjected to a refined system of indirect taxation on flour called the *piquet*, the proceeds from which go to a small number of anonymous and ubiquitous *fermiers*, whose abolition is being called for in every list of grievances. But the first two orders are opposing the use of these lists by the future representatives. When Mirabeau gets back to Aix, it becomes easier to understand his reticence in the face of the people's enthusiasm. True, he is plainly going to be able to get himself elected, but as a representative of a region in which "the cost of labor is too high; industry is shutting all the doors of its outlets; penury is widespread; the poor are dying off by thousands in the hospices; despair is driving others to crime."[1]

What is the point of all these Messieurs assembling to elect representatives to the Estates General, when most of the people who count in the region have made it very clear that exactly nothing will be changed as a result? Too much hope is turning into too much indignation.

In the first half of February, there was a rumor in Marseilles that the people were going to revolt for an allowance on bread and meat, if nothing else. M. de La Tour, First *Président* of the Provence *parlement*, wrote in his memoirs that "the native population, mingled with an assortment of foreigners, chiefly Genoese, Neapolitan and Catalonian sailors, were even talking of firing the ships in the port."[2]

A letter is picked up a month later by the fork of the postal censorship office, written by a lesser personage, a trader named Joseph Amelin: "At the end of February we should certainly have had a revolt in this town, because of the local mayors and consuls who, not content with looting the people for thirty years and more, wanted to raise the price of bread and meat again."[3]

Why the conditional tense? Because in the meantime Mirabeau comes back, to make an attempt of which he fails to measure either the scope or the folly until March 16: with no qualifications and no resources other than his spectacular overnight popularity, he tries to interpose himself between a people who are counting on him for everything and the rigid narrow-mindedness of the privileged.

At first he imagines that all he'll have to do in the coming elections is choose between Aix and Marseilles, and can in fact put off a final choice until the elections are over, because under Necker's regulations candidates can stand for election for whichever order wants them in more than one constituency, provided they opt for a single one in the event of their being elected to represent several places at the same time. Everything indicates that Mirabeau should stand for the third estate in Aix, where he is already so well known. Better than he wants to be, perhaps. The nobles of that town loathe him and he returns their loathing with interest; and he's been told that Marseilles may be able to offer something fresh and new despite its commonalty, which is a drawback by comparison with elitist Aix.

It's worth a second look. On Monday, March 16, he covers the eight-odd leagues separating the two towns and reaches his new hunting ground that evening. It looks good. The town comes out to meet him like a blushing bride. He's still a little overwhelmed the next day when, according to eye-witnesses, the busiest trading town in the south of France really does give itself to him before he's had time to ask it for anything. He stays at the Hôtel des Ambassadeurs on rue de Beauvau; its windows are hung with banners of every hue and size, borrowed from ships in port. He has a hard time getting to sleep because of the ruckus, and it's worse the next day. Mirabeau treats himself to a description of certain aspects of this peaceful conquest in a letter to the Comte de Caraman, one of his cordial enemies:

"Picture to yourself, Monsieur le Comte, 120,000 people in the streets of Marseilles,* the whole town, so busy and industrious, losing a day's work; spaces at the windows hired out for one or two louis, and as much for horses; my coach covered with palm fronds, laurel and olive branches; people kissing the wheels; women holding their children up to me; 120,000 voices, from cabin boys to millionaires, cheering and shouting '*Vive le Roi!*' and four or five hundred youths from the best families in town riding before me, three hundred carriages behind."[4]

"We deem it a most extraordinary piece of good fortune that there was not a single mishap. A host of people followed Monsieur de Mirabeau in vehicles, on horseback and on foot. . . . The people look upon him as their

---

*What an optimist! That is roughly the total population of the town.

savior and father and are counting upon his concern and efforts to lower the prices of essential foodstuffs."[5]

All day Tuesday and all day Wednesday he walks around like a conquering general, up and down the big town with its fifteen thousand houses and through the port where four thousand ships anchor every year. He is shown the Exchange, which has caryatids carved by Puget; he is made to hear a sample of the ring of the bells and the drums that announce its sittings; he is welcomed almost as an honorary canon to the cathedral church, "the oldest of the Gauls."[6] One wonders if he has time, while touring the port, to glance out to the isle of the Château d'If, where he was imprisoned fourteen years before.

He goes to the theater, where the military commander, on his own initiative, orders the Vexin regimental band, lit by sixty torches, to play a special salute to him when he enters. As an additional homage, he is assigned two young and pretty Marseillaises of good family to sit beside him—Mademoiselle Noble on his left and Mademoiselle Thiers* on his right.

He asks them if they like the play. Mademoiselle Noble is speechless, but Mademoiselle Thiers gallantly replies, "What we like most is for both of us to be in the company of the bourgeois gentleman."[7]

The authorities begin to worry. The presence of this colossal nuisance could send the people into an uncontrollable state of excitement. Beginning on the nineteenth, the experience becomes one of those mixtures of heady delight and cliff-hanging nerve that appear to be his specialty. After such manifestations of mass infatuation it seems a foregone conclusion that he will outdistance everyone in the elections; but now he learns that a man of national stature, one whose reputation has been established for many years, is almost certainly going to stand for the same order: Abbé Raynal himself, the famous author of the *Histoire des Deux Indes*, who has made a discreet comeback after the seven years of exile forced upon him by Diderot's "aggravated" edition of his great work. Taking advantage of Necker's liberal policies, looking for a springboard that could propel him into a position as founding father of a new France, here he is again.

Just in case, Mirabeau immediately writes and publishes an anonymous pamphlet that might be used as his electoral platform for Marseilles and in which he leaves no room for any other fans to glorify his efforts. Who else could reach such heights of modesty in self-portrayal as we read in this *Lettre d'un citoyen de Marseille à un de ses amis sur Monsieur de Mirabeau et l'abbé Raynal?*

After a cursory salute to the latter, he grows positively intoxicated with himself. He sketches the main lines of his literary career and points out that

---

*The future aunt of Adolphe Thiers, who tells the story later.

in Prussia he became "the organ of the people, the farmer, the merchant, the soldier. . . . For fifteen years, he has been inditing, in works that will endure as long as bronze and brass, the most sacred rights of man, liberty and equality. . . . Provence was enslaved, the Comte de Mirabeau came and restored its freedom. Using the national Estates as a pretext, the aristocracy of the nobility was crushing the commons; he brought down this Gothic edifice, and equality and liberty will shortly be the sole foundations of a new constitution."[8]

The windup is Homeric, almost in the literal sense of the word: "Lastly, this good citizen is also the most eloquent man of his century; his voice dominates in public assemblies as thunder outroars the howl of the sea; his courage is more arresting even than his talents; there exists no human agency that can force him to abandon a principle."[9]

He thinks he's made such good use of his time in Marseilles that he departs on March 20, leaving his candidacy to finish cooking by itself, with or without Raynal's.* It may be that the very vehemence of the Marseillaises' surge in his direction has given him pause and that he has had a premonition of its imminent metamorphosis into fury.

Whence the sharpness of his exchange with the Comte de Caraman. To the man who has just drawn him so delirious a picture of his stay in Marseilles, the military commander of Provence sourly replies, "You are too fond of order not to feel the consequence of such a multitude of gatherings at a time when the most terrifying agitation prevails. You can give no greater proof of your love for the King than to calm people's minds."[10]

Mirabeau is in no mood to put up with a scolding. On March 22 he retorts:

"The general discontent that you qualify as agitation has arisen on grounds too notorious to leave you in any doubt.

"Firstly, the people are starving to death; there is one ground.

"The main representatives of authority in the province are accused of highway robbery in wheat, over a span of forty years; there is another ground."[11]

Acting on what has become a sort of reflex in the last few months, he then publishes and circulates this exchange of letters in Aix and Marseilles.

So, for ten days, he rocks back and forth from euphoria to provocation.

Marseilles, Monday, March 23: first combustion point, a bald level space at the end of Meilhan Boulevard, if you're coming from the sea, which is

---

*Raynal is not anxious to run the risk of a second exile, and is so affected by the hullabaloo in Provence that he decides not to run for election.

known as the Saint-Michel Plateau or, more simply, the "plains." Gatherings
of all kinds take place there, it's where the Marseillaises launched their first
aerostats. Today, five to seven hundred angry men and women assemble
there in the afternoon, most of them armed with sticks, a few carrying guns.
They're out to get a poor fellow named Rebuffet, an *adjudicataire* or wholesale
butchery administrator who has been accused of pushing prices up and confiscating meat to sell for personal profit. Some friends have managed to warn
him, and he and his wife have just fled in disguise.

The rioters decide to demolish his house. The only thing that stops them
from razing it to the ground is a small group of brave young men from the
"lower third estate" who boldly try to calm them. Hereafter Marseilles is
inhabited by two separate but conjoined whirlwinds: the "little people" on
the rampage, and the *petits bourgeois,* with a few more sophisticated leaders
who know how to make use of the uprising and channel it to their own ends.
One of these is a stevedore named Armand, who roars out to the crowd that,
starting tomorrow, the price of meat will be seven sous a pound instead of
ten. The danger is considerable: the whole crowd surges to the town hall,
where the mayor, aldermen and many of the wealthy bourgeois are meeting
in preparation for the next day's elections and are now summoned by nearly
two thousand people to confirm the new prices. What else can they do?
According to a timeworn tradition, no military forces can enter Marseilles
except on the King's express orders. At seven in the evening the municipal
authorities give way and issue a decision setting the price of mutton at seven
sous, beef at six, and bread at two sous a pound. The town criers are dispatched to the street crossings to announce the news and the storm subsides,
with an occasional flare-up around the homes of the most unpopular dignitaries.[12]

During the night the Comte de Caraman turns up, with the few soldiers
custom allows him for personal protection. He finds the atmosphere so
unhealthy that he promptly leaves again for Aix, after advising the mayor
and first alderman to flee, which they immediately do, to Hyères.

Caraman having explained away his faintheartedness as a wish to let
Marseilles calm down "and the evil be cured by the inhabitants," 100,000
people have now been abandoned to themselves. On the morning of the
twenty-fourth, although essential foodstuffs are distributed at the promised
lower prices, groups gather anew, less numerous but more threatening than
before; they finish off the demolition of the Rebuffet house and lay a kind
of siege to the few minor but courageous magistrates who have remained in
the town hall.

In the afternoon, the most resolute "young liberals" decide to meet in
the main room of the Arquier Tavern on Meilhan Boulevard. At the insti-

gation of stevedore Armand and Jean-François Lieutaud, a young ironmonger who is described as "bourgeois" in official papers and who seems to have energy and influence, they decide to form themselves into a militia. Could they have succeeded in controlling the situation if the news of Mirabeau's return hadn't spread like wildfire?

Having organized themselves into several units, the youths immediately name one the Mirabeau Company. They go to the town hall in a picturesque and disorganized procession, their only uniform being a red feather in their hats. There they meet the authorities, who have recovered their courage and are marching ahead of them in gowns and hoods, preceded by the town criers and guarded only by the stevedores' corporation. Everybody proceeds to hug everybody else as the people, now quiet, look on, unaware that they have just witnessed the spontaneous creation of the first National Guard of France.

Responsibility for keeping order, which has escaped from the hands of an evanescent nobility, is taken over by the bourgeoisie of Marseilles.

No long speeches to the crowd, no time wasted in gesticulations. Mirabeau pitches camp in one of the rooms and communicates with the crowd through a score of the new militiamen, the most sensible and willing, whom he spots with a shrewd eye.

In a few hours, and without the slightest authorization or qualification, he does the work of the vanished intendant and military commander alike. He orders wheat distributed the next day, sets up a committee of twelve bourgeois to serve as a provisional municipal government, organizes patrols in all districts and finds time to write a short, somewhat scornful note to allay the fears of the Comte de Caraman, whom he met going the other way as he came into town. Nobody can ever reproach him for neglecting the King's representatives.

On the morning of the twenty-fifth he gets the bishop, Monseigneur du Belloi, to order the priests in every parish to call their flocks together and urge them to remain calm. In this they are so successful, invoking the name of Mirabeau, that on March 26 he can begin to act like a statesman, by taking the risk of reversing the economic measures adopted four days before.

Nobody else could have done that. Four days after the spectacular drop in prices, Mirabeau pushes through a decision raising the price of bread and meat by one or two sous. It takes a whole afternoon of debate by the municipal council, representatives of the different corporations and even a few members of the clergy and nobility, who are beginning to reemerge. The mere fact of Mirabeau's presence (he's careful not to take the chair and simply gives his opinion from his seat) is enough to change the very soul of the discussion. Owing to a chronic lack of organization, one of the biggest towns in France has a scant week's supply of provisions on hand, especially since this last extremely harsh winter. If the price is too low, people will grab up everything. Wagons are already creaking hurriedly up to the storehouses to buy two weeks' worth of wine and flour, but the bakers in the center of the town have nothing to bake. The only way to stave off famine is to raise the prices to a reasonable level, an average of the rates obtaining in the rest of the country.

Yes, but how are we supposed to explain this to the people, who were quieted three days before by the announcement that prices were going down? Mirabeau then gives a fine example of what thoughtful communication between authorities and public opinion can achieve:

"The bourgeois patrols took responsibility for everything. . . . Hired applauders were placed everywhere, to stimulate public joy. Moreover, I took the very wise precaution of asking the leaders of the bourgeois patrols to make the proclamation. In any other circumstances it would have been dangerous to attempt a crisis at half past eight in the evening; but I thought it even more dangerous to allow people's minds to turn in a different direction. Public notice was therefore given everywhere by torchlight, and cheered everywhere in the streets, from the balconies and at the windows, and the people were more grateful for having obtained a moderate price, that is, the real price of the thing, than for a lower price which they knew well enough could not last. People only want, and must have, reasonable things; governments will have made some progress when they understand that."

He prolongs the impact of this strange night by a little self-indulgence, sending people out to post all over town an *Avis de Mirabeau au peuple de Marseilles*,[13] in which he delivers a succinct lecture in political economy to thousands of people who, only four days before, were aware of only one thing—rage at paying one sou too much for their food.

He has no time to enjoy his success in Marseilles. A few hours of rest, and he learns that most of the rest of Provence is burning.

While Marseilles was aboil, so was Toulon, fifteen leagues away. The scenario there is the same, and the process is also the same, from penury to fury at the contempt of penury expressed by the great. The three days of rioting in Toulon are more violent, more dangerous than in Marseilles, where, paradoxically, the absence of troops kept people from feeling that they were being driven to the wall. Toulon, on the other hand, is an army town, although only half the size of Marseilles. Almost four thousand soldiers guard the Arsenal, where half the King's ships are built. There the rioters collide with the serried ranks of the men of the Dauphiné regiment. A large number of workers in the Arsenal join the peasants and craftsmen and threaten to set fire to it. Monsieur de Coincy, in command of the land army, is old and ailing, while Commander Albert de Rioms, the chief naval officer, is able and intelligent, but both of them are paralyzed by the orders that Necker has issued to military chiefs all over France to follow in the event of uprisings: passive resistance but no damage, and no firearms save in extreme cases.

Albert de Rioms has sense, and a few lines from him to his minister sum up the whole situation: "We ought to have foreseen the effects of the fermentation caused by the obstinacy of the enfeoffed lords in upholding the Provençal constitution, . . . thereby bringing the whole province to revolt; the peasants saw their lords as harsh men who, in all kinds of ways, were trying to oppose the good that the King wants to do for them; unfortunate circumstances, such as a long and harsh winter, the high cost of provisions of all sorts, and the loss of employment resulting from it, have helped to make the people more apt to flare up. And that is how, almost instantaneously, rebellion has broken out in the four corners of the province."[14]

A good analysis, coupled with a very cool head. For two days Albert de Rioms strives hard to keep the crowd from massacring the mayor, a few of the municipal authorities, some Arsenal officers, and above all the Bishop of Toulon, Elléon de Castellane, who has made himself conspicuous in the last two years by his hostility to change of any kind and his defense of the high clergy. Rioms contrives to hide the prelate inside his cathedral but is unable to prevent the looting of the episcopal residence, the slaughter of his horses and demolition of his carriage.

Order is restored on the twenty-fourth by a demagogical announcement of a price reduction and a loan of twenty thousand écus made to Rioms by a Monsieur Mallard, a progressive and wealthy bourgeois. The money is used to pay the Arsenal workers, who have had no wages since January. Soldiers patrol the town, showing no zeal but doing their duty, and peace and quiet gradually return.

The rest of the province is in the throes of a series of small-town jacqueries, which promise the best and unleash the worst, but always in relation to the electoral assemblies. At La Seyne, the seneschalsy judge opposes the third-estate electors; the people nearly dismember him. At Peynier, 150 employees from the soap works besiege the local seigneur, an octogenarian marquis, in his château, and force him to relinquish his seigneurial rights in front of a notary, whom they drag before him with knocking knees. At Salernes, peasants attack the home of the steward of the Marquis de Gallifet (the friend of Mirabeau's Émilie), take eight thousand livres in ransom money from him and drive their flocks to graze in his wheatfields. At Aups another noble, Brouilhomy de Montferrat, fires upon his assailants: he is killed and hacked to pieces on the spot. At Solliès the Marquis de Forbin has his mills and château destroyed. The Bishop of Riez looks on while piles of faggots, or rather brushwood, are heaped around his residence, and saves it by paying fifty thousand livres on the spot, but he cannot stop the mob from making a bonfire of his archives. On March 25 the larger town of Hyères is invaded by a crowd of peasants from La Crau, who destroy the buildings of the Ferme or tax collection agency, then the town hall and, after emptying it, the wheat storehouse. Similar scenes, give or take a few details, are enacted at Barjols, Brignoles, St. Maximin, Le Bausset, Le Luc and elsewhere, until, following the example of Marseilles, the bourgeois who have stayed put and not incurred the hatred of the peasants or laborers manage to set up militias and impose order. Their task is facilitated by the resumption of the electoral process, which has lost none of its importance in the public eye. The news of Mirabeau's election extinguishes the dying embers of the fire; he, meanwhile, imagining that he has won the day in Marseilles, finds that he has worse to face in Aix. There, too, blood has been shed.

Almost as soon as he turned his back and galloped off to Marseilles, the situation became explosive in Aix, where the Comte de Caraman has a whole regiment at his disposal, the Lyonnais, still disciplined and well in hand.

Breathing easier after his scare in Marseilles, Caraman thinks he can now devote himself to his assigned task, which is to guarantee a peaceful electoral assembly.

He quickly finds himself in the thick of a melee, however, on the Hôtel de Ville square, where the action is concentrated. The crowd has been gathering since morning. All eyes are raised to the beautiful seventeenth-century facade with its life-size statues of Charles of Anjou, Louis XI and Louis XIV.* To the south, the public granaries, three stories tall and vaulted, can hold enough wheat to feed the town for more than a year; to the northwest, the great clock tower that looks like a belfrey. Hour after hour, idlers keep turning up to watch, but there are also demonstrators emerging from the ten streets that make the square look like a sort of star.

The crowd, which already fills the square, is edgy with impatience; one magistrate says it is composed mainly of "women, peasants, picklocks, vagrants, strangers, Italians, or men with a reputation for audacity and brutality," like André, called the Butcher, or Blaise Jean, nicknamed Lou Damnat [The Damned].[15] Very few are armed. Flocks of children tag at their heels. Their intentions are not positively hostile, but they can be swayed by any provocation.

Monsieur de La Fare provides it. First Consul, firmly committed to the pretensions of the nobility, he enters the town hall and a few peasants try

*Destroyed during the Revolution.

to follow him into the meeting chamber. He brushes them away with an imperious gesture and tells them that the people of their class are supposed to meet in the church of the Collège Bourbon. This raises a volley of hisses and boos. La Fare is not a coward and awkwardly tries to prove it, imagining he can appease the press around him by tossing a handful of écus in their faces. But this is no baptism or wedding. One woman takes his coins as an insult and tells him so in a shout, whereupon La Fare retorts, loud and clear, that all she's made for is to eat horse manure.

The group surges at him. La Fare has to beat a hasty retreat inside and order all the doors shut. Every pane of glass is shattered within seconds.

Riot.

Outside, a furious mob; inside, the terrified municipal authorities, except for a handful who, like La Fare, reach for their swords.

At this point Caraman rides onto the scene, having rustled up fifty men, whom he places in front of the doors the mob is trying to break down. He attempts to harangue the assailants, who, in a paroxysm of rage, are all screaming *"Vive le Roi!"* and who might have listened to him if he had turned up alone. But a hail of stones falls on his soldiers and two of them are killed; without waiting for orders, their comrades open fire on the crowd. How many dead and injured? The families carry most of them away, but at least three are picked up where they fall. Caraman himself is wounded, his son more seriously, and his aide-de-camp fatally.

There, too, a few last-minute newcomers save the day—two or three of those consuls who get elected now and then because they have a way with people as much as for their professional abilities. One is named Perrin and another Gabriel. Garbed in their long robes, they order the main doors thrown open and go out to talk to the mob and keep it occupied while La Fare is being hoisted through a back window. However, they have to give the granary keys to the rioters' leaders, and that keeps most of their aggressors busy for a while: it takes a good three hours for them to remove the two thousand loads of Sicilian wheat inside. For good measure, they tear off the granary doors and locks as well, and one woman and two children are smothered in the process.

On the morning of March 26, Aix-en-Provence is abandoned by its First Consul and its military commander, who has gone to nurse his wound at the barracks where he has concentrated his troops. The insurgent crowd is master of the town. But the worst is not to come, for lo! Mirabeau rides again!

Arriving on the afternoon of the twenty-eighth, he moves in with Caraman to show that he is on good terms with the King's representatives. He receives all the Notables, especially the young, who come to him as to a providence-sent savior. It looks almost as though Marseilles was only a rehearsal. In two days he raises a bourgeois guard and puts it in charge of the nerve centers previously held by the soldiers, whose presence would soon be getting on the people's nerves; and he makes several tours of the town, his pockmarked face almost an advantage now, because nobody can mistake him for anybody else. Checks are made to ensure that grain is circulating freely, and the regular Saturday market is held, a thing considered impossible only a few hours before; but no market would have meant a hungry town. On March 29 he's done it—the bourgeoisie has taken over in Aix, in the King's name and in agreement with the troops, who return to their barracks. In this town the Revolution starts the way Mirabeau has always wanted it: without too much damage, and speedily brought under control. He can afford to leave town, draped in the gratitude of the Notables, who were spitting at and insulting him a month ago.

His fidgets bring him back to Marseilles, where he still thinks he'd rather be elected. But to be on the safe side he also gives his candidacy to some reliable friends in Aix.

But what a week!

The rest is mere formality. In his presence in a pacified Marseilles, the process of drawing up the lists of each of the three orders, and gradually identifying the names of the representatives considered most desirable, takes place initially through discussion and feigned politeness, rather than the comparison of written texts and lists of names on ballots. Each order meets separately from morning to night, usually in churches, of varying degrees of opulence depending on the caste inside them. During these first days of April the same thing is happening in most of the towns of France. Between March 30 and April 5, while all the jockeying for position is going on, Mirabeau doesn't stir, but the news from Aix infuriates him, because he has just saved the skins of the "haves" in that town by imposing order upon a people who trusted him, but is unable to prevent those same haves from taking their revenge and reverting to their nastiest habits the moment his back is turned. The Caramans, La Tours, etc., order some of the "hunger looters"—the men who emptied the granaries—placed under arrest. Then, more than five hundred bourgeois and craftsmen sign a petition asking that the culprits be turned over to the provost for judgment.

On the twenty-seventh, the *parlement* hastily judges and sentences André the Butcher, even though he helped Mirabeau to get the riot under control. The man's legal assassins are so scared of Mirabeau turning up again in Aix that they don't even take time to put up a gallows. They hang the "rebel" from the limb of a tree on the Cours on March 29.

When he hears the turn things have taken in one of the two towns he has just pacified, he's so upset that his habitual self-aggrandizement momentarily deserts him. Everywhere, on the evening of the twenty-fifth, people were telling him those words that were so flattering,* "Ah, if only Monsieur de Mirabeau were here, we would have justice and they wouldn't be killing us!" I weep as I write the words. . . . Women, men, children moistened my clothing and footsteps with their tears and proclaimed me their savior, their god. . . . I was obeyed like a beloved father.

But do you know what has come of it all? The moment everything was calm again, the nobility, who hadn't been seen for thirty-six hours, reappeared in arms, insolent, arrogant, demanding the places that the bourgeoisie had just taken over and shouting, "It's Monsieur de Mirabeau who has done all the harm!" . . . So, between Aix and Toulon in flames, Marseilles, where I went during a riot at the request of Monsieur de Caraman, is quiet and serene. And it is I who am supposed to have stirred up Aix and Toulon, where I never set foot! . . . A curious logic is the logic of hatred.

But that is nothing in comparison to the revenge being prepared now. They want the provost's justice, they want hangings, they want victims from a wretched people whose first crime is to have cried out against Monsieur de La Fare, a people who have been insulted and outraged and told to eat horse manure as the only food fit for them. . . . And today the people themselves almost seem to be crying for revenge. They also have to have hangings. Such is the human heart! I begin to feel a loathing for human nature.[16]

This letter seems to imply that he would rather be elected in Marseilles, where at least nobody has been hanged. Mirabeau has consistently expressed a strong aversion to torture and capital punishment. So he waits hopefully for the last laborious counts to be completed and a list of ninety names to be compiled, from which a series of votes will eventually select four.

At noon on April 5 three merchants—Roussier, Lejean and Delabat—are declared the winners. But wait—the Comte de Mirabeau has exactly as many votes as the man in fourth place, so there will have to be another ballot to choose between them, and this Mirabeau wins by a nose.

In fourth place, behind three merchants? Him? That same day he gets a letter telling him that more or less similar electoral proceedings in Aix have declared him the first winner there, on the first ballot. He politely thanks the agents of the third estate of Marseilles and assures them that he will always think of himself as their representative in spite of everything, but that he gladly resigns his fourth place to the merchant with whom he was tied before the final vote.[17]

Marseilles, farewell. See you later, Aix. This consecration by the people, this signal authority he has acquired in a feverish and ailing region, is his

*From a letter to one of his best friends in Aix, the Advocate Brémont-Julien.

revenge for forty years of failure. Now it's up to him to use, in Versailles and Paris, the strength he has husbanded. On his trip up to the Estates General he will be treated to a little Roman-style triumph, on a scale not experienced by a single one of the thousand other representatives now converging upon the capital from all over France. The eyewitness with the delectable style who follows the stages of this voyage is his faithful Figaro, Aimé Legrain, the thirty-seven-year-old Picard, valet, accomplice and friend who wedded himself to his master's service in 1782 and whom we have already seen at his side in Pontarlier, when he was starting life over yet again.

"He left Marseilles in the evening, accompanied by four hundred youths on horseback, each carrying a torch, and his coach was decorated with laurel and oak leaves. . . . You could see as clear as at midday, and in Aix everybody was afoot although it was the middle of the night. . . . We stayed several days before going on to Paris. Always a great party, until departure.

"He told me, 'Legrain, order the post horses for two in the morning, but don't place the order until eleven in the evening, so that nobody will know anything.' . . . And even though I had not told anyone, there was a flood of people to accompany him out of town. . . . The crowd was such, wherever we went, that all he could get for his breakfast was hot milk and a little coffee with milk in it, and no dinner until Avignon, where we had the same flood of people, even crossing Dauphiné."

ROBESPIERRE

64

APRIL 26, 1789

Let Us Grasp the Unique Moment

The election of Maximilien de Robespierre, at the other end of France, takes place in very different circumstances. The studious, sober, punctual young advocate who divides his time between work on his cases, hearings at the courts and a social circle confined to a few relatives and his sister Charlotte— who has kept house for him since his return from school at Louis-le-Grand— permits himself no recreation other than the meetings of the Academy of Arras, the somewhat freer but still circumspect evenings at the Société des

Rosati and walks in the country to satisfy his innate and powerful love of nature.

The chief obstacle to his election is his relative poverty, which prohibits such things as evenings out in town, theaters and entertainment, luxurious clothes and servants. Also, he has to overcome the hostility of a portion of his colleagues, who take a dim view of the often daring, sometimes provocative cases he tends to prefer, starting with the "lightning-rod trial," which won him his first local fame and the congratulations of Franklin.* During the five long years that followed, Robespierre has been trying to find his voice. Until now, he has kept out of politics. He goes to mass. He adheres sedately to his little place in the law court ritual. No unfavorable report about him reaches the desk of intendant or governor. He has a pleasant disposition, despite the aftereffects of a forlorn childhood. He makes up for the modesty of his dress by scrupulous cleanliness, fastidiously rolled and powdered hair and great politeness of manner. "He was almost always smiling," writes Charlotte.[1]

The conditions of his election are similar to almost all of the ones then taking place in France. In many places one can perhaps observe an antagonism between the more conservative lawyers and those who, like Robespierre, believe in the possibility of change in a society the rigidity of which they feel impelled to denounce. Even in the third estate, the electoral assemblies held this spring reflect these oppositions of class and temperament, although here the clashes are only verbal, and for the most part courteous; the "people," kept at a careful distance from the chambers in which the electors are gradually making their choices and compiling their lists of grievances, are very curious, very hopeful, but quite unexcited. They do not yet feel directly concerned. Hence the importance of the exceptions, Brittany and Provence.

For the last two years Charlotte and Maximilien have been living in a little house (still standing in 1987) on the rue des Rats-Porteurs.† It was high time they left the home of their aunt and uncle Carraut; they'd had enough of it. Meanwhile, their younger sister Henriette had died of "pulmonie," while Augustin, nicknamed Bonbon, had gone to Louis-le-Grand to sit in the place his brother had left nicely warmed up for him.

---

*On Robespierre's youth and family, his years in Arras and Paris, the strange disappearance of his father after his mother's death, his beginnings as a lawyer in Arras and, in particular, the lightning-rod trial, see Volume III.

†Which the municipality renamed rue Robespierre only a few decades ago. There is no other tribute to his memory in his native town, not even a statue.

He worked a great deal and spent much of the time he was not in the courtrooms in his study. He would get up at six or seven and work until eight. Then his wigmaker came to dress his hair. After that he would eat a light meal, consisting of some dairy product, and go back to work until ten, when he dressed and went to court. After the hearing he would come home to dine; he ate little and drank nothing but reddened water; he expressed no preference for any particular food. Many times I [Charlotte] asked him what he wanted to eat for his dinner and he replied that he had no idea. He was fond of fruit and the only thing he could not forgo was a cup of coffee. After dinner he would go out and walk for an hour, or make a call. Then he would come home and shut himself up in his study again until seven or eight o'clock; he spent the rest of the evening either with friends or with his family. . . .

When we played cards or talked of insignificant things, he would withdraw to a corner of the room, lean back in an armchair and muse, as though there were no other person present. He was naturally cheerful, however, and could sometimes joke and laugh until he wept. . . .

Sometimes he was so absentminded that one day he came home to dinner before the table was quite set; the soup was already on the table, he took a chair, sat down to the table and, not noticing that there was no plate in front of him, served himself a ladleful of soup onto the tablecloth.[2]

So he has lived eight years of this gray life, and there is no indication that he ever complained of it. At most, we can find a few signposts, between his appointment by the Council of Artois as advocate to the *parlement* and his election to the Estates General. His father has already died, in Munich in 1776, but he doesn't know that and never will. He defends between twenty and twenty-five cases a year. And if one of his first had not been that of the famous lightning rod, his name would still not be known much beyond the narrow circles of the Artesian bar.

In 1785 he is admitted to the Arras Academy and enters into a diffident relationship with Dubois de Fosseux, but there is nothing to indicate that he had any knowledge of the letters of Babeuf.

February 1786: he is elected annual director of the Academy and thus becomes more intimately aware of the literary competitions that are weaving back and forth throughout the country. He has already submitted, to the Amiens Academy, an *Éloge de Gresset,* a minor poet whose fame did not travel much outside Picardy. But Gresset also wrote plays. The new kind of theater that Diderot and Sedaine had recently brought before the public has aroused fierce criticism from champions of the classical style. There are a few lines by Robespierre in his *Éloge de Gresset* that are like a defense lawyer's plea for a development as reprehensible, in the eyes of the conservatives, as those newfangled political innovations. He is distinctly in favor of the new style:

"I do not know what mania has driven a host of critics to declaim against the new style with a sort of fanaticism. These fiery censurers, convinced that nature contains nothing but comedies and tragedies, take any dramatic work that does not bear one or other of those qualifications to be a literary monster . . . ; as though nature had only two colors and there were no middle ground for us, between the sallies of merriment and the transports of the most furious passions . . . . Vainly have they sought to persuade us . . . that it is permissible to feel compassion only for the catastrophes of kings and heroes; while they write books against the plays, we are hurrying to the theater to see them performed, and feeling that our tears may flow as sweetly for other woes than those of Orestes and Andromache."[3]

That same year comes the first ripple on these seemingly still waters: the Royal Society of Metz held a competition on the question, "What is the origin of the opinion that assigns to every member of a family some share of the shame attaching to the penalties involving loss of civil rights inflicted upon a guilty person?" Robespierre speaks out vigorously against what he calls "an abominable prejudice" and reads his essay to the Arras Academy with such good effect that he then elaborates upon it, expands it and publishes it, and in 1786 receives from the Royal Society of Metz a medal and prize of four hundred livres. The average minor notable would think that was glory enough, but it is only the second prize and Maximilien does not consider it an honor. Perhaps he went a little too far for the judges, in the passage in which he calls for equality of punishment for all citizens, including nobles, "whose crimes are always less excusable than those of the wretched, driven to evil by poverty."[4]

He makes a speech to the Arras Academy on the legislation governing the rights and status of bastards, in which he attacks a few of the more shocking features of that legislation, which situated bastards (the word was current in legal terminology) somewhere between serfs and livestock. They could not marry without the consent of their lord, they could not engage in trade, or save money, or travel, and even if they married "legally," any children they might have were still regarded and treated as bastards.

Like the rest of Robespierre's legal writings, this text is heavy, indigestible and full of rhetoric. He's no Mirabeau, no Brissot, nor yet a Barnave or Sieyès. Yet the theory defended from beginning to end is unfailingly largehearted. Bastards have the same rights as all other citizens and should be given the same treatment, from birth until death.

"Everything hangs together, everything corresponds, in politics as in morality. Politics itself is nothing but public morality. The prime object of legislation, and at the same time the most sublime effort of human wisdom, is to create agreement by means of a just combination of the various principles forming the elements of social harmony. The first of these principles, the authentic bases on which the public welfare rests, are the eternal laws of justice and the immutable rules of natural law. The lawmaker who sacrifices these to any particular consideration is like an architect removing from the foundations of his building the materials he needs to repair it."[5]

These considerations, which may appear rather abstract, are prompted by the law, then still in force, that obliges unmarried women who are pregnant to declare their pregnancy to the magistrates: "Ah, what worse fate could befall them than to be reduced to revealing this fatal mystery?" We should add that if a "girl mother" gives birth prematurely and before complying with the law, she is instantly tried for infanticide and hanged. In the few lines Robespierre devotes to this predicament we find a perfect example of his irrepressible indignation, and of his intellectual process, which is to move from the particular to the general, from the fate of the serving-woman made pregnant by her master to a universal view of the relations obtaining between human beings. In support of these last lines he cites Beccaria, whose *Traité des délits et des peines* is beginning to undermine the medieval structures of justice throughout Europe: "Infanticide is the almost inevitable effect of the appalling situation of a hapless woman who has succumbed to her own weakness, or to violence; the only choice allowed her by law is between infamy and the destruction of an insentient creature: how can anyone doubt that she must prefer the alternative that preserves her from shame and wretchedness and the unhappy fruit of her pleasures?"[6]

Between 1784 and 1787 the number of cases he defends falls by almost a third, and in that connection we discover another component of his character: money does not interest him. Rather than bowing to the little Arras clique, which he might easily have disarmed with a return to conformity, he boldly attacks one of the two reigning religious communities in a marathon trial (it lasts from 1782 to 1787). His client is François Déteuf, a ropemaker, and he is defending him against Dom Brognard, one of the highest dignitaries of the Anchin monks, who had been abbey paymaster and, in that capacity, the administrator of substantial sums, which rumor was accusing him of mishandling for profit.

Brognard's superiors prudently remove him from office, but in the meanwhile he lends eight hundred livres to Déteuf, whose little business is on the brink of bankruptcy. It would appear that the "loan" is actually a rather special sort of gift, intended to persuade Déteuf to urge his sister Clémence to yield to the dirty old monk's attentions. In any event, Déteuf does not return the money, and Brognard's successor is demanding not only repayment of the original sum but damages of three thousand livres from the debtor, under threat of forfeiture of his civil rights.

Robespierre has never gone so far before in a defense that is really an accusation, directed not so much against the monks themselves as against the system that allows them almost invariably to win the cases in which they are involved: "I see a host of unhappy persons, in a thousand similar instances of which no one has the least suspicion, all shattered against the bloody shoals of our criminal jurisprudence, and I feel that it is necessary to amend the force of justice and humanity of the succor denied them by the imperfection of the laws."[7]

The monks of Anchin lose the Déteuf case, but on January 30 the Artois Council orders "that all terms prejudicial to the authority of the law and of jurisprudence, and all terms injurious to the judges, shall be deleted from the printed account of the case signed by Robespierre, advocate."

Some thread in the weave of his life has snapped. At a public ceremony a man named Le Sage, one of the governor's deputies, calls him "depraved and a little squirt, and waved his fist in his face withal." The highest authorities won't let him sit near them. His clientele melts away; in 1788 he has only ten cases to plead, while other, less noted advocates have thirty-three, fifty-two, as many as seventy-seven.

Not that he is accursed by the town. People still speak to him in the streets and a few loyal colleagues whose minds run along somewhat the same lines as his continue to associate with him. Yet he feels that he is no longer quite at home in Artois. He thinks seriously of going to Paris; but how, without capital, and this time, without the help of the Arras Benedictines?

This last peaceful winter has not been a happy one for him. It shows in his first anonymous writing, *Lettre adressée par un avocat au Conseil d'Artois à son ami avocat au Parlement de Douai*. It's a vindictive piece of work and shows signs of a sort of neurasthenia. According to him, the advocate's profession is bad news from start to finish. Progress in the career is slower than a snail's pace; its practitioners are dependent upon the attorneys and obliged to beg cases from them. Also, he has such a grudge against his town, having no experience of any other, that he castigates it angrily: "There may be no other town less congenial to the advancement of young athletes competing in the arduous career of the bar. It is necessary to practice eight or ten years to be what is known as abreast of things, and even then one is very lucky to get one's turn."[8]

To offset this text, he also publishes, a little later but under his own name, a eulogy to a man he regards as the living example of what he would like to be himself, another man whose career paid the price of his courage. Robespierre's *Éloge du président Du Paty* is known to very few people at the time, because it is published just as the storm begins to break over France.

"Du Paty was concerned for the class of citizens whose worth is not reckoned in society, for which it sweats and labors; wealth looks down upon it with disdain, pride calls it the dregs of the people, but justice owes it particular protection, especially as it has no other mainstay, no other prop to lean upon."[9]

So is he going to spend the rest of his life defending servants accused of theft, insolvent debtors and deserting soldiers? News of the meeting of the Estates General has revived his fighting energy and made him want to play, for the whole of France, the political role he could not dream of filling in Artois. In response to Brienne's appeal of August 8, 1788, he seizes his pen, like so many others, and produces an *Appel à la nation artésienne,* which he publishes in February 1789 as a prelude to his candidacy.

Even here, opinion is beginning to turn in the preliminary gusts of the great gale. The first positive sign for him in a long while: on February 4, 1789, he is elected president of the Academy of Arras.

According to his *Appel,* the present system of representation of the third estate in the towns and villages of Artois is a perfect example of the institutional lie. Delegates to the local assembly are "elected" by the municipal authorities of ten towns in the province. But these Notables, who were themselves elected in conditions of relative freedom back in the days of the imperial occupation, have, since the middle of the reign of Louis XV, been appointed, like simple officers, by the governors.

What an outcry, from this man who is no orator! "Ah, let us grasp the unique moment that Providence has reserved to us in the course of centuries, in order to recover those imprescriptible and sacred rights! . . . The better citizens eschew such gatherings and give free rein to the ambitions of a handful of aristocrats, ever watchful to remove anyone who is suspected of possessing a soul, so that they may establish without impediment their ascendancy over the wretchedness and abasement of all."[10]

Robespierre doesn't confine himself to general ideas; he also gives a painstakingly documented catalog of the scores of injustices, largely fiscal, suffered by nine out of ten Artesians. However, the conclusion of his eighty-three pages tries to offset the impression that this enumeration is wholly pessimistic. Robespierre places great hopes in the decisions taken by Necker, whom he praises almost immoderately, because by granting double representation to the third, he has taken a small first step toward equality in national representation. Hang on, good people of Arras! "The time has come when the sparks from the sacred fire shall restore life, courage, happiness, to all."[11] On condition, it goes without saying, that the third estate be composed of a majority of men who believe in the new ideas. The pamphlet never mentions Robespierre's candidacy, but it is written between the lines.

As he begins to make active preparations for his campaign, he pleads the last case he will ever defend as an advocate, that of Hyacinthe Dupond, a former deserter riddled with debt who lives in the bailliage of Hesdin just next to Arras and is being pursued by a pack of creditors. A *lettre de cachet* has been issued against him and is preventing him from receiving the little income he has from his property. Robespierre makes time to write a copious defense for the poor man,* ending with ten pages of dithyrambic praise of Louis XVI, whom he compliments to the skies for abolishing *lettres de cachet,* although the King has by no means forsworn the principle and nothing has actually been done as yet. In passing, he takes the opportunity to write a vibrant appreciation of d'Eprémesnil, too, whom he will soon be seeing more of, he trusts, in the great assembly.[12]

Here we see Robespierre still cherishing attitudes that can be termed provincial. He is about to meet a Paris in which Louis XVI's popularity is already shaky and that of d'Eprémesnil as far in the past as ancient Greece; and he'll have to get used to it.

The third estate of Arras holds its first electoral meeting on March 27; it is marked by sharp altercations between the *ex officio* members, with Robespierre as spokesman, and the municipal officers appointed under the previous system, almost all of whom withdraw within three days.

March 30: first fully free meeting of all the delegates from the towns, burgs, parishes and communities of the principal bailliage of Artois. Maximilien is one of the forty-nine commissioners appointed to compile a summary of their lists of grievances.

April 3: Robespierre is elected thirteenth out of eighty-four electors.

April 20: opening of the general meeting of the three orders in the cathedral, with a speech by Monseigneur de Conzié, the bishop, the very man who got Robespierre his scholarship to Louis-le-Grand.

From April 20 to 26, each order functions separately again. The clergy elects four bishops and the nobility four seigneurs (including Comte Charles de Lameth). It remains for the twelve hundred electors of the third estate to choose eight representatives, which they slowly proceed to do between the twenty-fourth and twenty-sixth, each vote being for only one representative. It is not until Sunday, April 26, that Maximilien de Robespierre is elected, in fifth position, as representative of Arras to the Estates General.

His thirty-first birthday is five days later.

With two other delegates of the third, he sets out almost at once for Versailles, by stagecoach. No text of his remains to show what he thinks that day, not even the moment when he bids farewell to Anaïs Deshorties, a distant cousin who, according to Charlotte de Robespierre, is full of grace and gaiety and in whose company he has spent so much time in the last few months that they are widely supposed to be engaged.

*Released three years later by the Arras district court.

Many of his friends from the Rosati and the Academy stand by to cheer as he climbs into the coach. One is missing, though—Lazare Carnot, for whom Maximilien composed a frivolous ditty not long ago, which even contains an allusion to Dubois de Fosseux. It's called "The Empty Cup":

> Friends, from all these worn-out words
> Let us conclude that we must drink
> To our friend Carnot.
> This very moment I must drink
> To you, dear Fosseux.
> To the whole merry, jolly group
> Again, I must drink.[13]

RÉVEILLON RIOT

65

APRIL 27–28, 1789

In Paris People Were Cutting Each Other's Throats

Struggling through the haps and mishaps of the great thaw, the washed-out bridges and the flooded roads and sodden fields, one thousand representatives of France are converging upon the capital as fast as their horses can convey them, some traveling three or four to a post chaise.

Their haste is wasted. The date of the opening session of the Estates General has already been set back several times between January and March, and notwithstanding the present schedule it will be postponed yet again, until May 5. More time lost. To justify the delay, the government pleads the construction work needed to put the Menus Plaisirs building in order and the fact that, owing to a special election procedure there, no delegates have yet been chosen to represent the city of Paris. In reality, "the princes' party" has been engaging in a last-ditch maneuver designed to persuade the King to give up the whole idea of the Estates, and disappointment over this fresh delay has something to do with the uprising that is about to tear the capital apart. The delegates have been looking forward to a great civic festivity, and what they encounter is a narrow escape from a social St. Bartholomew's Day:* the Réveillon riot.

On April 27 the sudden explosion of the Saint-Antoine faubourg shakes people so badly that even Bookseller Hardy, who's usually mewed up in his shop with his ears flapping to catch every passing shred of news and gossip, actually steps out his door to see for himself what has put the town into such an uproar:

"In the afternoon, the Parisians were much affrighted, even shutting up their shops in some places, by a sort of insurrection that spread through the Saint-Antoine faubourg to the vicinity of Notre-Dame. It involved a considerable portion of the workers supposedly of that faubourg, whom some rogues had stirred up against a man named Réveillon, a wealthy manufacturer of printed wallpapers, and another man, also quite rich, named Hanriot, a saltpeter manufacturer, the two men being friends and living in the same part of town. The workers were marching, armed with sticks, and doing no harm to anybody; I met a detachment of about five or six hundred of them on the rue de la Montagne-Sainte-Geneviève, heading . . . toward the Saint-Marceau faubourg with just one drum; one of the men was carrying a gibbet over his shoulder, from which hung the effigy of a man painted on a piece of cardboard."[1]

Two names scribbled across the cutout explain, to a crowd whose scapegoat they have suddenly become, like Brienne and Lamoignon nine months before (except that they were already famous), that it is meant to represent Réveillon and Hanriot, two brave burghers of Paris whose names have been virtually unknown hitherto outside the Saint-Antoine faubourg.

What's it all about? The two ministers were governing 24 million people when their riots took place; whereas the first of these two poor fellows, whose names Hardy only learns today, has been governing 350 employees in his factory, and the second about half that number.

"The popular uprising against Réveillon, the rich dealer in wallpapers from the Saint-Antoine faubourg, would seem to indicate an incipient antagonism between bourgeoisie and proletariat.† But the incident has remained an obscure and probably inexplicable enigma. . . . In any event, I note that this ambiguous scene had no echo. Later, the people take revenge for the Champ-de-Mars massacre, but I can find no reference anywhere to the Saint-Antoine shootings and the hanging of the assailants. . . . It is as

---

*Massacre of French Protestants, beginning August 23, 1572, in Paris.

†According to Jean Juarès. The word he uses was not yet current but this passage in his book highlights the exceptional character of these two days. Even before the imminent and foreseeable conflict between the three orders, a sort of freak cyclone within the third estate itself heralds the social troubles of the nineteenth century.

though these gibbets somehow stand outside the field of history, even though they are on the very borderline of the Revolution."[2]

The villages on the east side of town follow the Seine down into Paris; they were brought under the administrative jurisdiction of the minister of the King's Household and lieutenant of police toward the end of the reign of Louis XV. They're an amalgam of bourgeois houses—often standing on rented ground, five or six stories tall as is the new fashion—and manufacturers, many of them new, wherever there's room for them. In these outlying districts, the adventure of the second branch of the great middle class is just beginning: the "bosses," as distinct from the men of law who congregate around the Palais de Justice.

Saint-Antoine is not the poorest part of the Paris conglomerate, which is why, following Colbert's doctrine, it was attached for essentially fiscal reasons to a center that would soon be producing nothing but court rulings, arts and literature, whereas in the course of the previous century several thousand producers of a different type had settled in the suburbs: carpenters, cabinetmakers, coppersmiths and tinsmiths, manufacturers of mirrors, pottery, porcelain, velvet, pewter and, in the present instance, painted papers and cloths.

The neighboring faubourg of Saint-Marceau is inhabited more by tanners and skinners, trades that make use of the many little arms of the Bièvre, which in those days flowed freely into the Seine. Wages are lower there, there's less space, and there is also a large population of relatively unskilled workers, conveyors of floating timber and water vendors. Day laborers.

Both districts have been affected by the same unrest as their inhabitants begin to realize that although they were allowed to settle there more or less in peace, the system gives them no freedom to choose for themselves, even as regards their living conditions. The wave of pamphlets published in the last six months has sharpened the discontent of a body of men who feel themselves left out of all these preparations for a renovated realm. They see segregation developing among themselves even now; those with money may be able to move in among the people in power, but the poor will remain chained to their destiny.

Nobody has considered their lot, not even the Parisian "thought clubs" or the Parisian electors; this storm is brewing underground. Also, the aftereffects of the hard winter have brought a stream of the unemployed into Saint-Antoine, men who are no longer able to make a living in the fields or mills. Although a placid man by nature, de Crosne, the police commissioner, has written to his minister, "In this faubourg of Saint-Antoine we have over forty thousand workers; the high price of bread and other foodstuffs may lead to movements in the faubourg, where there have already [on April 24] been a few rumbles."[3]

Perhaps we need look no further for the key to the enigma. Why do these two areas rise at the wrong political moment, and why against their two leading employers? Why Réveillon? This may be just one of those historical misunderstandings that touch off pointless battles and riots.

Because if Réveillon's name spreads like wildfire through the people's discontent, beginning around noon on the twenty-seventh, it may simply be because he is the best-known "taker on" of labor in Saint-Antoine, where he appears to have been one of the rare employers to give work to at least a few of the excess labor force around. He has recently explained his actions to the electoral assembly of the Sainte-Marguerite faubourg, whose list of grievances he helped to compose. The text ascribed to him is a perfect example of the kind of words that, taken out of context, produce an effect exactly the opposite of the one intended. All he was asking for was a reduction of the tax imposed upon goods leaving the faubourg daily through the porte Saint-Antoine and parading past the Bastille on their way to embellish new buildings in the capital: "Let us ask that the fruit of our labor no longer be taxed at the entrances to Paris, and once we have obtained satisfaction on that point, then we employers will be able gradually to reduce [the wages of] our workers, which will in turn bring about an equally graduated reduction in the price of manufactured goods."[4]

It may be at that point—although he always insists he didn't name the figure—that he proposed cutting some workers' wages to fifteen sous a day.... Monsieur Jourdain invented prose; has paper-manufacturer Réveillon invented deflation?

But it so happens that his regular workers are earning, on average, twenty-five sous a day, and some of them are already grumbling about having to make room for new workers, even though the new ones are being paid less. Solidarity has not yet become their strong point, we see; and since roughly the same proposals are attributed to Hanriot, the saltpeter manufacturer* in the Enfants Trouvés district, two opposing interpretations arise, and persist: either the "big bosses" in the faubourg mean to cut their workers' rates so that they can generously employ more of them, or they're in a conspiracy to lower wages so that they can make more profits for themselves.

"Fifteen-sou-Réveillon" is the nickname that sticks to him from now on. It should be noted, however, that very few of the slain, wounded and condemned on record after the two days of violence are employees of his.[5] The riot does not originate in his works. He is not much loved in the factory,

---

*Not to be confused with the drunkard who is briefly in command of the armed forces of Paris on 9 Thermidor in year II, whose inebriation contributes to the success of the conspiracy against Robespierre.

though; he is criticized for his rough ways and sharp speech, the tones of a person who is proud to be a "self-made man" and imagines that behavior of this kind is proof of his capacity for leadership. It is also possible that his workers were afraid of being laid off.

The short statement he makes when it is all over and he's trying to justify himself is not without an element of pathos:*

> I, who started out in life earning my way by the work of my hands! I, who know from my own experience . . . how greatly the poor are in need of benevolence! I, who remember, and who have always taken it as an honor, that I was once a manual laborer and day-earner; it is I who stand accused of paying laborers and day-earners fifteen sous a day!
>
> Never has calumny been more unjust, and never have I felt it to be more cruel. One word, it seems to me, should have been enough to justify me.
>
> Of all the workers employed in my shops, the majority earn thirty, thirty-five and forty sous a day; several of them get fifty; the lowest-paid get twenty-five. How should I have set the workers' wages at fifteen sous?†

> It is exactly forty-eight years since I began, as an ordinary worker, in the shop of a paper manufacturer.
>
> After three years of apprenticeship I found myself, for some days, without anything to eat, any roof over my head, or almost any clothing to wear. I was in the state of despair that arises from so appalling a situation. I was perishing of suffering and starvation. A friend of mine, a carpenter's son, came upon me; he was without money, but he had a tool of his trade with him, which he sold to buy me some bread . . . .
>
> At first the tradesman to whom I was introduced wanted nothing to do with me, because of the sorry state I was in, but then he agreed to let me stay a few days with him. He saw that poverty does not always mean misconduct. He kept me, grew fond of me, and I benefited from his teaching.
>
> In 1752 I was still earning only forty écus a year; my savings, when I parted from that tradesman, amounted to eighteen francs.
>
> Having become my own master again, I preferred to work for myself.[6]

It emerges from this brief autobiography that a small dowry, acquired through a felicitous marriage, enabled him, in 1760, to set himself up in the manufacture of velvet-surface paper, eventually to graduate from ten workers to eighty, and then to acquire, in the Saint-Antoine faubourg, a part of the

---

*The document, of which historians of the Revolution do not seem to have made much use, was published in the *Mémoires* of the Marquis de Ferrières and is based on a statement Réveillon made but was unable to get printed.

†The account books and relevant documents of the Réveillon works were destroyed, so there is no way of verifying these statements, which have been challenged by others.

Folie-Titon, a large tract of land being auctioned off by some great seigneur, on which Réveillon built himself a proper little château—the one that has just been demolished.

> A five-acre plot provided a suitable location for the huge workshops I was planning to build. I could already see a community of workers employed and fed by me and assisting me in my work; I cherished the idea, and imagined how, by working to make my own fortune, I would be providing bread for two hundred families.

For several years Réveillon lived a life he thought of as happy: medals from ministers, a monopoly over woven paper "in imitation of the English," the designation of his factory as a "royal manufacture," and the building of the first balloons to float over Paris. He was reaching the heights, and in passing gives a sketch of the already compartmentalized classes that are beginning to develop within the larger trades. At the top, draftsmen and engravers (fifty to one hundred sous a day), then the printers, plain-color sizers and coaters and carpenters (twenty-five to fifty sous); then the carriers, grinders and dressers, packers and sweeps (twenty-five to thirty sous) . . . and he unblushingly owns that "in the fourth class" he uses children aged twelve to fifteen (eight to fifteen sous).

> I see that they have time to receive religious instruction befitting their years. Similarly, I allow Protestant workers to work on holidays. . . .
> How could I expect that the people would treat me as an ogre, heedless of the misery of the poor?[7]

What are we to believe? On April 28, a worker in a china factory swears, before the provostship agents, that "he and the other workers in the neighborhood had a grudge against [the employer] because he said in the assembly of the third estate at Sainte-Marguerite that workers could live on fifteen sous a day, that he employed men who earned twenty sous a day and had watches in their pockets and would soon be richer than he." Testimony confirmed by that of another china-factory employee, named Olivier, who also attended the assembly: "Then Réveillon is said to have been insulted and quickly ran away, pursued by the howls of the people present, who took out their knives and started shouting, 'Kill him! Kill him!' "[8]

Singular contrast: that same day (April 28), the police commissioner is informing the King that the capital is apparently calm, the people are conducting themselves with unwavering respect toward the nobility, the electoral assemblies of the third estate are proceeding uneventfully, attendance at them is relatively small but one of them has just elected, as first-level electors, the academicians Suard, Marmontel, Target, Bailly and Dussaulx, plus Guillotin the physician, Lacretelle the advocate . . . and Beaumarchais.

By April 27 the dough has risen, and the collective explosion of a population that considers itself outraged by its "new seigneurs" leads to the hundreds of men Hardy meets on the streets about three in the afternoon. They are marching from Saint-Antoine to Saint-Marceau in order to incite their fellows on the other side of the Seine to bestir themselves and rise up.

In the absence of any inspired leaders, the insurgents in both faubourgs tread water until evening, looting a few wood storehouses which nobody is defending because no organized forces of law and order have yet been sent for. While Monsieur de Crosne confers with the Duc du Châtelet, the colonel of the French Guards, and Besenval, the colonel commanding the Swiss Guards, the rioters invade, pillage and burn Hanriot's house on the rue de Cotte, leaving him just time to escape with his family and servants. His house is harder for the handful of men of the watch to protect than Réveillon's large estate behind its wrought-iron fence, outside which the captain on duty in the faubourg that evening deploys the only detachment of French Guards to turn up in time.

During the night of the twenty-seventh, Officer Gueullette writes his report on what remains, or rather does not remain, of the saltpeter-maker's home. Will that be the end of the matter?

"In the middle of the street we found a fire in which the rioters burned all the furnishings, objects, linen, clothes, vehicles, carts, cabs and in general everything contained in the premises occupied by Monsieur and Madame Hanriot, which premises are utterly devastated."[9]

The only disappearances noted are those of the seven horses in the stables, the rooster, fourteen hens and fourteen ducks from the coops.

The authorities finally realize that anything might happen on the morrow. De Crosne doesn't get near his bed that night, holds conference after conference, calls up a hundred horsemen from the Royal-Cravate regiment quartered at Charenton and the Swiss companies from Courbevoie. On the morning of the twenty-eighth, the police commissioner's unshakable optimism moves him to write the King that the worst has been avoided, since the mobs seem to have dispersed.

Imagine his surprise, then, to see how furiously and even more, how widely, the riots resume in the course of the morning. How is it possible that folks carrying no arms more lethal than sticks, running hither and thither without any leader or plan, should not retreat at the mere sight of these superb soldiers dressed in white and equipped with that most deadly of weapons, the double-firing musket, not to mention the half-armored horsemen on steeds bred to combine the mass of workhorses with the speed of racers? Besides, once the forces are decently organized, the terrain is favorable for putting down a riot, because the troops can charge from the porte Saint-Antoine and from a broad intersection where four streets, wider than most of those in Paris, meet to form a star: la Roquette, Charonne, faubourg Saint-Antoine and Charenton.

But something certainly seems to have changed since the Flour War, and even since the anti-Lamoignon riots. When he emerges from the *Parlement* with a paternally severe proclamation signed by the King, in which he stamps his foot and orders his good people back to their homes, Monsieur de Crosne learns that once matters have reached a certain point this kind of threat is more likely to have the opposite effect: the flood only surges more powerfully than before. Hanriot's house was just a curtain raiser, it seems. Now you'd think they were crawling out from under the paving stones, ten against one, and every one of them obsessed with the idea of getting Réveillon. This is no riot, this is a revolt, its only comic aspect being that it unfurls to repeated shouts of *"Vive le Roi! Vive Monsieur Necker! Vive le Tiers État!"*

Around midday, the three men responsible for keeping order in town see what they have to do, even if it means a reprimand from Necker—the only thing that will stop this turmoil is steel.

De Crosne writes to Louis XVI again about five o'clock: "The rebels, joined by others from Saint-Marceau and elsewhere, are displaying such determination that Monsieur le Duc du Châtelet and Monsieur de Besenval have found themselves obliged to give their troops orders to use sabers and firearms."[10]

At this stage he still hopes he can save most of the buildings in the Folie-Titon. Two hours later it's all over. From de Crosne, again to the King:

"The disturbance increases by leaps at every moment, the audacity and temerity of the people have reached an extraordinary degree, fresh throngs keep arriving .... The guards posted outside the home of Monsieur Réveillon have been broken through, the house is being looted, everything inside it is being thrown from the windows and burned."

At the end of the statement he embarked upon with such self-satisfaction, all Réveillon has left are his eyes to cry with:

"In vain, a large number of guards were called up to defend me. In their very presence the most dastardly rogues forced open my gates and rampaged through my gardens .... They set three fires and into them threw, first, my most precious belongings, then every last stick of my furniture, even my food and the very fowl I was feeding, my linens, vehicles, my books and accounts ....

"This fit of rage lasted nearly two hours; then the troops, which they had actually dared to attack, fired upon the madmen, and they scattered and dispersed."[11]

He saves his own skin that night, and his family's, by having himself driven . . . to the Bastille, where he is lodged for several days.

Hanriot, meanwhile, is hiding out—in the tower at Vincennes, where he goes in disguise. Maybe the King's prisons have their good side after all. . . .*

This account would seem to imply that the troops don't fire upon the crowd until the damage is done—after, that is, and not before the sacking of Réveillon's houses. Yet the soldiers are at their posts when the gates are smashed open. One might think poor Réveillon simply got it wrong, but the end of de Crosne's last note to the King makes it clear that the shooting actually does take place *a posteriori*.

Why does a large body of armed soldiers stationed at the entrance yield without a fight at three in the afternoon? There are a hundred guards, and they've carried their precautions outside Réveillon's garden to the point of building barricades with the odds and ends lying around. There they stand, leaning against them and aiming their guns at the rioters, who, however numerous they may be, are not eager to be mowed down by running fire. So the first part of the afternoon is spent in a lengthy and not always abusive verbal altercation.

But, there is horse racing at Charenton today, and part of the Parisian nobility climbs into its carriages and heads for the track, totally unperturbed by rumors of a "spot of trouble" because totally unable to measure its intensity. After all, quite a lot has been going on in Paris these past months, and so far no noble has been personally molested. The fastest road from the porte Saint-Antoine to the racetrack is down the rue de Charonne. Trot on, coachman, you can see that some of the churls are even doffing their caps to us! Just one obstacle: the barricade of soldiers blocking the road opposite Réveillon's. Well, move them away and let us through! The flustered officers are not prepared to bar the road to seigneurs, chief among whom, and leading the cortege as is proper, is the Duc d'Orléans himself, the most popular man in the upper nobility. The troops move aside to let his carriage and those behind it through, the Duke and Duchess show themselves at the windows and the Duke speaks a few pacifying words in his customary mumble. Some people even swear they heard him say, "Now, now, friends, be calm! Keep the peace! Happiness is within our grasp."[12] An allusion to the opening of the Estates General next week. At the same time, he distributes the contents of his purse to the people crowding around his coach and cheering, *"Vive notre père d'Orléans!"*

---

*Jacques Godechot adds that Réveillon, after this, does not become a delegate to the Estates General but emigrates to Belgium, where he dies of illness. Nobody knows what happened to Hanriot.

The distribution is not universally appreciated by the other highnesses in the cortege, who are forced to follow suit and who regard this spontaneous gesture as a political maneuver—something of which the Duke is utterly incapable. One of the people present sets the tone: "Now that the Duke has reviewed his troops, the game can begin."[13]

So the barricade of soldiers stands respectfully aside to let the row of carriages through. But as they trot away toward Charenton, a compact mass pours past behind them, roaring imprecations against Réveillon. There may never have been a scene quite like it: a party of nobles cheered on by a mob of starvelings on the rampage against a commoner whom they accuse of betraying them.

Things really start to go wrong in the evening, when the tide of "smashers" begins to ebb. They're feeling fairly pleased with themselves, but most of them are also drunk. This lot, unlike the assailants of the Hanriot house, don't just stave in the barrels in the cellars; they also drink the equivalent of two-thousand-odd bottles of fine wine inside them. And they're sorry they did not get their hands on Réveillon himself.

The moment has come when the troops must either take action or get out, abandoning the two insurgent areas to the rioters. De Crosne affirms: "The main street of Saint-Antoine is so full of people that nobody can enter it. Fifty men of the Royal-Cravate regiment [i.e., cavalry] have been brought up . . . . Another battalion of the French Guards [i.e., infantry] has just reached the scene; the Swiss from Courbevoie are also on the march."[14]

Further: "The people have climbed onto the roofs and are hurling a stream of tiles, stones, etc., down on the troops. They have even thrown pieces of chimneys and beams, and although they have been fired upon several times, it has not been possible to gain control of them yet."[15]

The military riposte—violent, massive and swift—falls upon the day like a curtain of blood. Earlier, the horsemen from the Royal-Cravate showed little ardor in defending the factory, perhaps because they're in sympathy with the people's cheers for the King and Necker. But now they move forward in an orderly manner and, at first, push back the crowd without undue brutality. They are flanked on either side by the French Guards and Swiss. There might still be a chance of a peaceful disengagement, but when they reach Sainte-Marguerite, the crowd in the street is so dense that one side or the other must give way, if only because both sides will otherwise be asphyxiated. Some stones, even a few shots, issue from the people. The officers order their men to fire at will, and because they're at point-blank range, their fire is deadly. The crowd, their panic increased by alcohol, can escape the repeated salvos only by plunging into any building that is not shut against them. They can't just run away, because of the solid mass of people behind them.

Their only defense, then, is to bombard the soldiers with anything they can lay their hands on, mostly tiles and slates from the roofs.

Some of the projectiles hit their targets among the horsemen, who become furious. The officers fall upon the people and begin slashing with their swords, and a fair number are knocked down and trampled.[16] By virtue of the superiority of their weapons, the suddenness of their onslaught, and their unity, the royal forces totally overwhelm a crowd that far outnumbers them. By six or seven in the evening, the streets of the faubourg are clear and empty, except for the dead and wounded lying in them.

But what seeds have been sown there for the days to come! More groups form that night, and continue for another two weeks, "in different parts of Paris, such as the Pont-Neuf, the Pont au Change, around the boulevards, and in the Saint-Antoine faubourg," which must not be as well-muzzled as it looks. Peace and quiet have been restored, but it's only skin-deep, and the entire Royal-Cravate regiment, now fully manned, is posted in the faubourg indefinitely, along with most of the available Swiss, who set up eight case-shot cannon in firing position at the points reckoned to be the most dangerous.

As for statistics: of all the "revolutionary days," this is the hardest to give figures for. Even bookseller Hardy is vague about the number of dead. In the absence of any long-term and accurate investigation, it continues to fluctuate between twenty-five (the figure given by the Châtelet police) and nine hundred (according to the Marquis de Sillery, whose chief sources of information were the gardens of the Palais-Royal). The only sure numbers are those pertaining to the military: twelve men killed and eight injured. From which one can infer at least ten times that many civilian casualties. Only thirty or so are recorded in the hospitals, most of whom die there, but these are isolated cases or persons of no known identity, because those with families are not anxious to expose their kin to further reprisals and bury their dead in their parishes, which keep no statistics. A few years later, sixty or so bodies dating from that time, almost all with gunshot wounds, are found where they were dumped in a heap in the catacombs of Paris.

These few data, cross-checked against other sources of information, would seem to indicate that the "Réveillon riot" accounted for about three hundred lives.*

---

*This is the viewpoint of Jacques Godechot. If true, it means that this was one of the deadliest days of the entire Revolution, in Paris. The worst of all are August 10, 1792 (about one thousand dead), the first day of the September massacres that same year (about nine hundred), and Bonaparte's hecatomb of the royalist sections on 13 Vendémiaire (October 4) year IV. On July 14, 1789, there are ninety-eight deaths among the people, plus the massacre of Launay, Flesselles and six military.

In Versailles the next day, the government is much exercised. Should they go for large-scale repression and multiple convictions, or should they wipe the slate clean and pretend not to take too much notice of this sudden rise in temperature? The best men in France are about to congregate in Paris. Are we going to parade the deputies past serried rows of gallows? Necker pleads indulgence. The princes, Orléans excepted, would gladly burn half the city. The King's nonviolence leads him to arbitrate in favor of leniency. A "provost court," or *ad hoc* tribunal composed exclusively of magistrates from the Châtelet, will be convened at once; and that's all.

To it are committed, almost haphazardly, ten or so rebels arrested during the riots. Two of them are hanged, also pretty haphazardly: a roofer named Gilbert and a street porter named Pourrat. Their gibbet is erected at the foot of the Bastille on April 30.*

"They were escorted [according to Hardy] by substantial detachments of the foot and mounted watch . . . . Some people, seeing them go by, observed that the roofer, who was said to have a wife and four children, wore a resolute and insolent air; he stared boldly at the onlookers and took no notice of the priest, who was talking to him about eternity. He appeared to be about forty-five or fifty; but the other man, much younger, kept well-hidden in the vehicle so as to be seen by nobody; every aspect of him denoted suffering and repentance. The moment they reached the gallows, without having asked to go up to the Chamber [to make any last confessions], they were executed in turn, and their bodies removed an hour later, with the gallows."

Five other workers, picked up dead drunk in Réveillon's cellars, were sent to the galleys.

The Marquis de Ferrières, elected to represent the bailliage of Samur, has arrived from his province equipped with a keen sense of curiosity and a sharp eye for observation. He means to keep a diary while in town and begins it by noting that "while in Paris people were cutting each other's throats, in Versailles they were deciding the details of the delegates' attire."[17]

---

*One month later a public scribe named Mary is also hanged, and a woman, Jeanne-Marie Trumeau, is sentenced to die but reprieved because she is pregnant.

66

APRIL 30, 1789

Ground Which Has Never Been Trodden Before

"I have had my day . . ."

Washington wrote that to La Fayette at the close of the Marquis's triumphal tour of the United States in 1784.* In his farewell to the young French nobleman who had adopted him as a father and fought under his orders in the American army all the way to Yorktown, Washington, who has cultivated a native flair for neat turns of phrase, was referring to nothing more than the great day of the English capitulation. Once the peace was signed, almost the moment the closing formalities were completed, he headed back to his estate, and the commander-in-chief of the victorious army became a wealthy gentleman farmer again. Politics were repugnant to him, or at least that was the impression he wanted to give. He was a military man by nature and training, and it was as a military man, simply a better leader than the rest, that he put together and gave structure to the American army, and, with the help of France, won the war. He considered that his job was done; let the others, the John Adamses, Jeffersons, Franklins, Hamiltons, etc., do the rest without him.

But his name had gone around the world; his Cincinnatus-like retirement fitted him better than anyone else to meet the wishes of his newborn people, who were in search of a unique man, one who would not be a king but who would be able to make the others stick to what really mattered in their domestic disputes and difficulties, acting in the name of a new form of authority, and one who would at the same time embody America and represent it with the necessary dignity.

"I have had my day . . ." He may be repeating those words to himself

---

*See Volume III for the last meeting of the two men. Other material relating to Washington is in Volume II.

now, at noon on April 30, 1789, as he stands on a specially built balcony of the Federal Hall in New York, a huge edifice hastily put up on the corner of Wall and Nassau streets by a French architect named Lenfant, to house the gathering of congressmen and electors anxious to escape the traditional preeminence of Philadelphia that has always been imposed upon them in the past. This is the first time a major political event in the American Revolution has taken place in New York, formerly the site of purely military transactions and for long, the last large town in the Republic to be occupied by the British. There's a sense of redemption in the holding of the new president's inaugural ceremony there. It suddenly raises New York the accursed, or at least the unloved—if only because so many of its inhabitants remained loyal to the British Crown for so long—to a level of political equality with the other two big towns in the United States, Boston and Philadelphia.

This adds an edge to the crowd's delirious excitement that day, the universal roar of happiness that greets President George Washington when the leader of Congress withdraws the Bible on which he placed his hand to swear his oath of office. The men wave their hats and the women their kerchiefs. All of America has wanted this man for president and nobody else. In the whole history of the country he is the only one elected without opposition, although twenty of the seventy electors did vote for John Adams just to respect the rules of this unprecedented ballot. It was almost a tacit arrangement between them and Washington's supporters, however, since, for another few elections, and until an amendment to the Constitution decides otherwise, the vice president, the person who is to take the president's place if he is unable to fill it himself, is the one who receives the second-largest number of votes.*

What a tidy little paradox: that the construction of the first republic of modern history should be completed within the same week as, on the other side of the ocean, the venerable system of the world's longest-lived monarchy is being shaken to its roots.

George Washington is fifty-seven years old on the day he solemnly swears,† in public, "that I will faithfully execute the office of president of the United States, and will, to the best of my ability, preserve, protect, and defend the Constitution of the United States."[1] That makes him relatively

---

*Under the amended law, the vice-presidential candidate is chosen by the candidate for the presidency, thus forming the "presidential ticket."

†The same ceremony, soon to be known as the president's "inauguration," has taken place every four years since then, almost to the day, except in the case of a reelection. The words of the oath have never changed.

young to be the head of a great state, but eyewitnesses agree that today he looks like an old man. He's white as a sheet and his hands are trembling so that he can't find his spectacles. For him, the slow trip full of acclamations and festivities from Mount Vernon to New York has been a long march toward the calvary of the unpredictable. He who has always sought to foresee every detail of every circumstance finds himself entrusted with a mission that no human being on earth has ever performed. He left home on April 16, and wrote in his diary that day, "About ten o'clock I bade adieu to Mount Vernon, to private life, and to domestic felicity; and with a mind oppressed with more anxious and painful sensations than I have words to express, set out for New York . . . with the best dispositions to render service to my country, in obedience to its call, but with less hope of answering its expectations."[2]

It's true that leaving Mount Vernon was in itself enough to wrench all peace from his bosom. The typically colonial style of this "château-house," three stories tall with nine windows on each story, is singularly expressive of the easy life to which the big landowners of America returned, once the wounds of war were healed. Surrounded by numerous outbuildings for servants (Washington kept almost a hundred slaves), livestock and stores, Mount Vernon is an ideal image of the discerning good life earned by labor. It might almost be a large ship, its white facade contrasting with the dominant green of this mild, moist region. The master's house, soberly furnished, contains no more than is strictly necessary for study, thought and neighborly visiting. On the far side of it is a terrace from which the visitor can savor a landscape at once romantic and wild, rolling gently down to the Potomac, which—this being in America, where there are a hundred streams as broad or broader—is as wide as the Seine or Loire in France.*

It may never have been more apparent that Washington's neurasthenia, the bedrock of his personality, has undermined his confidence in himself, in other humans and in destiny. He tries to offset it by a highly abstract religious conviction, but in reality he's not much of a believer. Beyond all doubt, his morose disposition, contrasting so sharply with the demonstrations of fervent enthusiasm washing up at his feet, has helped to invest him with a sort of fatalism and authority that many a monarch would sell his soul to possess. On the day he enters New York, escorted by a congressional delegation, in a longboat rowed by thirteen oarsmen representing the thirteen states, he writes in his diary, "The display of boats which attended and joined us on

---

*Religiously preserved by the Americans down to the last book in the library, Mount Vernon is a profoundly memorable destination for a pilgrimage; after a short hour's drive through the woods from the city that bears his name but did not exist in 1789, the visitor can clearly feel the spirit of the owner of the place.

this occasion, some with vocal and some with instrumental music on board; the decorations of the ships, the roar of cannon, and the loud acclamations of the people which rent the skies, as I passed along the wharves, filled my mind with sensations as painful (considering the reverse of this scene, which may be the case after all my labors to do good) as they are pleasant."[3]

A few days later, again:

"I walk, if I may so express myself, on ground that has never been trodden before. . . . There is almost nothing in my conduct that will not one day be invoked as a precedent; this thought inspires in me a great mistrust of myself."[4]

The gentleman farmer who has always been so fond of long horseback rides, whether at war or on his own land, establishes his new life-style the very next day, shutting himself in his study for ten to twelve hours of meetings and documents, which he abandons only to attend sittings in Congress. He shrugs off his wife and doctor, who are urging him to have a care for his health. He's nearly killed by a carbuncle . . . which would have given the first president of the United States a term of one month. To top it off, he learns that his mother has died. Before leaving home, he went to pay his respects to her, without any illusions as to their meeting again. A few of his advisers restore his health by suggesting that he make a long tour of the states of the Union in order to determine their needs at first hand. Not that his power over them is absolute; every state is its own master, and in this respect nothing has changed since the epic altercations preceding the adoption of the Constitution in 1787.

For example, it has taken almost two years for the Federal Constitution to be accepted by all thirteen states, so that they could put a roof on their building. The procedure for choosing the president has not been the least of the obstacles. He is to play a substantial part in the life of the nation, even if he cannot interfere in the domestic affairs of individual states; but he will have federal powers such that he can prevent the nation from disintegrating. Army, navy and diplomacy are his, except that he has to negotiate with Congress, which, since the Declaration of Independence, has been the safeguard against any incipient despots. But that's just the point; how is the man to be elected if he is elected by the big states only and not by the little ones? The dispute that nearly brought the Constitutional Convention to its knees in the preliminary stages is dragged out again. He must certainly not be elected by direct universal suffrage (one-man-one-vote), nor even by Congress, where the more populous states have more representatives and thereby a controlling voice in elections. In the end, the ploy that was devised was to create an ephemeral body of electors chosen in each state after complex calculations that should ensure that no individual state carried more than its fair weight. Each of these electors is formally instructed by the people to vote for a particular presidential candidate, after which, like winged ants, the *ad hoc* college would drop its prearranged ballots in the box on Election Day and vanish away into the mists.*

So that's why the president's inauguration has just taken place in New York, not Philadelphia. Also, Congress roams from one city to another every year, to prevent any one of them from becoming more important than the rest, while they wait for a team of French architects, brought over in Rochambeau's wagon train and headed by Major Lenfant, to build them a town with a special status that will not be tied to any state and will become the federal capital. In this, the Americans are unblushingly copying Tsar Peter, who had St. Petersburg built two centuries before.† A new city for a new empire.

In New York, fifty thousand people are trying to forget the hell they've recently been through, build new wharves and reconstruct over half the houses destroyed by bombardments from the ships that laid siege to them for so long. Many of those that are still standing are in the style of the Dutch houses built by the first Europeans to settle, 160 years before, in this port that they called Nieuw Amsterdam.

Until something better turns up, Washington moves into one of them as though he were pitching a tent. The aristocratic Virginians and distinguished Bostonians in his retinue purse their lips haughtily at this building-site town; its streets are too narrow for them, there are no sidewalks, things aren't as clean as they might be, they are constantly colliding with stray cows and pigs. The hospital cannot hold more than sixty patients, and many down-and-outs shelter for the night inside the twenty-two churches administered by almost as many sects. But those with longer vision see sure signs of a portentous future. Apart from two or three harrowing winter months, the climate is good; and although there is no ready-made bay or harbor, the great natural canal of the Hudson River, which flows down to the ocean, can carry ships of all tonnages.

"After Rhode Island, it provides the safest and most convenient shelter anywhere in the United States. No town of this republic has greater or more varied advantages for commerce, or is any more certain to grow and develop.

*The system has continued in operation in the United States until the present, but world opinion pays no attention to it and largely believes that the president is elected by direct universal suffrage. On the other hand, even in April 1789, the French of the revolutionary period take so much interest in the potential role of an intermediary electoral college that the various communes of their history can be said to be a result of it.

†The town gradually becomes habitable only after 1800, and in 1789 nobody knows that it will bear Washington's name. It remains predominantly the fief of the civil servants and military, and Congress and the president are permanently installed in it.

Access to the ocean is easy, open at all times and safe . . . . In a sense, it disposes of the entire mass of the production of the huge state to which it is the key, and receives foreign imports solely from the hands of its own merchants."[5]

So the biggest city and the biggest man in the United States start on their journey together, more or less, except that the latter tends to turn his back on the former, taking little or no part in its everyday life. In his head is a whole new world to be created; one new town more or less matters little to him.

Immediately upon arriving he establishes an almost obsessive life-style for himself and his family, if only to stave off the importunate. His door is shut to all supplicants, however warmly recommended. He consents as seldom as possible to preside at large social events, and when he cannot avoid them, "he would stand in a large reception hall dressed in black velvet and gloved in yellow, with powdered hair and buckles not just on his shoes but also at his knees. In one hand he would hold a tricorne adorned with a black plume, and a long sword in a white leather scabbard hung at his side. He bowed stiffly to his guests and never shook anyone's hand. He went through the streets in a magnificent carriage drawn by four or six white horses, with footmen in brilliant liveries . . . . He sincerely believed that this attitude was necessary, to preserve the dignity of his high functions. He was an aristocrat by nature, however, and could easily assume a dignity comparable to that of a European monarch."[6]

This isolation and hauteur enable him to make the first major decisions of his government with the same good sense and breadth of view he showed before, when Congress gave him supreme command of the armies. The Constitution allows him only four ministers, and there has been much guesswork as to whether he would take them all from the same party or simply choose men who are unconditionally attached to himself. What he does is summon, as secretary of state (chiefly responsible for foreign affairs), the "radical" Thomas Jefferson, now acting as ambassador in Europe, despite his distaste for Jefferson's extremism; he gives the Treasury to Alexander Hamilton, his former aide-de-camp, with whom he quarreled during the war and who could be said to represent the "aristocrats." To the other two essential offices he similarly appoints men of opposing opinions but undeniable ability: Henry Knox for War, and Edmund Randolph for Justice.

The motor of the United States can start to turn.

67

APRIL 30–MAY 4, 1789

God, Country, Fellow Citizens: All Had Become Myself

On May 2 Gouverneur Morris is invited to supper by some Parisian friends.* He's hardly been in France three months, but has already caught the right tone: "During the evening a gentleman entertains the ladies with the description of the hanging match last Thursday .... The Baron de Besenval, who gave the order for quelling it, seems vastly pleased with his work .... It is therefore agreed that the Baron is a great general—and as the women say so, it would be folly and madness to controvert their opinion."[1]

The two Parisians executed after the riot on April 30 are not the only victims of that week, and insurrection is not the only fever in Versailles: there is also an epidemic of last-minute building and decorating. The first sitting of the Estates General is only a week away, and the major alterations needed in the Menus Plaisirs have hardly been started, so that now work has to go on day and night, "despite the rigors of the weather then prevailing, which cost the life of several workers,† hurled from the scaffoldings and attics by snow and ice."[2]

The cold spell almost claims another, less likely victim: "We were terrified by the danger to which the King was exposed on April 4, when visiting the attics .... A workingman saved our monarch by catching hold of his clothes just as he was about to take a terrible fall. The King awarded him a pension of one thousand two hundred livres from his privy purse; on condition, however, that he does not leave his present estate."[3]

---

*He's preparing to take over from Jefferson, who hasn't yet left France. He has some political influence in New York and the French take him for a hero of the late war because he has an amputated leg, which is actually the result of a riding accident. He leaves some lively memoirs on the Revolution, which he abhorred.

†Two deaths and at least six injuries, according to Paris, the architect, and Vacquier, the chief contractor.

By the end of April, the workers having brought to pass as many miracles
of ingeniousness and camouflage as though it were a setting for a shoestring-
budget opera they were building, the chamber is ready.

But why? What is the reason for all the delays between December and
May? The Estates General were convened in August, Necker set the date
for the opening session at the end of December. But not only was it apparently
forgotten that the hall now has to hold twice as many deputies as there were
Notables in it before, but also part of the bric-a-brac of the "Plaisirs du Roi"
that had been moved out in December for the second Assembly of Notables
had been shoved back into it again. This inertia was in part the petty but
very real result of a last-ditch delaying tactic by the absolutists. If we look a
little closer, we see that not only Paris, the architect, but also Villedeuil, the
minister of the King's Household, and Thierry de Ville d'Avray, master of
the royal storehouses—the three men, that is, on whom all decisions relating
to the work depend—belong to the faction of the Comte d'Artois, who has
been driven into a sort of fury by the imminence of the Estates, coming after
the fiasco of the princes' letter.

The King's brother seems to have shed some of his customary nonchalance. Infuriated by the growing popularity of the Duc d'Orléans and by
Monsieur's ambivalent attitude toward the third estate, he has contrived a
sort of little conspiracy, designed to keep anything at all from happening.*

Artois's reasoning is as simple and silly as himself. So long as the Estates
do not sit in the King's presence, their deputies have no legal authority. And
if, when they get to Paris, there should be no public place to receive
them . . . The Queen and the Polignacs have become more friendly to Artois
of late. If, acting together, they can get the King to dismiss Necker, Montmorin and Puységur—the three ministers who have fused into an image of
a diabolical triumvirate in the conservatives' eyes—then the ineffable Barentin could stay in the government. And to him could be added Broglie,
Breteuil, Foulon. And the two princes, Condé and Conti, could be given
seats on the Council. And these stormtroopers would also be able to count
on Besenval, whom Marie Antoinette has just had appointed military governor of Paris and who'd like nothing better than to carry out a whole series
of little "cleanups" along the lines of his crushing of the Réveillon riot.

But who would take Necker's place and continue to doctor the ailing
Treasury? Artois and his friends are so out of touch that they actually persuade
themselves that a voluntary contribution from a hundred of France's greatest

---

*Historians of 1789[4] have paid scant attention to this ultimate maneuver, begun too late
and on too small a scale. But it did succeed in getting the Estates postponed again and again at
a time when every week counted; it paved the way for the events of July.

fortunes would be forthcoming if it were solicited by a miracle man whom the King would pull out of his hat—by the name of Guillaume de Machault.

Did they say *Machault?* The minister who was expelled from grace by Madame de Pompadour, the man to whom Louis XVI barely preferred Maurepas as mentor at the beginning of his reign, is ninety years old today. All that remains of him is a little breath. But he is so horror-stricken by all the portents of social change that in February, when the Prince de Condé in person comes to see him at his estate at Arnouville, acting on instructions from neither the King nor the Queen, who has been cautious enough not to commit herself fully to this escapade, he actually gives Condé a hearing.

If Machault had been thirty years younger, and if Monsieur had come out clearly against Necker, it might still have been possible to call a sudden halt to the whole procedure. All through April most of the diplomats posted to Versailles are informing their courts that something is in the wind "on the King's floor," where a score of courtiers are still able to imagine that they are turning the wheels.

On April 26 Ferrières writes to his wife, "You can't believe what a powerful movement there is afoot against Necker among the high-placed, the financiers, the *parlements:* calumny, pamphlets denouncing him to the King as the most dangerous man alive . . . . Nor is his daughter, Madame de Staël, being spared. The Comte d'Artois is said to have spoken most forcefully to the King, telling him that his crown and his very life were in danger, and that Necker was a second Cromwell."[5] No less.

The person who reacts most sensibly to this final sabotage attempt is probably Louis XVI himself, who is not too dismayed to hear cries of "Long live the King!" and "Down with the nobles!" when he passes. For him, it's a kind of revenge for the sly and respectful contempt with which his whole circle, including his wife, has invariably treated him. But he is upset by his initial perusal of the lists of grievances, which have been cunningly slipped onto his desk. They contain unanimous calls for a constitution. As though, in his eyes, France didn't already have one! Ever since Hugh Capet, the constitution of France has been its living king and it is in this sense alone that, like a second Philip Augustus, he would consent to become the King of the third estate. But that's not quite what the dozens of utopists have in mind, as they draft text after text, carefully dotting every *i*. So he pettishly returns to his hunting and takes no further interest in the preparations, in Versailles or elsewhere. But nor does he dismiss Necker, even though his minister's speeches at Council meetings bore him to distraction; and so the conspiracy falls apart for want of glue, when the moment comes actually to do something about the thousand deputies who are beginning to haunt the streets of Versailles.

It is hard to imagine the problems created by this invasion in a town of a scant fifty thousand souls, all crowding around the château that feeds them. They take a dim view of these people bursting in upon them from all over the country and setting themselves up to teach them a lesson.

Versailles is used to thinking that it is the only town in the kingdom that counts. From now on, it's only the first. It will become less.

At last the decision is taken to open the Estates; but between decision and execution another week goes by, filled with conflict and vexation, while the aftereffects of the riots in the faubourgs lie like a haze over everything. "The delay in opening the Estates General wearied many people," notes Biauzat, a representative of the third.[6]

"Just under eight hundred deputies* came here on the twenty-seventh to attend the opening of the Estates. They were profoundly shocked, on their arrival, to see the King departing for the hunt. The decision to postpone the opening ceremony was not announced until the very last moment."[7]

This final waiting period is filled with frustrations rather than convivial meetings. Two essential factors are involved: the dress imposed upon the deputies and the manner of their presentation to the King.

On April 27, when all the tailors in Versailles and Paris are already snowed under, a ruling from the Marquis de Brézé is issued to the clergy ordering the cardinals to come in red copes, the bishops in rochets, capes, purple cassocks and square caps, and all other clergymen in cassocks and long cloaks.

Deputies in the order of nobility are to wear coat and cloak of black material "of the season" with gold decoration on the cloak and waistcoat to match the decoration, black breeches, white stockings and a hat with white plumes turned up in the style of Henri IV. The ruling generously adds that it is not essential for coat buttons to be gold.

As for the third estate, its deputies are to be garbed in black from head to foot. All they're allowed is a muslin cravat, and their hats, turned back on three sides, must have no cords or buttons. This attire is felt to border on the punitive and provocative because, with the exception of the higher clergy, black is the dominant hue of the ceremony, as opposed to the variegated colors of the "lower classes." The costume imposed upon the third, for example, is the same as that worn by certain judges and councillors of state, which sets them apart and makes them respected in their own precincts. That of the lower clergy, which is pretty much the same, is no more humiliating in itself. But the aggressive opulence of the nobles' costumes, especially

---

*Two hundred fourteen for the clergy, including thirty bishops; 183 for the nobility; and 488 for the third. Three hundred and fifteen out of the expected twelve hundred delegates, thus, were still missing.

the gold decorations and white plumes, is seen by the others as a claim to superiority. Also, the men of the third estate are forbidden to wear the symbolic short sword to which they are customarily entitled, so as to scotch any mild notions they might have of pretending to the tiniest particle of nobility. And the lower clergy is no less annoyed to see itself robed in mere black, in contrast to the varicolored bishops, who belong to the same order as themselves.

The malaise created by these rulings about dress is intensified by the ones regulating the delegates' presentation to the King, who endures the parade of the first two orders in his chamber of state with both doors open, while the men of the third, after a long period of shuffling from one foot to the other, are permitted a brief glimpse of him in his study, with only one door open.

As usual, because of his nearsightedness, Louis XVI watches them file past with about as much interest as he would bestow upon a flock of sheep. Also, the doorkeepers have been told to get it over with as quickly as possible, and deport themselves like sheepdogs, chivying the people along. According to Delandine, a deputy from Anjou, "Neither provinces nor bailliages were announced aloud. This is what was called acquainting the monarch with the nation's representatives."

The King's only reaction comes when one representative of the third, a big farmer from Rennes, casually turns up in a colored outfit, the one he wears on Sundays. At last Louis XVI brightens, slaps him on the shoulder, and says, "Hello there, my good man!"* He's known thereafter as "Old Gérard."

Mirabeau, newly arrived from Aix, does nothing to attract attention during the etiquette-ridden ceremony, which he scorns: "Today we are mere individuals, whose lips have not been unsealed by the legislator [the King, that is]: ah, when once we are allowed to speak, we shall most certainly address ourselves to graver matters than the nomenclature of the staircases and drawing rooms through which the master of ceremonies has conducted us."[8]

These little outbreaks of spitefulness and hurt feelings do lead to bickering, however, and further delays in the proceedings, including those on Monday, May 4, which everybody was awaiting as the great day of concord.

---

*Proof that the dress regulations did not come from himself but from his circle. Louis XVI was a simple man and did not care about frills. If he had had more to do with the preparations, some of the affronts to the third might have been avoided. "Old Gérard" remains in the assembly until the end of the Constituent and gives his name to a popular almanack published by Collot d'Herbois in order to broadcast revolutionary ideas through the countryside.

When people learn that Louis XVI has asked the Archbishop of Paris to organize a solemn procession that day, in which the sovereigns and princes will precede the deputies from one church in Versailles to another, the optimists begin to hope that the age of contention is over and the Estates General are about to begin under God's gaze with a general reconciliation.

But the arrangement of the procession and placing of people in the ceremonies are seen, on the contrary, as provocations. This is the first time that all these outlandish costumes are seen together, looking like nothing so much as an opera bouffe.

For instance, the installation of the deputies in the Cathedral of Notre-Dame of Versailles is held up almost half an hour by an argument touched off—who could believe it?—by dear old La Révellière-Lépeaux. Instead of following the rules for the uniform of his order, he has donned what he calls "a fine outfit," and buckled on his sword. Nobody notices him in the first church, while they're waiting for the King, but then part of the third happen to sit in the places reserved for the nobility, who get to come in last.

"Just as we had taken our places, we saw that the nobility who were following us suddenly stopped, instead of taking their seats, as we had done, in all the rows of benches. A handsome young man came up, tall and well built, in a coat all glittering with gold and precious stones, his fingers covered with diamonds and his head beplumed with feathers of dazzling white. An ebony baton with an ivory pommel, which he was wielding gracefully, was the mark of his high office . . . . This fair star was the Marquis de Brézé, grand master of ceremonies.*

" 'What is this, gentlemen?' the gorgeous courtier says to us. 'Are these your places?'

" 'Who are you, sir,' I retorted, 'to speak to the representatives of the French nation in such a tone?'

"Whereupon, I seated myself on one of the pews in the main nave, saying that I would not move from there."⁹

Can a scene be avoided? The nobles refuse to sit next to a bourgeois. It takes all the persuasion of La Révellière-Lépeaux's colleagues to convince him to accompany them to their assigned seats. Oh, well, this is such a great occasion; and this day, which has not happened in France since 1614, promises to be so glorious. . . .

The swell of the organ drowns conversation, and everybody waits for the King, who, today, is coming out to his people. Around eleven o'clock the trumpets herald his arrival, in his ceremonial carriage, surrounded by his

---

*Twenty-seven years old; his name goes down to posterity after Mirabeau makes his celebrated remark to him on June 23, 1789. He emigrates and resumes office under Louis XVIII, dying in 1829.

Life Guards on their splendid mounts and, for the last time in history, his Grand Falconry, which adds to the solemnity of his official movements. A Swiss spectator, not accustomed to so much pomp, writes to a friend in Geneva of his stupefaction at seeing thirty horsemen, commanded by the Comte de Vaudreuil, draw up around the cathedral porch, every one "with a well-armed falcon on his wrist. The poor animals looked most astonished to find themselves being taken to Notre-Dame."[10]

The King is greeted, along with his brothers, nephews, the Duc de Chartres and the other princes, his cousins, who have entered the church before him—except Orléans, who has made himself conspicuous by getting elected as a deputy for the nobility of Crépy-en-Valois and has accordingly declined all princely prerogatives for this day and those to come. All we're waiting for now is the carriage of the Queen, accompanied by Madame Elisabeth and their ladies-in-waiting.

The notes of the *"Veni Creator"* are the signal for departure of the procession, which everybody, including the sovereigns, follows on foot, behind the dais of the Holy Sacrament, for the few yards leading to the old cathedral, lopsided and deformed by the repeated enlargements and alterations that have transformed the everyday church of a largish village into the first church of royalty.

The departure is almost upset by a final incident, when the upper clergy refuse to let mere parish priests walk alongside them. Brézé deftly slips a group of musicians between the prelates and the common priests, who then feel themselves relegated to the condition of the third estate.

But now the moment comes when, in a surge of mingled religious and political excitement, the thousand actors in the procession and the ten-thousand-odd onlookers, some of whom have come out from Paris the day before and spent the night in their coaches, experience an unforgettable emotion.

Even the Good Lord joins in: the claws of the cruel winter have dug in until the very last night, when it rained so hard that they had to sand the paving stones. But an unexpected sun now clears the sky, illuminating, warming. Gouverneur Morris pays the price: "This has been so fine a day that walking about without my hat has got my face scorched exceedingly and both my forehead and eyes are inflamed."[11]

The procession may calm the ruffled feathers. Two kinds of harmony are at work: a harmony of colors, in the tapestries brought out of the King's storehouses and the swags of precious stuffs hanging at all the windows and across some of the streets; and a harmony of the royal, i.e., military, musicians, but also of the church choirs. Among so many others, Ferrières remembers these images and chants to his dying day.

"The regiments of the French Guards and Swiss Guards formed a line from Notre-Dame to St. Louis . . . . Joy shone in every eye; clapping hands, expressions of the most affectionate concern, gazes preceding us and following us still, after we were out of sight. . . . A ravishing, enchanting tableau . . . . Tears of joy streamed from my eyes. God, country, fellow citizens: all had become myself."[12]

The installation of all these people inside St. Louis gives rise to the same mixture of pomp and irritation as before, yet they are only an hour behind schedule by the time they have all found their proper places, including the deputies, who are hard-pressed to avoid setting fire to one another with the 1,043 tapers they've been handed, not counting another 286 more luxurious ones which have been distributed to the lords and ladies of Court.

Monseigneur de Juigné, archbishop of Paris, carries the Holy Sacrament beneath a canopy borne by the princes of the blood. Finally, about four o'clock, he goes to the altar to celebrate high mass. Then they're all going to have to endure the inevitable ordeal, the solemn sermon that everybody hopes will be brief and momentous. Juigné would have liked to give it, but it is customary for someone other than the celebrant to do so. It was up to the King to choose, and nobody knows why his choice fell upon Monseigneur de La Fare, who has been bishop of Nancy for barely a year. He's thirty-seven; like Talleyrand, he belongs to the new generation of bishops and seems adroit enough to be liked by all factions.

He talks, according to the gazettes, for "seven quarter hours."* As he proceeds, his audience can do no better than imitate the King, who, for once, is not the only person nodding. Mirabeau listens to enough of it to write that "never was a finer opportunity more utterly wasted."[13]

There is no danger that a prelate of this caste will give an evangelical sermon. He announces his major theme at the outset: "Religion makes the happiness of empires; religion makes the strength of empires."[14] His sermon, thus, is political, "religion" being taken as the supreme abstraction that ought properly to govern the world, in opposition to the "criminal new doctrines" now setting out to destroy society. More than half his remarks are a settling of scores with the Enlightenment, as though he were speaking twenty years earlier; there is absolutely no connection between what he says and the immense event he is inaugurating.

Duquesnoy, representing Bar-le-Duc, and one of the best witnesses to those days, is aghast: "All in all, his speech was weak, full of padding and declamations; a rhetorical style, without method or grace. He did not rise to the level of his subject, not by a long, long shot—an affected homily . . . . He lacks taste and his sermon was too long. He did not know how to end it."[15]

---

*He emigrates in 1791, attaches himself to the little Court of Louis XVIII and, returning to France with him, dies in 1829 covered in honors.

Mirabeau, again: "His speech seemed overlong and cobbled, without any plan or ideas or style or effects. People were waiting for a very different movement, a very different inspiration . . . . It embraced every possible commonplace, from the baptism of Clovis to the illness of Louis the Beloved in Metz, from exhortations on extravagance to assaults upon philosophy."[16]

La Fare is astute enough, however, to include among his "exhortations" a few relating to extravagance and ostentation, and these, occasionally, arouse his audience even to applause, a thing never before permitted in the presence of the Holy Sacrament. Under pressure from his electors in the bailliage of Nancy, no doubt, and with an eye to the future, "he compared the opulence of the Court with the destitution of the countryside. He asked how it could be, under a thrifty and wise king, that expenditure should so increase. . . . And there, he painted a very faithful picture of the life of the Queen,* even to the point of saying that, weary of riches and grandeur, it had become necessary for her to seek pleasure in a childish imitation of nature, an obvious allusion to the Petit Trianon. This was greeted with wild applause, albeit inside a church; . . . not one hand from the Court applauded . . . . I noticed a small mark of displeasure about the Queen's mouth; for the rest, the greatest aplomb and most intrepid phlegmatism; the King was asleep."[17]

Once mass is over and the King and princes have gone, the audience make their way out of St. Louis as best they can. Their numbers are already diminished by the departure of some of the "free" spectators, fearing death by tedium during the sermon. Among them is the young advocate Camille Desmoulins, who writes to his father, about La Fare, "The man did not seem to be in harmony with himself."[18]

The King is cheered as he finally climbs into his carriage again, despite his sullen air. Even the Queen, who could hardly have been expecting them, is given a few *Vivats!* The crowd is silent, on the other hand, as the princes go by, except for the ever-popular Duc d'Orléans.

Night falls on the contradictions and splendors of the religious day.

Tomorrow, make way for the secular.

*This is according to Duquesnoy, again, who undoubtedly heard what he chose to hear rather than the exact words that were spoken. However, the publication of the sermon is forbidden in 1789, which means that some passages in it must effectively have contained criticisms. When La Fare returns to France in 1818, he publishes it, disencumbered of any remarks liable to displease the Queen's daughter, the Duchesse d'Angoulême, whose chaplain he then is.

LOUIS XVI AND THE
ESTATES GENERAL

68

MAY 5, 1789

An Exaggerated Desire for Innovation

According to the cards issued by the grand master of ceremonies, the deputies
are to convene at eight in the morning, Tuesday, May 5. But considering
that a large proportion of them, in particular those from the third estate, of
course, will have to squeeze through the narrow doors of the hall of the
Menus Plaisirs almost in single file and will not be able to sit down inside
until around eleven, and considering that they are going to have to stay there
and behave themselves for another eight hours more, on top of the strain
and fatigue of the previous day, one might justifiably contend that this type
of overblown ceremony belongs rather to the realm of military maneuvers.
But there they are at last, crowded into the hall. It looks about the same as
the chamber that housed the Notables on two previous occasions except that
it is twice the size, because, in addition to the twelve hundred deputies who
are to sit there during plenary meetings, it also has to contain, along the
sides, three tiers of balconies for the "free" public.

On May 5 there are at least three thousand people in the room. It is
decorated mainly in white, its imperfections hidden by three hundred tapestries from the Gobelin works, illustrating, as ordered by the attentive works
managers, profane subjects only,* meaning shepherds and shepherdesses,
battles and political events ranging higgledy-piggledy from Antiquity to the
Age of Henri IV. Over 150 benches and 1,300 straight-backed chairs and
armchairs, all covered in green, have been mustered hastily. It would have
been impossible to get it all done in such a short time except by mobilizing
hundreds of unemployed workers at the last minute and paying them top
wages, and by using materials so flimsy that the builders are dreading any
agitation, or even a bad storm.

---

*Except for the room reserved for meetings of the clergy, where such subjects are pro-
scribed.

But the chamber that most of the deputies of the third will call the "national chamber" puts up a good front today, which is much to the credit of the people who put it together, especially as, at the same time as they were creating this huge room on the ground floor, they also had to produce two smaller ones on the floor above it for the representatives of nobility and clergy when they would be meeting by order—the theory from which Louis XVI and even Necker have still not departed.

Today, however, the great chamber is accommodating all three orders at once, not to mention the two thousand spectators who have turned up at dawn in order to be sure of a seat. People take their places in indescribable confusion owing to the lack of authority of Dreux-Brézé, whose crew is hopelessly inadequate: twelve ushers and heralds-at-arms to seat the whole crowd. At noon, though, under an enormous oval ceiling veiled in white taffeta, it offers a handsome enough spectacle, once everybody has sat down and the royal pair and princes are notified that they can finally take their places on a wide platform "surmounted by a splendid dais," in the words of Meister's *Correspondance littéraire,* which gives the rest of Europe the best account of the session. Everyone stands and their cheers swell kingward with a good heart, for they all give him the credit for this sensational idea that nobody would have dreamed of three years before. Also, when the two Assemblies of Notables met, there was not a female in sight, and this time the Queen and princesses are there, as well as any other woman who could get an invitation to a seat on the public benches.

So the whole morning passes in a muddle of pushing, shoving and ex-clamations of wonderment. There are squabbles, as yesterday, over which deputies are to sit where; there is excitement among the invited audience, who are aware that they are witnessing a unique event. In theory, all of them have been invited, by the Duc de Guiche, who is captain of the Life Guards this term, but that has not prevented strangers from slipping in among them, or lofty personages, e.g., certain members of the diplomatic corps, from failing to find a seat.

The style is half medieval reminiscence and half innovation. To the right of the platform, in three or four rows, are the men of the first order, the clergy, where the bishops are determined to get front seats; to the left is the second order, the nobility, identically aligned; and, facing the royal platform, from the back of the chamber to the middle, the representatives of the third, equaling the total of the first two orders. Most of the problems are created by the clergy, since the nobility follow their age-old hierarchy with the higher ranks in front of the lower, while the deputies of the third go to the places assigned to their respective bailliages and occupy them without a fuss.

Because of Vizille, there is some applause from the balconies when the

Dauphiné deputies turn up, more at the arrival of the deputies from Brittany (except for the nobles, who have all refused to come after the events in Rennes), and a mixed reception at the entrance of Mirabeau, whom most of the people here judge in terms of his past reputation, whereas he is actually arriving fresh from his triumphs in Provence. Germaine de Staël, who is sitting with the ministers' families, notes that "when Mirabeau appeared, a murmur ran through the entire assembly. He understood what it meant, but, moving proudly across the room to his seat, looked as though he was getting ready to stir up enough trouble in the state to confound both those who admired him and those who did not."[1]

The deputy who gets most applause, today as yesterday, is the Duc d'Orléans, who slips into place with his feigned humility among his colleagues in the nobility of Crépy-en-Valois.

By some miracle, and in spite of all the improvisation, all these people get themselves into their seats without any serious mishap, so the King is able to take his place a scant half hour behind schedule, beneath the vast canopy that really looks more like a tent, because of its size and golden hue. He remains standing a long moment in front of the chair reserved for him, more throne than chair, in fact, with a back so high it looks like the wall of a small house. The whole Court moves to either side of him on the platform just as a second miracle brings out the sun and illuminates the entire chamber, which abandons itself to enthusiastic clapping and cheering. Whatever happens afterward, the people who see this scene never forget it. For the first time since his coronation, the King and all his kin (except Orléans) can be encompassed in a single glance, wearing costumes of unbelievable splendor.

Louis XVI himself has on the great cloak of the Order of the Holy Spirit; on his head, a plumed hat with a diamond-studded border, the largest stone in which is also the largest stone in the world, known at this stage in its career as the Pitt.* He's thirty-six; he's put on weight, and his complexion has turned a uniform crimson. This is the Louis XVI that thousands of prints are to introduce to the whole of France, in the wake of the ones showing him young and almost handsome on his coronation day. But there is still majesty and good-fellowship in his bearing.

At that moment the King is the only man wearing a hat, while the whole assembly stands bareheaded before him. He briefly doffs his plumes in greeting to his audience, replaces them on his head and sits, while everybody else, the Queen included, wearing a gorgeous silver and blue paniered gown, remains standing to listen to his speech.

---

*It is later called the Regent, but in 1789 it bears the name of the person who sold it to the Court of France, an ancestor of the great English statesman.

Theoretically, everything is still possible for him. He is master of the law, of right, and of power. But if he thwarts the hopes of a whole people, the vast majority of whom believe in his justice and goodness, he will set off one of the greatest battles of all time, between tradition and innovation.

Among the people who listen to him, and who grasp the immense importance of his speech, are a few of those who are about to become the actors in the scenes to come, the "Men of Liberty" whose backgrounds this book has been exploring since Louis XVI's twentieth birthday. Many of them aren't here, others are known but still far away and a lot have not yet been heard of.

One woman: Germaine de Staël,* but only as spectator, and her father, Jacques Necker.

The few men with enough prestige and lung power to dominate the opening skirmishes: Mirabeau, La Fayette, Abbé Grégoire, Talleyrand, Barnave, Mounier, Malouet, Rabaut Saint-Étienne.

Little by little, others will take over from them, such as Robespierre, Barère, Dupont de Nemours, the brothers Alexandre and Charles de Lameth, Volney, Buzot, La Révellière-Lépeaux.

A few will prove unable to play the roles their past lives seemed to cast them for: Le Pelletier de Saint-Fargeau, Fréteau de Saint-Just, d'Eprémesnil, Coigny, Broglie, Lauzun-Biron, Lubersac,† d'Antraigues, Beauharnais, Lally-Tollendal, Vaudreuil, Sillery, Bergasse.

Others are still lost in the anonymous crowd of deputies, but we shall be hearing from them in due course: Pétion, Gobel, Batz, Custine, Menou, Boissy d'Anglas, Camus, Cochon de Lapparent, Régnier, Dubois-Crancé, Lanjuinais, Merlin de Douai, Mollien, Vadier.

Bailly isn't here today. He and Duport are among the ten or fifteen Parisian representatives who, like Sieyès, don't get elected until around May 15.

Nobody may speak before the King, and so much is expected of his speech that his opening words are engraved in every memory:

"Gentlemen, this day that my heart has long been awaiting has finally come, and I see myself surrounded by the representatives of the nation which it is my pride to command."[2]

---

*I am not counting the Queen, princesses and their suites.

†The Cardinal de Rohan is elected for the clergy of Alsace but never attends the Assembly, on grounds of "ill health": this is not the moment for him to show his face, because Jeanne de La Motte, after escaping from La Salpêtrière, has just published some very hot *Mémoires* in London.

As usual, the speech is short, and read in the "Bourbon style," slowly and heavily. The sonorous voice that Louis XVI has cultivated since childhood as a duty inherent in his office carries to the very back of the hall—something of a performance. It's true that in the last two days, before compiling his final text, he has been poring over the different versions he asked his advisers and the princes to submit. It's a success, in this chamber in which nobody has had a thought for the acoustics, and about which Mirabeau says "that only a stentorian voice can make itself heard. But by confining ourselves to strong lungs, we deprive ourselves of many strong heads."[3]

He even brings the unsentimental Gouverneur Morris to tears: "The tone and manner have all the *fierté* that can be expected or desired from the blood of the Bourbons. He is interrupted in the reading by acclamations so warm and of such lively affection that the tears start from my eyes in spite of myself."[4]

Even about his delivery, however, there are some reservations, in particular from Duquesnoy who, although a total royalist, writes that the speech was given "in a voice that was strong but had no grace or harmony; it was harsh and brusque. He was applauded several times. I tried to see why, for certainly there were no grounds for it. I was told that the first time the clapping interrupted him, he seemed upset when he began to speak again. I saw nothing of this and do not believe it."[5]

As for the contents of the speech, its sole merit is its conciseness. It offers a succinct blending of vague benevolence and intimidation.

At worst, it is more like an administering of admonitions by the principal of a wayward school than a speech by a sovereign to whom people are looking for liberalization in the future. Many listeners must wince when they hear him bemoaning the fact that "widespread unrest and an exaggerated desire for innovation have caught hold in people's minds and would mislead their opinions utterly if all haste were not made to stabilize them by a meeting of wise and moderate counsel."

There is one admission: "The state debt, which was enormous when I came to the throne, has grown still greater during my reign. The cause of this was an exorbitant but honorable war, and increased taxation has been the necessary consequence; so that inequalities in the collection of taxes have become more strongly felt."

Does he then announce that something is going to be done to reduce "inequalities in the collection of taxes"? Oh, no; on the contrary, he lavishes compliments upon the nobility and clergy for the imaginative efforts they have made: "I am touched to see that my confidence has been justified by the disposition shown by the first two orders to forgo their pecuniary privileges."

Where does he get that idea? The truth is exactly the opposite. So far,

they're sticking to them like limpets. As for the radical cuts advocated even
by Calonne in the ruinous budgets of the Households of the King, Queen
and princes, "I have already ordered substantial reductions in expenditure."
(Oh, yes, Mirabeau writes; "the reduction of the wolf-hunt and the elimi-
nation of a few falconers.") Magnanimously, the King adds, "You will submit
further ideas to me in this respect, which I shall be eager to receive; but
whatever the resources accruing from the most rigorous savings, I fear, gentlemen, that I may not be able to relieve my subjects as speedily as I should
desire."

But in that case, what are the Estates General going to *do?* The speech
ends in a swamp of propitiatory pronouncements and an appeal for universal
agreement—on what?

Many people think that all is not yet lost, because Necker is still to
come.

But before he does, the audience has to endure some more ceremonial
sideplay and a dreary display from Barentin. The King resumes his seat and
instructs a herald-at-arms to authorize the deputies to assume theirs, at long
last. The nobles don their handsome plumed hats; their side of the hall
suddenly looks like a strong breeze passing through a herbaceous border.
Protocol commands the third estate to remain bareheaded, but several
hundred of its members now cover their own pates. Whereupon Louis XVI,
who is occasionally capable of conceits of this sort, removes his hat and
pretends to fan himself with it. The others have no choice but to copy him,
so the entire assembly will now undergo an ordeal lasting several hours, hats
in hand.

For the Keeper of the Seals this is truly a day of mourning, but he makes
his audience pay for it to the limit by delivering an interminable and insipid
lecture "in so low, nasal and repulsive a voice," according to Duquesnoy,
"that he cannot have been heard by one-tenth of those present."[6] It's a
sequence of dithyrambic hymns to Louis XVI viewed as a reincarnation of,
inter alia, Charlemagne, St. Louis and Louis XII, who is deigning, out of
pure goodness of heart, to inform the Estates of the benefits he intends to
heap upon his people's heads. Even in the days of Louis XV, obsequiousness
in addressing the King never reached such summits as this.

Not until four o'clock does the only man at the ministers' long table
beneath the feet of the sovereign dressed in black—a black coat strewn with
golden sequins—rise, bow a request for permission to speak and turn to face
the Assembly, which finally shakes off its torpor. Jacques Necker is about

to obey the last sentence spoken some time back by the King: "The director general of my finances will describe their condition to you."

Although humility is not his besetting sin, Necker's opening words show that he is aware of the magnitude of the circumstances: "Gentlemen, when one is called upon to present oneself, to make oneself heard in so august and imposing a gathering, a feeling of reticence, a rightful mistrust of one's forces, are the first emotions one experiences."[7]

He's hardly more audible than Barentin. Necker's voice doesn't carry, and he has never been an orator. He's a banker, an economist-author if you like, and his style is heavy enough at the best of times. He has none of the qualities needed to sway people with the spoken word.

His speech, which lasts over three hours, is a vast plain of platitudes, badly composed, full of repetitions and containing no explicit statement of policy.

Soon aware that nobody can hear him, he asks the King's permission to have the rest of his discourse read out by Broussonet, one of his assistants, a man from Languedoc with a resonant voice, and returns to sit at the table like a punished schoolboy. The secretary does his best and is at least audible, but sounds more like an interpreter reciting a translation.

The speech is primarily an account of the financial situation of France, surely the most honest ever presented to the country—including Necker's first try in 1781. It shows that on May 1 the famous deficit, which has been the subject of so much argument since Calonne, stands at fifty-six million livres, and he explains this in exhaustive detail. The total expenditure of the royal and princely households accounts for thirty-three million of it, but it is only fair to point out that this sum includes a large number of pensions and annuities granted in olden days, by which the budget is encumbered. As it stands, however, there is nothing catastrophic about it.

Mirabeau, who entertains few illusions about Necker, picks up one or two phrases in the speech that seem to hint at a heart, in particular his condemnation of the slave trade and a sudden avowal of the anguish he is striving to hide: "Ah, gentlemen, in certain crises, and in the throes of his labors and pains, the feelings of which a minister has greatest need from others are compassion and pity."

He'd better not count on getting any from Mirabeau, after this tidal wave of banalities, reiterated homages to the King, and marks of graciousness toward the first two orders, from whom he, too, is asking for only voluntary sacrifices. The next day, in the newspaper he tries to launch on the Estates General, Mirabeau tears him to shreds: "Intolerable tedium, innumerable repetitions, trivialities pompously uttered, unintelligible things, not a single principle, not one indisputable affirmation, not one statesman's resource, not even one financier's expedient, no plan of restoration . . . ; and how could a man create, let alone consolidate, a different order of things, when he does not dare utter the word constitution?"[8]

We might suppose Mirabeau's fulminations to be the product of purely personal animus; but Duquesnoy, too, is appalled. "His speech was by no means satisfactory to all: he praised the King in every line; no new ideas about administration or finance . . . , everlastingly repeating that the King did not summon the Estates because he needed them, but out of his own good pleasure. In a word, it all seemed prejudiced in favor of the King and the two first orders."[9]

In the middle of this endless turkey, one sentence opens the gulf beneath Necker's feet that will lead to his downfall: "There is every indication, gentlemen, that if one part of this assembly were to request that the first topic of your debate should be a motion that votes be taken by name . . . , the result would be a schism such that the progress of the Estates General would be halted or at least suspended for some time." In other words, he has thrown his lot in with the people who hate him and are trying to prevent him from doing anything innovative. Perhaps his sparing treatment of the privileged is an attempt to show what he and the King have in common: a horror of confrontations and a strong sense of class hierarchy and its usefulness.

As a former clerk in the Thélusson Bank, Necker has always had something of the parvenu's coquettish attitude toward all princes. He shies away from the decisive role he is expected to play. He does not want to be seen as the leader of a people's party.

This is the beginning of Necker's political suicide. And he'll get no thanks for it from the people he's treating so gently, whereas the disappointment of the third estate is plainly shown in the silence that follows the end of his speech, even though he does make the effort to take his text back from Broussonet and finish it off himself, with the enumeration of the details of the budget.

"Looking back, I cannot think without bitterness of the way in which my expectations were deceived [he later writes, in his *Mémoires*] when, so happy to be able to inform the Estates General how little basis in fact there was for all the rumors going around about the deficit . . . , and rejoicing in advance at the impression this unexpected news would make upon the Assembly, I perceived nothing but chill and silence."[10]

So the first meeting of the Estates seems likely to end in a deathly hush, since nobody in the other two orders is applauding either.

Then what is the source of these refreshing ovations and clappings of hands, transforming the general gloom into gladness? Why, it's the King— the King, who rises, bows to everyone and leaves, followed by his family, at a distinctly more sprightly pace than is his wont.

The reason for this half flight is his terror of Mirabeau, although he hardly knows the man. But part of the Court is dreading some sort of ad lib action by the ogre. There have been rumors that he means to ask the King to consent at once to the convening of the three orders on a permanent basis and to voting by name. This would be an inconceivable scandal, as nobody is supposed to speak in front of the King without being invited to do so by him. But Mirabeau is too anxious to keep his options open for the future and can't take the plunge. Among his papers, however, is a text he thought of placing at the feet of Louis XVI that evening, if he found an opportunity, imploring him "not to entrust to the prejudice of the orders that which should be determined by the reason of all. Do not jeopardize the fruit of the finest action of your reign."[11]

This speech, which long remains undisclosed, would truly have set Mirabeau up as the anti-Necker. But it would seem that fame is teaching him patience. He opts for silence and applauds the King like a good boy, along with everyone else: "We were drunk with longing to applaud, and we applauded our fill and more."[12]

MALOUET

69

MAY 6–JUNE 11, 1789

Let Us Cut the Cable

What next? Next . . . nothing.

Much is anticipated on the morning after this solemn opening, however disappointing it may have been. France is still pinning its hopes on the Estates General.

But what happens is exactly what nobody had foreseen. The Estates are stricken with catalepsy. The first event of the Estates General is that for more than a month there is no event. It's as though some spell has put the historic gathering to sleep in its opening hours.

Between May 6 and June 11 the deputies circle in a holding pattern, unable to proceed because of a problem that could have been settled in a week: the validation of their credentials as elected representatives.

This means that the representatives sent by the different bailliages and seneschalsies must reciprocally attest to one another's election, which is almost as simple as holding out a passport or letter of introduction, and made easier by the fact that almost all the members of the delegations know one another within their respective orders and regions. They all know how they themselves and their colleagues were appointed, and they have come bearing the piece of parchment needed to authenticate their positions, duly signed by the presidents and secretaries of their electoral assemblies. To move from the local to national level, all they have to do is collate these documents.

It's so simple, in fact, that when the tabulation finally is made, hardly a single name is challenged. How could some stranger try to pass himself off as a deputy without being instantly denounced by other deputies from his locality?

But everything bogs down in questions of formality, because the first two orders want to validate their credentials unobserved, and invite the third to follow suit. But the third, put on their guard by the champions of the individual vote, chiefly Mirabeau, do not fall into the trap. Fine, let's validate credentials, but all of us together. If the bourgeois give way on this matter, voting by order will be a foregone conclusion. There will be three assemblies instead of the great collective merging the kingdom wants. Hence the deputies of the third, most of whom insist upon calling themselves "members of the commons," dig in their heels in the great hall downstairs, which has to be left to them anyway, while nobility and clergy cloister themselves in their rooms upstairs.

The next morning, May 6, the nobles set straight to work on their self-validation, despite the protests of 47 liberals, including La Fayette, who propose that they join the others in the only room that can hold them all. But they're opposed by 180 deputies in their own order.

The clergy decide to imitate the nobles, but by a smaller margin—133 to 114; which shows that the "little priests" are not prepared to let themselves be pushed around by the bishops.

As for the third, it merely resumes the seats it was occupying the day before, provisionally appoints the oldest member present to serve as interim chairman and folds its arms. It doesn't even send a delegation to call upon the other two orders, so as not to seem to consent to their separation.

If the others come to join it, they'll be welcome. No animosity is expressed toward them within the third. But it rejects the idea of acknowledging them within a structured difference and makes not the slightest move to validate its own credentials. Similarly, not wanting to stand out as it accuses the other two orders of doing, it makes no move in the direction of King or ministers.

Somewhere around three in the afternoon, after being kept waiting an eternity to get back to their places in "their" hall (the whole morning is wasted because of the incoherence of the heralds-at-arms and the removal of a number of benches needed upstairs), the gentlemen of the third, their tempers already none too sweet, open what can't really be called a sitting, but more a sort of indefinitely extended club debate. Pending the meeting of the body as a whole, the only right they allow themselves is the right to perorate.

But as for peroration, Lord in Heaven, how they go at it! What consummate windbags they are! For six solid weeks a flood of eloquence pours through the hall and out over the rest of the country.

The two speakers on the crest of the first wave of this oratorical inundation are Malouet and Mirabeau, the latter impressing his colleagues with the clarity of his initial summary:* "Until our credentials have all been validated together, we must look upon ourselves only as a collection of individuals who may confer informally but have no capacity to act. Respect for this principle must be absolute, to the point of refusing to open letters addressed to the commons and handed into this chamber. Let us give the privileged orders time to consider."[1]

Malouet's position is less radical,† while Mounier supports Mirabeau. These first leading speakers outline the two positions that engender much division and (at least apparent) confrontation within the third, many of whose members find Mirabeau's verbal superiority hard to take and who quite wrongly blame him for the hardening of the positions adopted by the third and the Court.

At this point, one deputy announces that he has just been told that the other two orders have opted definitively for separate validation. All that remains for the third estate is to leave the room, but not before deciding to meet there again the next day—but only to talk . . . to talk, if need be, until the end of the world.

---

*Most of the early speeches do not survive, as no arrangements had been made to record the debates—they hadn't even engaged a secretary, and the stenographic process known as logography does not come into use until later. Also, most of the individual voices are lost in the ambient roar, and when any speakers' words do emerge, it is only because they have them printed themselves and because a handful of journalists are on the job, in particular the team of Panckouke, who is preparing to launch the *Moniteur* [an early form of Congressional Record] and who issues a series of "reconstructions" at the end of the year.

†Formerly intendant of the navy, he has just been elected for the third estate of Auvergne, and the moderate tendencies he shows in this first debate increase as time goes on. For example, he does not oppose the idea of sending a delegation from the third to the other two orders just to make contact. See Volume I for his role in Guyane in 1777. He served as intendant of Toulon for some time, but chose Riom as the springboard for his political attempt.

On May 7, Malouet talks for a good hour in favor of some sort of contact with "the people above." Mirabeau tackles him head-on. Mounier, who is listened to by virtue of the authority vested in him at Vizille and Romans, "presents a middle way," suggesting that a few representatives go, in a personal capacity, to find out what the others are up to.

On the eighth, Rewbel, an Alsatian deputy from Colmar, shows a practical turn of mind by proposing "regulations for the collection of votes" and the appointment of some of their colleagues to take turns as secretaries.*

On the eleventh, the clergy makes up tasks for itself by appointing "conciliatory commissioners," whom the third listens to politely but without vouchsafing the slightest reply; the Comte de'Antraigues, who always has an eye to his popularity rating, leaks a long speech outside the walls of the nobility, but he has already changed the color of his coat and now stands as a vigorous champion of his order's special rights.

On May 13 it's the turn of a delegation from the nobility, headed by the Duc de Praslin, to draw a blank with the third. It also draws a stinging apostrophe from Mirabeau:

"Is it not a favor that the gentlemen of the nobility are conferring upon the other orders when they appoint commissioners to consult with them? .... Who is preventing them from going further, from making a constitution, settling the finances, enacting laws? Are not the nobles everything in France, alongside a corporation of twenty-four million persons who are not worth reckoning with?"[2]

Beginning that day a few "new" voices are heard from. Bishop Gobel, coming from the clergy, strives very hard but to no avail.† Two men of good will, Rabaut Saint-Étienne and a Breton, Le Chapelier, vainly try to revive the move toward some compromise.

On the fifteenth, Boissy d'Anglas,‡ a deputy from Languedoc, flaunts an extremist position he will not long hold: "The people's prayers are orders; its grievances are laws, and it is truly the nation; whereas the other orders are no better than its dependents."[3] Volney tries his puny voice, also to propose some form of contact, if only exploratory.

On the eighteenth, the front-line speakers, Malouet and Mirabeau, come to verbal blows again on the same question, and Mirabeau does not spare

---

*He keeps pretty much out of the limelight during the acute phase of the Revolution, is one of the last members of the Directoire, does not follow Bonaparte, and dies in 1810.

†This is the first appearance of the future revolutionary archbishop of Paris, who performs a spectacular self-defrocking in the Convention and is guillotined with the Enragés.

‡As *president* of the Convention, but after Thermidor, and after becoming a moderate, he is conspicuous for his courageous attitude during the riot of Prairial year III (May 20, 1795).

Rabaut Saint-Étienne while he's at it. He has shifted a little, however: "Send to the clergy, gentlemen, but do not send to the nobility, for the nobility orders and the clergy negotiates."[4]

Would this be the thin edge of a détente? Mirabeau can't seriously hope that the clergy are going to evolve so rapidly, perhaps even separate themselves from the nobility, in spite of the growing pressure being put upon them, not only by the parish priests but also by a number of prelates who are exasperated by the stiffening of the second order. Champion de Cicé, archbishop of Bordeaux, and Lubersac, bishop of Chartres, would gladly volunteer to promote a meeting with the third. But it's still a long way off.

For both Mirabeau and even the most vehement of the nobles, however—Lally-Tollendal, for instance, or d'Eprémesnil—the need to end the stalemate is being made imperative by pressure from public opinion, which is sending angry and impatient echoes from the provinces, where food shortages are as acute as ever and have led to dozens of local riots, and where the administration has broken down pending some action by someone somewhere.

The one prerequisite for the joint meeting of all three orders is that it should be commanded by the King, but without seeming to have been extorted from him by the third. Mirabeau is not the only one toying with the idea of another "royal sitting," in which the sovereign might fill the holes left in the one on May 5 and instruct all the representatives to merge into a single assembly. The idea is floating around in Necker's group as well. He is too well informed not to realize that, as Malouet has just said, France is "on the edge of the precipice."

But there's more than meets the eye in these initial gestures of Mirabeau in the direction of the clergy and in the remarks being exchanged in Madame Necker's drawing room and even by a few ministers on the Council. They speak in the presence of the King, but he has yet to express his real ideas on the subject, if any. Almost another month is consumed by a misunderstanding which is the chief cause of the first failure of the "royal revolution."

The interminable speechifying reflects only the surface of things. Almost all the actors whose names are beginning to occupy the foreground are hiding most of their cards and intentions. Mirabeau's asseverations, despite their ferocity, are often a smokescreen thrown up before his unswervingly monarchistic position. Now, having so copiously splattered him with mud, he is looking for a way to make contact with Necker, who scorns and fears him but can gauge his influence on opinion. At least three men at Court—Montmorin, Puységur and Saint-Priest—share this temptation. And many of the people around Mirabeau, who are trying to shout as loudly as he, are also half-listening for the first footfalls of reconciliation. Mounier, for example, Buzot, Volney, Boissy d'Anglas.

If access to the King were not made so difficult by the Barentins, Brézés and Breteuils who form a living rampart in front of him and call it etiquette, a few hours of audience might produce the desired arrangement. Who knows?

There are only two groups who are not trying to look both ways at once and who oppose any "arrangement" to the last.

At Court, longing only to unsheathe their swords and start hacking, are the "party" of the Queen and Artois, who will never yield. They have realized that the only way to regain control is to persuade the King to dismiss Necker and disband the Estates. But they are only a handful. And opposing them like a living retort are some new faces, floating to the surface on the benches of the third: Barnave, for instance, a deputy from Arras whom the first printed accounts insist upon calling Robert Pierre,[5] whenever the scribes can catch his weak voice in the tumult. Or, no less hard to hear but making himself felt by his reputation and terseness of speech, the man who will become the spokesman of those whom people are starting to call "republicans," although they don't yet merit the name, Emmanuel-Joseph Sieyès.

Sieyès has only just turned up at the Estates, one of the last of the stragglers. Rejected by the clergy of Chartres because of his notorious lack of faith, he has managed to get himself elected as number twenty-one—a supernumerary, thus—on the roster of the third estate from Paris. He is a rare example of a man who has been elected for what he has written, meaning his famous pamphlet. Bailly, who is number one in the Paris delegation, rightly observes that the ranks of the third estate are crowded with lawyers and "owners" but that there are virtually no writers in the entire assembly,[6] Condorcet, Beaumarchais and Marmontel having all been eliminated in the preliminary phases of the election.

But with the exception of these two extreme groups, everybody else really would like to come to an agreement—some out of personal ambition, more because they are in a hurry to get on with the business they are supposed to be conducting. When more is known of their offstage behavior, it becomes clear that nothing in their notions of what that business is raises any insuperable barrier between them, and that the "moderators," whose views are not always moderate and whose voices begin to be heard more insistently toward the end of May, when they grow bolder and begin to discern possible allies, will almost be capable of setting in motion the process that would bring the three orders together. Rabaut is their best exponent. But who would have thought that Mounier, with the aggressive reputation he acquired in Dauphiné nine months before and his first words before the "commons," which seemed to rival Mirabeau's for pugnacity, is also longing to make peace with Necker and spare the nobility?

In the end, the differences among all these men of the third are no broader, or very little, than a split hair. Necker is still their great man, and their one tangible hope remains the King, exactly insofar as they sense the danger of violent reaction by the Queen and princes.

Unable to speak openly to each other without losing face, they're compelled to continue their verbal escalations, which prevent the misunderstanding from being cleared up and give a foothold to the *real* extremists. On June 10, Sieyès is cheered to the skies when he calls out, "Let us cut the cable. It is time!"

But it's a near miss. Nothing irrevocable has taken place, not only between "commons" and King but also between the three orders. This is at least partly the doing of Mirabeau, who dons his fire-eating eloquence like a coat, only because he wants to be sure of the Court's ear when the Court gets around to wanting to listen to him. Therein lies the difference—as he himself acknowledges in a speech made on June 15[7]—between Sieyès, Robespierre and himself.

That day, fuming with contempt for the theoreticians of advanced subversion, he issues a dazzling definition, which is no less valid today as far as politicians are concerned:

"The difference between the metaphysician, who, while meditating in his study, apprehends the truth in its energetic purity, and the statesman, who is compelled to reckon with antecedents, difficulties and obstacles, is this: The former is concerned with what might be, while the latter is concerned with what can be. . . . The former is primarily the people's teacher, while the political administrator deals solely with the present . . . . Traveling around his globe, the metaphysician sails smoothly over every obstacle, is not hindered by mountains or deserts or rivers. But when the point is to reach the objective, then it must constantly be borne in mind that we are walking on earth and are no longer in some ideal world."

This might be seen as just another of his bits of brilliant wordplay, but in reality it's a coded message for the other camp—notwithstanding the miscarriage, on June 11, of a meeting brought about by Malouet between Necker and Mirabeau. This incident, which long remains secret, might have changed many things; its failure is one of the aggravating factors in the situation.

The incompatibility between the minister and the great orator hardens into granite because of Necker's frosty, almost insulting treatment of Mirabeau on this occasion. He can't forget the journalist's lampoons of him or the recent scandal over his book on Prussia. Mirabeau, on the other hand, for all his faults, is incapable of harboring a grudge.

Malouet's mistake is in not insisting upon being present at the interview, where his talents as a plain-dealing conciliator might have been put to good use. In Necker's mind the situation is quite simple: the only object Mirabeau can have in coming to him is to ask for a few thousand louis and his instructions. "As if Monsieur de Mirabeau were a man to sell himself in such a stupid and cowardly fashion!" groans Malouet, when he sees him arrive next morning, red with rage and snapping, "Your man is a fool. He'll hear from me!"[8]

Necker greets him with his eyes on the ceiling, "as was his custom . . . . He carried his head very high, tilted backward in fact, and there was affectation in the posture, for the degree of upward tilt of his head reflected the temperature of the political situation."[9]

"Monsieur Malouet has told me, Monsieur le Comte, that you wished to put proposals to me. What are they?"

"My proposal," rejoins Mirabeau, picking up his hat, "is to wish you a good day."[10]

BAILLY

70

JUNE 10–17, 1789

I Assumed the Uniform of a Deputy

Almost at the start of his *Mémoires,** Bailly relates his last day of peace as a scientist and his arrival at the "commons," following his election. It reads like the prelude to the reminiscences of a civilian who suddenly embarks upon the ship of politics only to become, almost immediately, its admiral.

On May 23, "Was to the meeting of the Academy of Sciences to read a report on the need to remove the slaughterhouses [open ones, in the streets] from inside the capital . . . . After that, left straightaway with Madame Bailly

---

*Which are not rightly so-called, because in them Bailly is trying to give an account of his political activity; hence they relate largely to his role in the Constituent and as mayor of Paris. He says nothing of the time before his election, and the Terror prevents him from saying anything of later days.

for Versailles and was set down in rue des Bourdonnais, where I had rented an apartment . . . .

"On May 24, I assumed the uniform of a deputy, black coat and cloak, long hair and cravat."[1]

So he uncomplainingly conforms to the imposed form of dress against which so many of the third estate deputies have protested, and he explains why he does so in a whole page of text from which he emerges as a man of order despite his allegiance to the universal desire for change. "An inviolable deputy, a legislator, is an object of public veneration, so it is good to proclaim him and make him known everywhere by some outward sign . . . . He must always be respected by the people, who are persuaded by their eyes, especially in a system of civil equality."[2]

Such, now, is Jean-Sylvain Bailly, the only "new man" to be revealed to France in the opening weeks of the Estates General.

He comes already enhaloed by the Paris electors, having been chosen first of twenty after a month of fine-honed debate. When he finally does turn up, "it could be said that the Assembly was quite directionless in its progress . . . . The Assembly in Paris must have been more regular and methodical in its proceedings than the others; for, taught by it, I brought the commons hope of a degree of order hitherto unknown to them. I was encouraged to establish that order and found myself, to my own surprise, strong and firm. But in fact, I am always strong when there is a law."[3]

Bailly is no Condorcet or Volney, but perhaps it is the fact that he has already passed the halfway mark of a life as a scholar and, on occasion, man of letters, that prompts him to take what is for him such an astonishing plunge, into the heart of the first great tremors. Who knows, perhaps he was a little bored with his astrolabes, laborious calculations on astral mechanics, and the occasional philanthropic activities in which he had been associating, for some years, with Dr. Guillotin, another newly elected deputy. (We must not forget a third representative sent by the nobility of Paris, who has been involved in politics for over a year now—Adrien Duport. But he hardly, if ever, opens his mouth during his first month in the Estates.)

Bailly is primarily an astronomer—a member, thus, of a resuscitated body of scholars who, after so many centuries during which the men of the West stared up at the stars solely in search of God and destiny, are now lurching haltingly between their still-uncertain observation of astral bodies and the rediscovery of the secrets of the universe first revealed by the Egyptians and almost wholly neglected ever since.

Caricaturists immediately begin drawing him in the guise of the astronomer from one of La Fontaine's fables, who gives a lecture to a man who has fallen down a well instead of helping him to get out of it. But although the caricature does fit his outer personality, it does not correspond to his deeper concerns, in which the fate of his fellows bulks very large indeed.*

He wears a white wig, well powdered but plain, and under it his rather immobile face, with regular features and the large eyes some people find empty, gives him something of the "noble father" look that both intimidates and inspires confidence.

He ought to have been an artist, except that he proved to have no gift for the manipulation of pencil and brush and thereby broke with a family tradition rooted in four generations of Baillys, through which he was brought into the world on September 15, 1736, in one of the apartments of the higgledy-piggledy gypsy encampment that was the Louvre in those days.

In the Bailly family the title of "painter to the King" was handed down from father to son, as generations of men in other families were officers or magistrates. His own father, Jacques, however, "authorized painter to the King" at thirty-six and inspector of the royal collections, showed more talent for keeping catalogs and criticizing other people's works than for creating his own. In this capacity, he had been given a comfortable apartment in part of the Grand Gallery and hoped his son would take it over from him. But in the course of Jean-Sylvain's training, and in spite of his family, the chain somehow broke. So what's the use of being born next door to Greuze?

The Baillys were an easygoing family and tyranny did not reign in their midst, which is presumably why Jean-Sylvain did not have to go through a period of revolt or become a temperamental youth. As was usual with a child about to climb a step or two up toward nobility—which was the case of those in his environment—he learned his abc's at home while his father was spending most of his time at the tavern and at least a little of it with actresses. The next phase of his education was entrusted to Abbé Rollin: Latin, history—ancient much more than national—and a taste for the Classical century. Not much in the way of mathematics; what use would that be to a boy being brought up to discover that he was a painter?

Bailly himself was neither lazy nor a libertine. To overcome the bashfulness that had always troubled him, literary creation occurred to him as a means of self-expression, and he began to study it under masters more skillful than Abbé Rollin. They succeeded in discouraging him, after the perpetration of two abysmal tragedies, a *Clotaire* and an *Iphigenie en Tauride*. Abbé Lacaille, a scholar of merit who was not above giving boys lessons at home even though he was a member of the Academy of Sciences, is Bailly's man of destiny, guiding him first to mathematics and then to the exploration of a universe that could at last be scrutinized without fear of persecution by the

*The best portrait of him is in the Musée Carnavalet. It dates from 1789, but Bailly doesn't change, whatever happens to him and whatever the ordeals by which he may have been branded, until his death by the guillotine on 28 Brumaire year II.

Church. At the same time he formed his pupil's style, or at least turned it
into solid, hefty prose. Jean-Sylvain is no more a novelist than a dramaturge
but at thirty he knows how to express himself, whether in praise of Corneille
and Molière or in giving form to the increasingly substantial results of his
scientific research. He remains devoted to the "great Lacaille," his "good
father" figure.

At twenty-seven, that same increasingly substantial research enables him
to be elected to the vacancy in the Academy of Sciences created by Lacaille's
death.

At forty, his abilities and conscientiousness are thought so highly of by
his colleagues in the Academy that they entrust him with one or two missions
which turn his footsteps, involuntarily, in the direction of politics. For instance, he is a member of the commission appointed to judge Mesmer and
his famous tubs, which he condemns firmly but without contempt.

In 1786 he publishes his report on the possible construction of a new
Hôtel-Dieu, confirming a leaning toward service to the ailing poor; in the
"old Hôtel-Dieu" they were still rotting three or four to a bed.

Unlike his father, and possibly because of his father's bad example, Bailly
has never cared much about women. But in 1787, at forty-two, he marries
a widow of his own years named Jeanne Le Seigneur. They are faithful and
attached to each other, and remain so.[4]

His *Mémoires* are like himself: honest, exact, boring. As a supplement
to the reconstructions that are published later, and to Mirabeau's *Lettres à
ses commettants,* they make it possible to follow almost hour by hour the
events of the storm that comes after the lull and hardens the extremist
position at the beginning of the Revolution far beyond what most people
were imagining, between June 17 and July 14.

It is not necessarily a coincidence that things start to happen after the
arrival of the deputies from Paris. Their absence from the aborted reconciliation efforts in June is unfortunate. The Parisians would have shaken the
assembly out of the sort of paralysis into which it had sunk.

It's not the King's fault that things go wrong again this time, or even
the Queen's. On June 4, at Meudon, the Dauphin dies. So, with less than
full ceremonial, the sovereigns retreat temporarily into their grief at Marly,
and ten more days of status quo ensue. On June 6, the third, again left to
its own devices, simply elects Bailly to act as its doyen in place of its oldest
member, who has already thrown in the towel. But in this case "doyen"
should rather be taken to mean "president," because Bailly is much more
than the "oldest member present."

"It cannot easily be conceived how greatly I was afflicted and altered by this decision. Seeking to decline, I stammered out some excuses that were not listened to . . . . What weakened my resistance was my feeling that the chief reason for the choice was a desire to honor the delegation from Paris."[5]

However that may be, Jean-Sylvain, who, three months before, was light-years away from politics, has now become the first man of the third, in the sense that he represents more people than anybody else. The "commons" now have someone to be their incarnation on the great occasions when they have to stand up to the other two orders and the King, who is not too unhappy about his election because he quite likes men of learning and is acquainted with some of Bailly's work, and he also knows him to be a moderate who may be able to act as a conciliator. Besides, the fellow cut quite a decent figure when first presented to him, and again when he came with some other deputies to "sprinkle holy water" on the poor little Dauphin's coffin.

That does not prevent the sovereigns from feeling sincerely hurt by the almost universal indifference with which their subjects greet the news of his death. Louis XVI is shocked by the persistence of the third estate, only a few days after his loss, in seeking an audience and asking him to hold another royal sitting as soon as possible. He retreats toward the princes and nobles, refuses to see the people from the "commons" (and has never accepted that name for them) and drifts away from Necker. This in turn provokes the third into giving free rein to its exasperation, which Bailly has certainly done nothing to encourage.

On June 13, it's the lower clergy's turn to lose patience. Every man in the third is on his feet, and some have tears in their eyes, when three priests from Poitou—the abbés Lecesve, Ballard and Jallet—come to join them. Abbé Grégoire misses this opportunity, but he makes up for it the next day, bringing five more members of the first order with him.

On June 15, the pace of the debates begins to accelerate.

After a speedy validation of the credentials of everybody present, the third proceeds to burn its bridges. It has to give itself a name and impose that name on King and country. But it doesn't get one without a rather comical lexical battle, in which both Mirabeau and Sieyès break a few spears. Back on May 29 the former, in the course of a speech on some other subject, used the expression "national assembly." He now proposes "representatives of the French people," while the latter suggests "representatives of the nation," which Bergasse wants to expand into "known and validated representatives of the nation." Mounier proposes "legitimate assembly of the representatives of the greater part of the nation acting in the absence of the lesser part," while Barère tries "representatives of the very great majority of the French in the national assembly." Target: "representatives of almost the whole of the French people"; Biauzat: "representatives of twenty-four million men"; somebody named Pison du Galland: "active and legitimate assembly of the representatives of the French nation."

On the evening of June 16 an obscure deputy from Berry named Legrand takes advantage of everyone else's fatigue to achieve simplicity: "National Assembly."

Discussion is adjourned until the next day, when Sieyès, realizing that he has missed the boat, seconds Legrand but acts as though the words are his own offering. Bailly calls for a vote on "the motion of Abbé Sieyès," which is approved by 491 to 90, and sends notice to the King "informing him of the decision. Then [according to one account] repeated cries of '*Vive le Roi!*' were heard."[6]

They're off.

JEU DE PAUME ASSEMBLY

71

JUNE 18–23, 1789

Well, Dammit, Let Them Stay!

The next day Bailly notes, in reference to the motion of June 17, that "from this moment, the commons disappeared; there is no longer anything but a National Assembly."[1]

What a relief for historians [and translators] who are compelled, when talking about the events of these last months, to hesitate between a whole family of names, not only "commons" but also "third order," "third," and "third estate." Bailly's first act is to clear up his own title. More legalistic than ever, he submits his resignation as doyen, which term similarly disappears from Assembly usage, while the body itself quickly reelects him as its head, but with the title of "president."

The only problem is, and the shrewder heads are apprehensive of the consequences, that on the morning of June 18 the Assembly is all alone in its new state, and neither the first two orders nor the Court and its ministers have ratified its decision. It comes at the wrong moment, just when, in the too-well-guarded secrecy of the royal study, the plan for the forthcoming "royal sitting" is being drawn up and Necker thinks he is home free. He has just submitted to the King the drafts of speeches and decrees that ought to give some satisfaction to the third. But he is not about to propose that Louis XVI command the three orders to meet together and is not in favor of the idea himself. So even he is nettled by the proclamation of June 17, and he's the first to observe the stiffening it produces in the King, who has adhered relatively faithfully thus far to his assigned role as arbiter. He's the first, but the new Assembly will soon observe it too.

Not that they don't try to be nice to the sovereign when they vote their "notice" informing him of the decision they have adopted, "whereupon repeated shouts of *'Vive le Roi!'* were heard."[2] But these shouts don't clear the palace gates. Louis XVI plays deaf and merely deigns to write, on June 18, "to M. Bailly, doyen of the order of the third estate," that he will not receive the delegation that the Assembly has sent him, and adds, "I disapprove of the repeated use of the expression 'privileged classes' as employed by the third estate in referring to the first two orders."[3]

So they want a royal sitting? Well, they're going to get one. Its original purpose was to effect a reconciliation, but now its goal is to satisfy the nobility and upper clergy only—so there.

Until it takes place, the two little worlds on which the whole of France depends operate as though they were on different planets. On one side is the Assembly, which gleefully flings itself into the legislative activities for which its members have been thirsting. On the other is the Court party, in which the Queen, Artois, Barentin and nearly all the ministers believe that the "third order" has just given them an undreamed-of chance by making the King feel they are trying to force his hand. Necker, entangled more deeply than ever in his ambiguous role, is still the only person in Versailles to make any effort to patch things up. But he's feeling increasingly isolated, on the verge of disgrace, and is thinking of resigning before he gets dismissed; and as early as June 19, people are beginning to be aware of this. That evening Thibaudeau is (incorrectly) informed, as are several other representatives, that some form of arbitrary action is being planned against them, or against their most noticeable members. "Forced dissolution was feared, an order for the Estates General to disband; several colleagues did not sleep at home that night."[4]

That does not prevent the Assembly from setting up several committees during its first "real sitting" that afternoon, each with a membership of twenty. The first formed, at the urgent request of Barère, who is alarmed by news of a growing famine, is the committee on provisions, which is to consider how to end the scarcity and reduce the high price of cereals. The next to be set up are a committee on validation and disputes, a drafting committee for official texts—in other words, the embryo of a secretariat—and a committee on rules of procedure, "for the order and dispatch of business," according to Bailly, whose position as president has abruptly brought him face to face with the joys of "parliamentary debate"—a phenomenon he is now inaugurating in France, in conditions of indiscipline and discourtesy that deeply shock the English traveler Arthur Young. Used to the starchy formality of debate in English assemblies, Young is now watching nearly a hundred speakers all talking at once and cutting each other off without listening. The poor astronomer-president on his platform is finding all these unruly lawyers something of a handful. This is certainly not the Academy of Sciences . . . .

"There was a great deal of noise and disruption. The Assembly had as yet no ushers to make people be quiet . . . . All I had was my bell, which was often ineffectual. One time when it was not heard, despairing at my inability to restore order and silence, I let escape the words, 'Gentlemen, you will be the death of me!' "⁵

And this is only the first day! Bailly will see more and worse before he's through, but at this point he is immediately consoled by the discovery of another facet of the French personality: its mutability. "My words produced instant and deep silence, followed by universal evidence of consideration. In those days, we were living in union and sharing the most brotherly sentiments . . . . Indeed, I think the happiest time of my life was when I was first president of the National Assembly."

He fixes a time for their meeting the following morning, to continue their work. But the following morning—

"This day [June 20] is the second memorable day that must be inscribed in the nation's annals [according to Bailly]. At half-past six in the morning a friend . . . came to my home announcing that, having gone to the chamber as he did every day, he had been refused entry. He asked if I had given any orders; I told him no. For several days we had been hearing that there was to be a royal session, but it was no more than a Versailles rumor and had no substance at all. I sent to the chamber for news. I was informed that it was surrounded by French Guards."

Bailly does not dwell upon the size of the military deployment brought in during the night, which, according to Ferrières, "presented all the loathsome appearance of a bed of justice."⁶ It isn't just French Guards, it's also army detachments, both French and mercenaries, who are beginning to come in from the east and could give the Versaillese reason to fear that their town is about to be besieged. A notice has been posted all around the Menus Plaisirs, the gist of which Bailly learns, the way everybody else does, by reading it on the walls. Its heading, which the palace still believes has a magical effect, leaves no room for doubt: "By order of the King." The text beneath it reads, "The King having determined to hold a royal session at the Estates General on June 22, the preparatory work to be done in the three chambers being used for the assemblies of the orders necessitates the suspension of those assemblies until after the royal session. In a further proclamation His Majesty will announce the time at which He will attend the assembly of Estates on Monday."[7]

A letter is eventually delivered from Dreux-Brézé, telling him the same thing and advising him, with presumably unintentional irony, "to instruct the secretaries to put their papers in a safe place lest they go astray. Kindly inform me, sir, of their names, so that I can give orders to have them admitted."[8]

In the meanwhile Bailly has dressed, bemoaning the "ministry's strange conduct: it shows what little notion it had of the body with which it was dealing and the proper way to deal with it."[9]

It is true that the "ministry," as Bailly says, always refusing to implicate the King, is only giving tit for tat. The Court was not told about the motion of June 17 until after it was adopted, so it responds by informing the "so-called Assembly" after a calculated delay.

But the Assembly did not evict the other orders, or anybody from the Court, whereas when Bailly turns up on the avenue de Paris he is met by a scene of desolation. Blocked in front by the military cordon, and pressed from behind by more than a thousand of their regular sympathizers come to sit in the galleries, about five hundred deputies are stamping their feet and shivering in one of the most torrential rainfalls of the month, which feels like an additional punishment. And the rain lasts all day.

All these people, suddenly finding themselves in the street, are in a dreadful stew, and Bailly, whose inclination is always to find a peaceful way out, understands that they're looking to him to take some initiative. He tries to go in through the main door but is stopped and forced to parley with the poor duty officer, the Comte de Vossan, who hasn't a clue about anything. All he is allowed to do is look at the chamber, accompanied by two secretaries, who take the opportunity to grab all the papers in sight. He observes that men are actually at work getting the chamber ready for the royal session. He and the secretaries are still inside sorting their papers when the officers come and beg him to intercede between the evicted deputies, who have grown even more incensed at being prevented from following their president inside, and the military, who are hardly able to contain the crowd and will soon be compelled to use force. The more excitable members of the crowd—possibly only onlookers—are making all kinds of wild suggestions: they should go to Marly, where the King is said to be hunting today, and hold their meeting near the estate; but if they learn that he's in Versailles this morning, then they should all go in a body to the place d'Armes and do the same thing there. A cozy meeting it would be, too, in this driving rain! Especially if they're imagining that the King will bestir himself for them at Marly or at Versailles now that they've been, so to speak, excommunicated.[10] Bailly has only been president for three short days; his sole authority is his title, and here he is saddled with the heavy responsibility of mediating between the men who elected him and a deaf and blind armed force.

Fortunately, at the last minute his friend Guillotin hits upon the saving idea. He points out that only a stone's throw away in the same avenue there is a space quite large enough for the homeless deputies, and it's free today. It's the Tennis Court.*

Off to the Tennis Court! Bailly sets out at the head of a lugubrious procession. "Fearing that entry might be denied us on some pretext, I asked five or six deputies to go on ahead and occupy the premises. The master of the Tennis Court welcomed us with joy and hastened to procure us every facility he could."[11]

The next day the newspapers are calling it "the Comte d'Artois's Tennis Court," which is incorrect. The premises are available for elegant matches played for pleasure by people with time and money to use them. It's true that Artois goes there more often than most, but anyone wanting the court has to book it in advance.

The deputies can barely squeeze themselves in. Fearing an invasion by the spectators left outside, Bailly asks a few colleagues to guard the doors.

"So here is the National Assembly of France in a tennis court, a place ordinarily given over to exercises and games, but which was about to witness the destinies of empire. Its walls were barren and bleak, and there was hardly a seat to sit down on. I was offered an armchair but refused it. I would not be seated in front of a standing Assembly and thus I remained for the whole arduous day. During the entire session we had no more than four or six benches and one table to write at."[12] As for the spectators, they get no galleries today. By means of acrobatic contortions, a fraction of them contrive to fasten themselves to the latticework around the walls, but all of them have suddenly become good as gold. Their anger has melted away, since that is the wish of their venerated Assembly.

Unwittingly and unintentionally the Assembly is about to perform the

---

*Of course the only people involved in this are the ones who were still being called the "third estate" a moment ago; the nobility and clergy have been given early warning and don't turn up, although a small minority of the former and a large portion of the latter are not in agreement with the palace's handling of the situation.

first symbolic act of the Revolution in a highly appropriate setting: like nothing on earth. Four utterly bare walls around which, close to the floor, runs a sort of crib in which the balls, nets, and rackets employed in interminable volleys are stored. And, in the angle of the flat ceiling, six or seven times a man's height, are the vast lattice-covered openings that let in the light and have, today, been transformed into balcony seats for the intrepid.

Nothing else. No assembly or *parlement,* even in the direst days of the wars of religion or the Fronde, ever "sat" in such total austerity.*

And what are we going to do with this session, now that Bailly has read out the letter from Dreux-Brézé? A few members, their affront still undigested, propose that they issue public protestations and perform various other actions, the very thought of which fills Bailly with horror. For example, that "the Assembly transfer its sittings to Paris and set out at once, on foot and in a body. One member was already drafting the motion. All would have been lost had we followed this violent course. Mounted troops might have been brought up to stop our march. And in any case we should have been separating ourselves from the King, and that would have had the most serious consequences."[13]

Mounier saves the day by proposing a solemn oath. Nobody was thinking of such a thing when they first entered the Tennis Court except maybe himself, already scribbling away at a rough draft. (Although it's true that eleven months before, back in Vizille, he got the Dauphiné Estates to swear an oath too.) Supported by Bailly and also by his "disciple" Barnave, along with Le Chapelier and Target, he adroitly makes it the focus of debate and *raison d'être* of the day. First, to pacify the extremists, he adds his voice to the chorus of protest; then, once he's captured the attention of the house, he makes his proposal. All he has to do is read out two short paragraphs, and it is unanimously approved.

The National Assembly,
Whereas its business is to establish the constitution of the realm, effect the regeneration of social order and sustain the true principles of the monarchy, it follows that nothing can prevent it from continuing its deliberations in whatever place it may be compelled to establish itself; and whereas, in whatever place its members are met, there is the National Assembly,†

*The Tennis Court still exists. In 1889 it was littered with busts and statues relating to the event, and David's famous painting was hung in it. In 1987, work was begun to restore it to its original state in time for the bicentennial.

†Paradoxically, Mounier, whose prime claim to fame is his authorship of the Tennis Court Oath, subsequently disowns his progeny. Soon sick of the Revolution, he returns to Grenoble in late 1789 and then emigrates. Shortly before August 10, 1792, he writes that he bitterly

Resolves that all the members of this Assembly shall swear forthwith a solemn oath never to part, and to gather wherever circumstances shall require, until the constitution of the realm has been established and set up upon firm foundations; and that, the oath being sworn, all the members, and each of them severally, shall confirm by their signatures this unbreakable resolution.[14]

An enthusiastic Bailly leaps upon the text. "I read it out in so loud and clear a voice that my words were heard by all the people outside in the street . . . , and universal, repeated shouts of *'Vive le Roi!'* rose up from the Assembly and the crowd."

So they are still hoping to reconcile the irreconcilable. Since June 17 they haven't stopped cheering a King whose powers they are steadily eroding. It looks like a ritual of piety.

After reading out the oath Bailly asks that he and the secretaries may be the first to swear it, "which was done on the instant. Then the Assembly swore the same oath between the hands of its president,"[15] meaning that the representatives are called by name, following the alphabetical order of the bailliages, provinces and towns, and come up to sign at the table. Almost all of them do, including Mirabeau, who's oddly silent these days, perhaps because he's jealous of Mounier or wants to keep some chance of a hearing by the Court.

One comical incident takes place that is worth noting, because it compels these budding democrats to consider the difference between unanimity and majority. Camus, one of the secretaries, looks up from the sheets he has been examining and announces that Martin d'Auch, representing Castelnaudary, has written "opposed" after his signature. "A general cry of indignation rose up,"[16] and Bailly has to prevent them from lynching the man. He pleads with them at least to listen to him, and Martin d'Auch stubbornly "declares that he does not believe he can swear to take part in deliberations that have not been sanctioned by the King." Bailly manages to calm the deputies somewhat, but still has to hustle the sole objector to the Tennis Court Oath out through a back door to protect him from the crowd outside, which is now rumbling again.

The Assembly can then adjourn until Monday the twenty-second, when the royal session is scheduled, but not before deciding that if the session takes place in the Menus Plaisirs, the deputies will remain in it after the King's departure and carry on with their regular work. Premeditation or presentiment?

.   .   .

---

regrets having proposed what he claims was ultimately an attack upon the rights of the King and the first step toward the acquisition of authority by a single assembly.

But the royal session does not take place on the twenty-second. That morning the Assembly learns, again unofficially, that it is being postponed until the following morning, June 23. The cause of this final delay is a series of feverish debates in the Council, at which Necker, abandoned by everybody except Montmorin and Saint-Priest, valiantly struggles to preserve some fragments of the draft speeches he submitted to the King. But the news of the Oath, brought to Louis XVI while he was out hunting, and coming on top of the proclamation of June 17, sends the royal blood pressure through the roof. Since the twentieth, the King has been working with unwonted perseverance. He is determined to teach a lesson to these upstarts who, he imagines, have now twice defied his authority. He needs time to carry out a radical revamping of Necker's texts, and doesn't finish until the early hours of Tuesday morning.

As it turns out, the delay is a very good thing for the Assembly, to which, on Monday, destiny makes a present it couldn't have been expecting so soon. During the last compulsory day of waiting the majority of the clergy come over to its side. Third crucial event of the Estates.

Since the seventeenth, the adoption of its name, its determination, and the commencement of its legislative activity have turned the Assembly into a sort of magnetic pole, an irresistible force of attraction to the men in the other two orders, who are fed up with being presumed to think the way everybody else does.

Where to meet? The Menus Plaisirs is still closed, of course, and the Tennis Court has now been closed, owing to a shabby trick by the Comte d'Artois, who simply booked it for the entire week. After approaching the Recollects, who are less than hospitable, the deputies decide to move into St. Louis, the church from which the procession set out on May 4. Father Jacob, the incumbent priest, doesn't dare refuse them. It can hold over a thousand people, as we already know, and it's going to have to. And in this way, as Target says with his customary lyricism, "the temple of religion is to be converted into the temple of the fatherland,"[17] a thing nobody could have foreseen a week earlier.

The representatives get the glad tidings around noon. A delegation of five bishops comes to notify them that the majority of the clergy have decided that morning to ally themselves with the Assembly and will join their meeting "if the Assembly will be good enough to make room for them." Good enough? Oh, we might be able to manage it. . . . Bailly is jubilant, and he's not the only one. They quickly vacate the best seats at the top of the nave, then sixteen deputies go to greet the incoming stream of ecclesiastics. There are 148 of them, give or take a couple, and they enter in majestic order, surrounded by joy and delight unbounded and led by two prelates—the Archbishop of Vienne and Champion de Cicé, archbishop of Bordeaux—

who have been hoping for a long time that things would turn out this way, if only to give the Church a chance in the subsequent negotiations.

Bear hugs and congratulations. Bailly finds the right words, and even contrives to be brief about it: "This is a day of happiness for the National Assembly. If I may be permitted to express a personal feeling, the day on which I saw this meeting take place will always be the finest day of my life."[18]

Almost shyly, two members of the nobility, the Marquis de Blacons and the Comte d'Agoult, edge in behind the priests, but are led up to the front row. They're the vanguard of a minority of nobles, which is also growing but often, as with La Fayette, remains hamstrung by coercive election promises.

Anyway, it's all over now; the division into three orders is about to become sheer pretense.

It is high time the King held this session—he who, on the contrary, is now firmly siding with the Queen and Artois. But how could he understand, in his ivory tower, that it's already too late? On the morning of the twenty-third, a great military spectacle is arrayed along his route from the château to the reopened Menus Plaisirs, in which protocol has repeated the gorgeous stage setting of the previous occasions. The soldiers turn back the public, who are not allowed into the galleries today, and it all begins in a sort of dream for the people of the Court.

Before it does, however, they inflict the obligatory insult upon those whom they alone now describe as "the third," namely a long wait outside (and in the rain again) while nobility and clergy take their places in the seats of honor. Bailly has a hard time preventing his colleagues from turning their backs and departing, leaving the King alone with the privileged orders. At last, around eleven, the members of the Assembly are brought in through a small door, two by two, to find everybody else comfortably settled.

The King turns up at noon with the princes and people of his Household. He looks even redder in the face than usual, sulky and restless. Not one cheer rose up from the people of Versailles as he passed. It's as though the gaze of the "royal town" has also shifted.

The ministers are seated in their usual places behind the long table at the King's feet, but the audience reels when it observes that one of the ministerial stools remains unoccupied. Necker isn't there. The mutter that rolls around the room at this discovery is so persistent that the sovereign has to wait for silence to fall before he speaks.

The reason why Necker has decided to stay away, after hesitating all night long, is that he has submitted his resignation, and the letter announcing it is awaiting Louis XVI at the château. He has avoided tendering it sooner for fear of being commanded to attend a meeting that in his view cannot fail to be a disaster, and he does not want to witness it. His absence, unexpected even by the King, is the first event of the day. "Amidst all this theatrical pomp and ceremony, people were struck by nothing so much as the minister who could nowhere be seen."[19]

Louis XVI must have been hit where it hurt, because in the past he has invariably confined his oratory to a short harangue whereas today he speaks on three separate occasions. Between speeches he has a secretary read out the lists of decisions of which he has come to give them notice.

Speech number one: a warning. "I owe it to the commonweal of my kingdom, I owe it to myself, to make you cease your fatal dissensions."[20]

The ensuing "catalog," containing fifteen articles, is a call to order, and accordingly it begins: "The King desires that the old distinction of the three orders in the state be preserved in every particular, as an essential part of the constitution of his realm." And so on. The King does deign to consider the possibility of an occasional joint meeting, but specifically excepts, in Article 8, "matters relating to the three orders, the form to be given to the forthcoming Estates General, feudal and seigneurial possessions, and the honorary prerogatives of the first two orders."

The fifteenth and final article announces that the public will no longer be permitted to watch meetings from the galleries; the deputies are to conduct their business in private.

The audience are still frozen by this first cold shower when the King, in his second speech, revives their hopes a little with his introduction of the second catalog, containing no fewer than thirty-five articles, which is supposed to set out "the benefits he has planned." He adds, modestly, "I may say, without illusion, that never has a King done so much for any nation . . . . Those who, through exaggerated pretensions, would further delay the enforcement of my paternal intentions, would render themselves unworthy of being looked upon as French."

This *Déclaration des intentions du Roi* is listened to attentively by those who hope to find in it at least some trace of the reforms that they have so earnestly longed to see and that Necker is known to have wanted. And in fact it does mention the abolition of the *taille,* and the annual vote by provincial assemblies of other forms of taxation on a more equitable basis . . . but only for the bourgeoisie because "the first two orders of the state shall continue to be exempted from personal levies" (Article 13). The text also consents to consider "the abolition of the orders known as *lettres de cachet,*" but later, later.

As though these trifling concessions were enough in themselves to undermine his power, the last article in this catalog stipulates that "His Majesty . . . desires to preserve, in every particular and without any impediment, the organization of the army, together with all authority, supervision and power over the military, such as have invariably been enjoyed by the French monarchs."

By way of conclusion, the King's third speech makes it plain that this is indeed a declaration of war. "If, through some fatality of which I cannot even conceive, you were to abandon me in so excellent an undertaking, then, alone, I should benefit my peoples; alone, I should consider myself to be their true representative."

It is the irony of fate that this is the only sentence left of the text originally proposed by Necker, but now being used for a totally different purpose. The minister meant it as an argument to compel the first two orders to relinquish their privileges; now it is being addressed solely to the third.

All eyewitnesses note that the King's voice is rather shaky, and that he leaves the room visibly perturbed. The unbroken silence of those who now comprise the National Assembly is felt by him as an affront. This time there is not a single *"Vive le Roi!"* to hail him, whereas there were so many when he wasn't there to hear them. What a change in atmosphere since the previous royal session! Only a few nobles applaud, halfheartedly, as the sovereign withdraws after a final injunction: "I command you, gentlemen, to disperse at once and to go tomorrow, each to the chamber intended for your particular order."

The deputies of the nobility, and a minority of the clergy, do as their sovereign has ordained, but the rest remain as though bolted to their seats.

At first people think they've been paralyzed by the tongue-lashing they've just received, but they soon learn that the whole thing was pre-arranged.

The session that follows is not a real working meeting and it doesn't last very long. But it counts. Bailly walks over to the ministers' table and composedly assumes his presidency. Dreux-Brézé returns and reminds him of the King's order. Bailly replies, "Sir, the Assembly was adjourned until after the royal session. I cannot order it to disperse until it has deliberated."[21] For his colleagues' sake he adds, "I do not believe the Assembly can be given any orders."

To Mirabeau, who has been sizzling in his seat for some time, this is not strong enough. He hurls after the vanishing master of ceremonies a vengeful apostrophe, several versions of which exist, but the word "bayonet" occurs in all of them. Most of his biographers, as well as the high school textbooks, have him say, "Go tell those who sent you that we are here by the will of the people and will be removed only by the force of bayonets."[22]

Bailly, whose memory is usually accurate, hears, "Go tell those who sent you that the force of bayonets can do nothing against the will of the nation."[23]

He turns to drive away the workmen who have been ordered to start dismantling the hall, while Camus, Barnave, Gleizen (from Rennes), Pétion, Buzot and Abbé Grégoire speak along the same lines as Mirabeau.

They let Sieyès have the last word: "Gentlemen, we are today what we were yesterday. Let us deliberate."[24]

When he is told that the National Assembly refuses to go away, Louis XVI doesn't know what to do. He has just received the worst affront ever inflicted upon him. His circle, always the same and decidedly impervious to anything emanating from the public even though the public has for the first time shown hostility to the King himself, on his return from the hall, urges him to call out the army against this hornets' nest of black-garbed lawyers. But Louis XVI has a more accurate sense than they of what is possible in the immediate future. The regiments have indeed been called in from the provinces, but there are still not enough of them on hand. And more than half of those present—the French, as distinct from the mercenaries—are not reliable.

He shrugs: "They want to stay; well, dammit, let them stay!"[25]

But he's got a plan; he'll get back at them another day. Then, to top it all off, at the end of this longest day of his reign he has to summon Necker and, almost humbly, refuse his resignation. In a few short hours the minister's absence from that session has restored all the glamour to his tarnished popularity, because he would not compromise himself by attending it. A swelling crowd, rowdy enough to impress even the Queen, is threatening to break down the château gates, which are not yet sufficiently guarded. So Louis XVI promises Necker to pay more attention to him in future and give him more help in carrying out his task—a promise made of the same stuff as those he has given in the past to so many of his ministers, from Turgot to Brienne. In the past, though, he was sincere, at least when he was making the promises, although he systematically failed to keep them afterward. But this time his promise is combined with the telling of his first major, conscious lie. That same afternoon he sends for Broglie in Normandy and gives instructions that the "loyal" regiments now marching toward Paris are to speed up. If he has anything to do with it, this Assembly is not going to remain in place one second longer than Necker. He just has to buy a little time.

So June 23 ends with the explosion of joy that people have been waiting for in vain since morning. It encompasses the death and resurrection of Necker, vanished at sunrise, triumphant at sunset.

For seventeen more days. . . .

72

JULY 11−13, 1789

How Quickly the Fire Spread Then!

On Saturday, July 11, Necker's dinner guests notice that their host seems a little preoccupied. His brother, Necker de Germany, is there, as is Madame de Staël. To the one he is silent as the grave, as an oyster to the other. Around six in the evening, accompanied only by his wife, he leaves Versailles, ostensibly to visit some lady friend . . . and vanishes. In reality, he hurries to his house at Saint-Ouen to pick up a few things, and, after sending word to his daughter, heads for Belgium.

He's been fired. Early that afternoon he received a letter, brought by his fellow minister La Luzerne, wearing his stiffest air, in which the King informed him of his decision and asked "that withdrawal be prompt and secret. It is important to your integrity and reputation that there should be no cause for stir or commotion."[1]

Not three weeks ago he was being implored to stay. He had assumed he was going to be able to get back to work and restore the bankers' confidence, which was sorely needed. There he was, slaving away, and now comes the thunderbolt. Never has a dismissed "principal minister" shown so much stoicism in the face of the most flagrant injustice. By the time the news of his disgrace begins to spread through the night, traveling by word of mouth through Versailles and on to Paris (it is not customary to make an official announcement of a minister's dismissal), Necker is already far away.

On the morning of the twelfth, in Arras, he informs the Court, via a letter scrawled on a table in an inn, that "in order to avoid passing through Paris or crossing Burgundy and Franche-Comté, the provinces in which people's minds are most agitated, and in order to find myself out of the kingdom as promptly as possible, I have chosen to head toward Brussels,"[2] which he reaches on the morning of the thirteenth. He will stay there until his daughter and son-in-law join him and then leave for Switzerland, which he hopes to reach around the twentieth.

His respect for the monarchy is so great that he is behaving as though he actually deserves what has been done to him.

Necker should have listened more closely to the rumors going around the last few days. Louis XVI has been working out the details of a "first-strike" government that he hopes will help him to dissolve the Assembly, which he decided to do on June 23. In his usual way, but with more than his usual determination, the King has made his plans secretly, letting people think that his decision to yield was for real. On June 27, he carries his Machiavellianism to the point of instructing the nobility and clergy to join the National Assembly, which has been working in a state of euphoria ever since and, on July 7, assumes the full title of National Constituent Assembly. It at once sets up a committee on a constitution and vows to give the country the fruit of its labors in a hurry.

Early on July 11, La Fayette, faithful to his American-born dream and hoping at last to play a part worthy of himself, places on the Assembly desk his preliminary draft of *Declaration of the Rights of Man and of the Citizen*— which the group doesn't have time to discuss for many a week. It was all too good to be true; they ought to have been on their guard. The news of Necker's dismissal hits them in the midriff, and that's not all. The Assembly also learns that Montmorin and Saint-Priest have been jettisoned, too, for the crime of siding, more or less, with Necker.

They are further informed, unofficially as usual, that there is not to be any "principal minister." The Baron de Breteuil, as head of the Conseil des Finances, will act in that capacity. "Under him" will be "M. Foulon, for the details," as the King writes to the Maréchal de Castries,[3] informing him at the same time that he has given Foreign Affairs to La Vauguyon and asking him to replace La Luzerne at the Navy, because La Luzerne is not conservative enough to suit him.*

This is clearly a ministry set up for a clean sweep, and its worst element will not be Louis-Auguste Le Tonnelier, Baron de Breteuil, despite "his big boom of a voice, like sheer energy," as Germaine de Staël puts it, and his habit "of making a great noise as he walks, stamping his feet as though he would cause an army to rise up out of the earth."[4] During the Assemblies of Notables he even showed tact and wit—of a sort. But the team he's being given now—especially Foulon, who is the protégé of the daughters of Louis XV—seems likely to be quite equal to the task being set for it by the Queen and her party.

Since June 23, Louis XVI has devoted all his time to making preparations

---

*But Castries, who sees things more clearly from his vantage point in Languedoc, politely declines.

for his new government, putting Besenval in command of all the troops in Paris and working out the details of his military arrangements.

But the King is laboring under a delusion. He should have moved at least two months earlier, and from Metz, as he had been advised to do. The trap laid for the Assembly is going to catch the Court instead.

July 12 is a Sunday. Many Parisians are out in the streets and public gardens. The weather is sultry and sickly and continues that way all through the week, punctuated by violent thunderstorms.

Food shortages have grown worse. "Every bakery was surrounded by huge crowds, to whom bread was being doled out most parsimoniously . . . . And yet this bread, so laboriously gained, was by no means a healthful nutriment. As a rule it was blackish, clayey, bitter, and caused inflammations of the throat and pains in the gut . . . . The people of Paris believed the entrance duties to be partly to blame for the high price of bread, so there were groups at the duty barriers trying to bring foodstuffs through by force without paying the duty."[5]

These barriers, outside the city tollhouses, have been threatened so constantly since the beginning of the month that as soon as the Royal-Allemand horsemen reach Paris from the north, under the command of the young Prince de Lambesc, they are deployed to protect the collectors and force the draymen to pay.

Inside Paris there has been a steady succession of scuffles and skirmishes between the hungry people and the forces of law and order. The focal point of the disturbances has been the Palais-Royal, where, beginning on July 6, some of the extempore orators have grown so violent that on several occasions the ever-popular Duc d'Orléans has thought it behooved him, as master of the place, to go in person and exhort them to keep the peace. He enters the gardens and, "speaking them fair and mildly, asked all the persons . . . gathered into groups and crowds to be good enough to disperse or remove themselves elsewhere."[6] He is cheered, but disobeyed. He has to send for the watch on his very doorstep, but asks it not to make a fuss. So the troops duly request the loiterers, "with great civility and much consideration, kindly to retire to their homes."*

Until July 12 the unrest in Paris remains sporadic, an inflammable atmosphere rather than actual rioting. People still pin so much hope on Necker that even the most miserable contain themselves. But the news of their idol's

---

*The Court's hostility toward Orléans is so intense that, with a tactic it has employed more than once before, it turns his actions inside out. He was urging the people to keep calm; they accuse him of fanning the flames of discontent.

dismissal reacts on the Parisians like a hot coal tossed into a powder keg.

Between nine o'clock and noon the rumors from Versailles spread through town. The gardens of the Palais-Royal are soon teeming with men and women, several thousand of them, so many that the very limbs of the trees begin to sag "under the weight of the people perched upon them."[7]

Scores of speakers have clambered onto the tables of the Café du Foy, one of the few establishments to set them up outdoors, and each is trying to shout his protests louder than the next. The tone has become shriller, too, since some of the Parisians have learned that the city is threatened by a ring of troops, as though about to lay siege. Several times a new cry rings out, one the people have never uttered before: "To arms!"

One of the speakers with a large audience, the largest of all according to himself, is Camille Desmoulins.

Already more journalist than lawyer, he's tried not to miss a trick in the balconies of the Menus Plaisirs, where, having failed to get himself elected by his hometown of Guise in Picardy, he has been gleaning information and attempting to approach some of the celebrities of the day. Despite a difficult childhood as the eldest of seven children and a shortage of cases to plead because of his poverty and tendency to stutter, he feels—he knows—that he is made for great things. The rickety table onto which he climbs now outside the Café du Foy, is surely about to bring them within his grasp.

To hear him tell it, not only is he the one who ignites the whole crowd in the Palais-Royal but it is also he who really begins the Revolution single-handed.

His great gifts as a writer enable him, by indulging in the exaggerations he never resists, to convince his friends that he's right. And this is not the least of his shortcomings. Fortunately, his bragging is tempered by a quick sense of irony. He certainly is not the only orator in the Palais-Royal that day, but at least he keeps a record of what he says and gives his first account of it only four days later, in a letter to his father:*

"I went about three to the Palais-Royal. I was deploring our faintheart-edness in the middle of a group when three young men went by, hands clasped, shouting, 'To arms!' I joined them. My fervor was noticed, I was surrounded, urged to get up on a table. Within the minute I had six thousand persons around me.†

---

*He was born at Guise in March 1760 and is guillotined, with Danton, on April 5, 1794. He attended Louis-le-Grand school, where he knew Robespierre slightly. He is, along with Marat, one of the best pamphleteers of the Revolution.

†At their utmost, the gardens of the Palais-Royal could hold four thousand. This letter is a good example of Desmoulin's need to prove himself to a father with whom he has been in psychological conflict since childhood.

" 'Citizens,' I said then, 'you know that the nation asked for Necker to be left to it, for a monument to be raised to him. He has been turned out! Is there any more insolent way to defy you? After this, they will stop at nothing, and this very night they are plotting a St. Bartholomew for all patriots!' "[8]

What's happened to his stutter? "A host of ideas were assailing me, choking me; I was spilling them out pell-mell.

" 'To arms,' I cried, 'to arms!' Let us all wear cockades of green, the color of hope .... The infamous police are here. They can take a good look, observe me closely. Yes, it is I who call my brothers to liberty.'

"And, raising a pistol, 'At least they will not take me alive, and I shall know how to die gloriously. The only misfortune that could befall me would be to see France enslaved.'

"Then I got down, I was embraced, stifled with hugs and kisses. 'My friend,' they all told me, 'we shall form a guard for you, we shall not abandon you, we shall go wherever you say ....'

"I took a green ribbon and tied it to my hat first. How quickly the fire spread then!"

He hands out all the green ribbon he has, and when he runs out, people tear off the lower leaves of the trees in the garden, fasten them to their hats, and form one of the countless parades that are beginning to stream through Paris—Camille may not even have remained at the head of the one he has just started. Who cares if the pistol becomes two pistols in a later version of his recital, or that he insists to the death that he remained in control of the whole uprising? Written almost as it happened, his letter is a good summary of the things that are shouted through Paris in the next two days.

With or without him, the crowd now rushes about forcing all the theaters to close, the Opéra included, on the grounds that performances would be blasphemous on this day of mourning.

One of the biggest of the processions wends its way to the boulevard du Temple, where a man of German origin named Curtius, who makes wax figures, eagerly presents it with a bust of Necker he has just completed. As a bonus, he throws in a bust of the Duc d'Orléans, even though nothing nasty has been done to him. But at least Curtius saves his studio.

Behind the two busts this huge mob, waving black flags to connote mourning, proceeds along the boulevards to the place Vendôme, where a detachment of dragoons, vastly outnumbered, is forced to retreat. The demonstrators then march on to the place Louis XV and invade the Tuileries gardens. It is there that the first collisions take place between the people and the Royal Allemand horsemen who have been brought up as reinforcements. But the physical damage is still minimal when Besenval, acting on reports brought by mounted courier to the Champ de Mars, where he has set up his headquarters, orders Lambesc to charge the crowd and clear the Tuileries. Lambesc and his mercenaries, who haven't the slightest idea what's going on, are caught in a hail of stones and other projectiles. Several times he orders a charge, and several times has to fall back, but not before killing the day's first victims. The shattered remains of the two busts are left where they fall, along with a few dead bodies, perhaps, which no one ever records. An unsubstantiated rumor runs through Paris, to the effect that the Prince de Lambesc himself ran one old man through with his saber.

The insurrection is already in control of most of the right bank of the Seine. Besenval's forces are holding the left, but what's the point? And it emerges during the day that few of them, except the Germans and the Swiss, are really reliable. The French troops are either hesitant or, in some cases, beginning to join the rebels—the French Guards, for instance, some of whom have flatly refusd to march against the people for the last two weeks. To set an example in the time-honored authorized manner, the authorities throw a dozen of them into the prison of St. Germain Abbey, where a large body of workmen go to force the doors and release them, as comrades, under the indulgent eye of the soldiers on guard. Among these newly freed prisoners are two noncommissioned officers who are about to get themselves talked about: Elie and Hulin.

And yet on July 10 the plan for the concentration of forces that Broglie submitted to the King looked sound enough for him to decide to make his move, beginning with Necker's dismissal. More than three thousand fully armed men are stationed in their assigned places between Charenton and Marly. But the only ones Besenval can count on are the mercenaries.

On July 8 the Assembly, shaken from its rosy fog by the news of this mobilization, which it feared was aimed primarily at itself, sent the King a communication, respectfully requesting that he remove the troops from the vicinity of Paris. Mirabeau added his own little touch, pointing out that "the soldiers, if brought close to the center of discussion, may forget that an enlistment made them soldiers and remember that nature made them men."[9] Louis XVI waited three days to send his answer, when he thought he was strong enough to make it a tough one. According to him, the troops were there only to put down or prevent further disorder, but "if, however, their necessary presence on the outskirts of Paris were still to cause umbrage, I should proceed to transfer the Estates General to Noyon or Soissons and should myself go to Compiègne." Reading between the lines, we sense that the dissolution of the Estates is imminent.

The night of July 12–13 is insane; Paris has not known its like for many a year. Thousands of people spend the whole night in the streets. Lost wages or no lost wages, nobody thinks of going to work the next day. Too late, Besenval orders one of the few regiments that are worth anything, from his point of view—the Salis-Samade Swiss—to cross to the right bank and protect, at least, the main arms depots there. But its commanding officer, the Chevalier de Bachmann, carries out his orders about as absurdly as anyone could, perhaps because he's intimidated by the crowds. Instead of marching calmly over the Pont-Royal, which is completely clear, he embarks his men in a fleet of ferries as though he were trying to cross the Rhine or Danube. His regiment doesn't get itself organized on the place Louis XV until sometime around midnight, and this "landing" has tipped the scales in the rioters' minds, convincing them, as Camille Desmoulins urged that afternoon, that they must arm themselves at once. So far, all they have managed to do is loot various gunsmiths' shops, and since most of them don't know how to use a gun, they are turning back to the tollhouse barriers to work off their anger there.

By dawn forty out of fifty-four barriers have been set on fire. The last major work of Claude-Nicolas Ledoux goes up in smoke. In several places, the toll wall itself is breached.

The position has become untenable for the Swiss, so Besenval orders them to withdraw to the Champ de Mars. Which they do, in a pitiful state, while the general tries to concentrate the troops that are still loyal around him there.

On July 13, Paris awakens to the sound of the tocsin. The city is in the hands of the insurrection.

Before anything else, find food! Serious looting starts early. The convent of Saint-Lazare is the first to go. Its reputation for vast wealth is confirmed by what the people find in it, without even looking very hard, as soon as the monks have run away: seventy-six hogsheads of Burgundy and eighteen of Roussillon, not to mention several hundred bottles of other wines, kegs of beer, vinegar and oil, twenty-five whole wheels of Swiss cheese, five casks of melted butter and fifty-three cartloads of wheat.[10]

Here, the prisoners of "ill repute," those considered unworthy of the best prisons, are released. In 1784 the King put Beaumarchais there after the first performance of *The Marriage of Figaro*. It was only for a few days, but the author was deeply marked by them.

Until noon, the crowd circles, with no goal and no leader. The usual rabble mix in with the steadier elements, and looting continues haphazardly while the sharper heads, certain that the royal forces will soon be back, keep a lookout for firearms.

What we need here is a little organization. Whereupon, the most important event of the day occurs. At the Hôtel de Ville, Flesselles, the new provost of traders, sees a handful of bourgeois in black edging forward. They come early, and at first they're a little sheepish and few in number, looking like anything but swashbucklers. But they are about to show considerable initiative and a courage of which they would not have thought themselves capable. The voters of Paris are about to take over the vacated seat of authority. In the last analysis, it is they who elected the Parisian delegation of the third, and here, as in a few towns in the provinces, they have continued to meet from time to time, to keep abreast of events. And since they feel a very strong need to protect their property, on the one front, from "the dregs of the people," and their town, on the other, from Besenval's battle-scarred old veterans, they proceed to form, without any premeditation, the first Commune of Paris.

By and large, they are respected by those beneath them on the social scale, and many of them know how to use a gun.

Flesselles is uncooperative. By tradition, the provost of traders is a confirmed royalist. When the burghers first find him, he's contending with a mob that has just ravaged the stores, but all he agrees to issue are three hundred guns from the cellars of the Hôtel de Ville. The burghers organize their distribution, along with thirty-five kegs of powder confiscated from a boat moored off the Grève.

They immediately set up a standing committee, which stays at the Hôtel de Ville and meets there uninterruptedly from now on. Then they divide themselves among their respective parts of town and proceed to institute a bourgeois militia,* which is needed so desperately that its membership rises in one day from twelve to forty thousand men. Only "known citizens" are taken, meaning that, under the burghers' supervision, the men engaged are all "decent people": students from the school of surgery, law clerks, etc. Sewing-women hastily produce the only uniform possible on such short notice, a cockade for their hats. The green brandished by Desmoulins the day before is not chosen; instead they opt for the old colors of Paris, blue and red.

Thus, with no sounding of tambours or trumpets, the Paris bourgeoisie fills the place left empty by the nobility and gradually begins to take over the running of the town, while in Versailles all the Assembly can do is send a plaintive motion to the King deploring Necker's dismissal and venturing to request that he be recalled. It is slapped down smartly by Louis XVI, who still believes that his scheme will be carried out any moment now. "It is for myself alone to decide, and I can make no change."[11]

When night falls upon a Paris still almost wholly in a state of insurrection, except that its energies are now beginning to be channeled, the big question

*It is not called the National Guard until some days later.

is still how to find arms. The people decide to wait until the next day, when they can get them where they're plentiful, namely in the Arsenal and Invalides. So far, the name of the Bastille has not been mentioned.

THE BASTILLE

73

JULY 14, 1789

The Greatest Revolution

Not a single deputy witnesses these days in Paris, not even the fourteenth of July. They're all immobilized in Versailles by order of the King, who has just told them they may not send a delegation to entreat the Parisians to calm down. They are beginning to feel a little like prisoners in their hall, in which they decided on Monday to meet nonstop. But the Court is worried lest their popularity turn them into the leaders of the uprising.

Mirabeau is even less visible than the rest because on July 14 he is attending the funeral of his father, who died three days before in his daughter's home, at the end of his emotional and financial destitution. But not before writing one last letter, on the eighth, to his brother, complaining about a situation he really was not capable of understanding: "Twelve hundred legislators, none with the slightest experience of any kind of administration, all of them unable to manage their own affairs, are surely going to turn out a wondrous state constitution, with a dunce's cap at the top and the man with the blue tales [Necker; a pun on *contes* = "tales" and *comptes* = "accounts"] for guide."[1]

But on July 14, Paris gives no more of a fig for the National Assembly than does the King. The search for arms resumes at six in the morning, after another sleepless night during which rumors announce at almost hourly intervals the return of Besenval's troops. Just in case, a few barricades have been thrown up in the streets to protect the Hôtel de Ville, which contains the assembly of electors spontaneously generated by the town.

In front of it, the place de Grève is looking like a sort of fairground heaped with food, bolts of cloth, and materials of every sort dumped by the wagons, which now pass the tollhouse ruins without impediment before being led docilely to the standing committee to be inspected by the tax-collection committee and paying whatever taxes they offer it—voluntarily, since taxes are no longer compulsory and the rates are much lower anyway.

The bourgeois militia, with backing from some French Guards—only a few because, after all, they'll face a firing squad if things go back to what they used to be, but the few are precious by virtue of their military know-how—are guarding the banks, the Caisse d'Escompte and the Royal Treasury.

A wind from the southwest, unusual in the capital, is pushing heavy clouds through a stormy sky when the first great flood of Parisians, chaperoned by militiamen wearing red and blue cockades, gathers outside the Invalides. Over thirty thousand guns are stocked there, meticulously serviced and arranged in vast chambers. Sombreuil, the governor, had a good idea that this was coming. He has asked in vain for orders and assistance from Besenval, whose troops are still encamped a stone's throw away in the Champ de Mars, whence they never budge. All Besenval has done is advise the governor to render the guns unfit for firing by removing the ramrods and unscrewing the hammers. But the only men he has to do the job are a score of crippled veterans whose sympathies are with the uprising and who are so unenthusiastic about their work that at the end of six hours they have managed to dismantle barely twenty guns. Sombreuil knows he can't count on his little garrison of lame ducks but he's loaded his cannons anyway and placed their gunners behind them, holding lighted but useless matches.

Over a thousand people are chafing and rumbling more and more loudly outside, when Corney, an attorney whom the electors have decided to send to the governor, turns up to mediate.

So the new bourgeois authorities are boldly adopting a position in opposition to the Court, trying to get Sombreuil to commit what in ordinary times would be no less than an act of high treason—this from a man who has been responsible for one of the King's most important edifices for years.

Sombreuil tries to gain time and asks Corney to persuade the Hôtel de Ville to have a little patience. He's allowed to leave unmolested, but the crowd piles in before the gates can close behind his carriage. The governor can count himself lucky to keep his own hide in one piece.

Meanwhile, even if Besenval had wanted to act, it's too late. The colonel of one of the few French regiments still thought to be loyal has just informed him, "with tears in his eyes," that his men will not obey. Besenval's braggadocio of two days past has become irrelevant. A few days later, he admits that "his generals were agreed from that moment that it was impossible to subdue Paris and that the only prudent course was to retire."[2] And he's going to have to hurry to do even that if he wants to stop the human hemorrhage that is emptying his camp. The first minutes written by the standing committee state that, beginning on the morning of the thirteenth, "a considerable number of soldiers, dragoons, and infantry from the different regiments encamped in the vicinity of Paris were presenting themselves with arms and baggage and declaring that they had come to serve the nation."[3]

During the morning, the guns taken from the Invalides are conveyed to the place de Grève by hundreds of rebels temporarily transformed into ants. There the electors try to distribute them, in as orderly a manner as they can, to those they consider capable of using them.

Yes, but what about gunpowder—gunpowder again? They know at least one place where there's plenty of it: the Arsenal, that old building in which, not so very long ago, it was manufactured as well as stored, and in which cannons were cast, too, along with quite a few of the statues standing in the grounds at Versailles. The forge is no longer in operation, and gunpowder is being made by more modern methods these days, at La Salpêtrière, but the Arsenal is still the largest powder depot for the King's armies. Human whirlwinds sweep toward it, their hopes high because they know it is not well guarded.

The high hopes are dashed. There's hardly a flake of powder left in the Arsenal because Besenval's first act, three days before, was to have 30,000 pounds of it, in 250 barrels, transferred to the Bastille, which is not far away and should be able to withstand all amateur attacks. So it is not until late in the morning of the fourteenth that the cry is born, first at the Arsenal and then all over Paris, that becomes the cry of the day: *"À la Bastille! À la Bastille!"* It flies spontaneously from hundreds of mouths and its paternity can be claimed by no one in particular.

Around midday the bulk of the insurrectionists begin to assemble around the awesome fortress whose towering walls, almost totally blank, crush the far end of the faubourg Saint-Antoine, defending the entrance to Paris as they have done since it was built in the reign of mad King Charles VI. The Bastille has repulsed many an assault in its day, especially during the Wars of Religion but also later, in the Fronde, and it has never been captured. Whence its reputation of invincibility and the almost holy terror people feel for it, even if, since Louis XIV, it has served only to house the King's "compulsory guests," in lots of forty, then thirty, then, on average, twenty a year. A few of them became and remain famous, such as Fouquet, or the mysterious man in the iron mask. But there was also Voltaire, twice, and Latude, a big-time crook who escaped several times and has recently published some memoirs about the place. More recently, the Cardinal de Rohan was locked up in it, with kid gloves, and Cagliostro, and the Marquis de Sade, who was transferred to Charenton at the beginning of the month.

There have been many rumors about another kind of prisoner there, the unknown and often forgotten kind, most of whom were put away by *lettres de cachet* originating in their own families.

In fact, under Louis XVI, the Bastille is simply surviving as a prison— one in which, when the winters are harsh, the inmates are often treated very considerately. They have servants and meals brought in by caterers, and are handled relatively gently by their wardens. Nowadays it has more staff than prisoners: in addition to the governor, who gets sixty thousand livres a year, there are officers, physicians, surgeons, apothecaries, chaplains, cooks, etc.[4] But its intimidating military potential still frightens people. And at this moment it is almost recast in its old role as defender of the capital, against an attack that nobody was expecting to see.

The crowd has no thought of releasing the prisoners, all of whom are unknown to it, and isn't even aware that there are only seven of them left, mostly insane. It shouts itself hoarse demanding powder and cartridges, which Launay, the governor, has no intention of giving. The men in his family are governors of the Bastille from father to son, the way other families hold their estates. He was born there, in 1740, and his loyalty to the King is part of his unpretentiously mediocre character, neither cruel nor kind. The only thing is, he is almost pathologically indecisive and on July 14, when he has to face the first serious threat the Bastille has known since he has had the keeping of it, this trait is his undoing.

Launay is expecting the ordeal that Sombreuil has just gone through at the Invalides, but he's trusting to the fifteen formidable cannons he has had drawn up to the crenels in the towers—his first blunder, precipitating the first salvo of irritation directed at him by the assailants. He's also trusting to the thickness of his walls, certainly more than to his rudimentary army: eighty cripples, many of whom are known in the neighborhood and are also beginning to turn the "wrong way." To reinforce them, he's just acquired thirty Swiss sent over by Besenval from the Salis-Samade regiment. Not much to fend off thousands of furious Parisians. But he posts his men within the inner courtyards, which can be reached only after crossing two drawbridges, which he had drawn up that morning.

Although he is shaken by the size of the crowd, he doesn't seriously believe that the King's finest fortress, even defended by so few soldiers, will yield to any sort of attack by carpenters and cabinetmakers, locksmiths, chiselers and cobblers, wine vendors, hatters and dyers who never saw fire before.*

The governor's reasoning is not unfounded because for over an hour all the crowd can do is shout louder and louder on the far side of the famous

---

*A list of just under a thousand names is published later; they call themselves the "Conquerors of the Bastille" and form an association.

walls, seemingly deaf and blind. Launay would in all likelihood have been able to wait until their throats wore out and they went away, except for one unforeseen incident, which is the cause of the day's great misunderstanding.

There is no assault; there never will be. But two inventive youths have an idea, and that starts the blood flowing just as Launay, complying with the request of an elector named Thuriot, who's been sent over by the standing committee, is pulling his cannons back out of sight.

Around three in the afternoon two day laborers named Davanne and Danain, operating from the roof of a perfume shop, contrive to force the gates from what is known as the Avancée, a sort of agglomerate of small houses and shops. The first drawbridge falls, and some axes, brought along by a few bold spirits, break down the doors leading to the outer courtyard, of no real importance because all it contains is the governor's house. A very different order of power would be needed to get from that courtyard into the next, where the soldiers are.

The trouble is that very few people are aware of the two lads' exploit because the Avancée can't be seen from the faubourg, where the crowd imagines that Launay has simply given orders to open the gates. A vigorous surge thrusts some of them into this outer courtyard which is of no use to them if they can't get past the second drawbridge into the heart of the fortress.

Thus far not a single shot has been fired. Who orders the Swiss to open fire on these people who have already come farther than they ever expected? Almost certainly not Launay. More likely it's the commanding officer of the Swiss, who, within three minutes, impelled by what or whom will never really be known, lay out ninety-eight corpses on the paving stones of the outer courtyard. The people draw back, carrying the wounded with them, and the cry of "Treason!" lashes out at the governor, who is now thought to have let the people enter solely in order to shoot them down at close range.

The raging crowd almost forgets that its main reason for being there is to get gunpowder. Now, for vengeance and for honor, the capture of the Bastille becomes the objective.

A brief hour of skirmishing ensues, with isolated shots fired from the faubourg and Avancée but doing very little damage to the massive towers, now mute again. And if a determined group of deserting French Guards led by Elie and Hulin had not turned up then, dragging six cannons confiscated from their barracks, the towers would have had nothing worse to fear than that. The men position their cannons to answer fire from inside the building, but they don't even need to use them because the fortress is being under-mined from within by Launay's staff, who are appalled by the Swiss volley and tell the governor that he must surrender.

Launay's last reflex is to head for the cellars with a torch, meaning to set fire to the powder there. If he succeeds, he may well blow up not just the Bastille but one whole district of Paris. Again, he is stopped by his own staff of cripples.

Elie and Hulin, finding themselves quite unintentionally at the head of the insurrection in spite of their lowly rank (they're second lieutenants), see a piece of paper being poked at them through an opening near the second drawbridge, signed Launay and dated "the Bastille, five o'clock in the afternoon, July 14, 1789." It says that he agrees to surrender on condition that nobody inside the fortress is killed. It's like a fairy tale.

If people would only stick to the facts, there would never be any talk of "storming the Bastille," only of a surrender without a fight. It gives itself up.

The second drawbridge goes down and the crowd, this time with some circumspection, spreads in growing numbers through the rooms, fraternizing with Launay's men. One of the first Parisians to reach the top of a tower waves his hat and is almost fired on from below because he's taken for a defender. The French Guards do their utmost to keep their promise and protect the governor, whom they conduct to the Hôtel de Ville, but they are powerless against the fury of the friends and relatives of the victims of the first courtyard, who look upon him as their murderer. Launay is massacred, along with five of the Swiss whom the troops can't manage to hide. Even at the Hôtel de Ville the cry of "Treason!" has grown so strong that it is hurled at Flesselles as well and he is shot down on the spot.

Besenval, meanwhile, aghast at the reports that are coming in, commands a general retreat of his remaining troops and abandons the Champ de Mars. The King is not told until the middle of the night, and it takes him another twenty-four hours to realize that his plans have misfired and that if he wants to save his throne, he, too, is going to have to capitulate and come to terms with Paris, whose electors ask nothing more.

On the sixteenth the Duke of Dorset, ambassador from Great Britain, writes to his government, "Thus . . . the greatest Revolution that we know anything of has been effected . . . . From this moment we may consider France as a free country, the King a very limited monarch and the nobility as reduced to a level with the rest of the nation."[5]

Notes

I

1. Docteur Robinet, *Condorcet, sa vie, son oeuvre, 1743–1794* (Paris, n.d., Librairies-Imprimeries Réunies), complete text of the marriage act (Appendix A, p. 332).

2. *Mémoires de Bachaumont,* December 28, 1786.

3. A. Guillois, *La marquise de Condorcet* (Paris, Ollendorf, 1897), p. 65.

4. Marquise de La Tour du Pin, *Mémoires* (Paris, Mercure de France, 1979), p. 73.

5. A. Guillois, *La marquise de Condorcet,* p. 2. Madame du Paty's remarks are on p. 3.

6. Expilly, *Dictionnaire,* IV, p. 727, entry on "Meulan." *Ibid.* for the following quote.

7. Archives of the du Paty de Clam family, quoted by A. Guillois, p. 59. Letter from Mme. de Grouchy to her brother-in-law, the *président.* See also the note on p. 61, on the testimony of Condorcet's friend, the scholar Jérôme de Lalande. "It was when he saw Sophie taking such affecting care of du Paty's young son, who had been bitten by a rabid [*sic*] dog, that Condorcet fell in love with her." It may be added, in connection with the du Paty de Clam family (the last name being that of a château in the Bordeaux district), that it was one of the *Président's* de-

scendants who made such an unfortunate name for himself a hundred years later by being involved in the attempts to hush up the Dreyfus affair.

8. Louis Amiable, *La Franc-Maçonnerie et la Magistrature* (Aix, Remondet-Aubin, 1894), p. 34.

2

1. A. Guillois, *La marquise de Condorcet,* p. 74. See the delightful pastel of Sophie, by herself, which belonged to her daughter and is reproduced as a frontispiece to Charles Leger's book, *Captives de l'amour* (Paris, Gaillandre, 1933).

2. Biographical notes on Mme. de Condorcet by Mrs. O'Connor, née de Condorcet, given to the academician Arago in 1841 and published in full, p. 369, in Robinet's *Condorcet,* Appendix I.

3. Vicomte de Gabrielly, *La France chevaleresque et chapitrale* (Paris, 1786), p. 87. Other particulars relating to the canonesses are from the same source.

4. Letters from Adélaïde du Paty to the *Président,* dated June 8 and August 4, 1785, in the family archives; quoted by Guillois, p. 38.

5. *Ibid.,* Sophie to Madame du Paty, August 10, 1785.

6. There is a portrait of du Paty engraved by Gerser in 1786, in the

frontispiece of Louis Amiable's book (see chap. 1, n. 8, above).

7. From du Paty to his wife, from Neuville, on September 4, 1785; family archives. *Ibid.* for the following quote.

8. *Ibid.*, from Madame du Paty to the *Président*, August 25, 1785.

9. *Ibid.*, from Sophie to the *Président*, on September 7, 1785.

10. *Ibid.*, n.d.

11. Same source as for 9; *ibid.* for the following quote.

12. C.J.B. du Paty, *Lettres sur l'Italie en 1785* (Paris, Verlière, 1824), II, letter 81.

13. *Ibid.*, letter 86. The first edition of these letters was published in 1788, which shows the degree of freedom of speech that was tolerated by the censors on the eve of the Revolution.

3

1. Diderot, *Oeuvres complètes* (Paris, C.F.L., 1971), VIII, p. 214.

2. A. Wattinne, *L'affaire des trois roués* (Mâcon, Protat frères, 1921), p. 8.

3. From an anonymous pamphlet published in Béziers in 1788; A. Wattinne, p. 31.

4. Expilly, *Dictionnaire,* II, p. 302.

5. Malouet, *Mémoires* (Paris, Plon, 1874), I, p. 189. Malouet, who was then the King's intendant [something like a provincial viceroy or governor] in Toulon, adds, "The deplorable end and last words of these unhappy men drove me to despair."

6. A. Wattinne, p. 57.

7. *Mémoire justificatif pour trois hommes condamnés à la roue* (Paris, Imprimerie de Philippe-Denys

Pierres, 1786); the author is anonymous, of course, but everybody knows it was du Paty.

8. *Ibid.*, pp. 221–224.

4

1. Chateaubriand, *Mémoires d'Outre-Tombe* (Paris, Garnier frères, 1947), I, p. 135.

2. *Ibid.*, p. 137.

3. *Ibid.*, p. 162.

4. *Ibid.*, p. 63. The remaining quotes relating to Chateaubriand's presentation are from the same source.

5. *Ibid.*, p. 164.

6. *Ibid.*, p. 167.

5

1. *Mémoires d'Outre-Tombe* contains no reference to the Assembly of Notables, although it opens five days after Chateaubriand's "royal hunt."

2. Abbé Georgel, *Mémoires pour servir à l'histoire des événements de la fin du XVIIIe siècle* (Paris, Alexis Eymercy, rue Mazarine, 1817), II, p. 277.

3. *Discours prononcé de l'ordre du Roi et en sa présence par M. de Calonne, contrôleur général des finances, dans l'Assemblée des Notables tenue à Versailles le 22 février 1787* (Versailles, Imprimerie P.-D. Pierres, 1787), p. 3. Other excerpts from Calonne's speech are taken from the same pamphlet.

6

1. Grimm and Meister, *Correspondance littéraire* (Paris, Garnier, 1879), XV, p. 32.

2. Antonina Vallentin, *Mirabeau avant la Révolution* (Paris, Grasset, 1946), p. 407.

3. *Dénonciation de l'agiotage au Roi et à l'Assemblée des Notables* by the Comte de Mirabeau, 1787, p. 111.
4. *Ibid.*, p. 17.
5. Duc de Castries, *Mirabeau*, p. 249.
6. *Ibid.*, p. 250.
7. *Dénonciation de l'agiotage*, p. 78.
8. G. Susane, *La tactique financière de Calonne* (Paris, Arthur Rousseau, 1901), p. 249.
9. *Dénonciation de l'agiotage*, p. 96.
10. A. Vallentin, *Mirabeau*, p. 407.
11. *Correspondance littéraire*, XV, p. 35.

7

1. Goethe, *Voyage en Italie* (Paris, Honoré Champion, 1931), p. 183. [There is an English translation by W. H. Auden and Elizabeth Mayer, 1962.—*Trans.*]
2. *Ibid.*, p. 169.
3. *Ibid.*, p. 171.
4. *Ibid.*, p. 173.
5. *Ibid.*, p. 174.
6. *Ibid.*, p. 175.
7. *Ibid.*, p. 185.
8. Richard Friedenthal, *Goethe, sa vie et son temps* (Paris, Fayard, 1967), p. 207.
9. *Ibid.*, p. 229.
10. *Ibid.*, p. 222.
11. *Ibid.*, p. 181.
12. *Ibid.*, p. 203.
13. *Ibid.*, p. 225.
14. *Ibid.*, p. 234; *ibid.* for the following quote.
15. *Ibid.*, p. 233.
16. *Ibid.*, p. 205.
17. *Ibid.*, p. 257.
18. *Ibid.*, p. 249.
19. Goethe, *Voyage en Italie*, p. 210.
20. Walter Sichel, *Emma, Lady Hamilton* (London, Archibald Constable,

1907). [Retranslated from the French.]
21. Joseph Turquan and Jules d'Auriac, *Lady Hamilton, ambassadrice d'Angleterre, et la révolution de Naples* (Paris, Émile-Paul, 1913), p. 16.

8

1. Article by Alfred Begis, *"L'Emprisonnement de Saint-Just sous Louis XVI,"* in *Curiosités Révolutionnaires* (1892, B.N., Ln 27/40675), p. 31.
2. *Ibid.*, p. 26.
3. *Ibid.*, p. 27, to Evry again.
4. *Ibid.*, p. 34.
5. D. Centoré-Bineau, *Saint-Just* (Payot, Paris, 1936), p. 35.
6. See the "publisher's notes," written by Saint-Just himself, at the end of the first edition of *Organt* in 1787 (B.N. 8°, La 32, 817).
7. Saint-Just, *Organt*, p. 6.
8. *Ibid.*, p. 39.
9. *Ibid.*, p. 66.
10. *Ibid.*, p. 76.
11. *Ibid.*, p. 54.
12. *Ibid.*, p. 80.
13. *Ibid.*, p. 170.
14. *Ibid.*, p. 12.
15. *Ibid.*, pp. 25–26.
16. *Ibid.*, p. 68.
17. *Ibid.*, p. 172.

9

1. *Correspondance littéraire*, XV, p. 36.
2. Louis-Sébastien Mercier, *Paris pendant la Révolution ou le Nouveau Paris* (Paris, Poulet-Malassis, 1862), I, p. 184.
3. F.A. Aulard, Preface to the *Mémoires de Louvet de Couvray sur la Révolution Française* (Paris, Li-

brairie des Bibliophiles, 1889), p. 5.

4. Mme. Roland, *Mémoires. Édition critique* by Claude Perrous (Paris, Plon, 1905), I, p. 161.

5. From a letter by Louvet, analyzed by Étienne Charavay in his *Catalogue d'une précieuse collection de lettres autographes* (Paris,1886); cited in Aulard's preface to Louvet's *Mémoires*.

6. *Romanciers du XVIIIe siècle* (Bibliothèque de la Pléiade, Gallimard, 1965), II, p. 601.

7. *Ibid.,* p. 684.

8. *Ibid.,* p. 419.

9. *Ibid.,* p. 481

10. *Ibid.,* p. 586.

10

1. M. de Lescure, *Correspondance secrète sur Louis XVI, Marie-Antoinette, la Cour et la Ville, de 1777 à 1792* (Paris, Plon, 1866), II, p. 115.

2. *Ibid.,* p. 116.

3. Robert Lacour-Gayet, *Calonne, financier réformateur contre-révolutionnaire* (Paris, Hachette, 1963), p. 127.

4. Charles Maurice de Talleyrand-Périgord, *Mémoires* (Paris, Jean de Bonnot, 1967), I, p. 95.

5. R. Lacour-Gayet, *Calonne,* p. 123.

6. *Ibid.,* p. 131.

7. Besenval, *Mémoires,* II, p. 209, in Jean Egret, *La pré-révolution française* (Paris, P.U.F., 1962), p. 40. [Egret has been translated into English, but has been retranslated from French throughout, in this book.—*Trans.*]

8. Lescure, *Correspondance secrète,* p. 112.

9. Archives Nationales, M 788 (57):

letter to the Comtesse de Gramont.

10. Pierre Jolly, *Calonne* (Paris, Plon, 1949), p. 183.

11

1. *L'Assemblée des Notables de 1787. La Conférence du 2 mars;* published text, with an introduction and notes by Pierre Renouvin (Société de l'Histoire de la Révolution française, 1920), p. 1.

2. P. Jolly, *Calonne,* p. 171.

3. *L'Assemblée des Notables de 1787,* p. 39.

4. *Ibid.,* pp. 41–44.

5. Adrienne Koch and William Peden, eds., *The Life and Selected Writings of Thomas Jefferson* (Modern Library, New York, 1944), p. 414. Article by Jean Egret, *"La Fayette dans la première assemblée des notables,"* p. 3, in *Annales Historiques de la Révolution Française,* XXIV, 1952.

6. J. Egret, *"La Fayette,"* p. 6.

7. *Mémoires, correspondance et manuscrits du général Lafayette,* published by his family (Paris, H. Fournier aîné, 1838), II, p. 165.

8. Bibliothèque de l'Arsenal, Ms 4546, p. 54.

9. *Journal de l'Assemblée des Notables de 1787* by the Comte de Brienne and Charles de Loménie de Brienne. Introduction and notes by Pierre Chevallier (Paris, Klincksieck, 1960), p. 76.

10. P. Jolly, *Calonne,* p. 189.

12

1. Malouet's *Mémoires,* quoted by J. Egret, *La pré-révolution,* p. 54.

2. *Mémoires de Weber, frère de lait de*

Marie-Antoinette (Paris, Firmin-Didot, 1860), p. 102.

3. *Journal de l'Assemblée des Notables,* p. 32.

4. *Ibid.,* p. 33 (reminiscences of the Vicomtesse de Loménie).

5. François-Aubert de la Chenaye-Desbois, *Dictionnaire de la Noblesse* (Paris, Reprint Editions, Berger-Levrault, 1980), VI, p. 275.

6. Brienne, *"Mémoire à la Commission des réguliers sur les religieux du diocèse de Toulouse,"* in Pierre Chevallier, *Loménie de Brienne et l'ordre monastique* (Paris, J. Vrin, 1959), p. 278.

7. Dom H. Leclerq, *Vers la fédération* (Paris, Letouzey, 1929), p. 263. See also Archives Nationales, D, XIX, No. 1–12; B.N. Ms No. 13857–58.

8. H. Leclerq, *Vers la fédération,* p. 264.

9. Marmontel, *Mémoires,* III, p. 131, quoted by J. Egret in *La pré-révolution,* p. 68.

10. Duc de Montmorency-Luxembourg, *Mémoires,* p. 269, quoted by J. Egret, *ibid.,* p. 68.

11. Joseph Perrin, *Le cardinal de Loménie de Brienne* (Sens, Paul Duchemin, 1896), p. 15.

12. J. Egret, *La pré-révolution,* p. 69; the specific reference is to *La Gazette de Leyde.*

13. Louis Gottschalk, ed., *The Letters of Lafayette to Washington, 1777, 1799* (Philadelphia, American Philosophic Society, 1976), p. 23.

14. Bibliothèque de l'Arsenal, Ms 3976, p. 960.

15. La Fayette, *Mémoires de ma main* (dictated by L. F. in 1828), II, p. 177.

16. *Ibid.,* p. 201.

17. Lescure, *Correspondance secrète,* II, p. 145.

13

1. Josefina Rodriguez de Alonso, *Le siècle des lumières conté par Francisco de Miranda* (Paris, France-Empire, 1974), p. 297. I am grateful to Ms. Rodriguez de Alonso, cultural attaché in the Venezuelan embassy in France, for sending me this book, the product of an exhaustive study of the Miranda archives, which are kept in twenty-four folios in the National Academy of History in Caracas. Her investigation has brought to light a great many little-known aspects of Miranda's life. Subsequent references to this work will be identified as Alonso-Miranda.

2. Alonso-Miranda, p. 88. *Ibid.* for the following quote.

3. According to C. Parra-Perez, *Miranda et Madame de Custine* (Paris, Grasset, 1950), p. 21, his date of birth was March 28, 1750. This author adds that, owing to the prevailing uncertainty about Miranda's background (the French in those days called him Peruvian, or Mexican, or even Portuguese), it took him a great deal of research to determine this date. I also had a hard time untangling my sources, because of a baptismal record relating to a brother of Miranda's who was four years younger than he and died in infancy; Miranda apparently made use of this record on occasion, as though it were his own.

4. Jean Descola, *Les libertadors* (Paris, Fayard, 1957), p. 191.

5. Miranda's *Diary*, quoted in Alonso-Miranda, p. 36.

6. C. Parra-Perez, *Miranda et la Révolution Française* (Paris, Pierre Roger, 1925), p. 14.

7. Alonso-Miranda, p. 49.

8. *Ibid.*, p. 65.

14

1. Descola, *Les libertadors*, p. 207.

2. Prince de Ligne, *Mémoires*, quoted by Henri Troyat, *Catherine la Grande* (Paris, Flammarion, 1977), p. 383.

3. Quoted by Parra-Perez, *Miranda et la Révolution Française*, Affaires Étrangères, Spain, vol. 619, fo. 383.

4. Descola, *Les libertadors*, p. 181. *Ibid.* for the next quote.

5. James Lloyd of Boston, quoted in Alonso-Miranda, p. 100. [Retranslated from the French.]

6. Quoted by Parra-Perez, *Miranda et la Révolution Française*, Vienna, State Archives, *Russia*, 44.

7. Catherine II just wrote this to Dr. Zimmerman; quoted by H. Troyat, *Catherine*, p. 375.

8. Comte de Ségur, *Mémoires, souvenirs et anecdotes* (Paris, Eymery, 1827), III, p. 44.

9. Victor Tissot, *La Russie et les Russes* (Paris, Plon, 1884), p. 142.

10. Ségur, *Mémoires*, p. 8.

11. The whole trip is wonderfully related by H. Troyat in *Catherine*, in particular see pp. 380–85.

12. Ségur, *Mémoires*, III, p. 8.

13. Peuchet, *Dictionnaire universel de la géographie commerçante* (Paris, Blanchon, Year VIII), V, p. 492.

14. Claude Pasteur, *Le prince de Ligne, l'enchanteur de l'Europe* (Paris, Librairie Académique Perrin, 1980), p. 163.

15. *Ibid.*, p. 162, quote by Ségur.

16. Comte Roger de Damas, *Mémoires* (Paris, Plon, 1912), I, p. 41.

17. *Ibid.*, p. 40.

18. Alonso-Miranda, p. 324. *Ibid.* for the next quote.

19. Ségur, *Mémoires*, III, p. 65.

20. *Lettres l'amour de Catherine II à Potemkine*, published by Georges Oudard (Paris, Calman-Lévy, 1934), p. 168.

15

1. Alonso-Miranda, p. 76. Unless otherwise mentioned, all other references to Miranda's Grand Tour are from the same source.

16

1. *Correspondance littéraire*, XV, p. 95.

2. Albert Babeau, *Paris en 1789* (Paris, Firmin-Didot, n.d.), p. 122.

3. *Ibid.*

4. *Correspondance littéraire*, XV, p. 95.

5. Beaumarchais, *Oeuvres complètes* (Paris, Furne, 1835), p. 234.

6. *Ibid.*, p. 257.

7. *Ibid.*, p. 231; Preface to *Tarare*.

8. *Ibid.*, p. 233; Preface to *Tarare*.

9. *Ibid.*, p. 231; Preface to *Tarare*.

10. *Ibid.*, p. 229; Preface to *Tarare*.

11. *Ibid.*, p. 239; *Tarare*.

12. From Bachaumont's *Mémoires secrets*, quoted by Adolphe Julien in *La cour et l'Opéra sous Louis XVI* (Paris, Librairie Académique Didier, 1878), p. 238.

13. Louis de Loménie, *Beaumarchais et son temps* (Paris, Calman-Lévy, 1879), II, p. 406. From a letter Salieri wrote to Beaumarchais's daughter, dated October 5, 1805.

14. *Ibid.* This quote alone is enough to make nonsense of the gratuitous allegation that in 1791 Salieri engineered the death of Mozart. In this connection, see Jean and Brigitte Massin, *Wolfgang Amadeus Mozart* (Paris, Club Française du Livre, 1959), p. 566.

17

1. Henri Cordier, *Bibliographie des Oeuvres de Beaumarchais* (Paris, Quantin, 1881). The Kornman affair is the subject of a large proportion of the entries, nos. 378 to 443. (Quoted by Frédéric Grendel, *Beaumarchais,* Paris, Flammarion, 1973).
2. Gudin de la Brennellerie, *Histoire de Beaumarchais* (Paris, Plon, 1888), p. 367.
3. *Correspondance littéraire,* XV, p. 70.
4. Étienne Lamy, *Nicolas Bergasse, 1750–1832* (Paris, Librairie Académique Perrin, 1910), p. 44.
5. *Beaumarchais et son temps* (Paris, Furne, 1835), II, p. 388.
6. É. Lamy, *Nicolas Bergasse,* p. 40.
7. Beaumarchais, *Oeuvres complètes,* p. 477.
8. *Ibid.,* p. 490.
9. *Ibid.,* p. 479.
10. *Ibid.,* p. 489.
11. *Ibid.,* p. 490.
12. É. Lamy, *Nicolas Bergasse,* pp. 1–60. One or two particulars relating to Bergasse, and all quotations by him, have been taken, with precaution, from this book, which is so fiercely antirevolutionary as to be absurd.
13. *Ibid.,* p. 30.

14. Beaumarchais, *Oeuvres complètes; Tarare,* p. 253.

18

1. The full text of the King's *lettres de provision* for Danton was published in the September 1901 issue of the *Revue de la Révolution Française;* the original is in the Archives Nationales, VI 529.
2. Hermann Wendel, *Danton* (Paris, Payot, 1978), p. 9.
3. In my efforts to pin down the few uncertainties of Danton's youth and marriage, I have compared the data in Louis Madelin, *Danton* (Paris, Hachette, 1914); Jacques Herissay, *Cet excellent M. Danton* (Paris, Fayard, 1960); Frédéric Bluche, *Danton* (Paris, Librairie Académique Perrin, 1984). See also the *Annales Historiques de la Révolution Française,* 1946, 1951, 1955.
4. Gabriel Pioro, *"Sur la fortune de Danton, d'après les minutes inédites des notaires parisiens"* (*Annales Historiques de la Révolution Française,* 1955), p. 328.

19

1. Alexandre Capitaine, *La situation économique et sociale des États-Unis à la fin du XVIIIe siècle* (Paris, P.U.F., n.d.), p. 11. *Ibid.,* pp. 11–14, for Philadelphia.
2. André Maurois, *Histoire des États-Unis* (Paris, Albin Michel, 1943), p. 194.
3. *Ibid.,* p. 195.
4. *Ibid.,* p. 194. [Retranslated from the French.]
5. Letters from Jefferson to Madison (January 30, 1787) and to Colonel Smith (November 13 of the same

year), both from Paris; *The Life and Selected Letters of Thomas Jefferson,* pp. 413 and 436.

6. A. Maurois, *Histoire des États-Unis,* p. 196.

20

1. Alexander Hamilton, *The Federalist* (Oxford, Basil Blackwell, 1948), p. 10.
2. Nathan Schacher, *Alexander Hamilton* (New York, Appleton-Century, 1946), p. 190.
3. According to E. Laboulaye, *Histoire des États-Unis* (Paris, Charpentier, 1867), III, p. 218.
4. A. Hamilton, *The Federalist,* p. xxv.
5. James Madison, *Debates in the Federal Convention of 1787,* I, edited by G. Hunt and J. B. Scott (Buffalo, Prometheus Books, 1987), pp. 14–15.
6. E. Laboulaye, p. 244.
7. *Ibid.,* p. 245.

21

1. Quoted by Peter Friedmann in his introduction to the selected writings of Mably, *Sur la théorie du pouvoir politique* (Paris, Éditions Sociales, 1975), p. 53; this excerpt is from *Des droits et des devoirs du citoyen.*
2. *Journal d'une bourgeoise pendant la Révolution,* published by her grandson Edouard Lockroy (Paris, 1881), p. 126.
3. Letter dated February 3, 1777, quoted in the *Petite Revue des Bibliophiles Dauphinois,* 1951.
4. Mably, *Oeuvres,* XV, p. 131, quoted by Peter Friedmann, p. 24. The next quote is from *Principes de morale,* in *Oeuvres,* X, p. 244.

5. *Correspondance littéraire,* XIII, p. 264.
6. Mably, *Sur la théorie du pouvoir politique,* p. 255.
7. *Ibid.,* p. 253.
8. See Mably's *Testament,* in the Archives Nationales, Mx XLV, 589.
9. Mably, *Sur la théorie du pouvoir politique,* p. 255.
10. Charles Francis Adams, *The Works of John Adams,* V (Boston, Little and Brown, 1851), p. 491. *Ibid.,* pp. 492–96, for the excerpts that follow.
11. Bernard Faÿ, *George Washington, gentilhomme* (Paris, Grasset, 1932), p. 266.
12. D. Pasquet, *Histoire politique et sociale du peuple américain* (Paris, Picard, 1924), I, p. 287.

22

1. *Correspondance de Babeuf avec l'Académie d'Arras 1785–1788,* published under the direction of Marcel Reinhard (Paris, P.U.F., 1961), p. 91.
2. *Ibid.,* letter dated March 21, 1787, p. 71. Georges Lefebvre and A. Saitta, two of the Revolution's greatest historians, have seen in this passage the first tremor of Babeuf's communist utopia.
3. The memorandum was published in 1770, 29 pages 8vo (B.N. 80 LK 9, 20).
4. *Correspondance de Babeuf,* letter dated June 5, 1787, p. 92.
5. Antoine Pelletier, *"Babeuf feudiste"* in *Annales Historiques de la Révolution Française,* January–March 1965, p. 33.
6. Jean Bruhat, *Gracchus Babeuf et les Égaux* (Paris, Librairie Académique Perrin, 1978), p. 49.

7. M. Marion, *Dictionnaire des Institutions,* p. 533.
8. A. Pelletier, *"Babeuf feudiste,"* p. 32.
9. Written in 1793, quoted by J. Bruhat, *Gracchus Babeuf,* p. 25.
10. Maurice Dommanget, *Sur Babeuf et la conjuration des Égaux* (Paris, Maspéro, 1970), p. 14.
11. *Ibid.*
12. It is an engraving by Bonneville and can be seen, *inter alia,* on the cover of M. Dommanget's *Sur Babeuf.*
13. G. Bertin, *Babeuf à Roye,* quoted by J. Bruhat, *Gracchus Babeuf,* p. 85. *Ibid.* for the following quote relating to his passport.
14. Victor Advielle, *Histoire de Gracchus Babeuf et du babouvisme,* I, p. 10; quoted by M. Dommanget, *Sur Babeuf.*
15. M. Dommanget, *Sur Babeuf,* p. 18.
16. Expilly, *Dictionnaire,* VI, p. 628.
17. Maurice Dommanget, *Pages choisies de Babeuf,* p. 108.
18. *Le Tribun du peuple ou le Défenseur des Droits de L'Homme,* No. 29, dated 1 Nivôse, Year III.
19. Undated text by Babeuf, from the Dommanget collection and from V. Avielle, I, p. 47. This reference is from *"Babeuf et les problèmes du babouvisme,"* Stockholm International Colloquy (Paris, Éditions Sociales, 1963), article by M. Dommanget, p. 39. *Ibid.* for the next quote.

23

1. With support from the CNRS, Léon-Noël Berthe published a substantial volume in this connection, in Arras, in 1969, with a preface by Marcel Reinhard: *Dubois de Fosseux, secrétaire de l'Académie d'Arras, 1785–1792, et son bureau de correspondance.*
2. L. N. Berthe, *Dubois de Fosseux,* p. 383.
3. The frontispiece to L. N. Berthe's book.
4. *Correspondance de Babeuf avec l'Académie d'Arras,* p. 22. *Ibid.* for the following unreferenced quotes.
5. This prospectus, fictitiously identified as originating in London in 1786, has been reproduced by EDHIS, reprinters of rare texts, 10, rue Vivienne, Paris. Léon Centener, head of the firm, has deserved history's thanks for many years.

24

1. *Archives Parlementaires* (Paris, Paul Dupont, 1879), I, p. 231.
2. *Ibid.*
3. Evelyne Lever, *Louis XVI* (Paris, Fayard, 1985), p. 401.
4. *Archives Parlementaires,* I, p. 232.
5. *Ibid.,* p. 233.
6. *Ibid.,* p. 234.
7. *Ibid.*
8. *Ibid.,* p. 236.
9. *Ibid.,* p. 238.
10. *Ibid.,* p. 244.
11. *Ibid.*
12. Target's Journal, quoted by Georges Michon in *Essai sur l'Histoire du parti feuillant. Adrien Duport* (Paris, Payot, 1924), p. 12.
13. *Correspondance secrète du comte de Mercy-Argenteau avec l'empereur Joseph II et le prince de Kaunitz,* published by the Chevalier d'Arneth and J. Flammermon (Paris, 1891), II, p. 112.
14. *Archives Parlementaires,* I, p. 246.
15. *Ibid.*

16. *Ibid.*
17. *Ibid.*, p. 247.
18. Bookseller Hardy's journal exists in manuscript form in the Bibliothèque Nationale, and because of its gargantuan size the complete text has still to appear in print. However, Robert Laffont's iconographic service has kindly procured a few of the essential pages for me—in this instance, sheet 164, dated August 6, 1787.
19. *Archives Parlementaires,* I, p. 249; *ibid.* for the next quote.

25

1. Aimé Chérest, *La chute de l'Ancien Régime* (Paris, Hachette, 1884), I, pp. 244–45.
2. G. Michon, *Adrien Duport,* pp. 1–3. Other unreferenced particulars relating to Duport are from the same source.
3. According to Lacretelle, quoted by Michon, *Adrien Duport,* p. 2.
4. Hardy's journal, sheet 164, dated August 7, 1787.
5. *Ibid.*
6. *Ibid.*, sheets 164 and 165.
7. *Nouvelles extraordinaires de divers endroits,* Leyden, August 14, 1787; *ibid.* for following quotes.
8. *Ibid.*
9. G. Michon, *Adrien Duport,* p. 10.
10. Hardy's journal, sheet 177.

26

1. André Kaspi, *L'Indépendance américaine, 1763–1789* (Paris, Gallimard, Julliard, 1976), p. 188.
2. Bernard Faÿ, *Benjamin Franklin,* II, p. 273.
3. Mark Van Doren, *Benjamin Franklin* (Westport, Greenwood Press, 1973), p. 755.

4. *The Declaration of Independence and the Constitution of the United States of America* (Washington, D.C., Government Printing Office, 1956), pp. 23–24.
5. James T. Flexner, *Washington* (Boston, Little, Brown & Co., 1974), p. 209.
6. A. Maurois, *Histoire des États-Unis,* p. 197. The following analysis of the proceedings at the Convention is taken from the same source, but also from Henry William Elson's *Histoire des États-Unis* (Paris, Payot, 1930), p. 332.
7. A. Maurois, *Histoire des États-Unis,* p. 201. [This does not appear in Madison's record, and I do not know where it can come from; things very much like this, if not these exact words, were certainly said, however.—*Trans.*]
8. *The Declaration of Independence,* pp. 11–22.

27

1. In this first approach to Fouché, I chiefly follow the book by Louis Madelin, *Fouché* (Paris, Plon, n.d.) and that of Henry Buisson, *Fouché, duc d'Otrante* (Bienne, 1968). A battle of historians has been waged over the last century in regard to the exact date of Fouché's birth and hence his age. Buisson gives May 27, 1760, but it would seem, on the strength of a registration of baptism in the Pellerin town hall, that Madelin has come closer to the mark by moving the date back a year. It is likely that the origin of this not very significant dispute lies in a copyist's mistake in the offices of the Oratory.
2. *Mémoires de Joseph Fouché, duc*

d'Otrante, ministre de la Police Générale (reprint by Jean de Bonnot, Paris, 1967), p. 7.

3. Expilly's *Dictionnaire*, V, p. 610.

4. J. Caille, *Fouché, d'après une correspondance privée inédite,* quoted by L. Madelin, p. 10.

5. H. Buisson, *Fouché, duc d'Otrante,* p. 50.

6. Letter from the Duc d'Otrante to the Comte de Fleaux, Prague, November 30, 1816, quoted by L. Madelin, p. 6.

7. H. Buisson, *Fouché,* p. 50.

8. Archives Nationales, M 592, quoted by L. Madelin, p. 11.

9. Georges Hamel, *Histoire de l'abbaye et du collège de Juilly* (Paris, Jules Gervais, 1888), p. 5.

10. *Ibid.,* p. 7.

28

1. Jan Potocki, *Le Manuscrit trouvé à Saragosse.* Text prepared and presented by Roger Caillois (Paris, Gallimard, 1958).

2. These references, sometimes out of order, come from pp. 123–48 of the *Voyages en Turquie et en Égypte, en Hollande, au Maroc* by Jan Potocki (introduction and notes by Daniel Beauvois, Paris, Fayard, 1980).

3. Mirabeau, *Oeuvres complètes,* V, *"Aux Bataves, sur le stathoudérat,"* p. 96. Other unreferenced quotes by Mirabeau in this chapter are from the same source, a text written in January 1788.

4. Pierre de Witt, *Une invasion prussienne en Hollande en 1787* (Paris, Plon, 1886), p. 4.

5. *Ibid.,* p. 5.

6. Pieter Geyl, *La Révolution batave (1783–1798)* (Paris, Société des

études robespierristes, 1971), p. 72.

7. Marquis of Carmarthen to Sir James Harris, quoted by P. de Witt, *Une invasion prussienne,* p. 227. [Retranslated from the French.]

8. Mirabeau, *Oeuvres complètes,* V, *"Lettre sur l'invasion des Provinces-Unies,"* p. 279.

9. P. de Witt, *Une invasion prussienne,* p. 261.

10. Louis Gottschalk, ed., *The Letters of Lafayette to Washington,* p. 331.

11. Henry de Peyster, *Les troubles de Hollande à la veille de la Révolution française (1780–1795)* (Paris, Picard, 1905), p. 114. *Ibid.* for the next quote, from a remark made to one of his friends.

12. Conrad de Mandach, *Le comte Guillaume de Portes (1750–1823)* (Paris, Librairie Académique Perrin, 1904), p. 98. Other unreferenced quotes by the Comte de Portes are from the same source.

13. Mirabeau, *Oeuvres complètes,* V, *"Lettre sur l'invasion des Provinces-Unies,"* p. 283.

14. Jan Potocki, *Voyages en Turquie,* pp. 144 and 146.

29

1. *Correspondance de Babeuf avec l'Académie d'Arras,* p. 129.

2. *Ibid.,* p. 146. Babeuf's long, despairing letter to Dubois, from which the following quotes are also taken, is dated November 22, 1787.

3. *Ibid.,* pp. 146 and 147.

4. *Ibid.,* p. 148, footnote, citing M. Dommanget.

5. *"Description des épidémies qui ont régné"* (Paris, 1783), a text quoted

in an article by Jean-Pierre Peter in *Médecins, climat et épidémies à la fin du XVIIIe siècle,* a collective work by the École Pratique des Hautes Études (Paris, Mouton, 1972), p. 162. The text translates, for modern readers: "in other words, flu, serious pulmonary ailments, malaria, typhoid, typhus, smallpox and dysenteries."

6. *Correspondance de Babeuf avec l'Académie d'Arras,* p. 148.

7. *Ibid.*

8. E. Coet, *Babeuf à Roye* (Péronne, 1865), quoted by J. Bruhat, *Gracchus Babeuf et les Égaux,* p. 39. Needless to say, no text, of whatever persuasion, can be found to give credit to this affirmation.

30

1. Rather oddly, the text of the *Édit de tolérance* is not in the first volume of the *Archives Parlementaires;* it is quoted at length by Pierre Grosclaude in *Malesherbes, témoin et interprète de son temps* (Paris, Fischbacher, 1961), p. 765, and also by Jean Egret, *La prérévolution,* p. 140.

2. Robert Mirabaud, *Rabaut Saint-Étienne* (Paris, Fischbacher, 1930), p. 85. Other unnumbered particulars relating to his early years are from the same source.

3. *Lettre-rapport de Saint-Étienne à MM. Les Membres du Comité de Bordeaux (1788),* Bibliothèque Consistoriale de Nîmes, Reg. B. 33.

4. P. Grosclaude, *Malesherbes,* p. 765.

5. *Lettre-rapport de Saint-Étienne.*

6. The complete text of the edict is given in the first edition of the *Oeuvres* of Rabaut Saint-Étienne (Paris, Laisné frères, 1826), II, p. 108.

31

1. R. Mirabaud, *Rabaut Saint-Étienne,* p. 9.

2. Edmond Hugues, *Histoire de la restauration du protestantisme en France au XVIIIe siècle* (Paris, Michel Lévy, 1875), II, p. 76. *Ibid.* for further particulars relating to Paul Rabaut.

3. Quoted by R. Mirabaud, p. 10; *ibid.* for the following quote.

4. Rabaut Saint-Étienne, *"Lettre sur la vie et les écrits de M. Court de Gébelin, adressée au Musée de Paris,"* in *Oeuvres,* II, p. 355. *Ibid.* for the following quotes.

5. Letter published in the *Bulletin de la Société du Protestantisme français,* XXVIII, 1879, quoted by R. Mirabaud, p. 16.

6. Quoted by Charles Dardier, *Rabaut Saint-Étienne, enfance, éducation* (Paris, Fischbacher, 1886), in R. Mirabaud, p. 19.

7. Letter from Jeanbon, dated May 16, 1788, to Saint-Étienne, quoted by Léon Lévy, *Le conventionnel Jeanbon Saint-André* (Paris, Felix Alcan, 1901), p. 9.

8. R. Mirabaud, *Rabaut Saint-Étienne,* p. 22.

9. According to Boissy d'Anglas, quoted by R. Mirabaud, p. 24.

32

1. Rabaut Saint-Étienne, *Oeuvres,* II. These are the opening lines of *Le vieux Cévenol,* which is published there in full. Other excerpts from the text are from the same source.

33

1. Expilly's *Dictionnaire,* IV, p. 801. When the future Henri IV was still king of Navarre, he was fond of the town and used to go there often. It became one of the main Protestant strongholds in the southwest and withstood long sieges by Richelieu's armies, who never succeeded in bringing it completely to its knees, even after the capture of La Rochelle farther north.

2. Léon Lévy, *Jeanbon Saint-André,* p. 3. See also the *Encyclopédie des Sciences Religieuses,* XI, p. 250.

3. Particulars given by L. Lévy, *Jeanbon Saint-André,* p. 6, from references in Sainte-Beuve's *Nouveaux Lundis* (he seems to have had access to documents that have since been lost), as well as from a "regional" biography by Michel Nicolas, *Jeanbon Saint-André, sa vie et ses écrits,* published in Montauban in 1848.

4. The certificate of his consecration is kept in the Archives of the Consistory of Castres; it is given in full in L. Lévy, p. 9.

5. On a trip home, before going to Castres, Jeanbon witnessed some of the events there, which opened his eyes to the incipient opposition between a predominantly Catholic factory proletariat that considered itself exploited and its small-time Protestant employers. See Jeanbon's letter to a man named Julien de Verdeilhan, dated June 24, 1773, quoted by L. Lévy, p. 50.

6. Léon Lévy, p. 11.

7. From Jeanbon's letter to Julien de Verdeilhan (see n. 5 above), in L. Lévy, p. 12.

8. See, in regard to this "ideological" shift, the numerous references given by L. Lévy, pp. 14–17.

9. Letter written by Jeanbon, dated July 1, 1778, quoted by L. Lévy, p. 20.

10. Letter found among Rabaut's papers, dated June 17, 1779, quoted by L. Lévy, p. 22.

11. Letter by Paul Rabaut, quoted by L. Lévy, p. 23.

12. L. Lévy, p. 23.

13. *Ibid.,* p. 24.

14. Letter from Jeanbon to Saint-Étienne, dated May 24, 1780; *ibid.,* p. 28.

15. Letters from Jeanbon to Rabaut senior and junior, written in spring 1782 and quoted by L. Lévy, p. 32.

16. L. Lévy, p. 23.

17. Published by M. Nicolas, pp. 275–310; quoted by L. Lévy, p. 33.

18. Letter from Jeanbon to Paul Rabaut, May 1, 1782, quoted by L. Lévy, p. 33.

19. Quoted by L. Lévy, p. 37.

20. *Ibid.,* p. 34; and *ibid.* for the next quote.

21. Rabaut Saint-Étienne's second *Mémoire,* published in the texts of the Academy of Nîmes, Seventh Series, XVI, p. 226; quoted by L. Lévy, p. 38.

22. A. Chérest, I, p. 390.

23. *Ibid.,* p. 391.

24. Joseph Droz, *Histoire du règne de Louis XVI* (Paris, Renouard, 1860), II, p. 38.

25. Léon de la Brière, *Madame Louise de France* (Paris, Reteaux, 1900), p. 331.

26. Lescure, *Correspondance secrète,* II, p. 212.

27. Dispatch by Baron de Staël, in *Gustave III et la Court de France,* quoted by A. Chérest, I, p. 391.

28. Avignon and Paris, 1787, 45 pp. 8vo, Bibliothèque Nationale, Ld 176, no. 707. *Ibid.* for the next quote.

29. All that can be found relating to her is, in the Montauban town hall, a death certificate designating her as "daughter of the late Henry Desuc and Marguerite Ferran," entered in 1812. She was born in Roquecourbe, just outside Montauban. See L. Lévy, p. 43.

34

1. J. Egret, *La pré-révolution,* p. 64.
2. Comte de Ségur, *Le Maréchal de Ségur* (Paris, 1895), p. 319.
3. Quoted by J. Egret, *La pré-révolution,* p. 64. The Comte de Virieu was a nobleman of liberal leanings from the Dauphiné; he wrote this in his *Dialogue sur l'établissement et la formation des Assemblées provinciales,* 1787, p. 45.
4. Besenval, *Mémoires,* III, p. 294, quoted by A. Chérest, I, p. 327.
5. A. Chérest, I, p. 335.
6. In August 1787, Brissot published an anonymous pamphlet called *Point de banqueroute ou Lettres à un créancier de l'État,* quoted by J. Egret, p. 182.
7. A. Chérest, I, p. 333.
8. Louis-Sébastien Mercier, *Tableau de Paris,* II, p. 4, and IV, p. 240.
9. Lamoignon's reply to the advocate general Séguier, quoted by J. Egret, p. 189.
10. *Archives Parlementaires,* I, p. 264. *Ibid.* for the following quote and the excerpts from Lamoignon's speech.

11. *Ibid.,* p. 269.
12. According to Sallier's *Annales françaises,* p. 133, quoted by A. Chérest, I, p. 352.
13. J. Droz, *Histoire du règne de Louis XVI,* II, pp. 30–31.
14. J. Egret, p. 189.
15. According to Sallier's *Annales françaises,* p. 128, quoted by J. Egret, p. 190.
16. *Archives Parlementaires,* I, p. 269.
17. Auguste Ducoin, *Monographie* (illustrated) *de Philippe d'Orléans-Égalité* (Paris, Dentu, 1845), p. 38.
18. Talleyrand's *Mémoires,* p. 193.
19. According to Sallier's *Annales françaises,* p. 128, quoted by J. Egret, p. 191.
20. *Archives Parlementaires,* I, p. 269.

35

1. The complete text of Napoleon's brief manuscript was published by Frédéric Masson and Guido Biago, *Napoléon, manuscrits inédits 1786–1791* (Paris, Albin Michel, 1927), pp. 21–23. These manuscripts are a curious batch of notebooks from Napoleon's early youth, which he unearthed and gave to his uncle, Cardinal Fesch, presumably during the Hundred Days, i.e., twenty years after writing them. Rediscovered by Frédéric Masson after a further period of oblivion and published under the general heading *Fonds Libri,* some of these writings throw a singular light on the youthful vaticinations, many of them tinged with romanticism, of Napoleon's mind.
2. Lecture by A. M. Franck, given in Valence in 1897, on *"Valence en 1785 et le lieutenant Bonaparte,"* quoted by Louis Garros, *Quel*

roman que ma vie, Itinéraire de Na-poléon Bonaparte (Paris, 1947), p. 29.

3. J. B. Marcaggi, *La Genèse de Napo-léon* (Paris, Perrin, 1902), p. 127.

4. *Napoléon, manuscrits inédits,* pp. 10–15: *"Réfutation de Roustan."*

5. René Heron de Villefosse, *L'Anti-Versailles ou le Palais-Royal de Philippe-Égalité* (Paris, Jean Dullis, 1974), p. 201.

6. *Napoléon, manuscrits inédits,* pp. 21–23. See also *La Jeunesse de Na-poléon* by Arthur Chuquet (Paris, Armand Colin, 1898), *La jeunesse inédite de Napoléon* by Paul Bartel (Paris, Amiot-Dumont, 1954) and *Les années de jeunesse de Napoléon Bonaparte* by Baron Thiry (Paris, Berger-Levrault, 1975).

36

1. Details of Merlin de Thionville's youth come from a rough draft of his memoirs, which he did not have time to take up to the Revo-lution but which were published in his great-grandson's book, *Merlin de Thionville, d'après des documents inédits,* by Roger Merlin (Paris, Felix Alcan, 1927); here, I, p. 35. Other unnumbered particulars are from the first thirty pages.

2. See the miniature by L. Boucher, a pupil of Louis David, repro-duced as the frontispiece in R. Merlin, *Merlin de Thionville.*

37

1. J. L. David, *Le Peintre Louis David,* B.N. fol. La/27, 31763, p. 53.

2. Louis Hautecoeur, *Louis David* (Paris, La Table Ronde, 1954), p. 17. I have found the largest
number of confirmed biographical details about David in this book.

3. A few historians have disputed the relationship—remote, no doubt, but proved by L. Hautecoeur, p. 17.

4. Letter from David to Cochin (sec-retary of the Academy of Paint-ing), quoted by L. Hautecoeur, p. 31

5. Quoted by J. L. David, p. 5. *Ibid.* for the rest of the tale of his "sui-cide."

6. *Ibid.,* p. 8.

7. Quoted in L. Hautecoeur, p. 46.

8. L. Hautecoeur, p. 68; *ibid.,* p. 64, for d'Angiviller's words in praise of Pécoul. The portraits of David's parents-in-law are in the Louvre.

9. From a letter written by Drouais to his aunt, quoted by L. Haute-coeur, p. 76.

10. Quoted by J. L. David, p. 43.

38

1. Jean François-Primo, *La jeunesse de Brissot* (Paris, Grasset, 1932), p. 218.

2. In the entry entitled *"Nègres, con-sidérés comme esclaves dans les colonies de l'Amérique,"* written by one M. Forney in vol. XI of the *Ency-clopédie* (1765 edition, pp. 76–83). *Ibid.* for the following quotes.

3. J. François-Primo, *La jeunesse de Brissot,* p. 216. *Ibid.,* p. 223, foot-note. [Title of essay retranslated from French.]

4. *Ibid.,* p. 218. [Retranslated from French.]

5. The letter was published by Claude Perroud in *Correspondance et papiers de Brissot* (memoranda and documents relating to the eighteenth and nineteenth centu-

ries, B.N., 80 L45, 78), p. 167. *Ibid.* for the following excerpts from the letter.

6. Jacques-Pierre Brissot, *Mémoires,* published by Claude Perroud (Paris, Picard, n.d.), II, p. 73.

7. *Ibid.*, p. 83.

8. B. Combes de Patris, *Valady* (Paris, de Boccard, 1930), p. 3.

9. Letter written by Valady to Thomas Taylor, quoted in B. Combes de Patris, p. 33.

10. B. Combes de Patris, *Valady,* p. 34.

11. *Correspondance et papiers de Brissot,* p. 175.

12. Aubert de Vitry, *"Souvenirs d'un Girondin,"* an article in *La Chronique de Paris* of March 29, 1835, quoted by B. Combe de Patris, p. 39.

13. Brissot, *Mémoires,* II, p. 83.

14. *Correspondance et papiers de Brissot,* p. 173.

15. Brissot, *Mémoires,* II, p. 75.

16. *Ibid.*, p. 78.

17. Julian T. Boyd, ed., *The Papers of Thomas Jefferson,* XII (Princeton, Princeton University Press, 1955), pp. 577–78.

18. Brissot, *Mémoires,* II, pp. 77–78.

19. J. François-Primo, *La jeunesse de Brissot,* pp. 165–66.

20. According to C. Perroud in the *"Notice sur la vie de Brissot,"* which prefaces the *Correspondance et papiers de Brissot,* p. 46.

21. Claude Perroud, *"Brissot et les Roland,"* in *La Révolution Française,* XXXIV (January–June 1898), p. 408.

22. The complete text is in Condorcet, *Oeuvres* (Paris, Firmin-Didot, 1847), VII, pp. 61–140. All subsequent quotes by Condorcet in this chapter are from the same source.

39

1. According to Simon Askenazy, author of the fullest biography, *Le Prince Joseph Poniatowski, maréchal de France* (Paris, Plon, 1921), p. 5. Other unnumbered details and quotes given subsequently are from the same source.

2. *Ibid.*, p. 14.

3. *Ibid.*, p. 18.

4. *Ibid.;* S. Askenazy makes a synthesis, here, of a number of correspondences and memoirs emanating from the refined society around Joseph II.

5. *Ibid.*, p. 13.

6. *Ibid.*, p. 15.

7. *Ibid.*, p. 20.

40

1. G. de Saint-Foix, *Wolfgang Amedée Mozart* (Paris, Desclée de Brouwer, 1939), IV, pp. 316–23.

2. *Ibid.*, p. 324.

3. *Avant-Scène Opéra,* no. 24 (November–December 1979), an issue devoted to Mozart's *Don Giovanni.* Here Mozart is quoted by Jean-Alexandre Ménétrier, p. 10.

4. *Ibid.* Article by Philippe Olivier, p. 14.

5. *Ibid.*, p. 15.

6. J. and B. Massin, *Mozart* (Paris, Club français du livre, 1959), p. 477.

7. *Ibid.*, p. 464. The Massins add, "Impelled by their growing poverty, they were about to resume their peregrinations from one lodging to another in the four corners of the city."

8. *Ibid.* Otto Jahn, one of Mozart's

first biographers, claims that after greeting Beethoven with initial indifference, Mozart sensed the youth's great talent and prophesied that "the world would hear from him." The Massins contest this.

9. *Ibid.*, p. 466. *Ibid.* for the following quote.

10. *Avant-Scène Opéra*, article by Philippe Olivier, p. 15.

11. *Ibid.*, p. 16.

12. Lorenzo Da Ponte, *Mémoires et livrets* (Paris, Livre de poche, 1980), p. 142; foreword and notes by Jean-François Labie. The details relating to the *Tree of Diana* come from one of his notes.

13. *Ibid.*, p. 143.

14. Goethe's correspondence, quoted by G. Saint-Foix, p. 276.

15. According to the introductory text in *Avant-Scène Opéra*.

16. From Albert Camus, *Le Mythe de Sisyphe*, quoted in the periodical *Obliques* nos. 4–5, on *Don Juan* (Les Pilles, Nyons, Borderie), p. 42.

17. Da Ponte, quoted by the Massins in *Mozart*, p. 479.

18. *Ibid.*, p. 480.

19. According to J. F. Rochlitz, quoted by the Massins, *Mozart*, p. 481.

20. Previously cited text by Jean-Alexandre Ménétrier, in *Avant-Scène Opéra*, p. 10.

21. According to J. F. Rochlitz, quoted by the Massins, *Mozart*, p. 481.

41

1. Letter dated November 23, 1787, *Correspondance secrète du comte de Mercy-Argentau*, quoted by J. Egret, p. 184.

2. J. Egret, *La pré-révolution*, p. 192.

3. Letter from Abbé Morellet to Lord Shelburne, quoted by J. Egret, p. 192.

4. In Condorcet, *Oeuvres*, IX, pp. 95 and 143.

5. *Mémoires* of Weber, Marie Antoinette's milk brother (Paris, Firmin-Didot, 1860), p. 123.

6. *Archives Parlementaires*, I, p. 273.

7. *Ibid.*

8. A. Chérest, p. 377.

9. According to J. Droz, *Histoire du règne de Louis XVI*, II, p. 39. *Ibid.* for the details of Church livings in 1788.

10. G. Michon, *Adrien Duport*, p. 20.

11. E. Dard, *Hérault de Séchelles*, p. 77.

12. These are some of the names that recur in Léonce Lavergne, *Les Assemblées provinciales sous Louis XVI* (Paris, Michel Lévy, 1863).

13. B.N. L6/39, no. 530, in A. Chérest, p. 456. *Ibid.* for the next quote.

14. *Archives Parlementaires*, I, p. 284.

15. J. Droz, II, p. 40. *Ibid.* for material relating to Goislard de Montsabert.

16. Weber, *Mémoires*, p. 124.

17. For the sum of five hundred louis, apparently, according to an unsubstantiated tradition that has survived in the d'Eprémesnil family, and in which there was even a touch of romance, the typesetter's wife having allegedly been quite attractive. For this and other particulars, see two articles by Henri Carré, *"Un précurseur inconscient de la Révolution, le conseiller Duval d'Éprémesnil,* in *La Révolution française*, XXXIII, 1897, pp. 349 and

450. Carré thinks it more likely that the texts of the edicts came to d'Eprémesnil by way of Councillor Sémonville, who might have betrayed a secret entrusted to him by Brienne.

18. *Ibid.,* p. 352; see also J. Egret, p. 150, in particular with reference to the opinion of Hérault de Séchelles.

19. On March 10, 1781, d'Eprémesnil violently condemns Beaumarchais's publication of the *Oeuvres complètes* of Voltaire: "Thus we are to assemble all these scattered limbs into a single body, in order that all the poison may be brought together and nothing escape contagion, and the infidel may be provided with plenty of ammunition to use against religion." Quoted in *Correspondance littéraire,* XII, p. 489.

20. Brissot, *Mémoires,* II, p. 54.

21. Weber, *Mémoires,* p. 125.

22. According to the article by H. Carré, p. 405; other details relating to the arrest of the two members of the *Parlement* are from the same source, but are also in A. Chérest, beginning on p. 475, and in *Archives Parlementaires,* I, beginning on p. 288.

23. Barère, *Mémoires,* p. 341, quoted by Robert Launay, *Barère de Vieuzac* (Paris, Tallandiere, 1929), p. 17. *Ibid.,* p. 28, for the following quotes.

24. Hardy's journal, sheet 422 (dated May 5, 1788).

25. According to Beugnot, *Mémoires,* p. 102, quoted by J. Egret, p. 157.

26. J. Egret, p. 158.

27. Pasquier, *Mémoires,* I, p. 64, quoted by J. Egret, p. 158.

28. Hardy's journal, sheet 422.

29. Weber, *Mémoires,* p. 126.

30. *Ibid.,* p. 127; *ibid.* for the next two quotes.

31. *Archives Parlementaires,* I, p. 290; *ibid.* for the next four quotes.

32. Hardy's journal, sheet 423.

33. *Archives Parlementaires,* I, p. 290; *ibid.* for the next two quotes.

42

1. *Archives Parlementaires,* I, p. 290.

2. *Ibid.,* p. 291.

3. *Ibid.*

4. A. Chérest, p. 482.

5. Hardy's journal, sheet 425.

6. *Archives Parlementaires,* I, p. 291; *ibid.* for the next two quotes.

7. A. Chérest, p. 482.

8. J. Egret, p. 253.

9. *Archives Parlementaires,* I, p. 291; *ibid.* for the following quotes.

10. Hardy's journal, sheets 426 and 427. Other details of this event are from the same source.

11. *Archives Parlementaires,* I, p. 293. *Ibid.* for the next quote.

12. *Ibid.,* p. 316; *ibid.* for the next two quotes.

13. J. Droz, II, p. 50.

14. *Archives Parlementaires,* I, p. 301.

15. *Ibid.,* p. 316; *ibid.* for the next two quotes.

16. Hardy's journal, sheet 428.

17. Launay, *Barère,* p. 28.

18. Hardy's journal, sheet 430.

19. Weber, *Mémoires,* p. 135.

20. Besenval, *Mémoires,* quoted by A. Chérest, p. 503.

43

1. These are the opening words of an unfinished record of the trip kept by Lapérouse and published in full by Admiral de Brossard (Paris,

1965) with the title *Voyage de Lapérouse autour du monde pendant les années 1785, 1786, 1787, et 1788.* All unreferenced quotes by Lapérouse in this chapter are from this source.

2. Quoted by Admiral Brossard in his preface to *Voyage*, p. 17.

3. According to Buache himself, quoted by Pierette Girault de Coursac, *L'Éducation d'un roi, Louis XVI* (Paris, Gallimard, 1972), p. 199.

4. According to Evelyne Lever, *Louis XVI*, p. 411.

5. See in this connection the excellent dissertation by Jean-Étienne Martin-Allanic, *Bougainville navigateur et les découvertes de son temps* (Paris, P.U.F., 1964), 2 vols.

6. According to Admiral Brossard's preface to *Voyage*, p. 15.

7. The full text is in Diderot, *Oeuvres complètes* (Paris, Club Français du Livre, 1971), X, p. 197.

8. The account by M. de Vaujuas was copied in full in the last letter from Lapérouse, to whom it was sent; *Voyage*, p. 369.

9. J. E. Martin-Allanic, *Bougainville*, p. 1494.

10. *Ibid.*, p. 1495.

11. *Voyage pittoresque autour du monde, publié sous la direction de M. Dumont d'Urville* (Paris, L. Tenré, 1835), II, p. 138.

12. The Tomb of the Maras, now covered by luxurious vegetation, was photographed by Admiral de Brossard in 1964. All of the conclusions set out in this chapter have been confirmed by John Dumore, *Lapérouse* (Paris, Payot, 1986).

44

1. Stendhal, *Vie de Henri Brulard* (Paris, Nouvelle édition with commentary by Henri Martineau, Le Divan, 1949), p. 36. *Ibid.* for the following unnumbered quotes by Stendhal relating to the Day of the Tiles.

2. Weber, *Mémoires*, p. 141.

3. Expilly, *Dictionnaire*, III, p. 663, entry on "Grenoble."

4. Octave Chenavas, *La révolution de 1788 en Dauphiné* (Grenoble, Gratier, 1888), p. 65.

5. Chevalier de Mautort, *Mémoires* (Paris, Plon, 1895), p. 361. The "little Picard chevalier" I mentioned in Volume II in connection with the failed invasion of England in 1779 is slowly mounting the military ladder in a regiment that has been transferred from naval to land army.

6. *"Relation des troubles de Grenoble par le Parlement"* (B.N. Lb 3, no. 5881), quoted by O. Chenavas, *La révolution de 1788 en Dauphiné*, p. 76.

7. Eyewitness account sent to Brienne on June 8 and discovered by Jean Egret among the Minister's papers in the Archives Nationales, Box 4AP 188. J. Egret published the letter in full in *Annales Historiques de la Révolution française*, 1957, XXIX, p. 71. See also, by the same author, *Le Parlement du Dauphiné et les affaires publiques dans la deuxieme moitié du XVIIIe siècle* (Grenoble, 1942), pp. 223–39. Subsequent quotes from the same letter are identified as *Papiers de Brienne.*

8. *Papiers de Brienne.*

9. *Ibid.*

10. Weber, *Mémoires,* p. 142.

11. Details of the events of the day have been taken from Chenavas; Chérest, II, pp. 9–17; and vol. II of Stendhal's *Vie de Henri Brulard,* which contains Henri Martineau's notes (in this instance, nos. 253 and 254). Martineau, disagreeing with the somewhat theatrical version given in the account written that same evening by *Président* de Bérulle, says that no military were killed and only about a score injured and that there were only two or three deaths in all, one of them a child of twelve and another the hatter's assistant observed by Stendhal, "Alexis Gay, age thirty, buried at Saint-Louis on June 11." According to the research by J. Egret, there were actually four deaths on the "people's" side.

12. *Papiers de Brienne.*

13. Stendhal, *Vie de Henri Brulard,* p. 46.

14. Again according to Stendhal, *ibid.,* p. 70, who adds, obviously from hearsay, "the present [1835] King of Sweden, a being no less noble than Marat but far more skillful. Lefèvre, a wigmaker and friend of my father, often told us how he saved his life when he was hard-pressed at the back of an alley-way." There is no means of verifying this.

15. In the last years of his reign in Stockholm, old Charles Jean Bernadotte, always more of a Gascon than a Swede, tried to make the French believe, in a muddled memorandum he wrote as a rough draft for his memoirs (they were never written up), that he personally saved the Duc de Clermont-Tonnerre's life. The Clermont-Tonnerre family had a no less muddled oral tradition that half-put the words into his mouth (see T. T. Hojer, *Bernadotte, maréchal de France* [Paris, Plon, 1943]). See also, in regard to Michelet and Thiers, Gabriel Girod de l'Ain, *Bernadotte, chef de guerre et chef d'état* (Paris, Perrin, 1968). Even Désirée Clary [a onetime fiancée of Napoleon and wife (1798) of Bernadotte] put her oar in, at the end of her life, again by hearsay. None of this is to be taken seriously.

16. Girod de l'Ain, *Bernadotte,* p. 34. The dust jacket of the book shows a striking portrait of Bernadotte as a general during the Revolution, by Johann-Lorenz Kreul (Musée Bernadotte in Pau).

17. According to Girod de l'Ain, p. 22; in passing, the author sets straight a slur made up by Napoleon regarding Bernadotte's "Arab blood," together with some aberrant claims found in anti-Semitic writings—beginning in Germany in 1910 and taken up by Roger Peyrefitte in 1965—concerning his hypothetical Jewish origins.

18. Bernard Nabonne, *Bernadotte* (Paris, Albin Michel, 1940), p. 13.

19. Quoted by Girod de l'Ain, p. 38

20. Quoted by Chérest, II, p. 13.

21. *Papiers de Brienne.*

22. Quoted by Chérest, II, p. 15.

23. Besenval, *Mémoires,* III, p. 325, quoted by Chérest, I, p. 505.

45

1. Jean-Jacques Chevallier, *Barnave ou les deux faces de la Révolution* (Paris, Payot, 1936), p. 42.

2. Quoted by J. J. Chevallier, p. 43. I have followed his summary. The pamphlet itself was never reprinted, or included in Barnave's *Oeuvres,* but an incomplete manuscript is kept in the Grenoble library, Fonds Barnave, U 5216.

3. Berenger de la Drome, *"Notice historique sur Barnave,"* at the beginning of Barnave's *Oeuvres* (Paris, Chapelle et Builler, 1843), p. xxvii.

4. O. Chenavas, *La Révolution de 1788 en Dauphiné,* p. 90.

5. Quoted by O. Chenavas, p. 93.

6. Jules Michelet, *Histoire de la Révolution Française,* quoted by O. Chenavas, p. 124.

7. Brienne's mandates, quoted by O. Chenavas, p. 88.

8. Chérest, II, p. 14.

9. Records kept in the Grenoble library; the full text of the proceedings is quoted in Chenavas, p. 99.

10. Barnave, *Introduction à la Révolution Française* (Paris, Cahiers des Annales, Armand Colin, 1960), p. 58.

11. Berriat Saint-Prix, *Éloge de M. Mounier, conseiller d'État fait en 1806,* quoted by J. Egret, *La Révolution des Notables: Mounier et les monarchiens* (Paris, Armand Colin, 1950), p. 10.

12. Saint-Didier, *Mounier, son caractère et son rôle* (Grenoble, 1898), p. 23.

13. Stendhal, *Vie de Henri Brulard,* I, p. 78. Stendhal adds, but by hearsay, "The strength of M. Mounier's son was his character, but his intelligence was not equal to his determination."

14. Christian Puel, *Un constituant: Jean-Joseph Mounier* (Bordeaux, Piquot, 1934), p. 15.

15. F. Vermale, *"Documents inédits sur les années de jeunesse de Mounier,"* article in the *Annales Historiques de la Révolution française,* 1939, p. 5. Other details of Mounier's education are from the same source.

16. The Grenoble library has nine briefs written by Mounier during those years; see L. de Lanzac de Laborie, *Jean-Joseph Mounier, sa vie politique et ses écrits* (Paris, Plon, 1887), p. 6.

17. F. Vermale, p. 22.

18. Berriat Saint-Prix, *Éloge,* quoted by J. Egret, *La Révolution des Notables,* p. 9.

19. *Ibid.,* p. 11.

20. According to Gaultier de Biauzat, a member of the Constituent Assembly, in his *Correspondance,* quoted by J. Egret, *La Révolution,* p. 11.

21. O. Chenavas, p. 113.

22. *Ibid.,* p. 111.

23. *Ibid.,* p. 115.

24. *Ibid.,* p. 118.

25. Reported by Augustin Perier, quoted by O. Chenavas, p. 123.

46

1. Pierre Barral, *Les Perier dans l'Isère au XIXe siècle* (Paris, P.U.F., 1964), p. 23.

2. From a letter he wrote to Trudaine in January 1768, quoted by P. Barral, *Les Perier,* p. 24.

3. According to Charles de Rémuzat, quoted by P. Barral, *Les Perier,* p. 25.

4. Isère departmental archives, II c 98.

5. The original of the minutes is in the B.N., Lb 39, 614.

6. Isère departmental archives, II J 27(31): anonymous memoir dated

1769, quoted in the catalog of the handsome exhibition held there in 1894 and entitled "The Periers, a Bourgeois Dynasty in the French Revolution."

7. O. Chenavas, p. 172. Chenavas also reprints the whole text of the minutes and letter to the King, which were first brought to light in the catalog of the Perier exhibition, see p. 42.

8. Barnave, *Oeuvres,* I, p. 97. *(Introduction à la Révolution française.)*

9. Bertrand de Molleville, *Histoire de la Révolution française,* quoted by Lanzac de Laborie, p. 15.

47

1. From the *Mémoire sur la situation présente des affaires,* written by Malesherbes in late July 1788, given to the King in August, never made public, and found in the archives of the Rosanbo family (Box 18, file A) by Pierre Grosclaude, *Malesherbes, témoin et interprète de son temps,* p. 660.

2. *Ibid.,* p. 656.

3. *Ibid.,* p. 654, also from box 18 of the Rosanbo archives, which contains the two memoranda written by Malesherbes that summer, the first relating specifically to the grounds for his resignation and the second, more general text, on "the present state of affairs."

4. *Ibid.,* p. 655.

5. *Ibid.*

6. *Ibid.,* p. 653.

7. According to a confidence made to Bertrand de Molleville, quoted in the latter's secret *Mémoires,* III, p. 21.

8. *Motifs de la demande que j'ai faite,* quoted by Grosclaude, p. 653.

9. *Ibid.,* p. 652.

10. *Ibid.,* p. 654.

11. According to an addition in Malesherbes's hand, in box 18 of the Rosanbo archives (Grosclaude, p. 655).

12. *Mémoire sur la situation présente,* quoted by Grosclaude, p. 652.

13. *Ibid.,* p. 661.

14. *Ibid.,* p. 663.

15. According to Grosclaude, p. 654.

16. Quoted by Chérest, II, p. 64.

17. According to the *Journal* of the Abbé de Véri, as reported by the Duc de Castries in *La Revue de Paris,* November 1963.

48

1. The complete text of Grégoire's long letter has been published by P. Grosclaude, p. 647.

2. *Ibid.*

3. At this point the text is still confidential, but it is printed early in 1789 by Claude Lamort in Metz and goes on sale simultaneously at two bookshops in Paris and one in Strasbourg. It was reprinted in 1968 by Éditions EDHIS, Paris.

4. As reported by Roederer, Malesherbes's friend and confidant, who repeated the remark in an article in the *Journal de Paris* on 5 Nivose year V; quoted by Grosclaude, p. 631.

5. Jean Tilde, *L'abbé Grégoire* (Paris, Nouvelles Éditions latines, 1946), p. 10.

6. *Mémoires de Grégoire, ancien évêque de Blois* (Paris, 1840). The two volumes published under this title nine years after his death are really a collection of conversations and papers compiled by one of his faithful admirers, Hippolyte Car-

not, the son of Lazare Carnot, who is also politically active in the "Republican left wing" under Louis-Philippe and the Second Republic. Grégoire's comments on his birthplace are on pp. 342 and 325 of vol. I.

7. From Grégoire's *Mémoires,* quoted by J. Tilde, *L'abbé Grégoire,* p. 9.

8. *Ibid.,* p. 10.

9. *Mémoires de Grégoire,* p. 326; *ibid.* for the following quote.

10. J. Tilde, *L'abbé Grégoire,* p. 11.

11. *"Les Juifs et la Révolution française,"* symposium led by B. Blumenkranz and A. Soboul (Toulouse, Privat, 1976); text by F. Delpech, p. 6.

12. H. Grégoire, *Essai sur la régénération des juifs,* p. 390.

13. *Ibid.,* p. 226.

14. *Ibid.,* p. 13.

15. *Ibid.,* p. 15.

16. *Ibid.,* p. 127.

17. *Ibid.,* p. 128.

18. Grosclaude, *Malesherbes,* p. 648.

49

1. *Archives Parlementaires,* I, p. 387.

2. Weber, *Mémoires,* p. 151.

3. *Lettres de Mirabeau au major de Mauvillon,* quoted by A. Chérest, II, p. 71.

4. Mirabeau, *Mémoires et correspondance,* V, p. 187, letter dated August 16, to M. Levrault in Strasbourg, quoted by A. Chérest, II, p. 171.

5. J. Droz, *Histoire du règne de Louis XVI,* II, p. 58.

6. *Archives Parlementaires,* I, p. 377.

7. *Ibid.,* p. 378.

8. J. Perrin, *Le cardinal de Loménie de Brienne,* p. 23.

9. Weber, *Mémoires,* p. 145.

10. Germaine de Staël, *Considérations sur la Révolution française,* I, p. 100. *Ibid.* for the following quote, p. 104.

11. A. Chérest, II, p. 111. Figures from the *Annuaire du Bureau des longitudes,* article by M. Faye, 1877, p. 483.

12. *"Discours de Dupont de Nemours devant l'Assemblée nationale, sur les banques en général"* (Paris, November 1789), p. 30, quoted by J. Egret, *La pré-révolution,* p. 313.

13. La Fayette, *Mémoires,* II, p. 234.

14. Letter from Marie Antoinette to Mercy-Argenteau, August 19, 1788, quoted in *Le comte F.D. de Mercy-Argenteau, ambassadeur impérial à Paris sous Louis XV et sous Louis XVI,* by the Comte de Pimodan (Paris, Plon, 1911), p. 234.

15. Loménie de Brienne, *Mémoires,* quoted by J. Egret, *La pré-révolution,* p. 316. *Ibid.* for the next quote.

16. Letter from Necker to Mercy-Argenteau, August 21, quoted by J. Egret, *La pré-révolution,* p. 316.

17. Letter quoted by J. Egret, *La pré-révolution,* p. 317.

18. H. Taine, *Origines de la France contemporaine, Ancien Régime,* chap. IV, quoted by J. Perrin, *Loménie de Brienne,* p. 21.

50

1. Mme. de Staël, *Correspondance générale* (Édition de Béatrice W. Jasinski, Paris, J.-J. Pauvert, 1962), pt. I, p. 245.

2. *Ibid.,* p. 250.

3. J. Necker, *De l'administration des finances de la France,* 3 vols. (1784).

4. J. Necker, *De l'importance des opi-*

nions religieuses (London and Lyons, 1788).

5. *Correspondance secrète de Mercy-Argenteau,* published by d'Arneth and Flammermont (Paris, Firmin-Didot, 1875), I, p. 189; letter to Joseph II, September 14.

6. Mme. de Staël, *Correspondance générale,* pt. I, footnote on p. 250.

7. *Ibid.,* p. 248.

8. Hardy's journal, year 1788, sheet 63; *ibid.* for the next quote.

9. Mme. de Staël, *Correspondance générale,* pt. I.

10. Quoted by J. Egret, *Necker, ministre de Louis XVI* (Paris, Champion, 1975), p. 215.

11. La Fayette, *Mémoires,* II, p. 237.

12. *Gazette de Leyde,* September 9, 1788; *ibid.* for the next quote.

13. Hardy's journal, August 28, 1788, sheet 61; *ibid.* for the next nine quotes.

51

1. A. Chérest, II, p. 133. See also J. Egret, *La pré-révolution,* p. 319, with particular reference to Lamoignon's "suicide" as seen by his friend Marmontel.

2. A. Wattinne, *L'Affaire des Trois Roués;* the complete text is on p. 208.

3. *Ibid.,* p. 151.

4. *Ibid.,* p. 154.

5. *Ibid.,* p. 158.

6. *Ibid.,* p. 159.

7. *Ibid.,* p. 164; *ibid.* for the next quote, taken from Bachaumont's *Mémoires secrets.*

8. Hardy's journal, sheets 87 and 88; *ibid.* for the following quotes.

9. A. Wattinne, p. 173.

10. Weber, *Mémoires,* p. 157.

11. A. Chérest, II, p. 133.

12. Hardy's journal, sheets 79 and 80.

13. *Ibid.,* sheet 82.

14. *Ibid.,* sheet 82. *Ibid.* for the next quote and footnote on the page.

15. *Ibid.,* sheet 85. *Ibid.* for the next three quotes.

16. *Archives Parlementaires,* I, p. 326.

17. *Ibid.,* p. 327.

52

1. J. Droz, II, p. 84.

2. Weber, *Mémoires,* p. 158.

3. *Correspondance de Marie-Antoinette avec Joseph II et Léopold II,* published by von Arneth (Leipzig, Paris, Vienna, 1966), p. 112.

4. Quoted by Françoise Kermina, *Fersen* (Paris, Perrin, 1985), p. 133.

5. *Ibid.,* p. 114; letter from Catherine II to Joseph II.

6. *Ibid.,* p. 115; letter from Fersen to his father.

7. Alma Soderjhelm, *Fersen et Marie-Antoinette* (Paris, Kra, 1930), p. 118.

8. *Ibid.,* p. 123, letters to his father, December 10, 1788, and January 2, 1789.

9. Saint-Priest, *Mémoires,* quoted by E. Lever, *Louis XVI,* p. 476.

10. A. Soderjhelm, p. 121.

11. Quoted by E. Lever, *Louis XVI,* p. 476.

12. Pierre de Nolhac, *Le Trianon de Marie-Antoinette* (Paris, Calman-Lévy, 1924), p. 266. Details relating to the Queen's hamlet and other unnumbered quotes on the subject are from the same source.

13. Continuation of Marie Antoinette's letter to Joseph II (see n. 3).

14. Quoted by F. Kermina, *Fersen,* p. 107.

53

1. Remark reported by Sallier (in the *Annales françaises,* II, p. 125), quoted by J. Egret, *Necker,* p. 222.
2. La Fayette, *Mémoires,* II, p. 237.
3. Jacques Necker, *Sur l'administration de M. Necker, par lui-meme* (Paris, 1791), p. 28; *ibid.* for the next quote.
4. J. Egret, *Necker,* pp. 226–28.
5. Jacques Necker, *De la Révolution française par M. Necker* (1796), I, p. 45.
6. J. Necker, *Sur l'administration,* p. 31.
7. Malouet, *Mémoires,* I, p. 217.
8. G. de Staël, *Considérations sur la Révolution française,* quoted by A. Chérest, II, p. 141.
9. Letter from Mirabeau to Major de Mauvillon, November 8, 1788, quoted by A. Chérest, II, p. 176.
10. Statement reported by Sallier, quoted by A. Chérest, II, p. 186.
11. *Archives Parlementaires,* I, p. 391.
12. La Fayette, *Mémoires,* II, p. 238; letter, date and addressee unspecified, but probably written on October 6 or 7, 1788. La Fayette was being overoptimistic, because the Notables do not meet until November 6 and do not disband until December 12; and although the elections certainly do take place during bad weather, it's the bad weather of the following spring.
13. A. Geffroy, *Gustave III et la Cour de France,* II, pp. 474–75 (Dresden Archives).
14. G. Michon, *Adrien Duport,* p. 29. These few lines give an excellent

idea of Duport's quality. Michon adds, "Duport inculcated into the cream of the nobility, clergy and third estate a habit of looking always to the larger interest, of ceasing to think as noble, clergy or bourgeois and beginning to think as a citizen of a great country" (p. 30).
15. Mirabeau, *Mémoires* (published by his adoptive son) (Paris, A. Guyot, 1834), V, p. 199.

54

1. *Archives Parlementaires,* I, p. 391. *Ibid.* for the other aspects of the ceremonial protocol and excerpts from Necker's speech, p. 393.
2. Louis Guimbaud, *Auget de Montyon 1733–1830* (Paris, Émile-Paul, 1909), p. 198. See also Paul Morand's witty speech to the Académie Française, at the annual public sitting of December 16, 1971, published by Gallimard the following year.
3. The text of the *Mémoire présenté au Roi par Monseigneur, comte d'Artois, M. le prince de Condé, M. le duc de Bourbon, M. le duc d'Enghien et M. le prince de Conti* was published in full in *Archives Parlementaires,* I, p. 487.
4. The harangue that Conti read to Monsieur at a meeting of the latter's committee on November 28, and the bittersweet note that Louis XVI sent to Monsieur the following day by way of a tap on the wrist to be passed on to Conti, are published in *Archives Parlementaires,* I, pp. 402–3. Unintentionally, however, the King virtually issued an invitation to the princes to write their "letter" when he

said in his note that "M. le Prince
de Conti, like the other princes of
my blood, must address what he
has to say to myself [in other
words, not to Monsieur] and I
shall always be pleased to listen to
them."

5. From the edition of *Qu'est-ce que le
Tiers État?* annotated by Abbé
Morellet, quoted here by A. Chérest, II, p. 206. *Ibid.* for the following quote by Sieyès.

6. Quoted by Béatrice Jasinski, from
a letter from Mme. de Staël dated
January 21, 1789, in *Lettres de jeunesse*, I, pt. 2, p. 274.

7. *Archives Parlementaires*, I, p. 480.
Ibid., p. 487, for the next quote.

8. Entry on Necker in the Michaud
biography, signed Lally-Tollendal,
who says he saw the sentence
written in the minister's hand;
quoted by A. Chérest, II, p. 213.

9. Abbé Morellet, *Mémoires*, quoted
by A. Chérest, II, p. 214.

10. A. Chérest, II, p. 214 (from the
Michaud biography).

11. H. Taine, *Les origines de la France
contemporaine* (Paris, R. Laffont,
1986), p. 281.

12. *Mémoire autographe de Monsieur de
Barentin sur les derniers conseils du
roi Louis XVI* (Paris, Campion,
1944), p. 63. *Ibid.* for the next
quote.

55

1. *Archives Parlementaires*, I, p. 563;
introduction to the list of the main
writings catalogued. *Ibid.* for the
next quote.

2. G. Michon, *Adrien Duport*, p. 34.

3. According to the executor himself,
quoted, p. xli, in the fullest edition (that of Jean-Louis Lecercle)

of *Des droits et des devoirs du citoyen*, published in Paris in 1792
by Marcel Didier. The autograph
manuscript is in the library of the
National Assembly, and the
quotes from Mably that follow are
taken from it.

4. Rabaut Saint-Étienne, *Oeuvres*, I, p.
281 (at the opening of his *Précis de
l'Histoire de la Révolution française*).

5. All the titles mentioned and the
quotes taken from them come, except where otherwise specified,
from three sources: *Archives Parlementaires*, I, pp. 566–89; A. Chérest, *La Chute de l'Ancien Régime*,
II, pp. 252–79; J. Droz, *Histoire
du règne de Louis XVI*, II, pp.
203–10.

6. Lauraguais, *Recueil de pièces historiques sur la convocation des États
Généraux, et sur l'élection de leurs
députés* (Paris, 1788), p. 114.

7. The few things known about these
five toughest years of Marat's life
were uncovered by Jean Massin,
Marat (Paris, C.F.L., 1960), pp.
65–67.

8. Charles Vellay, *Les pamphlets de
Marat* (Paris, Fasquelle, 1911), p.
2. *Ibid.* for the following quote on
the third estate, p. 9.

56

1. Text reprinted in full by EDHIS,
Paris, 1967.

2. *Ibid.*, 1976.

3. Weber, *Mémoires*, p. 161.

4. It contains 279 pages and includes
conscientious appendices enumer-
ating every name of the representatives of Languedoc at the Estates
of 1484 (Tours), 1576 (Blois) and
1614.

5. Weber, *Mémoires*, p. 161.

6. D'Antraigues, *Mémoire sur les États Généraux*, p. 61.

7. And apparently forged a score of letters, allegedly signed by Rousseau. On the Comte d'Antraigues's already ambiguous early years, his activities as a spy, and his death, see Jacques Godechot, *Le comte d'Antraigues, un espion dans L'Europe des émigrés* (Paris, Fayard, 1986).

8. D'Antraigues, *Mémoire sur les États Généraux*, p. 251.

9. All seven texts are published, in order, in vol. IX of Condorcet, *Oeuvres*, pp. 125–364. The following quotes are taken from that source.

10. Franck Alengry, *Condorcet, guide de la Révolution française, théoricien du droit constitutionnel et précurseur de la science sociale* (dissertation published in Paris in 1904), quoted by Jeanine Bouissounouse, *Condorcet* (Paris, Hachette, 1962), p. 134.

11. Mirabeau, *Mémoires*, V, pp. 122 and 145.

12. *Ibid.*, p. 187, to Levrault. The following quote is from a letter to Lauzun, p. 188.

13. *Ibid.*, p. 189, to Levrault.

14. *Ibid.*, p. 209 (of the pamphlet).

15. *Ibid.*, p. 205, footnote.

16. Paul Bastid, *Sieyès et sa Pensée* (Paris, Hachette, 1970), p. 47.

17. *Ibid.*, p. 43.

18. Mme. de Staël, *Considérations sur la Révolution française*, II, p. 248.

19. According to Sainte-Beuve in his writings on Sieyès, quoted by Paul Bastid, p. 56.

57

1. *Correspondance littéraire*, XV, January 1789, p. 383.

2. *Ibid.*

3. Louis Jacob, *Fabre d'Églantine, chef des "fripons"* (Paris, Hachette, 1946), p. 45. Other details of his career and quotes by Fabre are from the same source, except those from the pamphlet.

4. According to papers found at Robespierre's after 9 Thermidor, quoted by L. Jacob, p. 54. Proof of Fabre's notoriety, in 1793, in the Dantonist party.

5. These are excerpts from the unique and original text of the *Lettre de M. Fabre d'Églantine à Monsieur de ***** relativement à la contestation survenue au sujet du Présomptueux ou l'Heureux Imaginaire, et les châteaux en Espagne.* The publication bears no mention of publisher or place and is dated January 12, 1789, but must have come out about the end of the month. There was little response.

6. Quoted by L. Jacob, p. 66.

58

1. Pierre Naville, *D'Holbach et la philosophie scientifique au XVIIIe siècle* (Paris, Gallimard, 1967), p. 133. Subsequent unnumbered particulars relating to d'Holbach are from the same source, in particular the excerpts from material in the appendices so arduously compiled by Pierre Naville.

2. *Correspondance littéraire*, XV, by Meister, March 1789, p. 418.

3. Abbé Morellet, *Mémoires*, chap. VI, quoted by P. Naville, p. 47.

4. *Correspondance littéraire*, XV, March 1789, p. 417.

5. *Ibid.*, p. 416.

6. *Mémoires secrets de la Cour et de la Ville,* February 19, 1770, quoted by P. Naville, p. 109.

7. *Correspondance littéraire,* X, January 1773, p. 174.

8. Letter from Galiani to Mme. d'Épinay, September 8, 1770, quoted in the appendices to P. Naville's book, p. 481.

9. *Correspondance littéraire,* XVI, December 1790, p. 131, headed: "From the manuscripts of the late M. le Baron d'Holbach."

59

1. According to Jean Gaulmier, *Volney, un grand témoin de la Révolution et de l'Empire* (Paris, Hachette, 1959), p. 10; unnumbered details relating to Volney are from the same source.

2. Quoted by J. Gaulmier, p. 18.

3. François-Yves Besnard, *Souvenirs d'un nonagénaire, Mémoires* (Paris, Champion, 1880), I, pp. 188 and 191; *ibid.* for the following four quotes.

4. The original document is kept in the Mayenne Archives.

5. The collection of all five issues of *La Sentinelle du peuple,* published from November 10 to December 25, 1788, is in the B.M., L/2, C. no. 100.

6. Quoted by J. Gaulmier, p. 76.

7. The description is from Augustin Cochin, *Les sociétés de pensée et la Révolution en Bretagne (1788–1789)* (Paris, Champion, 1925), I, p. 277 and *passim.* The occasionally brilliant and extremely detailed descriptions sprinkled throughout this big book are the most useful and precious part of it to researchers, together with the numerous biographical particulars, especially those relating to "ordinary" people. Its author was led by his political bias to elaborate, upon a basis of fact, a perfectly abstract theory of a huge ideological conspiracy instigated by Freemasons and even atheists, aimed at proving that events in Brittany, and the whole Revolution to come, followed some great global plan worked out in the shadows of the philosophical societies; regrettably, A. Cochin inflicts his growing and ever more improbable obsession upon the reader.

8. *Ibid.,* pp. 275–76.

9. *"Relation authentique de ce qui s'est passé à Rennes les 26, 27 et jours suivants du mois de janvier 1789,"* an anonymous text published in *Archives Parlementaires,* pp. 522–28. Other unnumbered details and quotes on these events are from the same source.

10. According to A. Cochin, p. 382, this scene was more or less dreamed up by the "patriots"; the victim was very slightly injured, was himself a nurse, and the official account makes no mention of a wife or children.

11. *Voyages en France de François de La Rochefoucault (1781–1783)* (Paris, Champion, 1933), I, p. 89. *Ibid.* for the next quote.

12. A. Cochin, p. 385, and *Archives Parlementaires,* p. 525.

13. Hardy's journal, sheet 222; sheet 225 for the following particulars.

14. *Archives Parlementaires,* p. 526.

15. *Ibid.,* p. 530; *ibid.* for the next quote.

16. J. Gaulmier, p. 77; *ibid.* for the following quote.

17. Larevellière-Lépeaux, *Mémoires* (Paris, Plon, 1895), I, p. 65.

60

1. Letter from Mirabeau to his father, quoted by A. Vallentin, I, p. 477.
2. Letter from the Marquis de Mirabeau to his brother the Bailli, quoted by A. Vallentin, I, p. 475.
3. Portalis, *"Mes souvenirs politiques,"* in *Séances et travaux de l'Académie des sciences morales et politiques,* XLVIII, pp. 365–67.
4. Fauris de Saint-Vincent, quoted by J. Egret, *La pré-révolution en Provence (1787–1789),* in the *Annales Historiques de la Révolution française,* XXXVI, 1954, p. 113.
5. Letter from Mirabeau to his sister Caroline du Saillant, January 20, 1789, quoted by Georges Guibal, *Mirabeau et la Provence* (Paris, Albert Fontemoing, 1901), I, p. 239; other unreferenced details in this chapter are from the same source.
6. Quoted by A. Vallentin, I, p. 479. *Ibid.* for the following quotes by the son, then the father, p. 482.
7. Quoted by Guy Chaussinand-Nogaret, *Mirabeau* (Paris, Seuil, 1982), p. 133. In looking at the rest of Mirabeau's Provençal "campaign," it is useful to compare the books of Guibal and Vallentin with this comprehensive and much more recent work.
8. A. Vallentin, I, p. 482; *ibid.* for the next four quotes.
9. Bouches-du-Rhône Archives, B 3268, quoted by G. Guibal.
10. Archives Nationales, H 1240, letter from M. de La Tour to Necker, quoted by G. Guibal, p. 253.

11. Quoted by G. Chaussinand-Nogaret, p. 133.
12. A. Vallentin, I, p. 488.
13. Letter from d'Esterno to Montmorin, February 17, 1789, quoted by Henri Welschinger, *La mission secrète de Mirabeau à Berlin* (Paris, Plon, 1900), p. 510. In this book all of Mirabeau's "mission" letters are presented, including those he did not publish in his lifetime. They are preserved in the Archives of the Ministry of Foreign Affairs.
14. *Ibid.,* from the same to the same, August 4, 1789.
15. H. Welschinger, p. 97.
16. A. Vallentin, I, p. 491.
17. H. Welschinger, p. 63.
18. A. Vallentin, I, p. 493.
19. H. Welschinger, p. 64.
20. *Correspondance littéraire,* XV, p. 392.
21. Mirabeau, *Mémoires,* V, p. 269.
22. The descriptions of Mirabeau's triumphant return are taken from G. Chaussinand-Nogaret, G. Guibal and A. Vallentin.
23. Mirabeau, *Mémoires,* V, p. 274; *ibid.* for the next quote.
24. According to an anonymous account, dated March 7 and found by the publishers of Mirabeau's *Mémoires,* V, p. 275.
25. *Guide pittoresque du Voyageur en France* (Paris, Firmin-Didot, 1836), II, p. 20.
26. See note 24 above; *ibid.* for the following quote.

61

1. Bernard de Lacombe, *Talleyrand, évêque d'Autun, d'après des documents inédits* (Paris, Perrin, 1903), p. 70; further unnumbered partic-

ulars and the liturgical formulae, excerpts from sermons and list of grievances written by Talleyrand are all from the same book, which covers every detail of the few but decisive weeks that Talleyrand spends as bishop of Autun.

2. Letter from Mirabeau to the Comte d'Antraigues, April 28, 1787, quoted by G. Lacour-Gayet, *Talleyrand* (Paris, Payot, 1933), I, p. 81.

3. Arnault, *Souvenirs d'un sexagénaire,* quoted by G. Lacour-Gayet, I, p. 103.

4. Archives of the Seminary of Saint-Sulpice, quoted by Lacour-Gayet, I, p. 89.

5. Thirteen 8vo pages, no place or date, quoted by B. de Lacombe, p. 108.

6. B. de Lacombe, p. 117.

62

1. Marcel Reinhard, *Le grand Carnot* (Paris, Hachette, 1950), I, p. 131.

2. From his *Mémoire au sujet des places fortes,* August 1788, quoted by M. Reinhard, p. 130.

3. M. Reinhard, p. 137.

4. Letter from the Chevalier de Bouillet, published by Alfred Bégis, *Carnot, membre du Comité de Salut Public; son emprisonnement sous Louis XVI à Béthune* (Paris, Les Amis des Livres, 1900), p. 26. Other unnumbered references relating to this little-known episode are from the same publication, the author of which berates Carnot as though he had committed some great crime. *Ibid.* for the following quote.

5. *Ibid.,* pp. 25–26.

6. The complete text of the two me-morials is in A. Bégis, *Carnot,* pp. 29–39, from which phrases quoted in the body of the text are taken.

7. Letter to Mme. Tiffet de Saint-Romain, written in Béthune on November 28, 1789, and pub-lished as an appendix to vol. I by Marcel Reinhard, pp. 322–25. *Ibid.* for other quotes from the letter.

8. A. Bégis, *Carnot,* p. 44.

9. Letter to Mme. Tiffet de Saint-Romain, in M. Reinhard, p. 325.

63

1. From a brochure published in Jan-uary in Marseilles, by M. Blanc-Gilly (subsequently elected admin-istrator of the Bouches-du-Rhône Département), *"Plan de révolution concernant les finances,"* p. 62; quoted by G. Guibal, *Mirabeau et la Provence,* I, p. 294. Details of the economic situation of Pro-vence given here are also from G. Guibal.

2. *Ibid.,* p. 295.

3. *Ibid.*

4. Marseilles Municipal Archives; registry of written letters, fo. 32; quoted by G. Guibal, I, p. 321.

5. *Ibid.;* this file contains other letters by the mayor and aldermen, con-firming Mirabeau's impressions.

6. M. Reichard, *Guide des voyageurs en Europe,* II, p. 55; *ibid.* for the following three quotes.

7. G. Guibal, I, p. 320.

8. A. Vallentin, I, p. 496; to my knowledge she is the only author to have unearthed this singular text.

9. *Ibid.,* p. 497.

10. Mirabeau, *Mémoires,* V, p. 286.

11. G. Guibal, I, p. 323.

12. Material and quotes relating to the riots in Provence are taken from the books cited above, in particular Guibal, I, pp. 329–47, and vol. V of Mirabeau's *Mémoires*, pp. 287–306.

13. Published in full as an appendix to vol. V of Mirabeau's *Mémoires*, p. 411.

14. *Archives Parlementaires*, X, p. 532; the neighboring pages contain a complete file of Albert de Rioms's exhaustive communications on the disturbances in Toulon.

15. Archives of the Bouches-du-Rhône, quoted by G. Guibal, I, p. 360.

16. Mirabeau, *Mémoires*, V, p. 304.

17. An account of the various phases of the voting and Mirabeau's letters to the third-estate agents are given in *Mémoires*, V, pp. 301–7, and appendix. The passages from his valet Legrain's letters are from the same source, p. 511.

64

1. *Mémoires de Charlotte Robespierre sur ses deux frères* (Présence de la Révolution, Paris, 1987), p. 44.

2. *Ibid.*, pp. 38–40.

3. See in this connection Max Gallo's writings on this period of his life, in *L'homme Robespierre* (Paris, Perrin, 1968), pp. 48–52. The excerpt from the *Éloge de Gresset* is quoted by E. Hamel (see next note).

4. Ernest Hamel, *Histoire de Robespierre* (Paris, 1867), p. 52.

5. Maximilien Robespierre, *Les droits et l'état des bâtards* (Arras, 1971), p. 68; *ibid.* for the following quote.

6. From chap. 31 (*Des délits difficiles à prouver*), quoted by Robespierre in *Les droits et l'état des bâtards*, p. 69.

7. Quoted by Max Gallo, *Robespierre*, p. 56; *ibid.* for the next two quotes.

8. Gerard Walter, *Robespierre* (Paris, Gallimard, 1961), I, p. 59.

9. Quoted by Karl Brunnemann, *"Maximilien Robespierre,"* in *Les Cahiers de la Quinzaine* (Paris, 1879), p. 25.

10. E. Hamel, *Robespierre*, p. 69.

11. *Ibid.*, p. 73.

12. The full text of Robespierre's defense of H. Dupond is published in vol. I of his *Oeuvres complètes* (edited by the *Revue Historique de la Révolution française*).

13. E. Hamel, *Robespierre*, p. 30.

65

1. Hardy's journal, sheet 297, April 27, 1789.

2. Jean Juarès, *Histoire socialiste de la Révolution française* (Paris, Éditions sociales, 1978), I, pp. 208 and 210.

3. Quoted by Jacques Godechot, *La prise de la Bastille* (Paris, Gallimard, 1965), p. 175 [also available in English].

4. *Ibid.*, p. 174.

5. According to Alexandre Tuetey's excellent introduction to the material on the Réveillon riots in vol. I of his *Répertoire général des sources manuscrites de l'histoire de Paris pendant la Révolution française* (Paris, Imprimerie Nouvelle, 1890), pp. xix ff.

6. Document appended to the *Mémoires* of the Marquis de Ferrières (Paris, Baudouin frères, 1821), p.

428; *ibid.*, p. 431, for the next two quotes.

7. *Ibid.*, p. 435.

8. Testimony recorded by agents Grandin and Le Blanc, and confirmed, give or take a few details, by Verpy, a carpenter, and Deldeveis, a stone carver; Tuetey, *Répertoire général*, p. xxi.

9. Officer Gueullette, quoted *ibid.*, p. xxv.

10. Quoted *ibid.*, p. xxvi. *Ibid.* for the next quote.

11. Marquis de Ferrières, *Mémoires*, p. 436.

12. J. Godechot, *La prise de la Bastille*, p. 182.

13. *Ibid.*, p. 183.

14. Quoted by A. Tuetey, *Répertoire générale*, pp. xxvii and xxviii.

15. *Ibid.*, p. xxvi.

16. Hardy's journal, sheet 299; *ibid.* for the following quote.

17. Marquis de Ferrières, *Mémoires*, p. 18.

66

1. Stefan Lorant, *The Presidency* (New York, Macmillan, 1952), p. 20. The unnumbered particulars that follow are taken from Jacques Fernay, *Georges Washington, fondateur de la République des États-Unis* (Paris, Charavay, 1886).

2. D. Jackson and D. Twohig, eds., *George Washington, Diaries,* V (Charlottesville, University of Virginia Press, 1979), p. 445.

3. *Ibid.*, p. 447.

4. [The translator has been unable to locate this statement in *ibid.* or *Letters,* so it has been retranslated from the French.]

5. J. Peuchet, *Dictionnaire universel de la géographie commerçante* (Paris, An VIII), V, p. 743.

6. Henry William Elson, *Histoire des États-Unis* (Paris, Payot, 1930), p. 339. [Retranslated from the French.]

67

1. Anne Cary Morris, ed., *The Diary and Letters of Gouverneur Morris* (New York, Scribner, 1888), I, p. 71.

2. *Recueil des documents relatifs aux séances des États Généraux, mai–juin 1789. Vol. I: Les Préliminaires. La séance du 5 mai.* Presented by G. Lefebvre and Anne Terroine (Paris, Éditions du C.N.R.S., 1953). Most of the unnumbered details in this chapter are from the same book, the last to be produced by G. Lefebvre. Excerpts from speeches have been taken from the same source.

3. M. de Lescure, *Correspondance secrète inédite sur Louis XVI, Marie-Antoinette, la cour et la ville,* II (Paris, Plon, 1866), p. 342.

4. According to G. Lefebvre; it emerges from his extremely clear introduction to the collection cited above (note 2) that a full-fledged conspiracy was being fomented against Necker and his reforms just when, and perhaps because, most of their champions were in the provinces getting themselves elected and everything looked as though it would be smooth sailing ahead. See pp. 92–97 of his work. Contrary to most people's ideas, the final postponement of the first meeting of the Estates definitely cannot be attributed solely to the "Réveillon riot." Who knows, it

may actually have provided more ammunition to the diehard saboteurs.

5. Marquis de Ferrières, *Correspondance inédite, 1789, 1790, 1791;* presented by Henri Carré (Paris, Armand Colin, 1932), p. 29.

6. G. Lefebvre, *Recueil de documents,* I, p. 104.

7. Lescure, *Correspondance secrète,* II, p. 350.

8. G. Lefebvre, *Recueil de documents,* I, p. 113.

9. La Révellière-Lépeaux, *Mémoires,* I, p. 67.

10. University Library of Geneva, Ms F 153 C, quoted by G. Lefebvre.

11. Gouverneur Morris, *Diary,* I, p. 74.

12. Marquis de Ferrières, *Mémoires,* pp. 18 ff.

13. No. 1 of Mirabeau's ephemeral newspaper, *Sur les États-Généraux,* p. 10. Quoted in the article by C. Constantin in *Annales Historiques de la Révolution francaise,* V, 1928, p. 25.

14. *Ibid.,* p. 23.

15. Adrien Duquesnoy, *Journal* (Paris, Picard, 1894), I, p. 4.

16. Mirabeau, *Sur les États-Généraux,* p. 9.

17. Duquesnoy, *Journal,* p. 5.

18. Letter by Camille Desmoulins, quoted by G. Lefebvre, *Recueil de documents,* I, p. 143.

68

1. Quoted by A. Vallentin, *Mirabeau,* II, p. 12.

2. The texts of his speech and the following ones by Barentin and Necker are published by G. Lefebvre in *Recueil de documents,* I, starting on p. 281. All three were widely circulated at once by newspapers in France and elsewhere in Europe; the only one they all publish in full is the King's, if only because it is so short.

3. A. Vallentin, *Mirabeau,* II, p. 9, from no. 1 of his *Journal des États-Généraux.*

4. Gouverneur Morris, *Diary,* I, p. 75.

5. Quoted in Richard Cobb and Colin Jones, eds., *The French Revolution, 1789–1795* (London, Simon & Schuster, 1988), p. 48.

6. *Ibid.,* p. 7.

7. The complete text is in G. Lefebvre, *Recueil de documents,* I, pp. 292–358.

8. A. Vallentin, *Mirabeau,* II, p. 14. As often, Mirabeau is a shade over the top here: the word "constitution" does appear toward the end of Necker's speech, but in passing, without definition or proposals.

9. Quoted in R. Cobb and C. Jones, *The French Revolution,* p. 48.

10. A. Vallentin, *Mirabeau,* II, p. 15.

11. *Ibid.,* p. 13. The text was found long afterward among the papers Mirabeau left to his friend Frochot, who is prefect of the Seine under Napoleon.

12. Quoted *ibid.,* p. 16. From the first issue of his *Journal des États-Généraux.*

69

1. *Archives Parlementaires,* VIII, p. 28.

2. *Ibid.,* p. 36.

3. *Ibid.,* p. 38.

4. *Ibid.,* p. 43.

5. E. Hamel, I, p. 103, and *Archives Parlementaires,* VIII.

6. Bailly, *Mémoires* (Paris, Baudouin

frères, 1821. Geneva, Slatkine Reprints), I, p. 53.

7. *Archives Parlementaires,* VIII, p. 112.

8. A. Vallentin, *Mirabeau,* II, p. 44.

9. Malouet, *Mémoires,* p. 279.

10. *Ibid.,* p. 282.

70

1. Bailly, *Mémoires,* I, p. 68.

2. *Ibid.,* p. 69.

3. *Ibid.,* p. 100.

4. Most of the biographical details I have just given come from Fernand Laurent, *Jean-Sylvain Bailly, premier maire de Paris* (Paris, Boivin et Cie, 1927).

5. Bailly, *Mémoires,* I, p. 89.

6. *Archives Parlementaires,* VIII, p. 127.

71

1. Bailly, *Mémoires,* I, p. 161.

2. *Archives Parlementaires,* VIII, p. 127.

3. *Ibid.,* p. 129.

4. Quoted by G. Lefebvre in *Recueil de documents,* I, p. 14.

5. Bailly, *Mémoires,* I, p. 176; *ibid.* for the next quote.

6. Ferrières, *Mémoires,* p. 58.

7. Bailly, *Mémoires,* I, p. 181.

8. *Archives Parlementaires,* VIII, p. 137. Quotes relating to the Tennis Court Oath come from the same source.

9. Bailly, *Mémoires,* I, p. 181.

10. It is not known which, if any, of the deputies put forward these proposals; they are reported only by the *Moniteur,* which gives the fullest account of events relating to the Tennis Court Oath: no. 10, June 20–24, 1789, p. 89. No names are mentioned but various *mémoires* confirm that the proposals were actually made.

11. Bailly, *Mémoires,* I, p. 187.

12. *Ibid.*

13. *Ibid.,* p. 189.

14. *Ibid.,* p. 190; *ibid.* for the following quote.

15. *Archives Parlementaires,* VIII, p. 138; the complete list of signers is on the same and following pages.

16. *Ibid.,* p. 139; *ibid.* for the next quote.

17. Bailly, *Mémoires,* I, p. 142.

18. *Ibid.,* p. 201.

19. *Histoire de la Révolution de 1789 et de l'établissement d'une Constitution en France, par deux amis de la liberté* (Paris, 1790), I, p. 234; quoted by J. Egret, *Necker.*

20. *Archives Parlementaires,* VIII, p. 143. The other excerpts from the royal speeches are from the same source, ending on p. 146.

21. Bailly, *Mémoires,* I, p. 214. *Ibid.* for the next quote.

22. A. Vallentin, *Mirabeau,* II, p. 54.

23. Bailly, *Mémoires,* I, p. 215.

24. *Archives Parlementaires,* VIII, p. 146.

25. According to the *Mémoires de l'abbé Jallet,* quoted by G. Lefebvre, *Recueil de documents,* I, p. 74.

72

1. The record of this letter is in the Archives Nationales, C 185.

2. *Ibid.*

3. In a letter published by the Duc de Castries in his book *Le Maréchal de Castries,* p. 160.

4. *Considérations sur la Révolution*

française, quoted by J. Egret,
Necker, p. 309.

5. According to Montjoy's paper
"*L'Ami du Roy,*" III, quoted by
J. Godechot, *La prise de la Bastille,*
p. 229.

6. Quoted *ibid.,* p. 230; *ibid.* for the
following quote.

7. *Ibid.,* p. 235.

8. The fullest excerpts from this letter of July 16 are given by René
Farge, *Un épisode de la journée du
12 juillet 1789: Camille Demoulins
au Jardin du Palais-Royal* (Paris,
Ernest Leroux, 1914), pp. 10–11.
Ibid. for the next quote.

9. Quoted by J. Godechot, *La prise*

de la Bastille, p. 229. *Ibid.* for the
King's reply.

10. *Ibid.,* p. 243.

11. *Ibid.,* p. 251.

73

1. A. Vallentin, *Mirabeau,* II, p. 61.

2. Besenval, *Mémoires,* quoted by
J. Godechot, *La prise de la Bastille,*
p. 269.

3. Quoted *ibid.*

4. Jacques Hillairet, *Évocation du
vieux Paris,* I (Paris, Éditions de
Minuit, 1951), p. 33.

5. R. Cobb and C. Jones, *The French
Revolution,* p. 68.

Index

A NOTE ABOUT THE AUTHOR

Claude Manceron was born in 1923, the son of a French naval officer and a Greek princess. His formal schooling ended after he was crippled by polio at age eleven, but he continued to read and became a teacher and a writer—at first of historical novels. His research, undertaken to make the characters' backgrounds authentic, led him to give up fiction and become a historian. He has been working on the French Revolution since 1967, and so far has completed four of ten projected volumes; this volume is the fifth. M. Manceron has given up teaching to devote himself full time to this work. He and his wife, Anne, live in a small village in the south of France, where they do research and write.

A NOTE ABOUT THE TRANSLATOR

Nancy Lipe Amphoux was born in Rockford, Illinois, and was educated by the cornfields there, at Vassar and Carnegie-Mellon, and in Europe, where she has lived since 1959. Her interests and activities include teaching and social work, horses and tropical fish, and Zen. Some of the books she has translated are Henri Troyat's biographies of Tolstoy, Pushkin, and Gogol; Edmonde Charles-Roux's biography of Chanel; François Ponchaud's *Cambodia Year Zero;* and an earlier volume in The French Revolution series, *The Wind from America.* She now lives in Strasbourg, France.